EXAMPLES & EXPLANATIONS

The Law of Torts

EXAMPLES & EXPLANATIONS

The Law of Torts

Seventh Edition

Joseph W. Glannon
Professor of Law
Suffolk University Law School

ASPEN PUBLISHING

To contact Customer Service, e-mail customer.service@aspenpublishing.com, call 1-800-950-5259, or mail correspondence to:

Aspen Publishing
Attn: Order Department
1 Wall Street
Burlington, MA 01803

1 2 3 4 5 6 7 8 9 0

ISBN 979-8-8890-6269-1

Library of Congress Cataloging-in-Publication Data

Names: Glannon, Joseph W. author
Title: The law of torts / Joseph W. Glannon.
Description: Seventh edition. | Burlington : Aspen Publishing, 2026. |
Series: Examples & explanations | Includes bibliographical references and index. |
Summary: "This book is based on the common sense premise that students encountering complex legal issues for the first time will appreciate a book that provides clear, straightforward introductions to these issues, together with examples that illustrate how these principles apply in typical cases"—Provided by publisher. Identifiers: LCCN 2026000283 (print) | LCCN 2026000284 (ebook) | ISBN 9798889062691 paperback | ISBN 9798889062714 epub | ISBN 9798889062707 ebook Subjects: LCSH: Torts—United States | Torts—United States—Problems, exercises, etc.
Classification: LCC KF1250.Z9 G58 2026 (print) | LCC KF1250.Z9 (ebook)
LC record available at https://lccn.loc.gov/2026000283
LC ebook record available at https://lccn.loc.gov/2026000284

ABOUT ASPEN PUBLISHING

Aspen Publishing is a leading provider of legal education content and digital learning solutions in the United States and globally. Our innovative products and platforms—designed based on best practices in learning science—engage students and enhance outcomes. From textbooks and audiobooks authored by renowned experts to digital platforms and products like LEAF, Connected eBooks, Connected Quizzing, PracticePerfect, and JD-Next, we empower the next generation of legal professionals with innovative, trusted, and accessible resources.

The Aspen Casebook Series, affectionately known as the "red and black" casebooks among law faculty and students, includes hundreds of highly regarded textbooks across more than 80 disciplines. These range from foundational courses like Torts and Contracts to emerging electives such as Sustainability and the Law of Policing. Our study aids, including the popular *Examples & Explanations* series, help law students master complex topics with clarity and confidence.

Aspen's expertise extends to undergraduate education with our Paralegal, Criminal Justice, and Business Law series, offering the same hallmark quality to a broader audience. JD-Next, our groundbreaking online law school prep course and admissions test, provides a realistic preview of law school, equips students with essential skills for academic success, and evaluates their readiness for legal studies.

Aspen Publishing Is Proud to Be a UWorld Company

Since 2003, UWorld has been a global leader in developing high-quality learning tools for students preparing for high-stakes exams. With a commitment to excellence, UWorld has helped millions of students in undergraduate, graduate, and professional programs in fields such as medicine, nursing, finance, and law achieve their academic and career goals.

Founded by Chandra S. Pemmasani, M.D., during his medical residency, UWorld began focusing on medical education and has since expanded into various academic fields, including law. In 2020, UWorld launched its Legal vertical, starting with its comprehensive Multistate Bar Exam (MBE®) Question Bank, followed by the acquisition of Themis Bar Review, which integrated resources to provide a complete bar exam preparation experience. In 2024, UWorld expanded its offerings by acquiring Aspen Publishing, enhancing its suite of legal education products.

Today, UWorld offers an unparalleled range of study materials that blend active learning methods with expert content, ensuring students and educators can access the most effective resources. From bar preparation to law school success, UWorld is committed to supporting the next generation of legal professionals. Learn more at uworld.com.

I dedicate this book to my wife, Annie.

Contents

Preface to Students

This book is based on the common sense premise that students encountering complex legal issues for the first time will appreciate a book that provides clear, straightforward introductions to these issues, together with examples that illustrate how these principles apply in typical cases.

I have good reason to believe that this premise is valid. Some years ago, I wrote a book on civil procedure, entitled *Civil Procedure: Examples and Explanations*, which uses the same approach. The book has been widely used in law schools across the country. Not only do many faculty members assign or recommend it, but many students have found their way to the book on their own or on the recommendation of other students who have found the approach helpful.

Each chapter of this book includes a brief introduction to the topic, followed by a set of examples that apply the concepts to particular fact situations. After the examples, I have included my analysis of each example. Unlike the typical questions found in the casebooks, which are often either too hard to answer or downright unanswerable, the examples here tend to start with the basics and move on to more sophisticated variations. If you study the readings for your Torts class and the introductions in this book, you should be able to respond effectively to most of the examples. Trying your hand at them and comparing your analysis to mine should help to deepen your understanding of the concepts and your ability to think critically about legal issues in general. It may also help to convince you that you are capable of learning the law, a type of feedback that law school seldom seems to provide.

You will also want to use the book to review the course toward the end of the year. Most casebooks contain representative cases and provocative questions and notes, but they do not explain the state of the law or provide much context for the issues raised. Reading these chapters and reviewing the examples should help you to test your understanding of the topics covered and fill in the gaps left by your casebook.

The last part of the book includes three chapters that will be particularly helpful in preparing for exams. The first chapter explains the type of analysis that law professors are looking for on a Torts essay exam (or any other first-year exam, for that matter). The second analyzes common mistakes students make in taking essay exams. The third includes several exam questions, with sample answers and some comments on strategy. Law exams are quite different from others you've taken. These chapters will help you to understand the analytical approach that most law professors want to see in the merry month of May.

Like every author, I hope that this book will go through many more editions. If you have comments or suggestions for improvement, drop me a note at Suffolk University Law School, 120 Tremont Street, Boston, MA 02108. Or, send me an e-mail at jglannon@suffolk.edu.

January 2026 *Joseph W. Glannon*

Acknowledgments

I appreciate the permission granted by the American Law Institute to reproduce various sections, comments, and illustrations from the First, Second, and Third Restatements of Torts and the Second and Third Restatements of Agency.

Finally, I thank the many students who have sent me comments, corrections, and suggestions for improvement. Keep 'em coming.

Special Notice

For several frequently cited treatises, I have used shortened forms after the initial citation to the work. These are as follows: Dobbs, Hayden & Bublick, *The Law of Torts,* cited as Dobbs' Law of Torts; Harper, James & Gray, *The Law of Torts* (2d ed. 1986), cited as Harper, James & Gray; Prosser and Keeton, *The Law of Torts* (5th ed. 1984), cited as Prosser & Keeton; Minzer, Nates, eds., *Damages in Tort Actions,* cited as Minzer, Nates; Schwartz, *Comparative Negligence,* cited as Schwartz; and Speiser, *Recovery for Wrongful Death and Injury,* cited as Speiser.

PART I

Intentional Torts

CHAPTER 1

Fundamental Protections: The Tort of Battery

INTRODUCTION

The primitive world must have been a fairly scary place. Our ancestors had to cope not only with the awesome forces of nature, impossible to predict or control, but also with another unpredictable danger—other human beings. Doubtless, one of the primary reasons they decided to become "civilized" was to ensure physical security from each other.

Medieval England, from which our tort law evolved, sought to deter physical aggression through a criminal remedy, the "appeal of felony," for physical assaults and other invasions of personal interests. Harper, James & Gray, The Law of Torts §3.1 (3d ed. 1996). If the defendant was found guilty, she would be fined; that is, she would have to pay a sum of money or forfeit her goods to the crown. The appeal of felony helped to enforce the King's peace, but it did nothing to compensate the injured victim for her injury.

Over time, the English courts also developed civil tort remedies to compensate victims of physical aggression. This tort remedy differed according to the nature of the defendant's invasion. For example, the tort of battery authorized damages for deliberate, unwanted contacts with the plaintiff's person. Assault allowed recovery for placing the plaintiff in fear of an unwanted contact. False imprisonment was the remedy for unwarranted restraints on the plaintiff's freedom of movement. This chapter examines the action of battery, that most basic of tort remedies for invasion of the most basic of personal rights, the right to freedom from unwanted bodily contact.

It seems as though this ought to be a very short chapter. Even the law, with its tendency to overanalyze, can only complicate a seemingly simple matter so much. And battery seems like a simple matter. Jones hits Smith: She has invaded Smith's right to freedom from physical aggression and should be liable for any resulting injuries. All that is left to decide is how much Jones should pay.

Sometimes it is that simple, but often it is not. Jones may have bumped into Smith because Lopez pushed her, or she may have collided with Smith while jumping out of the way of an oncoming car. Perhaps she pushed Smith in order to prevent the car from hitting *her*, or while thrashing around in an epileptic seizure. Each of these cases involves an unauthorized contact with Smith, but Jones should not be required to compensate Smith for such blameless—or even helpful—invasions of Smith's physical autonomy.

Since the courts have refused to condemn all unwanted contacts, they have struggled to craft a definition of battery that limits recovery to those types of contacts the law seeks to prevent. Most courts define battery as the intentional infliction of a harmful or offensive contact with the person of the plaintiff. See Restatement (Second) of Torts §13. Under this definition the defendant must act, her act must be intentional (in the restricted sense peculiar to tort law), the act must cause a contact with the victim, and the intended contact must be either harmful or offensive to the victim. These requirements are discussed in detail below.

THE INTENT REQUIREMENT

As this definition indicates, battery protects against *intentional* invasions of the plaintiff's physical integrity. No contact is intentional if it is not the result of a voluntary act. If Lopez faints and falls on Jones, Lopez is not liable for battery, because she has not caused the touching by a voluntary act. It hardly seems fair to require her to pay damages to Jones for something she didn't "do" in any meaningful sense, that is, something that was not the result of her voluntary conduct. Similarly, if Smith pushes Lopez into Jones, Lopez has not acted, and would not be liable for battering Jones. See Restatement (Second) of Torts §2 (defining an act as an "external manifestation of the actor's will").

Even if the defendant has acted, however, in the sense of making a voluntary movement, that act may not be intentional as that term is used in the context of intentional torts. Suppose, for example, that Chu fails to look carefully in stepping off a bus, does not see Munoz coming along the street, and bumps into her. Chu's act of stepping off the bus is intentional in the sense that it was deliberate: She certainly intended to put her foot down and move off the bus, but she did not intend to cause the resulting contact with

Munoz. To commit a battery, the defendant must not only intend to act; she must act *for the purpose of* inflicting a harmful or offensive contact on the plaintiff, or realize that such a contact is *substantially certain* to result.

> The word "intent" is used . . . to denote that the actor desires to cause consequences of his act, or that he believes that the consequences are substantially certain to result from it.

Restatement (Second) of Torts §8A. This definition lets Chu off the hook in the bus case since her act was not intentional in the intentional tort sense. She did not act for the purpose of hitting Munoz, nor was she substantially certain that she would. The contact resulted instead from her failure to take proper precautions (such as looking where she was going) to avoid hitting Munoz. Chu may be liable for negligence, but she has not committed a battery.

Indeed, the purpose of the intent requirement is to confine intentional tort liability to cases in which the defendant acts with a higher level of culpability than mere carelessness: where she acts with a purpose, or with knowledge that the act will cause harmful or offensive contact to the victim. If Chu pushed Munoz to get her out of the way, she would meet this intent requirement since she would be substantially certain that Munoz would find such a contact offensive. She would also meet the intent requirement if she pushed her to embarrass her in front of a friend—an offensive contact—or to cause her to fall in front of a car, an obviously harmful one.

The intent requirement in the Restatement is disjunctive; that is, it is met *either* by a purpose to cause the tortious contact *or* substantial certainty that such a contact will result. Suppose, for example, that Smith heaves a stone at her enemy Jones, though she thinks Jones is probably beyond her range. She is not substantially certain that she will hit Jones, but she acts with the desire to do so. This satisfies the intent requirement; if the stone hits Jones, Smith has committed battery.

Under this definition, an actor can possess tortious intent even though she bears the victim no ill will whatsoever. If Chu sees Jones walking along the street below and deliberately throws a bucket of water on her from a second-story window, it is no defense that she was simply emptying the scrub bucket and did not mean to offend Jones. In intentional tort terms, she intends those contacts that she is substantially certain will occur, as well as those she desires to see happen. Indeed, a battery can be committed with the best of motives. In *Clayton v. New Dreamland Roller Skating Rink, Inc.*, 82 A.2d 458 (1951), for example, the defendant's employee attempted to set the plaintiff's broken arm, against her protests. While the employee was only trying to help, he knew (because the victim told him so) that she found the contact unwelcome, and consequently met the intent requirement for battery.

SINGLE v. DUAL INTENT

The intent requirement as described above requires not only that the actor intended to make a contact with the receiving party, but also that she intended the contact to be either a harmful contact or an offensive contact. Many cases apply that test: If the actor intends a contact, but not one that is harmful or offensive, she does not have the intent necessary for battery.

A number of jurisdictions, however, appear to apply a "single intent" test for battery claims. These courts hold that the actor need only *intend to make the contact*, not intend a harmful or offensive contact. If the contact *turns out to be* harmful or offensive, the actor is liable. Here's a case that illustrates the distinction:

In *White v. University of Idaho*, 797 P.2d 108 (Idaho 1990), a piano teacher, a guest in Mrs. White's home, tapped out a rhythm on her shoulder while they were discussing piano music. Unexpectedly, she suffered serious injury from the contact, requiring surgery.

Under dual intent analysis, the teacher would very likely not be liable, since he did not intend either a harmful or offensive contact—his touching would likely be acceptable between music enthusiasts under the circumstances in which he made it. But the teacher clearly *did* intend the contact, which turned out to be harmful to Mrs. White. The court held—applying the single intent theory—that this touching constituted battery. The Third Restatement of Torts endorses this approach. Restatement (Third) of Torts: Intentional Torts to Persons, Tentative Draft No. 4 1§102 cmt. b. Other courts, however, continue to apply the dual intent approach. See, e.g., *White v. Munoz*, 999 P.2d 814 (CO. 2014) (en banc).

This distinction, while it made all the difference in Mrs. White's case, very seldom arises in the case law. In the vast majority of cases that lead to a lawsuit, the contact was clearly intended to be either harmful or offensive. In such cases the actor is liable under either theory.

TRANSFERRED INTENT

Although intentional tort law requires a very specific type of intent, that standard may be met if the actor intends to commit a battery on one person and actually inflicts one on somebody else. Suppose, for example, that Chu throws a rock at Smith, hoping to hit her, but her aim is bad and she hits Lopez instead. Chu would argue that she cannot be held liable to Lopez, since she had no intent to hit her—she was aiming at Smith.

Although Chu had no tortious intent toward Lopez in this example, she *did* have tortious intent toward Smith. In such cases, courts hold that the tortious intent to hit Smith *transfers to* Lopez. Restatement (Second) of Torts §16(2). Thus, where the actor tries to batter one person and actually causes a harmful or offensive contact to another, she will be liable to the actual victim.

Obviously, transferred intent is a legal fiction created to achieve a sensible result despite lack of intent toward the person actually contacted. The rationale for the doctrine is that the tortfeasor's act is just as *culpable* when her aim is bad as when it is good; it would be unconscionable if she were exonerated just because she hit the wrong person. Under transferred intent, she will be liable whether she hits her intended victim or someone else.

The transferred intent fiction also allows recovery where the actor attempts one intentional tort but causes another. If, for example, Chu tries to hit Smith with a hammer but misses, placing Smith in fear of a harmful contact but not actually causing one, her intent to commit a battery suffices to hold her liable for assault. Conversely, if she tries to frighten Lopez by shooting near her, but the bullet hits her instead, she will be liable for battery even though she intended to commit an assault instead.

HARMFUL OR OFFENSIVE CONTACT

Not all intentional contacts will support a claim for battery. It would make little sense to allow Jones to bring a battery suit against every subway passenger who jostled her during rush hour. This kind of contact is an accepted fact of city life. Similarly, if Smith taps Jones on the shoulder to tell her that she dropped a glove, it is reasonable for Smith to expect that this touching is acceptable to Jones, as it would be to most of us.

To distinguish between such common, socially accepted contacts and actionable batteries, courts require that the defendant intend to cause either a harmful or an offensive contact. *Harmful* suggests broken arms, black eyes, and the like, but a great deal less will do. Section 15 of the Restatement (Second) of Torts defines *bodily harm* as "any physical impairment of the condition of another's body, or physical pain or illness." Of course, if the harm is minor, the plaintiff will recover very little, or be limited to nominal damages, but the courts will still have vindicated her right to physical autonomy.

Even if the contact is not harmful, it is tortious if it is offensive. If Smith chucks Jones under the chin in a demeaning manner, or spits on her, she has caused an offensive contact. Allowing a battery suit for such offensive contacts not only deters such personal invasions, it also provides Jones with a civilized alternative to retaliation. Since offensive acts are particularly likely to provoke retaliation, it is appropriate to provide a battery remedy for such contacts instead.

Of course, people don't all react the same way to every contact. If Smith goes around slapping folks on the back at the office party, Jones may find it obnoxious, but Cimino may be flattered by the attention. If the definition of offensive contact depended on the subjective reaction of each plaintiff, Smith would not know whether her conduct was tortious until she saw the reaction to it. Smith should have some way of determining whether a contact is permissible *before* she acts. To allow such advance judgments, courts use an objective definition of offensive contact. The Second Restatement, for example, defines a contact as offensive if it "offends a reasonable sense of personal dignity." Id. at §19.

Under this test, a contact is offensive if a reasonable person in the circumstances of the victim would find the particular contact offensive. An actor is not liable under this definition for a contact that is considered socially acceptable (i.e., that would not offend a "reasonable sense of personal dignity"), even though the victim turns out to be hypersensitive and is truly offended. On the other hand, if she makes a contact that the reasonable person *would* find offensive, it is not a defense that she did not mean to give offense, or that she did not realize that the victim would be offended.

What the reasonable person would find offensive varies greatly with the circumstances. Often a prior course of conduct between the parties indicates that they accept contacts that would ordinarily be considered offensive. Suppose that Burgess and Munoz routinely engage in horseplay at work, including backslapping, arm locks, bear hugs, and the like. A stranger would undoubtedly find such contacts offensive, but Burgess and Munoz expect these contacts from each other. Burgess would be justified, given their previous interactions, in inferring that Munoz will not find such contacts offensive, though they would offend the "reasonable sense of personal dignity" of a new employee.

THE DIFFERENCE BETWEEN CONTACTS AND CONSEQUENCES

It is crucial to distinguish the intent to cause a harmful or offensive contact from the intent to cause a particular consequence which results from that contact. Suppose, for example, that Brutus decides to humiliate Cassius by tripping him as he leaves the Senate building. Unfortunately, Cassius suffers a freak fall sideways over a railing and down a flight of stairs, causing a severe concussion. While Brutus intended to trip Cassius, he certainly did not intend the resulting freak injury. He did not act with a purpose to cause this unusual train of circumstances, nor was he substantially certain that tripping Cassius would result in serious injury.

However, Brutus did commit a battery on Cassius, and is therefore liable for all of Cassius's injuries. Brutus acted with the purpose to trip Cassius, which is surely an offensive contact. He succeeded in causing that contact when Cassius tripped. At that point, the battery was complete, and the law holds Brutus liable for all the consequences of the battery. Cassius may suffer no injury at all, or more injury than Brutus expects, or less, but if the contact itself is a battery, Brutus is liable for the resulting harm, whatever its extent may be.

The language of §8A of the Second Restatement is a bit confusing on this point: It states that the actor must intend "the consequences" of the act. However, the consequence to which §8A refers is the harmful or offensive contact itself, not the injuries that result from it. In our example, Brutus intended to trip Cassius; because he intended that "consequence," he is liable for the unintended fall down the stairs as well.

Perhaps another example will help to make this important distinction clear. In *Lambertson v. United States*, 528 F.2d 441 (2d Cir. 1976), an inspector ran up behind a worker in a meatpacking plant, jumped on his back, and pulled the worker's hat over his eyes. The worker stumbled forward, struck his face on some meat hooks, and sustained serious injuries. Evidently, the inspector in *Lambertson* acted in the spirit of horseplay; there was no suggestion that he intended the worker to hit the meat hooks or suffer serious injuries. Yet the court concluded that the inspector had battered the worker when he intentionally jumped on his back, since the reasonable person in the victim's circumstances would find that contact offensive. Since he battered the worker when he jumped on him, the inspector could be held liable for the consequences of that battery—the facial injuries—though he did not intend to cause them.

It is not hard to see the reason for this seemingly draconian rule: Batteries are intentional invasions of others' right of personal security. One purpose of intentional tort law is to deter such unauthorized contacts from the outset. Imposing the cost of all resulting injuries on the actor should serve this deterrent purpose. After all, intentional torts are eminently avoidable: Because they require a *deliberate choice* to invade another's rights, the actor need only restrain herself to avoid the invasion. Where she fails to do so, it seems appropriate to impose all resulting damages—even unintended damages—on her rather than the innocent victim.[1]

1. This is a wee bit of an overstatement. See Chapter 2, Example 12, which suggests that there is a limit—albeit a limited limit—to liability for unexpected consequences of an intentional tort.

THE CONTACT REQUIREMENT

Even the seemingly self-evident requirement of a contact requires some explanation. Suppose Smith doesn't touch Jones at all, but pokes her with a ten-foot pole or stretches a wire across the sidewalk as Jones approaches, causing her to fall. Surely the underlying policy of protecting physical autonomy supports liability in these cases. In each, Smith invades Jones's physical integrity in one way or another and intends to do so under the definition discussed above.

Although no part of her body has touched Jones in these examples, Smith has imposed an unauthorized *contact* on Jones. The defendant need not actually touch the plaintiff at all, or even be present at the time of the contact, to commit a battery. For example, setting the wire out for Jones, knowing that she will trip over it later, will satisfy the contact requirement. An actor is liable, regardless of whether she uses her fist, a nightstick, or a city bus to cause the contact, if it is intended to cause a harmful or offensive contact to the victim.

The contact requirement has also been extended to include objects intimately associated with the victim's body. Chu's sense of personal space can be breached as effectively if Lopez pulls her coat lapels or knocks off her hat as by a direct touching to the skin. Extending the sphere of personal autonomy to include such items protects against intrusive contacts that are very likely to be offensive, thus raising the ante in physical confrontations. Obviously, however, there are limits; if Lopez kicks the fender of Chu's vintage Ford Mustang, the contact requirement is probably not met, even if Chu is sitting in the back seat.

The following examples illustrate the elements of battery. In analyzing them, assume that the Restatement definitions apply and, unless otherwise noted, that the court applies the dual intent approach to the intent requirement.

Examples

The Bard, Updated

1. Romeo likes to drive his souped-up Trans Am around the high school parking lot, racing the motor, accelerating rapidly, and stopping on a dime. He arrives at school one winter morning, speeds across the parking lot, and screeches to a halt in a parking space, hoping to impress the ladies with his hotshot driving. Unfortunately, the parking lot is icy; the rear end of the car skids out of control, jumps the curb sideways, and knocks Thibault to the ground. Has Romeo battered him?

2. When Romeo gets out of the car to apologize, Thibault yells, "What's the idea?" and gives him a push. Romeo slips on a patch of ice, hits his head on one of the mag wheels of his Trans Am, and suffers a serious concussion. Is Thibault liable for Romeo's injuries?

3. Romeo and Juliet are an item, "going steady" as they said when I was in high school. Romeo comes up to Juliet in the school parking lot on Monday morning and gives her a hug, as he is accustomed to doing each morning. Unfortunately, Juliet is standing on a patch of ice and Romeo's embrace causes her to fall and fracture her arm. Is Romeo liable for battery?

4. In an effort to make amends, Romeo starts to help Juliet up. Thoroughly annoyed, Juliet growls, "Don't touch me." Romeo, determined to be gallant, helps her up anyway, despite her efforts to pull away. Is this a battery?

Introducing Judge Fudd

5. Romeo and Thibault are bitter rivals for Juliet's favor. After gym class, Romeo leaves a bar of soap on the floor of the shower Thibault usually uses, hoping that Thibault will slip and fall. He does, suffers injury, and sues Romeo for battery. At trial, Judge Fudd, a well-meaning but sometimes inartful jurist, instructs the jury as follows:

   > If you find that, when the defendant acted, he did not know that his act was substantially certain to cause a harmful or offensive contact to the plaintiff, you must find for the defendant.

   a. Which party will object to Judge Fudd's instruction, and what is wrong with it?
   b. Can you write a more accurate instruction on the issue of intent?

6. Romeo is sitting on a wall in front of the school. He sees Thibault wandering across the lawn, with his nose in a book, toward a trench recently excavated for some utility work. Cheering silently, he watches as Thibault ambles absentmindedly toward disaster. To his delight, Thibault walks right into the trench, suffering minor injuries and considerable humiliation. Thibault sues Romeo for battery. What result?

No Offense Intended?

7. Romeo considers himself irresistible. He is accustomed to flirting with the girls at will. He comes up to Ophelia, a new student, on her first day in the school and, by way of introduction, gives her a hug. She sues him for battery. Is he liable?

8. Romeo is a sprinter on the track team. At the first meet of the season, he is nosed out by Mercutio, the star of the visiting team. In a burst of good sportsmanship, he goes over to Mercutio, slaps him heartily on the back, and says, "Great run, Mercutio!" Mercutio, who, it turns out, is very sensitive about being touched by strangers, reacts with rage at the contact. Is Romeo liable for battery?
   a) Is Romeo liable to Mercutio for battery under the dual intent theory?
   b) Is he liable to Mercutio under the single intent theory?

9. Romeo and Mercutio meet again at the regional finals. This time Romeo ends up the victor. After the race, he turns to Mercutio on the track, punches his shoulder playfully and says, "Well, Mercutio, turnabout is fair play!" The humorless Mercutio sues him for battery. Is he liable this time?

10. Romeo races Mercutio again in the state finals, and loses. Infuriated, he takes his track shoes and hurls them into the crowded stands. They hit Polonius, causing facial lacerations. Can Polonius sue Romeo for battery?

Star-Crossed Lovers

11. Alas, poor Romeo. He still holds a candle for Juliet, and she won't even talk to him anymore. He finds her asleep at one of the carrels in the school library. A confirmed romantic, he slips up to her and kisses her on the cheek. Malvolio, the school sneak, later tells Juliet.
   a. Upset, she heads for court. Battery?
   b. You have recently passed the bar and hung out your own shingle. Juliet brings her sneaky-kiss case to you and asks you to sue Romeo for her. Would you take the case?

Some Touching Cases

12. Romeo gets the idea that Juliet is seeing Thibault. He decides to get even. Which of the following vengeful acts makes Romeo liable for battery?
   a. He confronts Thibault in the cafeteria and makes some very offensive allusions to his moral character.
   b. At the prom, he laces Thibault's lemonade with 100-proof vodka. Thibault drinks it.
   c. He laces Thibault's lemonade with vodka, but the gallant Thibault gives his drink to Juliet, who drinks it.
   d. He throws his own drink at Thibault. Unfortunately, Mr. Merola, the Vice Principal for Discipline, steps through the door at that moment and is hit instead.

e. Just before the science fair, Romeo deliberately sits on Thibault's latest science project, an elaborate geodesic representation of an international space station, built from 5,000 toothpicks and Elmer's glue. Thibault is watching at the time.
f. He blows cigarette smoke in Thibault's face.
g. He shocks Juliet by offering to show her a photo of her favorite rock group but shows her some pornographic pictures instead.
h. A motel manager rents a room to Thibault, even though he knows that the bed is infested with bedbugs.

13. Regan and Goneril, two teenagers, decide to while away the afternoon standing on a bridge over the interstate, watching the traffic. Regan takes a mirror from her pocket and starts to shine it in the eyes of oncoming drivers. Cordelia, driving under the bridge, is temporarily blinded, swerves out of control, and hits the bridge. Is Regan liable for battery?

Explanations

The Bard, Updated

1. Romeo has done a dumb thing, a clearly negligent thing, but he has not committed a battery. A battery requires an intent to cause a harmful or offensive touching. While Romeo certainly *did* cause a harmful contact, he didn't intend to under the Restatement definition. He did act intentionally in the sense that he deliberately drove his car across the lot. However, while this act was voluntary, he did not act with the purpose of hitting Thibault or with knowledge that he was substantially certain to do so; he was headed in another direction entirely. Nor, the facts suggest, was he trying to frighten Thibault or another student, which might support an argument for transferred intent. He was just showing off. Thus, his act was not intentional in the limited sense in which courts use that term for defining intentional torts.

   In analyzing battery cases, always distinguish the intent to act from the intent to cause a harmful or offensive contact. Battery requires more than a deliberate act. It requires a deliberate act done for the purpose of causing a harmful or offensive contact, or which the actor knows to a substantial certainty will cause such a contact. If only a deliberate act were required, battery would encompass many cases where the actor intended no harmful or offensive contact. For example, a driver would commit a battery if she looked away from the road and got in an accident, even though she did not intend to hit the plaintiff. Or, a joker would be liable for battery for throwing a snowball at a tree, if a pedestrian unexpectedly stepped into the snowball's path. In both of these cases, the actor did a voluntary act. But these acts—like Romeo's in the example—were *not* done with the state of mind necessary to commit an intentional tort: either purpose or substantial certainty that a harmful or offensive contact would result. They may be negligent acts, if the actor failed to exercise due care, but they are not intentional torts.

2. Although Thibault is justly angry with Romeo, that does not give him a license to retaliate against him. He has intentionally inflicted a contact that Romeo will find offensive, and perhaps harmful as well, and he is liable to him for battery.

   But is he liable for the unanticipated and unintended concussion? As in the Brutus example in the introduction, Thibault is fully liable for all harm resulting from the battery. Although he had no intent—as that term is used in either the Restatement or everyday life—to cause Romeo's concussion, he did intend to push him. Since he committed a battery by doing so, he is liable for all the resulting injuries, even unexpected ones.

   This rule, that a defendant who commits an intentional tort is liable for all the resulting harm, does not apply in negligence cases. Under negligence law, liability is limited to the foreseeable consequences of the defendant's act. See Chapter 12. However, because intentional torts are deemed more culpable, the courts generally hold the defendant liable for all the ensuing consequences, foreseeable or otherwise. This rule imposes very severe damages on Thibault for what seems like a relatively innocuous act—but it didn't turn out to be innocuous, did it? The Solomons of tort law have concluded that the loss in such cases should fall on the actor rather than the victim.[2]

   For an extreme example of this, see *Baker v. Shymkiv*, 451 N.E.2d 811 (Ohio 1983), in which a defendant's trespass to land (an intentional tort) led to an argument with the owner. During the argument, the owner had a fatal heart attack. The trespasser was held liable for it as a consequence of the intentional tort.

3. Given their relationship and Juliet's past acceptance of Romeo's embraces, Romeo is justified in inferring that Juliet will not find his customary hug offensive. The reasonable person in Juliet's circumstances would not be offended by a hug from her boyfriend. But surely she finds falling down and breaking her arm harmful or offensive. Even if Romeo's hug isn't a battery, isn't causing her to fall on the ice one? (Remember that the contact need not be with the defendant; it can be with the ground or anything else.)

---

2. But see Chapter 2, Example 12, which suggests that there is *some* limit to this extended liability.

In this case, Romeo did not act with the intent of causing a harmful or offensive contact to Juliet. He had no reason to believe she would find the contact he intended—the hug—offensive, due to their relationship. And the contact she found harmful—the fall—he had no intent to cause: He did not act with a purpose to cause Juliet to fall or with substantial certainty that she would. While Romeo may be liable for negligence, for hugging her where the footing is slippery, he is not liable for battery.

Distinguish this case from Example 2. In that case, Thibault intended a harmful contact—the push. Thus, he committed a battery and was held liable for all the resulting harm, even though it was greater than he reasonably would have anticipated. Here, since Romeo did not intend a harmful or offensive contact, he did not commit a battery and consequently is not liable for battery even though the contact itself turned out to have harmful consequences.

4. Poor Romeo; he was only trying to help. Maybe he even *was* helpful. But he still committed a battery.

   In analyzing battery cases, it is important to distinguish between intent and motive. The motive for Romeo's act was honorable, but he still intended to cause a contact to Juliet that he knew she would find offensive because she told him so. The elements of battery do not include acting from a malicious motive, nor will a virtuous motive prevent liability if those elements are present. The plaintiff has the right to decide for herself which contacts are beneficial; she need not submit to the prodding of any Romeo who wishes to be gallant. Juliet may prefer the higher risk of slipping to the touch of the klutzy and out-of-favor Romeo. That decision is hers, not his. Where Romeo substitutes his judgment for hers, he is liable for battery.

   Because of the fundamental value placed on physical self-determination, courts have held defendants liable for battery even though their motives were pure and their contacts beneficial. The classic example is *Mohr v. Williams*, 104 N.W. 12 (Minn. 1905), in which a doctor was held liable for battery when he operated on the plaintiff's left ear after the plaintiff had consented to surgery only on the right. Although the left ear was diseased, and the surgery was successful, the court concluded that the doctor had violated the patient's "right to complete immunity of his person from physical interference of others. . . ." Id. at 16.

Introducing Judge Fudd

5. a. Thibault will object to the instruction, and rightly so. If Judge Fudd's instruction were correct, Romeo would not be liable. Although he hoped that Thibault would slip and fall, and put the soap there for that purpose, he could hardly be substantially certain that he would

cause Thibault to fall, since he did not know that Thibault would use that shower or that if he did, he would slip on the soap. However, the intent requirement is satisfied either by an act done with substantial certainty that the contact will result *or* by an act done with the purpose to cause the contact.

In the practice of law, a word can make a world of difference. Here, the word "or" indicates that either substantial certainty or a desire to cause the result will suffice to establish intent. Since Romeo acted with the purpose to cause the contact, he cannot defend by arguing that it was a long shot that his plot would succeed. Judge Fudd's instruction is wrong. Thibault's lawyer should object to it and have it corrected before it leads the jury to return an erroneous verdict.

b. How about this:

> If you find that, when he left the soap in the shower, Romeo acted either for the purpose of causing Thibault to fall or with substantial certainty that he would cause him to fall, then you should find that Romeo had the intent necessary to commit a battery.

This instruction tells the jury to find the intent requirement met if Romeo acted with either of the states of mind required for an intentional tort.

6. If desire can make a battery, Romeo has surely committed one since he fervently hoped Thibault would fall in, and was delighted when he did. And we know that Romeo need not directly touch Thibault to batter him: Contact with the trench suffices to meet the contact requirement. And certainly Thibault found the contact both harmful and offensive.

But Romeo is still not liable to Thibault. He has not done anything to cause the contact. To incur liability, he must *act;* he must inflict the contact, not simply hope for it. This contact results from the acts of others, not from Romeo.

No Offense Intended?

7. Obviously, Romeo is of the opinion that no woman in her right mind would object to his attentions. However, the question is not whether Romeo finds his conduct offensive. It is not even whether Romeo thinks that Ophelia will. As the introduction points out, the question Romeo must ponder before his dalliance with Ophelia is whether the reasonable person in Ophelia's circumstances would find it offensive. The answer to that question is almost certainly "yes." Most teenagers don't like being hugged by strangers, even attractive strangers.

So, offensiveness is determined by an objective test—whether the contact would be offensive to the reasonable person in the victim's circumstances. But isn't it true, even if Romeo's hug is "offensive" under this definition, that Romeo must *intend* an offensive contact, not just cause one? And, if Romeo genuinely believed that the new girl in school would welcome his attention, how can he be said to have intended an offensive contact?

Very likely Romeo will be held liable, even if he is too conceited to realize that this contact is offensive under the Restatement definition; the law will attribute to him an understanding of what the reasonable person finds offensive. Otherwise, he could avoid liability based on his testimony that he didn't think it would be offensive. Such a test would allow social boors to escape liability simply because they have poor judgment—or lie about what they understood—even though they inflict unwanted contacts on others.

8. a. Romeo has again acted with good intentions, but we saw in Example 4 that good intentions will not negate a battery if the elements of the tort are established. However, those elements are not met here, since Romeo has no reason to believe that his slap will be offensive to a reasonable person under these circumstances: Congratulatory hugs and slaps are common among athletes on such occasions.

   The requirement that the contact "offen[d] a reasonable sense of personal dignity" (Restatement (Second) of Torts §19) allows actors to make contacts with others that the ordinary person will not find offensive, without fear of a suit for battery. This requirement places the burden on the party with unusual sensibilities, such as Mercutio, to inform people of his susceptibility. Until he does, those who interact with Mercutio are protected if they conform to generally accepted standards of behavior.

   If actors were liable to hypersensitive plaintiffs for generally accepted contacts like this, many everyday interactions would entail the risk of liability. Under that rule, Romeo could be sued for tapping a stranger on the shoulder to tell her she had dropped her umbrella, or brushing past a fellow passenger on the subway. To avoid liability, he would have to avoid all contact. The world might be a marginally safer place for the hypersensitive, but a great deal of spontaneity would be sacrificed.

   b. It is tempting to conclude that Romeo is liable here, because he intended the contact and it turned out to be offensive to Mercutio. However, Romeo is probably not liable for battery, even under the single intent theory because the contact he made was not one "offensive to a reasonable sense of personal dignity." So the contact is not offensive . . . even if Mercutio finds it so! Here is some authority from the Third Restatement:

> If plaintiff has an unusual sensitivity to offense of which the actor is unaware, and if the actor's conduct does not satisfy the objective requirement of offending a reasonable sense of personal dignity, then the actor is not liable for an offensive battery.

Restatement (Third) of Torts s. 103 cmt. a. The apparent rationale for this conclusion is that contacts that do not meet the tort standard of "offensive" should not support liability. However, this approach appears to contradict the logic of the single intent theory since the contact did turn out to be offensive. The outcome in the *White* case can be distinguished—the teacher's contact there clearly turned out to be harmful under the tort definition of that term.

9. This example is like the last, except that here Romeo is aware before he acts that Mercutio is sensitive to physical contacts, even those generally accepted by others. The issue is whether the actor is liable for contacts that are not offensive under the Restatement's "reasonable-sense-of-personal-dignity" standard, but which the actor knows *will be* offensive to a particular hypersensitive individual.

   The Second Restatement declined to take a position on whether there should be liability in a case like this, but the Third Restatement guardedly approves it if the actor knows that the contact is "highly offensive to the other's sense of sense of personal dignity, and the actor contacts the other with the primary purpose that the contact will be highly offensive." Restatement (Third) of Torts: Intentional Torts to Persons (Tentative Draft No. 4 §3(b)).

   This small concession to Mercutio's sensitive nature strikes Your Humble Author as unduly restrictive. Surely the values underlying battery support liability in this case: The purpose of battery is to protect individuals from unwanted intrusions on physical security. Where an actor knows that another *accepts* contacts that others would find offensive (e.g., friends who routinely engage in rough horseplay), his actual knowledge protects him, despite the objective standard usually applied. Conversely, where he knows that another rejects contacts others would tolerate, that knowledge, not the objective standard, should govern his liability. Here Romeo knows this intrusion will be offensive to Mercutio, and he ought to avoid it, even if others would accept the contact.

10. Romeo will doubtless argue that he had no intent, in the battery sense of the term, to hit Polonius. He did not desire to hit him, nor did he know to a substantial certainty that he would hit him—the shoes could have hit anyone.

    Clearly, this is an anemic defense. As long as Romeo knew to a substantial certainty that the shoes would hit *someone*, he knew his act would cause a harmful or offensive contact to the person of another. It should not negate the tort that his act had a large number of potential victims. If that were the case, a terrorist who threw a bomb onto the mezzanine at O'Hare International Airport would not be liable to the strangers he injured, since he couldn't be sure which ones would be hurt, and wished no ill will to any one of them in particular.

This is not really a case of transferred intent. It is not a situation in which he threw at a specific victim and hit another instead. Rather, it is a case in which the actor knows at the outset that he will cause a harmful or offensive touching to someone, but does not know who the victim will be. However, as in transferred intent cases, the intent requirement should be considered met since Romeo's culpability is just as great here as if he had thrown at a particular victim.

Star-Crossed Lovers

11. a. Romeo's romantic gesture would be tortious if Juliet were awake because it is an intentional contact that he knows she would find offensive. But can it be a battery if she doesn't even know about it?

    One need only contemplate examples like the lecherous dentist and the anesthetized patient to confirm that battery must lie in this case. The underlying purpose of battery, to prevent invasions of physical security, will not be fully served if such conduct escapes liability. Juliet's right to be free of unpermitted touchings is infringed just as clearly when she is asleep as it would be if she were awake.

    Romeo will probably argue that she did not find it offensive, since she was not even aware of the contact at the time. The argument will not fly. The requirement of offensive contact is met if it is a contact that the reasonable person in Juliet's circumstances would reject if given the choice. If immediate awareness of the contact were essential, a surgical patient could not be battered, even if the doctor gave her a nose job instead of the contemplated appendectomy. *Mohr v. Williams*, the case in which the doctor operated on the wrong ear, clearly indicates that the unconscious patient can be battered.

    b. There is no requirement to prove damages in order to establish liability for battery. Proving that Romeo intentionally caused an offensive contact establishes Juliet's right to a judgment in her favor. Getting a jury to say that Romeo battered her may even meet Juliet's purpose for bringing the action, to assuage her sense of the invasion of her person.

    However, while a plaintiff has a theoretical right to sue for even a trivial invasion of her person, the majesty of the law is tarnished somewhat by practical realities. While damages are theoretically unnecessary in an intentional tort case, they are crucial as a practical matter. Most lawyers take tort cases on a contingent fee basis, under which they receive a percentage of the damages recovered as their fee. When there is little prospect of recovering substantial damages, the plaintiff will have a hard time finding a lawyer to take her case. Consequently, victims seldom recover for minor batteries, even if they are clearly actionable.

Some Touching Cases

12. a. This is not a battery. It is offensive contact, not offensive conduct, that is required.

 b. This is a case of indirect contact. Romeo did not touch Thibault but has intentionally caused him to come into contact with the alcohol because he acted with the purpose that Thibault would pick it up and drink it after he laced it. This is no different from lacing his drink with poison, although the effect is less drastic. So long as the reasonable teenager at the prom would find this offensive (a debatable issue, perhaps), this is a battery.

 c. Romeo's intent was for Thibault, not Juliet, to drink the vodka. He did not desire nor was he substantially certain that he would cause a contact with Juliet. However, under the doctrine of transferred intent, a party who attempts a battery on one person but actually contacts another is liable for battery. Since Romeo intended to batter Thibault, he is liable if he causes a harmful or offensive contact to Juliet instead.

 This fiction furthers the underlying purpose of battery law, to protect victims of acts intended to cause unwelcome or harmful touchings. Romeo is just as culpable when his plot goes awry as if it hits his intended target. Under the transferred intent doctrine, liability follows in either case.

 d. In this example, Romeo does not even know that Mr. Merola is around when he acts—presumably he would have restrained himself if he had. However, he acted with tortious intent toward Thibault. That intent will transfer to the unintended victim, even if the actor did not know that the unintended victim was there. Romeo tried to cause an offensive touching, and he did; he is liable for it under transferred intent.

 e. This is doubtless pretty upsetting to Thibault, but it is not a battery. Battery requires an intentional harmful or offensive contact to the person, not to one's property. No matter how proud Thibault is of his construction, this doesn't fit the elements. It would, however, constitute trespass to chattels, a distinct intentional tort involving interference with another's personal property.

 f. There is no doubt that Romeo's act here was intentional and meant to offend. The issue is whether Romeo has caused a contact with Thibault. Clearly, if he spat on Thibault, or took pebbles in his mouth and shot them at him, this would be a battery. But smoke? Why not? Smoke is a substance, the particulate products of burning. Why should it matter if the contact is with small particles propelled through the air, instead of a large rock propelled through the air? Although smoke is (arguably) less harmful, it is equally likely to offend, and was clearly meant to in this case. And isn't it equally likely to provoke a breach of the peace?

Advocates for the rights of nonsmokers have long argued that there should be a battery remedy for smoking. See A. Brody & B. Brody, The Legal Rights of Non-Smokers 75-80 (1977); O. Reynolds Jr., Extinguishing Brushfires: Legal Limits on the Smoking of Tobacco, 53 U. Cin. L. Rev. 435, 456-458 (1984). However, the case law on the point is contradictory, and fails to apply battery analysis consistently. For example, *McCracken v. Sloan*, 252 S.E.2d 250 (N.C. App. 1979), found no battery where the defendant smoked in his office during a meeting with the plaintiff:

> Consent is assumed to all those ordinary contacts which are customary and reasonably necessary to the common intercourse of life. Smelling smoke from a cigar being smoked by a person in his own office would ordinarily be considered such an innocuous and generally permitted contact.

252 N.E.2d at 252. The reasoning in *McCracken* is probably outdated, but a more recent case finds no battery from secondhand smoke on even more dubious reasoning. In *Pechan v. Dynapro, Inc.*, 622 N.E.2d 108 (Ill. App. 1993), the plaintiff was continuously exposed to the defendant's smoke, had protested repeatedly, and allegedly was made ill by it. However, the court dismissed her battery claim with the following anemic reasoning:

> [T]he act of smoking generally is not done with the intent of touching others with emitted smoke. [The plaintiff] has not alleged that any of the office's smokers intended that she be exposed to their smoke, or that reasonable persons should have known that their smoke would have contacted [her] in sufficient quantity to reasonably cause the damages claimed.

622 N.E.2d at 119. This analysis blatantly ignores the substantial certainty prong of intent, as well as the maxim that damages are not an essential element of the battery tort.

In *Leichtman v. WLW Jacor Communications, Inc.*, 634 N.E.2d 697 (Ohio App. 1994), the court held that smoke can constitute contact for purposes of battery, where the defendant purposely blew smoke in the face of an antismoking advocate. "Furthermore, tobacco smoke, as 'particulate matter,' has the physical properties capable of making contact." 634 N.E.2d at 699. However, the court inconsistently distinguished the secondhand-smoke situation:

> We do not, however, adopt or lend credence to the theory of "smoker's battery," which imposes liability if there is substantial certainty that exhaled smoke will predictably contact a nonsmoker.

Id. Compare *Golesorkhi v. Lufthansa German Airlines,* 1997 WL 560013 (4th Cir. 1997) (dismissing claim under Virginia law for lack of a "physical touching").

The dubious reasoning in these cases reflects the discomfort courts encounter in extending a traditional tort like battery to new situations. If smoke is held a contact, how about obnoxious horn honkers, the odor of greasy french fries, or loud football spectators? Or, as one student nicely pointed out in my class, how about air pollution from Midwestern power plants? Taking matters further, if courts accept that smoke is contact, and that substantial certainty of that contact constitutes intent, will it recognize a right of secondhand-smoke victims to use self-defense? These problems make courts reluctant to follow the seemingly inevitable logic of smoke as battery. As Justice Holmes famously declared, "The life of the law has not been logic: it has been experience." The Common Law 1 (Little, Brown 1881).

g. The battery action is not a general remedy for obnoxious behavior, but a limit on physical invasions of the person. Here again there is no contact, unless the court were to stretch the contact requirement to include light waves. If it did, battery would lie in every case in which an unpleasant scene was foisted on the unwilling eye. The courts will leave the plaintiff to other remedies on these facts, such as infliction of emotional distress.

h. Here, the motel manager presumably had nothing against Thibault; he simply wanted the benefit of his patronage. But he rented Thibault a room with substantial certainty that Thibault would suffer an offensive contact—with the bedbugs. Judge Posner (a former Torts professor) suggested in *Mathias v. Accor Economy Lodging Inc.,* 347 F.3d 672 (7th Cir. 2003), that such contact would constitute battery. Judge Posner cited "the famous case of *Garratt v. Dailey* . . . which held that the defendant would be guilty of battery if he knew with substantial certainty that when he moved a chair the plaintiff would try to sit down where the chair had been and would land on the floor instead." 347 F.3d at 675.

For another interesting case involving the "substantial certainty" prong of intent and an unusual contacts argument, see *Swope v. Columbian Chemicals Co.,* 281 F.3d 185 (5th Cir. 2002). In *Swope,* the plaintiff was an employee of a chemical company. He alleged that he was exposed at work on a daily basis to excessive levels of ozone, and that the company knew of the exposure and that it caused various health problems. The court held that these allegations stated a battery claim against the company. It noted that the victim need not be aware of the contact at the time it happens. Id. at 196.

In many states, employees cannot bring negligence suits for injuries suffered during their employment—they are limited instead to workers' compensation benefits. However, many workers' compensation statutes do allow suits against employers for *intentional* torts in the course of employment. Students often wonder why we should fuss over the distinction between intentional tort and negligence. *Swope*, in which the plaintiff's lawyer asserted an intentional tort claim to recover a significantly larger award, illustrates one reason that the distinction matters.

13. On first glance, this seems to be a battery because the plaintiff crashed into the bridge abutment. That's a contact if there ever was one.

However, Regan did not have the necessary intent to cause that contact. She did not either desire or know to a substantial certainty that Cordelia would crash into the wall. Presumably, she merely meant to annoy drivers, not to cause a crash, and it is far from substantially certain—though clearly possible—that this brief distraction would cause Cordelia to crash.

Regan did, on the other hand, intend to flash the mirror in Cordelia's eyes: She desired to cause that result, even if she was not substantially certain that her aim would be good enough to hit such a small moving target. But, of course, for battery, there has to be a *contact*, and that means the court would have to conclude that the light rays constitute "contact."

One reader sent me the following e-mail, arguing that the light here satisfies the contact requirement.

> The physics of light is divided into particle theory and wave theory. Although it is certain that light behaves as a wave, physicists more often describe it using particle theory. A particle of light is a photon imparting energy to a surface that it strikes. Under this theory, light is analogous to the smoke of example [12f]. Lasers are highly focused beams of photons having extremely high energy. The difference in a laser and reflected sunlight is a matter of degree, not nature.

This may be good science, but I'm not sure that it would persuade a court that calling light a contact would be good law. Accepting the argument opens the door to slippery-slope arguments in the horn honking and other cases. If Regan had used a high-powered laser that burns through steel, the court would doubtless find a contact. On these facts, however, the court might conclude that there was no contact, and therefore no intentional tort. However, some cases appear to extend the contact requirement to similar scenarios. For a remarkable case on this arcane point, see *Eichenwald v. Rivello*, 318 F.Supp.3d 766 (D. Md. 2018). In *Eichenwald*, the defendant sent the plaintiff—who the defendant knew had epilepsy—a tweet that projected "an animated strobe image flashing at a rapid speed." 318 F.Supp.3d at 769. Viewing the image caused the plaintiff to suffer an epileptic seizure. The court concluded that

> Plaintiff has alleged that light waves emitted from the GIF [Graphic Interchange Format] touched Plaintiff's retina, generated an electric signal, and caused a seizure. Taking Plaintiff's allegations as true . . . there was physical contact.

318 F.Supp.3d at 774. See also *Adams v. Commonwealth*, 534 S.E.2d 347, 351 (Va. Ct. App. 2000) (contact through laser held a battery where it "result[ed] in some manifestation of a physical consequence or corporeal hurt").

If Regan's act was not a battery here, it surely was recklessness or gross negligence, which, of course, gives rise to tort liability as well.

CHAPTER 2

The Action for Assault: A Tort Ahead of Its Time

INTRODUCTION

Historically, tort law has been reluctant to protect mental tranquility alone. For example, courts have not allowed recovery for insult, or for disturbing the plaintiff's peace of mind through distasteful behavior or voicing unpopular opinions. True, some courts have recently begun to redress limited forms of psychic injury, such as infliction of emotional distress and invasion of privacy. But these have gained currency only in the last few decades. If the duration of the common law were an hour, this would represent only the past few minutes.

Assault, however, is an exception to this general principle. The action for assault, which has been with us virtually since the inception of the common law, does allow recovery for interference with peace of mind, even where there is no physical invasion of the victim's person or property. Unlike battery, which requires a tangible, physical invasion, assault protects one form of mental tranquility, the right to be free from fear or apprehension of unwanted contact. In this sense, assault has truly been a tort ahead of its time.

> One of the most important objects to be attained by the enactment of laws and the institutions of civilized society is, each of us shall feel secure against unlawful assaults. Without such security society loses most of its value. Peace and order and domestic happiness, inexpressibly more precious than mere forms of government, cannot be enjoyed without the sense of perfect security. We have a right to live in society without being put in fear of personal harm.

Beach v. Hancock, 27 N.H. 223, 229 (1853). Assault, like battery, protects this right of personal security by authorizing damages for threatened invasion of the person. However, assault is definitely not a general remedy for interference with mental tranquility: It only protects against one narrow type of mental distress, the apprehension of immediate physical aggression.

THE RESTATEMENT DEFINITION

Because assault is an ancient remedy applied in many jurisdictions, the cases vary somewhat in describing its elements. In *Cucinotti v. Ortmann*, 159 A.2d 216, 217 (Pa. 1960), for example, the court held that "an assault may be described as *an act* intended to put another person in reasonable apprehension of an immediate battery, and which succeeds in causing an apprehension of such battery." Compare *Western Union Tel. Co. v. Hill*, 150 So. 709, 710 (Ala. App. 1933): "To constitute an assault there must be an intentional, unlawful, offer to touch the person of another in a rude or angry manner under such circumstances as to create in the mind of the party alleging the assault a well-founded fear of an imminent battery, coupled with the apparent present ability to effectuate the attempt. . . ." Despite such differences, the essence of these definitions is quite similar. The Third Restatement defines assault as follows:

An actor is subject to liability to another for assault if:

> (a)(i) the actor intends to cause the other to anticipate an imminent, and harmful or offensive, contact with his or her person, or
>
> (ii) the actor's intent is sufficient under §110 (transferred intent);
>
> (b) the actor's affirmative conduct causes the other to anticipate an imminent, and harmful or offensive, contact with his or her person . . .

Restatement (Third) of Torts, Tentative Draft No. 1 §105. Under this definition, the defendant must (1) act with intent (2) to place the victim in apprehension of a harmful or offensive contact or to make such a contact, and (3) the victim must reasonably be placed in apprehension of such a contact. These requirements are discussed in detail below.

THE INTENT REQUIREMENT

Assault, like battery, requires intentional conduct, and in the same restrictive sense. The defendant must act with the *purpose* to cause apprehension of a contact or *substantial certainty* that the apprehension will result. Restatement (Second) of Torts §8A. Thus, as in a battery case, the defendant may not avoid liability by claiming that he did not mean to place the plaintiff in fear of an unwanted touching, if he knew to a substantial certainty that fear of a touching would result. Suppose that Owens throws a shot put across the infield while Jackson is standing in the landing area. Owens cannot avoid liability for assault by arguing that he was just warming up for the decathlon. If Jackson was looking at him, Owens must have known that Jackson would reasonably fear being hit. Thus his act is intentional under the Restatement definition, even though he did not do it for the purpose of placing Jackson in fear.[1]

On the other hand, many cases in which plaintiffs are placed in fear of a touching are not intentional as that term is used in intentional tort law. If Jackson loses control of her car on Main Street, and careens over the curb in Owens's direction, Owens will doubtless be placed in fear of being run down. However, Jackson has not acted with a purpose to frighten Owens, or with substantial certainty that the act will frighten him. Jackson may be liable to Owens for negligence, but she has not assaulted him.

Even if Jackson acts intentionally in the sense that she *deliberately* swerves toward the curb, she lacks intent in the intentional tort sense if she does not desire or know to a substantial certainty that she will hit Owens (or place him in apprehension that she will hit him). For example, if Jackson suddenly realizes that her brakes have failed, and steers for the curb to stop the car, her act is intentional in the sense that it was a voluntary, deliberate act, but it would not be an assault if she did not know that Owens was there and would be placed in fear of being hit.

The Restatement definition also provides that one who attempts to batter the plaintiff but misses is liable for assault if the plaintiff is placed in apprehension of a blow. Restatement (Third) of Torts Tentative Draft No 1 §110(b). Suppose, for example, that Rose, infuriated by Owens's bragging that he won more Olympic medals than she did, throws a shot put at him but misses. Even though Rose tried to commit a battery rather than an assault, she is liable to Owens for assault if he sees the shot put coming and is placed in fear of being hit. (On the other hand, if Owens is looking the other way and doesn't know of her act, he is not placed in fear of a harmful touching and has no tort claim for assault.)

This principle, that the intent to batter can also suffice for assault, is obviously akin to the transferred intent doctrine illustrated in Chapter 1. See Example 12c from that chapter, in which Romeo tried to batter Thibault

1. The analysis in this chapter applies the dual intent theory, not single intent. As noted in Chapter 1 (see p. 6), most intentional tort cases would come out the same under single or dual intent analysis.

by lacing his drink, but Juliet drank it instead. In that example, Romeo was liable for battery, even though he had no intent to cause a harmful or offensive contact to Juliet. He intended to batter someone, and did, though by mischance he ended up battering someone other than the intended victim. Somewhat analogously, Rose is liable to Owens for assault, even though she tried to batter him instead. She had the intent necessary to commit an intentional tort, and she did commit one, though by mischance she accomplished assault rather than battery.

Because assault only protects against fear of a harmful or offensive contact, the plaintiff must prove that she feared the type of contact that would support a battery claim if it actually occurred. Thus, the analysis in Chapter 1 of the meaning of *harmful or offensive* is also necessary in assault cases. If a contact would not have been harmful or offensive had it been made, the threat of that contact is not an assault either. If Leonard and Spinks often slap each other on the shoulder in jest before sparring, their contacts are not offensive and do not constitute battery. Thus, if Spinks moves to slap Leonard, he does not commit an assault, since Leonard anticipates a touching, but not a harmful or offensive one.

NOTHING TO FEAR BUT APPREHENSION ITSELF

Actually, the word "fear," though it is often loosely used in the cases, is not quite accurate. The Restatement definition requires that the defendant cause "apprehension" of a harmful or offensive contact. *Apprehension* as used here means the perception or anticipation of a blow rather than fright. Assault protects not only against the fear of an unwelcome contact, but also against the mere expectation or anticipation of one. If Dillard threatens to spit on Baxter's shoes, Baxter will anticipate, or apprehend, an unwelcome and demeaning contact, which would be a battery if it actually took place. This anticipation is sufficient for an assault claim, even though Baxter is not frightened in the usual sense of that term.

The Restatement definition also requires that the apprehended contact be *imminent*; that is, the defendant's act must cause the victim to expect that he is about to be touched. This imminence requirement obviously raises slippery-slope problems. Since the dawn of the Socratic method, Torts professors have tortured (no pun intended) students with barely distinguishable assault hypotheticals: Dillard swings an axe at Oda from a foot away, from four feet away, through a window, from across the room, from the end of the street, but he's a faster runner than Oda, and so on. The Restatement suggests that "imminent"

> does not mean immediate, in the sense of instantaneous contact, as where the other sees the actor's fist about to strike his nose. It means rather that there will be no significant delay. It is not necessary that one shall be within striking distance of the other, or that a weapon pointed at the other shall be in a condition for instant discharge. It is enough that one is so close to striking distance that he can reach the other almost at once, or that he can make the weapon ready for discharge in a very short interval of time.

Restatement (Second) of Torts §29 cmt. b.

This explanation still leaves line-drawing problems in applying the imminence requirement. However, the fact that there will be close cases (again, no pun intended!) is hardly a fatal criticism of the requirement. Close factual issues of this sort will be decided by the jury, under careful instructions as to the meaning of assault. The jurors' practical intuition about what actions are likely to cause reasonable apprehension will lead to a just decision in most cases. On the other hand, it is clear that fear of a *future* contact will not support liability for assault. "If you try out for the Olympic team next month, I'm going to bust your nose" is not an assault since the threat is not of an imminent contact.

Perhaps such threats for the future *should* be assaults. They are reprehensible, and may be very unsettling to aspiring athletes. Realistically, however, the law can't protect everyone from everything; it has to pick its targets. Such general, future threats suggest possible, vaguely formed (and hence, changeable) intention, perhaps even mere braggadocio. Consequently, they are likely to be less intimidating than the raised fist of an incensed assailant. In addition, future threats leave the victim time to take other steps to prevent the harm, such as going to the police or avoiding the assailant. Thus, they are less likely to provoke immediate retaliation by the victim.

Sometimes a defendant may place the reasonable person in apprehension of an unwanted contact even though he could not actually batter her. Suppose, for example, that Landy brandishes a realistic-looking toy pistol at Oda. It may reasonably appear to Oda that the pistol is real, and that Landy intends to shoot her. Even though Landy could not actually accomplish a battery with the toy pistol, this is assault since she had the "apparent present ability" to cause an unwanted contact. Put another way, assault turns on whether the defendant's act would place a reasonable person in apprehension of an unwanted contact, not whether the aggressor is in fact able to make the threatened contact. Assault protects the victim's right to be free of meaningful threats of unwanted touchings. Landy's threat obviously could be mighty disturbing even if she could not actually shoot Oda. (On the other hand, if Oda knows the pistol is a toy, she will not apprehend such a touching, and Landy will not be liable for assault.)

THE "MERE WORDS" PROBLEM

The requirement that the victim anticipate an imminent battery has led many courts to hold that *mere words* alone cannot constitute an assault, because they do not sufficiently show the defendant's purpose to immediately batter the victim. For example, a defendant who growls at the victim, "I'm going to wring your neck!" might be held not to commit an assault, but if he extracts a rope from his pocket and proceeds to wind it around his hands, his act provides the necessary evidence of an imminent intent to batter the plaintiff.

This problem of assault by words alone is intractable. The requirement that the defendant go beyond mere words to commit a threatening act is meant to distinguish between bluster and real aggression. Some cases have been quite strict in requiring such an act. In *Cucinotti v. Ortmann*, 159 A.2d 216 (Pa. 1960), for example, the plaintiffs alleged that the defendants confronted them and threatened that they would commit "immediate bodily harm upon the plaintiffs, and would strike the plaintiffs with blackjacks and would otherwise hit them with great force and violence." Id. at 218. The court held that the complaint did not state a claim for assault since no threatening act was alleged. The *Cucinotti* court even held that an allegation that the defendants produced the blackjacks and showed them to the plaintiffs would not state a claim for assault. Id. at 218-219.

The Second Restatement of Torts, however, suggests a more flexible approach to this problem:

> Words do not make the actor liable for assault *unless together with other acts or circumstances* they put the other in reasonable apprehension of an imminent harmful or offensive contact with his person.

Restatement (Second) of Torts §31 (emphasis added). Accord: Restatement of the Law (Third): Intentional Torts to Persons (Tentative Draft No. 1) §105 cmt. g. The italicized clause suggests that circumstances may suffice to make words actionable as an assault if they reasonably cause the victim to fear an imminent contact. Courts are likely to be realistic in assessing the defendant's intent; where the circumstances clearly indicate that he is about to strike, very little more than words—such as a step, a rolling up of sleeves, or a drawing back of fists—will suffice to take the case to the jury. Even without that, courts may allow recovery based on the words and surrounding circumstances alone, if those circumstances are compelling enough. For example, some courts, relying on §31 of the Second Restatement, would probably allow recovery on the facts of *Cucinotti*. For cases finding assault despite the absence of an obvious aggressive act, see *Gouin v. Gouin*, 249 F. Supp. 2d 62 (D. Mass. 2003) ("you can either do it my way or I can beat you half to death") and *Vetter v. Morgan*, 913 P.2d 1200,

1204 (Kan. App. 1995) (threat to pull plaintiff from van sufficed under the circumstances).

CONDITIONAL THREATS

Other factors may also undermine the imminence element of assault. Suppose that Oda snarls at Rudolph, "If you hadn't fouled out of the hundred-meter competition, I'd beat you to a pulp." Here, Oda's own threat defeats the assault since her words indicate that she does not plan to carry it out. Her comment is still unpleasant and unwelcome, but it is not likely to make Rudolph anticipate immediate invasion of her physical security. Similarly, the defendant who states, "If you were not an old man, I would knock you senseless," does not assault the plaintiff since his own words negate the intent to cause a harmful contact.

Some threats, however, will constitute assault even though they are conditional. Suppose that Oda snarls at Rudolph, "If you don't get off this track, I'll kick your tail into next week." This folksy threat is conditional, in the sense that Rudolph can avoid the threatened battery by leaving. At least in theory, she need not fear a blow, because she holds the means of avoiding it. Obviously, however, this should still be an assault. Otherwise, Rudolph could be forced to abandon her right to walk the streets (or run the track) in order to avoid battery. Bullies would be able to impose their will on others by the threat of force, yet incur no liability. One need only pose a slightly more extreme hypothetical ("If you don't go to bed with me, I'll throw you out this window") to make clear that the imposition of a condition that the assailant has no right to impose will not defeat an assault, even though the plaintiff can avoid being struck by complying with the unlawful demand.[2] See, e.g., *Holcombe v. Whitaker*, 318 So. 2d 289, 294 (Ala. 1975) (liability for conditional threat where no right to impose the condition).

CRIMINAL ASSAULT DISTINGUISHED

Since the early days of the common law, assault has been recognized not only as a tort, but as a crime as well. However, the crime of assault has not

2. On the other hand, if the defendant *does* have a right to make a conditional threat, he is not liable for doing so. "If you don't get off my land, I will put you off," threatens physical force, but the owner has a right to use reasonable force to eject a trespasser. Restatement (Second) of Torts §77. Even if this frightens the trespasser, it is not an assault, since the statement is privileged.

always been equated with the tort of assault. Historically, criminal assault was usually defined as an attempt to commit a battery. *Pope v. State,* 79 N.Y.S.2d 466, 471 (1948), *aff'd,* 99 N.Y.S.2d 1019 (1950) (defining assault as "an unlawful offer or attempt with force or violence to do corporal hurt to another"); W. LaFave, Criminal Law §16.3. This definition does not specify that the victim must anticipate the blow; the mere attempt to batter suffices. Under this criminal law definition, if Haines throws a javelin at Mathias, intending to injure him, he commits a criminal assault, whether or not Mathias sees it coming. However, this would not constitute the civil tort of assault if Mathias were unaware of the oncoming javelin, since he would not be placed in apprehension of a blow.

By contrast, if Owens pretended to throw the javelin at Mathias simply to frighten him, without intending to release it, this would be an assault in the tort sense of the term (if Mathias saw him do so), since it would doubtless place Mathias in fear of being skewered. But it would not be criminal assault under the traditional approach if Owens had no intent to throw, since he had not in fact attempted a battery. Similarly, if an assailant has no ability to cause the battery, as where Mathias threatens Owens from a distance with an empty gun, he does not commit a criminal assault under the traditional definition, but would commit the tort of assault.

In recent years, many states have amended their criminal statutes to make conduct that constitutes assault in the tort sense punishable as a criminal assault as well. A majority of states now make either act—attempted battery or placing in anticipation of a battery—a criminal offense. W. LaFave, Criminal Law §16.3(b). But the historical distinction lingers in the form of confusing statements in the cases, such as the oft-repeated statement that "every battery includes an assault." *Western Union Tel. Co. v. Hill,* 150 So. 709, 710 (Ala. App. 1933). That is clearly untrue in the tort context: If the defendant kicks a sleeping plaintiff, he commits the tort of battery, but not the tort of assault, since he has not placed the defendant in fear of the contact.

The following examples probe the various elements of assault. In considering them, assume that the Restatement definition applies. After the examples, there is a brief discussion of how to plead the elements of assault and battery, together with an illustrative complaint.

Examples

Fear and Trembling

1. Hennie, an Olympic figure skater, is about to perform her final routine in the women's individual skating event. She brings her music CD, meticulously edited and carefully guarded over four years of preparation, into the arena and puts it on the table by the CD player. Wilson, a sports cartoonist with a sick sense of humor, puts the CD on the floor and pretends

to jump up and down on it while Hennie looks on from across the ice. Hennie is terrified that it will be broken. Can she sue Wilson for assault?

2. The malicious Wilson crawls into the grid above the rink and loosens a heavy Olympic banner. He drops the banner as Hennie skates under him, but it sails a bit and lands ten feet behind her. She then turns and sees the banner lying on the ice and is shocked to think how close she came to being injured.
   a. Does she have an assault claim against Wilson?
   b. Is Wilson guilty of the *crime* of assault?

3. Wilson lets the banner go, aiming for the unsuspecting Hennie, who is concentrating on her routine. As the banner falls, she looks up, sees it coming, and skates to safety. Is this an assault?

4. Assume that Hennie sees the banner coming, but she can't get out of the way in time. Hennie is hit, though not injured. Can she sue for assault?

5. Wilson crawls up into the grid, sees a skater below, thinks it's Hennie, and drops the banner. However, the skater is actually Thomas, who looks up, sees the banner falling, and barely escapes being hit. Can Thomas sue Wilson for assault?

Some Variations

6. Button, Hennie's partner in the doubles competition, is sitting in the stands and sees the banner fall toward her. He is terrified that she will be hit. He sues Wilson for assault. What result?

7. Suppose that Button was warming up at the same time as Hennie. Wilson, while climbing across the grid to loosen the banner, knocks an iron clamp off a beam. Button, alerted by a spectator, looks up in alarm and sees it coming at him, but manages to duck out of the way. Is Wilson liable to him for assault?

8. Wilson, a fan of the Russian sprinters, approaches the U.S. track coach. He shakes his fist and snarls, "If you run Ashford on the anchor leg of the women's four-hundred-meter relay tomorrow, I'll see that you never walk again." Is this an assault?

Judge Fudd at the Olympics

9. Hennie is practicing for her routine while the Zamboni (that big machine that grooms the ice) circles the rink. As she gracefully executes a backward glide, Wilson yells to her, "Watch it! You're going to hit the Zamboni!" Although Hennie is startled, the Zamboni is actually on the other end of the rink. Hennie sues Wilson for assault.

a. Whether Wilson is liable for this conduct will depend on how the jury is instructed on the definition of assault. Consider the Restatement definition and the definition in the *Cucinotti* case, both quoted at p. 26. If you represented Hennie, which would you ask Judge Fudd to use in instructing the jury, and why?
b. If you represented Wilson, what other argument would you raise that Hennie could not meet the prima facie elements of an assault claim?
c. Gibson, the driver of the Zamboni, realizes that Hennie is still somewhere on the ice, but starts grooming the ice anyway. Coming around the end of the rink, Gibson suddenly reverses direction, turning quickly back the way she had come, and nearly hits Hennie, skating behind the Zamboni. Is this an assault?

The Impossible Dream

10. Corbett, a four-foot-nine-inch gymnast, approaches Press, a 250-pound shot-putter who has just beaten out the American favorite in the shot put competition. Shaking her fist at her, she growls, "Press, wipe that smile off your face, or I'll wipe it off for you!" Press sues Corbett for assault. Is she liable?

11. Press, as it turns out, is a sensitive type. She is so upset by Corbett's threat that she develops a phobia about competition and goes into therapy to overcome it. She sues Corbett for a substantial sum for these consequences. Is Corbett liable for them?

Outrageous Fortune

12. Mathias, a rival of Weismuller, decides to upset him before the finals. While Weismuller is warming up, Mathias runs at him suddenly, startling Weismuller, who turns to run and sprains an ankle. Weismuller is taken to the hospital. While he is being treated, there is a fire in the hospital and Weismuller is burned. Is Mathias liable for his burns?

Explanations

Fear and Trembling

1. In this example, Hennie clearly would be traumatized by Wilson's conduct, but would not succeed in an action for assault. Assault addresses only one narrow form of emotional distress, apprehension of a contact with the person of the plaintiff. That is not what Wilson has threatened in this case. Wilson did not intend to touch Hennie, nor did she fear that he would. Since assault only protects against threatened contacts with the plaintiff herself, this is not an assault.

It surely is obnoxious behavior, though. Hennie ought to have a remedy for such conduct, even if it can't be shoe-horned into the elements of assault. If it isn't assault, it must be *something*, or else the law ought to make it something and give it a name so Hennie can recover. Traditionally, the common law did not provide a remedy for such antisocial acts—the courts did not attempt to redress all grievances, but confined themselves to the most venal. Only recently have the cases begun to develop the tort of infliction of emotional distress, which allows recovery for acts that cause severe distress, regardless of whether a physical threat was made. See also Restatement (Second) of Torts §870 (supporting liability for intentional infliction of harm that does not fit the elements of traditional intentional torts). But the assault tort, too hoary with age to learn new tricks, only applies to threats to the plaintiff herself.

2. a. When Hennie turns and sees the banner, she realizes that she might have been hit and is justifiably upset, but this is still not an assault. There is a difference between apprehending an imminent injury and realizing, after the fact, that you have narrowly escaped one. The elements of assault require that the plaintiff be placed in apprehension of an imminent contact. Hennie's post hoc awareness that the banner almost hit her may be equally disturbing, but it isn't an assault.

   As in the last case, our instincts tell us there should be a remedy for this kind of behavior. If there is, however, it will have to be under the rubric of intentional infliction of emotional distress or some other cause of action such as "prima facie tort" (see Restatement (Second) of Torts §870), not assault. The assault cause of action is too arthritic to be stretched this far.

   b. Under the traditional criminal law approach, an attempted battery is an assault. Wilson's act would constitute criminal assault if, as the example suggests, he acted with a purpose to hit Hennie when he dropped the banner. But the *tort* of assault is not synonymous with attempted battery; it requires that the actor place the plaintiff in apprehension of an impending, not a past, touching.

3. In this case, Wilson tried to hit Hennie, not frighten her. Indeed, the success of his scheme probably turned on her ignorance of the peril since she could skate away if she knew it was on the way. Thus, Wilson may try to argue that he did not intend to cause Hennie to apprehend an imminent contact, only to make the contact itself.

   The argument fails under the Restatement definition of assault. Although Wilson only tried to commit the battery itself, he is liable for assault since he acted with tortious intent and placed Hennie in apprehension of a harmful touching. Under Restatement (Third) of Torts, the intent requirement is met if Wilson was trying *either* to cause the contact (as he was in this case) or to cause Hennie to apprehend it, and she actually suffers such apprehension.

4. Since the banner actually hit Hennie, this is a battery, even though she suffered no injury. Only an unwelcome touching, not resulting harm, is necessary to complete the battery. But Hennie suffered an assault as well since she saw the banner coming and was placed in apprehension that she would be hit by it. The torts of battery and assault often occur together, though of course the elements of each must be separately satisfied.

   If Hennie had not seen it coming, she would have suffered a battery but not an assault, since she would not have experienced apprehension of the impending contact, but only the contact itself.

5. The twist in this example is that Wilson made a mistake about who the skater was. Clearly, his act should be an assault. Wilson had the necessary intent to cause an assault (or a battery, which would also suffice), and he actually did place the skater in apprehension of a harmful touching. Yet, he had no intent to assault *Thomas*.

   While this example looks a little like a transferred intent case, transferred intent does not apply. Wilson did not aim at one person and hit another: He aimed at Thomas and she is the one who suffered the apprehension. The problem is that he made a mistake about her identity.

   In the law of intentional torts, this is analyzed under the aptly named doctrine of mistake. Generally, a tortfeasor will be liable to a victim even if mistaken about her identity. After all, Wilson saw Thomas, aimed at her, and meant to hit her. He's a bad actor; he *ought* to be liable! Imagine that he had shot Thomas, thinking she was Hennie. It would be outrageous if he could defend on the ground that he thought she was someone else. He can't. As the aggressor, Wilson is liable for his tortious act whether the victim is the person he thought she was or not.

   There's a lovely old case on mistake, *Ranson v. Kitner*, 31 Ill. App. 241 (1888), in which the defendant shot and killed the plaintiff's dog, thinking it was a wolf. In *Ranson*, the court held the defendant liable, throwing the risk of the mistake on the defendant. It seems appropriate, where the actor acts for the antisocial purpose of causing a harmful or offensive touching, to place the risk of mistake on him. Another example is the intentional tort of trespass to land: Tort law holds an actor liable for trespass if she enters land of another, even if she mistakenly believes it to be her own. See Dobbs, Hayden & Bublick, Dobbs' Law of Torts §50 (cited hereafter as "Dobbs' Law of Torts"). The intent requirement is met since the actor intended to enter the land; the law places the risk of mistake as to ownership on the actor.

Some Variations

6. In this example, Button has been placed in fear that Hennie will suffer a harmful or offensive contact. This is not assault, however, because assault protects only the intended victim from threats of bodily contact, not bystanders who fear for the victim's welfare. Restatement (Second) of Torts §26 cmt. a.

   Since threats to physical security are considered so antisocial, and are so easily avoided by a little self-restraint, why not allow Button to recover on facts like these? Broadening the right to recover would further deter assaultive conduct, and remedy real infringements of Button's mental tranquility.

   Perhaps so, but if we allow Button to recover, why not Hennie's manager—or her boyfriend, or anyone in the audience, or anyone who sees it on TV? Naturally, Button has more at stake than some of these bystanders, but each may suffer real distress from the fear that Hennie will be injured. Opening up the tort to third persons may not be worth the candle, since in most cases the truly distressed person will be the intended victim.

7. Wilson has placed Button in fear of a harmful or offensive contact with the clamp, but he has not acted intentionally in the restricted intentional tort sense. He may have carelessly knocked the clamp down, but he did not do it for the purpose of hitting or frightening Button, nor was he substantially certain at the time that it would do so.

   At the time of the act, however, Wilson was on his way to commit an intentional tort on Hennie by dropping the banner on her. Can Button's counsel make a transferred intent argument based on this? It seems not; transferred intent applies where a specific act is done with tortious intent and misfires. Here, the act of knocking down the clamp was not done with intent to hit or frighten anyone. Button cannot prove intent by showing that Wilson was planning to commit a tort later on someone else. He must focus on the act that placed him in apprehension of a harmful touching. That act may have been negligent, but was not done for the purpose or with substantial certainty that it would cause such apprehension.

8. In this example Wilson has threatened the coach with physical violence if he does not comply with Wilson's demands. Naturally, Wilson has no right to tell the U.S. track coach who to run in the relays, so the fact that the coach can avoid the threat by doing as he is told does not prevent this from being an assault. However, it isn't an assault anyway, since Wilson has not threatened the coach with an imminent contact. A threat to do something tomorrow almost certainly is not imminent; a future threat, while reprehensible, does not satisfy the imminence requirement.

Judge Fudd at the Olympics

9. a. It would be crucial for Hennie to convince the judge to instruct the jury in terms of the Restatement definition instead of that given in the *Cucinotti* case. *Cucinotti*, if you read the definition carefully, requires that the defendant place the plaintiff in apprehension of a *battery*. Here, presumably Hennie anticipated an accidental collision with the Zamboni, not a deliberate battery by the driver. If apprehension of a battery is necessary, Wilson would not be liable.

   Under the Restatement definition, however, the defendant need only cause the victim to apprehend a harmful or offensive contact, not necessarily a contact by the defendant, or one which meets the elements of battery. See Restatement (Second) of Torts §25 (victim need not be placed in fear of a touching from the actor in order to constitute assault). Under the Restatement definition, Wilson could be liable, since he caused Hennie to fear a harmful contact, though not a contact with Wilson or one which would constitute a battery at all.

   There are many ways an actor can place a victim in fear of harmful or offensive touchings without threatening a battery. Consider the following:

   - When passing a construction site: "Watch out, a plank is falling on your head!"
   - While camping in the desert: "Don't move; there's a rattler next to your foot!"
   - While riding up in a ski lift: "Jump! The cable's about to snap!"

   Such obnoxious tricks can be mighty disturbing to one's mental tranquility. The drafters of the Restatement evidently concluded that inflicting such apprehension should be actionable. See Restatement (Second) of Torts §25 illus. 1 (actor liable for sounding a buzzer behind the victim in the desert, placing him in fear of a snake bite). However, your author has found no cases either imposing or denying liability in such circumstances.

   b. Wilson's counsel will doubtless argue that this is a case of mere words, without any act. Yet, as the introduction suggests, words together with circumstances can create reasonable apprehension of unwanted contact. The Second Restatement (§31 cmt. d) gives the example of a thief who stands in the dark road, holding a gun but without moving, and says, "stand and deliver!" These mere words, in context, certainly incite a fear of an imminent harmful touching; the discussion in the Restatement comment clearly suggests that the thief could be sued for assault. Accord: Restatement of the Law (Third): Intentional Torts to Persons (Tentative Draft No. 1) §105 cmt. g.

Similarly, here, it seems likely that Wilson's words and excited tone of voice, together with the circumstance that Hennie is skating backward while the Zamboni is grooming the ice, would reasonably cause her to fear hitting the machine, even if Wilson does not move a muscle. Under the Restatement's approach, a court would likely uphold a finding of assault on these facts.

c. Although Gibson has acted "intentionally" in the sense that she meant to turn the Zamboni, the example suggests that she did not know that Hennie was behind her. Thus, she did not act for the purpose of placing Hennie in apprehension, nor did she know to a substantial certainty that she would do so. Her act may have been negligent, but was not an assault.

The Impossible Dream

10. Perhaps your first response here is that Press would have to be dreaming to be at all intimidated by Corbett's threat. Given the disparity in their size, the reasonable shot-putter would not have feared a threat from Corbett, so arguably no assault occurred.

    However, while Press doubtless was *not frightened* by Corbett's threat, her conduct does cause Press to *apprehend* an unwelcome contact from her—surely Corbett has the present ability to attack Press, even if she was unlikely to cause her any substantial harm. The action for assault protects victims from the anticipation of unwelcome contacts, even where they are confident that they can adequately defend themselves. Put another way, assault turns on the acts and intent of the defendant, not on how good the victim is at self-defense. The strong have a right to physical autonomy as well as the weak, and should not be placed in the position of having to defend themselves from such invasions. Corbett is liable for assault.

11. In this example, the plaintiff reacts to the assault in an unexpected manner. Corbett's threat would be a minor annoyance to the average shot-putter, but Press is a hypersensitive soul who is really upset and permanently affected by it. The example is reminiscent of Example 8 in Chapter 1, in which Mercutio is upset by a good-natured slap on the back that other athletes would casually accept.

    Although it may be reminiscent of the Mercutio example, this case is different. In that example, Romeo did not commit a battery, since the reasonable person under the circumstances would not be offended by the contact Romeo made. Consequently, he was not a tortfeasor at all, and was not liable even though Mercutio was actually distressed. Here, however, Corbett did commit an assault, since she threatened a contact that would be offensive to the reasonable person. Consequently, she *is* a tortfeasor, and is liable for the damages Press suffers as a result of the tort—*all* the damages she suffers, even though they exceed the damage one would anticipate from the conduct.

The difference between these two examples is important to understand. In the Mercutio example, the fact that the reasonable person would not be offended by the contact goes to the existence of liability in the first place. In the Press example, because a reasonable person would find the impending contact offensive, the threat is tortious. Since Corbett has committed a tort, she "takes the plaintiff as she finds her." She is liable for the actual damages Press suffers, even if they are greater than the average shot-putter would experience from the tortious conduct.

Outrageous Fortune

12. In this example, Mathias clearly assaulted Weismuller. He will certainly be liable to him for the ankle sprain. But would a court go so far as to hold Mathias liable for the freak burn injury Weismuller suffered while at the hospital?

    It is often broadly stated that intentional tortfeasors are liable for all the consequences of their torts, even unintended consequences. For example, where Brutus tripped Cassius in Chapter 1, and Cassius unexpectedly fell down the stairs, I suggested that Brutus would be liable for all of Cassius's injuries, even though they are greater than Brutus intended. See p. 8.

    However, the result may be different where the subsequent injury is unforeseeable, as the burn injury is here. If Mathias had caused Weismuller's ankle sprain through negligence, the concept of proximate cause would probably bar Weismuller from recovering for the unforeseeable burn injury. See Chapter 12. While courts often impose liability for unexpected consequences on intentional tortfeasors, there is probably some foreseeability limit in intentional tort cases as well. The Third Restatement recognizes that there is a limit to the scope of liability even for intentional torts. See Third Restatement of Torts: Liability for Physical and Emotional Harm §33(b) (in considering whether to impose liability for unexpected harm from an intentional tort, the court should consider the moral culpability of the actor, the seriousness of the harm intended, and the degree to which the actor's conduct deviated from appropriate care). Here, Mathias's spur-of-the-moment act seems relatively mild compared to the severe consequences that ensued and the unexpected manner in which they occurred. Despite the occasional language in the cases suggesting that there is no proximate cause limit on intentional tort liability, the court would likely refuse to make Mathias pay for Weismuller's burn injury, even though he committed an intentional tort.

PLEADING CLAIMS FOR ASSAULT AND BATTERY

These two chapters have analyzed the substantive elements of assault and battery, that is, the basic facts the plaintiff must show to establish that the defendant is liable. It may be useful to see how these elements are presented to a court in a complaint for assault and battery.

The first step in seeking recovery for a tort claim is to file a complaint alleging that the defendant has committed a tort and demanding damages. A well-crafted complaint should allege a *prima facie* case, that is, the basic facts establishing that defendant's conduct fits the elements of the tort for which the plaintiff seeks damages. In an assault complaint, the plaintiff must allege facts that show that the defendant intentionally placed her in apprehension of a harmful or offensive touching. A battery complaint must allege facts that show that the defendant intentionally caused such a harmful or offensive touching. In addition, the plaintiff should allege the harm that resulted from the assault and the relief (usually money damages) that she seeks as compensation.

Often, a single incident will support claims for both assault and battery. Figure 2-1 is an example of such a complaint. Like most court papers, it is basically straightforward. It begins by identifying the parties (paragraphs 1 and 2) and then briefly setting forth the events that gave rise to the claim. See paragraphs 3-5. The complaint then recasts the facts in terms of legal causes of action, in individual *counts* or *claims for relief.* Paragraph 7 of Juliet's First Claim for Relief specifically alleges that Romeo's conduct satisfies the elements of an assault: an act ("threatened to strike her and shook his fist"), intent ("intentionally"), and resulting fear of a touching ("placing her in fear that he was about to strike her"). Paragraph 8 does the same for the second assault alleged. Paragraph 11 similarly alleges the elements of battery. Thus, the complaint demonstrates that the plaintiff claims she can establish the facts necessary to recover for each tort. In addition, it alleges the injuries suffered as a result of the defendant's tortious acts (paragraphs 9 and 12).

Finally, Juliet's counsel includes a demand for damages (the "wherefore" clause following paragraph 13). The damage demand here far exceeds the actual out-of-pocket costs Juliet incurred; a large part of the injury in intentional tort cases is intangible emotional harm, such as distress, pain and suffering, and humiliation resulting from the invasion. Such damages are genuine but hard to quantify; hence, plaintiffs often demand a good deal more than their out-of-pocket damages in cases involving such intangible elements as pain and suffering, emotional distress, interference with reputation, or other psychic injuries. Similarly, punitive damages, which may be awarded for intentional torts in some states to punish and deter tortious conduct, also may lead to an award of damages which far exceeds the plaintiff's economic damages from the tort.

2. The Action for Assault: A Tort Ahead of Its Time

STATE OF WEST DAKOTA

CONKLIN COUNTY, SS.	CIVIL ACTION NO. 25-7192
JANE JULIET, Plaintiff, v. RONALD ROMEO, Defendant	COMPLAINT FOR ASSAULT AND BATTERY

1. The plaintiff is an individual residing at 332 Ruiz Circle, Arlington, West Dakota.

2. The defendant is an individual residing at 11 Rolvag Way, Arlington, West Dakota.

3. On February 6, 2025, the defendant approached the plaintiff in the main hall of Arlington High School, in Arlington, West Dakota, raised his right arm with the fist clenched, and threatened to punch her if she did not stop seeing a classmate, Michael Mercutio.

4. When the plaintiff refused to agree, the defendant deliberately grabbed her by the arm, squeezed it hard, and knocked her to the ground.

5. As a result of the defendant's acts, the plaintiff suffered a bruised arm, and abrasions on both knees requiring medical treatment. She also suffered severe pain, fear, and emotional distress.

FIRST CLAIM FOR RELIEF—ASSAULT

6. The plaintiff repeats and realleges the allegations in paragraphs one to five of the complaint.

7. The defendant committed an assault on the plaintiff when he intentionally and without her consent threatened to strike her and shook his fist, placing her in fear that he was about to strike her.

Figure 2-1

8. The defendant committed a further assault when he intentionally and without her consent reached out to grab the plaintiff's arm, placing her in fear that he was about to strike her.

9. As a result of these assaults, the plaintiff suffered fear, humiliation, and emotional distress, and was unable to attend school or engage in other usual activities for two weeks.

SECOND CLAIM FOR RELIEF—BATTERY

10. The plaintiff repeats and realleges the allegations in paragraphs one to five of the complaint.

11. The defendant committed a battery upon the plaintiff when he intentionally and without her consent grabbed her arm and threw her to the ground.

12. As a result of the defendant's acts, the plaintiff suffered bruises and abrasions on both knees, extensive pain and suffering, fear, humiliation, and emotional distress.

13. As a further result of the defendant's acts, the plaintiff incurred $800 in medical expenses for treatment, and was unable to return to school or engage in other usual activities for a period of two weeks.

WHEREFORE, the plaintiff seeks the following relief:

1. Compensatory damages in the amount of $8,000.
2. Punitive damages in the amount of $10,000.
3. Interest from the date of judgment as allowed by W.D. Rev. Code §14:103.
4. Her costs of suit.

The plaintiff claims trial by jury in this action.

By her attorney

____

Luis Mendez
84 Main Street, Suite 4
Arlington, WD 58102
(901) 225-1093

Figure 2-1 (continued)

CHAPTER 3

Protecting the Right of Possession: Trespass to Land

INTRODUCTION

The tort of battery protects against unwelcome intrusions to the person, basically, touchings to the body. Assault protects against the anticipation of such intrusions. Trespass to land provides a legal remedy for intrusions upon one's real property, that is, on land owned or occupied by the plaintiff. We all know what a trespasser is — someone who comes on another's land without permission. As one of the casebooks suggests, "Trespassers tend to be thought of as fence-breaking, chicken-stealing no-accounts."[1] But to sue for trespass, a plaintiff still must prove a set of carefully defined elements of the tort.

THE ELEMENTS OF TRESPASS

Even stating those elements turns out to be a bit complex. The Second Restatement of Torts defines trespass as follows:

> §158. One is subject to liability to another for trespass, irrespective of whether he thereby causes harm to any legally protected interest of the other, if he intentionally

1. J. Henderson, R. Pearson, & D. Kysar, The Torts Process 439 (9th ed. 2017).

(a) enters land in the possession of the other, or causes a thing or a third person to do so, or

(b) remains on the land, or

(c) fails to remove from the land a thing which he is under a duty to remove.

Note some points about this definition. First, trespass is an intentional tort. In order to be a trespasser, the actor must act with a purpose to cause the intrusion on land, or with substantial certainty that she will cause it. Negligently causing entry on Astor's land will not support a claim for trespass . . . though it may support a claim for negligence. So the analysis of intent in Chapter 1 applies to trespass as well as to assault and to battery.

Various corollaries of intent analysis will also apply, such as the doctrine of transferred intent. If Connors gets mad at Lugo and hurls a rock at him, intending to batter him, but misses, and the rock rolls onto Parvi's land, Connor has committed trespass to land. He intended to cause a battery, but accomplished an unauthorized entry on the land of another, a trespass. He is liable for trespass under transferred intent.

Similarly, a mistake by the actor is treated the same way in analyzing intent for trespass as it is for battery or assault. An actor is liable for entry on property of another, even if she believes that she is on her own property, or some other property where she is entitled to be. Suppose that Ramone wanders back into the woods behind her house, believing she is still on her own land, but has actually drifted across the line into Wang's woods. She is a trespasser, even though she doesn't know it and didn't "intend" to be. She did intend to walk where she walked, and her intentional walking caused an intrusion on the inviolable grounds of her neighbor. She may be morally innocent, but from the tort point of view she takes the risk of her imperfect understanding of the boundaries of her lot. Restatement (Second) of Torts §164.

Note, too, that damage to the property is not an element of trespass to land: Under §158, the unauthorized entrant is liable "irrespective of whether he thereby causes harm to any legally protected interest of the other." This allows a court to award at least nominal damages for the intrusion, in order to vindicate an owner's right to sole possession of her property. Historically, this provided a legal vehicle for determining possessory rights in land. Lord Snobbin could sue Jack Sprat for trespass based on the mere fact that Jack walked on the property, even though he hadn't bent a blade of grass. The court would have to determine Snobbin's title to the property in order to determine whether Jack was a trespasser, and a judgment for Snobbin for nominal damages would confirm his title. Historically the tort of trespass to land was probably used as much for this purpose—to prevent trespassers from acquiring easements or adverse possession rights[2]—as it was to remedy significant economic damages to the property.

THE ROLE OF CONSENT

Suppose that Paredes invites Marshall to his birthday party. At the appointed time Marshall shows up and knocks on the door, and Paredes declares her a trespasser. Under §158 of the Second Restatement, Marshall appears to be a trespasser: She has intentionally entered Paredes land, and nothing in the Second Restatement definition excuses an actor just because she had permission to enter. But of course consent to Marshall's entry will defeat a claim for trespass. For simplicity's sake, let's think of it as a defense or privilege which, if established, defeats the right to recover, even though the prima facie elements—(1) intentional (2) entry (3) on the land of another—have been proved.

The Second Restatement tucked this point away near the end of its four-volume compendium of black letter tort principles:

> **§892A. Effect of Consent**
>
> (1) One who effectively consents to conduct of another intended to invade his interests cannot recover in an action of tort for the conduct or for harm resulting from it.

Under this principle, Paredes cannot sue Marshall for trespass to land if he consented to her entry. Consent is probably the most common defense to actions for trespass to land. Like the prima facie elements, however, it has its subtleties. For example, Paredes can consent to one intrusion on his property but not others. Although he invites Marshall to the birthday party, that does not mean she may use his property at will. Consent to entry on one occasion, or for one purpose, does not constitute a general consent to entry. If Marshall returns to fish in Paredes's pond a week later, she will be a trespasser if the reasonable understanding of the birthday invitation was that it limited entry to the party itself.

Similarly, consent may be limited in time. By inviting Marshall to the party, Paredes does not acquiesce to her staying for a week, even if she claims she is still celebrating. And, it may be limited to entry on certain areas of the owner's property. A store owner who invites customers to visit

2. Adverse possession, covered in the Property course, is a means of acquiring an interest in property by openly occupying it for a period of time.

his showroom does not consent to them coming upstairs to his apartment and watching TV.

It is clear, too, from the Restatement (Second) definition that a person may become a trespasser even though she entered the land with permission. If Marshall wanders off from the party and takes Paredes's horse for a ride, she will become a trespasser, though she entered the land with permission. Or, if Clements, a college student, leaves her trunk full of textbooks at Kobe's house for the summer, decides not to return to school, and never returns for the trunk, she becomes a trespasser by failing to remove the trunk at the end of the agreed time. The act of leaving the trunk—of not coming for it—is a trespassory act, although one might argue that it is no act at all.

Consent provides a defense not just to trespass to land, but to other intentional torts as well, such as battery or trespass to chattels. It is explored in more detail in Chapter 6.

Trespass Compared to Nuisance

I usually manage to get through my course in Torts without mentioning the word "nuisance." I do this because the concept is, well, a nuisance, a complex and slippery concept. But it is hard to discuss trespass to land without comparing it to the complementary protection that nuisance law provides to landowners. Trespass is generally viewed as a tort remedy for actual physical intrusions on land—throwing stones on the property, driving a truck across it, or mining gravel on it. The action for private nuisance, by contrast, provides a remedy for interference with the use or enjoyment of land that is less tangible, such as operating machinery on adjacent land that causes continuous vibrations, excessive noise, or foul odors.

The action for private nuisance, by contrast, provides a remedy for conduct that does not involve trespass on an owner's property, but substantially interferes with the owner's use and enjoyment of her property. Examples might include operating machinery nearby that involves excessive noise, vibrations, or odors that reach the owner's property. Such interference may support either a claim for damages or injunctive relief caused by the nuisance.

Here are some distinctions between trespass and nuisance that will help you decide which of these remedies for interference with land is likely to apply:

- Trespass requires an unauthorized direct or immediate intrusion on the owner's property, while nuisance typically involves interference with use and enjoyment over a period of time.

- Trespass usually involves the entry of a person or physical object, while nuisance usually involves more diffuse annoyances, such as smoke, noise, or vibrations. Typically, the nuisance defendant acts on nearby land, but the effects of her activity impact a nearby owner's quiet enjoyment of hers through some sensory interference. Nuisance "typically involves the indirect consequences to plaintiff's land of something done entirely on defendant's own premises."[3]
- A trespasser is usually liable even for trivial physical intrusions, such as a single harmless amble across a neighbor's lawn. Nuisance, by contrast, involves a weighing of the interest of the party creating the nuisance and the party who suffers from it. Sometimes, a court may conclude that some level of interference with the quiet enjoyment of adjoining property is reasonable, in view of the value of the activity that creates it, and therefore will not support recovery for nuisance.
- On the dividing line between nuisance and trespass lie cases in which invisible particles intrude on property. While there is no traditional interference with use and possession, as typically required for an action of trespass, some courts have allowed actions for trespass if the intrusion results in actual damage. See *Rhodes v. E.I. Dupont de Nemours and Co.*, 657 F. Supp. 2d 751, 771-772 (S.D. W. Va. 2009). However, plaintiffs typically rely on nuisance actions in such claims for environmental injury. S. Ferrey, Environmental Law: Examples & Explanations 30 (8th ed. 2019).
- Trespass is an intentional tort. The actor must act with intent—either the purpose to cause the intrusion or with substantial certainty that it will cause the intrusion. An actor may create a nuisance, however, without intending to impact the property of another. The gravamen of the nuisance claim is the interference defendant's activity causes to the plaintiff's use of her property, not intent to cause that interference. Restatement (Second) of Torts §822(b). An actor might not know, for example, that the noise from his cement plant will reach owners' property a half-mile away, but the noise can still constitute a nuisance to those owners.
- If a physical trespass is found that may recur, a court will grant an injunction against further trespasses. However, in nuisance cases courts balance the utility of the conduct against its interference with the adjacent owner's rights. If a court finds that the defendant has created a nuisance, it may choose not to enjoin the conduct, due to its importance to the community. In such cases, the court will permit the defendant to continue his conduct, while granting damage compensation to surrounding owners affected by the activity.

3. F. Harper & F. James, The Law of Torts 83 (2d ed. vol. 1).

The following examples should help you understand the elements and the limits of the claim for trespass to land.

Examples

No Putt Intended

1. Albers, a sometime golfer, goes golfing on Saturday. On the fourth hole he hits a smashing drive. While his drive has lots of height, it hooks badly, veers off the course, and breaks the window in Genet's bungalow adjoining the golf course. Does Genet have an action against Albers for trespass to land?

2. Dean, a teenager high on life, decides to impress his friends with his neat sports car. He speeds down the road adjacent to Genet's land at 75 miles per hour. When he encounters a sharp turn he loses control, skidding off the road onto Genet's lawn. Is he a trespasser?

3. Albers gets so mad at his golf score that he picks up a small stone and heaves it off the golf course onto Genet's lawn. The stone rolls across the lawn and into the woods. Genet wasn't home at the time, so did not see it happen.
   a. Has Albers committed trespass?
   b. Why would Genet bother to sue for trespass if he has suffered no significant injury?
   c. Albers's stone flies into Genet's driveway and smashes the windshield of his vintage Model T Ford, which had been handcrafted for Genet by an antique car specialist at a cost of $9,000. Is Albers liable for the loss?
   d. Albers goes out to play a round of golf after four serious drinks in the clubhouse. He is so soused that he grabs a putter to drive off the tee. Because of the shape of the putter the ball hooks erratically, goes off at a right angle to the green and into Genet's yard, where it hits Genet on the noggin. Is Albers liable for trespass?

Moving In

4. Albers buys a home with a large stand of maple trees toward the back of the lot. The real estate broker tells him that the trees are on the lot he is buying. After buying, Albers decides to thin the stand by cutting several trees. After doing so he is sued for trespass by Piaget, owner of the property behind his. It turns out that the maples are only partly on Albers's land, and the ones he cut were on Piaget's. Is Albers liable for trespass?

5. Same facts, except that Albers had a survey done before cutting the trees. The survey showed the whole stand of trees to be on Albers's land. But

the surveyor made a mistake in calculating the location of the property line. In fact, the trees were on Piaget's lot, and he sues for trespass. Is Albers liable?

A Ridiculous Question

6. Albers is irked by Piaget's trespass suit. He decides to cut down two *more* of Piaget's trees, but do it in the middle of the night, when no one will see him. He sneaks out one moonless eve and cuts two trees. He goes out the next day and discovers that in the dark he had actually cut a couple of his own trees. Unfortunately, he had bragged to Mercutio, the town snitch, that he was going to cut Piaget's trees, so Piaget learns of the escapade and sues him for trespass on a transferred intent theory. Is Albers liable?

Not So Funny

7. Berle, a jokester, tells Menlove that Snobbin, as a charitable gesture to those who live near his estate, has announced that anyone from the town may go in and pick strawberries from his strawberry patch. Menlove does so, but Snobbin's gardener catches him at it. Snobbin, less beneficent than Menlove gave him credit for, sues him for trespass.
   a. Has Menlove committed trespass?
   b. Has Berle?

8. Menlove was having breakfast at the local diner when he heard Janowski talking to a waitress. Janowski tells the waitress that she had heard that Snobbin was allowing people to pick his strawberries. After breakfast, Menlove heads for the strawberry patch and eats Snobbin's strawberries. Snobbin, learning that Menlove heard this rumor from Janowski, sues Janowski for trespass. Is she liable?

A Hard Case

9. On the snowy plains of West Dakota, local municipalities often erect snow fences next to roads, in order to prevent drifts from covering the roads. The town of Plainsville obtains permission from Frain, a local farmer, to place a snow fence along the edge of his field, to be removed by May 1 each year so he can farm the land. After the third winter, the town removes the fence, but leaves a metal anchor pipe in the field. Frain, mowing his field in July, is killed when the mower catches on the pipe and he is thrown under the machine. Is the town liable? Should Frain's survivors sue for negligence or trespass?

Nuisances and Trespasses

10. Arnez belongs to the Concord Minutemen, a group of ten would-be patriots who reenact Revolutionary War scenes. While practicing at Arnez's home, they set off their antique flintlock rifles twice. The reports of these ancient arms are noisy and produce a foul-smelling gunpowder odor that blows across Martell's next-door lot. Have Arnez and his Minutemen committed trespass or nuisance?

11. Chan is late for the train, which he sees pulling into the station. Since he needs to catch the train to make an important meeting, he cuts across Pasik's lawn to the station, saving enough time to make the train. No harm is done. Pasik is away, but learns about Chan's shortcut and sues.
    a. Should Pasik sue for trespass or nuisance?
    b. How will the court respond to Chan's argument that he had an important reason to cross Pasik's property, and caused no harm?
    c. Suppose that Chan was chased by a mugger with a knife, and ran across Pasik's land to reach the police station. Would he be liable to Pasik for trespass?
    d. While fleeing through Pasik's yard to avoid the mugger, Chan tramples Pasik's flower garden. Is he liable for the damage?

12. Conglomerate Chemicals Corporation manufactures chemicals at a plant in East Dakota. The processing of raw materials into chemicals involves a complex smelting process that gives off emissions containing trace amounts of various chemicals, including quasimonomethane. Over a period of years, the particles in these smokestack emissions settle on surrounding property. Green is an organic farmer who lives a mile from Conglomerate's plant. In 2008, he learns that he cannot get the vegetables grown on his land certified as organic anymore, due to traces of quasimonomethane the plants have absorbed from the soil on his farm. He wishes to sue Conglomerate.
    a. Conglomerate argues that it is not liable for trespass, because it had no intent to deposit chemicals on Green's property. If it moves to dismiss Green's case on this ground, how is the court likely to rule?
    b. Is Green's proper remedy in trespass or in nuisance?

Trespass Down Under

13. Zarvas owns an undeveloped lot in a growing neighborhood. Two years ago his neighbor Fox developed his property. To do so, he had to lower the water table, so he dug a drainage ditch near the border between his property and Zarvas's. A perforated pipe was set in the ditch, which was covered back over. Water under the property would run out through the

pipe and off into a stream, keeping the ground water below the level of the pipe.

Zarvas decides to sell his lot and has it surveyed. The surveyor informs Zarvas that Fox's pipe actually runs under a corner of his property. It isn't doing any harm down there (it may even be keeping Zarvas's lot dry), but it is on his property. Removing the pipe would be quite expensive, especially since Fox has put in expensive plantings above it. May Zarvas obtain an injunction ordering the pipe removed from his property?

Owners and Occupiers

14. Shepherdson keeps sheep on his land in rural Nebraska. A fence—entirely on Shepherdson's property—keeps them off farmland next door. The farmland is owned by Grangerford, and this year he had leased the acreage to Farmer, who was growing grain on it.

    It was a dry year, and Shepherdson's sheep were struggling, while Farmer's field of grain, thanks to constant irrigation, was thriving. One night, Shepherdson slipped out and pulled back a section of his wire fence, and then went to visit his brother for the weekend. While he was away, his sheep took the hint; they wandered into Grangerford's field, where they ate a lot of Farmer's grain as well as destroyed a bunch of ornamental shrubs along the edge of the field.

    a. Is Shepherdson liable for trespass?
    b. If so, to whom?

Explanations

EXPLANATIONS

No Putt Intended

1. Albers is not liable for trespass, because he did not act with intent to cause an entry on Genet's land. He did not have a purpose to do so, nor did he know to a substantial certainty that his ball would veer off into Genet's yard. Certainly, if he is a mediocre golfer, he will recognize that this is a possibility. But possibilities do not make an intentional tort; intended intrusions do. Here, when Albers acted, he did not have either of the states of mind that would support intentional tort liability—purpose to cause the intrusion or substantial certainty that he would. He may be liable for negligence, but that's another tort, requiring a different type of fault.

2. Here, Dean acted "intentionally," in the sense that he meant to speed down the street. And, as with Albers, he could foresee the danger of losing control and veering onto adjacent property. But he still has not acted with the intent—either purpose or substantial certainty—to enter

Genet's property. Genet will have to sue him for negligence, not trespass (so long as Dean does not linger on the property after his car stops).

3. a. Certainly he has, as long as he meant to throw it on Genet's lawn. Although he has not entered the property himself, he has caused the stone to do so. In the language of §158 of the Second Restatement, he has "caused an object" to enter the land without permission, interfering with Genet's right of exclusive possession.

   It didn't interfere very much, though, did it? The stone rolled off into the woods, joining a thousand others just like it. But damage is not an element of trespass: The intruder is liable for nominal damages for making the intrusion even if it causes no harm. The unpermitted interference with exclusive use is itself tortious, with or without resulting harm to the property.

   Nor is there any requirement that the landowner be aware of the intrusion at the time it happens. The common law has always placed a high premium on the right to exclusive use of property, including the right to use it for nothing or leave it entirely alone. If Genet spends 11 months a year in another state, he still enjoys the right to keep his local property free of intrusions by others while he is away.

   b. Most of the time, owners don't sue for trivial trespasses to land. But if they happen continually, they may, seeking injunctive relief—that is, a court order to the defendant to cease the intrusions. If Trujillo crosses Genet's land every day to get to the bus stop, he may not damage Genet's land. But he does interfere with the right to exclusive enjoyment that we associate with land ownership. Genet may sue, not because he has suffered economic damage but to keep Trujillo and others from entering his land.

   If Genet ignores these trespasses, they could at some point ripen into an easement—the right to cross his land to reach the bus stop. So it is important, in terms of confirming title, for Genet to have a right to sue even though he has not suffered damages from the trespass.

   c. Albers threw the stone out of pique, not because he had a purpose to injure Genet's property. But he did have the purpose to throw the stone at his lot, and this deliberate intrusion led to the windshield damage. By deliberating throwing the rock onto Genet's property, he became a trespasser, and as a trespasser, he will be liable for resulting damage, even damage he had no desire or expectation that he would cause.

   d. Albers has not committed trespass, because he had no purpose to cause the ball to enter Genet's yard, nor did he know that it would. However, he clearly was negligent. Under basic negligence law he will be liable for Genet's injury. On the other hand, if the ball had bounced on Genet's lawn and rolled off his property, Albers would not be liable. In an action based on negligence—unlike one based on trespass—the plaintiff must establish that the entry caused damage. If the ball rolled harmlessly away, it probably did not.

Moving In

4. Yeah, Albers is liable. He intentionally entered on Piaget's land and cut the trees. "But he didn't know they were on Piaget's land," you say. True, but they were. Albers acted in good faith, but he still intentionally went on his neighbor's land and cut the trees. Will Piaget miss the trees any less knowing that Albers "didn't mean to" cut *his* trees?

   This is a classic "mistake" case: Albers believes he is on his own property but in fact is not. Someone has to take responsibility for the mistake. . . . Should it be Piaget, who lost his trees, or Albers, who cut them down? Trespass law places the loss in these cases on the person who caused it. One rationale is that this rule gives actors like Albers an incentive to investigate fully before venturing forth with a chain saw.[4]

5. In this case, Albers responded to the incentive that trespass law provides: He used all care to make sure he did not intrude on his neighbor's lot. But he still entered Piaget's property and cut his trees, and he is a trespasser. Very likely, he would not be liable for criminal trespass; criminal prosecution generally requires a *mens rea* element lacking in examples like this. See, e.g., 18 Pa. Cons. Stat. Ann. §3503 (requiring knowledge that the actor lacks license or privilege for criminal trespass). But the tort of trespass to land protects against unauthorized entries, even if not morally reprehensible.

   In *Serota v. M. & M. Utilities, Inc.*, 285 N.Y.S.2d 121 (N.Y. Dist. Ct. 1967), an oil company had a delivery contract with a homeowner. The homeowner sold the property but didn't tell the oil company, so they duly appeared to refill the heating oil tank, but spilled some oil because the tank had been filled. The company was held liable to the new owner as a trespasser. "Obviously, the defendant intended to come upon plaintiff's land and make an oil delivery and did not intend to commit a trespass or intentionally to cast oil upon plaintiff's land. His innocence and his mistaken belief that his visit was authorized is of no moment since his intent is clearly shown to have been to deliver oil. This unauthorized act, resulting in whatever damages which may have occurred, rendered him liable." 285 N.Y.S.2d at 124.

4. Albers might have a claim for indemnification from the real estate broker, since her negligent (or intentional) misrepresentation led to the trespass.

A Ridiculous Question

6. Albers had tortious intent—he planned to and tried to cut Piaget's trees. But he didn't. The intent to commit a trespass will not support liability, without causing an actual intrusion on the land of another. Ridiculous question, indeed.

   Put another way, there isn't a tort of attempted trespass. Just as an actor would not be liable for battery if he threw a rock at someone and missed,[5] Albers is not liable if he does not actually cause an intrusion on Piaget's property.

Not So Funny

7. a. Even if we assume that Menlove's mistake was a reasonable one, it is unlikely to protect him from a trespass action. If Albers's reasonable mistake about whether he was on Piaget's land was no defense in Example 5, Menlove's mistake about consent to entry will presumably be equally ineffective. This is the position taken by the Second Restatement: Section 164 declares that an entrant is a trespasser even though he acts under a mistaken belief that the owner has consented.

      This approach places the risk of mistake on the party who acts, and is in a position to take additional steps to confirm his right to do so. Suppose Menlove thought he had consent to cut a stand of trees, and did cut them. Snobbin should not go without recompense for this unconsented harvest, even if Menlove acted in good faith. Very likely, a court would take a very hard line here. For example, comment a to §164 of the Second Restatement states that an entrant would be liable for trespass even if, "due to the advice of the most eminent of counsel," he believed that he was on his own land. See also §164 illus. 5 (entrant a trespasser though assured by another that he has permission to enter).

   b. Berle is a trespasser under the Second Restatement definition of trespass. Even though he never entered Snobbin's land, he caused Menlove to do so. Section 158(1)(a) expressly provides that one who causes another to trespass is liable for the entry. Of course, Berle must still act with intent to cause the entry. Assuming that, as a jokester, he acted for the purpose of causing Menlove to pick Snobbin's strawberries, he would have the necessary intent.

8. Here, Janowski's loose talk led Menlove to trespass, so one can argue that she caused the trespass. However, trespass is an intentional tort. Janowski did not act for the purpose of causing Menlove's entry, nor with substantial certainty that she would. She is not liable to Snobbin for trespass.

5. If the victim saw it coming at him it would be assault, however.

A Hard Case

9. This example is based on a Michigan case, *Rogers v. Board of Road Commissioners*, 30 N.W.2d 358 (MI 1948). The farmer's survivors sued for wrongful death, based on negligence and trespass theories. The court held that the complaint stated a claim for trespass. The commissioners had permission to put the fence in for the winter, but by not removing the anchor pipe in the spring, committed trespass. The court relied on Restatement (Second) of Torts §160, which provides that

   > A trespass, actionable under the rule stated in §158, may be committed by the continued presence on the land of a structure, chattel or other thing which the actor or his predecessor in legal interest therein has placed thereon
   >
   > (a) with the consent of the person then in possession of the land, if the actor fails to remove it after the consent has been effectively terminated . . .

   In this case, no one entered Frain's land with tortious intent—they had permission to erect the fence. All the Plainsville employees did was forget to remove the pipe. But the fact that the pipe remained on the land after permission had terminated still constituted a trespass, supporting recovery.

   Although the resulting harm in this case was personal injury, not harm to the property, the defendant could still be liable for it. Section 158 of the Second Restatement suggests that a trespasser is liable for "harm to any legally protected interest of the other," not just for property damage caused by the intrusion.

   This case illustrates why it is important for tort lawyers to think carefully about their potential remedies. Frain's survivors might sue for negligence in this case, based on the employee's negligent failure to pull up the pipe. However, cities and towns often have limited liability or immunity for acts of negligence by their employees. The *Rogers* court held that, whether or not a negligence claim could be brought, public immunity did not bar the claim for intentional tort.

Nuisances and Trespasses

10. Probably neither. Trespass requires a physical intrusion on property, and the few puffs of smoke from these colonial flintlocks will probably not be considered a sufficient physical invasion to constitute a trespassory entry. Nor is this event likely to constitute an actionable nuisance. It was a single event, not an ongoing interference with Martell's quiet enjoyment of his property. If they did this every day, and fired 56 times at each practice, Martell would likely have a case for nuisance. But this single event is probably not substantial or continuous enough an interference to support liability.

If single-shot annoyances sufficed, too many of life's vicissitudes might lead to neighborly litigation, such as an occasional noisy car repair, a dance party, or burning the fall leaves. The requirement that the interference be substantial eliminates many such annoying cases about annoyances.

11. a. Pasik's claim is for trespass, Chan's intentional physical entry onto his property. It's a one-shot thing, and it involves actual entry by Chan, so trespass is his proper remedy.
    b. Reasonable people might view Chan's decision as a reasonable one, but his need to make the train will not provide a defense to trespass. He still intentionally entered Pasik's property, and will be liable for trespass. Owners, in our ownership-oriented society, have a right to exclude others, even if those others might have good reasons to enter.
    c. Although the common law generally worships the sanctity of private property, it thankfully recognizes some limits to the right to exclude. This example illustrates one. The law recognizes a privilege to enter the property of another if necessary to avoid serious harm to the person.

Restatement (Second) of Torts §197 Private Necessity

> (1) One is privileged to enter or remain on land in the possession of another if it is or reasonably appears to be necessary to prevent serious harm to (a) the actor, or his land or chattels. . . .

The Restatement offers several examples of such privileged entries. In one, a canoeist encounters a violent storm and ties up to B's dock to save his life and his canoe. In the other, a pilot with sudden mechanical trouble makes a forced landing in B's field. Restatement (Second) of Torts §197 illus. 1, 3. In each of these cases, the actor was privileged to enter, though he intentionally entered on private property.

    d. The previous example indicates that Chan was privileged to enter to save himself from his pursuer. However, the few cases on the point suggest that, while there is a privilege to enter under these circumstances, it does not excuse the entrant from the obligation to pay for any resulting harm to the land. See, e.g., *Vincent v. Lake Erie Transp. Co.*, 124 N.W. 221 (1910). So Chan will have to pay for the trampled flowers. While he may grumble about that now, it's a deal he gladly would have made at the point of deciding to run through the garden.

And it makes sense, really. He has made use of Pasik's property for his own benefit, and it is reasonable that he, rather than Pasik, absorb the resulting loss. As Professor Dobbs nicely puts it, "the skier who is lost in a snow storm may enter your cabin for shelter without liability. But if he burns the furniture to stay warm he must pay for its destruction."[6] In the (unlikely) event that Chan recognizes this possible liability as he flees his pursuer, it will give him an appropriate incentive to choose the least costly route of escape across Pasik's land. Thus, the privilege recognized here is sometimes referred to as an "incomplete privilege," because, while the actor is privileged to enter, she must pay for resulting harm to the property.

12. a. The court will likely reject the no-intent argument. Conglomerate's argument is like Romeo heaving his sneakers into the crowded stands at the track meet, and then arguing that he isn't liable when they hit a spectator, since he didn't know who would be hit. See Example 10 in Chapter 1. An actor has the intent necessary to commit an intentional tort if he acts for the purpose of causing the invasion of the other's interest, or with substantial certainty that he will invade it. Romeo knew that he would cause a harmful touching to *someone*. Here, Conglomerate knows that its smelting operation emits polluting chemicals. It may not know who Green is, or where his farm lies, but it does know that the pollutants will come to earth on nearby owners' property. It has intent to cause the intrusion, in the "substantial certainty" sense of the term.

    b. Green may be able to sue for both trespass and nuisance. Traditionally, trespass would lie for direct physical intrusions on property. If Consolidated lofted an errant steam boiler onto Green's land, that would be trespass. For interferences with use of property due to noise, vibration, or light, however, nuisance was the proper remedy. See Dobbs' Law of Torts §51.

    The facts in this example fall along the divide between the two remedies. The entry is by invisible particles, not a rock or a car. And the intrusion takes place over time; it is the accumulated amount of quasimonomethane that causes the damage, not one day's or week's emissions. But the intrusion is physical and causes actual deposits on the land. Traditionally, it would probably have been viewed as nuisance since the particles were so small as to be invisible as they arrived on Green's farm. Today, however, many courts would conclude that Conglomerate is liable both in nuisance and in trespass. See, e.g., *J.H. Borland v. Sanders Lead Co.*, 369 So. 2d 523 (Ala. 1979). It is trespass because there is a detectable physical entry that damages the property. The entry also constitutes a nuisance since it is based on continuous behavior and interferes with Green's use of his property.

    While modern courts may treat such invisible intrusions as trespass, they are likely to require proof of actual damage in order to

6. Dobbs' Law of Torts §117.

allow recovery. Admittedly, more traditional trespasses are actionable without proof of resulting damages. However, as one court noted, "no useful purpose would be served by sanctioning actions in trespass by every landowner within a hundred miles of a manufacturing plant." *Bradley v. American Smelting and Refining Co.*, 709 P.2d 782, 791 (Or. 1985). Requiring substantial damage to the property is different from traditional trespass law, which holds trespass actionable at least for nominal damages without proof of any resulting damage.

Not all courts agree with this trend to treat such pollution cases as trespass. In *Adams v. Cleveland-Cliffs Iron Co.*, 602 N.W.2d 215 (Mich. App. 1999), for example, the court rejected the trend to find trespass in cases like this, choosing instead to retain the distinction between trespass, which requires "an unauthorized direct or immediate intrusion of a physical, tangible object on land" (602 N.W.2d at 222), and nuisance, which lies if the plaintiff proves "*significant harm* resulting from the defendant's *unreasonable interference* with the use or enjoyment of property." Id. (emphasis in the original). See also *Johnson v. Paynesville Farmers Union Co-op Oil Co.*, 817 N.W.2d 693, 702-705 (Minn. 2012) (rejecting trespass claim based on pesticide drift particles).

The distinction may matter for several reasons. The limitations periods may differ for nuisance and trespass (usually trespass is longer). And, if the intrusion is short lived, nuisance may not provide a remedy at all. If only nuisance applies, a court may find some level of interference reasonable, and therefore not actionable.

Trespass Down Under

13. Zarvas is likely to obtain an injunction ordering removal of the pipe, even though it will be inconvenient and expensive for Fox to do so.

    Note that this is a subterranean trespass, which will only be actionable if Zarvas's exclusive right to use of his property includes the right to use of the property below the surface. Most courts hold that an owner's right to exclusive possession extends both above and below the surface of the property. See Restatement (Second) of Torts §159, which provides in part that "a trespass may be committed on, beneath or above the surface of the earth." Thus, ownership of property protects the right to subsurface mining as well as use of the property's surface and the immediate airspace above the property.[7] So Fox's laying of the pipe is a trespass, an invasion of Zarvas's right to exclusive use of his property.

    However, the pipe isn't bothering Zarvas, and it will be expensive to remove it. Still, the right to exclusive use of property is sufficiently

7. Section 159(2) provides an exception for aircraft flights above the "immediate reaches of the air space next to the land."

prized that a court will likely order the pipe removed. It is not a defense to trespass that the trespass isn't causing damage, or that terminating the entry will be costly. And, while the pipe isn't causing any problems now, it might interfere with Zarvas's use of the land in the future. For example, he might want to put a septic system along that property line at some point.

If Zarvas decides to be a good neighbor and let the pipe remain since it's not a present problem, he risks problems later. If he is aware of the trespass and does not seek to remedy it, Fox may acquire an easement for his pipe over time, and Zarvas may be stuck with it.

Probably the "right" outcome for a case like this is a settlement. The value to Zarvas of enforcing his right to exclusive possession is probably a great deal less than the cost to Fox of digging up the pipe. Hopefully Fox can convince him to sell him an easement to leave the pipe in place for an amount reflecting the diminution in value of his land rather than the exorbitant cost of terminating the trespass.

Owners and Occupiers

14. a. Shepherdson may argue that he did not intend to trespass, his sheep did. How is he to know that they will wander next door to eat all that juicy grass? Well, one might argue that Shepherdson was substantially certain that his sheep would head for Farmer's field, but the easier argument is that Shepherdson opened the fence for the purpose of having his sheep enter the field, so he has the intent necessary to commit a trespass. We know that Shepherdson need not enter himself; he may do so by causing a stone, a car, or a sheep to do so. Shepherdson is—and should be—liable for trespass.

    b. In this case two parties have an interest in the field—Farmer's right, as lessee for the year, has been infringed by the loss of his grass, and Grangerford's, as the owner of the land, by the damage to the bushes. Both of these interests seem worthy of protection against trespass. However, §157 of the Second Restatement provides that a person is "in possession of land" (and therefore able to maintain an action for trespass) if he is "in occupancy of land with intent to control it." This allows Farmer, who has full control over the land while he has leased it, to sue for trespass, to recover for the damage to his interest—the value of the grain consumed by Shepherdson's sheep.

    Traditionally, however, a party like Grangerford, with a reversionary interest in the land—that is, the right to possession at some later date, but not presently—could not sue in trespass, because the defendant had not interfered with his right to possession. However, in cases like this, in which the trespasser causes injury to an owner's interest in the property as well as the current possessor's, courts have allowed recovery for the damage to the owner's interest under one name or another.

> An action for trespass may technically be maintained only by one whose right to possession has been violated . . . however, an out-of-possession property owner may recover for an injury to the land by a trespasser which damages the ownership interest. . . . In our view, the inquiry in a case involving unlawful intrusion on property rights should focus upon the nature of the injury and the damages sought: If the right to possession has been abridged and possessory rights damaged, the possessor may complain by way of an action for trespass; if, on the other hand, an intruder harms real property in a manner which damages the ownership interest, the property owner may seek recovery whether the cause of action be technically labeled trespass or some other form of action, such as waste.

Smith v. Cap Concrete, Inc., 184 Cal. Rptr. 308, 310 (Cal. App. 1982). Under some such rubric, Grangerford would doubtless recover for the value of his bushes as well. See also *Motchan v. STL Cablevision, Inc.*, 796 S.W.2d 896, 898 (Mo. App. 1990) (owner has right to sue for damage to its reversionary interest as a result of trespass to land).

For an even clearer example in which both interests are infringed, imagine that Rollo backs a truck onto a neighboring lot and hits the corner of a house on the property. The lessee has to vacate the house until repairs can be made, and the owner suffers damage to the value of the house. Although their interests differ, both should have a remedy against Rollo.

CHAPTER 4

Dueling Remedies: Trespass to Chattels and Conversion

INTRODUCTION

The traditional intentional torts protect not only the inviolability of the body (through the action for battery) and possession of real property (through the action for trespass to land) but also a possessor's interest in personal property, such as a car, a couch, a book, or a cow. Such personal possessions are referred to as "chattels" under property law, pieces of tangible, movable personal property, as opposed to "real property" such as land.

Over time, several intentional torts evolved to protect against invasions to personal property. If an actor intentionally damaged an owner's personal property, or temporarily deprived the owner of possession, she was liable for trespass to chattels. If she intentionally deprived the possessor of an item of personal property, as by stealing it, she was liable for conversion. This chapter will discuss and compare these related causes of action for interference with personal property.

TRESPASS TO CHATTELS

The most basic distinction between trespass to chattels and conversion is that trespass to chattels provides a remedy for damage to personal property, or temporary interference with its use, even though the possessor is not permanently deprived of it. Suppose that Carter takes Puso's horse, Flora (conceived in law as a chattel, whatever Flora may think about it), for a three-hour ride, and then returns her to Puso's barn. Carter has probably committed trespass to chattels, but he is not liable for conversion. Carter has not permanently deprived Puso of Flora's use, nor is she damaged by the interference. Or, if Carter throws a rock at Puso's car and puts a dent in its door, he has committed trespass to chattels, by damaging the car, but not conversion, since Puso still has the car.

The Second Restatement addresses the elements of a claim for trespass to chattels in two sections. Section 217 defines the ways in which an actor can commit trespass to chattels:

> **Section 217. Ways of Committing Trespass to Chattel**
>
> A trespass to a chattel may be committed by intentionally
>
> (a) dispossessing another of the chattel, or
>
> (b) using or intermeddling with a chattel in the possession of another.

Oddly, §218 then addresses when an actor who commits a trespass to chattels *is liable to the possessor,* suggesting that sometimes one may commit the tort (under §217), but not incur liability for it, because none of the consequences described in §218 results from the trespass.

> **Section 218. Liability to Person in Possession**
>
> One who commits a trespass to a chattel is subject to liability to the possessor of the chattel, if, but only if,
>
> (a) he dispossesses the other of the chattel, or
>
> (b) the chattel is impaired as to its condition, quality or value, or
>
> (c) the possessor is deprived of the use of the chattel for a substantial time, or
>
> (d) bodily harm is caused to the possessor, or harm is caused to some person or thing in which the possessor has a legally protected interest.

When Puso took Flora for a ride, he used the horse, so he committed trespass to chattel under §217(b). Carter can sue him for the tort if he suffers one of the four consequences listed in §218. If Puso rode Flora for three hours, he is likely liable under §218(c) because he deprived Carter of her use for a substantial period of time. Or, if he rode Flora so hard that she developed shin splints,[1] he may be liable under §218(b). Unlike trespass to land, which is actionable without any resulting harm, §218 limits liability for trespass to chattels to those which cause resulting harm. If Puso sits down on the bumper of Carter's car, he has intermeddled with Carter's

1. What are shin splints, anyway? Do horses get them?

personal property under §217, but under §218 he is not liable if he causes no damage to the car. For example, suppose that D releases the brake on P's car, and pushes it forward a few feet to make space to park behind it. If no harm is done, D is not liable, since he did not dispossess P of the car or cause any damage to it. Restatement (Second) of Torts, §218 Ill. 3.

Note several things about this definition. First, §217 requires intent, as that concept is analyzed in Chapter 1. As with battery, assault, and other intentional torts, the actor must act for the purpose of causing the trespass, or with substantial certainty that the trespass will result. Negligent interference with personal property will not support recovery for trespass to chattels.

Second, note that, under §§217 and 218(a), one who totally deprives a possessor of a chattel is liable for trespass to chattels. This is puzzling because total deprivations of a chattel are usually treated as a conversion. To some extent, the two remedies overlap, so that conduct constituting conversion may also support recovery for trespass to chattels.

Note also that the definition speaks of a "possessor" of the chattel, not an owner. Usually, the owner will be the possessor of the property, but not always. If Burstein borrows his neighbor Konegin's lawn mower, and Goliath comes over and smashes it with a sledge hammer, Burstein will have an action against Goliath for trespass to chattel. His interest as a borrower suffices to constitute "possession" for purposes of recovering for Goliath's interference with the mower. Section 219 of the Second Restatement provides that one who damages or takes a chattel is liable to an "immediate possessor," such as a bailee. Section 220 provides that the tortfeasor is also liable to a "person entitled to future possession"—the owner Konegin, in the mower case—for any damage to his residuary interest in the chattel.

CONVERSION COMPARED

Historically, conversion evolved from the early form of action for "trover," and provided a remedy for dispossession of a chattel. The major distinction between trespass to chattels and conversion is that conversion provides a remedy for a deprivation sufficiently serious that the tortfeasor is liable for the full value of the property. It "requires very substantial exercise of control or dominion inconsistent with the plaintiff's rights." Dobbs' Law of Torts §61. If the property is merely damaged, or possession is temporarily interfered with, the claim is usually for trespass to chattels, not for conversion. If the property is stolen, or even used for a substantial period of time, however, the actor will likely be liable for conversion. "The significance of conversion lies in the measure of damages, the recovery of the full value of the goods, and that the tort is properly limited to those wrongs which justify imposing it." W. Prosser, The Nature of Conversion, 42 Cornell L.Q. 168, 173 (1957).

Here is the Second Restatement's attempt to define conversion:

> **Section 222A. What Constitutes Conversion**
>
> (1) Conversion is an intentional exercise of dominion or control over a chattel which so seriously interferes with the right of another to control it that the actor may justly be required to pay the other the full value of the chattel.

Of course, trespass to chattels also involves interference with possessory rights in the chattel. Here are a few examples that may help you to distinguish these two related tort claims.

- Horton, leaving a restaurant, picks up Cobble's hat from a coat hook, thinking it is his own. When he reaches the street he realizes that he has the wrong hat and returns it.
  — This is not conversion, because the dispossession is brief and does not cause damage to the property. See Restatement (Second) of Torts §222A illus. 1. It probably isn't trespass to chattels either, since the deprivation is so brief, and there is no indication that Cobble tried to find the hat while it was away.
- Horton takes Cobble's hat, again thinking it his own. As he is leaving, he is frustrated that it won't fit right, and pushes it down on his head, tearing the hat band inside it. Then he realizes it isn't his and returns it to the coat hook.
  —This is likely trespass to chattels since the hat is damaged. See Restatement (Second) of Torts §218(b). If the hat were damaged to the point of being useless, Horton would be liable for conversion.
- Horton takes Cobble's hat by mistake and wears it home. He doesn't look at it again until the following winter, when he realizes that the hat is not his. He returns it to the restaurant.
  —Cobble will have a claim for conversion since he has been deprived of his hat for such a long period of time.

Suppose on the facts of the last example that Cobble did return to the restaurant to ask about his hat, and they gave it to him. What would Horton be liable for? The Restatement takes the position that he is liable for conversion, due to the length of time for which Cobble has missed his hat. Restatement (Second) of Torts §222A illus. 2. But this fits the definition of trespass to chattels as well since Cobble has been deprived of the use of the hat for "a substantial time." Restatement (Second) of Torts §219(b). In these cases, it appears that trespass to chattels and conversion overlap. If I were Cobble, and wanted to recover from Horton, I would assert claims for both conversion and trespass to chattels, and let the court sort it out.

In the last two examples, Horton is a tortfeasor, though he had no malicious intent. But he did have *intent* in the sense needed for an intentional tort: He meant to assert dominion over the hat, and did, by the act of taking it. Although he was mistaken about the character of his act, tort law places the consequence of his mistake on him.

Admittedly, the line between trespass to chattels and conversion is hazy. The Second Restatement recognizes that there is no single bright line distinction that classifies the cases. Instead, it suggests several factors courts should consider in determining whether conversion is the proper remedy.

Section 222A

(2) In determining the seriousness of the interference and the justice of requiring the actor to pay the full value, the following factors are important:

(a) the extent and duration of the actor's exercise of dominion or control;

(b) the actor's intent to assert a right in fact inconsistent with the other's right of control;

(c) the actor's good faith;

(d) the extent and duration of the resulting interference with the other's right of control;

(e) the harm done to the chattel;

(f) the inconvenience and expense caused to the other.

This section attempts to make sense of centuries of somewhat contradictory case law, by basing liability for conversion on a number of factors. In some cases conversion may lie because the property has been completely destroyed or sold, perhaps even if the actor acted in good faith. In others, it may lie because the tortfeasor acted with conscious intent to interfere with possessory rights, or knew that his interference would cause severe consequences to the possessor. Sometimes, brief exercise of control over the chattel may support a conversion claim; in other cases, based on the other factors in §222A, it will not.

If conversion is found, the defendant is liable for the full value of the chattel at the time of conversion. Restatement (Second) of Torts §222A cmt. c. If the defendant commits trespass to chattels, the damages are the diminished value of the chattel or damages for the deprivation of use.

Perhaps the examples below will help you to get a handle on these two intentional torts.

Examples

Insults and Injuries

1. Romeo is joking around with Benvolio, exchanging slaps before class. Benvolio steps backward to avoid a slap, and falls on Thibeault's science project, a model of an international space station made from 5,000 toothpicks and Elmer's glue. It is demolished. Is Romeo liable for trespass to chattels? For conversion? How about Benvolio?

2. Cody sees Woof, his neighbor Fred's dog, walking down the sidewalk next to his property. He throws a rock at Woof, but misses. Fred sees this from his window. What tort may he sue Cody for?

Hat Tricks

3. Cobble is wearing a hat with a peace sign on it. Horton grabs it off his head and throws it to the ground. The hat is not damaged. What tort, if any, has Horton committed?

4. Horton grabs Cobble's hat, which is sitting on the fender of Cobble's car, and heaves it up in the air. Cobble retrieves it immediately, but Horton's greasy fingers have left a stain on the brim. The cleaning bill is 15 dollars. Is Horton liable for it? What tort should Cobble sue for?

5. Horton grabs Cobble's hat, which is sitting on the fender of Cobble's car, and heaves it behind him. It lands in the street, where it is run over by a steamroller, reducing it from three dimensions to two. What tort?

6. Horton sees Cobble's hat on a shelf near the door of a restaurant. Mistaking it for his own hat, he puts it on and walks out. It doesn't feel right, so he looks more closely at it, realizes it isn't his, and returns it to the shelf, none the worse for wear (so to speak). What tort has he committed?

7. Horton sees Cobble's hat on the shelf. He decides to steal it, grabs it, and starts out the door. However, he sees a police officer nearby, so he slips back in and places the hat back on the shelf. What tort has he committed, if any?

Horse Play

8. Wongsun lives next door to Brooks, who has a stable where she keeps horses. Wongsun learns that Brooks is going away for the weekend. While she is gone Wongsun takes Flora, one of her horses, for a two-hour ride through the woods. He returns Flora before Brooks comes home, but

Malvolio, a sneak, tells Brooks about it. Has Wongsun committed conversion? Has he committed trespass to chattels?

9. Wongsun takes Flora for that ride, and Flora steps in a rabbit hole, breaking a leg. The horse must be shot. What tort has Wongsun committed?

10. Wongsun borrows Flora while Brooks is away, with Brooks's permission. While Flora is grazing in his backyard, Interloper, a passing motorist, stops and offers to buy Flora for an excellent price. Wongsun sells Flora to her and spends the proceeds gambling on the lottery. Is Wongsun liable for conversion? Is Interloper?

At Sea

11. a. Sailor keeps a mooring for his sailboat in a local harbor. (A mooring is a large floating buoy anchored to the harbor floor that you tie a boat to so it won't float away.) Sneaky Pete sails into the harbor for the night and finds Sailor's mooring empty since his boat is in dry dock having the barnacles scraped off the hull. Pete ties up to Sailor's mooring for the night. He leaves the next morning. Has he committed trespass to chattels?
    b. Same facts, but Sailor shows up to use the mooring late in the evening and finds Pete there, so he can't tie up.
    c. Section 217 provides that an actor commits trespass to chattels by certain conduct. But §218 provides liability for damages for such conduct only if the trespass leads to damage or deprivation of use. If B sits on the fender of A's car for half an hour, he commits trespass to chattels under §217. But if he does no damage, and does not interfere with A's use of the car, he is not liable for trespass to chattels under §218. What is the point of declaring certain conduct tortious if it will not support an action for damages?

A Clever Ploy

12. Cain and Abel, two brothers, both have a fondness for a painting of an apple orchard done by their mother, Eve. It is only worth 50 bucks on the open market, but has great sentimental value to both brothers. Mom leaves it to Cain. Abel, a first-year law student and usually the Goody Two-shoes of the family, studies conversion in Torts and hatches a scheme. He will borrow the painting and just keep it. If Cain sues for conversion, Abel will pay him 50 bucks. So he will end up with the painting through an "involuntary sale." What do you think?

Quick Takes

13. Consider, in each of the cases below, whether the actor would be liable for trespass to chattels, conversion, both, or neither.
    a. Mephisto, having a grudge against Plaintiff, shoots her horse Flora.
    b. Mephisto slashes the front tires on plaintiff's car.
    c. Mephisto rents a car, misses a turn, and hits a tree, causing damage to the fender.
    d. Mephisto, a medical researcher jealous of a colleague, contaminates her cell cultures, ruining her experiment.
    e. Mephisto borrows Plaintiff's horse Flora for a ride, with Plaintiff's permission. Flora steps in a rabbit hole and is permanently lamed.
    f. Mephisto sneaks over and takes Flora, while Plaintiff is away, to ride into town. On the way Flora nibbles a poisonous bush and is sick for three hours.
    g. Mephisto performs a risky surgery on Secretarius, Plaintiff's race horse. The surgery is not successful, leaving the horse unable to race.
    h. Mephisto, a rival of plaintiff in an auto-racing event, dumps a truckload of dirt at the end of his driveway. Plaintiff cannot get his car out in time to compete in the race.
    i. Muir, an environmental activist, chains himself to a giant logging machine owned by Monumental Paper Company, to prevent the company from logging old-growth forest in a national park. Work is stopped for a day while the police dispose of Muir.
    j. Zenger, a reporter, is waiting to interview Carnegie, a corporate executive accused of wrongdoing. He notices that Carnegie has left his papers out on a desk in his office, while conferring with his lawyers in a nearby conference room. Zenger slips into the office and takes photos of Carnegie's papers with his cell phone. He later publishes a story based on the documents.

Cyber Chattel

14. Compu-Drive is an Internet service provider. Its computers provide access to the Internet, both for e-mail and the World Wide Web, for subscribers who establish accounts with Compu-Drive. Spam Spreader Incorporated is in the business of sending "spam," thousands of unsolicited e-mail advertisements to people with e-mail accounts. Many of these unwanted e-mails are sent through Compu-Drive's servers, placing a burden on the servers and slowing down access to the Internet and e-mail for customers. Compu-Drive sues Spam Spreader for trespass to chattels. Does its complaint state a claim upon which relief can be granted?

Explanations

Insults and Injuries

1. Romeo is probably not liable for either trespass to chattels or conversion. Both are intentional torts, and Romeo probably has not acted with the intent necessary to commit an intentional tort. If he and Benvolio are used to this kind of horseplay, as the example suggests, they consent to it, so Romeo was not assaulting Benvolio by aiming the slap at him: He had the intent to make a touching, but not a harmful or offensive one. While Thibeault's creation is smashed as a result, he will have to sue for negligence, not intentional tort. Similarly, Benvolio has not acted with the intent to damage the science project. He may be negligent for fooling around next to it, but he is not an intentional tortfeasor.

2. However mean-spirited Cody may be, he has not committed a tort. Woof may be a chattel, but Cody hasn't converted Woof, nor has he trespassed upon him. He may have acted with the intent (in the "purpose" sense here) to injure Woof, but he didn't injure him.

   Since Fred saw this, he may have been upset to think that Woof would be injured. But that isn't an assault, which requires apprehension of a harmful or offensive touching to one's person, not one's dog. I know of no tort for being subjected to the apprehension (but not the fact) of injury to property. I don't think Cody is liable.[2]

Hat Tricks

3. Cobble should probably sue for battery. As noted in Chapter 1 (see p. 10), contact with an object intimately associated with a person's body will satisfy the "contact" requirement for battery. Grabbing Cobble's hat should suffice. Which is good because Cobble should have a remedy, and conversion and trespass to chattels will probably not provide one. Horton has not converted Cobble's hat, since he has only taken it for a moment. And he hasn't damaged the hat, though he has "intermeddled" with it. So he is probably not liable for trespass to chattels. The essence of his invasion here is his intrusion on Cobble's person, so battery is the most appropriate claim and likely to apply. Recall that for battery (unlike trespass to chattels), Cobble need not suffer any resulting harm to have a claim; the intrusion itself is actionable.
4. Horton's intentional meddling with Cobble's hat constitutes trespass to chattels. See §217 of the Second Restatement (trespass to chattels is

2. In extreme cases, acts like this might give rise to a claim for intentional infliction of emotional distress, if they were committed with the intent to cause distress to the plaintiff. See Restatement (Second) of Torts §46. But Cody's act very likely does not rise to the level of extreme and outrageous conduct.

committed by intentionally intermeddling with another's personal property). And, since he has caused damage to the hat, §218(b) provides that he is liable for the resulting impairment of its condition. Horton should pay Cobble's cleaning bill.

5. Horton is liable for conversion. He acted with intent to exercise control over Cobble's chapeau, if only temporarily. That satisfies the intent standard for conversion. And, as a result of his intentional act, the hat has been destroyed, making it reasonable that Horton should be treated as an involuntary purchaser liable for the full value of the hat.

   True, Horton did not intend to demolish the hat, only to pull a prank. But Horton intended to take the hat, which makes him an intentional tortfeasor. Since he acted with intent to interfere with Horton's property, he is liable, even though the damage caused is more extensive than he intended.

6. This example is used as an illustration in the Second Restatement. See Restatement (Second) of Torts §222A illus. 1. The illustration says it is not a conversion, presumably because there was only a brief interference with Cobble's possession of his hat. However, Cobble may have an action for nominal damages for trespass to chattels since Horton did "dispossess" Cobble of the hat for a brief period, even though he did not damage it in any way. See Restatement (Second) of Torts §218 cmt. d (even minimal loss of possession supports recovery for nominal damages).

   Horton might also argue that he did not have the intent to commit a tort, since he made an innocent mistake. That would not be a good defense. Horton did intentionally take control of the hat. Just as a trespasser who thinks he is on his own land is liable for trespass to land, Horton would be liable for trespass to chattels if he damaged the hat or lost it after taking it by mistake.

7. In Example 6 Horton did much the same thing as he did here. Where he did it by mistake, the Restatement concludes that he has not converted the hat. On these facts, however, the Second Restatement takes the position that Horton has converted the hat. Restatement (Second) of Torts §222A illus. 4.

   What's the difference? While the interference with Cobble's dominion over his hat in this case is again brief, factors (b) and (c) of §222A(2) support liability for conversion: Horton clearly had the intent to "assert a right in fact inconsistent with [Cobble's] right of control" (factor b) and did not act in good faith (factor c).[3]

3. "There seems to be no doubt that any taking with knowledge of the plaintiff's rights and an intent to deprive him of them permanently is a conversion." W. Prosser, The Nature of Conversion, 42 Cornell L.Q. 169, 175 n.29 (1957).

If Horton is liable, what are the damages? Presumably Cobble still wants his hat, and doesn't want to involuntarily sell it to Horton. So the ordinary measure of damages for conversion—the fair market value of the converted property—doesn't apply. Perhaps Horton will be liable for punitive damages. If not, there seems little point to bringing suit. This will be the case in many minor trespass to chattels and conversion cases.

Horse Play

8. Wongsun is probably not liable for conversion, based on the factors listed in Restatement (Second) of Torts §222A. He only used Flora briefly, during a time when Brooks was away, so he hasn't substantially interfered with Brooks's horsey rights. He hasn't damaged Flora, as far as the facts tell us. He hasn't caused Brooks any inconvenience or expense. He did deliberately take Flora, just as Cobble took Horton's hat in Example 7, but his intent was to use her briefly, probably a crucial distinction from Example 7.

   He might be liable for trespass to chattels, however. He has used Flora, which constitutes trespass to chattels under Restatement (Second) of Torts §217. Section 218 provides that he is only liable to Brooks if he has dispossessed her of Flora, interfered with Flora's use for a substantial period of time, damaged the horse, or caused personal injury by his use. He hasn't dispossessed Brooks of Flora, since he only used her briefly. Has he deprived her of Flora's use (§218(c)) if Brooks doesn't even know Flora is missing and had no intent to use the horse during the period that it is missing? I don't know, and haven't found any definitive authority on the point. Liability would have to be premised on his interference for a period of time with Brook's use of Flora. If Brooks were home, and Wongsun took Flora for a 12-hour ride, this damage would be shown. But where Brooks was away, and the ride is fairly short, it is not clear that Wongsun would be liable.

   However, Wongsun may have committed trespass to land when he entered to take Flora. That intentional tort is actionable without a showing of resulting harm, at least for nominal damages.

9. Wongsun has committed both trespass to chattels and conversion. Under Restatement (Second) of Torts §217, he has taken Brooks's horse, and as a consequence caused damage to it. Restatement (Second) of Torts §218(b). One might also argue that he has "dispossessed" Brooks of Flora since the horse had to be shot.

   Wongsun has also committed conversion—in this case both remedies apply. He has exercised control over Flora inconsistent with Brooks's ownership, which has led to Flora's loss. And the factors in Restatement (Second) of Torts §222A strongly point to liability for conversion. Taking

Flora was inconsistent with Brooks's right of control (§218(b)), and led to her complete loss (§218(e)), causing serious expense and inconvenience to Brooks (§218(f)). Wongsun's deliberate commandeering of Flora also shows bad faith (§218(e)). This would support liability for conversion as well as trespass to chattels.

10. Wongsun is liable for conversion since he has completely deprived Brooks of her horse and acted in bad faith. It would be hard to find a clearer case for conversion. Most jurisdictions would also hold Interloper liable as a converter. She has taken Flora, and obtains no right to possession by buying her from Wongsun, since Wongsun had no right to tell her. Although Interloper acted in good faith, she still deprived Brooks of her property. Here's the Restatement's position on such cases:

> **Section 229. Conversion by Receiving Possession in Consummation of Transaction**
>
> One who receives possession of a chattel from another with the intent to acquire for himself or for a third person a proprietary interest in the chattel which the other has not the power to transfer is subject to liability for conversion to a third person then entitled to the immediate possession of the chattel.

Put another way, buyer beware. This position is consistent with the treatment of mistake in other intentional tort cases: Here, as there, Interloper is "innocent" in some sense, but the law places the burden of her mistake on her rather than on the party who loses her property. The Restatement suggests that one who becomes a converter in such cases may reduce the resulting damages by returning the chattel unimpaired. Restatement (Second) §229 cmt. f.[4]

At Sea

11. a. Pete has committed trespass to chattels, but probably isn't liable to Sailor. As in Example 9, Pete has intermeddled with property, but caused no damage to it. He has used it for 12 hours or so, but it is hard to say that he has deprived Sailor of its use since Sailor's boat was not even in the water, and Sailor was not planning to use the mooring. Again, it is unclear whether a claim exists for such deprivation of use when, as here, the owner has no intent to use the property during the period when it is interfered with.

    The Restatement offers an example in which A leaves his car on the street, and B, for a joke, pushes it around the corner. A spends an

4. Interloper might recoup any damages she pays to Brooks from Wongsun, in an action for fraud or misrepresentation.

hour finding it. Restatement (Second) of Torts §218 illus. 4. Under the Restatement, B has committed trespass to chattels. However, this example is distinguishable since, in the Restatement illustration, A tried to use his car and was deprived of its use. It's hard to make that argument here.

b. On these facts, Pete is liable for damages under §218 since he has deprived Sailor of the use of the mooring for a substantial time. Restatement (Second) §218(c). Sailor could sue . . . but realistically, would he? What lawyer would take this case for a contingent fee (a percentage of the recovery)?

c. Even if some trespasses to chattels do not support an action for damages, defining such intrusions as tortious may give the possessor other rights. For example, tort law creates a limited privilege for a possessor of chattels to use force to recapture them. See Restatement (Second) §§100-110. This privilege would presumably apply if the taker had committed trespass to chattels under §217, even if he had not caused damages compensable under §218.

In addition, commission of the tort might support an action for an injunction, even if the trespasser had not caused damages. If Sneaky Pete regularly uses Sailor's mooring, Sailor might seek an injunction, even though he could not establish that he had planned to use the mooring at any time when Sneaky Pete tied up. See, e.g., *Buchanan Marine Inc. v. McCormack Sand Co.*, 743 F. Supp. 139, 142 (E.D.N.Y. 1990) (approving injunctive relief in a similar case).

A Clever Ploy

12. You can see Abel's reasoning here, can't you? If the tortfeasor interferes substantially with the right of possession, conversion law treats him as having "bought" the chattel. "Suits me," says Abel, "I'll pay the 50 bucks and keep the painting." Surely this is not going to work. Apart from potential criminal liability, a court would order return of the painting. (Traditionally the plaintiff could bring an action for *replevin* to recover the painting. See generally D. Dobbs and C. Roberts, Law of Remedies Third ed. 2018 §5.16.) Some courts might also grant punitive damages. Conversion is not meant to give tortfeasors an option to commandeer property as long as they are willing to pay for it. It is meant to make them pay its value as damages for major interference with the owner's possessory rights.

Quick Takes

13. a. Here, Mephisto has never taken possession of Plaintiff's property; instead, he destroyed it. He might argue that he is not liable for conversion because he did not "exercise . . . dominion or control"

over Flora. The argument won't fly. Surely, killing an animal is a way of exercising control over it. Mephisto is liable for conversion since he has destroyed, not damaged Flora. Restatement (Second) of Torts §222A illus. 17.

b. Mephisto has converted the tires, since he has rendered them useless by his intentional interference. He is also liable for trespass to chattels with regard to the car, since he has intermeddled with it (Restatement (Second) of Torts §217), resulting in an impairment of its condition. Restatement (Second) of Torts §218(b).
c. Mephisto is not liable for trespass to chattels or conversion, since he did not act with intent to cause harm to the car. He may be liable for negligence.
d. This is conversion. Mephisto intended to interfere with Plaintiff's property (Restatement (Second) of Torts §222A(2)(b)), caused extensive interference to it (§222A(2)(d), (e)), and certainly did not act in good faith. In *United States v. Arora*, 860 F. Supp. 1091 (D. Md. 1994), on which this example is based, the court held that the defendant had converted the cell line, which was destroyed by his interference.
e. This is neither conversion nor trespass to chattels. Mephisto had permission to use Flora, so his taking is not a dispossession. And he had no intent to cause the harm Flora suffered.
f. Trespass to chattels. Mephisto has intermeddled with Flora, but only caused temporary damage, not serious enough to treat him as a converter.
g. Neither conversion nor trespass to chattels. Presumably Plaintiff agreed to the surgery, understanding the risk that Secretarius would never run again. Thus, Mephisto would have consent to perform it, defeating a claim for intentional interference. Any claim would have to be based on negligence instead.
h. This is trespass to land, not to chattels. Mephisto has come upon plaintiff's property and deposited dirt on it, a clear trespass. He is liable. The more complicated question is what the damages are. Plaintiff's damage is consequential loss of economic opportunity, which is not your typical damage from trespass. Frankly, I don't know if Mephisto is liable for that. He is liable for trespass, regardless of whether he caused *any* damage (Restatement (Second) of Torts §163)), but naturally plaintiff wants damages for losing the chance to compete. Perhaps he will recover punitive damages based on Mephisto's reprehensible conduct.
i. Though Muir's motives may be lofty, he has committed trespass to chattels by intermeddling with Monumental's logging machine. As a result Monumental has been deprived of its use for a substantial

period of time—loss of a day's logging with these huge machines is likely a significant economic hit. See *Huffman and Wright Logging Co. v. Wade*, 857 P.2d 101 (Or. 1993) (affirming verdict for compensatory and punitive damages for trespass to chattels on similar facts).

j. Zenger is probably not liable for either trespass to chattels or conversion. He has not deprived Carnegie of the use of his papers for any length of time, much less permanently, so he isn't liable for conversion. Nor is he likely to be liable for trespass to chattels. He has "intermeddled" with Carnegie's papers, so arguably he has committed trespass to chattels. But he hasn't damaged Carnegie's papers, or dispossessed Carnegie of them in any way, so it appears that he would not be liable to Carnegie under §218. A much more likely remedy is a claim for invasion of privacy, which is the real gist of Carnegie's complaint. See *Pearson v. Dodd*, 410 F.2d 701 (D.C. Cir. 1969) (denying recovery for trespass to chattels or conversion on similar facts).

Cyber Chattel

14. In *Compuserve Inc. v. Cyber Promotions, Inc.*, 962 F. Supp. 1015 (S.D. Ohio 1997), the court held a spammer liable for trespass to chattels on similar facts. Cyber Promotions argued that it did not cause any injury to Compuserve's servers by its e-mail transmissions, but the court, citing Restatement (Second) of Torts §218 cmt. h, noted that a defendant who interferes with a chattel can be liable for trespass even though it does not harm the chattel. The spamming in this case caused multiple problems for Compuserve, including the burden of excessive traffic and the costs of trying to circumvent the defendant's misuse of its electronic facilities. The court entered a preliminary injunction barring Cyber Promotions from sending spam messages through Compuserve's network. See also *eBay Inc. v. Bidder's Edge, Inc.*, 100 F. Supp. 2d 1058 (N.D. Cal. 2000) (granting preliminary injunction against use of "web crawler" technology challenged on a trespass to chattels theory); *America Online Inc. v. IMS*, 24 F. Supp. 2d 548, 550-551 (E.D. Va. 1998) (defendant who sent 60 million unauthorized e-mail advertisements through Internet service provider's network liable for trespass to chattels).

CHAPTER 5

False Imprisonment: Protecting Freedom of Movement

INTRODUCTION

Battery and assault protect the right to be free of physical intrusions on the person. Trespass allows redress for intrusions on private property. False imprisonment safeguards an equally fundamental value, the right to be free of restraint on one's freedom of movement, the right to "go freely through the world,"[1] the right not to be confined against one's will. Physical confinement is a drastic intrusion on personal liberty, as well as a humiliating blow to a person's sense of dignity and independence. It isn't surprising that the tort of false imprisonment dates to the very early days of the common law.

The Elements of False Imprisonment

The law of false imprisonment in most states fairly closely reflects the formulation in the Restatement of Torts.

> **Section 35. False Imprisonment**
>
> (1) An actor is subject to liability to another for false imprisonment if

1. M. Shapo, Principles of Tort Law §10.07.

> (a) the actor intends to confine the other within a limited area, or the actor's intent is sufficient under §11 (transferred intent);
>
> (b) the actor's affirmative conduct causes a confinement of the other, as provided in §§8 and 9, or the actor fails to release the other from a confinement despite owing a duty to do so;
>
> (c) the other is aware that he or she is confined or the other suffers bodily harm as a result of the confinement; and
>
> (d) the other does not consent to the confinement, as provided in §12.

Restatement of the Law (Third) Torts: Intentional Torts to Persons (Tentative Draft No. 3) §7.

Note that false imprisonment again requires intent, in the same sense as required for other intentional torts. Carelessness is not enough; the defendant must have acted with a purpose to cause the confinement, or with substantial certainty that his acts will cause it. Here, as with battery and assault, one may act *deliberately* but not intentionally. If Peterson, a zookeeper, closes up the tiger cage and goes to bed, not realizing that Stanley is still in there feeding the tigers, he has not committed the tort of false imprisonment. Although he acted deliberately, in the sense that he meant to close the door, he did not close the door with the purpose to confine Stanley, or with substantial certainty that he would. Any remedy against Peterson will be for negligence, not intentional tort.

Second, the defendant's intentional act must cause confinement of the plaintiff. The essence of the tort is restraint of the plaintiff's freedom of movement, so she must establish confinement to recover. Not all restraints on a plaintiff's freedom of movement constitute confinement. If Munoz blocks the door of her store, refusing to let Maxwell in, she has not committed false imprisonment. Preventing the plaintiff from going to one particular place does not "confine" her, even though it restricts her freedom of movement in some degree. Similarly, blocking the plaintiff's way in the street will not support recovery for false imprisonment, as long as plaintiff can go some other way. Even if Munoz blocks an exit from her store while Maxwell is inside, she has not confined Maxwell, if some reasonable means of getting out remains. If the side door is open, and Maxwell knows it, he is not confined, just frustrated. If, on the other hand, he can only escape by slipping out through a hatch into the sewer system, he has no reasonable means of escape.

Confinement must be within a limited area. Threatening to kill Bertucci if he goes into outer space would not be actionable: No court would view a restriction to wandering the earth as confinement to a bounded area. One court wisely found Taiwan too spacious to constitute a "bounded area" (see *Shen v. Leo A. Daly Co.*, 222 F.3d 472, 478 (8th Cir. 2000)), but another suggests that "if Denmark was a dungeon to Hamlet . . . we suppose Illinois could be a prison to [the plaintiff]." *Albright v. Oliver*, 975 F.2d 343, 346 (7th Cir. 1992). See also *Helstrom v. North Slope Borough*, 797 P.2d 1192, 1199 (Alaska 1990) (preventing plaintiff from leaving Barrow, Alaska, could constitute false imprisonment). Obviously, most of the cases involve confinement within a much more limited space, such as the four walls of a house, an office or a prison, or in a car or other vehicle.

Consent by Coercion

Confinement does not always entail physically locking the plaintiff up. If store personnel confront a customer in the aisle, accuse her of theft, and threaten her with physical harm if she leaves, she suffers confinement, even if the door is open. "The restraint may be by means of physical barriers, or by threats of force which intimidate the plaintiff into compliance with orders. It is sufficient that he submits to an apprehension of force reasonably to be understood from the conduct of the defendant, although no force is used or even expressly threatened." *Dupler v. Seabert*, 230 N.W.2d 626, 631-632 (Wis. 1975). Similarly, an actor can confine the plaintiff by confiscating significant items of personal property, or by other threats that would cause a reasonable person to submit to confinement.

Cases often involve the question of whether the plaintiff was really forced to remain, or simply responded to psychological or economic pressure that we all experience at times. Consider the common false imprisonment scenario involving a customer in a store who is brought to the office and accused of theft. The customer may choose to stay in the office for a variety of reasons. She may believe that she is not free to leave, and will be subjected to physical restraint if she does. As the *Dupler* case suggests, this suffices to constitute confinement. Or, the customer may believe that, if she leaves, store personnel will keep her purse, or her purchases. The cases hold that staying to avoid loss of personal property also constitutes confinement. Or, the customer may believe that, if she refuses to cooperate and leaves, store personnel will call the police, or tell others that she had stolen from the store. Choosing to remain in scenarios like the last one, which involves forms of pressure that the defendant has a right to use, generally will not constitute confinement.

Such cases pose close factual issues concerning what threats were made or why the plaintiff submitted to physical restraint. These cases, of course, raise questions of fact for the jury, as to whether the plaintiff stayed because she reasonably apprehended physical force or loss of valuable property, or stayed for other reasons, such as to clear matters up, or to avoid arrest or dismissal from employment.

As with other intentional torts, the plaintiff generally need not show any physical injury or other damage in order to recover for false imprisonment.

The Restatement draft quoted above (pp. 79–80) provides that damages need not be proved unless the plaintiff was unaware of the confinement. The plaintiff may recover at least nominal damages by proving the fact of the false imprisonment itself. However, few plaintiffs bring lawsuits solely to have the court declare that they have been wronged. Almost always, they hope for an award of substantial damages. A jury might find substantial damages if the plaintiff has suffered psychological injuries as a result of the confinement. In one case, for example, a store clerk accused of theft testified that the incident caused her throat to swell so that she couldn't breathe, and that she could no longer work in a store, for fear of making mistakes and being subjected to similar treatment. Such consequences could support a substantial award. In some states punitive damages may be available, providing an additional incentive to sue even if physical or economic damages are small.

COMMON PRIVILEGE DEFENSES TO FALSE IMPRISONMENT

Many false imprisonment cases turn on whether the defendant had a privilege to commit acts that otherwise would constitute false imprisonment. The three most common privileges asserted in false imprisonment cases are consent, the privilege to detain a customer to investigate apparent shoplifting, and the privilege to arrest.

It isn't entirely clear whether these privileges constitute defenses, or whether the plaintiff must prove the absence of such privileges as part of her prima facie case. Logically, these privileges probably should be viewed as defenses to false imprisonment, which a defendant must plead and prove to avoid recovery. The definition of false imprisonment in Restatement (Second) of Torts §35 did not include lack of consent as an element. However, authorities often speak of the tort as applying to confinement "without a lawful privilege." Harper, James, & Grey, The Law of Torts §3.7. The proposed Third Restatement will apparently include lack of consent as an element of false imprisonment (§7(d)), which likely reflects the trend in the cases. See id. at cmt. k.

The privilege of consent, addressed in Chapter 6, is frequently asserted in false imprisonment cases. If a party consents to enter a three-week drug treatment program, he cannot sue for false imprisonment if he is kept for three weeks.[2] Similarly, a store clerk who consents to remain in the security office to discuss a claimed theft cannot sue for false imprisonment. But

2. Unless, of course, he validly revokes consent during the period.

consent can be limited. The clerk might have consented to a brief detention, but not five hours. The drug user might have consented to three weeks' treatment, but not five months. The issues here tend to be—as in other consent cases—whether there was true consent, as opposed to coercion, and whether the defendant exceeded the scope of the consent freely given.

A common false imprisonment scenario involves detention of a person suspected of stealing from a store. Under the traditional common law approach, a merchant who detained a person suspected of stealing goods risked liability for false imprisonment, particularly if it turned out that the person had not stolen the merchandise. Some courts, recognizing the dilemma this poses for merchants, have recognized a privilege to detain a person to investigate theft. This privilege is often referred to as the "shopkeeper's privilege." The Second Restatement recognizes this privilege, though it has not been universally adopted by courts:

> One who reasonably believes that another has tortiously taken a chattel upon his premises, or has failed to make due cash payment for a chattel purchased or service rendered there, is privileged, without arresting the other, to detain him on the premises for the time necessary for a reasonable investigation of the facts.

Restatement (Second) of Torts §120A. Under the Restatement, the privilege is not limited to the police or similar security officers. It may be exercised by a store manager or a clerk. But note several limits on the privilege: The actor must have a reasonable belief that the theft has taken place, and the detention must be limited to the time necessary for a reasonable investigation. Many states now have statutes that codify this privilege. See, e.g., Calif. Penal Code §490.5(f)(1), which provides in part that

> A merchant may detain a person for a reasonable time for the purpose of conducting an investigation in a reasonable manner whenever the merchant has probable cause to believe the person to be detained is attempting to unlawfully take or has unlawfully taken merchandise from the merchant's premises.

Another common affirmative defense to false imprisonment claims is the privilege of arrest. This is too complex an area to get into in detail here . . . the Second Restatement offers some 34 sections on the privilege of arrest.[3] It involves a good many complex distinctions, such as arrest by private persons vs. police officers, arrest with or without warrants, and arrests for felony vs. arrests for lesser offenses. The issue is further complicated by constitutional guarantees and statutory variations. Suffice it to say here that in many circumstances there is a privilege to arrest a person based upon a warrant or reasonable suspicion that the person has committed a crime, but

3. See Restatement (Second) of Torts §§112-145.

that where the privilege does not apply, an arrest constitutes actionable false imprisonment (though often referred to as false arrest).

EXAMPLES

Examples

Probing the Elements

1. Lewis, a school bus driver, completes her route, returns the bus to the lot, locks the door, and heads for home. Unbeknownst to her, Gretel, a small first grader, had fallen asleep curled up in a back seat, and wasn't visible from the front of the bus. Lewis had looked to the back before getting off the bus, but did not see her. Gretel awoke and was terrified. She was not discovered until the following morning. Her parents bring suit on her behalf for false imprisonment. What result?

2. Tough and Thug meet Milquetoast, a hiker and nature lover, on a grassy hill, with a view for 60 miles in each direction. Furious that Milquetoast won the school spelling bee, they order him to sit down in the grass and stay put, threatening to beat him to a pulp if he moves. Milquetoast sits. After Milquetoast sits in the grass for seven minutes, enjoying the view, they let him go. Can Milquetoast sue for false imprisonment?

3. Tough and Thug accost Milquetoast on a city street late at night. Thug pulls a knife and demands that Milquetoast take them to an ATM to withdraw money. They walk seven blocks to the ATM, but Tough and Thug run away when they see a police officer nearby. Are they liable to Milquetoast for false imprisonment?

4. Clevinger refused to pay the bill for repairs on his car, claiming they were inadequate. Parrish, the owner of the garage, had him bring the car in from his farm, 40 miles out of town. When Clevinger arrived, Parrish put the car on the lift and raised it in the air. He then refused to bring it back down until Clevinger paid his bill. Clevinger sues for false imprisonment, claiming he could not return home without his car. What result?

5. Alston gets on the bus to go downtown and starts talking politics with Felix, the bus driver. Unfortunately they don't see eye to eye on such matters, and end up in a violent argument. When they get to Alston's stop, Felix refuses to let Alston off the bus until he apologizes for insulting his favorite politician. Alston sues for false imprisonment. Can he make out a good claim?

Confinement and Compulsion

Many close false imprisonment cases involve the issue of whether the plaintiff was really forced to remain, or chose to for reasons of her own. Here are a few examples that explore the problem.

6. Xavier meets Quentin on the street. He steps in front of Quentin and orders him to stop. Quentin had just broken up with Xavier's sister, and she was devastated. Xavier demanded an explanation, and showed every sign of making a scene if Xavier didn't discuss the matter with him. Quentin, anxious to avoid a scene, stops. The confrontation lasts 20 minutes. Quentin later sues Xavier for false imprisonment. Does he have a false imprisonment claim?

7. Here's a nice example from the Second Restatement. "A is naked in a Turkish bath. B locks the door into the dressing room but leaves open the door to the general waiting room where persons of both sexes are congregated." Restatement (Second) of Torts §36 illus. 5. Has B confined A?

8. Mulvey, as a joke, locks Maroney in his (Mulvey's) apartment while he is sleeping off a hangover. Maroney gets up and tries the doors but can't get them open. When sued for false imprisonment, Mulvey argues that Maroney was not confined, because all the windows were unlocked and the apartment was on the first floor. What result?

9. Montez has just broken up with Hurley. She agrees to go for a drive with Hurley to discuss their relationship, if he will bring her back to the house. He brings her back, but then begins to coast slowly down the street. Montez could escape by jumping from the car, but doesn't. Instead, she sues for false imprisonment. Has she been confined?

10. Griffin pays a visit to a former boyfriend, Clark. Clark offers to drive her home, but she refuses, saying she will take the train to her home 30 miles away. Clark grabs her suitcase and puts it in his car. Meanwhile, the train leaves the station. Rather than spend the night in a strange town, Griffin reluctantly gets into Clark's car. En route, there is an accident due to the negligence of another car, and Griffin suffers personal injuries. What arguments would you expect Clark to make to avoid liability for Griffin's injuries?

11. Consider this example from the Second Restatement:

    > A, a small and weak man, takes hold of B's coat for the purpose of detaining him against his will. B is a much larger man and could, with little exertion, free himself at once. B submits. A has confined B.

    Restatement (Second) of Torts §39 illus. 2.

    a. Would B have a privilege to use force to free himself?
    b. Why, if B has a privilege to escape, and easily could, do the drafters of the Restatement treat this as confinement?

False False Imprisonment

12. Ruggiero, a store security officer, sees Li walking out of the store with four pairs of Levis, which still have the security tags attached. (These are typically removed when items are rung up on the cash register.) He asks Li if he can examine the Levis. Li gives them to Ruggierio, who then announces that Li will have to come to the office to discuss the matter. Li, unwilling to part with the Levis, goes along. In the office he is interrogated by the manager for 20 minutes before he is allowed to leave.
    a. Assume that Li had paid for the Levis, but the clerk had failed to remove the tags. Since he was not a shoplifter, could he sue for false imprisonment?
    b. Rudansky, a customer, follows Li out of the store and grabs him, ordering him to return to the store and pay for the goods. Is he covered by the shopkeeper's privilege articulated in §120A of the Second Restatement (see p. 83)?
    c. Suppose that Ruggiero, the security officer, was told that a tall male customer had run out of the store with unpaid merchandise, and ran out and grabbed Li, a tall male, in the store parking lot. However, it turns out that it was another tall male who had taken the goods. Is Ruggiero liable for false imprisonment?

Cabin Fever

13. In *Abourezk v. New York Airline, Inc.*, 705 F. Supp. 656 (D.D.C. 1989), the plaintiff was a passenger on a plane set to fly from Virginia to New York. Due to flight delays, the plane sat on the tarmac for several hours. Since he could no longer make his appointment in New York, Abourezk demanded to be let off the plane, but the pilot refused. His subsequent lawsuit for false imprisonment was dismissed by the federal district court. Why isn't this a good claim for false imprisonment?

Explanations

Probing the Elements

1. Gretel will lose this case since Lewis did not act with tortious intent. She did act "intentionally," in the sense that she deliberately locked the bus before leaving. But she did not act with a purpose to confine Gretel, or with substantial certainty that she would.

    Lewis may have been negligent, for failure to walk to the back of the bus and check for sleeping kids; this doesn't seem like a totally unlikely scenario. If so, Gretel may have a claim for negligence against her. But false imprisonment is an intentional tort, which means that Gretel can only recover for it if she proves that Lewis acted with a purpose to confine or with knowledge to a substantial certainty that her act would confine her. That isn't true here.

2. Even though Milquetoast is confined in the open, with a 60-mile view, he is confined. He is forced to remain where he is, whether he wants to or not. He is confined within a bounded area, the spot where he sits. The area may not have walls, but it doesn't have to. One can be confined in the open as well as in a room, and experience the same indignity and humiliation from deprivation of the freedom of movement. Milquetoast has a good cause of action for false imprisonment.

   Seven minutes is not a very long confinement, but even a very brief confinement suffices for false imprisonment. The fact that the confinement was short may affect the extent of the damages, but does not avoid liability for the tort itself.

3. This is false imprisonment. Tough and Thug didn't make Milquetoast stay in one place, but they did confine his freedom of movement, forcing him to go where they order him to. (Similarly, one can be confined by being carjacked, for example.) They have committed assault as well since they have placed Milquetoast in apprehension of being knifed if he does not comply with the illegal condition of going where they order him to.

4. This example, loosely based on *Warrem v. Parrish*, 436 S.W.2d 670 (Mo. 1969), does not constitute false imprisonment. While Clevinger was prevented from driving home, he was not prevented from going home in some other way, or from going any other place. He was not "confined." His remedy will have to be for conversion of the car, or infliction of emotional distress, but not for false imprisonment.

   Admittedly, this case looks a lot like the case in which a store manager grabs a customer's purse and tells her to stay in the store while they investigate whether she stole merchandise. But in that case, the defendant confiscates the purse to coerce the plaintiff to *stay*, that is, restricts her right to leave by taking property. In *Warrem*, the station owners did not bar the car owner from leaving; they just told him they would keep his car.

5. Even though Alston got on the bus voluntarily, he did so with the understanding that he could get off at any stop. The driver has a duty to let Alston off at his stop. By refusing to do so, the driver has intentionally confined Alston in the bus. His indignation at Alston's political views does not give him any privilege to confine him. Alston has a right to get off, and is detained against his will. This is a good claim.

   As the case illustrates, a defendant can commit false imprisonment by refusing to release another as well as by initiating confinement. In a well-known case, the defendant induced the plaintiff to travel on his yacht, agreeing to let her off when they got to Maine, but refused to provide a boat to take her to shore when they arrived. Because he had a duty to assist her in disembarking, the defendant was liable for false imprisonment. See *Whittaker v. Sandford*, 85 A. 399 (1912).

Confinement and Compulsion

6. A plaintiff can reasonably respond to various threats by submitting to confinement, including threats of physical force, threats to her property, or threats to a member of her family. But staying to avoid the prospect of "a scene" does not suffice to constitute confinement. Life is full of awkward situations that put us to difficult choices. Not all can be redressed by tort law. Quentin may choose to avoid embarrassment by staying to talk to Xavier, but the law does not protect him from "scenes." Similarly, the choice to stay in a place to clear one's name, to resolve a dispute, to avoid being reported to the police, or for similar reasons will not make out a case of false imprisonment.

7. This example, like the last, probes the types of threats that may reasonably lead the plaintiff to consider himself confined. The Restatement states that a person is not required to take a means of escape "if the circumstances are such as to make it offensive to a reasonable sense of decency or personal dignity." Restatement (Second) of Torts §36 cmt. a. The Turkish bath example is a clear example of such a situation. A may sit tight and sue for false imprisonment.

8. This might be a good defense. One is not confined if there is a reasonable means of escape. Surely Maroney should consider the windows, shouldn't he? I would think so. If he had to jump ten feet to get out, this would not be a reasonable means of escape. But if they are fairly close to ground level, there is a strong argument that he was not confined.

9. First, the fact that Montez agreed to get into the car initially does not prevent her from suing for false imprisonment. One can consent to one thing without consenting to another. Here, Montez consented to go for a ride with Hurley, not to remain in the car afterwards. So Hurley's consent defense will not fly.

   As stated in the Introduction, a plaintiff is not confined if there is a reasonable means of escape from the confinement. But jumping from a moving car, even a slowly moving car, is not a reasonable means of escape. So Montez is confined in the car, and may sue for false imprisonment for the period after they returned from the drive. Hurley's driving away forces her to remain, constituting false imprisonment.

10. In this example, loosely based on one of the classic cases, *Griffin v. Clark*, 42 P.2d 297 (Idaho 1935), there is no suggestion that Clark drove negligently. Thus, Griffin could not sue him for negligence; she would have to recover based on his false imprisonment of her instead. Clark might argue that she was not forced to skip the train; she did so to retrieve her bag. But coercion through seizure of personal property can constitute false imprisonment, so that argument will not fly.

    Clark might also argue that she consented to ride with him since she got into Clark's car. But here too, if she did so under compulsion, she could still claim that she was imprisoned in the car. This is like the customer who willingly goes to the office in a store after her purse is confiscated by security guards. There is no true consent to the detention, because it is done under duress. See Restatement (Second) of Torts §40A (submission under duress makes consent ineffective to bar action for false imprisonment). Whether she has been coerced is a factual question: Certainly if Clark said he would leave with her things if she did not come along, this would constitute coercion, vitiating her consent.

    Perhaps Clark's most interesting argument would be that his false imprisonment was not the proximate cause of Griffin's injuries in the accident. Even though he acted intentionally in falsely imprisoning her, he did not do so for the purpose or with substantial certainty that she would suffer resulting personal injuries in the accident. Very probably, however, a court would hold Clark liable for this extended consequence of his tort. Intentional tortfeasors are generally liable for the consequences of their deliberately tortious behavior, even unexpected consequences. While there is probably some limit to this (see Chapter 2, Example 12), an accident is a reasonably predictable consequence of forcing Griffin to ride in the car. Thus, she is likely to recover for it on a false imprisonment theory.

11. a. Yes, B would have the privilege of self-defense since A, by grabbing him, is committing a battery. Also, if A's grabbing constitutes false imprisonment, the common law recognizes a privilege to use self-defense to prevent it. Restatement (Second) of Torts §68. So, B *could* use force here, but the Restatement *gives him the choice not to.* He may submit and sue for false imprisonment, and A will not be able to argue that he did not commit false imprisonment because B could have broken loose.

    b. As a policy matter, the Restatement position makes sense. Otherwise, B would be required to use self-defense, by breaking loose from Milquetoast-like assailants, since he would not have the alternative of submitting and suing for false imprisonment. (Either way, he could sue for battery, but the two torts protect different invasions.)

Requiring B to use self-defense would encourage escalation of the conflict.

If the tort rule only allowed B to submit and sue for false imprisonment when the assailant is stronger, B would have to make difficult judgments when accosted with physical force. In many cases, it won't be clear who is the weaker party. Suppose that A and B are more evenly matched, or B doesn't know that A is a karate instructor (or mistakenly thinks that he is)? The position taken by the Restatement should (if anyone in such circumstances considers tort law) discourage violence by allowing B to acquiesce and later sue for false imprisonment.

False False Imprisonment

12. a. The facts suggest that Li was coerced into going to the office and remaining there during the interrogation. As the Introduction states, one can be confined by coercion, and confiscation of personal property can constitute coercion. This makes out a prima facie case of false imprisonment.

    However, while Li makes out the elements of a false imprisonment claim, the facts suggest that Ruggierio and the manager can establish the "shopkeeper's privilege" as a defense to it. They had reasonable cause, based on the fact that the tags remained on the jeans, to believe that Li had taken them without paying. Thus, they probably had a sufficient basis to detain Li for a reasonable period to investigate the possible theft. Although the reasonableness of the length of the detention depends on the facts of each case, 20 minutes is probably a reasonable time to detain a customer to resolve most shoplifting disputes.

    In this case, of course, Li turns out *not* to be a shoplifter. The Second Restatement suggests that the privilege arises where the person exercising it "reasonably believes" that the other has stolen the goods. In these situations, as with the privilege of self-defense, the actor must act based on reasonable appearances. "If there were no such privilege, he must either permit the suspected person to walk out of the premises and disappear, or must arrest him, at the risk of liability for false arrest if the theft could not be proved." Restatement (Second) of Torts §120A cmt. a. It seems that the privilege should apply, even if further investigation establishes that no theft has taken place.

    b. Probably not. Section 120A refers to taking of chattels "upon his premises," pretty clearly creating a privilege for merchants, but not a roving privilege for anyone who may think someone else has stolen goods. Customers or bystanders are not likely to be as aware of the details of a transaction, so would likely make more mistakes. In addition, they are not used to dealing with such cases, so might more frequently provoke violence. Evidently, the section does not support a privilege for such vigilante intervention.

c. This is a tough question. Suppose that Tough and Thug decide to hold Milquetoast for ransom, and lock up Jessup, who looks like Milquetoast. Their mistake of fact will surely not prevent them from being liable to Jessup, just as a mistake about ownership of property will not bar an action for trespass. But if a mistake about *whether* there was a theft does not negate the shopkeeper's privilege (as suggested immediately above), why should a reasonable mistake about *who* committed a theft?

   Tort law is often more tolerant of mistakes in assessing privileges than it is in applying the basic elements of intentional torts (see *Prosser & Keeton on Torts*, (5th ed. 1984) at 111), so the privilege may well apply to this mistake in asserting a privilege. In many states this will depend on the wording and intent of the statute codifying the shopkeeper's privilege. For example, there is a strong argument that the California statute quoted at p. 83 protects the detention of a person to investigate, even if it turns out that she has been mistaken for someone else.

Cabin Fever

13. Abourezk makes out a good prima facie case of confinement. He was confined within the airplane by the deliberate refusal of the pilot to let him out, after he had repeatedly expressed his desire to leave. Naturally, the pilot had good reasons; he couldn't very well let him walk out onto the runways, and it was dangerous for a vehicle to come out to the plane. But he clearly was confined.

    The defense, it seems, should be consent. Passengers, by contracting for transportation with the airline, consent to the airline's reasonable procedures incident to providing transportation, including restrictions on movement in situations like this. Surely, if passengers were ordered to stay in their seats with their seatbelts fastened during turbulence, that would not constitute false imprisonment, even of the most vociferously objecting passenger.

CHAPTER 6

The Far Side of the Coin: Classic Defenses to Intentional Torts

INTRODUCTION

The preceding chapters describe the elements a plaintiff must prove in order to recover for various intentional torts. These elements, it is said, are necessary to establish a "prima facie case," that is, a showing sufficient to allow a jury to conclude that the tort has been committed. However, the case is not over once the plaintiff has presented evidence to establish these prima facie elements. The defendant must be heard from, and very likely, she will offer another side to the story.

The defendant may defend by simply negating one or more of the prima facie elements of the tort. For example, she may present evidence in a battery case that she never touched the plaintiff, that she did so unintentionally, or that the touching was not one that the reasonable person would find offensive under the circumstances. In other cases, however, the defendant takes the position that, *even if* the prima facie elements of the tort are shown, she is not liable anyway, because of additional facts that allow her to avoid liability. Such additional facts are often referred to as *affirmative defenses.*

Some affirmative defenses have nothing to do with the underlying incident itself. For example, if Jones sues Smith for battery, Smith might defend on the ground that the claim is barred by the statute of limitations, the statutory period within which suit must be brought on a claim. This defense asserts that, even if Jones can prove that Smith intentionally inflicted a harmful or offensive touching on her, she is not liable, because the suit was brought too late. Or, Smith might plead that Jones had signed a release from liability (a contractual agreement not to sue on the claim, usually given for a sum of money paid in settlement). Again, this defense does not rely on a showing that no battery occurred, but rather on additional facts that demonstrate that there is no longer a right to sue for the claim.

Other affirmative defenses, however, relate more directly to the events that give rise to the claim. The classic example is self-defense. In Jones's action for battery, for example, Smith might plead that she hit Jones because she was warding off a blow from Jones. If she acted in self-defense, she was privileged to inflict the harmful or offensive touching on Jones, and will not be held liable for doing so.

Another common affirmative defense to intentional tort is consent. Courts generally hold that the victim's consent bars recovery for touchings that would otherwise constitute batteries. If Jones proves that Smith slapped her in the face, Smith might plead that she and Jones were rehearsing for a play, and that Jones consented to the slap as part of the script. If this is true, Smith's act was privileged; she will not be liable even if the slap was offensive and intentional.

A number of other privileges may also constitute defenses to battery and assault claims. Police officers enjoy a privilege to use reasonable force in the course of arrest. An actor who causes an intentional invasion of another's property interests may sometimes assert the defense of *necessity*, that an otherwise tortious act was privileged because it was done to prevent a greater harm. Teachers and parents enjoy a limited privilege to use force in disciplining children. And there are other privilege defenses. This chapter, however, focuses on self-defense and consent as examples of the effect of privileges on tort liability.

THE PRIVILEGE TO USE FORCE IN SELF-DEFENSE

Self-preservation, they say, is the first law of nature. It is not surprising, then, that the law of torts has long recognized the privilege to use force to protect oneself from an aggressor. An actor who is privileged to use force in self-defense incurs no liability for doing so, in some cases even if she inflicts serious bodily injury or death upon her assailant.

However, self-defense is a limited privilege. It is not a general license to attack an aggressor, or to respond to unwarranted provocation, or to give blow for blow; it only authorizes the use of force to prevent an impending battery or to stop one which is in progress. Suppose, for example, that Jones slaps Smith on the face and announces, "There, now we are even." Smith has no privilege of self-defense on these facts. She does not need to use force in her own defense, because she is no longer threatened with a battery. True, she has been the *victim* of one, and may sue for it, but self-defense does not authorize a tort victim to respond to force with force. It is a privilege to forestall an impending battery, not to retaliate for prior ones.

Similarly, there is no right to attack another simply because the other may deserve it. Smith may not strike Jones because she makes derogatory statements about Smith's lineage or her politics. Nor may she invoke self-defense against threats of future harm, such as a threat to attack her at a later time. In such cases, Smith has peaceful legal remedies, and is required to resort to them rather than "taking the law into her own hands" by immediate physical force.

Even where the privilege arises, it is limited: The victim of an aggressor may only use reasonable force in self-defense. The victim is not licensed to extract an "eye for an eye," but only to use the force that she reasonably believes is necessary to avert the threatened harm. Smith may not knife Jones in the ribs to avoid a slap in the face, though she would certainly be privileged to block the blow or push Jones away. Smith may not even be privileged to use the same level of force used by the initial aggressor, if less will do to prevent the contact. Remember that the purpose of self-defense is not to remedy the wrong already inflicted; such redress should be sought through criminal prosecution or intentional tort damages. Self-defense is authorized solely to prevent a further intrusion that cannot be avoided by waiting for legal redress.

On the other hand, the victim will sometimes be privileged to use *more* force than was necessary to avert a threatened battery. The privilege to use force in self-defense turns on the victim's *reasonable belief* that force is necessary, even if, in fact, it is not. If Enemy Jones raises a knife before her, Smith has no time to conduct an investigation of Jones's motives before forestalling the blow. Smith would be privileged to strike Jones if she reasonably concluded that Jones was about to stab her, even if Jones actually intended to scratch his back with the knife. Restatement (Third) of Torts: Intentional Torts to Persons (Tentative Draft No. 5) §21 cmt. h.

The limits on the privilege of self-defense reflect a policy of minimizing the use of force as a means of self-protection. Arguably, this goal would be furthered by always requiring victims to retreat—that is, to run away—before using self-defense. However, courts have refused to create a duty to retreat (even if it can be done with perfect safety) before using *nondeadly* force in self-defense. Such a duty would require the victim of threatened violence to relinquish her right to walk the streets. Our culture places a high premium on personal choice and independence; consequently, a "duty to run" has not met with public or judicial acceptance. Thus, at least where nondeadly force is threatened, the victim is privileged to stand her ground and use nondeadly force in self-defense, even if retreat is feasible. Restatement (Third) of Tort: Intentional Torts to Persons (Tentative Draft No. 5) §22 cmt. g.

DEADLY FORCE IN SELF-DEFENSE

While all courts recognize a limited right to self-defense, most impose additional restrictions on the right to use deadly force, that is, force "by which the actor intends, or which a reasonable person would view as likely, to cause either death or serious bodily harm." Restatement (Third) of Torts: Intentional Torts to Persons (Tentative Draft No. 5) §23 cmt. c. The Third Restatement draft (§23) provides that an actor may only use deadly force in self-defense if

> The actor reasonably believes that:
>
> (1) the other [i.e. the assailant] is intentionally inflicting or about to intentionally inflict unprivileged force upon the actor, and the actor is thereby put in peril of death, serious bodily harm, or forcible rape, which the actor can safely prevent only by the immediate use of deadly force.

Under this widely accepted approach, there is no right to use deadly force in response to the lesser threat of nondeadly force. If Smith raises her hand to slap Jones, Jones may not shoot her dead, or swing at her head with a hammer. Jones may use nondeadly force, or retreat, or suffer the slap and sue for battery, but she is not privileged to escalate the conflict by using deadly force.

Jones may not even be privileged to use deadly force if she is attacked with deadly force. Some jurisdictions, and the Third Restatement, require a victim of deadly force to retreat if it is safe to do so before using deadly force against the assailant. See Restatement (Third) of Torts: Intentional Torts to Persons (Tentative Draft No. 5) §23(b). The Restatement offers this rationale for imposing a duty to retreat:

> the interest of society in the life and efficiency of its members and in the prevention of the serious breaches of the peace involved in bloody affrays requires one attacked with a deadly weapon, except within his own dwelling place, to retreat before using force intended or likely to inflict death or serious bodily harm upon his assailant, unless he reasonably believes that there is any chance that retreat cannot be safely made.

Restatement (Second) of Torts §65 cmt. g. Both Restatements recognize, however, that the victim need not retreat unless it is clearly safe to do so. If the victim has any doubt of that (as most will), she may use deadly force in self-defense against deadly force.

A majority of jurisdictions appear to reject the Restatement approach, however. Instead, they hold that the victim of an assault with deadly force is privileged to stand her ground and use deadly force in self-defense, even if retreat is feasible. Dobbs' Law of Torts §81. Even the Restatement recognizes that one threatened with deadly force in her home need not retreat. This obviously reflects the widely shared view that one's home, if not quite a castle, ought at least to be an inviolable place of refuge.

DEFENSE OF OTHERS

Interesting problems arise when an actor defends others rather than himself. Suppose, for example, that Sir Galahad comes around the corner and sees Goliath taking a swing at David. Inferring that Goliath is about to batter David, he punches Goliath. Is he protected from liability by a privilege of "defense of another"?

The basic premise in the cases has been that an intervenor such as Galahad has the right to use the same force to defend David that David could use to defend himself. Dobbs' Law of Torts §84. Thus, if Goliath is about to batter David with nondeadly force, Galahad (like David) could use reasonable nondeadly force to prevent that battery. If Goliath was using deadly force, Galahad could use deadly force in defense of David, if necessary to forestall the battery.

But suppose that Galahad, when he comes around that corner, misconstrues the situation. Suppose that David had just reached into his pocket for a knife, and Goliath's impending blow was a privileged act of self-defense against an assault by David? Galahad may reasonably interpret the scene as an assault by Goliath, but suppose he is wrong?

The cases have taken two approaches to this "mistaken defense of other" problem. Some take the position that Galahad has a privilege to act upon his reasonable perception. Thus, if it reasonably appears to Galahad that Goliath is the aggressor, he may defend David from Goliath's blow, even if he is wrong. After all, we give *David* that privilege—to act upon his reasonable perception that he is being attacked, even if he is not. So why not give the same privilege to Galahad, the virtuous intervenor? Under this approach, Galahad may use reasonable force to protect David so long as he reasonably believes that David is about to be the victim of a battery by Goliath. Restatement (Third) of Torts: Intentional Torts to Persons (Tentative Draft No. 5) §24.

Other courts have taken what is sometimes called the "shoe-stepping" approach to defense of others. Under this view (evidently a minority position), Galahad only has a privilege to defend David if David *actually* was privileged to defend himself. So, when Goliath swings at David in self-defense against the knife threat, but Galahad, arriving on the instant, mistakenly perceives Goliath as the aggressor, Galahad would not be privileged to defend David, because David, as the initial aggressor, would not be privileged to defend himself. In a jurisdiction that takes this approach, Galahad acts at his own risk. If he is wrong about who the aggressor is, and defends the actual aggressor, he "steps into the shoes" of the aggressor (David, in our example). He would not have a privilege to defend David, because David would not be privileged to defend himself from a blow by Goliath in self-defense. This approach suggests that intervenors should "look before they leap," while the reasonable mistake approach places a higher priority on Galahadism.

THE "DEFENSE" OF CONSENT

A second common affirmative defense to intentional torts is *consent*. Tort law generally accepts the maxim *volenti non fit injuria* ("to one who is willing, no wrong is done"). Prosser & Keeton, The Law of Torts §18 at 112 (5th ed. 1984). If the victim of a harmful or offensive touching manifests consent to the contact, the defendant is usually not liable for causing it. This is an example of the premium our society places on the individual's right to craft her own fate, to choose for herself, even to make choices most of us would consider stupid or self-destructive.[1]

Although consent avoids liability, it may not be entirely accurate to call it a defense. If an element of battery is the unwelcome nature of the contact, arguably the plaintiff's consent negates a basic element of her prima facie case. On this reasoning, *lack of consent* should be an element of the plaintiff's prima facie case of battery, and the plaintiff should include an allegation of lack of consent in her complaint.[2] There is considerable authority that this is so. See Dobbs' Law of Torts §105. The draft Third Restatement suggests that "the predominant view" is that the plaintiff bears the burden to establish lack of consent (Restatement (Third) of Torts: Intentional Torts to Persons (Tentative Draft No. 4) §[cite] cmt. e), yet some cases treat consent, like most privileges, as an affirmative defense that must be raised and proved by the defendant if she claims that the plaintiff consented to the contact. See, e.g., *Sims v. Alford*, 118 So. 395 (Ala. 1928).

This somewhat scholastic pleading question is less important than understanding what constitutes consent, and when it is effective to protect the actor from liability. Largely, common sense dictates the scope of consent. Common sense tells us that a person may consent to one touching but not another. Smith's acceptance of a "kiss in the moonlight" does not authorize

1. Another example is the negligence doctrine known as "assumption of the risk," discussed in Chapter 23.

2. Note that Juliet did include this allegation in her complaint for assault and battery in Chapter 2. See Figure 2-1, p. 42, paragraph 7, and p. 43, paragraph 11.

Torres to have intercourse with her, nor does Vega's agreement to a fistfight with Jones authorize Jones to use a shotgun if he fares poorly in the battle. Common sense also tells us that one can manifest consent to a touching without signing a contract, or even uttering a word. Smith may agree to Torres's kiss with a look or a blush—and may similarly refuse without speaking.

Naturally, difficult factual issues will often arise as to whether the victim consented to the contact. However, paradoxically, the privilege does not turn on *actual* consent. Most courts hold that the defendant is privileged to make a contact where the plaintiff's words, gestures, or conduct reasonably manifest consent to it, even if she was not actually willing to be touched. See Restatement (Third) of Torts: Intentional Torts to Persons (Tentative Draft No. 4) §16(a). The classic case for this proposition is *O'Brien v. Cunard S.S. Co.*, 28 N.E. 266 (Mass. 1891), in which the plaintiff received a shipboard vaccination prior to entering the United States. Although she later testified that she was unwilling to be vaccinated, she had stood in a line of 200 women waiting to be vaccinated, had watched those in front of her receive their vaccinations, and had held up her arm to receive the shot. On these facts, the court held that the doctor was "justified in his act, whatever her unexpressed feelings may have been. In determining whether she consented, he could be guided only by her overt acts and the manifestations of her feelings." Id. at 266.

Common sense also suggests that consent that is based on a fundamental misunderstanding of the facts does not evidence true acceptance of a contact. This is illustrated by two recurring scenarios. In one, a doctor obtains a patient's consent to an examination by representing that it is for treatment purposes, but actually is seeking sexual gratification. In another, the defendant obtains the plaintiff's consent to sexual intercourse without revealing that she has a communicable venereal disease. In both cases, the plaintiff's consent is invalid because, due to the defendant's misrepresentation (or, in the second case, failure to reveal crucial facts relevant to the plaintiff's choice), he did not appreciate the true nature of the intended contact and thus did not meaningfully consent to it.

Where the legislature has barred conduct to protect a disadvantaged class, even the plaintiff's *actual* consent may not create a privilege. For example, it has been held that consent to intercourse by a minor under the legal age of consent does not bar the minor from suing for battery. Statutory age-of-consent laws are intended "to protect a definite class of persons from their own immaturity." Harper, James & Gray §3.10 at 3:49-3:50. They prohibit the defendant's conduct *regardless of the minor's consent* since the minor is deemed incapable of making a proper judgment about whether to engage in the conduct. Consequently, the defendant (the party who induces the minor to engage in the conduct) is subject to criminal prosecution even if the minor consented. To reinforce this legislative policy, courts hold that the defendant should also be barred from raising the minor's consent as an affirmative defense in a tort action based on the same conduct. See Restatement (Second) of Torts §892C(2).

CONSENT TO MEDICAL TREATMENT

Consent issues often arise in the context of medical treatment since even therapeutic touchings have been viewed as batteries if the patient has not consented to them. Thus, the medical cases illustrate in one frequently recurring context the consent issues discussed more generally above.

For example, the treatment cases mirror the common sense principle that consent may include one touching but not another. In *Mohr v. Williams*, 104 N.W. 12 (Minn. 1905), *overruled on other grounds by Genzel v. Halvorson*, 80 N.W.2d 854 (Minn. 1957), a physician obtained a patient's consent to operate on her right ear, but, finding the left more seriously diseased, operated on it instead. Although the surgery was carefully done, it was held a battery since the doctor's touching went beyond the scope of contact to which the patient had consented.

Mohr was a pretty clear case of exceeding consent, but many medical consent situations are more ambiguous. A recurring scenario is the surgeon who, after commencing surgery with the consent of the patient, encounters unexpected conditions which require extension of the procedure beyond that approved by the patient. For example, the surgeon might find it necessary, in an operation on the intestine, to remove part of it, or, in an operation for ovarian cysts, to remove the ovary. In a heart bypass operation, the surgeon might find it necessary to make an unanticipated incision in the patient's arm to locate a suitable artery for the bypass procedure.

It would be nice if surgeons could satisfy the law's sense of propriety by waking the patient in such cases to obtain consent to the extension of surgery, but that would usually be impracticable or even dangerous to the patient. Ideally, such complications should be anticipated and addressed in advance, by obtaining the patient's consent (or refusal) to various predictable scenarios the surgeon may encounter. However, this is often not possible, because there is no reason to anticipate the extension. It is common practice for physicians to seek consent from a relative of the patient in such situations. Such "substituted consent" or "proxy decision-making" may also be authorized by state statutes. See, e.g., WA St. 7.70.065. Substituted consent is generally honored by the courts. In addition, patients are much less likely to challenge a decision in which their family members have concurred. Thus, this practice greatly reduces the likelihood that suit will be brought based on lack of consent.

If no relative is available, the cases support a limited privilege to extend the surgery within the area of the initial incision, unless the extension involves the destruction of a bodily function, such as the amputation of a limb or loss of reproductive function.[3] See Prosser & Keeton at 118. While it is sometimes said that there is implied consent to such extensions (see Dobbs' Law of Torts §115), this privilege is not really based upon consent—which, by definition, has not been given. It arises from the exigencies of the situation, which allow the surgeon to choose for the patient based upon what the reasonable patient would consent to if she could be consulted.

A related issue is the emergency privilege to treat an unconscious patient, for example, the victim of an auto accident who requires immediate treatment, but is unconscious due to her injuries. If no relative is able to consent, the cases recognize a privilege to render such treatment if the reasonable person would consent to it, if there is no reason to believe that the particular patient would not, and if delay would involve a risk of death or serious bodily harm to the patient. See, e.g., *Shine v. Vega*, 429 Mass. 456, 464-465 (1999); see generally Dobbs' Law of Torts §115.[4]

The examples that follow explore the application of self-defense and consent to some fairly straightforward cases—and a few be-Fuddling ones as well.

Examples

Self-Defense Basics

1. In which of the following cases was the assailant's blow a privileged act of self-defense?
   a. Rollins makes a disparaging comment about Okina's husband. She slaps him in the face.
   b. Rollins goes to knock off Okina's hat. She pushes him back hard.
   c. Rollins punches Okina in the stomach and turns to go. Okina hits him with the umbrella she is carrying.
   d. Rollins, on the facts of the last example, sees Okina coming at him with the umbrella and pushes her away as she swings it.
   e. Rollins pushes Okina. She stabs the sharp point of her umbrella at his face.

3. Even here, the surgeon may be privileged if delay would itself lead to death or loss of a bodily function.

4. Here again, there may be a stricter standard if the treatment involves destruction of a major bodily function, as, for example, an amputation. In such cases, the privilege may only attach if delaying treatment would risk death or very serious consequences to the health of the patient. Prosser & Keeton §18 at 117-118.

f. Zilla sees Enemy Kong running toward her excitedly. Fearful of an attack, she punches him in the chest. As it turns out, Kong had had a religious conversion and was rushing up to Zilla to apologize for past transgressions.
g. Zilla sees Enemy Kong rushing at her with a bat. She throws a brick at him and hits Cusack, a bystander.

2. Zilla is standing on a street corner when Kong, an old enemy, spies her. Kong advances toward her, shaking his fists and threatening to knock her down. Zilla, who is bigger, pushes at Kong with both hands as she is about to be hit, knocking Kong down. Unexpectedly, Kong falls on the stub of a metal post that had been cut off several inches above the sidewalk, and is gouged in the back. The wound requires 18 stitches and lands Kong in the hospital for three weeks. Is Zilla liable to him?

Never Sound Retreat

3. Zilla is sitting in the front seat of her car with the door open. Kong, an old enemy, sees her from 100 yards down the street and charges at her with a knife. Zilla steps out of the car with a baseball bat, swings hard at Kong with the bat, and hits him.
   a. Assume that the principles of the Third Restatement §23, requiring retreat in certain deadly force cases, apply. Who is liable, and for what?
   b. Assume that the incident takes place in a state that does not require retreat before the use of deadly force. Is Zilla liable to Kong?

4. Goliath meets David, who is considerably smaller than he is, on the street. Goliath objects to David's coat, which has a picture of the American flag covered over with a peace sign. He threatens to tear the flag right off the coat while it is on David's back, and moves toward him in obvious anger. David, convinced that it is his only means of self-defense, stabs Goliath with a pitchfork he is carrying.
   a. Is either party liable to the other, and if so, for what?
   b. On the same facts, assume that Goliath sees the pitchfork coming. To prevent being impaled, he picks up a two-by-four and hits David on the head with it. David suffers a concussion. Is Goliath liable for the injury to David?
   c. Assume that David defended himself against Goliath's assault by pushing at Goliath with his arms outstretched, in an effort to knock Goliath down. Goliath, surprised by David's aggressive response, swings at him, knocking him down. Who is liable to whom?

Into the Fray

5. Assume, on the basic facts of the last example, that Lancelot comes on the scene and sees David rushing at Goliath with the pitchfork after Goliath

rushes him to grab the flag. To protect Goliath, he swings at David with a crowbar, hitting him on the head and injuring him. Is Lancelot liable to David?

6. Suppose that Lancelot happens on the scene, and sees David about to push Goliath to prevent him from grabbing the flag on his jacket. Lancelot hits David in the stomach. Is Lancelot liable to David for battery?

Judge Fudd on the Cutting Edge of the Law

7. Zilla is sitting on the bench at a softball game when she sees Kong bearing down on her with a knife. Unable to retreat, Zilla wards off the blow by hitting Kong with a baseball bat. On later examination, it turns out that the knife Kong was carrying was a child's toy, made of soft rubber.

   Kong sues Zilla for battery. The case arises in a jurisdiction that does not require retreat before the use of deadly force in defense against deadly force. At trial, Judge Fudd instructs the jury as follows:

   > You are instructed that the defendant was privileged to use that level of force reasonably necessary to defend herself from a threat of bodily harm.
   >
   > If you find that the defendant was attacked with nondeadly force, then the defendant was only privileged to use nondeadly force in self-defense. If you find that the defendant was attacked with nondeadly force, and that the defendant used deadly force in self-defense, then you must find for the plaintiff.
   >
   > If you find that the defendant was attacked with deadly force, then the defendant was privileged to use that level of force reasonably necessary for her self-defense, which may include deadly force.

   Who will object to the instruction, and why?

Macho Consent

8. Franken approaches Stein in the street and threatens him: "If you don't hightail it out of here, I will give you two black eyes." Stein refuses to budge, and Franken socks him in the eye. Has Stein consented to the touching?

9. Hulk, a wrestler, brags to his friends at a bar about how strong he is. He braces himself and invites them to "just try to push me over." Brower, with a mighty shove, pushes at Hulk with both hands. Hulk loses his balance, stumbles backward, and falls against the footrest in front of the bar. He suffers a separated shoulder, which ends his wrestling career. He sues Brower for battery. Is Brower liable?

What You Don't Know . . .

10. Rodriguez meets Alvord in a bar. They chat. One thing leads to another. They end up back at Rodriguez's apartment, and go to bed together.

A month later, Rodriguez discovers that she has contracted a sexually transmitted disease from Alvord, and sues him for battery. If the evidence shows that Alvord did not know at the time of their tryst that he had the disease, will he be liable to her?

11. Alvord meets Rodriguez and they have several dates. In their conversations Alvord articulates his desire to "settle down." Rodriguez, who is anxious to get married, pursues the relationship, including going to bed with Alvord. It turns out Alvord is not interested in settling down. When she discovers this, Rodriguez sues him for battery, claiming that her consent was ineffective because it was based on a unilateral mistake.

Taking Aim

12. Manny and his brother Paul go out with their buddies to play paintball, a game in which two teams with paintball guns stalk each other and "kill" opponents by hitting them with a paintball. When a player is hit, the paintball explodes, leaving a colorful splat that shows that the opponent has been hit. Players agree to aim for the enemy's body rather than his head.
    a. Manny and Paul are on opposite teams. He shoots at Paul, who was on the opposite team, but his shot goes a little high, hitting Paul in the neck and leaving a bruise. Is Manny liable for battery?
    b. As they are suiting up at the outset, Manny sees Paul across the field, leaning over to tie his shoe. His large derriere is a tempting target, and Manny can't resist planting a paintball on it. Is he liable for battery?

13. Dr. Langone is scheduled to do surgery on Carella. On his way into the operating room he grabs the chart for a different patient, which had been put in the wrong spot. Langone starts to do an incision for a gallbladder surgery rather than the planned appendectomy. The mistake is caught; they sew up the incision and reschedule the surgery for the next day. Carella sues for battery. Assuming the mistake was reasonable on Langone's part, is she liable?

You're the Doc

14. Seaman is about to have exploratory hip surgery by Dr. Langone. Langone stops in to obtain consent, and to discuss the risks and possible side effects with Seaman. Seaman stops her. "Doc," he says, "I'm a businessman; I know stocks and bonds. You're my doctor; you know surgery. I trust you. Just do what has to be done for me and that'll be fine with me."

    During the surgery, Langone extends the surgery by doing a full hip replacement. Seaman, upset with the result, sues for battery. Will the defense of consent apply?

Consent-less Consent?

15. Wenner is sunning himself on the beach when he sees Fiori, a swimmer, flailing wildly and about to go under the waves. He dives in, pulls Fiori to shore, and begins to do CPR. Wenner had been trained in CPR 15 years before, but he had never actually performed it and did not remember much from the training. In the process of trying to stimulate Fiori's heartbeat, he breaks three ribs. Is he liable for battery?

16. Carella is brought to the emergency room unconscious after an accident, in need of immediate surgery. Dr. Langone recognizes that immediate surgery is necessary, and is much less dangerous if blood transfusions are given. Giving blood during the surgery would be good medical practice, and would be accepted by "the reasonable patient." Carella, however, is wearing a medical alert bracelet stating that he does not wish to be given blood transfusions.

    Since Carella cannot be awakened to seek his consent, Dr. Langone performs the surgery and gives Carella six pints of blood. Is she liable for battery?

There Must Be Some Privilege Here!

17. Wedge is walking past a hotel and sees a large chair falling from the fifth-floor balcony toward Janus, a pedestrian. He lunges forward and pushes the unsuspecting Janus out of the way. She falls and breaks her arm. If she sues Wedge for battery, what defense would Wedge raise and would it be accepted?

Explanations

EXPLANATIONS

Self-Defense Basics

1. a. Okina's blow is not in response to a threat of an unwanted physical contact; rather, it is in retribution for an insult. The privilege of self-defense authorizes physical force to forestall an invasion of the victim's person, not to respond to insults or to "get even." Okina's blow is a battery.

   b. Here, Rollins has threatened an offensive contact to Okina's hat, not a physically harmful contact. However, his act, if completed, would be a battery—the unconsented contact with objects intimately associated with the body satisfies the contact requirement. So Okina is privileged to use reasonable nondeadly force to prevent the intrusion. Since her push probably constitutes reasonable force, the privilege of self-defense applies.

c. This is clearly retaliation rather than self-defense. Rollins's battery is over, he's leaving, and Okina therefore has no need to protect herself from an impending battery. Since she is not privileged, her blow is a battery. (Of course, Rollins's blow was as well.)

d. Even though Rollins committed a battery himself when he punched Okina, her later effort to strike him with the umbrella is an independent battery, as explained in the prior example. Because Okina's threatened blow with the umbrella is not privileged, it is an assault, and Rollins has a right to use reasonable force to defend himself against it. His push is therefore privileged.

e. Rollins commits battery when he pushes Okina, which gives rise to a right on her part to use self-defense if she expects Rollins to continue to do so. However, she only has the right to use reasonable, nondeadly force in response to a nondeadly assault. Stabbing a sharp point into Rollins's face may well be excessive force because it is "likely to cause death or serious bodily harm," such as putting out Rollins's eye. Her stab is likely an assault, and if it lands, battery.

f. Here, Zilla thought that Kong was going to attack her, and therefore punched him in self-defense. However, she was wrong about the need to use self-defense since Kong actually had no intent to attack her.

   Zilla's act was privileged, even though she was mistaken about the need to use self-defense. Where she must act immediately, and reasonably believes that she is about to be battered, the privilege will apply. After all, what would *you* do? Right, you'd defend yourself, just as she did. Zilla is not "at fault" for acting on her reasonable understanding of the facts rather than waiting meekly for Kong's blow to fall. Thus, most courts allow the privilege of self-defense, so long as the victim reasonably believed that she was about to be battered. Dobbs' Law of Torts §82.

g. Here, Zilla is threatened with deadly force, and responds with deadly force. Her act would be privileged in most jurisdictions, which allow a victim to use deadly force in self-defense against deadly force without any duty to retreat. (In a jurisdiction that followed the Restatement (Third) §23(b), Zilla would not be privileged to use deadly force against Kong if she could safely retreat from Kong's attack.) Assuming her throw would have been privileged if the brick hit Kong, is it privileged when it hits Cusack, an innocent bystander? Who should this unfortunate loss fall upon—the innocent Zilla or the innocent Cusack?

   Analytically, Zilla has not committed battery on Cusack; she did not intend to cause a harmful or offensive touching to him. But, she *did* intend to cause one to Kong, so shouldn't the intent transfer to Cusack? No; to hold someone liable under the doctrine of transferred intent, you must first show that the actor's original intent in striking the blow was tortious. Here, if Zilla had a privilege to hit Kong in self-defense, her blow was not tortious toward Kong and therefore cannot be if it hits Cusack.

On a policy level, there may be stronger arguments for holding Zilla liable for Cusack's injury. If she invited Kong's attack, for example, it seems fairer to place the loss on her than Cusack. On appropriate facts, a court could reach that result by finding Zilla negligent for inviting a dangerous brawl in a crowded place.[5]

2. This example is reminiscent of several from the first two chapters, in which the actor intends a blow, but it causes more injury than she expected it would. Here, Zilla intended the push, but she did not intend to impale Kong on the metal post. As in the earlier examples, Zilla's liability turns on whether she committed a tort in the first place. If she did, she is liable for the resulting harm, though greater than anticipated. If her act was not tortious, she is not liable, although serious injury resulted.

   Here, whether Zilla's act is tortious turns on whether she was privileged to push Kong down in self-defense. It certainly appears that she was. She was threatened with nondeadly force, a push, and responded with appropriate nondeadly force to ward off the blow. Since she was privileged to push Kong, the touching is not a battery, and Zilla is not liable, even though serious injury resulted.

Never Sound Retreat

3. a. Section 23 of the Third Restatement requires a person attacked with deadly force to retreat, if she may safely do so, before responding with deadly force in self-defense. The facts here suggest that Zilla could have retreated by closing the car door and driving away. If this is true, she would not have a privilege to defend herself with a baseball bat. If her blow is not privileged, it is a battery, so Zilla would be liable to Kong for the injury she inflicts.

      Kong would also be liable to Zilla. His charge down the street with the knife is clearly an assault—Zilla's overreaction doesn't change that fact, though it makes Zilla liable as well.

   b. As the introduction indicates, many states do not require retreat before the use of deadly force. Yet Zilla might be liable even in a jurisdiction that takes this view. A threat of deadly force does not automatically authorize the use of similar force in self-defense. Rather, it gives the victim a privilege to use force she reasonably believes necessary to

5. Kong would be liable to Cusack as well on a negligence theory since it is foreseeable that his attack on Zilla would cause injury to bystanders.

prevent the threatened battery. That may include deadly force if such force appears necessary, but here Zilla could presumably have prevented the battery by simply closing and locking the car door. If so, she is not authorized to do more simply because Kong's attack threatens more serious harm.[6]

4. a. Goliath is liable to David for assault. He has no right to redesign David's jacket, and his move toward David reasonably puts David in fear that he is about to do so by force. But Goliath's assault does not justify David's use of deadly force in self-defense. The threat to David was of nondeadly force. Such a threat does not authorize him to use deadly force in self-defense. Thus, David is also liable to Goliath since he exceeded the scope of his privilege of self-defense.

   The facts suggest that David, a smaller man than Goliath, used the only means at his disposal—his pitchfork—that would avoid the invasion of his person. However, this does not change the result. David is not authorized to use deadly force to prevent the threat of nondeadly force, even if his only alternatives are to run or submit to the battery. See Restatement (Second) of Torts §63 cmt. j. While this may be humiliating to David, the policy reason for this conclusion appears sound: It is better that David suffer temporary humiliation and be vindicated later in court, than cause a serious injury or death to Goliath to prevent a fairly minor intrusion on David's rights.

   This presupposes, of course, that David does not fear anything beyond having his coat ripped. If Goliath's conduct leads David to reasonably fear serious bodily injury himself, he would be entitled to use similar force in self-defense.[7] In order to determine the scope of David's privilege, it is necessary to characterize the type of force *Goliath* has threatened—or, more accurately, the type of force David reasonably anticipates. It is often difficult to say after the fact that the victim was unreasonable in perceiving a threat of deadly force, even if the assailant really intended something less—which is a forceful argument for aggressors to think twice before striking.

   b. Here, Goliath is the initial, nondeadly aggressor, and David overreacts by using deadly force to protect himself from nondeadly force. By overreacting, he becomes a batterer himself, and would be liable to Goliath for any injuries resulting from his excessive force.

---

6. Might a court hold that Zilla need not close the door because that would constitute "retreat"? Probably not; by closing the door, Zilla is not running away (a loss of face that many jurisdictions refuse to compel), but simply blocking the battery without directly exerting force against the aggressor.

7. Unless he has a duty to retreat, as he might in jurisdictions following the Restatement (Third) of Torts §23.

If Goliath is now the victim of a battery, it follows, doesn't it, that Goliath has a privilege to use self-defense against David's battery? Frankly, I'm not sure that it *should* follow: Goliath is the original aggressor here. Had he not provoked the fight, he would have had no need for self-defense. If Goliath is privileged to respond to the pitchfork with deadly force, he might provoke a quarrel fully expecting David to overreact, and then use his privilege to injure or kill him. It seems like poor policy to authorize Goliath to do that. On the other hand, it hardly seems sensible to require Goliath to meekly accept his fate at the tines of a pitchfork, either.

A middle ground would require Goliath, as the original aggressor, to retreat if possible before using deadly force against the victim-turned-aggressor. Apparently, some criminal cases have taken this approach. See Dressler, Understanding Criminal Law §18.02[B][2][b] (6th ed. 2012); see also Model Penal Code §3.04(2)(b)(i). The Second Restatement of Torts took the position that Goliath is privileged to use deadly force in self-defense once David converts the nondeadly quarrel into a deadly one.

> "One who intentionally invades or attempts to invade any of another's interests of personality, does not by his wrongdoing forfeit his privilege to defend himself by any means which would be privileged were he innocent of wrongdoing against any excess of force which the other uses in self-defense." Restatement (Second) of Torts §71(c) cmt. d.

c. This example is like the last, in that Goliath, the original aggressor, responds to David's self-defensive efforts by defensive efforts of his own. Here, however, David has not exceeded his privilege. He is using a reasonable method to ward off Goliath's initial attack. Thus, David is not a batterer; consequently, Goliath is not privileged to act in self-defense; he must either retreat or suffer David's blow. If he does more, he is liable, while David is not.

Into the Fray

5. Here Lancelot, an interloper, comes on the scene, concludes that David is the aggressor, and intervenes to protect Goliath. If his interpretation were correct, there would be no doubt of his right to come to Goliath's aid. Tort law provides a privilege to defend others threatened with battery as well as to defend oneself. Restatement (Third) of Torts (Tentative Draft No. 5) §24.

   However, here Lancelot is wrong; David is not the initial aggressor, he is acting in self-defense (but exceeding his privilege by using deadly force). Courts have taken two approaches to the situation in which an intervenor acts to protect an apparent victim of a tort (here Goliath) who was actually the initial aggressor. Some courts say that the intervenor may act on her reasonable belief that a battery is about to be committed. Under that rule, Lancelot's act would be privileged since it reasonably appeared to Lancelot that David's attack was a battery. Other courts say that the intervenor steps into the shoes of the apparent victim, in this case, Goliath. Under this approach, Lancelot would only be privileged to use deadly force to defend Goliath if Goliath were privileged to do so himself. If Goliath had no privilege of self-defense, Lancelot's intervention would be battery.

Even under this second, shoe-stepping rule, Lancelot's act may have been privileged. If Goliath had no chance to retreat, he was privileged to respond to David's pitchfork with deadly force, even though he was the initial aggressor. See Example 4b. If so, then Lancelot shares Goliath's privilege.

6. The outcome of this case will depend on the approach the jurisdiction takes to defense of a third person. If, under the relevant law, the intervenor is authorized to act on his reasonable perception, Lancelot would be privileged since David appeared to be the aggressor. If the law of the jurisdiction only gives Lancelot a privilege to defend Goliath if Goliath himself would have a privilege of self-defense (the "shoe-stepping" approach), Lancelot would not be privileged and would be liable for battery, because David's push was a privileged use of nondeadly force.

Judge Fudd on the Cutting Edge of the Law

7. Judge Fudd's instruction is incorrect for several related reasons that would seriously prejudice Zilla's case. First, the instruction suggests she must have *actually* been attacked with deadly force in order to have a privilege to use deadly force in self-defense. This is not always true: Zilla would have the right to use deadly force if she *reasonably believed* that she was threatened with deadly force. See Restatement (Third) of Torts: Intentional Torts to Persons (Tentative Draft No. 5) §23(a) (premising right to use deadly force on reasonable belief that assailant threatens deadly force).

   Second, Judge Fudd's instruction makes her privilege turn on whether the force she used was *actually* necessary to repel Kong's attack. Because Kong's knife was harmless, Zilla did not actually have to use deadly force to avoid it. However, she may have *reasonably believed* that such force was necessary for her self-defense, if she thought the knife was real. Because an assault victim has no time to verify her perceptions of the force with which she is threatened, the law allows her to act on her reasonable belief that deadly force is necessary. Because Judge Fudd's instruction does not allow the jury to consider Zilla's state of mind in determining whether she was privileged, it is improper.

Such distinctions may appear hypertechnical, but many verdicts in tort cases are reversed for such subtle mistakes in instructing the jury. The be-Fuddled instructions throughout this book should give you useful practice in reading jury instructions critically. If you acquire this skill, sometime down the road you will be glad that you did.

Macho Consent

8. This example is reminiscent of the conditional threat example (Example 8) in Chapter 2. As in that example, the aggressor here threatens to hit the victim if she does not comply with a condition. The condition ("high-tail it out of here") is one that the aggressor has no right to impose. In Chapter 2 we concluded that such threats are assaults. By the same logic, the aggressor commits a battery if she follows through on the threat.

   Obviously, this analysis of conditional threats compels the conclusion that Stein does not consent to Franken's punch by standing his ground. Franken has no right to force Stein to choose between his freedom of movement and a punch in the eye. His refusal to comply with this impermissible condition does not constitute consent to the ensuing blow, which is an obvious battery. Nor would the reasonable person construe his act of standing his ground as a manifestation of consent. The more logical inference is that Stein simply refuses to be bullied.

9. Forgive me for belaboring once again the distinction between *contacts* and *consequences*. Here, Hulk, for his own macho reasons, has invited his friends to try to knock him over. He is willing that they should try, though he does not expect any of them to succeed. He has consented to the exact contact that Brower has imposed, though he did not anticipate the harmful consequence (the separated shoulder) of the contact. Since he consented to the contact, it is not tortious, and Brower is not liable despite the ensuing injury.

What You Don't Know . . .

10. The Introduction explains that sometimes the mistaken understanding of a consenting party will render her consent ineffective because she acts without understanding the true nature of the contact she is accepting. For example, if Alvord knew that he had a sexually transmittable disease, and had sexual relations without telling Rodriguez, her acceptance of the contact would be based on a misunderstanding facilitated by his failure to reveal a fact central to her decision. His act would smack of misrepresentation by omission, and vitiate the "meeting of the minds" upon which true consent is based.

    Where Alvord does *not* know about his condition, however, there is no disparity in the understanding of the parties at the time of consent, and no misrepresentation by Alvord. True, Rodriguez didn't know all the facts when she consented to the contact, but neither did Alvord. They both consented to a contact that entailed some risks, as most do. The court would very likely find Rodriguez's consent effective and deny recovery on the battery claim.

11. Rodriguez's claim of mistaken consent will probably fail. She did consent to the sexual contact that took place. Her complaint is really that she was deceived, not about the nature of the contact, but about other facts that influenced her decision to engage in it. If a court accepted this argument, it is easy to imagine myriad cases in which a party is mistaken—or deceived—about collateral matters that influenced the decision. Suppose Alvord had claimed he made $100,000 a year, or graduated Phi Beta Kappa from Stanford, or has a great idea for the next generation of software? (Suppose he just thought his software idea was great, but it really wasn't? or claims that he only told her that he *hoped* it was great idea??) For fear of a plethora of such slippery-slope cases, courts are likely to confine the concept of mistaken consent fairly closely to mistakes central to the transaction itself, such as that in the previous example.

Taking Aim

12. a. This is a clear case of consent. The participants understand that the object of the game is to hit the other side's players with paintballs, and thus consent by their participation to that contact.[8] Although players are required to aim for the body, having a shot go astray is clearly within the expectations of the players, so Paul has consented to the contact even though he is hit in the neck and suffers pain and a bruise.

    b. Although Paul has consented to being hit by some paintball shots, this one is beyond the scope of his consent. A player's reasonable expectation would be that he might be hit during the game, not by random shots some joker can't resist before it starts.

    I suppose Manny might assert the "brother privilege," that it's OK to do anything to your brother if it's funny and doesn't cause permanent disability. This privilege is not recognized by any of the prominent authorities. Manny's best argument would be that he and Paul have a history of physical-contact practical jokes, so Paul consents to this type of brotherly assault. But nothing in the question suggests such a history.

8. Doubtless they sign a pregame contractual release of liability as well, but that would protect the operator, perhaps not other participants.

13. This example is reminiscent of some in earlier chapters, in which an actor caused interference with person or property due to a mistake. Even if his mistake was reasonable, Langone will be liable for battery, for intentionally making an unwanted touching to Carella. See Restatement (Second) of Torts §51 illus 1. As in the trespass cases (see Chapter 3), intentional tort law places the risk of making an unconsented intentional intrusion on the actor, who can take steps to avoid the mistaken intrusion. The same would be true if Langone started the right operation on the wrong patient.

You're the Doc

14. Here Seaman has effectively delegated the decision-making to his doctor. There is no bar to a patient doing that; presumably the autonomy to make decisions about one's body includes the right to designate another to do it for you. This is commonly done in substituted consent situations, in which a patient designates another to make health care decisions for him if he is incapacitated.

    But there is still an issue as to *what* decisions Seaman has delegated to Dr. Langone. Surely, she couldn't give him a new nose or insert a pacemaker while he is under the knife. A court would have to consider the *scope of the consent* that he had given. Surely, common extensions of the expected surgery were within the contemplation of the parties, and perhaps even the new hip. The case poses a question of fact for the jury as to whether this extension was within the reasonable expectations of the parties, given their discussions, his presenting condition, and the purpose of the surgery.

Consent-less Consent?

15. Wenner did cause a harmful touching to Fiori by breaking his ribs. But did he intend to cause one? He had a virtuous motive for acting, but one can commit battery with a pure heart. See *Mohr v. Williams*, 80 N.W.2d 854 (Minn. 1957), in which the doctor placed the patient under anesthesia to operate on the right ear, but found the left one worse and operated on it instead. While the operation was successful, the doctor was held liable for battery, for invading the patient's body without consent.

    Here, absent the exigent circumstances, anyone would find a stranger pounding on his chest to be an offensive contact, even without the broken ribs. Wenner will rely on "implied consent" as a defense, arguing that he had a privilege to render emergency assistance to save Fiori's life. This privilege is not based on consent at all, but a privilege to render emergency assistance to an unconscious or endangered person. The Third Restatement addresses such emergency interventions without advance consent in a section entitled "Emergency Doctrine":

> If an actor engages in otherwise tortious intentional conduct for the purpose of preventing or reducing a risk to the life or health of another, the actor is not liable to the other, provided that:
>
> (a) the actor reasonably believes that:
>
> (i) his or her conduct is necessary in order to prevent or reduce a risk to the life or health of the other that substantially outweighs the other's interest in avoiding the otherwise tortious conduct; and
>
> (ii) it is necessary to act immediately, before it is practicable for the actor to obtain actual consent from the other or from a person empowered to consent for the other, in order to prevent or reduce the risk to life or health; and
>
> (b) the actor has no reason to believe that the other would not have actually consented to the conduct if there had been the opportunity to do so.

See Restatement (Third) of Torts: Intentional Torts to Persons (Tentative Draft No. 4) §17. Under this section Wenner will be likely be protected from liability even though he is rusty on his CPR skills. If there are three lifeguards standing around, his clumsy intervention might not be reasonable, but if he is the only other person on the beach, it would be. If we could ask Fiori, he would very likely accept CPR from Wenner over probable death without an attempt at resuscitation. Who knows, maybe he did save Fiori's life while breaking those ribs.

Note that nothing in §17 restricts such emergency treatment to doctors, nurses, and EMTs. There may not be one of these types around when a waitress is confronted with a choking diner; if there isn't, the tort rules should protect the waitress's choice to perform the Heimlich maneuver to save the diner's life.

16. As the previous example indicates, tort law recognizes a limited privilege to provide generally acceptable emergency treatment to an unconscious person. The logic for the privilege is that most people would accept such treatment, so going ahead will probably implement *this patient's* choice too. However, in this case Carella's bracelet informs Dr. Langone that he does not accept a treatment that others would. The bracelet rejects this touching just as clearly as if Carella sat up on the table and said, "Hey, no transfusions!" Dr. Langone must honor this choice, despite her disagreement with it, even if she

expects it may prove fatal to Carella. If she does not, she will be liable for battery.[9]

There Must Be Some Privilege Here!

17. Wedge has caused a harmful touching to Janus. Absent any privilege, the push itself would be a battery, let alone the broken arm. One might label the privilege "necessity." But if so, it would be private necessity, and in those cases the courts hold that the actor, while privileged to interfere with property or person, must pay for resulting harm. That doesn't seem like the right result here.

    How about "defense of other?" A person may defend another under the same circumstances that the other could defend herself. But it again seems awkward to think of Janus here as "defending" herself from the falling chair. Typically, "defense of other" involves defense against another person, not a chair.

    Isn't this example covered, though, by the privilege in §17 of the Third Restatement, quoted just above in the analysis of Example 15? While the obvious applications of that section concern emergency medical treatment, it is written much more generally and certainly appears to cover this example.

9. Might Dr. Langone give the transfusions anyway? Perhaps she would choose to save Carella's life even at the risk of being sued. How much would a jury award Carella under these circumstances, especially if the evidence suggests that Carella would have died without the transfusions? Probably not much. But ignoring Carella's directive disregards a solemn value choice by the patient about contacts with his person. As a practical matter, hospital policy will almost certainly mandate compliance with such directives.

PART II

The Concept of Negligence

CHAPTER 7

That Odious Character: The Reasonable Person

INTRODUCTION

Surely the most common basis for tort liability is negligent conduct. This chapter is about the meaning of negligence.

Let's begin by clarifying our terminology. Courts often speak of a "claim for negligence." In this sense, negligence is a tort with four elements: (1) a duty of reasonable care, (2) breach of that duty, (3) causation, and (4) resulting damages. A plaintiff must prove all four of these elements to "recover on a claim for negligence." But courts also use the term "negligence" in a related but more limited sense, to refer to the failure to live up to the standard of due care. In this sense, "negligence" refers to the *second element* of a claim for negligence, breach of the standard of due care. To say that the defendant "was negligent" is to say that he failed to exercise reasonable care under the circumstances.

Since courts do not always distinguish these two meanings of "negligence," students often get confused between the tort of negligence and the concept of negligence as a breach of the standard of due care. A defendant may be negligent without necessarily being "liable for negligence" (if, for example, the plaintiff does not suffer damages from the defendant's failure to exercise due care). It is important to distinguish the *tort* of negligence from the second *element* of that tort. This chapter is about the latter meaning, the failure to live up to the standard of reasonable care.

THE STANDARD OF REASONABLE CARE

The basic premise of negligence law is that we generally owe our fellow citizens a duty to exercise reasonable care in the conduct of our own affairs. This duty does not require that we avoid all injury to others, but only that we avoid injuring others by carelessness. That duty is breached (element #2 of a negligence claim) by failing to exercise reasonable care.

> Negligence is the omission to do something which a reasonable man, [sic] guided upon those considerations which ordinarily regulate the conduct of human affairs, would do, or doing something which a prudent and reasonable man [sic] would not do.

Blyth v. Proprietors of the Birmingham Waterworks, 156 Eng. Rep. 1047, 1049 (1856). See also Restatement (Third) of Torts: Liability for Physical and Emotional Harm §3 (to avoid being negligent, actor must "exercise reasonable care under all the circumstances"). While the *Birmingham Waterworks* case goes back a century and a half, you could go into courtrooms across the United States and hear juries in negligence cases instructed in very similar terms today—though the reference would be to the gender-neutral "reasonable person."

Who is this "excellent but odious character,"[1] the Reasonable Person? He is a model of propriety and common sense, a person of sound judgment who acts at all times with "ordinary prudence, . . . reasonable prudence, or some other blend of reason and caution." Prosser & Keeton §32 at 174.

> He is an ideal, a standard, the embodiment of all those qualities which we demand of the good citizen . . . He is one who invariably looks where he is going, and is careful to examine the immediate foreground before he executes a leap or bound; who neither stargazes nor is lost in meditation when approaching trapdoors or the margin of a dock; . . . who never mounts a moving omnibus and does not alight from any car while the train is in motion, . . . and will inform himself of the history and habits of a dog before administering a caress; . . . who never drives his ball till those in front of him have definitely vacated the putting-green; . . . who uses nothing except in moderation, and even while he flogs his child is meditating only on the golden mean.[2]

Odious indeed, the Reasonable Person is a fiction, an impossible creature who always exercises proper self-restraint and weighs appropriately not only his own interests, but those of others as well in regulating his affairs.

1. A. P. Herbert, Misleading Cases in the Common Law 12 (7th ed. 1932).
2. Herbert, supra n.1 at 9-11.

HOW THE REASONABLE PERSON THINKS

The reasonable person standard seems self-evident, even tautological: Of course we should all act reasonably to avoid injury to others. But the standard is also desperately vague. It hardly projects the majesty of The Law to admit that every year hundreds of millions of dollars in damages turn on such a homespun, commonsense idea of fault. Yet, courts obviously cannot prescribe more specific rules in advance as to what is reasonable in every situation: The variety of human experience is much too great to allow such a catalogue of proper behavior. It is possible, however, to describe in a general way the factors that the reasonable person considers before acting, and how he weighs those factors.

First, in deciding whether a course of conduct is appropriate, the reasonable person considers the *foreseeable risks of injury* that that conduct will impose on the community. This does not suggest that the reasonable person avoids all conduct that creates risks to others: We all accept the fact that people must act, and that most activities impose some risk on the community. But the reasonable person considers those risks in light of the *utility* of the conduct. For example, lighting a fire in dry woods near a town imposes a risk that the fire will spread. It may be reasonable to impose that risk to prevent a brush fire from spreading, but not to toast marshmallows. Similarly, rapid release of a large volume of water from behind a dam imposes a risk of downstream property damage or personal injury. That risk might be reasonable to prevent a collapse of the dam, but not to lower the water level to facilitate dredging.

The reasonable person also considers the *extent* of the risks posed by her conduct. Restatement (Third) of Torts §3. Conduct may be reasonable if it threatens minor property damage, but unreasonable if it creates a risk of serious personal injury. The dam release, for example, might be appropriate if it risks minor flooding of grazing land but not if it threatens to drown campers down river. Placing a gas tank in a particular place on a truck might be reasonable if it poses a risk of stalling the engine, but unreasonable if it could cause the tank to explode in a collision. And, since a risk is greater if it exposes many to a risk of injury than if it endangers a few, our odious paragon considers that too.

The reasonable person also considers the *likelihood* of a risk actually causing harm. It often makes sense to do a useful thing that imposes low-probability risks, but may not if the risk is greater. Placing the gas tank in a particular place may be reasonable if it risks a one-in-a-million explosion, but not if one in a thousand will blow up. Distributing a vaccine may be a reasonable choice if an adverse reaction will happen to one patient in 10,000, but not if one in ten will suffer it. Restatement (Third) of Torts §3 ("likelihood that the person's conduct will result in harm" a primary factor in determining negligence).

Our Model of Propriety also considers whether *alternatives* to her proposed conduct would achieve the same purpose with lesser (or greater) risk. Restatement (Third) of Torts §3 cmt. 3. If a live vaccine poses a risk of serious injury to one patient in 10,000, but a dead vaccine achieves the same protection with injury to only one in a million, it may be unreasonable to use the live vaccine. On the other hand, if there is no alternative to the live vaccine, the one-in-10,000 risk may be reasonable, given the benefit to the other 9,999 users.

It must also be admitted that this obnoxious paragon of ours is a little bit cold-blooded: He also considers the *costs* of various courses of action in determining what is reasonable. He does not take every precaution which might reduce the risk of injury, but only those which are "worth it" in the sense that the injuries avoided outweigh the cost of the extra precaution. If it would cost $15 to add a kill switch to a $50 circular saw, and the switch would prevent a hand injury to one in 20,000 users but would also substantially impede the operation of the saw, it would likely be reasonable to leave off the switch. Adding the switch would increase the costs of the machine by $300,000 for each injury avoided ($15/saw×20,000 saws) and reduce its efficiency for all users. The "trade-off" to avoid one hand injury doesn't seem worth it.

Similarly, if a live vaccine that risks side effects to one in 10,000 costs $1 per dose, while a dead vaccine that will only injure one patient in 100,000 costs $25, the drug manufacturer may be "reasonable" to market the live form, even though it will mean, statistically speaking, nine more injured kids per 100,000 users. This economic dimension to reasonableness analysis is hard to swallow—one of those kids might be yours—but there is little question that it exists. Otherwise we would all drive tanks instead of vulnerable automobiles.

THE "HAND FORMULA"

While it is useful to identify the factors the reasonable person considers in contemplating action, it is more difficult to specify exactly how he weighs those factors, or what conclusion is reasonable on a given set of facts. One estimable jurist, Judge Learned Hand, endeavored to do so in the famous case *United States v. Carroll Towing* Co., 159 F.2d 169 (2d Cir. 1947). Judge Hand postulated that the defendant's duty in controlling its barge in that case was

> a function of three variables: (1) The probability that [the barge] will break away; (2) the gravity of the resulting injury, if she does; (3) the burden of

> adequate precautions. Possibly it serves to bring this notion into relief to state it in algebraic terms: if the probability be called P; the injury L; and the burden B; liability depends upon whether B is less than L multiplied by P; i.e., whether B is less than PL.

Id. at 173. This celebrated "Hand formula," B < PL, is meant to suggest not only the factors the Reasonable Person considers, but how he balances those factors in reaching a judgment. The reasonable person, Hand postulates, takes a precaution against injury if the burden of doing so is less than the loss if the injury occurs multiplied by the probability that the injury will occur. To illustrate, suppose that a safety catch costs $20 per machine, that one in 100 of the machines will cause an injury without the catch, and that the likely damages from the injury if it happens are $1,000. The Hand formula suggests that the reasonable person will not attach the safety catch. It will cost $2,000 to put the guard on 100 machines, but will only prevent $1,000 in injury costs. On the other hand, if the guard cost $5 per machine, the formula would compel the conclusion that the reasonable person would add it.

The Hand formula has been applauded particularly by economic theorists, who see negligence law as a means of regulating social conduct to promote efficiency. See, e.g., R. Posner, A Theory of Negligence, 1 J. Legal Stud. 29, 32-34 (1972). But it is also very easy to criticize. What, for example, does "L" really mean in the formula? A single risk, such as a bald tire on the defendant's car, could cause a wide variety of losses, from a broken axle to a nine-car collision with multiple fatalities. How is the reasonable person to apply the formula where such a range of "L"s is possible? And, of course, *valuing* even a known loss is a very speculative business. How is the defendant, in deciding whether to drive on the bald tire, to assign a value to a serious personal injury if he does not know the age, employment, susceptibility to pain, family circumstances, or other characteristics of his future victim? Similarly, assigning probabilities to particular types of risks is a highly speculative business. The defendant may have a vague sense that bald tires are a bad idea, but that is a far cry from assigning a meaningful quantitative value to "P" in the Hand formula.

The formula, standing alone, also fails to consider other possibilities, such as adopting an entirely different method of achieving a given result. It may be prohibitively expensive to design an alarm system which would eliminate a small risk of a release of a poisonous gas used in a certain manufacturing process. If so, the Hand formula suggests that it is reasonable to conduct the operation without such a system. But the reasonable person would also consider other alternatives: It may be possible to change the process to eliminate the gas entirely, and ordinary prudence may dictate that course if the danger cannot otherwise be adequately reduced. In other cases where precautions to eliminate a risk are too expensive, the only reasonable choice may be to *forgo the conduct entirety*, a possibility not accounted for in Hand's calculation.[3]

Such criticisms of the Hand formula are valid, but they may miss the point. Judge Hand never viewed his formula as a mechanical solution to the complex human problem of reasonableness. He made no attempt to quantify the elements of the formula in *Carroll Towing*, and suggested elsewhere that it is in fact impossible to do so. *Moisan v. Loftus*, 178 F.2d 148, 149 (2d Cir. 1949). But Judge Hand's formula does highlight basic factors that the reasonable person considers in making choices about risk-creating conduct. In an intuitive, impressionistic way, reasonable people do consider, in deciding upon a course of conduct, the extent of the risks posed by that conduct, the type of injury likely to result from those risks, the utility of the conduct, and the cost of avoiding the risk. Juries in negligence cases will not be instructed in strict Hand formula terms ("the reasonable person takes precautions against risk if the burden of doing so is less than the probability of an injury multiplied times the loss that will be suffered if the risk materializes"). But a jury might well be instructed that, in considering whether the defendant acted reasonably, they should consider the likelihood of an accident happening, the burden of taking precautions to prevent an accident, the utility of the conduct, and the nature and extent of the injuries likely to result if an accident occurs.[4]

APPLYING THE REASONABLE PERSON STANDARD: THE RELEVANCE OF PERSONAL "CIRCUMSTANCES"

While the reasonable person is a fictitious construct, people are not. Each individual possesses unique physical and mental characteristics. How can this artificial, uniform standard of good judgment account for our individuality—or should it?

To some extent, the negligence standard does account for the personal characteristics of the actor. One's duty is to act as a "reasonable person under

3. Other more global criticisms have been leveled at the formula as well. For example, the formula appears devoid of any moral content, suggesting that tort law is a purely economic calculation rather than a system to compensate victims, to punish unacceptable conduct, or to deter injurers. Beyond that, of course, lies the plain fact that people simply don't think in formulas, and won't be made to by judges.

4. The Third Restatement of Torts expressly endorses Hand formula analysis in determining negligence: "Primary factors to consider in ascertaining whether the person's conduct lacks reasonable care are the foreseeable likelihood that the person's conduct will result in harm, the foreseeable severity of the harm that may ensue, and the burden of precautions to eliminate or reduce the risk of harm." Restatement (Third) of Torts: Liability for Physical and Emotional Harm §3.

the circumstances." Some individual characteristics of the actor are considered part of "the circumstances" in determining reasonableness. For example, it is generally held that a person with a physical disability is required to act as a reasonable person *with that disability* would act. Thus, it is not negligent for Lear, a blind person, to walk the streets, though he will occasionally bump into others. The blind have to live in the same world as the rest of us, and it is reasonable for them to impose the risk of occasional sidewalk collisions (and more serious motor vehicle accidents as well) in order to do so. It might be a closer case if Lear ventured forth without a cane, but the important point is that his conduct will be judged against that of other actors in the same "circumstances," not against the population at large.

While allowance is made for physical disabilities, no allowance is made for the "circumstance" that a person lacks good judgment, is hasty, awkward, or perennially oafish. This was well settled in the torts classic, *Vaughan v. Menlove*, 132 Eng. Rep. 490 (1837), in which poor Menlove argued that he had exercised his judgment to the best of his ability, and should not be held liable just because his "best" wasn't very good. If Lear is not held to the standard of a sighted person, why should Menlove be held to the standard of a person with good judgment? Isn't his obtuseness a "circumstance" that the law should take into account as well?

In the courts of heaven, Menlove's argument will doubtless weigh heavily, but as a legal standard his suggested test (whether he "had acted honestly and bona fide to the best of his own judgment" (Id. at 493)) would obviously be a disaster. Had Menlove's test been adopted, we would not have one standard of care for negligence, but a million. We would not try the defendant's *conduct* in negligence actions, but his character and intelligence. The perennially careless would enjoy the right to endanger their neighbors with impunity. By sticking with the "reasonable person under the circumstances" test, the courts have provided instead an objective test that allows impartial application, avoids subjective judgments about individual character, and allows some measure of prediction about the consequences of conduct.

This same refusal to consider individual personality is illustrated in the treatment of the mentally ill. The traditional rule, still generally accepted, is that the mentally ill are held to the same standard as everyone else, despite the "circumstance" of their illness:

> An actor's mental or emotional disability is not considered in determining whether conduct is negligent, unless the actor is a child.

Restatement (Third) of Torts: Liability for Physical and Emotional Harm §11(c). This is a harsh, perhaps indefensible rule. It holds a mentally ill adult to a standard that any psychology student will tell you he cannot meet. But it is at least consistent with *Menlove*, in the sense that it is based on a refusal to make the standard a subjective one, to account for individual personality in administering the negligence system. These rules send the same message to those who, due to mental illness or weak intelligence, may have trouble meeting the objective standard: "Since the law will not hold you to a lesser standard, you will have to curtail your activity or exercise particular self-restraint (or be restrained by others) in order to avoid liability."

This treatment of the mentally ill and those of weak judgment confirms that the reasonable person standard is a legal judgment, not a moral condemnation. Morally, we could hardly fault a Menlove for a judgment which was the best he could do, or a mentally ill defendant for conduct that was compelled by delusion or neurosis. But for legal purposes, we need a standard that defines "fault" in some predictable, universal way. The "reasonable-person-under-like-circumstances" test provides a neutral instrument for deciding disputes, not a value judgment about a person's character.

Given the refusal of negligence law to account for mental deficiencies, the application of the "reasonable person" standard to children may seem inconsistent. Children are *not* held to the adult standard of care, but rather the standard of a reasonable person of like age, intelligence, and experience under like circumstances. Restatement (Third) of Torts §10. Unlike the unitary adult standard of care, this child standard clearly *does* make allowance for their mental ability and development. The rationale is that children have to *learn* to be careful, and ought not be exposed to tort liability for conduct that is reasonable in light of their stage of development during the learning process. Adults, however, have had 18 years to become "reasonable"; if they don't make it by that age, they probably never will. They must then suffer the liability consequences or adopt a low-risk lifestyle to avoid causing injury to others.

The child standard does not mean that children cannot be found negligent. There is little doubt that most children of ten have developed the judgment to understand that setting a fire can burn a building, or shooting an arrow at a playmate can put out an eye. In many respects a child of 16 is as capable of due care as an adult (in crossing streets, stacking lumber, or playing football, perhaps) and will effectively be required to meet the adult standard of care. In addition, a good many cases hold children who engage in certain high-risk activities primarily engaged in by adults, such as driving, to the adult standard of care. See Dobbs' Law of Torts §137.

APPLYING THE REASONABLE PERSON STANDARD: THE RELEVANCE OF EXTERNAL "CIRCUMSTANCES"

While the personal characteristics of the actor are sometimes relevant to determining whether she acted reasonably, the external circumstances in which she acted are always relevant. Decisions about conduct are not made in a classroom or an armchair; rather, they are made in the hurly-burly of everyday events, in the factory, on the road, in the operating room. The reasonableness of the defendant's decision is always judged in relation to the unique context or "circumstances" in which she made it.

For example, a defendant may make a decision in the second before an impending accident that he would not have made if he had time to weigh the choices more carefully. In judging that decision, the jury should consider whether the decision was reasonable in light of the "circumstance" that the defendant had to act in a split second. The so-called emergency doctrine means no more than this, that in judging the reasonableness of conduct in an emergency, the "circumstance" that the defendant must act quickly is relevant.

Other circumstances are also relevant. It is relevant that the defendant acted as others customarily do in like circumstances. The fact that conduct is generally engaged in by those in a particular trade or profession at least suggests that such conduct is acceptable. For example, if a roofer is injured in a fall from the roof of a two-story building, it is relevant on the issue of his negligence that roofers ordinarily do not wear safety harnesses in reshingling two-story buildings (or that they do). If most roofers consider that an acceptable risk for the extra freedom of movement or time savings involved, it may well be that they are right.

However, while relevant, evidence of custom is not dispositive. In some circumstances, custom and reasonableness may diverge dramatically. To save costs, out of inertia, tradition, or for other reasons, a practice may continue long after thoughtful analysis would compel its rejection, or a new precaution may be ignored despite its obvious benefits. Seat belts offer a good example. Aware of the proven safety advantages of seat belts, our odious paragon doubtless buckles up every time he motors forth, although a substantial segment of the population refuses to follow his pious example.[5] Similarly, if some enterprising roofer develops a new easy-snap, no-hassle safety harness, it may be that the reasonable roofer would use it. Even if it is hard to teach old roofers new tricks, they may be unreasonable to follow the older custom under changed circumstances.

Another "circumstance" that commonly colors the reasonableness of conduct is whether a statute requires a particular course of action under the circumstances. Generally speaking, the reasonable person obeys the

5. Ironically, courts and legislatures have gone to considerable lengths to avoid the ineluctable conclusion that it is unreasonable to drive without buckling up. See, e.g., D. Westenberg, Buckle Up or Pay: The Emerging Safety Belt Defense, 20 Suffolk U. L. Rev. 867, 885, 923-943 (1986) (detailing statutes limiting use of evidence of failure to wear seat belt to prove negligence). These attitudes may be changing, however. See Restatement (Third) of Torts: Apportionment of Liability §3 cmt. b and illus. 3 (failure to wear seat belt treated as negligence).

law; thus, evidence that the defendant ignored a statutory standard will frequently suffice to establish that he was negligent. This problem, proving negligence based on violation of statute, is explored in the next chapter.

A further relevant circumstance is whether the actor has acted as an expert in a particular field. If you have a tax accountant prepare your taxes for you, you justifiably expect a higher level of knowledge and judgment than if your bookkeeper or your neighbor does. If you entrust your yacht to a licensed merchant marine captain, she should have a higher level of skill than a beach bum. This does not mean that persons with specialized knowledge are held to a higher *standard* of care than others: Their standard, like that of others, is reasonable care under the circumstances. But the fact that an actor is a professional or assumes the role of an expert in an activity is a "circumstance" that colors the meaning of reasonableness. A professional will be expected to possess and employ the skill and knowledge of her profession, not of the "ordinary reasonable person."

The facilities or resources available to the actor are also relevant to the reasonableness analysis. It may be reasonable to perform exploratory surgery in a community where less invasive methods of diagnosis are unavailable, but not in an area where they are. It may be reasonable for a general practitioner to litigate an antitrust case in northern Maine, where antitrust lawyers are hard to come by, but not in Washington, D.C., where several are lurking on every block.

Beyond these recurring types of relevant circumstances, there are the utterly miscellaneous facts of every individual case to be considered. Facts about weather, about what the parties knew, about how they observed events, about the condition and behavior of animals, vehicles, computers, or machines, about the purposes the actors hoped to achieve by their conduct and alternative ways they might have done so. Reality is infinitely diverse, and each case is unique. It is up to the parties to bring out the circumstances that conditioned the actors' choices, and argue the reasonableness of those choices in light of the flesh and blood context in which they were made. It is exactly this multifariousness of *facts* that requires the *legal standard* of negligence to be so frustratingly general, and makes the practice of negligence law so interesting.

The examples below explore the factors involved in the negligence calculus, and the process by which they are weighed.

Examples

Burdens and Benefits

1. Costard, owner of a large estate, throws an all-day party for a few hundred of his close friends. During the day, some of his guests wander through the woods and come to an abandoned quarry on the property, which has filled up with water. They opt for a dip. Trinculo is injured

when he dives into the quarry and hits his head on a submerged promontory only three feet under the surface. He sues Costard for negligence.

Costard argues that he was not negligent, since, though the injury was foreseeable, filling in the quarry was prohibitively expensive. In Hand formula terms, the burden was too great given the relatively low risk of injury to a wandering entrant on the property, which is normally not open to outsiders. What is the problem with this argument?

2. Suppose that, instead of a quarry, an abandoned well existed on the property, covered with some boards placed there a few years ago and now beginning to rot. Trinculo, wandering the grounds, does not see the well, which is covered with autumn leaves. He falls through, is injured, and sues Costard for negligence. Is he likely to prove negligence?

3. The town of Stratford is given a piece of vacant land adjacent to a quiet residential street. Since there is considerable demand for recreational space, and little open space in town, they build a baseball field on the parcel. The edge of the field is 30 feet from the road. In the course of a game, Feste hits a high foul ball, which is caught by the wind and angles into the street. Glendower, driving by, suddenly sees the ball coming, instinctively swerves away from it, and is injured when his car turns into a ditch. He sues the town for negligence in locating the field where it did. Do you think the jury will find the town negligent?

Risks and Reasonableness

4. The Leadville Railroad Company is putting in a new rail line. The line will cross Elm Street, a moderately busy street. The railroad's planners have to decide between a grade crossing (where the street simply crosses the tracks) and an overpass. Based on long experience they can predict that, even with gates and flashing lights, there will be (statistically speaking, anyway) two accidents at a grade crossing on a street like this every ten years. If they build an overpass for the street, the presence of the rail line will not cause any accidents. However, it will cost $25 million for the overpass, compared with $20,000 to install a grade crossing.

   The planners opt for the grade crossing. Feste is seriously injured when he fails to see the gate coming down and drives across the track into the path of an approaching train. Is the railroad negligent?

5. One of the early classics of negligence law is *Blyth v. Proprietors of the Birmingham Waterworks*, 156 Eng. Rep. 1047 (1856). In *Blyth*, the plaintiff's basement was flooded by a Birmingham Waterworks water line, which burst during a cold spell. Due to the cold, the frost had "penetrated to a greater depth than any which ordinarily occurs south of the polar regions." Id. at 1049. The court held that the waterworks was not liable

for failing to place their pipes deep enough in the ground to avoid bursting in such a frost.

a. Suppose that there had been a frost this bad 75 years ago. Would the waterworks be negligent for failing to set the pipes deep enough to withstand such a frost?
b. Suppose that there had been a frost this bad the year before, but it was the only one in recorded history and was considerably worse than any other recorded year. Would the waterworks be negligent if it continued to place its pipes at the shallower depth?
c. Let's think about *Blyth* in Hand formula terms. Suppose that placing the pipes one foot down would avoid most, but not all, flooding damages to abutters. It would cost the waterworks an extra $20 million to place the pipes two feet down, but the waterworks engineers can predict with confidence that going the extra foot would avoid $5 million in flooded basement damages to homeowners over the life of the system. What would the reasonable waterworks company do?
d. Assume that, after doing the calculation just described, the waterworks lays its pipes at the one-foot level. Two years later, a highly unusual, deep frost bursts a pipe and Blyth's basement is flooded. Is the waterworks liable to Blyth?
e. Assume that tort law holds waterworks companies strictly liable for all damages caused by their operations (that is, they must pay if the system causes damages, whether they conducted their operations with due care or not). Assume further that the waterworks had placed their pipes one foot down, knowing that in highly unusual years some pipes could burst and flood basements. In an unusual frost, a pipe bursts and floods Blyth's basement. Who pays?
f. Assume that strict liability applies, and that the waterworks knows that it will be strictly liable for all flooding damages from its system. If the numbers given in Example 5c apply, would the waterworks place its pipes at the two-foot level?

A True Story: Judge Hand at the Roller Rink

6. Once upon a time, a Torts professor took his daughter rollerblading. Kids of all ages were speeding around the rink, some more in control than others. To his dismay, the prof noticed that there was a wall around part of the rink, about three feet high, made of concrete blocks. Having always sought to emulate that odious paragon, the Reasonable Person, the prof approached the rink manager. "Why don't you hang some mats on the inside of that wall? One of these kids could lose control, go into the wall headfirst, and suffer serious injury." The manager coolly replied, "It hasn't happened in 17 years."

The next day, Jane, a nine-year-old daredevil, stumbles and goes into the wall, suffering a serious head injury.

a. Identify the Hand factors—probability, loss, and burden—in Jane's case.
b. If you were arguing those factors in front of a jury, which party would you think had the stronger argument?

Fudd and Foreseeability

7. Falstaff, anxious to get to a pub, passes a driver on a curve, and collides with Bottom coming the other way. Sued for negligence, Falstaff argues that he was not negligent, because the road was little traveled, and it was very unlikely that a car would come around the curve at the time he was in the wrong lane. Judge Fudd instructs the jury as follows:

> If you find that it was more probable than not that a car would be traveling in the opposite lane and collide with the defendant's car, then you should find that the defendant violated the standard of reasonable care in passing as he did.

What is wrong with Fudd's instruction? Can you write a more accurate one?

8. Barnardine, a roofer, is working on the roof of a townhouse on a narrow city street. Like most roofers, he is not wearing a safety harness, though effective safety harnesses are available. He is startled by a flying pigeon, steps back, and falls from the roof, hitting Elbow, a passing pedestrian.

In Elbow's negligence action against Barnardine, Judge Fudd instructs the jury as follows:

> If you find that it was customary in the trade for roofers to work on roofs such as the one in question without safety harnesses, then you must find that the defendant was not negligent for failing to wear a safety harness at the time of the accident.

a. Which party will object, and why?
b. Assuming that the evidence that most roofers don't use safety harnesses is admitted, how should Judge Fudd instruct the jury with regard to that evidence?

A Duty of Much Care

9. Gobbo, a gas station attendant, has just started a cigarette break when Mariana drives up for gas. He goes out to fill her gas tank with the cigarette in his mouth. Annoyed by a persistent bee, he takes a swipe at it and knocks the cigarette out of his mouth. It falls near the nozzle of the hose, causing an explosion that injures Mariana. She sues him for negligence.

At trial, her counsel asks the judge to instruct the jury that Gobbo, in dispensing the gas, owed her a duty of extreme care, due to the explosive nature of gasoline. Should the judge give the instruction?

An Almost Perfect Record

10. Dr. Quince operates on Peasblossom to remove a bony growth from her lower spine. During surgery, he accidentally contacts her spinal cord, causing partial paralysis of her left leg. Peasblossom sues him for negligence.

    At trial Quince seeks to establish that he exercised due care in surgery by offering evidence that he has an almost perfect record as a back surgeon. He has performed over 370 similar surgeries, and only twice come into contact with the spinal cord. His counsel argues that this proves that he is a careful surgeon.

    a. Does this evidence establish that Quince complied with the standard of reasonable care?
    b. How should Judge Fudd instruct the jury as to the standard of care Dr. Quince was required to meet in operating on Peasblossom?
    c. How is the jury to know what due care requires in this case?

Menlove in Reverse

11. Dogberry has been skiing since he was four, has participated in several skiing competitions, and is generally acknowledged to be a first-class skier. One morning, he is executing a turn on a moderate ski run, loses control, and slides backward into Portia, breaking Portia's ankle. She sues him for negligence. At trial, Portia argues that the jury should be instructed that Dogberry must exercise the level of care that would be exercised by "the reasonable expert skier under the same circumstances." Should the instruction be given?

An Elementary Example

12. Falstaff heads home after drinking nine beers at the local pub. Much the worse for wear, he is proceeding along at 28 miles per hour, just below the speed limit, within his lane of traffic, when a pickup truck, going the other way, makes a sharp stop in the opposite lane. Moth, a boy of five, is leaning over the side of the bed of the pickup and is thrown out immediately in front of Falstaff's left front wheel. Falstaff runs him down and is sued for negligence. Leaving aside possible contributory negligence of Moth, would Falstaff be liable?

Explanations

Burdens and Benefits

1. Costard has tried to take charge of the negligence analysis here by looking at one possible means of addressing the risk and applying the Hand formula with only that in mind. The argument might hold water (so to speak) if filling in the quarry were the only possible means of dealing with the risk. But other, less burdensome "B"s exist here. Costard could have fenced the quarry, or posted signs warning of the danger of rocks beneath the surface. The burden of taking these alternative precautions is much lower, and the balance of risk against cost of prevention is a great deal closer on these facts. This is not to say that Trinculo will necessarily win, but that it is important for his counsel not to let Costard frame the negligence issue only in terms of a prohibitively expensive precaution, since other means of prevention are possible.

2. In this case, Costard's negligence is clear because the burden of prevention is so low. Even filling in the well would likely be an appropriate precaution to eliminate the risk of serious injury from falling in. But much less would prevent most accidents. Building a fence around the well or capping it with a solid concrete cover would eliminate the risk at a clearly acceptable cost. Surely our Paragon of Propriety, the reasonable person, would have done so.

3. Stray foul balls like Feste's are certainly foreseeable; indeed, even an accident like Glendower's is foreseeable. But foreseeable risk is not the end of the analysis. The reasonable man eschews unreasonable risks, but not all risks. If the risk here was low enough, in relation to the utility of the activity, it is not negligent for the town to impose it.

   Here, that may well be the case. The facts suggest that there was little open land and a need for recreational facilities in the town. The town sited the field with a substantial margin beside the road. Certainly, a few fouls will still reach the road, but since it is a quiet street, most will not hit a car. Those that do will not usually cause much damage. In view of the value of the field to the citizenry, the lack of alternative sites, the relatively low risk of accidents, and the minimal damage likely if an accident does take place, a jury might well find the town's choice a reasonable one.

   One lesson of this example is that plaintiffs do not always win negligence suits just because an accident actually happens. The test is not whether injury was caused, or even whether injury was foreseeable, but whether the defendant's conduct was reasonable in view of *all* the circumstances, including the possibility of injury, the utility of the conduct, the alternatives available, and others.

The example also illustrates that the peculiar circumstances of every individual case really do matter. This case might come out differently if there were more alternatives to the site, if the space outside the foul line were only ten feet, or if the road were a busy high-speed freeway. *Facts* are ever so important to negligence cases because each fact colors the "circumstances" against which the defendant's conduct must be judged.

Risks and Reasonableness

4. My students often conclude that a defendant who foresaw a risk of injury but failed to prevent it will be found negligent. However, negligence law does not hold actors to that stringent standard, which would amount to strict liability. In this case, the railroad could foresee injuries if it chose a grade crossing, but went ahead anyway, based on the great expense of eliminating the risk and the small number of injuries likely to be caused by the grade-crossing option. This may well be a reasonable decision, even though the railroad knows, on an actuarial basis, that its decision will cause injuries to others. The railroad is not required to eliminate all risk of injury from its operations, only to conduct it with reasonable care. If the planners drew a reasonable balance here between risk and the expense of eliminating it, the decision to use a grade crossing will not be deemed negligent.

Analyzing the railroad's decision in Hand formula terms suggests that the decision may well be reasonable. If we assume that two injuries will be caused in a decade, that the average injury cost will be \$500,000,[6] and that the overpass will last 30 years, the injury cost will be \$3 million, compared to the \$25 million cost of averting the six likely accidents. In social terms, the investment to prevent these accidents may be more than society—through the mechanism of tort law—is willing to require.

It is true that the analysis here involves valuing human suffering against economic cost, but negligence law routinely involves such heartless but practical balancing. For example, the automobile causes immense human suffering, yet we accept—indeed, seem at times to worship—the automobile for the convenience it brings. It is not negligent to drive, even though resulting accidents are a statistical certainty. "There is essential truth . . . in the saying that the law of negligence privileges actors to kill and maim people carefully." Harper, James & Gray §16.9 at 478.

6. Yes, I know, this figure is bound to be a wild approximation. The actual accidents could be anything from a minor fender bender with no personal injuries to a school bus full of seriously injured children.

5. a. The waterworks is not necessarily negligent for failing to take precautions against this risk. Once in 75 years is a very small risk. A frost like that may not happen for another 75, or another 150. Even if it does happen again, the flooding damages are likely to be small compared to the cost of placing the pipes deeper. So the reasonable operator might well choose to ignore this very small risk in planning the water system.

   b. Logically, it shouldn't make any difference if the freak frost was 75 years ago or last week. In either case, the waterworks is on notice of this unusual risk, but the question remains whether they must act to avert it. As long as it is a very unusual risk, and as long as it will be very expensive to eliminate it, the decision not to eliminate it is probably reasonable.

      Of course, if the waterworks engineers had reason to believe that last year's frost shows that such frosts were becoming *more* common (if, for example, woolly mammoths have recently appeared in the streets of Birmingham), then the risk would be a more important factor in the equation. But if their best judgment is that the recent deep freeze was indeed off the charts, they may reasonably view it as too remote a risk to warrant expensive precautions.

   c. The Hand formula indicates that the reasonable waterworks company should not place the pipes lower. In economic terms, it is not reasonable to invest $20 million to avoid $5 million in economic losses. So, if we use Hand's formula as the measure of reasonableness, the waterworks company is not negligent for laying the pipes at the one-foot level.

   d. Assuming that the decision not to guard against this frost was a reasonable judgment on the part of the waterworks, it is not liable to Blyth. The whole point of a negligence liability rule is that you pay if your conduct was unreasonable, but not if it was reasonable, *even though others suffer harm from your reasonable conduct.*

      The irony of this example, of course, is that the waterworks saves $20 million by imposing $5 million in losses on the homeowners! Because negligence law tells the waterworks that it doesn't have to take precautions against this unusual risk, it doesn't. If the risk comes to pass, and floods Blyth's basement, the waterworks isn't liable to compensate Blyth, because it wasn't negligent.

   e. The difference between strict liability and negligence is that under strict liability the actor who causes harm pays the resulting damages, even if he acted with due care. Under this rule, the waterworks would have to pay for Blyth's flooded basement, even if it made a reasonable judgment not to avoid the risk of extreme frosts. Under negligence law, the cost of accidents often falls on an innocent victim—like

Blyth in the last example—as long as the person causing the harm acted with due care.

f. This example asks how the waterworks' conduct would be different if we change the governing tort principle to strict liability. A large organization like a waterworks, which expects to be around for a long time, may very well consider liability rules in planning its operations. Indeed, according to economic theorists, one of the goals of tort law is to design rules that will encourage socially desirable planning *in advance*, not just redistribute a loss after it happens.

In this case, however, the waterworks' conduct wouldn't be different at all. Using the figures in Example 5c, the rational waterworks would still put the pipes at the one-foot level. This would save $20 million. If a freak frost occurs, they will have to pay $5 million to homeowners, but that makes more sense than spending $20 million to save $5 million.

So here, the choice of the strict liability rule over a negligence rule does not affect the rational economic actor's level of precautions. However, it *does* make a difference: It requires the actor to internalize the accident costs it causes, even though it reasonably chose not to prevent them. There's something to be said for that result, both in economic terms and in person-in-the-street fairness terms. But strict liability is not the law in most accident cases. Negligence is.

A True Story: Judge Hand at the Roller Rink

6. a. This really is a classic Hand formula situation, isn't it? There is evidence of P—that the probability of an accident was quite low. "It hasn't happened in 17 years." Intuitively, I would have estimated that P was much higher: The combination of youthful exuberance, frequently coupled with inexperience and speed, suggests that accidents would be more common. Frankly, I think the rink was beating the odds.

There is also evidence about L, the likely loss if an accident happens. Of course, L could be low, a skinned knee or bruised shoulder, perhaps. But really serious accidents, possibly leading to profound brain injuries, are also quite predictable—and of course, those are the ones likely to end up in court.

On the other side of the formula, B, the burden of prevention, is very low: For a few hundred dollars the rink could pad that wall and drastically reduce the risk of a serious injury.

b. While the jury can't quantify the Hand formula terms, they could, in an impressionistic way, analyze this case intelligently in Hand formula terms. Can't you just hear Jane's lawyer's closing argument to the jury:

> An accident like Jane's was an obvious, very serious risk. They should have seen it coming and known that when it came it was likely to be a head injury, the most serious kind. All they had to do to prevent this from happening to Jane was to put some padding on the walls. The cost would be negligible—a few hundred bucks to avoid a catastrophic injury. The reasonable operator would have done it. They should have done it. If they had, Jane would be OK and we wouldn't be here today. You should send them a clear message to give safety a higher priority in running their business.

I would sure rather argue this case for the plaintiff than the defendant, wouldn't you? It would have taken so little to avoid the harm. Even if the accident was unlikely, the formula clearly suggests that that odious Reasonable Person would have taken precautions.

Fudd and Foreseeability

7. Fudd has grievously confused the burden of proof with the standard of care. His instruction suggests that Falstaff was negligent only if the accident was "more probable than not." In fact, Falstaff's act may have been negligent even if an accident was very unlikely.

In a civil case, the plaintiff must convince the jury that it is more probable than not that each of the elements of the claim is true. Here, most juries would conclude that it was more probable than not that Falstaff *was negligent*, even though the probability that his conduct would cause an accident was quite low. As the Hand formula suggests, a risk does not have to be *likely* to happen before the reasonable person avoids it. The reasonable person avoids even small risks if the resulting injuries, if they occur, are likely to be great. Since the damages from a head-on collision with an oncoming car are likely to be grievous, the reasonable driver in Falstaff's circumstances would not take that risk, even if it was a very small risk. In Hand formula terms, while P is low, L is very great, and B, the burden of avoiding the risk, is very low: Falstaff need only wait for a clear stretch of road before passing.

Opinions in negligence cases often state that conduct was negligent because injury was the "natural and probable consequence" of the defendant's act. This is promiscuous language; "probable" here really means *foreseeable*. A risk may be foreseeable, and worth avoiding, even though the chances are a great deal less than 50 percent that it will actually come to pass.

The Honorable Fudd would be better advised to instruct the jury along these lines:

> If you find that the defendant passed on the curve without being able to tell whether a car was coming the other way, and that the risk of a collision was sufficiently foreseeable that a reasonable person in the defendant's

> circumstances would not have acted as he did, then you should find that the defendant breached the standard of due care.

This instruction requires the jury to engage in the same balancing process that the Reasonable Person does, to weigh risks and advantages to determine what Falstaff *should have done* and then to compare that to what he actually did. In effect, the jury first decides what the standard means in the context of the facts (what is "reasonable" under *these* circumstances) and then decides whether the defendant acted that way or not.

8. a. Elbow's counsel will object to Fudd's instruction because it requires the jury to find that Barnardine was not negligent if he did what is customarily done in the trade. This instruction would elevate custom to a rule of law: Whatever is done in a trade or profession would automatically constitute due care, thus delegating to roofers the decision about what due care means on a roof. For various reasons, real roofers may not behave the way the reasonable roofer should. As Judge Learned Hand so eloquently explained:

> [A] whole calling may have unduly lagged in the adoption of new and available devices. It never may set its own tests, however persuasive be its usages. Courts must in the end say what is required. . . .

The T. J. Hooper v. Northern Barge Corp., 60 F.2d 737, 740 (2d Cir. 1932). Consequently, evidence of custom, what is usually done in a trade or profession, is admissible at trial—the jury is allowed to hear such evidence. However, they still must determine whether what was done, customary or not, comports with the negligence standard itself—ordinary care under the circumstances.

b. Judge Fudd should tell the jury that they can consider the evidence of what is customary in the roofing trade, but that they are not bound to find Barnardine reasonable if he did what most roofers do:

> There has been evidence introduced at trial about the extent to which roofers wear safety harnesses in working on jobs like the one that gave rise to this claim. If you find that it was customary in the trade to use a safety harness, or not to wear one, you may consider this evidence along with all the other evidence in determining whether the defendant acted reasonably under the circumstances that gave rise to this claim.

This instruction allows the jury to consider custom evidence, but indicates that the question for the jury is whether the defendant's conduct was reasonable under the general due care test.

If I represented Elbow, I would ask Judge Fudd to give the following further instruction:

> If you find that it was customary for roofers not to wear a safety harness, you may still find that the defendant was negligent for failing to do so. The standard you must apply is reasonable care under the circumstances, not what is generally done in the trade.

This instruction makes the point a little more emphatically from the plaintiff's point of view. However, the judge might refuse to give it. It basically repeats the general instruction above, and is perhaps a bit argumentative as well.

A Duty of Much Care

9. The judge should refuse the instruction. Negligence law holds defendants to a duty of reasonable care under the circumstances, not different duties depending on the degree of risk of each activity. The jury should be instructed that Gobbo owed Mariana a duty of reasonable care under the circumstances.

However, the circumstances here involve a high risk of injury. Reasonable care in the dispensing of gasoline undoubtedly requires a greater *amount* of care than dispensing ice cream sodas. But this is not a different *standard* of care; it is just what the reasonable person would do under *these* circumstances. It would be perfectly appropriate for the judge to instruct the jury as follows:

> If you find that dispensing of gasoline involves a high risk of explosion, and that the reasonable person in the defendant's circumstances would have known or should have known of that risk, then the defendant was required to exercise a high level of care commensurate with the high risk involved in that activity.

This instruction may be only subtly different from the one Gobbo's counsel requested, but it is different in an important respect: It states that the reasonable person, acting under the usual due care standard, exercises a higher *amount* of care if the circumstances involve high risk. The requested instruction wrongly suggests that a different *standard* of care applies.

The jury very likely won't catch the subtle distinction between these two instructions: They will just pick up on the fact that the defendant was required to be very careful. But getting the instruction right is still important, especially to Mariana. If the inaccurate one is given, her verdict may be reversed on appeal. The correct instruction will communicate much the same message to the jury, but without the risk of reversal for legal error.

An Almost Perfect Record

10. a. In baseball, .300 is a good batting average, and Quince is batting nearly a thousand. This tends to show that Quince is a careful doctor. If I were choosing a doctor, such information would make me more likely to choose Quince.

    But this case is not about whether Quince is a careful doctor: It is about whether he exercised due care *on this occasion*. We are not testing his general virtue or his career accomplishments; rather, we are testing his conduct in one particular operation. It is no answer to Peasblossom that Quince was careful in all those *other* cases; she claims—and is entitled to—the exercise of reasonable care in the performance of *her* operation.

    On the other hand, how can we hold Quince to a standard of perfection? We all make mistakes, and Quince makes fewer than most. How can we condemn him if the knife slips once?

    Well, we aren't condemning him. A finding of negligence is not a moral judgment passed upon a person, or a finding of incompetence, but a post hoc evaluation of a single event against an abstract standard set up by the law. Since that is all that we are doing, evidence of Quince's batting average, that he usually meets the standard of care in his operations, is beside the point, just as evidence that he had made mistakes on other patients would not establish that he was careless in Peasblossom's operation. See Fed. R. Evid. 404(a) (evidence of character generally inadmissible "to prove that on a particular occasion the person acted in accordance with the character or trait").

    b. Judge Fudd should not give the usual reasonable-care-under-the-circumstances instruction on the element of negligence. Here, the defendant was acting as a professional, a lumbar surgeon. By doing so, he has undertaken to apply the skill of a specialist, and will be required to meet that standard in Peasblossom's case. Fudd should instruct the jury along the following lines:

    > In performing the operation that gave rise to this claim, the defendant was acting as a specialist in the area of surgery. In determining whether the defendant was negligent, you must decide whether, in performing the operation, he committed some act that the reasonably competent physician engaged in the practice of surgery would not have done, or failed to do some act that the reasonably competent physician engaged in that specialty would have done.[7]

7. A good many states still apply a "customary practice" standard of care to doctors. See, e.g., *Purtill v. Hess*, 489 N.E.2d 867, 872 (Ill. 1986) (same reasonable care as "reasonably well-qualified physician" in same or similar medical community). This standard essentially

c. The average jury is made up of a cross section of individuals with varying educational backgrounds, professions, experiences, and values. Few, if any, will know anything about lower lumbar surgery. They are in no position, based on their general knowledge, to say what reasonable care requires in such operations.

   Thus, the parties will have to educate the jury not only about what the defendant did, but also about what the standard of reasonable care required under the circumstances in which he did it. Each side will offer expert evidence (doubtless from lumbar surgeons in Peasblossom's case) as to the proper way to perform surgery of this type. The jury will have to determine, after assessing the conflicting testimony of these experts, what the reasonable surgeon does in such cases. Having determined that, they will then have to decide whether Quince failed to meet that standard.

   In many cases, the jury's life experience will allow them to determine what reasonable care means without the testimony of experts. Jurors can pass judgment on the reasonableness of driving a car, operating simple machinery, controlling children in a classroom, crossing the street, or climbing a ladder, based on their general knowledge. But a great many cases require expert evidence in order for the jury to determine the standard of reasonable care. The proper way to reinforce a bridge, to pilot an ocean vessel, to analyze a financial statement, to ride a racehorse, to land a 747, or to treat a drug overdose, to name a few examples, are beyond the common experience of jurors. In such cases, trial must include an expensive "battle of the experts" on what reasonable care demands in those circumstances.

Menlove in Reverse

11. Portia can make a pretty good argument for holding Dogberry to the standard of care of an expert: He is a highly experienced skier who is probably capable of better control than your basic weekender on the slopes. Why should he be held to a lesser standard of care than he is able to meet?

    There is some force to the argument, but there are also problems with it. First, it tends (like Menlove's argument) to destroy the

---

equates what doctors generally do with acceptable medical practice, contrary to the more limited role that custom usually plays in proving reasonable care (see Example 8). However, the general reasonable physician standard reflected in this instruction appears to be gaining ground. See P. Philip, The Role of the Jury in Modern Malpractice Law, 87 Iowa L. Rev. 909, 913-917 (2002).

uniformity of the standard of care. If the argument were accepted, the jury would have to ascertain in each case just how good the defendant was at what he did before deciding what standard to apply to him. Should the jury "grade" the defendant as "expert," "very good," "good," or "average" before determining what standard he must meet? Suppose he is a subpar skier? Ratcheting the standard of performance up for the able seems to imply lowering it for the less able as well, yet *Menlove* certainly indicates that the court will not do that. If the goal is a single objective standard, it appears to make sense to stick to the reasonable-person-under-the-circumstances test for Dogberry, at least when he is engaging in ordinary maneuvers engaged in by skiers with a wide range of abilities.

It would be different if Dogberry were *acting as an expert* at the time of the injury. For example, if Dogberry were a member of the ski patrol in the course of a rescue, he would be acting as an expert and should be held to that standard. But in this example Dogberry is just skiing, like everyone else on the slopes, and should be held to the same standard of care as the reasonable skier under the circumstances. Similarly, a trucker driving his car to the movies may be an "expert" driver, but will be held to the general reasonable person standard for ordinary driving. See *Fredericks v. Castora*, 360 A.2d 696, 698 (Pa. Super. 1976) ("to vary the standard according to the driver's experience would render the application of any reasonably uniform standard impossible").

The result here is not entirely clear, however. Some authorities suggest that Dogberry should be held to the standard of an expert in this example. See Restatement (Third) of Torts: Liability for Physical and Emotional Harm §12 (particular skills and knowledge are circumstances to be considered in additional reasonable care). As a practical matter, of course, if the evidence shows that Dogberry is highly experienced, the jury is likely to demand more of him anyway, whether or not they are instructed to do so.

An Elementary Example

12. This chapter began by drawing the distinction between negligent conduct and liability on a negligence claim. We end with the same distinction. Falstaff was clearly negligent here in the sense that he breached the standard of due care by driving drunk. He failed to act as a reasonable person under the circumstances would. That satisfies Element #2 of the cause of action for negligence.

    But the *tort* of negligence has three other elements, and one of those is causation. Here, the facts suggest that Falstaff was not negligent in the way he handled the car, even though he was drunk. He was in his lane, driving below the speed limit. Because Moth fell right in front of the car, there was nothing Falstaff could have done to avoid hitting Moth; even if he had been sober, the accident would have happened the same way. Liability for negligence turns not just on *being* negligent, but upon negligent conduct *causing* injury.

But Falstaff's negligence did cause the harm, didn't it? He was negligent to be on the road *at all* while drunk, and his driving caused the accident. This argument proves too much. On this theory, Falstaff would be liable to Moth if he had bald tires, worn windshield wipers, or a loud muffler, and had the same accident, even though none of these conditions contributed in any way to the injury.

In order for a negligent act to be considered a cause of the plaintiff's injury, the risk that makes the conduct negligent must lead to the harm. Driving while drunk is negligent because it impairs the ability to control the car: It is only when this impairment contributes to the occurrence of the accident that the negligence becomes a "cause" of resulting harm. Falstaff would be liable if Moth fell far enough in front of the car that an unimpaired driver could have braked in time, and Falstaff failed to brake because of his inebriation. On those facts his negligence would have affected the outcome, and the causation requirement—Element #3—would be established. See generally Chapter 10 on cause in fact.

CHAPTER 8

Borrowing Standards of Care: Violation of Statute as Negligence

INTRODUCTION

As the previous chapter indicates, the plaintiff in a negligence case must prove four elements—duty, breach, causation, and damages—in order to recover in a negligence case. To establish the second element, breach of the duty of care, or negligence, the plaintiff must show that the defendant failed to act with reasonable care, to behave as the ordinary prudent person would under like circumstances.

This reasonable person standard has been criticized as too vague to provide any meaningful guidance to the jury in evaluating the defendant's conduct. Juries are supposed to find facts, not to establish the rules of law that determine whether the defendant is liable. Arguably, the negligence standard is so broad that it licenses the jury to find as they please, without constraining them by meaningful legal rules.

On the other hand, how can the rule be any more specific? The variety of human experience, the range of circumstances that may cause injury, is so great that it would be impossible for courts to formulate specific rules in advance to govern liability for all careless conduct. Since it is impossible to "particularize" the negligence standard, the jury is usually instructed under the reasonable person formula. The jurors are left to use their common sense, experience, and, where appropriate, expert testimony, to pass judgment on the defendant's conduct under this very general standard.

While courts cannot elaborate specific negligence rules to define how parties should behave in all circumstances, *legislatures* routinely enact statutes establishing standards of care for common situations. This chapter considers the role that such statutes play in proving the second element of a claim for negligence, that a party breached the standard of care or "was negligent."

LEGISLATIVE STANDARDS OF CONDUCT

Legislatures very commonly enact statutes that establish standards of care for private conduct. Many such statutes govern that ubiquitous, highly practical, but potentially lethal instrumentality, the automobile. Here are some hypothetical, but typical, examples:

> No person shall make a turn onto or off of a public way without signaling his or her intention to turn, either by hand or by an electrical signal device. West Dakota Ann. Laws Title V §12.
>
> No person shall drive a motor vehicle without a muffler or other suitable device to control excessive noise. West Dakota Ann. Laws Title V §212.
>
> No person shall drive an unlighted vehicle upon any public highway during the period from one-half hour after sunset until one-half hour before sunrise. West Dakota Ann. Laws Title V §94A.
>
> The driver of a vehicle on any public highway, traveling in any direction, shall stop before reaching any bus marked "school bus" and exhibiting flashing red lights. The driver shall not proceed until the bus resumes motion or the lights are no longer flashing. West Dakota Ann. Laws Title V §74.

Many statutes establish standards of care in other areas as well:

> No person shall enter upon or be employed upon the premises of an active construction site without wearing a construction helmet. West Dakota Ann. Laws Title IX §111.
>
> No person shall leave a refrigerator, freezer, or similar appliance in any unsecured area accessible to children, whether for disposal or otherwise, without detaching the door from said appliance. West Dakota Ann. Laws Title XXIV §51.
>
> Every owner or lessor of property used for rental purposes shall maintain every outside stair and porch in sound condition and good repair. West Dakota Ann. Laws Title XVII §19.
>
> No person shall operate any mobile piece of heavy construction equipment unless said equipment is equipped with a beeper which sounds at all times while such equipment is operating in reverse. West Dakota Ann. Laws Title XXIII §123.

Statutes like these are intended to promote safety by establishing standards of conduct for particular situations. They are legislative commands which, if applicable, every citizen is bound to obey. Usually, such safety statutes impose a small criminal penalty for violations of the standard, but do not say anything about whether violation of the statutory standard establishes negligence in a civil action for damages. Not surprisingly, however, persons injured due to a violation of such a statute usually claim that the defendant was negligent for failing to comply with the statutory standard of care.

Suppose, for example, that Bourjailly drives past a stopped school bus with flashing lights and hits Hellman, a child alighting from the bus. If the school bus statute quoted above applies, Hellman will argue that Bourjailly should be found negligent because he violated the statute. Or suppose that Updike is injured by a falling object on a construction site, and sues the contractor. If the helmet statute quoted above applies, and if Updike was not wearing one, the defendant would argue that Updike's violation of the statute proves, in and of itself, that he failed to live up to the standard of due care.

ARGUMENTS FOR AND AGAINST THE NEGLIGENCE PER SE RULE

There are some good arguments that a violation of a statute should be treated as "negligence per se," that is, negligence in itself. Where the legislature has decreed that certain precautions must be taken, or that certain acts should not be done, a person who violates the statute has ignored the standard of care established by the legislature. Arguably, reasonable people don't do that.

In addition, if the jury is permitted to find that the defendant acted with due care, despite his violation of a statutory standard of care, the jury is being licensed to disregard the command of the legislature. Suppose, for example, that the jury finds that Updike was not negligent in failing to wear a helmet. Doesn't this ignore the legislature, the voice of the people, which has barred such conduct? Shouldn't the standard of conduct enforced by the courts be the same as that established by the legislature, so that court decisions in negligence suits will reinforce rather than contradict the policy of the legislature?

There is much logic to these arguments, but the negligence per se cases vividly illustrate Justice Holmes's famous maxim, "The life of the law has not been logic; it has been experience." O. W. Holmes, Jr., The Common Law I (Little, Brown 1881). Automatic adoption of general legislative standards has proved too rigid. While it may be generally true that the reasonable person obeys the law, it is not always true. In unusual circumstances, it may be reasonable to disregard the statute, as where a driver swerves across the center line to avoid a child in the street, or stops in a no-stopping zone to attend to a seriously ill passenger. In other cases, it may be impossible to obey the law, despite the best will in the world, as where blizzard conditions overwhelm efforts to keep a street clear. Imposing liability in cases like these, simply on the ground that the defendant violated the statute, would look more like strict liability than liability based on fault.

Another argument against automatic adoption of the legislative standard is that most statutes that establish standards of care say nothing about what role the legislative standard should play in a tort action for damages. Since the legislature has not provided that violation of the statutory standard of care automatically establishes negligence, it is fair to infer that courts have some discretion to "borrow" that standard selectively.

Last, it is doubtful that the legislature intended blind adherence to statutory standards regardless of the circumstances. Legislators tend to be practical people, and practical people recognize that there are circumstances in which the ordinary rules do not pertain. If asked, no legislator who voted for a statute requiring drivers to keep to the right would testify that she intended them to run down small children in order to fulfill the statutory command, or to smash into a stalled oil delivery truck.

COMMON APPROACHES TO BORROWING STATUTORY STANDARDS

Some early cases appear to hold that violation of a statutory standard of care always constitutes negligence per se. Under this approach, if the defendant violated the statute, the jury would be required to find her negligent, without regard to any excuse she might offer. One of the classic cases, *Martin v. Herzog*, 126 N.E. 814 (N.Y. 1920), might be read to stand for this position,[1] and early cases from other jurisdictions appear to agree. See, e.g., *Decker v. Roberts*, 3 A.2d 855 (Conn. 1939); *O'Bannon v. Schultz*, 169 A. 601 (Conn. 1933); cf. *Zeni v. Anderson*, 243 N.W.2d 270, 281 (Mich. 1976) (noting that the negligence per se rule bars evidence of excuse). Under this approach, the only way the defendant could avoid liability would be to show that the statute did not apply under the circumstances (see, e.g., *Tedla v. Ellman*, 19 N.E.2d 987 (N.Y. 1939)), or that the violation, while admittedly negligence, did not cause the plaintiff's injury.

1. However, even *Martin*, despite its strong language, intimated that the violation in that case established negligence per se because it was "wholly unexcused." 126 N.E. at 815.

However, as Holmes's maxim portends, experience with the negligence per se doctrine has led virtually all courts to soften this Draconian stance. Most courts have adopted one of the following approaches, which allow the jury to *consider* the violation of a statutory standard of care in determining negligence, but avoid making it automatically determinative.

A. Negligence Per Se with "Excuse"

The most common approach to violation of statute as negligence is reflected in §14 of the Third Restatement of Torts: Liability for Physical and Emotional Harm. That section provides as follows:

> An actor is negligent if, without excuse, the actor violates a statute that is designed to protect against the type of accident the actor's conduct causes, and if the accident victim is within the class of persons the statute is designed to protect.

Under this provision, if an actor violates a relevant statutory standard of care, that violation will establish her negligence if no excuse is offered. Suppose, for example, that Bourjailly violates the school bus statute quoted above by passing a stopped school bus and hits Hellman, a student getting off the bus. Suppose also that Bourjailly offers no excuse for his violation (quite likely because he doesn't have one). On these assumptions, the jury would be instructed that, if they find that Bourjailly violated the statute, they must find that he was negligent.

However, the Restatement recognizes that there may be legitimate reasons for violating a relevant statute. Thus, the violator will be entitled to offer evidence of an excuse for the violation. Section 15 of the Third Restatement recognizes the following categories of "excused violations":

(a) the violation is reasonable in light of the actor's childhood, physical disability, or physical incapacitation;
(b) the actor exercises reasonable care in attempting to comply with the statute;
(c) the actor neither knows nor should know of the factual circumstances that render the statute applicable;
(d) the actor's violation of the statute is due to the confusing way in which the requirements are presented to the public; or
(e) the actor's compliance with the statute would involve a greater risk of physical harm to the actor or to others than noncompliance.

Under the Restatement, these listed excuses are not exclusive; Bourjailly would be free to offer some other reason for the violation as well.

Restatement (Third) of Torts: Liability for Physical and Emotional Harm §15 cmt. g.

Under the Restatement approach, Bourjailly would be deemed negligent if he violated the school bus statute and offered no evidence of an acceptable excuse. However, if he did present evidence of an excuse, the plaintiff's effort to prove negligence simply by proving a violation of the statute would fail. The jury would be instructed to determine whether Bourjailly acted reasonably under all the circumstances, including his violation of the statute, the reasons offered for noncompliance, and others. That sounds a good deal like a general reasonableness inquiry.

B. "Presumption" of Negligence

Some jurisdictions hold that proof of a statutory violation creates a "presumption" that the violator was negligent. The violator is still free, however, to rebut the presumption by showing that the reasonable person would have acted as he did. It is not clear that there is much difference between this approach and the Restatement approach. Under each, the plaintiff may use evidence of a statutory violation to establish negligence. Under each, the defendant may offer evidence of a good reason for her conduct. If she does not offer such evidence, the violation of the statute establishes her negligence. If she does offer evidence of an excuse, the jury is left to assess her conduct under a reasonable person standard, considering both the requirements of the statute and the violator's reasons for violating it.

Under both the Restatement and the presumption approaches, most courts hold that the burden of proof remains on the plaintiff.[2] The plaintiff can prove negligence by proving violation of a relevant safety statute, if the defendant does not offer evidence of an adequate reason for the violation. If evidence of an excuse is offered, the burden remains on the plaintiff to convince the jury that, in light of the violation and the reasons offered, the defendant did not behave as a reasonable person would under the circumstances. See, e.g., *Moughon v. Wolf*, 576 S.W.2d 603, 604-605 (Tex. 1978) (where plaintiff proves statutory violation and defendant offers evidence of excuse, plaintiff bears the burden to convince the jury that defendant's conduct was negligent under the reasonable person standard).[3]

---

2. A few cases appear to shift the burden of proof to the defendant to prove due care, once a violation of statute has been shown. See, e.g., *Resser v. Boise-Cascnde Corp.*, 587 P.2d 80, 84 (Or. 1978) (once violation is shown, burden shifts to violator to prove that he nevertheless acted reasonably). It is not always clear, however, whether these courts mean that the burden to produce evidence of excuse shifts to the defendant, or the actual burden of proof.

3. This chapter consistently speaks of the plaintiff invoking negligence per se. Clearly, however, defendants may invoke the doctrine as well to prove that the plaintiff was negligent.

C. Evidence of Negligence

The third common approach is to treat violation of a statutory standard of care as evidence of negligence. Under this approach, evidence that the defendant violated a statute is admissible at trial. The jury may consider it along with all the other evidence that the defendant did or did not exercise ordinary care. They may be persuaded (on that evidence alone, or along with other evidence) that the defendant was negligent. But they are not compelled to find him negligent, *even in the absence of rebutting evidence from the defendant.*

This is meaningfully different from the per se and presumption approaches. Under those approaches, if no excuse is offered, the judge should instruct the jury that they must find the defendant negligent if they find that she violated the statute. Under the evidence-of-negligence approach, proof of an unexcused violation would support a finding of negligence by the jury, but they would still be free to find that the defendant was not negligent, even if no excuse were offered. It is certainly conceivable that a jury would refuse to find negligence despite the violation: For example, a jury might well find that driving 57 m.p.h. on a clear dry day on a rural interstate highway is not negligence, even if the speed limit were 55 and the defendant had no excuse. Under the evidence-of-negligence approach, the jury would be free to reach that conclusion. Under the presumption or per se approaches, however, this violation would establish negligence unless an excuse were offered.

While negligence per se is widely applied, the Dobbs treatise makes a strong case for the evidence-of-negligence approach:

> *Evaluating the evidence of negligence rule.* The negligence per se rule has been criticized on numerous grounds. The main problems of rigidity, the costly efforts to avoid rigidity, and the displacement of factual evaluation, however, are resolved under the evidence of negligence rule. That rule is flexible and easy to administer. It does not generate litigation over excuses or over questions about what risks and harms were covered by the statute. The per se rule is often said to be justified in part on the ground that it creates more certainty, but it is far from clear that it creates as much certainty as it creates litigation and litigation strategy. So the evidence of negligence rule is a fair contender for support.

Dobbs' Law of Torts s. 149 (footnotes omitted).

THE REQUIREMENT OF RELEVANCE

As the foregoing section indicates, evidence of the violation of a statutory standard of care is usually admissible, and can be conclusive, on the negligence question. However, such evidence may not be used to establish breach of the duty of care unless the statute establishes a *relevant* standard of care. If Bourjailly causes an accident by turning into the path of Perelman's oncoming car, common sense tells us that it is irrelevant that he violated a statute requiring him to curb his dog, or even one requiring working windshield wipers (assuming the weather was dry at the time of the accident). Allowing evidence of these violations might prove that Bourjailly was a generally negligent person, but would not show that his negligence caused this particular accident.

Courts frequently state that a statute is only relevant in establishing negligence if it is meant to protect persons like the plaintiff from the type of harm which actually occurred. The dog curbing statute was not aimed at preventing intersection collisions, but the turn signal statute quoted at p. 146 clearly was enacted to protect other drivers from collisions with turning vehicles, exactly the type of accident which resulted from Bourjailly's failure to comply with the statute. This statute establishes a relevant standard of care because it was meant to protect drivers like Perelman from the type of harm—turning accidents—that resulted in this case. See generally Dobbs' Law of Torts §152.

This requirement is nicely illustrated by one of the classic cases on the point. In *Gorris v. Scott*, 9 L.R.-Ex. 125 (1874), the plaintiff's sheep were washed overboard while being transported by sea. The plaintiff tried to establish the carrier's negligence by proving that it had violated a regulation requiring that animals on shipboard must be kept in pens of a certain size. Had the defendant complied with the statute, the plaintiff argued, the sheep would not have been washed overboard.

The court refused to find negligence on the basis of the violation. The regulation, the court concluded, was not meant to protect animals from being washed overboard, but rather to prevent the spread of disease by preventing overcrowding. Since it was not aimed at preventing the type of harm that occurred, it did not establish a standard of care relevant to the circumstances, and could not be used to establish the shipper's negligence.

Another case which nicely illustrates the point is *Kansas, Okla. & Gulf Ry. Co. v. Keirsey*, 266 P.2d 617 (Okla. 1954), in which the plaintiff's cow entered a railroad right of way and ate itself to death. The plaintiff claimed that the railroad was negligent per se because it had violated a statute which required it to maintain fences to prevent animals from straying onto the right of way. The court refused to find negligence based on the violation since the statute was aimed at protecting farm animals from being hit by trains, not from eating too much grass.

Courts will also refuse to treat violation of a statute as negligence if the statute was not intended to protect the class of persons to which the plaintiff belongs. See Restatement (Third) of Torts: Liability for Physical and Emotional Harm §14, which provides

> An actor is negligent if, without excuse, the actor violates a statute that is designed to protect against the type of accident the actor's conduct causes, and if the accident victim is within the class of persons the statute is designed to protect.

For example, a building code might be intended to protect building occupants, not workers involved in the construction of the building. If so, the court would likely refuse to apply the building code standards to determine negligence in an action by a worker injured during construction since the legislature was thinking about a different group with a different set of expectations and different opportunities to protect themselves. Thus, the statute is not relevant on the question of proper precautions during construction. Another nice example is a firefighter injured fighting a fire in a building that lacks sprinklers required by statute. The court might refuse to allow the firefighter to establish negligence based on the lack of sprinklers since the statute was meant to protect occupants, not emergency personnel.

If the defendant successfully argues that the statute was not aimed at the type of harm the plaintiff suffered, or at protecting persons in the plaintiff's situation, violation of the statute will not be given per se effect and the jury will not hear anything about it. That does not mean that the plaintiff must lose the case. All it means is that she cannot prove the second element of her claim—breach of the standard of care—by proving a violation of the statute. Instead, she must shoulder the usual burden to show negligence under the reasonable person standard discussed in the previous chapter.

THE PERSUASIVE FORCE OF THE NEGLIGENCE PER SE ARGUMENT

It is easy to see why the negligence per se argument is attractive to lawyers. If Hellman can prove that Bourjailly was negligent just by showing that he violated the school bus statute, it substantially eases her burden of proof. It is a lot easier to prove that he didn't stop for the bus than to prove that his conduct was careless under the vague ordinary-prudence-under-the-circumstances standard. In addition, proving that Bourjailly violated the statute brands him as a "lawbreaker" in the eyes of the jury, which can't do his case a lot of good. Thus, using the violation to establish negligence has great tactical value for Hellman. Similarly, if the contractor in the second example can prove that Updike was negligent simply by showing that he wasn't wearing a helmet, its defense looks a good deal stronger than it would under a general negligence standard.

The use of statutory standards to prove negligence also reduces the likelihood that the jury will decide the case on grounds unrelated to the merits.

A jury sympathetic to the injured Updike in the helmet case might be tempted to ignore his negligence and find for him anyway. It will be harder for them to do that if they are instructed that they *must* find him negligent if they find that he did not wear a helmet. Indeed, if it were undisputed that Updike had no helmet on, the court might take the negligence issue from the jury entirely, on the ground that the undisputed and unexcused violation of the statute establishes his negligence as a matter of law.[4]

All this appears complex, but is pretty much a matter of common sense in actual operation. Perhaps the following examples will help.

Examples

Some Relevant Questions

1. A good place to start in any negligence per se situation is to ask whether the statute was intended to protect the plaintiff from the type of harm which she actually suffered. In which of the following cases do you think the court would find the statutory standard relevant to the plaintiff's claim?
   a. Porter, the town dog officer, quarantines a dog who had bitten a child. The officer allows the owner to take the dog after a week, in violation of a quarantine statute that requires him to hold the dog for 14 days. The next day, the dog runs in front of Jones's car. Jones swerves to avoid the dog and is injured.
   b. Oliver, a seven-year-old child, finds an abandoned refrigerator in a vacant lot, crawls in to hide, and suffocates. In an action for his death, the estate tries to prove the owner's negligence by showing violation of the statute quoted on p. 146, requiring removal of doors from appliances left in places accessible to children.
   c. Welty hits Capote broadside when she is driving down Main Street and fails to see Capote pulling out into the street at an intersection. Capote alleges that Welty was negligent because she violated the statute quoted on p. 146, requiring a working muffler on all motor vehicles.
   d. O'Neill leaves his dirt bike on the front porch of a general store while he goes in to buy some candy. When he comes out, he mounts the bike, rides off the end of the porch, and is seriously injured. He sues the store owner, claiming that she was negligent for violating a building code provision that requires "a wall or protective railing at least 36 inches high enclosing every porch more than 30 inches above the ground."

4. Even if instructed that the violation constitutes negligence, the jury in a comparative negligence jurisdiction would still have to determine Updike's percentage of negligence.

   e. A West Dakota statute requires a motel to have a lifeguard on duty at the motel pool during the hours of 8:00 a.m. to 10:00 p.m. On a particular day Welty, the lifeguard, was an hour late. Faulkner went down to the pool with his work clothes at 8:00, planning to have a quick swim, change, and go to work. While he was doing laps his wallet was stolen from his pants. Faulkner sues for financial losses due to massive charges on his stolen credit cards. He seeks to prove the motel's negligence based on its violation of its statutory duty to have a lifeguard on duty starting at 8:00 a.m.
   f. Austin, riding her bicycle down the street, approaches a truck parked in a loading zone. To clear the truck, she steers further into the street, and is hit by a passing motorist. She alleges that Porter, the owner of the truck, was negligent for violating a statute that limits parking in the loading zone to one-half hour during morning hours. Porter's truck had been there for nearly two hours.

2. After reading about the various ways in which the defendant may excuse a statutory violation, it may seem that the negligence per se doctrine is a toothless tiger. The plaintiff can use it to suggest negligence, but the defendant can rebut it, so it all comes down to general reasonableness anyway. Here are a few cases that illustrate that the doctrine can make a big difference in a negligence case. In each case, ask yourself why the per se negligence doctrine will make an important difference in the outcome.
   a. Salinger is driving east on a rural West Dakota highway when Ginsberg comes toward him from around a curve, driving astride the center line of the road. Their cars collide and Ginsberg is killed. Salinger sues Ginsberg's estate for negligence. To prove that Ginsberg failed to exercise due care, he testifies that Ginsberg violated a statute that requires vehicles to keep to the right of the center line.
   b. Salinger is injured when Ginsberg's car turns in front of him while he is driving down Maple Street. He seeks to establish Ginsberg's negligence by proving that Ginsberg failed to signal his turn, as required by the statute quoted on p. 146. Ginsberg claims that he did signal before turning.
   c. Perelman hits Woolf, a construction worker, while backing up a large bulldozer. Perelman was watching carefully, but (as he knew) the beeper on the bulldozer was broken, and had been for five days. The statute on p. 146, requiring a beeper on heavy construction equipment, applies.

3. Williams, a painter, is painting the exterior wall on a new five-story building. Although a statute requires that hard hats be worn on all active construction sites, Williams was not wearing one. He is injured when a two-by-four falls on him from a higher floor. Williams claims that he

lacked knowledge of the need to comply with the statute since he was unaware of the statute. Will this excuse the violation?

Statutory Enlightenment

4. Cheever owns a three-unit apartment building in Oakley, West Dakota. He fails to replace a burnt-out light bulb in the upstairs hall. O'Connor, a tenant, is unable to see the steps, trips, and falls down the stairs. She sues him for negligence, and offers to prove his negligence by showing that he violated West Dakota Stat. Ann. Title XVI §31, which requires landlords to maintain adequate lighting in all common areas of their buildings.
   a. Does the statute establish a standard of care relevant to the case?
   b. Assume that Cheever defends by offering evidence that the light was not out; thus, he does not offer any reason for failing to replace the bulb. Assuming that West Dakota applies the negligence per se doctrine, should the judge direct a verdict for O'Connor on the negligence issue?
   c. Assume again that Cheever claims the light was on, and that West Dakota applies the negligence per se doctrine. How should the judge instruct the jury on the negligence issue?
   d. If there were no statute establishing a relevant standard of care in this case, how would the judge instruct the jury on the negligence issue?
   e. Assume now that West Dakota takes the position that violation of a relevant statute is admissible evidence of negligence rather than negligence per se. If O'Connor claims that Cheever violated the statute, how should the judge instruct the jury on the issue?

5. Assume again that O'Connor relies on the violation of the lighting statute to prove Cheever's negligence. Cheever testifies that he was aware of the burnt-out bulb, but had asked Porter, another tenant, to replace it, and Porter had told him that he would do it right away. Assume also that West Dakota applies the negligence per se with excuse approach, but that it only recognizes the five excuses listed in the Restatement (Third) of Torts §15 (see p. 149). How will the negligence issue be resolved?

6. Assume that Cheever's building is in a high-crime area. Calisher, accosted on the street by a robber, runs into Cheever's building to escape. Because the light is out, she stumbles over a child's tricycle and is injured. In a negligence action, can she rely on his violation of the lighting statute to establish negligence?

Judge Fudd Rules Again

7. Calisher runs a small, low-budget theater in the round. Wharton, a patron, is injured when her seat collapses during a performance, evidently

because a bolt sheared off underneath it. In her negligence action against Calisher, Wharton introduces evidence that Calisher had violated West Dakota Ann. Laws Title LXI §21A, which requires that theater owners have their premises inspected and certified annually by the city building inspector.

a. Assume that West Dakota follows the evidence of negligence approach. Judge Fudd instructs the jury, in part, as follows:

> If you find that West Dakota Ann. Laws Title LXI §21A is intended to protect a class of persons including the plaintiff from the danger of injuries such as that suffered by her, and that the defendant violated that statute, then you are instructed that the violation is evidence, along with all the other evidence in the case, that you may consider in determining whether the defendant was negligent.

Can you spot a fundamental flaw in Judge Fudd's instruction?

b. Assuming that the statute establishes a relevant standard of care, what other basic problem do you see in Wharton's case?

Negligence Per Se, or Negligence Per Cent?

8. One more variation on Cheever's light bulb woes. Let's assume that the case takes place in a comparative negligence jurisdiction. Under comparative negligence, the jury not only decides whether the parties were negligent, but they also assign percentages of negligence to all parties who caused the accident. The plaintiff's damages are then reduced to account for her negligence. For example, if the jury found the defendant 60 percent negligent and the plaintiff 40 percent negligent, the plaintiff would recover 60 percent of her damages. (For a detailed treatment of comparative negligence, see Chapter 24.)

   Assume that O'Connor sues Cheever in a state that applies comparative negligence, and that Cheever has no excuse for violating the lighting statute. What would be the effect of the negligence per se doctrine in the case?

The Goose and the Gander

9. A West Dakota statute requires a fence at least four feet high around private pools. Beverly has such a pool, with a four-foot fence. Alice, a child of seven, climbs over the fence, jumps into the pool, and drowns. Alice's parents sue Beverly for negligence in failing to prevent children from entering the pool area.

   a. What will Beverly argue in her defense?
   b. How should the court rule on the defense?

Explanations

Some Relevant Questions

1. a. Clearly, this statute is aimed at protecting people from being bitten by diseased dogs, not at preventing dogs from running into the street, which could happen no matter when the dog is released. Since the statute is not meant to protect against the *type of harm* suffered by Jones, the court will not allow her to prove Porter's negligence by showing this violation.

   b. This statute was clearly aimed at exactly the risk that caused the harm here: A child getting caught in the appliance when the door closes on her. In the absence of an excuse, the violation of this statute would establish negligence in a per se or a presumption jurisdiction.

   c. In order to invoke the muffler statute to prove Welty's negligence, Capote will have to demonstrate that it was aimed, at least in part, at preventing the type of accident that took place here. At first glance, the statute appears aimed at preventing excessive noise that disturbs the public peace. But it is entirely plausible that it was *also* aimed at ensuring that drivers could *listen* for traffic hazards as well as see them. A statute may be aimed at preventing a variety of evils. So long as one purpose of the statute is to avert the type of injury suffered by the plaintiff, the violation should be considered relevant to the negligence issue.

      Often there is little legislative history to assist in determining what risks the legislature was trying to prevent by the passage of a statute. The court must infer the statute's purposes primarily from the provisions of the statute itself. Thus, courts exercise a good deal of judgment in determining whom the statute was meant to protect, and from what hazards.

      Of course, Welty's violation of the muffler statute would only establish liability if it *caused* the accident. Her noisy muffler would be irrelevant unless her inability to hear contributed to the accident. The evidence might show, however, that Capote had blown his horn to warn Welty, but that she was unable to hear due to the muffler noise. If so, Welty's violation of the muffler statute would be a cause of the accident.

   d. This example is based on *Matteo v. Livingstone*, 40 Mass. App. Ct. 658 (1996). In *Matteo*, the court held that when building code provisions "prescribe protective walls or rails, the consequence they are designed to prevent is that a person will fall off accidentally. Such regulations do not have as their object preventing bicycle acrobatics." 40 Mass. App. Ct. at 661. The court upheld the trial judge's refusal to allow the statute to be admitted in evidence to establish the store owner's negligence.

The regulation at issue in *Matteo* was not a statute, but a regulation promulgated by a state agency. The Third Restatement takes the position that negligence per se applies to "regulations adopted by state administrative bodies, ordinances adopted by local councils, and federal statutes as well as regulations promulgated by federal agencies." Third Restatement of Torts: Liability for Physical and Emotional Harm §14 cmt. a. However, this regulation was clearly not aimed at the type of harm the plaintiff suffered anyway.

e. Perhaps this one is debatable. However, the likely purpose of this statute is to prevent drowning, not to protect against theft of personal property. The court would probably not allow use of the lifeguard statute to establish the motel's negligence.

f. This statute is aimed at ensuring access to adequate parking for deliveries, not at preventing the type of accident Austin has suffered here. Austin does not claim the truck was too far out into the street, but only that it was *there*. She could just as well have suffered the same accident if the truck had only been there for ten minutes. Indeed, if Porter had left on time, another truck would likely have been there anyway. This statute is irrelevant to the case; Porter's violation of it should not be considered by the jury on the negligence question. See *Capolungo v. Bondi*, 224 Cal. Rptr. 326 (Cal. App. 1986) (rejecting negligence per se on similar facts).

2. a. Under either the per se or the presumption approach, Salinger's evidence of the violation will, if the jury believes it, establish Ginsberg's negligence, unless evidence of an adequate excuse is offered. Here, Ginsberg is not around to offer exculpatory evidence. He may have had a good reason for the violation, but if the proof is not offered, the presumption governs. The doctrine is very powerful in cases like this, where the violator is unable to offer the countervailing evidence that would rebut the presumption.

b. Here, instead of trying to prove a good reason for violating the statute, the defendant claims that he did not violate it. It is a little hard for the defendant to play both sides of the street (no pun intended) in these cases. Usually, she will have to either try to explain a violation or deny that it took place. If she stakes her case on the factual contention that she did not violate the statute, and the jury finds that she did, that finding will determine the negligence issue: Under either the negligence per se or the presumption approach, the violation establishes negligence, in the absence of any evidence of an acceptable excuse.

c. Here, the defendant violated the statute, which was clearly intended to prevent the type of accident which took place, and just has no acceptable excuse. In a per se or a presumption jurisdiction, the evidence that the beeper was not working will establish Perelman's negligence. The fact that he looked carefully will not avert a required finding of negligence, because the jury is not free to make a general finding on the negligence issue: If it finds that the statute was violated, and Perelman has no excuse, it must find that he breached the duty of due care.

This will doubtless be the situation in many negligence per se cases: The defendant simply has no excuse for the violation of the statute. (Given human nature, this happens a lot, right?) In such cases, the statutory negligence doctrine provides a powerful weapon for the plaintiff since it establishes the most ambiguous element which she must prove to recover: breach of the duty of due care.

3. No way. We are all held to know the law. It is one thing to be unaware of *facts* that give rise to a violation; it is quite another to be unaware of relevant statutes themselves. If a driver's taillight suddenly goes out while she is driving, she would have an excuse for violating a statute requiring working taillights. However, if she knew her light was out but was unaware that a statute required working taillights, she would have no excuse. The Third Restatement recognizes an excuse if the actor "neither knows nor should know of the factual circumstances that render the statute applicable" (Third Restatement of Torts: Liability for Physical and Emotional Harm §15(c)), but not if an actor simply isn't aware of applicable statutory requirements. The judge would not even allow Williams to offer this evidence, since the excuse is insufficient as a matter of law.

Statutory Enlightenment

4. a. The lighting requirement in the statute is clearly aimed at protecting tenants like O'Connor from the type of harm that she has suffered—injury while trying to negotiate the stairs in the dark. Thus, it establishes a standard of care relevant to the case, and it is appropriate to consider that standard in resolving the negligence issue.

b. The judge should not direct the verdict, even if the negligence per se doctrine applies. The violation of the lighting statute only establishes Cheever's negligence if the light *was* out. Whether it was out is a factual issue the jury must decide. Thus, the jury still has an important role to play, even in a negligence per se jurisdiction. But their task will be much more circumscribed than it would be under a general reasonable care standard since they need only decide whether Cheever violated the statute. If he did, and offers no excuse, his negligence is established under the negligence per se doctrine.

c. The judge should instruct the jury along the following lines:

> Under West Dakota law, the violation of a statute intended to protect against the type of harm suffered by the plaintiff establishes negligence. If you find in this case that the defendant violated West Dakota Ann. Laws Title XVI §31, by failing to provide adequate lighting in the hallway of the building, then you must find that the defendant was negligent.

Note that the judge would not instruct the jury on the effect of an excuse for the violation, since Cheever has not offered such evidence. He has staked his case on the position that he did not violate the statute.

d. If there were no statute relevant to the case, the judge would instruct the jury to consider whether Cheever was negligent under the usual reasonable person standard:

> Negligence is the failure to use that degree of care that an ordinary prudent person would use under the circumstances. If you find that the defendant exercised the degree of care that an ordinary prudent landlord would exercise in maintaining the common areas of the building, then you should find that he was not negligent. If you find that the defendant failed to exercise the degree of care that an ordinary prudent landlord would exercise in maintaining the common areas of the building, you should find that he was negligent.

It is not hard to see why O'Connor would prefer to see the jury given the instruction in Example 4c. That instruction narrows the issue from the general "throw-it-to-the-jury" due care standard to a very specific fact question, and requires the jury, if it finds the light was out, to find for O'Connor on the critical issue of negligence (assuming no evidence of excuse is offered). Thus, the adoption of the statutory standard of care substantially eases her burden of proof. It also brands Cheever as a "wrongdoer," which may color the way the jury looks at other issues in the case.

e. The judge should give the jury a general negligence instruction, such as the instruction in Example 4d. She should then add a further instruction along these lines:

> If you find that the defendant violated West Dakota Ann. Laws Tit. XVI §31, requiring adequate lighting in the common areas of apartment buildings, you may consider that violation together with all the other evidence in the case in determining whether the defendant failed to exercise reasonable care under the circumstances.

This instruction would leave it to the jury to consider the statutory duty along with all the evidence in deciding whether Cheever was negligent. The jury could conclude, under the ordinary reasonable person standard, that he was negligent. On the other hand, the jury would also be free to conclude that he wasn't, even if it finds that the light was out. This more flexible rule gives a good deal more latitude to Cheever to persuade the jury that he acted reasonably under all the circumstances, even if he violated the statute.

5. Most of the excuses listed in §15 of the Third Restatement would not apply. Cheever is not a minor or incapacitated; he was aware of the facts that violated the statute; there is no evidence that the statute was confusing or ambiguous; and there is no reason why complying—by replacing the light bulb—would pose a greater risk of harm than noncompliance. Cheever would presumably rely on §15(c), arguing that he had "exercise[d] reasonable care in attempting to comply with the statute" by asking Porter to replace the bulb. Alternatively, he might argue that the list of excuses in §15 is not exclusive, so that his "the-tenant-agreed-to-do-it" excuse should still be considered by the jury. Based on one argument or the other, presumably the jury would be allowed to consider whether Cheever's reliance on his tenant was an adequate excuse for the violation. Thus, the jury would have to decide, in light of the violation and Cheever's excuse, whether he exercised reasonable care.

6. To be relevant, a statute must not only protect against the harm suffered by the plaintiff, but must also be intended to protect a class of persons to which the plaintiff belongs. Certainly, the lighting statute was meant to prevent stumbling over obstacles in the dark, but it is questionable whether it was meant to protect *Calisher* from such risks. It was doubtless aimed at protecting tenants, and probably guests as well . . . maybe even meter readers. But it hardly seems that it was meant to protect passersby who enter unexpectedly to avoid a robbery. Thus, Calisher probably cannot use the statute to show a standard of care relevant *to her*.

Judge Fudd Rules Again

7 a. The problem here is that the jury is not the proper body to decide whether the standard of care established in the statute is relevant—Judge Fudd is. The jury is there to try the case, not the statute. Whether the statute was enacted to prevent a certain type of harm poses a question of law for the judge, not an issue of fact to be decided by the jury. When Wharton offers evidence of the violation at trial, the judge will have to decide whether the statute was meant to protect parties in the plaintiff's position from the type of harm suffered. If the judge concludes that the statute establishes a standard that is relevant to the case, evidence that it was violated will be admitted; otherwise, the jury will hear nothing about it.

b. Wharton may be able to convince the jury that the inspection statute was meant to prevent injuries by identifying safety problems on the premises. But she will still have a hard time establishing that the violation of the inspection statute *caused* her injury. It is extremely unlikely that an inspection would have revealed that a bolt underneath the chair was about to shear off. Presumably, most of the bolt is not even visible, and it may be impossible to spot this type of metal fatigue from a visual inspection anyway. It is doubtful that the inspector would get down and look underneath the chairs; probably she would check for major risks such as blocked aisles, inadequate emergency lighting, or broken sprinklers. Thus, Calisher will argue that, even if the required inspection had been done, the bolt problem would not have been detected. If this is so, the violation is not an actual cause of Wharton's injury.

That does not mean that Wharton must lose: It simply means that she must fall back on the general negligence standard to establish Calisher's negligence. Perhaps Calisher continued to use the seats beyond their useful life or after other similar accidents. Perhaps she was notified of this type of risk by the manufacturer, but failed to repair the seats. Maybe she replaced the bolt herself with one too small for the task. Any of these might show that Calisher was negligent under the usual reasonable person standard.

Negligence Per Se, or Negligence Per Cent?

8. At common law, negligence was an all-or-nothing decision. If the plaintiff was negligent, she lost, under the doctrine of contributory negligence. If the defendant was negligent, she was fully liable for the damages, unless the plaintiff was negligent as well. Thus, the negligence per se doctrine had particular force because in many cases it required the jury to find a party negligent.

Under comparative negligence, however, a finding that one or both of the parties was negligent has a less profound impact on the outcome. For example, even if the jury is instructed, under the negligence per se doctrine, that they must find Cheever negligent for failing to replace the light bulb, *the percentage of negligence* they attribute to him based on the violation is still up to them. If they don't think he was particularly faulty, they might ascribe 3 percent to him and 97 percent to O'Connor, which is pretty close to letting Cheever off the hook entirely.

However, the negligence per se doctrine still has a powerful impact in cases where the jury ascribes *no negligence* to the plaintiff. If Cheever violated the lighting statute, the jury would have to find him negligent under the per se doctrine. If O'Connor was not negligent at all, the jury must then ascribe 100 percent of the fault to Cheever, even if they don't think he was "very negligent" for violating the statute. Thus, the doctrine still forces the jury in these cases to find the defendant fully liable for the plaintiff's injury.

In addition, the doctrine still has important persuasive force in comparative negligence cases since it may lead the jury to ascribe a large percentage of fault to a party who has failed to follow an established statutory standard.

The Goose and the Gander

9. a. Beverly will argue that "what is sauce for the goose is sauce for the gander": If failure to comply with a statute constitutes negligence, *compliance* with a statute ought to constitute due care. Here, the statute required a four-foot fence. That, Beverly will argue, is the measure of due care, and she should be found "careful per se" for providing the security required by the statute.

   b. The argument has an immediate appeal but has generally been rejected. Standards of care imposed by the legislature are often minimum standards, intended to avoid the most dangerous practices but not to immunize persons who do the minimum from liability where more precaution is appropriate. It may be that it is unreasonable to ignore the minimum standards set by the legislature, but it does not follow that the reasonable person takes *only* those minimum precautions. See Restatement (Third) of Torts: Liability for Physical and Emotional Harm §16 (compliance with statute "does not preclude a finding that the actor is negligent . . . for failing to adopt precautions in addition to those mandated by the statute"). For example, a four-foot fence around a pool may suffice in some areas, but in others where many children live a reasonable person might conclude that a four-foot fence is insufficient to prevent them from entering.

   Speed limits provide another good example of this point. In setting a limit, the legislature may have concluded that it is dangerous to exceed a particular speed, but that does not imply that it is always reasonable to travel at that speed. In fog, snow, or heavy traffic, a slower speed may be called for and a rule that compliance with the posted limit absolves the defendant would be inappropriate.

CHAPTER 9

A Phrase in Latin: Res Ipsa Loquitur

INTRODUCTION

The last chapter considered the use of statutory standards of care to prove that the defendant breached the duty of due care or "was negligent." This chapter considers another means of proving negligence, through the mystic doctrine of res ipsa loquitur.

Sometimes proving negligence is straightforward. Suppose that Cisneros goes to the neighborhood garage to have the wheels of his Maserati balanced. After driving away, the right front wheel falls off. Cisneros gets out and looks around, but is only able to find three of the lug nuts that hold the wheel on. He returns to the station, where another customer tells him that he saw the mechanic leave the other lug nuts off. Negligence? No problem: What happened is clear from direct evidence, the testimony of the other customer, and a jury would almost certainly conclude that the mechanic was negligent in failing to replace all the lug nuts.

Would that all negligence cases were so easy. If they were, few negligence cases would be tried because cases in which liability is clear almost always settle before trial. The cases that reach the trial stage are likely to present substantial disputes of fact, in which proof of essential elements—particularly negligence—is more problematic.

THE DIFFERENCE BETWEEN DIRECT AND CIRCUMSTANTIAL EVIDENCE

In the Maserati example, Cisneros produces compelling evidence of the mechanic's negligence, direct testimony from a witness who observed the negligent act. However, negligence need not always be proved by direct evidence. In many cases, plaintiffs will have to rely on "circumstantial" evidence, that is, evidence of facts from which a jury could *infer* that the defendant was negligent. Cisneros might, for example, return to the garage and find two Maserati lug nuts sitting next to the wheel balancing apparatus. This might suffice to allow a jury to infer negligence on the part of the mechanic. The argument runs like this: If the wheel fell off shortly after Cisneros drove away, and if two Maserati lug nuts were sitting at the garage, and if Cisneros could only find three at the scene, it is likely that the mechanic only refastened three. Common experience tells us that leaving some of the lug nuts off creates an unreasonable risk that the wheel will come loose. Therefore, it appears probable that the mechanic was negligent in failing to secure the wheel.

Cisneros might have to rely on even less compelling circumstantial evidence to establish negligence. He might only be able to prove that the wheel fell off shortly after he left the garage, and that he was unable to locate all the lug nuts at the scene of the accident. This does not directly show that the mechanic failed to refasten them, but it again suggests (though less forcefully than the last scenario) that the likely explanation of the accident is the failure to refasten all the lug nuts. A jury could still reasonably infer from the facts Cisneros *has* proved that the accident more probably than not happened because the lug nuts were not refastened or were improperly fastened. Thus, proof of the circumstances allows an inference of further facts that would establish the mechanic's negligence.

Circumstantial evidence is commonly used in proving all sorts of tort cases. The plaintiff offers evidence of a pile of freshly cut maple logs in the defendant's backyard to establish that the defendant cut down his maple trees. Scratches or paint scrapings on the defendant's fender are offered to establish that it was his car that hit the plaintiff's. Evidence of large, unexplained deposits in defendant's bank account is offered to establish that he converted the plaintiff's funds. In each case, evidence of one fact is offered because it tends to establish another.

The "banana peel cases" offer a classic example of the use of circumstantial evidence to establish negligence. The plaintiff slips on a banana peel on the supermarket floor, and sues for his injuries. To establish negligence, he must show that the banana peel was there long enough that store employees should have seen and removed it. It would be ideal to introduce direct evidence, say, three customers who saw it on the floor over the course of several hours before the accident. Such direct evidence isn't likely to be available, however. If three customers had seen it, one would likely have told someone about it, or picked it up. (Similarly, in the Maserati case, if another customer had seen the lug nuts left off, he would likely have said something to the mechanic and averted the accident.)

Absent such direct evidence, banana peel plaintiffs usually offer circumstantial evidence to prove that the banana peel was on the floor long enough that store employees should have seen and removed it. The plaintiff will testify that the banana peel was black, or gritty, or trampled flat. From such facts, a jury could reason as follows: Most people don't hold onto old banana peels; they throw them away immediately after eating the banana. Therefore, if a black and gritty banana peel was on the floor, it was probably on the floor long enough to *turn* black and gritty. Common experience suggests that this takes an hour or so, and that's long enough that an employee should have found it and picked it up. Similarly, if the banana peel had been trampled, the jury could infer that it had been stepped on repeatedly over a period of time. Such evidence does not exactly provide an airtight case, but it will often be the best that the plaintiff can do, and may well convince a jury that it is "more probable than not" that the defendant was negligent.

FROM CIRCUMSTANTIAL EVIDENCE TO RES IPSA LOQUITUR

If circumstantial evidence is one step away from direct testimony, the classic doctrine of res ipsa loquitur is a further step beyond the traditional use of circumstantial evidence. The doctrine originated in the famous case of *Byrne v. Boadle*, 159 Eng. Rep. 299 (1863), in which the unfortunate plaintiff was hit on the head by a flour barrel that fell from the defendant's second-story window. While there was no evidence of what caused the flour barrel to fall on Byrne's boodle, the court allowed him to recover. "Res ipsa loquitur," the court opined, "the thing speaks for itself."

Dean Prosser offers the following whimsical response to this tautological logic: "*res ipsa loquitur, sed quid in infernos dicet?*" ("The thing speaks for itself, but what the hell did it say?") Schwartz, Partlett, Cardi, and Lahav, *Torts: Cases and Materials*, p. 313 (15th ed. 2024). Well, the *Byrne* judges took it to say that flour barrels don't just fall out of windows on their own; that when they do fall, the most likely reason is the negligence of the person in control of the premises. Thus, even though the plaintiff cannot offer direct or circumstantial evidence of exactly what caused the barrel to fall, he should be allowed to reach the jury on the issue of negligence by proving the circumstances of the accident itself because they "bespeak negligence" even without a more specific showing of the chain of events.

There is nothing particularly mystical or sophisticated about this idea. As Lord Shaw quipped: "If that phrase had not been in Latin, no one would have called it a principle." *Ballard v. North British Ry. Co.*, 1923 Sess. Cas. 43 (1923). Res ipsa is not really a separate principle, but rather a special form of circumstantial evidence. The underlying rationale of res ipsa loquitur, as of circumstantial evidence in general, is that facts can sometimes be inferred from other facts. In a case like Cisneros's tire problem, the circumstantial evidence allows the jury to infer *a particular negligent act*, failure to replace the lug nuts. In res ipsa loquitur cases, the circumstantial evidence allows the jury, based on evidence about the accident itself, to infer that it must have resulted from *some negligent act* by the defendant. In *Byrne v. Boadle*, for example, the circumstantial evidence that the barrel had fallen from the defendant's second-story window sufficed to allow a jury to conclude that some negligent act by the defendant had probably caused it to fall.

Here are some other examples of cases in which the plaintiff might use res ipsa loquitur to establish negligence.

- A railway company hires a contractor to install a temporary boarding platform for trains, and it collapses under Feinstein shortly after it is put into use. Even if the collapse makes it impossible to produce evidence of the exact cause, a jury might well infer that negligent construction caused the collapse.
- A brick falls from a roof where a chimney is being repaired and hits the plaintiff. Here again, the plaintiff may not be able to demonstrate what caused the brick to fall; indeed, the workers may not be able to either. Again, however, a jury might fairly infer that the brick probably fell due to some negligent act by the workers.
- An elevator stops abruptly between floors, throwing the plaintiff to the floor.

In each of these cases, there is no showing of exactly how the accident happened, but the fact that it happened at all suggests that someone was probably negligent.

A CRITIQUE AND A DEFENSE

We saw in Chapter 7 that the plaintiff must prove all the elements of a negligence claim in order to hold the defendant liable. Arguably, courts that apply res ipsa loquitur play fast and loose with the negligence element of the claim since they allow the jury to find for the plaintiff without proving any specific negligent act. In the platform case, for example, if the plaintiff merely offers evidence that the platform fell shortly after it was constructed, he has not "proved" any particular negligent act by the contractor. Similarly, in the brick case, evidence that the brick fell while the defendant's employees were working on the roof does not prove what negligent act (if any) caused it to fall. The jury cannot determine exactly what caused the brick to fall on the basis of such general evidence. How then, are they to know that there was negligence involved at all?

Well, they don't *know* that negligence was involved, of course. On the other hand, they don't *know* what caused the accident in the Maserati example, either; they simply make a reasonable estimate of the probabilities based on what they do know. Similarly, in res ipsa loquitur cases, the jury may not be able to reconstruct the sequence of events, but they may be able to make an educated inference that, whatever it was, it probably involved the defendant's failure to exercise due care in some respect. The inference may not be infallible, it may not be satisfying to the ruthlessly syllogistic mind, but it is accepted by the legal system as sufficient to satisfy the "more probable than not" standard of proof in negligence cases. Courts, as practical institutions, must face the fact that irrefutable proof is seldom available in practical affairs, that the system is imperfect by its nature and must settle for a reasonable balance of the probabilities.[1] "Res ipsa by its nature deals with mysteries and the efforts of imperfect legal processes to unravel them." M. Shapo, Principles of Tort Law 255.

Consider the alternative. The judicial system could send Byrne away empty-handed, explaining the result to him thus:

> Sorry, Byrne, about your busted boodle. But we aren't willing to make Boadle pay you unless you show that he did something wrong. You haven't met your burden of proof, because you haven't shown us what specific act Boadle did that was negligent. Unless you produce such evidence, you are not entitled to recover.

This reasoning sounds pretty good, but it doesn't comport with most people's sense of elementary fairness. Most people *would* make the inference that Boadle or his employees must have done something negligent for that barrel to get loose, even if we don't know exactly what it was. Similarly, most people would infer that the platform collapse was caused by faulty construction, or that the brick fell because of negligence. The res ipsa loquitur doctrine allows juries to make the same inference of negligence that most of us would make from our common experience.

---

1. "[A]s law is an instrument of governance rather than a hymn to intellectual beauty, some consideration must be given to practicalities." *Newman-Green Inc. v. Alfonso-Larrain R.*, 854 F.2d 916 (7th Cir. 1988).

THE "FOUNDATION FACTS" IN A RES IPSA CASE

Not every plaintiff can get to the jury by intoning the magic Latin, however. For the res ipsa doctrine to apply, the circumstances must support an inference of negligence:

> There must be reasonable evidence of negligence. But where the thing is shown to be under the management of the defendant or his servants, and the accident is such as in the ordinary course of things does not happen if those who have the management use proper care, it affords reasonable evidence, in the absence of explanation by the defendants, that the accident arose from want of care.

Scott v. London & St. Katherine Docks Co., 159 Eng. Rep. 665, 667 (1865). This early statement of the doctrine remains essentially intact. Most courts hold that the plaintiff can make a case for the jury under res ipsa loquitur by showing *first* that he was injured by an accident that would not ordinarily happen without negligence, and *second* that the negligence is more likely than not attributable to the defendant rather than to the plaintiff or a third party.

A. The Requirement That the Accident Ordinarily Would Not Happen Without Negligence

The first "foundation fact" in a res ipsa case is that the accident is of a type that ordinarily does not happen without negligence. Many accidents would not support an inference that negligence was involved. It is doubtful that a court would allow the jury to infer negligence from the fact that the plaintiff trips going down the defendant's stairs, or that the defendant's car skids into plaintiff on a rainy day. There are common explanations for such occurrences that do not involve negligence. But many other accidents, by their very nature, do support an inference of negligence. For example, most courts would conclude that the following accidents probably would not have occurred without negligence:

- a newborn baby is matched to the wrong mother in the maternity ward
- an airplane disappears without a trace in good weather
- a chunk of glass or a tack is found in a can of spinach
- oil spills from a tank truck on the highway

In each of these cases, common knowledge suggests that this is probably not an "accident" in the pure sense of the word; that someone's careless conduct is the likely explanation. That is not to say that negligence is the *only conceivable* explanation for the accident. It is always possible to hypothesize other causes—for example, terrorism in the airplane case, or an undiscoverable defect in the tank truck case. But the plaintiff's burden of proof in a negligence case is not to eliminate all possible alternative causes of his injury. His burden is to show that the *more probable* cause was negligence. In the example cases just given, a jury might reasonably conclude that it was.

B. The Requirement That the Negligence, If Any, Is Attributable to the Defendant

The second "foundation fact" in a res ipsa case is that the negligence is attributable to the defendant. It is not enough to show that someone's negligence probably caused the harm. The evidence must point to the defendant as the negligent party. Often this is obvious, as where a load of cement drops from the defendant's crane, or a scaffold just erected by the defendant falls. In these examples, the defendant is in control of the source of the accident and responsible for its safe operation. If an accident bespeaks negligence in these cases, it very likely bespeaks the defendant's negligence.

This attribution requirement is more difficult, however, where a product causes injury after leaving the defendant's hands. A frequent example is the explosion of a bottle of soda or beer in the hands of a consumer. Many courts have concluded that beverages bottled under pressure should not explode unless someone was negligent in filling or handling the bottle. Thus, the probably-would-not-happen-without-negligence element is met. But in these cases the bottle may have been handled by the distributor, the retailer, and the consumer after it left the bottler's hands. Thus, it is harder to show that the negligence, if there was any, was the bottler's.

The cases often state that this attribution requirement is not met in a res ipsa loquitur case unless the instrumentality that caused the harm was "under the defendant's control" at the time of the accident. This formula is clearly too narrow. For example, in the glass-in-the-spinach case, the canner was clearly not in "control" of the can when the plaintiff ate the spinach and was cut by the glass. Yet it is highly likely that the glass got into the can when the spinach was canned. Thus, a jury could reasonably infer that the negligence, if any, is attributable to the canner. Similarly, the collapsing railroad platform may not be in the "control" of the contractor who built it at the time of the collapse, but it is very likely that the negligence took place at the time of construction and is therefore attributable to the contractor. Although this "control" language is often found in the cases, most courts have not taken it so literally as to preclude use of res ipsa in such obviously appropriate cases.

The formulation of the res ipsa loquitur doctrine in the Second Restatement of Torts nicely avoids the misleading "control" language:

> (1) It may be inferred that harm suffered by the plaintiff is caused by negligence of the defendant when
>
> (a) the event is of a kind which ordinarily does not occur in the absence of negligence;
>
> (b) other responsible causes, including the conduct of the plaintiff and third persons, are sufficiently eliminated by the evidence. . . .

Restatement (Second) of Torts §328D. Under this statement of the doctrine, the plaintiff may invoke res ipsa loquitur even if the defendant did not have exclusive control of the source of the harm, so long as the plaintiff can demonstrate that the negligence was likely that of the defendant rather than himself or other parties.[2]

THE EFFECT OF THE PLAINTIFF'S CONDUCT

Courts often state that there is a third requirement for the application of res ipsa loquitur: that "the event must not have been due to any voluntary action or contribution on the part of the plaintiff." *Reber v. United States*, 941 F.2d 975, 978 n.1 (9th Cir. 1991). This is confusing because it suggests that a plaintiff who was partially at fault in causing an accident can never prove the defendant's negligence through a res ipsa loquitur inference.

That isn't so. Often, the circumstances will support an inference that a defendant was negligent, even if the plaintiff was too. Suppose, for example, that a contractor sets up a scaffold on the outside of a building, and it starts to topple. Merlini, rushing to a meeting inside the building, sees it sway, but dashes underneath, figuring that she can get inside before the scaffold falls. She doesn't make it, and is injured. Clearly, Merlini's negligence contributed to her injury. But shouldn't res ipsa still be available to

2. The Third Restatement of Torts: Liability for Physical and Emotional Harm §17 recasts the definition of res ipsa loquitur as follows:

> The factfinder may infer that the defendant has been negligent when the accident causing the plaintiff's harm is a type of accident that ordinarily happens as a result of the negligence of a class of actors of which the defendant is the relevant member.

Although this description may be accurate, it is hard to understand and is not likely to be used in instructing juries. In this chapter, Your Humble Author will stick with the Second Restatement formulation.

prove negligence of the contractor in causing the initial collapse? A scaffold should not collapse unless there is negligence in erecting it. And, if there was negligence, it was almost certainly the negligence of the contractor. Merlini should be able to use res ipsa to establish the contractor's negligence, whether she was negligent in rushing underneath or not. Her subsequent negligence should be accounted for under comparative negligence analysis, not by barring her from proving the other party's negligence through res ipsa loquitur.

This supposed third requirement is really only a corollary of the second: It is meant to reemphasize that the plaintiff must show that the negligence that created the initial danger (whatever it was) is attributable to the defendant rather than to her. If it is equally probable that the plaintiff's negligence created the danger, she has not "brought the negligence home to the defendant." But when the circumstances show that the negligence that created the initial danger was probably the defendant's, res ipsa should be available, even if the plaintiff was negligent in reacting to the danger. In the scaffold case, for example, there is a strong res ipsa loquitur case that the *collapse* was caused by the defendant's negligence. Merlini should be able to invoke res ipsa on that issue, even though she was negligent in running under the scaffold.

THE EFFECT OF THE DOCTRINE AT TRIAL

Even if a case is tried, a judge has the power to refuse to submit it to the jury if there is no credible evidence in support of one or more of the elements of the plaintiff's claim. Frequently, the defendant will argue that the judge should take the case from the jury (by "directing a verdict" for the defendant[3]) since the plaintiff has not produced proof of a specific negligent act by the defendant. The crucial impact of res ipsa loquitur is that it allows the plaintiff's case to go to the jury even though he has not proved a specific act of negligence. Naturally, plaintiffs are very keen to avoid directed verdicts and reach the jury; thus, the res ipsa doctrine is very popular with the plaintiff's bar.

If the plaintiff establishes the "foundation facts" discussed in the preceding section, the judge will allow the case to go to the jury. It will then be up to them to decide whether the accident was more probably than not the result of the defendant's negligence. They are free to infer that his negligence caused the accident, but they are also free to conclude, based

3. For a discussion of directed verdict practice, see J. Glannon, Civil Procedure: Examples and Explanations 493-501 (9th ed. 2023).

on the evidence presented, that the defendant's negligence is *not* the more likely explanation. The doctrine, in other words, permits the jury to infer negligence, but it does not require them to. Some cases suggest that res ipsa loquitur shifts the burden of proof to the defendant, or creates a presumption of negligence that requires a finding of negligence if not rebutted. Most courts hold, however, that the doctrine merely provides evidence sufficient to support an inference that the defendant was negligent, but does not compel a finding for the plaintiff even where there is no rebuttal evidence. See Restatement (Third) of Torts §17 cmt. j.

INSTRUCTING THE JURY ON RES IPSA LOQUITUR

Logically, it would seem unnecessary to confuse the jury by giving them specific instructions about res ipsa loquitur. It should suffice to tell them that the plaintiff must prove the defendant's negligence by the preponderance of the evidence, and that they are free to infer negligence or not, as they choose, from the evidence presented. The risk of resting on such general instructions, however, is that the jury will take a more technical view of the plaintiff's burden than the courts do, and find for the defendant simply because the plaintiff has not shown the exact cause of the accident. Thus, courts usually give specific instructions detailing the "foundation facts" for res ipsa loquitur and the effect of finding those foundation facts. Here is an example adapted (not quite *verbatim*) from a Minnesota case:

> When an accident is such that it would not ordinarily have happened unless someone was negligent, and if the thing which caused the accident is shown to have been under the exclusive control of the defendant at the time that the negligent act, if any, must have happened, then you are permitted to infer from the mere fact that the accident happened and the circumstances surrounding it that the defendant was negligent.

See *Bossons v. Hertz Corp.*, 176 N.W.2d 882, 886 (Minn. 1970). Note how this instruction tracks the elements of the doctrine. It tells the jury that they *may* conclude that the defendant was negligent, if they find that it was the type of accident that does not ordinarily happen without negligence, and that the thing which caused it was under the defendant's control at the time of the negligence. (This instruction, like many currently in use, does include the dubious "exclusive control" language, which has raised problems when taken too literally. However, it properly focuses on control at the time of the likely negligence rather than at the time of the accident.)

THE DEFENDANT'S CASE

The res ipsa doctrine may warm the hearts of plaintiff's counsel, but it places the defendant in a very difficult position. How is he to refute the plaintiff's proof of negligence, where plaintiff hasn't proved any specific negligent act? Certainly, the most effective way to rebut a res ipsa loquitur case is to prove the actual cause of the accident. For example, proof that the station platform collapsed because the transit authority was tunneling underneath it will completely undermine (excuse the pun) the res ipsa inference.

Short of that, the defendant can attack each of the foundation facts necessary to support res ipsa loquitur. He may question the second foundation fact by showing that other persons mishandled the product that caused the injury after it left his hands (e.g., the retailer in the exploding beverage case). He may undermine the required showing that the type of accident does not ordinarily happen without negligence, by showing other common, nonnegligent causes of this type of accident. A chain is only as strong as its weakest link; if the jury is not convinced that each of the foundation facts is established, it should refuse to infer the ultimate fact of negligence. If the defendant's proof on either of these points is strong enough, the judge may even direct a verdict for him, on the ground that the jury could not reasonably conclude that the proper foundation for the res ipsa doctrine has been established.

When the defendant does *not* have evidence of the exact cause of the accident, he may try to refute the res ipsa inference by proving that he generally exercised due care. In the case of the glass in the spinach, for example, the canner might produce evidence of the careful quality control measures it takes to avoid objects getting into the cans. The airline in the lost plane example might produce evidence of its careful training, maintenance, and inspection procedures. This does not conclusively eliminate negligence as the cause, but it could influence the jury's thinking about the probabilities. On the other hand, this can backfire: The more careful the defendant's procedures, the less likely that an accident would happen if they had in fact been followed. Thus, such proof could lead the jury to conclude that, had the procedures been followed, there would not have been an accident at all. For a fine example of this, see G. Fricke, The Use of Expert Evidence in Res Ipsa Loquitur Cases, 5 Vill. L. Rev. 59, 70-72 (1959), quoting cross-examination of a defendant's expert that very effectively showed that the accident could not have happened unless the usual precautions were omitted.

The cases often suggest that the plaintiff should be able to rely on res ipsa loquitur because the defendant has better access to evidence of the cause of the accident than the plaintiff does. It is certainly true that the doctrine creates a strong incentive for the defendant to produce any evidence it has that will rebut the inference that its negligence caused the accident. However, most courts do not restrict the doctrine to cases in which the defendant has better access to proof. See Restatement (Third) of Torts §17 cmt. i; Dobbs' Law of Torts §176. Often, the defendant has no better chance of explaining the accident than the plaintiff does. In the disappearing plane case, or the glass-in-the-spinach case, for example, the airline or the canner may have no idea what caused the accident, or any way of finding out. Yet the likely explanation of the accident may still be negligence. In such cases, the defendant should not be able to avoid res ipsa simply by showing that it knows no more about the cause of the accident than the plaintiff does.

The following examples should help you to understand the types of cases in which the res ipsa doctrine applies, and how this mystic doctrine assists the plaintiff in getting to the jury in those cases.

Examples

Victims of Circumstance

1. In which of the following cases do you think the plaintiff could reach the jury by invoking res ipsa loquitur?
   a. Lindsey's front tire blows out while he is driving down Sunset Boulevard. He sues Firewall Tire, the manufacturer of the tire.
   b. LaGuardia is injured while making a delivery to Acme Manufacturing Company's warehouse. He was raising a rolling garage door upward when the door stuck in the metal track and bounced back on his head. He offers evidence of multiple hammer marks on the track and a distortion in the shape of the track to show that Acme had negligently maintained the door.
   c. Young, a three-year-old toddler, comes home from day care. Throughout the evening, he complains of a sore arm. His parents finally take him to the emergency room, where an X-ray reveals that his arm is broken. The parents sue the day care center for negligence.
   d. Younger, a five-month-old baby, comes home from day care. Throughout the evening she shows obvious discomfort on her left side. Her parents take her to the emergency room, where X-rays reveal that her left arm is broken. The parents sue the day care center for negligence.
   e. Flynn is walking past a high-rise hotel when a beer mug falls on his head from one of the balconies above. He sues the hotel for negligence.
   f. While entering an interstate highway, Daley is injured when a stray Volkswagen engine suddenly appears in the roadway in front of him, causing him to crash. There is no sign of an ailing Volkswagen to be found in the area. Daley sues his insurance carrier, under a policy provision allowing recovery from the insurer for injuries negligently caused by an unidentified motorist.

g. White is injured when a large truck backs into a propane tank, causing an explosion. Lindsey, the trucker, claims that he hit the tank because Wagner, another trucker, waved him back too far. Wagner claims that the truck jumped suddenly at the last moment, presumably because Lindsey hit the accelerator instead of the brake. White sues them both, and invokes res ipsa loquitur.

Possibly Probable Negligence

2. Consider again Example 1c above, in which Young, a three-year-old toddler, came home from day care with a broken arm. Suppose that the only evidence before the court is the evidence of Young's injury. Suppose further that the judge recognizes that there is a good deal of uncertainty about the more likely cause of the accident. The judge believes that negligence on the part of the day care center may have been involved, but doubts that it was the *more likely* cause. Perhaps he views negligence as a 40 percent likelihood, and an accident resulting from the toddler's general exuberance a 60 percent likelihood. Should the judge direct a verdict for the day care center, or allow the case to go to the jury?

Firming Up the Foundation

3. Alioto makes up a yummy salad for lunch. He throws in some lettuce, a tomato, a can of artichokes, some mushrooms, and some sliced turkey. Then he pours Newton's Own Natural Russian Salad Dressing over the top. While enjoying the salad, Alioto bites into a piece of glass and breaks a tooth. He sues Newton's.
   a. Which of the foundation facts poses a problem here?
   b. How might Alioto strengthen the argument for applying res ipsa loquitur to the case?

4. Ulner undergoes leg surgery by Dr. Eastwood to correct an arterial problem in his thigh. After the operation, he notices that he has decreased sensation along the left side of the leg, which gets worse over the ensuing weeks. He sues Eastwood for negligence.
   a. What foundation fact raises problems in applying res ipsa loquitur to this case?
   b. In addition to the basic facts described above, Ulner presents a medical expert, who testifies that reduced sensation "does not ordinarily occur" as a result of the type of surgery Ulner had, if ordinary care was exercised. Should Ulner's case go to the jury on a res ipsa loquitur theory?
   c. Assume that Ulner's expert testifies that nerve damage of the type he suffered would not ordinarily happen unless the surgeon was negligent. Dr. Eastwood then offers an expert who testifies that such loss of sensation may result from a number of causes, including

the underlying medical problem, poor post-surgical nursing care, unavoidable surgical abrasion of the nerve, or negligence. Given the contradictory expert testimony as to the likelihood of negligence, should the judge allow the case to go to the jury on a res ipsa theory?

d. Suppose that after Ulner's expert testifies that the damage would not ordinarily occur without negligence, Dr. Eastwood takes the stand. He testifies that the surgery was unremarkable, that he followed standard procedure, and that he definitely did not touch, cut, or pinch any of the surrounding nerves. At the close of his evidence he moves for a directed verdict. How should the judge rule?
e. Assume instead that Dr. Eastwood takes the stand and testifies that during the surgery an artery in Ulner's leg began to hemorrhage, due to an unanticipated weakness in the artery wall. To prevent a life-threatening loss of blood, Eastwood was forced to clamp off the artery, which was directly in contact with the major nerve in the left side of the leg. This procedure risks damage to the nerve, but is unavoidable when such surgical complications arise. This evidence is confirmed by the surgical notes and by the assisting physician. After offering this evidence (which is not contradicted by the plaintiff), Dr. Eastwood moves for a directed verdict. Should it be granted?

Not for Attribution

5. Bradley, a guest at the Fontainbleau hotel, leaves his suite for dinner. A half-hour later there is a fire in the room. The evidence indicates that the fire started in a sofa in the sitting room of the suite. The hotel sues Bradley for negligence.

6. Atkins's house is destroyed in a fire following an explosion in a closet in the cellar. He offers evidence that two weeks before the fire, the gas company had installed a new gas line to his water heater, located in the closet. He argues that this evidence suffices to allow the jury to find negligence based on res ipsa loquitur.
   a. Would this evidence suffice to get to the jury on a res ipsa theory?
   b. After Atkins produces this evidence, the gas company puts on its case. Its evidence indicates that Atkins had taken the door off the closet and stored various combustible materials in the closet before the explosion, that no one had smelled gas during the two weeks before the fire, that Atkins had been working around the heater an hour before the fire, and that the wind was blowing at 80 miles an hour outside at the time of the explosion. Should the case go to the jury on a res ipsa loquitur theory?

7. Young is hit by a piece of wood that falls from the open third floor of a construction site. At the time, Koch and Alioto, two employees of

the Wagner Construction Company, the framing subcontractor, were the only workers on that floor.

a. Unable to discover exactly what caused the board to fall, Young sues Koch and Alioto. Can he invoke res ipsa?
b. Young has an easy alternative here; what is it?

Fudd Ipsa Loquitur

8. Assume that Judge Fudd tries the case described in Example 5, in which the hotel fire started in a couch in the defendant's room. Judge Fudd, after brushing up on his res ipsa learning, gives the following instruction to the jury:

> If you find that the fire in this case was not likely to have happened in the absence of negligence, and that the negligence, if there was negligence, was likely that of the defendant, then these facts give rise to an inference of negligence on the part of the defendant.

   What is the problem with the Honorable Fudd's instruction?

9. Farmer Jones decides to take a break from the spring plowing. He turns off the ignition and gets off his new tractor. Suddenly, the tractor unaccountably starts up with Jones standing next to it. Jones, perhaps ill-advisedly, jumps for the driver's seat to stop it, is thrown off and injured. He sues International Tractor Company, the manufacturer, alleging negligence in causing his injuries. At trial, he proves the above facts, and argues that he should get to the jury based on res ipsa loquitur.

   The defendant asks Judge Fudd to give the following jury instruction:

> No inference of negligence by the defendant is permitted, unless the plaintiff has shown that the injury-causing occurrence was not due to any contribution or voluntary activity on the plaintiff's part.

   Should Judge Fudd give the instruction?

Explanations

Victims of Circumstance

1. a. As the introduction states, res ipsa loquitur only applies where the nature of the accident indicates that it would not ordinarily happen without negligence. Most courts would probably hold that a tire blowout does not satisfy this requirement. Tires can blow out from a number of causes, including over- or underinflation, glass or other sharp objects in the road, excessive wear, a Chicago-sized pothole, and probably others as well. Of course, it could result from a defect in the tire, but given all the other potential causes, this accident is probably not the type that "ordinarily does not happen without negligence."

b. This isn't really a res ipsa case. LaGuardia has simply used circumstantial evidence to show a *particular negligent act*. The hammer blows and twist in the track indicate that the track had been damaged and someone had tried to fix it. From this a jury could infer that the repair had been poorly done, and that the distortion in the track had caused the door to stick and bounce back at LaGuardia.

   In a res ipsa case, the plaintiff usually doesn't have evidence of the particular cause of the accident. Rather, he tries to show that the general circumstances of the accident suggest that it wouldn't have happened if the responsible party had been careful. The plaintiff argues, "Hey, I can't explain exactly what happened here, but it's reasonable to infer that the defendant must have done *something* careless, or this accident wouldn't have happened." LaGuardia doesn't have to fall back on such general proof, since he has evidence—albeit, circumstantial evidence—of the specific act of negligence that caused his injury.

c. Surely any parent can testify to the fact that many toddlers are more enthusiastic than careful. They try new things, fall down a lot, bump into things. It seems quite credible that an active three-year-old would fall off a swing, trip, or get hit hard enough to break an arm, even if the day care personnel were exercising due care in supervising him. Thus, it is at least doubtful that a jury could infer negligence of the day care center from the mere fact of this accident. See, e.g., *Ward v. Mount Calvary Lutheran Church*, 873 P.2d 688 (Ariz. App. 1994), which refused to apply res ipsa on similar facts.

d. Although three-year-olds get around very well and consequently take some pretty hard knocks, a five-month-old can hardly navigate at all. It seems improbable that Younger could manage to break her arm all by herself; it is much more likely that someone dropped her, or left her unattended on a changing table. This case seems a much stronger candidate for application of res ipsa loquitur.

e. This accident is not likely to happen without someone's negligence. The problem is in attributing the negligence to the hotel owner. It is quite likely that a guest, rather than an employee, knocked the mug off a balcony railing. While hotels have a duty to exercise due care in controlling the conduct of guests, the hotel cannot have guards in every room to interdict every careless act of its guests. Thus, res ipsa will probably fail here because it is impossible to show foundation fact #2, that the negligence, if there was any, was attributable to the defendant.

f. This is a good res ipsa case. When an engine is found in the middle of an expressway, it probably didn't walk there. The facts strongly suggest that the engine must have fallen from a truck. Clearly, that shouldn't happen if the hauler has exercised reasonable care in securing the load.

But what of the second foundation fact—ascribing the negligence to a particular person? Here, Daley is relieved of the problem posed by the second res ipsa requirement. Under the policy provision, the insurer is liable as long as his accident was caused by the negligence of some unidentified motorist. Here the facts provide reasonable proof of that.

g. When I gave this fact pattern on an exam, a number of students said that White should invoke res ipsa since he is unable to tell which defendant's negligence caused the collision. However, this is not a res ipsa case. First, to invoke res ipsa, the plaintiff must show that the negligence, if any, was likely that of a particular defendant. Here, there are two, and White simply isn't sure which one was at fault. Res ipsa does not allow White to simply point the finger at multiple defendants and argue, "Hey, someone did it, so I can sue them all, prove that somebody was negligent, and recover." White still bears the burden of attributing the probable negligence to a particular person.

   In addition, this is not really an unexplained accident. It is clear what happened: The truck backed into the tank. The only problem is the conflict in the evidence as to which of two negligent acts caused it. That's simply a question of who is telling the truth.

Possibly Probable Negligence

2. This example raises a tough but important question. Here, it is a debatable proposition whether the accident was more probably the result of negligence or pure accident. The judge puts the probabilities at 40 percent negligence/60 percent pure accident, but recognizes that others (in particular, the jury) might disagree. Should he let the jury decide, or direct a verdict for the defendant on the ground that one of the foundation facts (that the accident "ordinarily would not have happened without negligence") has not been established?

   Presumably, if the jury could reasonably conclude that the accident "ordinarily would not happen without negligence," they should be allowed to decide. They are the factfinders, so presumably they decide the *foundation facts* as well as the ultimate issue of negligence. If they agree with the judge that negligence is not the more probable explanation, they should find for the defendant. But if they conclude that the accident does bespeak negligence (and that the negligence is likely attributable to the defendant), they would be entitled, under res ipsa, to make an inference that the defendant was negligent.

   Put another way, the judge's role is not to make findings himself that the foundation facts are established, but rather to determine whether the jury reasonably could conclude that those facts are proved. If there is evidence from which the jury could find that the foundation facts are probably true, they must be given the opportunity to do so, and (if they do) to decide whether to make the further inference that the defendant was negligent.

Firming Up the Foundation

3. a. It seems very likely that glass would not have ended up in Alioto's salad unless someone was negligent. The problem in the case, of course, is to decide whose negligence it was. The glass could have come from the mushrooms, the lettuce, the artichokes, perhaps even the sliced turkey, as well as from the salad dressing. It may also have fallen into the salad from a shelf or the kitchen counter. Thus, the circumstances do not of themselves demonstrate that the negligence is attributable to Newton's.

   b. Alioto may be able to shore up his res ipsa foundation against Newton's by eliminating other possible sources of the glass. He may be able to testify that he washed the lettuce, drained, washed, and cut up the artichokes, rubbed each mushroom before cutting it into the salad, and sliced the turkey on a clean cutting board. He may also be able to testify that he washed the counter before making the salad. Depending on the particulars, such testimony could lead the jury to eliminate the other items in Alioto's lunch as the source of the glass, leaving Newton's the likely culprit.

   It is quite common for plaintiffs to offer testimony to eliminate the negligence of others, including themselves, so as to satisfy the requirement that the negligence be attributable to the defendant. In an exploding bottle case, for example, the plaintiff will try to show careful handling by the retailer and himself, in order to prove that the negligence was likely that of the bottler. In a disappearing airplane case, the plaintiff will offer testimony that the weather was clear to bolster the inference that negligence, not weather, caused the plane to crash.

4. a. If there was negligence at all in this case, it was very likely attributable to Dr. Eastwood. However, it is not at all clear that this side effect results from negligence. It is very doubtful that a jury could conclude, from their general knowledge, that decreased sensation after thigh surgery bespeaks negligence of the surgeon. Thus, the jury is not in a position, based on the mere fact of the injury, to determine that the foundation for the res ipsa inference is established.

   b. Ulner's expert testifies that nerve damage does not usually result when the type of surgery Ulner had is carefully performed. However, it does not follow, just because this side effect doesn't usually occur, that when it occurs it probably results from negligence. There are many side effects of surgery that occasionally happen despite the exercise of due care. Surely, negligence should not be inferred just because such side effects are rare. For example, surgical patients rarely get infections from careful surgery, but this does not mean that, if a patient does get infected, the surgeon was probably negligent. In a small percentage of cases, it just happens anyway, despite all reasonable precautions.

Many courts state that res ipsa applies to "the type of injury that ordinarily would not occur if reasonable care had been used." *Wick v. Henderson*, 485 N.W.2d 645, 649 (Iowa 1992). However, this language is misleading. It is one thing to say that the type of accident does not ordinarily happen when the actor is careful. It is another to say that, *when the accident does occur,* it is more likely than not that negligence was the cause. Tire blowouts do not ordinarily happen if car owners are careful, but it does not follow that when tires *do* blow out, it is probably the result of negligence. People do not ordinarily fall down on the sidewalk, but when they do, it does not follow that negligence is the likely cause.

A better statement of this requirement is that the accident "would not ordinarily happen without negligence." (Note that Ulner's expert did not testify to that.) Res ipsa requires that the accident not only be unusual, but that it be unlikely to happen unless someone failed to exercise due care. If Ulner's expert testified that nerve damage does not occur in this type of surgery *unless the surgeon was careless,* his testimony would provide an evidentiary basis for the jury to conclude that his injury probably resulted from negligence. On that testimony, Ulner would be allowed to reach the jury on a res ipsa theory.

c. Here, Ulner's expert has provided testimony that would support the first "foundation fact." However, Dr. Eastwood has offered expert testimony that contradicts that testimony. Presumably, it is for the jury, as the factfinders, to resolve this conflict in the evidence. If they believe Ulner's expert, they may conclude that injuries of this type most likely result from negligence. They could then make the further inference that this one in fact *did* result from Dr. Eastwood's negligence. Compare Example 2. If they are convinced by Eastwood's expert, they will conclude that negligence is not the most likely explanation, and find for the defendant.

d. Eastwood's motion should be denied. Ulner's evidence suggests that this type of outcome likely results from negligence of the surgeon. Eastwood then testifies that he did not make the type of mistake which would likely explain Ulner's complications. If the jury believes Eastwood's testimony, they will presumably refuse to make the inference permitted by the res ipsa loquitur doctrine. They are free to do that, but they are also free to disbelieve Eastwood's testimony and make the res ipsa inference based on the evidence that such results usually do result from negligence of the surgeon, and the further fact that the injury did in fact occur. On this state of the evidence, the case is for the jury.

e. The res ipsa loquitur doctrine allows a jury to conclude that an unexplained accident more than likely happened due to negligence. But here, the defendant has offered an uncontradicted, fully corroborated explanation that the injury occurred without negligence. Unless there is some basis to conclude that the witnesses are lying, this accident is no longer unexplained, and there is no need for the jury to estimate the probabilities concerning an unexplained occurrence. Thus, res ipsa would no longer have a role, and the judge would likely direct a verdict for the defendant.

   If there were some basis in the evidence for the jury to disbelieve Eastwood's testimony concerning the ruptured artery, they would be entitled to do so. If they did disbelieve it, and the proper res ipsa foundation had been laid, they would be free to infer that negligence caused the problem.

Not for Attribution

5. This case is a strong candidate for application of res ipsa loquitur. Here, the evidence indicates that the fire started in a sofa, not a usual place for fires absent someone's negligence. In addition, it started shortly after Bradley left the room, which supports the inference that, if negligence led to the fire, it was his. See *Olswanger v. Funk*, 470 S.W.2d 13 (Tenn. App. 1970) (approving use of res ipsa loquitur in a similar case).

   In this case, further evidence may strengthen the inference of Bradley's negligence. If he locked the room, for example, this tends to eliminate vandalism as an alternative explanation. If Bradley is a smoker, that would greatly strengthen the inference that he had caused the fire.

6. a. Atkins has probably produced enough evidence to go to the jury on res ipsa. His evidence shows that the accident happened shortly after the gas company worked on the heater, that the fire resulted from an explosion, and that the explosion took place in the area where the gas company had done the work. A reasonable jury could infer from these facts that the accident probably resulted from a gas leak, and that the leak was probably caused by faulty work in installing the gas line. Atkins's case is hardly ironclad, but it supports a reasonable inference of negligence.[4]

   b. Sometimes res ipsa seems to leave defendants at the mercy of the jury as long as some inference of negligence can be made. But this

4. Of course, the gas company was not "in control" of the heater or the gas lines at the time of the explosion. But under the Restatement formulation of res ipsa this is not necessary. Atkins must simply show that the negligence is probably attributable to the gas company.

example, based on an actual case, *Nutting v. Northern Energy, Inc.*, 874 P.2d 482 (Colo. App. 1994), illustrates that defendants, through aggressive discovery, are often able to muster substantial evidence to undermine the foundation facts. In *Nutting*, the plaintiffs had to admit that they had been working around the heater, weakening the inference that the negligence, if any, was the gas company's. In addition, the weather records suggested yet another explanation for the fire—that the force of 80-mile-per-hour winds had caused a downdraft, blowing the burner flame outward, and igniting the combustible materials stored in the closet. On this state of the evidence, the court held that the plaintiffs had not made a case for one of the res ipsa foundation facts: that the negligence, if any, was likely attributable to the defendant. Consequently, the court refused to give the jury a res ipsa instruction.

7. a. This case resembles *Byrne v. Boadle*, the flour barrel case that gave rise to the res ipsa doctrine. As in *Byrne*, it seems fairly clear that a jury could find, based on their own experience, that this accident would not ordinarily happen without negligence. Someone must have left the board too near the edge of the building, or dropped it in the course of the work, or *something*.

   The problem is the other foundation requirement, attributing the negligence to a particular defendant. Granted, it is probably attributable to *one of the defendants*, but it is not clear which one. Even where the plaintiff relies on the general inference of negligence permitted by res ipsa, it must be an inference of a particular person's negligence, not just someone's. Otherwise, Young could simply sue all possibly negligent parties and argue that one of them must have been negligent.

   On these facts, most courts would refuse to send the case to the jury on a res ipsa theory.

   b. Young can rely on res ipsa loquitur in this case if he sues Wagner Construction Company. The accident is of a type that ordinarily would not happen without negligence. Wagner, as an employer, is liable for the negligence of any of its employees in the course of the work. See Chapter 23. Thus, it is liable regardless of which employee caused the board to fall. Even though Young could not invoke res ipsa against Koch or Alioto, he could show that the negligence must be attributable to someone for whom Wagner is responsible.

Fudd Ipsa Loquitur

8. Fudd's instruction tells the jury that, if they find the foundation facts established, "these facts give rise to an inference of negligence on the part of the defendant." This suggests to the jury that they *should* make the inference that Bradley was negligent if they find the foundation

established. Most courts hold that res ipsa permits, but does not require a jury to infer negligence where the foundation facts are shown. The instruction would be much improved if the Honorable Fudd told the jury that, if they find the foundation facts are established, they *may* but are not required to infer that the defendant was negligent.

One may well wonder if such subtle distinctions in a complex verbal instruction have any real meaning for a jury. If the jury understands the res ipsa instruction at all, they may well understand it as Judge Fudd mistakenly phrased it, to mean that they should find for the plaintiff if they find the foundation facts established. Jury instructions play an ironic role in the trial of cases. When they are correct, it is not clear that the jury understands them or pays them full attention. But when they are wrong, the losing party is very likely to appeal on the ground that the jury was given the wrong rules for decision. Thus, it may be more important not to get the instructions wrong than it is to get them right.

9. As the Introduction notes, you will very frequently see language of this sort in the statement of the res ipsa loquitur requirements. See, e.g., *Stillman v. Norfolk & W. Ry. Co.*, 811 F.2d 834, 837 (4th Cir. 1987). The rationale is apparently that, if the plaintiff contributed to the accident, the inference that the negligence leading to it was the defendant's is undermined. In addition, res ipsa dates from the era of contributory negligence, when any negligence by the plaintiff barred recovery even if the defendant was negligent.

   In this case, however, Jones should be able to invoke res ipsa loquitur even if he was a partial cause of his injury. Although Jones may have been negligent *after* the tractor started, for jumping on board, there is nothing to suggest that he contributed in any way to causing it to start. Thus, his conduct does not undermine the inference that any negligence that led to the tractor starting up was International's. Brand-new tractors should not roar into life on their own. When they do, a jury could reasonably infer that the manufacturer was negligent. The fact that Jones *reacted negligently to* the risk should not bar him from using res ipsa to establish the initial negligence of International. If Jones reacted negligently to the situation, and thus contributed to his own injury, this can be accounted for under comparative negligence by reducing his recovery.

   Thus, in instructing the jury, Judge Fudd should separate the issue of International's negligence in causing the initial problem from Jones's negligence in reacting to it. He should instruct the jury that they could infer negligence of International based on res ipsa loquitur, and further instruct them that, if Jones's subsequent conduct was also negligent, they should account for that under comparative negligence principles. See, e.g., *Giles v. City of New Haven*, 636 A.2d 1335, 1341-1342 (Conn.

1994) (allowing plaintiff to invoke res ipsa in a similar situation under comparative negligence).

This point is a bit confusing, but important, since comparative negligence has become the law in most states. Here is another example. In *Cramer v. Mengerhausen*, 550 P.2d 740 (Or. 1976), the plaintiff was having a tire changed at a repair shop when the truck started to slip off the jack. He grabbed the back of the truck, to try to keep it from sliding forward, and was injured when the truck fell. The court held that plaintiff could invoke res ipsa, even if he had been negligent as well, to establish the initial negligence of the repair person since trucks shouldn't fall if properly jacked. If plaintiff was negligent in reacting to the situation, this could be accounted for under comparative negligence by assigning him a percentage of negligence and reducing his damages accordingly.

PART III

The Causation Enigma

CHAPTER 10

Reconstructing History: Determining Cause in Fact

INTRODUCTION

As previous chapters have indicated, the common law has developed a consistent set of elements—duty, breach, causation, and damages—that plaintiffs must prove in order to recover in a negligence action. This chapter addresses basic aspects of the very difficult—and fascinating—third element, causation. The next chapter addresses several complex causation issues frequently encountered in the Torts course.

Although causation is often a difficult problem, fundamental fairness obviously requires that a defendant be held liable only for injuries he actually caused. If Jones, an electrician, wires Smith's house, and leaves exposed wires in the wall, which cause a spark and burn down the house, Smith's loss is a direct result of Jones's negligence. It would not have happened if Jones had been careful, and it did happen because Jones wasn't careful. It seems fair to shift the loss from the blameless Smith to the careless Jones. However, if the house burns down because Smith's toddler starts the fire, Jones did not cause the harm and should not pay, even if he was negligent in wiring the house.

To assure that liability will only be imposed where the plaintiff's loss is fairly attributable to the defendant's conduct, courts have developed two causation requirements, causation *in fact* and *proximate* or legal causation. Cause in fact, the subject of this chapter, requires that, as a factual matter, the defendant's act contributed to producing the plaintiff's injury. Proximate causation, considered in Chapter 12, deals with limits on liability for remote or unexpected consequences of tortious conduct.

It is often quite clear from the events themselves that the defendant's negligence was the cause in fact of an injury. Suppose, for example, that Wright drops a sheet of plywood from a building onto Sullivan's car, obscuring her ability to see the road, and she crashes into a parked car. There is little doubt that Wright's negligence "caused" the accident. Sullivan will doubtless testify that she swerved off the road *because* the plywood obscured her view. The accident would not have occurred otherwise. Similarly, if Darrow, a lawyer, draws a will for a client and fails to include one of the intended beneficiaries, it is clear that this omission is the cause in fact of the beneficiary's inability to take under the will. Common sense tells us that the problem happened because the beneficiary was left out, and would not have happened if she had been included. We would all accept that Darrow's mistake "caused" the beneficiary's damages, and so would any court.

In other cases, we could all agree, philosophers included, that the defendant's negligence did *not* cause the plaintiff's injury. Suppose that Pei's truck hits Gaudi on Maple Street. Investigation shows that the truck was carefully driven and in good working order, except that the windshield wipers were broken. However, the weather was dry at the time. No court will hold Pei liable for the accident because of the broken wipers. The wipers weren't needed; the accident would have happened the same way if they had been working. Even though Pei was negligent, his negligence was, in the language of the torts trade, "negligence in the air," negligence irrelevant to the injury that Gaudi suffered, and therefore not actionable.

THE TRADITIONAL TEST: "BUT FOR" CAUSATION

Traditionally, courts have used the "but for" test to determine whether the defendant's act was a cause in fact of the plaintiff's harm. Under the "but for" test,

> [t]he defendant's conduct is a cause of the event if the event would not have occurred but for that conduct; conversely, the defendant's conduct is not a cause of the event if the event would have occurred without it.

Prosser & Keeton at 266. Under this approach, the court asks whether the plaintiff would not have suffered the harm "but for" the defendant's negligence. In other words, if we go back and replay the accident, but take away the defendant's negligent act, would plaintiff have escaped injury? For example, in Pei's windshield wipers case, if the wipers had been working at the time of the accident, Gaudi would still have been injured in exactly the same way. So, Pei's negligence in failing to fix the wipers is not a "but for" cause of the harm. We cannot say that, but for the broken wipers, the accident would not have happened.

The plywood case, on the other hand, satisfies the "but for" test. But for the falling plywood, which obscured Sullivan's view of the road, she would not have swerved and hit the car. If we take Wright's negligence in dropping the plywood out of the scenario, the accident doesn't happen. Because the accident would not have happened without Wright's act, that act is a "but for" cause of the harm. Consequently, cause in fact is satisfied.

Another way of saying this is that the defendant's act must be a "sine qua non" of the plaintiff's injury. Sine qua non means "without which it is not; an indispensable requisite" (Ballentine's Law Dictionary 1182 (1969)), that is, that the injury would not have happened without the defendant's act. Again, the test invites us to look at what *did* happen and compare it to what *would have* happened if defendant had not been negligent. If the injury would not have resulted without the defendant's negligence, then the negligence is a sine qua non of the injury, and the cause-in-fact element is met.

Let's apply the "but for" test to two more straightforward examples. (We'll see more complicated ones soon enough.) Suppose that Rios, a pharmacist, mistakenly fills Paul's prescription for an antidepressant with pills that can lead to seizures. Paul takes the pills and has a seizure resulting in injuries. "But for" causation is clear: Paul had the seizure because Rios gave him the wrong pills. But for Rios's mistake, Paul would not have had the seizure. Rios's negligence is a cause in fact of Paul's injury.

Now the other example. Suppose that Mancuso works in a factory using a high-speed band saw. Phillips had removed the saw blade guard, which is meant to prevent workers' hands from contacting the blade. Mancuso is cutting a piece of plastic on the saw and has a severe allergic reaction to the plastic fumes. Here, although Phillips may have been negligent in removing the guard, his negligence is not a "but for" cause of Mancuso's injury. Presumably, the fumes would still have wafted up to Mancuso's nose if the saw had a guard, so the accident would have happened the same way if Phillips had not been negligent. His act is not, therefore, a cause in fact of Mancuso's injury.

THE PROBLEM OF MULTIPLE "BUT FOR" CAUSES

Accidents very frequently result from more than one negligent act. Suppose, for example, that the Edison Company negligently attaches a transformer to a light pole, and Gaudi negligently backs into the pole, knocking the loose transformer down on a child waiting for the school bus. Assume that the transformer would not have fallen, even though Gaudi hit the pole, if it had been tightly secured. Similarly, assume that the transformer would not have fallen, even though it was loose, if Gaudi had not negligently hit the pole.

If this is so, Edison might argue as follows: "Yes, it is true that I was negligent, but even though I was, the accident would not have happened unless Gaudi was, too. Even if the transformer was loose, it wouldn't have fallen unless he hit the pole. So Gaudi is the cause of the accident, not me." Of course, Gaudi can make a similar argument: "Well, I may have negligently hit the pole, but if the transformer were adequately secured it would not have fallen. So Edison's negligence is the cause of the harm, not mine."

Neither argument is sound. While it is true that either defendant's negligent act was not enough to cause the accident alone, each act was a necessary antecedent to the harm. Each cause contributed to the accident; if we take away the negligence of either defendant, the accident would not have happened, even assuming the negligence of the other. In cases like this, *both* negligent acts are causes of the injury under the "but for" test.

Put another way, it is no defense for one negligent actor that someone else's negligence also contributed to the accident. There is no requirement that the defendant's act be the *sole* "but for" cause of the injury, only that it be *a* "but for" cause.

> [A] tortfeasor is liable for all damage of which his tortious act was a proximate cause. "[He] may not escape this responsibility simply because another act—either an 'innocent' occurrence such as an 'act of God' or other [tortious] conduct—may also have been a [concurrent] cause of the injury."

Richards v. Owens-Illinois, Inc., 928 P.2d 1181, 1185 (Cal. 1997), quoting from *American Motorcycle Assn. v. Superior Court*, 578 P.2d 899, 903 (Cal. 1978). Thus, Edison cannot avoid liability because the transformer would not have fallen if Gaudi hadn't hit it. Although the loose transformer was not the sole cause of the accident, it was a "but for" cause, because if Edison had not been negligent, there would not have been an accident. The same is true for Gaudi. Both are "but for" causes of the accident.

This point is important enough to merit another illustration. Suppose Olmstead, a mason, is building a chimney on top of a city townhouse while pedestrians are using the sidewalk below. Richardson, the general contractor, was required to place a scaffold with a roof over the sidewalk to protect pedestrians from falling objects during construction, but failed to do so. Olmstead drops a brick and it injures Wren, who is walking on the sidewalk. On these facts, the negligent acts of both Richardson and Olmstead are "but for" causes of the harm. The accident would not have happened if Olmstead had not dropped the brick. It also would not have happened (even if Olmstead dropped the brick) if Richardson had put up the scaffold.

This logic applies both to negligent acts that take place at different times, as in the Edison example, and to negligent acts that take place simultaneously.

Suppose that Sullivan is driving down the street without looking carefully, and that Pei runs a stop sign coming out of a side street. Sullivan hits Pei, and his car careens into a pedestrian. The jury finds that the accident would not have happened if Pei had not run the stop sign. They also find that (even assuming Pei's negligence) the accident wouldn't have happened—even though Pei was negligent—if Sullivan had been keeping a proper lookout and stopped before hitting Pei's car. On this reasoning, both drivers' negligent acts are "but for" causes of the accident. Take away either one, and the accident would not have happened. Each is a sine qua non of the harm since that harm would not have happened without the negligence of each.

PROBLEMS IN APPLYING THE "BUT FOR" TEST: RECONSTRUCTING HISTORY

In the cases described above, applying the "but for" test is easy. In many cases, however, it involves a complex and speculative exercise because we can never know for sure what would have happened if history had been different. Suppose, for example, that a motorcyclist is killed when he pulls out in front of a bus that is going seven miles per hour over the speed limit. Or suppose that the plaintiff suffers chest pains, his doctor fails to diagnose it as a heart attack and provide suitable emergency treatment, and the patient dies of the heart attack.

In each of these cases, we know that the defendant was negligent, but we don't know whether things would have come out differently if the defendant had not been negligent. If the bus had been driving at the speed limit, could it have stopped before hitting the cyclist? If the doctor had provided timely treatment, would the patient have survived or died anyway? The defendant should not be held liable in such cases if the harm would have taken place regardless of the negligence. However, to determine whether the defendant's negligence affected the outcome, the jury must not only decide what actually happened, but must also speculate about a hypothetical alternative version of events: What would have happened if the defendant had not been negligent. In such cases, the "but for" test

> challenges the imagination of the trier to probe into a purely fanciful and unknowable state of affairs. He is invited to make an estimate concerning facts that concededly never existed. The very uncertainty as to what might have happened opens the door wide for conjecture.

W. Malone, Ruminations on Cause in Fact, 9 Stan. L. Rev. 60, 67 (1956).

However, while the "but for" inquiry involves a speculative comparison between actual events and hypothetical alternatives, that comparison still must be made, in order to distinguish injuries that would have happened anyway from those that were brought about, in whole or in part, by the defendant's negligent conduct. After all, the defendant's argument in these cases has much force: "I should not be held liable, even if I was negligent, unless my negligence made a difference, actually led to the plaintiff's injury."

Although this type of counterfactual inquiry is inherently speculative to some degree, the parties may be able to produce evidence that makes it less so. In the motorcycle example, the distance between the bus and the cycle when the cyclist pulled into the street will be critical in determining whether the excessive speed of the bus made a difference. Expert evidence about stopping distances at various speeds will also make the jury's task less speculative. In the heart attack example, the medical evidence may establish fairly clearly that the plaintiff would have recovered with prompt treatment, or, conversely, that death was inevitable even with immediate care. Although we can never achieve certainty about cause in fact, the jury can usually make a reasoned judgment as to whether the negligence contributed to the outcome.[1]

SOME COMPLICATIONS: THE "SUBSTANTIAL FACTOR" TEST

"But for" analysis has been the traditional basis for analyzing actual causation in negligence cases. A defendant's act is almost always a cause of the injury if the "but for" test is met. See Restatement (Third) of Torts §26 ("Conduct is a factual cause of harm when the harm would not have occurred absent the conduct"). However, there are a few quirky situations in which the "but for" test *is not* met, yet courts still think the defendant should be treated as a cause of the harm. In these situations, courts have created exceptions to the "but for" approach. Remember, however, that these *are* exceptions; in most circumstances, the defendant whose conduct was not a "but for" cause of the harm will not be liable.

One situation in which courts have created an exception to the "but for" rule is where two defendants act negligently, and either's act alone would suffice to cause the plaintiff's injury. In these cases, the plaintiff's injury is "overdetermined." That is, the act of either defendant was sufficient to

1. For an example of just how difficult such counterfactual analysis can be, consider the case of a plaintiff attacked by an emotionally unstable mental patient taking Prozac. Plaintiff claims that the drug caused the assailant's assaultive conduct, yet the very reason the patient was on the drug was for emotional problems. Even if the plaintiff shows that Prozac can cause aggressive behavior, it is a speculative enterprise indeed to show that it, rather than the patient's underlying condition, caused her assault.

cause the injury, but they operated together. In *Corey v. Havener*, 182 Mass. 250 (1902), for example, two motorcyclists roared past the plaintiff's horse-drawn wagon, scaring the horse and causing it to run away, injuring the driver. Very likely, the noise from either cycle would have caused the horse to run, so Cyclist #1 could argue that he was not a but for cause of the accident—if he hadn't been there making noise, the other cyclist would have caused the accident anyway. Inevitably, Cyclist #2 will make the same argument. If the court sticks with the "but for" test, neither would be liable, though both contributed to the noise that scared the horse.

Anderson v. Minneapolis, St. P. & S. St. M. Ry. Co., 179 N.W. 45 (1920), which lurks in most of the casebooks, presented a similar scenario. In *Anderson*, two wind-driven fires merged into one. After the fires merged, they reached the plaintiff's land and burned his property. Only one of the fires was due to the defendant's negligence. It was impossible to say that but for the defendant's fire, the plaintiff's barn would still stand, because the other fire would likely have caused the damage anyway. Yet the defendant's culpable act clearly contributed, and it seemed fair to hold the defendant liable for it.

In *Anderson*, the court rejected application of the "but for" test. Instead it held that the defendant would be a cause in fact of the damage if the jury found that its act was "a material or substantial element" in producing it. 179 N.W. at 46, 49. Under that test, the defendant was held liable even though the property would probably have been burned by the other fire anyway. This "substantial factor" test leaves it to the jury to decide whether each of the two actors was a substantial factor in causing the harm. The jury must make an intuitive judgment both as to what degree of causation is "substantial" and whether the defendant's negligence reaches that level. See Robertson, Powers, Anderson & Wellborn, Torts 141 (2d ed. 1998) ("substantial factor" test "incorporates no particular mental operation but appeals forthrightly to instinct"). It also appears to treat causation as a matter of degree rather than a "yes or no" proposition.

In the unusual situation illustrated by *Corey* and *Anderson* numerous courts have applied the "substantial factor" test. See Restatement (Second) of Torts §431(a). However, the Third Restatement of Torts suggests a different, quite sensible approach to this causation conundrum:

> If multiple acts exist, each of which alone would have been a factual cause under s. 26 of the physical harm at the same time, each act is regarded as a factual cause of the harm.

Restatement (Third) of Torts §27. Under this approach, the railroad would be liable as long as its fire was sufficient on its own to cause the harm that occurred. The drafters of the Third Restatement avoided the "substantial factor" language because it seems to introduce *proximate cause* concepts into actual cause analysis. It invites the jury to assess the extent to which the defendant's conduct contributed to the harm, which suggests a policy analysis rather than a judgment about actual causation. See Restatement (Third) of Torts §27 cmt. b. The Third Restatement approach is likely to supersede the somewhat ambiguous substantial factor approach to these overdetermined cases.

While these multiple-cause cases exist, they are rare, quirky exceptions to usual actual cause analysis. The casebooks bedevil first-year students with anomalous cases like *Anderson* and *Summers* (discussed immediately below), but in the vast majority of cases, remember that the "but for" test applies.

MORE COMPLICATIONS: SHIFTING THE BURDEN OF PROOF

Summers v. Tice, 199 P.2d 1 (Cal. 1948), illustrates another situation in which the "but for" test yields unsatisfactory results. In *Summers*, the two defendants fired their shotguns, and a pellet from one or the other injured the plaintiff's eye. Both defendants were negligent, but it was impossible for the plaintiff to show that it was "more probable than not" that either defendant's pellet had hit him: It was a 50/50 proposition that either defendant's shot had hit the eye. Under "but for" analysis, the plaintiff would lose.

The California Supreme Court was unwilling to see the plaintiff lose in *Summers*. It was clear that both defendants had committed the same act, that both were negligent, and that one or the other had injured the plaintiff. Given those facts, the court concluded that it would be unfair to let both of them off the hook simply because plaintiff was unable to pinpoint which hunter's shot had caused the harm. Instead, the court shifted the burden of proof to each defendant to show that he had *not* caused the harm. The defendants, of course, were no more able to prove whose pellet hit the plaintiff than he was. So, the result was that both were liable for the injury.

Summers v. Tice stands for the proposition that, where two (or perhaps more) defendants simultaneously commit similar negligent acts, one of which caused that plaintiff's injury, the burden of proof shifts to each defendant to show that he did not cause the harm. If they cannot make that showing, both will be held liable for the plaintiff's loss. This fairly narrow proposition has been followed by a number of courts. Others have rejected *Summers* entirely, leaving the plaintiff to establish causation under the traditional "but for" test. See, e.g., *Leuer v. Johnson*, 450 N.W.2d 363 (Minn. App. 1990).

However, be careful not to take the *Summers v. Tice* to stand for more than it does. *Summers* does *not* hold that every time the plaintiff sues more than one defendant, the burden of proof shifts to the defendants on the issue of causation. That is much too broad a reading of the case. *Summers* addresses a narrow anomaly in which "but for" analysis fails; it is not a general abdication of plaintiff's burden on the causation element of a negligence claim.

Suppose, for example, that Pablo is walking past a building where Wren and Farmer are reshingling a roof above the sidewalk. Pablo is hit by a hammer which clearly fell from the roof where the workers were doing the work. Pablo cannot sue Wren and Farmer and claim that the burden of proof shifts to each of them to prove that he did not drop the hammer. *Summers* does not apply in Pablo's case: It involved an unusual situation in which two actors did the same negligent act, and it is likely impossible to determine which of those acts caused the harm. In Pablo's case only one of the roofers was negligent, and it remains Pablo's job to prove which one it was.

RECONSTRUCTING HISTORY: PRACTICAL PROOF PROBLEMS IN ESTABLISHING CAUSE IN FACT

In many cases the act that caused the injury is clear, but the plaintiff faces a difficult causation problem in identifying the actor who did that act. Suppose in the plywood example that three subcontractors were working on the floor from which the plywood fell. Although the falling plywood clearly caused Sullivan's injury, Sullivan will have the very practical causation problem of proving who dropped it. Or, suppose that Fleming is injured when a crowbar she is using snaps in half, sending a splinter of steel into her eye. Here again, the mechanism that caused the harm is clear, but Fleming faces a formidable problem in proving who made the crowbar since crowbars look pretty much alike and may not carry any identifying marks. Or, suppose a fan throws a beer bottle from the stands at a football game, injuring a player. Negligence and causation are clear, but it may simply be impossible to identify who threw the bottle.

The causation issue in these who-done-it cases is not *conceptually* difficult, but poses the difficult practical problem of identifying the proper defendant. If we had an omniscient observer (we'll call him Solomon) and a time machine, we could send him back to review the relevant events and solve these identification problems. Without Solomon, however, plaintiffs must do the best they can to prove that the defendant was the negligent actor. In the real world of law practice, plaintiffs often lose cases because they cannot prove that the defendant committed the negligent act. In many other cases, the plaintiff never brings suit in the first place because she simply can't identify the negligent party. Students generally come to the Torts course with the preconception that a person who is hurt always recovers damages, but any torts practitioner will attest that practical realities often prevent worthy plaintiffs from recovering at all.

The examples below illustrate basic problems in determining cause in fact. In approaching them, assume that the "but for" test applies, except in situations such as *Anderson* and *Summers*, in which it yields unsatisfactory results.

Examples

Applying "But For" Causation

1. Perrone, a landlord, rents rooms in an apartment building to tenants. Despite repeated citations from city authorities for failure to install a required fire escape at the back of the building, he doesn't install one. Late one night, a fire breaks out that destroys the building. Swensson, a tenant with a room on the front of the third floor of the building, is found dead in his bed of smoke inhalation. Swensson's family sues Perrone for wrongful death, alleging that Perrone was negligent for failure to install the fire escape
   a. What causation problem do you anticipate in proving Perrone's liability for Swensson's death?
   b. Suppose Swensson's body was found halfway down the hall? How would that affect the causation issue?

2. Harper, while driving down Main Street, was tuning the radio dial instead of looking where his car was going. James, another driver, negligently failed to stop for a stop sign. Harper could have avoided a collision had he been paying full attention, but their cars collide, and Gray, a passenger in Harper's car is injured. Gray sues Harper and James for her injuries. Who is a cause of Gray's injury?

3. Gray is taken to the hospital, where Dr. Green negligently sets her arm. Consequently, it must be rebroken a week later and set again, causing Gray considerable pain and medical expense. Which actors are "but for" causes of the injuries to Gray?

Nature and Negligence

4. Corbusier, driving down a country road, comes around a curve, and encounters a deep puddle due to recent heavy rains. He tries to stop, but his brakes have been so poorly maintained that he cannot control the car. The car swerves to the left and hits Saarinen driving in the opposite direction, causing serious injuries. Is Corbusier liable under the "but for" test?

5. Dobbs is driving carefully to the store for a quart of milk when Fletcher pulls out of a side street without looking and crashes into Dobbs, who swerves into Schwartz on the sidewalk. Which driver's conduct is a "but for" cause of Schwartz's injuries?

6. Dobbs is driving to the store without his glasses, which he really ought to be wearing to drive safely. Fletcher pulls out of the side street without looking. Dobbs sees him too late, they collide, and Dobbs suffers a concussion in the resulting collision. What are the "but for" causes of the accident?

Revisionist History

7. Haines, a student, is beaten and robbed in a college dormitory. Investigation determines that the assailant, Gibbs, had been admitted to the dorm to visit another student. Haines sues the college, alleging that it was negligent in failing to hire enough security officers to assure adequate security.
   a. What is the nature of Haines's problem in proving causation in this case?
   b. What will the college argue on the causation issue?
   c. What will the plaintiff's counterargument be?

8. Smith applies to Jones, the Chief of Police, for a permit to carry a handgun. A statute requires Chief Jones to check with the state Department of Public Safety to determine whether an applicant has a criminal record before issuing the permit, and to refuse the permit if the applicant has a record. Jones fails to do so and issues the permit. Three days later, Smith shoots Doe on the street with the gun. Doe sues Chief Jones for negligence.
   a. Assume that Smith had no criminal record. Is cause in fact established?
   b. Assume that Chief Jones fails to check, and issues the permit to Smith even though Smith did have a criminal record. Can the plaintiff prove cause in fact?

Pestiferous Problems

9. Smith and Jones, two farmers, both sell tomatoes to a local market that have been sprayed with Icthar, a banned pesticide. The market puts the tomatoes out, together, in a bin. No other farmers' tomatoes are in the bin. Wren buys one and gets sick from the pesticide.
   a. If Wren sues the farmers, what type of causation problem will he face?
   b. How does the problem compare to the problem in *Anderson v. Minneapolis, St. Paul & St. Marie R.R. Co.*, the two fires case?
   c. Can this problem be solved by use of the "substantial factor" test?
   d. How will this case come out under *Summers v. Tice?*
   e. What is the best argument *against* the *Summers*'s court's solution to this type of problem?

But for Judge Fudd

10. Ortega is injured when he slips on a pencil on the office floor. The floor had been swept early that morning. The only other employees in the office that day are Chu, Abbrezio, and Tate. Ortega sues all three for his injury. Prior to trial, Ortega requests the following jury instruction on cause in fact at trial:

> If you find that the defendants Chu, Abbrezio, and Tate were at the office on the day in question, but that the plaintiff is unable to establish which of them dropped the pencil that caused her injury, you should find each of the defendants jointly liable for the injury. However, if any of the defendants establishes by a preponderance of the evidence that he did not drop the pencil, you should not find that defendant liable.

Should the Honorable Fudd so instruct the jury?

11. Markosky negligently fails to stop at a traffic light, and plows into Osteen's car. Osteen is shaken up but, after exchanging papers, heads home. On the way, the luckless fellow is rear-ended again, by Lugo.

    Later in the evening, Osteen's back begins to ache. X-rays reveal that he has a serious injury to a disk in his back. The causation problem, of course, is to determine which accident caused his injury.
    a. How is this case like *Summers v. Tice?*
    b. How does it differ from *Summers?*
    c. What are the court's options for choosing a causation rule for this case?

A Conundrum for Fun

12. Two farmers negligently start fires on a windy day, to burn brush off of their fields. Both fires escape, Farmer Jones's fire a bit ahead of Farmer Smith's. Jones's fire burns toward Menlove's barn, which burns to the ground. Just after it burns, Smith's fire arrives.
    a. Who is liable under the "but for" test?
    b. Who is liable under the substantial factor test?
    c. Applying a little common sense, who should be liable to Menlove?
    d. Can you think of a clever argument to limit Jones's liability?

An Elemental Example

13. Wright negligently runs down Morales in the street. Morales dies of his injuries. However, Morales had a terminal disease from which he was expected to die within a matter of weeks. Did Wright cause Morales's death? Should he be held liable, and if so, for what?

Explanations

Causation and Consequences

1. a. Perrone was clearly negligent in failing to provide adequate fire escapes for the building. Evidently a fire escape was required by law, so Perrone was likely negligent per se. However, proving Perrone negligent is not enough to establish his liability; Swensson's family will have to establish that Perrone's negligence caused Swensson's death. Yet it appears that Swensson died in his bed from smoke inhalation, without ever trying to escape from the building. If that is true, a dozen fire escapes would have made no difference in the outcome. We cannot say that, but for Perrone's failure to install a fire escape, Swensson would be alive today. It appears that Swensson would have died just the same if Perrone had not been negligent. If that is true, it will be impossible to establish that Perrone's negligence in failing to install a fire escape was a factual cause of his death.

   b. If Swensson is found in the middle of the hall, his family can argue that the lack of a fire escape did lead to the result, that it did "change history." If he was found in the hall, perhaps he made it to the back window, was unable to get out because there was no fire escape, and ran back toward the front. That would show that he died *because* of the lack of a fire escape, that "but for" the negligence of the landlord, Swensson would be alive today. That is the plaintiff's burden in establishing causation.

   Of course, this would still be a tough case on actual causation. The landlord will argue that Swensson never made it to the back window, so the lack of a fire escape did not cause the death, was mere "negligence in the air." It will be very difficult for the family to establish causation here without more evidence that the lack of a fire escape made a difference. But it is not necessarily impossible. For example, evidence that the back window was open, or that someone saw Swensson at the window (wouldn't the family's lawyer love to have that evidence!), could help to establish causation.

2. Both Harper and James are "but for" causes of the accident. If James had stopped at the stop sign, he wouldn't have run into Harper's car. If Harper had been looking at the road instead of the radio, he would have (the example assumes) been able to stop before colliding with James. They are both negligent causes of a single, indivisible injury to Gray, and each will be liable for it. Harper cannot argue that "if only James had been careful there would not have been an accident, so I am not liable." If that argument were accepted, James could make the same argument, in which case neither would be liable for an injury that they both caused.

3. Under "but for" analysis, Harper and James are both "but for" causes of Gray's initial injury, and also of his additional injuries due to Green's malpractice. But for each of their negligent acts, Gray would not have been in the hospital to begin with, and would not have suffered the additional injury due to Dr. Green's mistake. Consequently, they have caused the initial injury and the malpractice damages as well.

   Dr. Green, however, is not a cause of the initial accident. It would have happened the same way if we remove his negligence from the scenario. He is, of course, a "but for" cause of the injuries from resetting the arm. But for his failure to set it properly the first time, this enhanced injury would not have happened. So, he may be liable for the enhanced injuries but not those resulting from the initial collision.

   As we will see in later chapters, the traditional response of the common law to situations where more than one tortfeasor causes an injury is to hold them all liable for the plaintiff's damages. Under traditional tort law, Harper and James would be jointly liable for Gray's initial injury. Harper, James, and Green would be liable for the extra damages due to Green's missetting of the arm.

Nature and Negligence

4. This accident is caused by both Corbusier's negligent maintenance of his car and the puddle that created the dangerous condition in the road. Although only one of these causes is due to Corbusier's negligence, that negligence is still a "but for" cause of the harm. The accident would not have happened if Corbusier had not been negligent. True, it would not have happened *even if Corbusier was negligent,* if the puddle had not been there, but that does not exonerate him. It is not a defense for him that other circumstances, whether natural or negligent, also contributed to the accident, if his negligence was one of those causes.

5. This example makes a very basic point. Clearly, both Dobbs's and Fletcher's driving are "but for" causes of the accident. If Dobbs hadn't gone for milk, the accident wouldn't have happened; if Fletcher hadn't pulled out of the side street, the accident wouldn't have happened. However, the fact that they both *caused* the accident doesn't mean that they will both be liable to Schwartz. Dobbs caused the accident by nonnegligent conduct, while Fletcher was a negligent cause. In a tort case, the plaintiff must show that the defendant's *tortious conduct* caused the harm, not just that his act caused it. In analyzing cause in fact, then, be careful to ask the right question—whether the defendant's negligence caused the harm, not just whether his conduct caused it.

6. In this example, the plaintiff's negligence is one of the "but for" causes of the accident, along with the negligence of the defendant. There's nothing

unusual about that; it's just another multiple-cause case. Sometimes two parties are negligent and cause injuries to a third party, as in the typical joint tortfeasor situation like the Edison example in the introduction. At other times, two actors are negligent and their negligence causes injury to *one of them*, as in this case.

If the plaintiff's negligence is one of the "but for" causes of an accident, tort law has to decide what to do about that. As a matter of policy, we might decide to bar a plaintiff who was causally negligent from recovery entirely—the rule of contributory negligence. Or, we might reduce the plaintiff's damages to account for his negligence—the rule of comparative negligence. Last, we might hold the defendant fully liable anyway—the rule of strict liability. But these choices have nothing to do with the basic *factual* question of whose negligence caused the accident: It is perfectly clear under "but for" causation that the negligence of both Dobbs and Fletcher did.

Revisionist History

7. a. The causation problem here is to determine whether the defendant's negligence affected the result, that is, whether the plaintiff would not not have been assaulted if the college had provided adequate security. It requires the factfinder to compare what did happen to what *would have happened* absent the defendant's negligence.

   b. The college will argue that it should not be held liable, even if security was inadequate, because any inadequacy in security did not cause the assault. It will argue that having more security officers would not have affected the outcome, because the student did not slip into the dorm illegally; he was admitted through the ordinary procedures.

   There is certainly force to this argument. Gibbs did not break into the dorm, he entered openly for a legitimate reason. Consequently, inadequate security did not affect Gibbs's ability to get into the dorm. Even if there had been additional officers available, they would not have barred his entry and prevented Gibbs's actions.

   c. Haines will argue that, even if the inadequate security did not cause Gibbs's entry, it still caused the harm because, had Gibbs known that the dorm was well patrolled, he would have feared being caught and therefore would not have attempted the crime. This illustrates the speculative role of the jury in this type of case, in which they must try to get into Gibbs's mind and decide what he would have done under different circumstances.

8. a. This is another case that requires the jury to compare what actually happened to what would have happened if the defendant had not been negligent. Here, Jones's negligence in failing to check Smith's

criminal record was not a "but for" cause of Doe's injury. Had he checked, he would have discovered that Smith had no record; consequently, he would have issued the permit anyway. Thus, Doe cannot show that, but for Jones's failure to check the record, Smith would not have obtained the gun permit and shot Doe. Although that failure was negligent, it was not causal negligence.

b. The argument for causation is a great deal stronger in this case. If Jones had checked, he would have discovered that Smith had a record and refused the permit. But for his failure to check, the permit would not have been issued.

However, Smith might have carried the gun without the permit and shot Doe anyway. Perhaps the evidence would even show that he would have. But the evidence might also lead the jury to conclude that Smith would not have carried a gun without a permit, and that Doe would therefore not have been shot. The plaintiff need not show that Smith could not possibly have shot Doe without the permit; she need only convince the jury that it is more probable than not that she would not have been injured but for the police chief's negligence. Though there is certainly a measure of speculation involved, one can imagine facts on which the jury could reasonably reach that conclusion here.

Pestiferous Problems

9. a. These facts are closely analogous to the facts of *Summers v. Tice*, in which two hunters fired at a bird and shot from one of the guns injured the plaintiff. Here, as in *Summers*, we know what caused the harm—eating the tomato laced with pesticide—but we need to know whose tomato it was. It is a proof problem that Solomon could easily solve if he went back and watched the events carefully enough. But we don't have a Solomon and we don't have any way of determining which farmer's tomato Wren ate.

b. In *Anderson*, there were two causes of the harm, either of which was sufficient to produce it. Each defendant could argue that its negligence was not a "but for" cause of the harm, because the negligence of the other would have caused it anyway. However, each was clearly a sufficient cause of the fire. Here, by contrast, there was only one cause of the harm: Wren only ate one tomato, supplied by one of the farmers but not by the other. The problem—probably an insuperable one, as a practical matter—is identifying which defendant's tomato was the "but for" cause of his illness.

c. Using a substantial factor test for causation does not resolve this problem. Even under this test, there was only one "substantial factor" that caused the injury. The basic problem of tracing the tomato remains.

d. In *Summers*, the court resolved the dilemma posed by cases like this by shifting the burden of proof to the defendants since they were both negligent. This does not solve the identification problem; it simply places the risk of nonidentification on the defendants. Since the farmers here are no more able to show whose tomato caused the harm than the plaintiff, they will both be held liable, and will end up splitting the loss under contribution principles if both are solvent. This resolution of the dilemma may lack intellectual elegance, but it does provide a kind of rough-and-ready justice that courts must often settle for in real disputes.

e. The best argument against the *Summers* solution is that it guarantees that a defendant who did not cause any harm to the plaintiff will be held liable for her damages. Since neither farmer will be able to prove that Wren did not eat his tomato, each will be held jointly and severally liable. Presumably, one will pay Wren, and then seek contribution from the other, so they will end up splitting the damages. But Wren only ate one tomato, so only one farmer caused her any harm. Admittedly, the other was negligent, but traditional tort doctrine says that's not enough to support liability: The defendant's negligence must *cause injury* to support liability. Not so under *Summers v. Tice*.

While this is a departure from the traditional rules, it is one that a number of courts find more acceptable than the alternative: sending the plaintiff away empty-handed.

But for Judge Fudd

10. If I put this on my exam, many students would say that Judge Fudd should give the requested instruction since the case is vaguely like *Summers v. Tice*. They would justify that conclusion with reasoning like this: "If the plaintiff is unable to determine which defendant caused the harm, the court will shift the burden of proof to the defendants to show that they didn't cause it."

This is Fudd-led analysis because this case differs from *Summers* in important respects. First, in *Summers*, the plaintiff had proved that both defendants were negligent. Here, she hasn't proved that any of them were; she could have dropped the pencil herself. If it was one of the defendants, well, it was *one* of the defendants, and the others didn't do anything negligent. There is no justification for shifting the burden of proof to the defendants every time plaintiff sues more than one. The burden remains on Ortega to prove who dropped that pencil. Restatement (Third) of Torts: Liability for Physical and Emotional Harm §28 cmt. i.

But, how can she ever meet that burden of proof? Maybe she can't. But there is no rule of tort law that says injured plaintiffs must always win. The basic rules say she wins only if she proves all elements of her negligence claim, and—*Summers* or no *Summers*—the burden of making that proof generally falls on her.

11. a. The case is like *Summers* in that plaintiff can prove that both defendants were negligent. It is also like *Summers* in that plaintiff may be unable to establish by a preponderance of the evidence which defendant caused the resulting injury.

    b. The case differs from *Summers* in that here, unlike in *Summers*, causation is not necessarily an either/or proposition. In *Summers*, plaintiff's eye was hit by one pellet, either Tice's or Simonson's. One defendant had caused no harm at all; the other had caused the entire injury. In Osteen's case, one collision may have caused the entire injury, but it is also possible—indeed, likely—that the first collision caused some and the second collision caused some more.

    This type of case (in which two negligent defendants have probably contributed to an injury, but it is difficult or impossible to determine how much of the injury was caused by each) is much more common than the pure *Summers v. Tice* scenario. Osteen's case, unlike *Summers*, poses a proof problem that commonly arises in the practice of tort law.

    c. The court could take a number of approaches to this apportionment problem. One would be to stick to the traditional rules: make Osteen prove how much injury each defendant caused. If he couldn't, he loses. He may not be able to muster the necessary proof, but if not, that's life in the big Torts city. As indicated in the introduction, lots of plaintiffs go without compensation because they simply can't find the proof.

    A second approach is to shift the burden to the defendants, once Osteen establishes that they were both negligent, to show that they did not cause the injury, or to show what part of it they did cause. Most courts have taken this approach to the apportionment dilemma in these two accident cases. If the plaintiff proves that both defendants were negligent, and that he suffered an injury difficult to apportion, the burden shifts to the defendants to show which part they caused. If they can't separate the damages, they are held jointly liable for them all. Restatement (Third) of Torts: Liability for Physical and Emotional Harm §28 cmt. k and illus. 10; see generally Dobbs' Law of Torts §192.

A Conundrum for Fun

12. a. Farmer Jones will argue that the "but for" test does not apply, because if his fire had not burned the barn down, Farmer Smith's would have done so immediately thereafter. Clearly, Jones argues, the barn

would have burned down even if he had not started a fire; Smith's fire was adequate to do the job and would have.

A practical court would not accept that reasoning. Jones's fire did burn the barn. If his fire had not been there, perhaps Smith's fire would have. . . . or maybe not. If Chan runs over Miss Marple on the street, she is the "but for" cause of her injuries, even if fifty other negligent drivers were careening in her direction.

b. Any sensible jury should conclude that Jones's fire was a substantial factor in burning Menlove's barn. It *did* burn the barn, without any help from Smith's fire.

Presumably, Smith's fire was *not* a substantial factor in causing the loss—it made no contribution at all to the demise of Menlove's beloved barn. It certainly could have if it had had the chance, but the barn was gone when it got there.

c. This conundrum involves what might be called a "preempted cause," one that is sufficient to cause the harm, but never actually comes into operation. Smith's fire would have done the job, but didn't, because the other fire caused the loss first. Having the capacity to cause the loss ought not to substitute for actually causing it. Jones, whose negligence caused the damage, should be liable for it. Smith, who didn't cause it, shouldn't be liable, even though his negligence would have caused the harm if Jones had not preempted him.

This is like the case of Villain, who poisons his enemy's drink. Just as Enemy puts it to his lips, he is shot by Desperado. Villain tried to cause Enemy's death, and his means were sufficient to the purpose. But the poison never came into operation, since Enemy died without drinking. We might punish Villain for attempted murder at criminal law, but he is not the cause of Enemy's death.

d. Jones could argue that, while he burned down the barn, he only deprived Menlove of a few minutes of use of the barn. If he (Jones) had not been negligent, Smith's fire would have burned the barn several minutes after his did. So what damage has he actually caused to Menlove . . . just the use of the barn for the few minutes before Smith's fire arrived.

Surely, this argument must fail . . . I think. If it is accepted, Menlove recovers almost nothing from Jones, and nothing at all from Smith, though he is deprived of all use of his barn. Jones burned down *the barn*, and should pay for it, even if some other cause would have destroyed it later. Compare a case in which Ace and Deuce each go looking for Menlove, to shoot him. Ace finds him and shoots him, and Deuce arrives on the scene minutes later with evil intent. Who killed Menlove?

An Elemental Example

13. Of course Wright caused Morales's death; the example basically says so. Morales died of his injuries, not of the terminal disease. But for the accident, Morales would have been alive; because of the accident, he died. Wright is a tortfeasor and liable for Morales's death.

The fact that Morales was terminally ill is relevant, however, to the fourth element of the negligence claim, *damages*. The measure of damages in Morales's case will be the loss caused by Wright's tort. But for Wright's negligence, Morales would have lived, but only for a few weeks. Wright will be liable, but the damages for wrongful death will be limited by Morales's short life expectancy.

CHAPTER 11

Risks Reconsidered: Complex Issues in Establishing Factual Cause

INTRODUCTION

Most law students think of proximate cause as the Heartbreak Hill of the Torts marathon, the toughest problem in a course replete with tough intellectual issues. However, the real action today is in the cause-in-fact arena, where tort law is constantly butting heads against an intractable problem: the limits of human knowledge about cause and effect. There is a world of difference between a defendant causing injury to a plaintiff, on the one hand, and the plaintiff *proving* that she did, on the other. This chapter, for those of you courageous enough to press on, addresses a number of cutting-edge factual causation issues often encountered in the Torts course—and increasingly, in the practice of tort law.

CAUSATION IN DES CASES: WHO DONE IT?

The first complex causation problem is illustrated by the DES cases. DES is a drug that was widely prescribed for several decades to prevent miscarriage, but which has subsequently been shown to cause various medical problems in the daughters of women who took it during pregnancy. Because DES was marketed in chemically identical form by over 200 companies, a plaintiff injured by DES exposure faces a very difficult cause-in-fact problem: Even if all companies were negligent for marketing the drug, only one of them—the manufacturer that manufactured the DES pills her mother took—caused her injuries.

This is an enormously difficult proof problem, but there is nothing *conceptually* hard about it. Evidently, the health problems DES daughters experience are clearly traceable to DES exposure, so there is no difficulty in determining *what* caused their injuries. The problem is determining *who* caused it since so many drug manufacturers sold DES for use during pregnancy. If we could summon Solomon, our omniscient time traveler, he could solve this problem easily enough, by going back to watch the relevant events and jotting down the name of the manufacturer on the prescription filled by the plaintiff's mother.

Sometimes the plaintiff can solve it, too. She may be able to identify the manufacturer if her mother recalls the shape, color, or brand of DES she took.[1] In many cases, however, the evidence will show that the mother took DES, but not which manufacturer's pill it was. In such cases, the plaintiff will be unable to establish that a particular manufacturer caused her injury. If she is held to the usual burden to prove causation, she must lose.

While this result appears inexorable under traditional tort theory, the California Supreme Court in *Sindell v. Abbott Laboratories*, 607 P.2d 924 (1980), found it unacceptable. To avoid this outcome, the court fashioned the "market share" theory, which allows the plaintiff to sue a number of manufacturers and—assuming they are found at fault—hold each liable for part of the plaintiff's damages. Under the *Sindell* approach, each manufacturer's share of the liability is determined by the proportional share of DES it sold in the relevant market area.

Sindell does not solve the cause-in-fact problem . . . it redesigns it. Instead of asking who caused the particular plaintiff's damages, it asks who contributed to the creation of a general risk of injury, and distributes the damages among those risk creators in proportion to the amount of risk each created. It is entirely clear under *Sindell* that defendants will be held liable to a plaintiff *even though they did not cause her any harm*. If Sindell sues six manufacturers who sold DES in the relevant market, but her mother only took one brand of DES, five of them may be held partially liable without having caused the injuries for which she sues.

On the other hand, if all DES daughters sued all manufacturers under the market share approach, the manufacturers would, theoretically, pay in proper proportion to the injuries they caused. A manufacturer who made 10 percent of the DES sold would be held liable for 10 percent of each plaintiff's injuries. Since it actually caused *all* the injuries suffered by 10 percent of

---

1. The plaintiff hit a snag with this approach in *Krist v. Eli Lilly & Co.*, 897 F.2d 293 (7th Cir. 1990). Her mother testified repeatedly, under the defendant's examination, that the DES she had taken was a "little red pill." The defendant then introduced evidence that it had indeed sold DES in a little red pill, but that it had done so only *after* the mother's pregnancy.

DES daughters, this should work out about right in the aggregate. Of course, all plaintiffs will not sue all defendants for their DES injuries, nor have all states (or even a majority) adopted the market share theory. Consequently, while in theory there is logic to the market share approach, its effect is rather haphazard in practice.

Market share liability looks more like a legislative solution to the causation problem than a judicial one: The court fashions a remedy that encompasses not only the party that actually caused the plaintiff's harm but also other parties who contributed to the general risk that harmed her. While it serves several of tort law's basic goals—compensation for the plaintiff and deterrence of negligent conduct—it arguably goes beyond the traditional role of courts in tort cases, by holding parties liable who caused no harm to the plaintiff before the court. But complex problems of modern life have forced courts to fashion such nontraditional remedies in a variety of contexts. While it is easy to criticize the California court's approach, the alternative—leaving plaintiffs without a remedy for negligent conduct, and defendants without an incentive to avoid it—isn't very satisfying either. In lawsuits, unlike philosophy classes, courts have to decide. Refusal to refashion traditional doctrine in cases like *Sindell* usually means that the plaintiff loses.

Since *Sindell*, courts have created some interesting variations on the market share approach. Here are three.

- In *Martin v. Abbott Labs.*, 689 P.2d 368 (Wash. 1984), the Washington Supreme Court held that a plaintiff may sue one DES manufacturer only. (Of course, she is free to sue more if she wishes.) If she proves that that manufacturer sold the drug in the relevant market area (that is, where her mother purchased the drug), and that DES caused her injuries, that defendant will be liable for the plaintiff's injuries.

  However, the defendant may implead (that is, bring into the action) other DES makers. If it does, all makers before the court are *presumed* to have equal market shares. Thus, the plaintiff need not shoulder the difficult burden of establishing market shares. If the defendants offer no proof as to market share, they will each be held liable for a pro rata share of the plaintiff's damages. (If, for example, five are joined, each would be severally liable for one-fifth of the plaintiff's damages.) Any defendant that establishes that it had a smaller market share will pay according to that share. If this happens, the shares of the other defendants go up, so that plaintiff still recovers 100 percent of her damages.
- In *Abel v. Eli Lilly & Co.*, 343 N.W.2d 164 (Mich. 1984), the Michigan Supreme Court adopted an approach to DES liability modeled on *Summers v. Tice*. The court held that a plaintiff may recover by joining all defendants who might have sold the drug ingested by her mother.

Any defendant may avoid liability by proving that it did not manufacture the DES that injured the plaintiff. Any maker who does not make such proof would be *jointly and severally liable* to the plaintiff for her entire damages.[2]

- The New York Court of Appeals has taken the most radical approach to market share liability. In *Hymowitz v. Eli Lilly & Co.*, 541 N.Y.S.2d 941 (1989), the court held that a plaintiff who proves that she was injured by her mother's ingestion of DES recovers from any defendant who participated in the *United States* market for DES. Recovery is in proportion to national market share. If less than all makers are before the court—which will virtually always be so—the plaintiff will recover less than full damages since each maker pays only in proportion to its market share.

What makes New York's approach radical is that it uses national market share, *and bars any maker from proving that it did not make the DES that injured the plaintiff.* Suppose, for example, that Acme Drug Company proves that it never sold DES in New York, where the plaintiff's mother bought the drug. Or suppose it proves that its DES pills were blue, and the plaintiff's mother testifies that the pills she took were red. Under *Hymowitz*, Acme pays in proportion to its national market share, even though it conclusively establishes that it did not cause the plaintiff's injury:

> It is merely a windfall for a producer to escape liability solely because it manufactured a more identifiable pill, or sold only to certain drugstores. These fortuities in no way diminish the culpability of a defendant for marketing the product, which is the basis of liability here.

541 N.Y.S.2d at 950. This quotation from *Hymowitz* is enormously ironic. Common law courts for centuries have premised liability on causing the plaintiff's harm. Yet the *Hymowitz* court fairly casually concludes that it is "merely a windfall" to allow the defendant to avoid liability by showing it did no harm to the plaintiff!

Market share liability is a controversial doctrine. Some courts have refused to adopt any variant on *Sindell*. Rhode Island, for example, rejected it in a one-page rescript opinion. "We are not willing to adopt the market-share doctrine which has been accepted in the State of California in *Sindell v. Abbott Laboratories, Inc.*... We are of the opinion that the establishment of liability requires the identification of the specific defendant responsible for the injury." *Gorman v. Abbott Laboratories*, 599 A.2d 1364, 1364 (R.I. 1991). See also *Mulcalhy v. Eli Lilly & Co.*, 386 N.W.2d 67, 76 (Iowa 1986) ("awarding

2. The *Abel* approach may no longer apply, due to statutory abrogation of joint and several liability in Michigan. See *Napier v. Osmose, Inc.*, 399 F. Supp. 2d 811 (W.D. Mich. 2005).

damages to an admittedly innocent party by means of a court-constructed device that places liability on manufacturers who were not proved to have caused the injury involves social engineering more appropriately within the legislative domain").[3]

The examples that follow illustrate the application—and some of the problems—of the market share approach to actual causation. The explanations begin on p. 224.

Examples

Share, or Share Alike?

1. Sindell sues nine DES makers in California. At trial, she introduces some proof that the drug was that of Acme Drug Company. In the alternative, she relies on the market share theory. If the jury concludes that Acme made the drug her mother took, what should it do?

2. Sindell sues four DES makers in California. At trial, she establishes that all defendants were negligent for marketing DES, and that their individual market shares were as follows: Dl 10 percent, D2 20 percent, D3 30 percent. D4 proves that it sold no DES in the relevant market at the time. The jury finds Sindell's damages to be $100,000. Under the *Sindell* approach, how much should each defendant pay?

3. On the facts of Example 2, what happens if D2 is unable to pay its share of the total liability?

4. You represent Sindell, and have decided to proceed on a market share theory in California. What problems would you foresee in proving the market shares of the various defendants?

Absent Tortfeasors

5. Assume that Sindell's mother bought DES in New York, and Sindell sues there after *Hymowitz*. One defendant, the Acme Drug Company, establishes that it never sold DES in New York, but that it did have a 10 percent share of the national market for DES at the relevant time. Is it liable?

6. Assume that Sindell sues in New York after *Hymowitz*. Assume that the Acme Drug Company proves that it did not sell DES at all at the time that Sindell's mother took the drug, but the plaintiff establishes that it did have a 20 percent share of the DES market two years later. How should its liability be determined under *Hymowitz*?

---

3. Several states have also passed statutes barring adoption of market share liability. See Ga. St. §51-1-11(d) & (e); OH St. §2307.73(C).

7. Assume that Sindell sues one DES maker, the Acme Drug Company, in Washington State (Washington's approach to market share liability is described on p. 213). Acme brings three others, Beta, Gamma, and Phi Corporations, into the suit. Phi establishes that it never sold DES in the relevant market. Beta establishes that its share of the market was 6 percent. The other defendants offer no evidence on their market shares. Under the approach adopted by the Washington Supreme Court in *Martin*, what would each defendant owe?

8. Suppose on the facts of Example 7, that Acme proved its share was 15 percent, Beta proved its share was 6 percent, Gamma proved its share was 10 percent, and Phi proved it had no market share. How much would each defendant pay under the Washington market share approach?

CAUSATION IN MULTIPLE EXPOSURE CASES

A somewhat different problem is posed by cases of multiple exposure to a dangerous substance such as asbestos. Suppose, for example, that Corbusier worked as a pipe insulator in a shipyard for 30 years and was exposed over those years to various asbestos products sold by six companies. These products might include insulating materials, fireproofing, floor and ceiling tiles, and others. Eventually, he contracts asbestosis, a disease of the lungs which has been definitively linked to breathing asbestos fibers.

As in the DES cases, there is no problem here in ascertaining the mechanism that caused the harm. As the name indicates, asbestosis is a "signature disease"; medical experts can determine from a physical examination that Corbusier got his disease from asbestos exposure.[4] The problem here is another who-done-it problem, but of a different sort. Here *all* the defendants exposed the plaintiff to the injury-causing agent.

If it were clear that *cumulative* exposure to all the asbestos was necessary to cause Corbusier's disease, the "but for" test would dispose of this problem. The plaintiff could argue that, but for the negligence of each defendant, he would not have gotten asbestosis. Each would be liable under traditional causation principles.

In most cases, however, the evidence will *not* show that each defendant's product was essential to causing the disease. The plaintiff's expert will testify that breathing asbestos causes asbestosis and that the more you breathe, the greater the chances of contracting the disease, but that a fairly

4. Asbestos exposure also causes diseases, including cancer, that are not signature diseases (i.e., they have other causes as well, some known and some not known). In these cases, the plaintiff faces both a who-done-it problem and a what-done-it problem in establishing factual causation.

brief exposure can suffice. She will be unable to state in Corbusier's case how much was necessary, though she will state with certainty that asbestos exposure caused the harm. On these facts, each defendant can argue that "but for" causation is not established because, even if its product had not been at the site, Corbusier would have contracted asbestosis from the other defendants' products anyway.

In this type of multiple exposure case, most courts have invoked the "substantial factor" test for cause in fact. The jury is left to consider, based on the evidence of each defendant's contribution to the risk, whether its product was a substantial factor in causing Corbusier's disease. If the exposure to Company #6's product was minimal, the jury may conclude it did not meaningfully contribute to the harm. But if Company #6's product was there on a consistent basis and its asbestos particles were more than a minimal percentage of the exposure, they would be free to conclude that it had "caused" Corbusier's disease, even though he probably would have contracted it from the other manufacturers' products anyway. The test allows the jury to find the defendant liable if it contributed significantly to the *risk* of plaintiff's injury:

> We therefore hold that . . . in a trial of an asbestos-related cancer case, the jury should be told that the plaintiff's or decedent's exposure to a particular product was a substantial factor in causing or bringing about the disease if in reasonable medical probability *it contributed to the plaintiff or decedent's risk of developing cancer.*

Rutherford v. Owens-Illinois, Inc., 941 P.2d 1203, 1206 (Cal. 1997) (emphasis added).

Using the "substantial factor" test in such cases is hardly an intellectually rigorous solution to the problem. "The [substantial factor] test has become a default, resorted to when nothing else works, and juries are afforded virtually no guidance as to how much of a causal connection is necessary to satisfy the test." G. Boston, Toxic Apportionment: A Causation and Risk Contribution Model, 25 Envtl. L. 549, 630 (1995). The jury cannot determine which asbestos particles actually injured the plaintiff. Even Solomon with his time machine would have tough sledding trying to reconstruct the etiology of the disease. So the question is, what should tort law do in the absence of better knowledge about causation? On balance, holding the defendants liable under the substantial factor approach, based on evidence of a meaningful contribution to a general risk, is probably more satisfactory than denying liability simply because the other manufacturers' asbestos might have caused the disease anyway. See Restatement (Third) of Torts: Liability for Physical and Emotional Harm §27 cmt. g (in multiple exposure cases, each exposure is a factual cause of the harm, though minimal exposures may be held not liable on policy grounds).

Examples

Substances and Substantial Factors

9. Are the asbestos cases more like *Summers v. Tice* (discussed in the previous chapter at pp. 198-199) or *Anderson v. Minneapolis, St. Paul and St. Marie R.R. Co.* (discussed in the previous chapter at pp. 196-197)?
10. Why not use a market share approach to liability in the asbestos cases?
11. Suppose the plaintiff proves exposure to the asbestos products of five defendants, and the jury concludes that each was a "substantial factor" in causing his asbestosis. What would the plaintiff recover from each defendant?
12. Suppose that the evidence shows that Asbestos Products, Inc. contributed about 4 percent to the asbestos particles in the work area where the plaintiff worked during his years of exposure to asbestos. Should it be held liable to the plaintiff? Suppose it contributed one-tenth of 1 percent?

Comparing Causation

13. Five mining companies release saltwater into various streams that flow into Farmer Jones's pond. Over a period of time, the salt level rises to the point where his fish die.
    a. How is this like the asbestos cases?
    b. How would you argue that this is different from the asbestos cases?

CAUSATION IN TOXIC EXPOSURE CASES

A third thorny cause-in-fact problem arises in cases like the Agent Orange case, which involve exposure to toxic chemicals. The Agent Orange plaintiffs were veterans who were exposed to dioxin in Vietnam and subsequently developed a number of skin diseases they claimed were caused by the exposure. Medical science can sometimes establish that persons who have been exposed to toxic substances are more likely to contract certain diseases, but such evidence will not always establish causation in tort cases. Suppose, for example, that epidemiological studies demonstrate that individuals exposed to quasimegamethane are more likely to contract liver cancer. The studies might show, perhaps, that there are 10 cases of liver cancer per 100,000 among the general population, but 14 cases per 100,000 among those exposed to quasimegamethane. Suppose further that Wren was exposed to quasimegamethane and that he subsequently contracts liver cancer.

There are two problems with using this evidence to prove that quasimegamethane caused Wren's cancer. First, although liver cancer is *correlated with* exposure to quasimegamethane, this does not necessarily prove that quasimegamethane has the capacity to *cause* liver cancer. Here is a nice example to prove the point: Although production of pig iron in the United States and the birth rate in Great Britain followed the same linear increase, it is relatively clear that the one did not cause the other![5] Similarly, exposure to quasimegamethane could be correlated to liver cancer for many reasons, even though it did not cause the cancer. Perhaps the lives of factory workers are more stressful for economic reasons, so that they smoke more. Or perhaps they had poorer nutrition as children, and this increases their rate of liver cancer.

If studies are carefully done to correct for such extraneous factors, they may establish that quasimegamethane *can* cause liver cancer.[6] Doubtless, epidemiologists would accept strong correlations based on careful studies as proof of causal capacity. However, even assuming that the plaintiff establishes causal capacity, there remains the further question whether quasimegamethane caused *Wren's* cancer. The statistics given show that people also get liver cancer *without* being exposed to quasimegamethane. Indeed, of any 14 cancer victims in the group exposed to the toxin, presumably 10 contracted cancer from other causes: There is no reason to believe that the rate of cancer from background causes would be lower in the exposed group. Thus, even if quasimegamethane *can* cause liver cancer, this does not show that it *did* cause Wren's.

In the first two situations discussed in this chapter, the mechanism of harm was clear, but the identity of the proper defendant was problematic. In these cases, by contrast, the mechanism of harm is itself uncertain both on the general level ("Can quasimegamethane cause liver cancer?") and on the particular level ("Did quasimegamethane, rather than one of the other possible causes, cause Wren's cancer?"). This is a what-done-it problem, and a very difficult one indeed.

Sometimes the plaintiff in these cases can provide evidence to link her disease to a particular toxic agent. The medical evidence may establish that the agent can cause the disease, and that it runs a different course in patients who contract it from that agent, or that these patients have unique symptoms that support an inference that the agent induced it. She might show that the disease appears after an unusual latency period if it is caused by the defendant's chemical, and that hers did as well, or that the diseased cells

5. B. Black & D. Lilienteld, Epidemiologic Proof in Toxic Tort Litigation, 52 Fordham L. Rev. 732, 755 (1984) (citing G. Snedocor & W. Cochran, Statistical Methods 189 (6th ed. 1967)).
6. In the Agent Orange cases, the plaintiffs were ultimately unable to surmount even the first hurdle, proving that Agent Orange had the capacity to cause their illnesses.

actually look or act a little differently if they are caused by the chemical. Evidence of this sort allows the jury to infer that *this plaintiff* contracted the disease from the toxic exposure instead of other known causes for which the defendant is not responsible.

In other cases, however, the plaintiff is only able to show that she was exposed to a toxic chemical and that persons exposed to it contract the disease at an increased rate. Some courts would refuse to allow a jury to find the defendant liable based solely on such proof. Even if statistical evidence establishes a general causal relationship between the chemical and the disease, this does not establish that *this* plaintiff contracted the disease from the exposure. See, e.g., S. Gold, Causation in Toxic Torts: Burdens of Proof, Standards of Persuasion, and Statistical Evidence, 96 Yale L.J. 376, 379-380 (1986). If courts require "particularistic evidence" that the individual plaintiff's disease was caused by the chemical rather than background causes, the plaintiff may lose even though the exposure caused by the defendant substantially increased their risk of getting the disease.

This is a very tough problem. Some commentators have suggested a risk creation approach to it, analogous to *Sindell*'s approach to DES liability. Under this approach, the manufacturer would be liable to each liver cancer victim who had been exposed to quasimegamethane for a proportion of her damages, reflecting the probability that the exposure caused the disease. See, e.g., D. Rosenberg, The Causal Connection in Mass Exposure Cases: A "Public Law" Vision of the Tort System, 97 Harv. L. Rev. 849, 859 (1984) (advocating proportional liability in toxic exposure cases).

Most courts have not adopted a proportional approach, however, or automatically imposed or rejected liability based on statistical probabilities derived from epidemiological evidence. Instead, courts have generally admitted careful studies in evidence as relevant to the question whether the toxic substance is capable of causing the plaintiff's disease (general causation) and whether it actually did cause it (specific causation). Courts then look to expert testimony about the individual plaintiff that may undermine or strengthen the inference of causation based on the statistics. A plaintiff may bolster her case, for example, by showing (in addition to a statistical increase in disease due to exposure to the substance) that she lacks genetic factors suggesting alternative causes, that she has not engaged in other conduct (such as smoking) likely to lead to the disease, that she had extensive exposure to the toxic agent, or that the disease appeared within an expected "latency period" after exposure to the agent. Such testimony by the medical witnesses or experts may support an inference, beyond bare statistical likelihood, connecting the plaintiff's exposure to her injury. Courts are likely to find such "particularistic evidence" sufficient to allow the plaintiff's case on causation to go to the jury.

Examples

Science and Solomon

14. Quinn worked for 11 years at Acme Company's plant. During those years his hands often came into contact with the chemical pseudomonomethane. After he left Acme, he developed skin cancer on his hands. He believes that the cancer was caused by his exposure to pseudomonomethane. However, since pseudomonomethane is a rare chemical, no epidemiological studies have been done to determine whether it causes cancer. How will Quinn prove that Acme is liable?

15. Employees of Beta Corporation are exposed to quasimegamethane during their employment there, and later contract liver cancer. Suppose that a careful epidemiological study shows that exposure to quasimegamethane increases liver cancer rates by 40 percent. The disease strikes 10 people per 100,000 in the general population, but the study shows that 14 per 100,000 persons exposed to quasimegamethane contract liver cancer.
    a. If Nunez, one of the employees, sues for damages, should she be allowed to recover based on the study?
    b. Assume that the jurisdiction would not allow recovery to a plaintiff based on this evidence, unless she presented some proof that her individual disease was caused by quasimegamethane. If 14 Beta employees with liver cancer sued Beta and the study is the only evidence they have, how many would recover?
    c. Based on the scientific evidence, how many of these 14 plaintiffs can we deduce were harmed by exposure to quasimegamethane?
    d. If we view deterrence and compensation as major goals of the tort system, what is the problem with denying recovery to these plaintiffs?

16. Suppose we allow each of the plaintiffs in Example 16 to prove her case based on the study, and send each case to the jury with a "substantial factor" instruction. What should the jury do? What would you do if you were on the jury?

17. What would happen in these 14 cases if we used a percentage-risk approach to the problem, under which each plaintiff recovers in proportion to the risk that her disease was caused by Beta's conduct?

Double Indemnity

18. Suppose that the epidemiology study shows that exposure to quasimegamethane increases the risk of liver cancer by more than two? Suppose, for example, that there are 10 cases per 100,000 in the general

population, but 23 cases per 100,000 in the population of persons exposed to quasimegamethane. If 14 employees sued Beta for causing their cancer, how many would likely recover?

19. Suppose that Nunez produces a credible expert who testifies, with supporting evidence from the medical literature and her own experience, that liver cancer, when caused by quasimegamethane, attacks a particular part of the liver and follows an unusual disease pattern. Surgery shows that Nunez's disease follows this pattern. However, assume that the epidemiological studies indicate that quasimegamethane only increases the risk of liver cancer by 20 percent. Should Nunez be allowed to get to the jury on the issue of whether quasimegamethane caused her disease?

CAUSATION IN LOSS-OF-A-CHANCE CASES

Another difficult cause-in-fact problem is illustrated by medical malpractice cases in which the defendant's negligence has reduced a plaintiff's chances of survival or cure. In *Herskovits v. Group Health Cooperative of Puget Sound,* 664 P.2d 474 (Wash. 1983), for example, the decedent died of lung cancer. The evidence indicated that he had a 39 percent chance of surviving with prompt diagnosis of his cancer, but that the defendant's negligent delay in diagnosing it reduced his survival chance to 25 percent. The suit was for wrongful death.

Naturally, the defendant in cases like this will argue that he did not "cause" the harm. It is impossible to say that Herskovits would have lived but for the delay in diagnosis since, even if his cancer had been promptly diagnosed, chances were better than even (61/39) that he would have died.

This loss-of-a-chance causation problem, like other "but for" dilemmas, requires the factfinder to compare what did happen to what would have happened if the defendant had not been negligent. This is a very speculative endeavor: The statistics suggest that the outcome *might* have been different absent the defendant's negligence, but probably would not have been.[7] Yet the plaintiff takes little solace from these cold statistics. She still feels she has lost something very valuable, a significant chance that her husband would still be with her. In *Herskovits*, for example, the late diagnosis deprived the decedent of a 14 percent chance to survive.

The majority in *Herskovits* held that the causation issue should go to the jury under a "substantial factor" instruction. That is, the jury would be

7. Even Solomon with his time machine couldn't help much with this one. Going back to watch the events wouldn't answer the real question: What *would have happened* if the doctor had diagnosed the cancer at an earlier stage?

asked, based on this statistical evidence, to decide whether the late diagnosis contributed to the decedent's death or whether he would have died even if diagnosed immediately. This is not a very satisfactory solution to a vexing problem: How can the jury possibly place Herskovits in the 14 percent group that would have lived with earlier diagnosis, as opposed to the 61 percent who were doomed either way? The substantial factor approach simply licenses the jury to find for the plaintiff on intuitive grounds, despite the likelihood that the negligence did not change the outcome.[8]

There is an obvious relationship between this loss-of-a-chance problem and the toxic chemicals problem just discussed. There, the epidemiological evidence established an increased risk of harm, but could not show whether the chemical had injured the individual plaintiff. Here, the statistical survival evidence establishes that the defendant's negligence decreased the plaintiff's chance of survival, but cannot resolve the issue of whether she would have survived if promptly diagnosed.

Here, as there, some scholars have suggested a proportional approach to the problem: If a defendant reduced the decedent's chance of survival by 15 percent, she should be held liable for 15 percent of the wrongful death damages. See J. King, Causation, Valuation, and Chance in Personal Injury Torts Involving Preexisting Conditions and Future Consequences, 90 Yale L.J. 1353 (1981). In this group of cases, unlike the toxic exposure cases, this percentage solution has caught on with the courts. A good many have chosen to treat the injury as the *lost chance*, and allow the jury to value the damages in proportion to the chance lost due to the defendant's negligence.

This solution is subject to the same objection here as in the toxic exposure cases: It overcompensates in every case in which the decedent would have died anyway, and undercompensates in every case where the delayed diagnosis caused the death. The examples below explore the implications of the loss-of-a-chance approach.

Examples

Chance Occurrences

20. Sven goes to Dr. Kildare complaining of indigestion and tightness of the chest. Kildare negligently fails to diagnose a heart attack. Later that day, Sven goes to the emergency room and is diagnosed and treated for a heart attack. However, he dies three days later.

    The medical testimony establishes that Sven had a 40 percent chance of recovery had he been diagnosed when he first saw Kildare. However, by the time he went to the emergency room, the progress

8. Although the substantial factor approach appears logically dubious, it continues to gain some adherents. See *Estate of Frey v. Mastroianni*, 463 P.3d 1197 (HA 2020).

of the heart attack had reduced his chance of recovery to 15 percent. Sven's survivors sue Kildare for wrongful death.

a. If the court retains the traditional "but for" approach to causation, how will the case come out?
b. If the court sends the case to the jury under a "substantial factor" instruction, how will it come out?
c. If the court applies the "lost-chance" approach to the case, how will it come out?

21. Assume that Dr. Kildare made the same mistake on 100 patients, and the survivors of the patients who died sued in each case.
    a. How many would recover under the traditional causation standard?
    b. How many would recover under the loss-of-chance approach?

22. Assume that the medical testimony is that Sven would have had a 60 percent chance of recovery with prompt treatment, which was reduced to 40 percent due to the delay. Sven dies and his family sues Kildare. What will happen if the court applies the traditional causation standard?

Judge Fudd's Dilemma

23. Yamato goes to Dr. Kildare, complaining of a lump in her breast. Kilclare fails to take a biopsy. Later, after the lump has grown, Yamato goes to Doctor Rivera, who finds an advanced malignant tumor. The tumor is removed, and no sign of cancer is found in the surrounding tissue. However, Rivera advises Yamato that, because of the advanced stage of the tumor, she has a 50 percent risk of a recurrence. Had the tumor been taken out earlier (when she went to Kildare), the risk would have been 20 percent. Yamato sues Kildare, in a jurisdiction that has adopted the lost-chance approach to damages, seeking recovery for the increased risk of a recurrence due to Kildare's late diagnosis. Should the Honorable Fudd dismiss the case?

Explanations

Share, or Share Alike?

1. Obviously, the jury should find Acme liable for her full damages (assuming, of course, that they find Acme was negligent) and dismiss the claims against the other manufacturers. The market share theory provides a back-up alternative where the plaintiff cannot prove which maker caused the harm. If the jury finds that one defendant caused it, that defendant should pay, and the others should not.

2. Under *Sindell*, where the plaintiff sues defendants representing "a substantial share" of the market, they are liable in proportion to their market

shares, unless a defendant proves that it did not sell DES in the relevant market. Since D4 has made that showing, it is not liable. The other three, however, are liable for their market shares.

So what do they pay? There are two possibilities: They could each pay an appropriate proportion of $100,000, the total damages. Under this approach, Dl would pay 10/60ths of $100,000, D2 would pay 20/60ths, and D3 would pay 30/60ths. Sindell would recover fully, though she only sued four makers, and there are many more out there who could have supplied the drug.

Alternatively, *Sindell* may be interpreted to require each defendant to pay its market share percentage times the total damages. Here are the numbers:

Dl pays 10 percent of $100,000	=	$10,000
D2 pays 20 percent of $100,000	=	$20,000
D3 pays 30 percent of $100,000	=	$30,000
Sindell recovers		$60,000

It was unclear after *Sindell* which of these methods the California Supreme Court intended. In *Brown v. Superior Court of San Francisco*, 751 P.2d 470 (Cal. 1988), the court opted for the second. Under this approach, plaintiff does not recover her full damages, because the defendants found liable do not absorb the market shares of absent defendants.

3. The point of *Sindell* is that each maker would pay in proportion to the risk it created by marketing DES. Each is only *severally* liable for its share of the market; it is not liable for other defendants' shares. Thus, if D2 cannot pay, plaintiff loses this part of the judgment.

4. The first problem you would face is defining the market. Is the market the particular pharmacy plaintiff's mother bought from? The town where she lived? The metropolitan area? Or the state? The individual pharmacy seems like the best choice, but this information may not be available. If a local area is used, there will be serious proof problems: For example, many drug makers may have sold DES to wholesalers, who redistributed the drug to pharmacies. They may have filled orders with DES from various manufacturers, and may well have no remaining records of what was sold where. The same proof problems are likely if a state market area is used. To make matters worse, the plaintiff's mother may have bought the drug in a distant state. Thus, actually *proving* a market area under *Sindell* could be extremely complicated and expensive.[9] Doubtless, this entered into the thinking of the New York Court of Appeals in choosing a national

9. "The administrative costs of determining each defendant's market share have been distressingly disproportionate to the compensation provided." Restatement (Third) of Torts: Liability for Physical and Emotional Harm §28 cmt. p.

market area. The total national sales of various makers will be easier to reconstruct. And, once it has been done in a few cases, the parties in later cases will likely stipulate the market shares, thus dramatically simplifying the trial of most market share cases.

Absent Tortfeasors

5. Yes, it is. Even though Acme conclusively establishes that it could not have caused the plaintiff's injury, it will pay 10 percent of her damages. New York has chosen to impose damages based on the amount of risk each maker created, *nationally*, even where it is clear that some of them created no risk to the plaintiff personally or to New Yorkers. That is why defendants cannot exonerate themselves under *Hymowitz* by showing that they did not make the drug taken by the plaintiff's mother.

6. This example introduces another problem posed by the market share approach: Manufacturers entered and left the market for DES at various times. Here, Acme created a risk of DES injuries, but not at the time the plaintiff's mother ingested the drug. If a court decides to base liability on risk creation, rather than specific causation of the plaintiff's injury, it seems that Acme ought to pay in this case. Under *Hymowitz*, it pays even if it was not in the market at the particular *place* where the drug was sold. Why shouldn't it pay here, even though it was not in the market at a particular *time*, so long as it contributed to the overall risk posed by the sale of DES? As the *Hymowitz* court held, "[W]e choose to apportion liability so as to correspond to the overall culpability of each defendant, measured by the amount of risk of injury each defendant created to the public-at-large." 541 N.Y.S.2d at 950.

   If we are looking to the "overall culpability" of each defendant, it seems we ought to look at the total DES sold by each defendant over the entire period DES was marketed, and convert that to a percentage of the total DES sold by all makers during that entire period. Acme would pay that percentage, even though it did not sell DES at the time plaintiff's mother took it. Under this logic, Acme could be held liable, though it never sold DES in New York and never sold it anywhere when plaintiff's mother took the drug.

7. Phi Corporation owes nothing. By proving it did not participate in the Washington market at the relevant time, it establishes that it did not cause the plaintiff's injury. In Washington (unlike in New York), this bars recovery.

   Beta owes the plaintiff 6 percent of her damages. Under the Washington scheme, makers who prove their market shares pay in proportion to those shares.

The dicey part of the analysis concerns Acme and Gamma. Since they have not presented proof of their market shares, they are presumed to have equal market shares, and to have the entire market except for Beta's 6 percent. Thus, they are each presumed to have 47 percent of the market (one half of 94 percent). Each will pay 47 percent of the plaintiff's damages.

Note several points about this: First, under the Washington approach, the plaintiff doesn't bear the burden of proof on market share; the defendants do. If they don't shoulder that burden, they are presumed to have equal shares of the market. Second, unlike in California, the plaintiff recovers fully since the market shares of defendants who don't prove their actual share expand to cover the shares of makers who were not sued. Third, in Washington a plaintiff can sue just one maker. Defendants then have a strong incentive to implead other makers, to reduce their presumptive market shares.

8. Here, the defendants have overcome the presumption of equal shares, so each would pay according to its market share. Acme would pay 15 percent of the plaintiff's damages, Beta 6 percent, Gamma 10 percent, and Phi would pay nothing. Plaintiff would recover only 31 percent of her damages. However, if she could locate one defendant unable to establish its market share, that defendant would be liable for the remaining 69 percent.

Substances and Substantial Factors

9. These cases are closer to *Anderson* than to *Summers*. In *Summers* there was only one cause, but the plaintiff was unable to prove which hunter it was. In *Anderson*, there were two sufficient causes of the harm, and the defendant argued that he should get off because the plaintiff would have suffered the same harm if his fire had not been present. The harm was "overdetermined," in the sense that, if the one fire hadn't caused it, the other would have.

   Similarly, in the asbestos exposure cases, the plaintiff's injury is also overdetermined. If any one defendant's asbestos had not been at the worksite, the others would probably have sufficed to cause the plaintiff's disease anyway. The problem is, if we let any one defendant off the hook on this basis, they all get off. *Anderson's* substantial factor approach avoids that unpalatable result.

10. In the DES cases, all defendants marketed exactly the same product, and the plaintiff's mothers (presumably) only took one defendant's pill. The problem is simply identifying which defendant made the offending product. It can be said, with approximate fairness, that each created risk to the public in direct proportion to its market share.

In the asbestos cases, however, the plaintiff's injury was usually caused by cumulative exposure to the asbestos in the products of several defendants. In addition, asbestos products are quite different, and impose quite different risks. For example, in some products the asbestos is permanently fixed in tiles or other adhesives, and is seldom released into the atmosphere. In others, however, the particles are "friable," that is, easily broken up and released, posing a much greater risk.

Last, asbestos exposure takes place over time, often decades. Over such long periods asbestos products entered and left the market, or a particular workplace. Thus, it would be virtually impossible to reconstruct a single "market" for asbestos. For these reasons, courts have generally rejected market share analysis in asbestos cases.

11. If the jurisdiction retains joint and several liability, under which each defendant that caused the harm is fully liable, the plaintiff could recover his entire damages from any one of the five defendants.[10] This is in marked contrast to market share liability, which holds each defendant severally liable only in proportion to its percentage of the market.

12. Under the substantial factor standard, this defendant probably could be held liable. Most courts have not set a threshold minimal percentage requirement for finding a defendant liable under the substantial factor test. Indeed, it would be hard to ascertain such a percentage, given the variety of asbestos products involved, the differences in their toxicity, and the great difficulty in reconstructing working conditions decades after the fact. Some courts have required the plaintiff to establish that they worked regularly in proximity to the defendant's product to get to the jury against that defendant. See, e.g., *Sholtis v. American Cyanamid Co.*, 568 A.2d 1196, 1206-1208 (N.J. Super. Ct. App. Div. 1989). Other courts have rejected even this requirement, in light of evidence that a minimal exposure can cause asbestosis.[11]

    At some point, however, a defendant's contribution to the risk may become so small that it is inappropriate to hold it liable, even though it did contribute to the risk that caused the injury. The substantial factor test allows the jury to reach that result; they can simply conclude, if Asbestos Products contributed one-tenth of 1 percent of the asbestos, that its product was not a "substantial factor" in causing the plaintiff's disease, and render a verdict in its favor.

---

10. In most states, if Defendant #1 paid the judgment, it would have a right to contribution from the other defendants, so that the judgment would be redistributed among them all.

11. See B. D. Masi, Comment, The Threshold Level of Proof of Asbestos Causation: The "Frequency, Regularity and Proximity Test" and a Modified *Summers v. Tice* Theory of Burden-Shifting, 24 Cap. U. L. Rev. 735, 748-751 (1995).

The Third Restatement of Torts would reach the same result by a different analysis. It would conclude that such a trivial contribution to the risk is not a legal cause of the resulting harm. Thus, it would reject liability on proximate cause grounds rather than actual cause grounds. The drafters reason that this defendant's product may in fact be an actual cause, though a minor one. The reason to exonerate Asbestos Products is that its conduct was a trivial contributing factor, which is a judgment about the appropriate contours of legal responsibility, not a judgment about factual causation. See Restatement (Third) of Torts: Liability for Physical and Emotional Harm §36 and illus. 1.

Comparing Causation

13. a. This case is like the asbestos exposure cases, in that all the defendants have contributed to the exposure that caused the plaintiff's harm. All released salt into Jones's pond, though perhaps in varying amounts.
    b. In the asbestos cases, any one of the defendants' asbestos could have caused the harm even if the others were not present. We don't know—and never will—which defendant's asbestos actually caused it, or if they all did together. In this case, by contrast, the facts suggest that the harm resulted from the *cumulative* exposure to salt, so we can say that they all contributed to cause an indivisible harm: When the combined discharges reached a certain level, the fish died. Thus, the defendants would probably all be liable even under a "but for" standard.

Science and Solomon

14. Quinn probably won't recover from Acme. He bears the burden of proof, yet the evidence to tie the chemical to his disease simply doesn't exist. Scientists can't study everything, and they simply haven't gotten around to pseudomonomethane. In the absence of proof that it causes cancer, it is hard to see how Quinn can win, even if the chemical really did cause it.

    As the introduction suggests, Quinn will probably offer medical testimony that his cancer was caused by exposure to pseudomonomethane. Although courts have noted that scientific studies are not always necessary to support a finding of causation (*Ferebee v. Chevron Chemical Co.*, 736 F. 2d 1529, 1535-1536 (D.C. Cir. 1984)), Quinn's expert will have to support her view on some accepted medical basis. If she could show that the symptoms are different if linked to pseudomonomethane, that would allow an inference of causation. But they probably aren't, or if they are, no one has shown that they are since there are no studies on the drug. She might make the causal link by showing that the disease progresses differently, or appears sooner, or whatever, but how will she make such a showing without supporting scientific studies?

How about the fact that Quinn's disease appeared after his exposure to pseudomonomethane, and in the area where he sustained that exposure: Would that suffice to allow the jury to infer causation? Probably not, since this is a "post hoc, ergo proper hoc" argument: Because it occurred after the exposure, it must have been caused by the exposure. The argument has some force, but may not suffice to make a prima facie case. See, e.g., *Conde v.Velsicol Chemical Corp.*, 804 F. Supp. 972, 1020-1023 (S.D. Ohio 1992), in which the plaintiffs showed that their home was treated with Chlordane, that they became sick after the exposure, and that their symptoms abated when they moved out of the house. The court held that they had not established that Chlordane caused their injuries, in the absence of medical evidence that Chlordane could cause the symptoms they alleged. But see *Alder v. Bayer Corp.*, 61 P.3d 1068, 1089-1090 (Utah 2002) (temporal sequence, together with other evidence, supported proof of causation).

15. a. Here, there is no individual proof that any plaintiff's disease was caused by quasimegamethane, as opposed to the general background causes of liver cancer. Solomon might be able to go back and find the answer, but logically there is no way for the jury, based on the study, to conclude that Nunez's disease was more likely caused by quasimegamethane than by the other, nontortious causes of the disease. Indeed, chances are 10 out of 14 that it was caused by something other than the defendant's conduct. If the only proof before the court was the statistical increase, it seems that a verdict should be directed for Beta.
    b. If particularized proof is needed, none of these plaintiffs will recover. Each plaintiff will face the same problem, lack of individualized proof that *her disease* resulted from the defendant's conduct. The 40 percent increase in disease associated with exposure to quasimegamethane is not sufficient (even in a purely statistical sense) to establish that any plaintiff's disease was "more probably than not" caused by the exposure. (To establish that, as a matter of statistics, the increase would have to exceed 100 percent; exposure would have to more than double the risk of contracting the disease.)
    c. The studies support an inference that 4 out of every 14 cases of liver cancer in persons exposed to quasimegamethane are caused by that exposure (the 14 cases minus the 10 expected from general causes). Thus, statistically speaking, we can say that 4 of these plaintiffs' injuries were caused by Beta's conduct.
    d. If each of these plaintiffs loses her case for lack of particularized proof that her cancer was caused by the chemical, neither of these

goals is served. Refusing recovery to each of these plaintiffs will lead to "under-deterrence" of tortious conduct since Beta caused four cases of liver cancer, but is held liable for none. In addition, four deserving plaintiffs who suffered injury from Beta's conduct go without compensation.

16. This is not a viable solution to the causation enigma. There is simply no way for the jury to reach a reasoned verdict using a substantial factor test. They should probably, if acting rationally, find for the defendant in each case since there is no logical way to conclude that its conduct probably caused any one of these cases of liver cancer.

    More likely, they will find for the plaintiffs in all 14 cases since Beta was negligent and caused harm to some. If so, then Beta's conduct will be overdeterred since they probably only caused 4 cases of the disease. In addition, the 10 plaintiffs who contracted the disease from background causes instead of quasimegamethane will be overcompensated.

17. Under this approach, the manufacturer should pay each plaintiff 4/14ths of her damages. If each plaintiff suffered $100,000 in damages, each would recover $28,571.

    Arguably the manufacturer would pay the "right" amount in damages under this formula. The study shows that it caused 4 of these cases of liver cancer, for a total in damages of $400,000. It ended up paying 14 plaintiffs $28,571 each, which comes out to $400,000. Thus, this approach works well in terms of deterrence.

    However, it does not work so well in serving tort law's compensatory purpose. Ten of these plaintiffs collect $28,571 too much, while four of them (those actually harmed by defendant's chemical) collect $71,429 too little.

Double Indemnity

18. In this example, the study shows that exposure to the chemical more than doubles the risk of contracting liver cancer. Thus, the jury can reasonably conclude—at least statistically speaking—that it is more probable than not that the exposure caused each plaintiff's disease. It seems likely that a court would allow the jury to find for each of the 14 plaintiffs on this evidence. See, e.g., *Merrell Dow Pharmaceuticals, Inc. v. Havner*, 953 S.W.2d 706, 715-719 (Tex. 1997); see generally Restatement (Third) of Torts: Liability for Physical and Emotional Harm §28 cmt. c(4).

    This result is not inexorable, however. The plaintiff has still only presented purely statistical proof, not any evidence about her own disease. Some courts would probably still deny recovery, absent particularized proof about each individual plaintiff's disease, such as testimony about the extent, nature, and duration of the plaintiff's exposure to quasimegamethane, the exact nature and timing of each plaintiff's symptoms, or the absence of other risk factors for the disease.

If the court allows each plaintiff to recover based on the study alone, the defendant will pay some plaintiffs who did not get the disease from exposure to its chemical. Presumably some of these cases (roughly 10 out of 23) were caused by other causes, not by quasimegamethane.

19. In the last example, the statistical evidence demonstrated that exposure to quasimegamethane more than doubled the risk of contracting liver cancer. In this example, however, the studies alone would certainly not support a finding that Nunez "more probably than not" contracted the disease from exposure to quasimegamethane, since exposure only increases the risk of liver cancer by 20 percent.

But here, while the statistics suggest that exposure to quasimegamethane only increases the risk of getting liver cancer by 20 percent, Nunez has evidence that strongly suggests that she is one of that 20 percent. The fact that the disease originated in an unusual spot, and followed an unusual pattern characteristic of quasimegamethane poisoning, provides "particularistic" evidence that Nunez contracted liver cancer from that chemical. Even if the studies suggest that people exposed to quasimegamethane are not very likely to contract liver cancer, they also support a conclusion that the agent is *capable of causing* liver cancer, and does so in about 20 percent of the cases. And Nunez has clinical evidence suggesting that it did lead to her disease. Thus, even though exposure to quasimegamethane does not "double the risk," her diagnostic evidence, together with the epidemiological evidence of "general causation," would likely suffice to make a submissible case that exposure to quasimegamethane caused her disease.

Chance Occurrences

20. a. Under the traditional approach, Sven's survivors would not recover. The chances are better than even (60 percent) that he would have died even if Kildare had diagnosed him immediately. Thus, a jury could not rationally conclude that it is "more probable than not" (the standard of proof in a civil case) that Sven would have survived with prompt treatment. If the medical evidence is to be believed, he probably wouldn't have.

b. Who knows what the jury will do if the judge instructs them under the substantial factor test? They may take a sober look at the case, conclude that he probably would have died even if treated immediately, and find for Kildare. But they may also decide that Kildare injured Sven by depriving him of a very significant chance of recovery, and find Kildare liable. If they do, it appears, based on the majority opinion in *Herskovits*, that Kildare would be liable for full wrongful death damages.

c. Under the lost-chance approach, the jury would determine the chance that Sven lost due to Kildare's negligence, and value that. To do this, they would determine full wrongful death damages and discount them by the percentage chance Sven lost due to Kildare's negligence. If damages for his death were $100,000, they would find Kildare liable for $25,000 (25 percent × $100,000), because Kildare's late diagnosis deprived Sven of a 25 percent chance of recovery.

21. a. Presumably, all plaintiffs would lose because none can show that their decedent's death was more probably than not due to the negligence of Kildare, since in each case the chance of dying was 60 percent before the patient sought treatment. The irony, of course, is that with a hundred cases, we can say (with statistical confidence, anyway) that Kildare caused 25 deaths.

b. Under the lost-chance approach, the survivor in each suit would recover $25,000 (assuming, again, that damages in each case were $100,000). There will be 85 suits (remember, statistically speaking, 15 percent of Kildare's victims will survive even with delayed diagnosis). Kildare will pay $25,000 × 85, or $2,125,000 in damages.

If we could identify the 25 patients who died due to delayed diagnosis, each family would recover $100,000 from Kildare. So he would pay 25 × $100,000, or $2.5 million. So he saves a little, but pays something like the full damages he has caused.

Once again, however, the approach looks dubious in light of tort law's compensatory goals. If all 100 families sue, 60 of them recover $25,000, even though Kildare caused no harm to their decedents—the 60 who would have died even with prompt diagnosis. The other 25 families, who have each suffered $100,000 in damages, recover only a quarter of that.

22. a. Under traditional causation analysis, Sven's family apparently would be able to recover full wrongful death damages in this case. If Sven had been diagnosed promptly, he would have had a better than even chance of recovery (60 percent), but he died with late diagnosis. It appears that, prior to the development of the loss-of-chance doctrine, most courts would have sent this case to a jury under a traditional "but for" causation instruction. See, e.g., *Wilson v. Horton*, 2004 WL 2913562 (loss-of-chance theory inapplicable where initial chance of survival was 60 percent).

However, note that in this example Kildare deprived Sven of a smaller chance of recovery than in the prior examples. It is at least quizzical that Sven's family would only be entitled to a percentage recovery in Example 20c000, yet here, because the numbers hover around the 50 percent mark, his family recovers full wrongful death damages.[12] At least one court has recognized that it is awkward to allow full recovery in a case like this, and opted for a lost-chance approach even though the initial chance of recovery exceeded 50 percent. See *DeBurkarte v. Louvar*, 393 N.W.2d 131, 137-138 (Iowa 1986).

Judge Fudd's Dilemma

In this example, the plaintiff has incurred a 30 percent increased risk of *future* harm due to Kildare's negligence. However, she has not yet sustained the injury itself, just incurred the risk. How can the plaintiff sue without having suffered an injury?

If a court adopts the loss-of-chance approach to cases like those just discussed, it is really compensating the plaintiff for incurring the risk, not for the disease itself. Thus, it ought not to matter that the risk is a future risk instead of a past risk. In both cases, the injury is the exposure to risk. To be consistent, shouldn't Judge Fudd allow Yamato to recover 30 percent of the damages she would incur from a recurrence of the cancer?

The cases in this chapter illustrate that some courts have recognized risk exposure as a harm in several contexts. Yamato's counsel should argue that she has incurred an increased risk of future disease, and is entitled to recovery for that harm. See, e.g., *Cudone v. Gebret*, 821 F. Supp. 266 (D. Del. 1993) (approving submission of an increased risk claim to the jury under Delaware law).

Many courts would probably refuse to do this, even if they had adopted the lost-chance approach. After all, the plaintiff has not suffered the actual underlying harm—malignancy—just a risk of it. These courts might hold Yamato's suit premature, but allow her to sue later if her cancer recurs. Then, the case becomes a regular lost-chance case.

What would happen if the court allowed recovery, and then Yamato later did have a recurrence? Presumably, she would be barred from a second action, under traditional principles of res judicata. Even if she could bring one, presumably her recovery should be a loss-of-chance recovery (since the late diagnosis only increased the risk by 30 percent) and she would already have received that in her earlier action.

---

12. If we assume that Kildare reduced the chances of recovery of 100 patients from 60 to 40 percent, the families of all who died—there should be 60 of them—would recover under the traditional standard. Statistically speaking, however, he would only have injured 20 patients.

CHAPTER 12

Drawing a Line Somewhere: Proximate Cause

INTRODUCTION

One of the nice things about the inch is that virtually everyone who has anything to do with one agrees about what it is. While it is a purely human construct, an *idea*, we have achieved such wide consensus about its meaning that we can use the term effectively without wasting energy arguing about its definition. This is probably true for the vast majority of concepts we manipulate through language. If it weren't, language wouldn't communicate much and people would rebel and vote in a new one.

Unfortunately, proximate cause is the exception that proves the rule (please excuse the pun). A great deal of confusion persists about what the term "proximate cause" is meant to convey. Students find this very frustrating: Justifiably, you would like some answers, some solid ground on which to base an understanding of a difficult concept.

Yet, if exact definition eludes us (as it does, of course, for other useful concepts, like "negligence" or "justice"), we can still achieve a working knowledge of the problem sufficient for most purposes. This chapter seeks such a working knowledge of "proximate cause."

THE CRUX OF THE PROBLEM

Despite differences in approach to proximate cause, all courts agree that the crux of the problem is that defendants cannot be held liable for every consequence of their conduct, even if that conduct is negligent. Here are a few examples in which courts would likely balk at imposing liability:[1]

- Defendant store owner leaves a box lid on the sidewalk. Plaintiff stumbles over it, skins her knee, and stops to get first aid. Consequently, she misses her train and gets a later one. She is injured when that train crashes into another at a crossing.
- Defendant, a short-order cook, leaves a box of rat poison on a shelf near the stove that is used to store food. Although the cook had no reason to expect it, the poison explodes due to heat from the stove, injuring a customer.
- Defendant drives negligently, and collides with plaintiff, causing him injuries. Plaintiff is taken to the hospital, where he is further injured three days later when the hospital burns.
- Defendant leaves his car unlocked, with the keys in the ignition. A terrorist steals the car, loads it with explosives, and sets off an explosion at a foreign embassy, injuring a passerby.

In each of these cases, the defendant was negligent, and in each, that negligence was on actual cause of the resulting harm. Yet most courts, perhaps all, would deny recovery, on the ground that the plaintiff's injury is too unusual, too far removed from the type of harm to be anticipated from the defendant's negligence to warrant imposing liability.

It is important to emphasize at the outset that this is not based on a lack of *actual* causation. If the only issue were cause-in-fact, the defendant would likely pay in all of the examples since her conduct was a necessary antecedent of the plaintiff's harm in each. If the store owner had not left out the box lid, the pedestrian would have gotten the earlier train and would not have been injured in the crash; if the restaurant owner had not placed the poison on the shelf, it would not have exploded, and so on. Indeed, unless actual causation is found, there is no need to consider issues of proximate cause at all. If the defendant was not a cause-in-fact of the harm, the court will dismiss the case without reaching the complex policy question of whether liability should follow. For this reason, courts often describe the proximate cause problem as one of "legal cause," or "scope of liability" to emphasize that the issue is whether, as a matter of policy, liability should be imposed,

1. Many of the examples in this chapter are drawn from cases discussed in Judge Robert Keeton's helpful book, Legal Cause in the Law of Torts (1963).

not whether the defendant's act was a cause-in-fact of the plaintiff's harm. "An actual cause question asks, 'What happened?'; a legal cause question asks, 'What shall be done about it?'" C. Morris, On the Teaching of Legal Cause, 39 Colum. L. Rev. 1087, 1089 (1939).

Certainly, courts must impose some further limit on liability, apart from the cause-in-fact requirement. Otherwise it is too easy to come up with absurd hypotheticals. Reynolds, not looking where he is going, bumps Carpenter on the sidewalk, knocking her down. Carpenter then walks to the corner and meets Dias, an old boyfriend, crossing the other way. They have dinner, end up at Dias's apartment, and Carpenter contracts a venereal disease. Reynolds's negligence is a necessary historical antecedent of the harm; had he not delayed Carpenter, she would not have spotted Dias, and so on. Yet no system could countenance holding Reynolds liable for Carpenter's disease. As a matter of policy, the relation between the negligence and the injury is too tenuous, the consequence too far removed from the fault, to make Reynolds pay.

Here's another example that makes the point. A doctor negligently performs a vasectomy. As a result, the patient later fathers a child. At the age of six, the child sets fire to the plaintiff's garage.[2] Here, as in the last case, the doctor's negligence is clearly a "but for" cause of the plaintiff's loss. If he had done the operation right, the patient could not have conceived a child, etc. If the defendant were held liable for all injuries caused by her negligence, the doctor would pay here. But no court would hold the doctor liable for this. All courts agree that a line must be drawn, *somewhere*, to limit liability for the consequences of a negligent act. The problem, of course, is how to define that limit.

EFFORTS TO DEFINE PROXIMATE CAUSE

Courts have labored for over a century to articulate such a definition, to draw a defensible line between consequences of negligence that are actionable and others too remote to support liability. Perhaps it is a mistake to try; proximate cause decisions, even within a single jurisdiction, often appear inconsistent or hard to predict based on previous precedents. It may be like pornography, of which Justice Stewart said that perhaps he could not define it, but "I know it when I see it." *Jacobellis v. Ohio*, 378 U.S. 184, 197 (1964). Most courts, however, have felt obliged to try to define some proximate cause limits, in order to guide litigants and lower courts in future cases.

2. This example is taken from Dobbs' Law of Torts §198.

A. An Early Approach: The Direct Cause Test of *In Re Polemis*

An early proximate cause case, *In Re Polemis and Furness, Withy & Co.*, 3 K.B. 560 (1921), held that the defendant is liable if his conduct is the "direct cause" of the plaintiff's injury, as opposed to a "remote" cause. In *Polemis*, a workman dropped a board into the hold of the plaintiff's ship, which caused a spark and ignited petrol vapors in the hold, destroying the ship. Although the explosion was deemed unforeseeable, the court held that the defendant was liable since the negligent act of its employee was the "direct cause" of the harm. Although the English court questioned *Polemis* in *Overseas Tankship (U.K.) Ltd. v. Morts Dock & Engineering Co., Ltd. (The Wagon Mound)*, A.C. 388 (1961), direct cause language still appears in some proximate cause cases.

The problem with the direct cause test is that it is "not responsive to the decisions either as a test of inclusion or exclusion." W. Seavey, Mr. Justice Cardozo and the Law of Torts, 52 Harv. L. Rev. 372, 389 (1939). In other words, it simply does not explain the results in real cases. It is often more restrictive than the cases: Since "directness" suggests the lack of a later cause after the defendant's negligence, it suggests that liability would be cut off where subsequent conduct contributes to the accident. Yet courts often conclude that the defendant should be liable despite intervening forces. For example, where one driver is negligent and another then negligently fails to avoid the accident, the first driver would typically be held liable, even though a later, independent act of the other driver also led to the accident. But if this is direct, just what does direct mean?

In other cases, we would all agree that the defendant's act led directly to the harm, yet we would not think she should be held liable. The act of the short-order cook in leaving the rat poison near the stove appears to be a direct cause of the explosion in that case. The placement of the poison led it to become hot and blow up. Yet many courts would be uncomfortable imposing liability for that unexpected consequence of the cook's negligence. Thus, it is hard to escape the conclusion that "direct" is just a word rather than a method of analysis. It does not in itself help judges or juries to draw the line between consequences the defendant should be held responsible for and others he should not.

B. Perhaps as Good as It Gets: Foreseeability/Scope of the Risk

Perhaps the most helpful approach to proximate cause considers whether the defendant, at the time that he acted, could foresee the risk that injured the plaintiff. Under this foreseeability/scope-of-the-risk approach, the court considers what the risks were that made the defendant's conduct negligent in the first place. If the defendant should have anticipated a particular risk at the time he acted, and he negligently failed to avert that risk, he would be liable if that risk caused the plaintiff's harm.

The Third Restatement of Torts rather nicely articulates this approach:

> **Section 29. Limitations on Liability for Tortious Conduct**
> An actor's liability is limited to those harms that result from the risks that made the actor's conduct tortious.[3]

In other words, an actor is negligent for ignoring foreseeable risks. When those risks cause injury, liability follows because ignoring those risks was negligent. But if some bizarre result happens, a risk that a reasonable person would not have foreseen, the actor is not liable, because failing to avoid a risk you would not foresee was not negligent. The Third Restatement, by the way, generally avoids the phrase "proximate cause." Instead, it refers to the "scope of liability," which is certainly a more accurate expression for the concept covered in this chapter.

For example, in the terrorist bombing case, a reasonable driver should realize that leaving the keys in the car creates a risk that children would be injured tampering with the car, that a thief would take it and drive negligently, or that vandals would damage it. But it hardly seems that the reasonable person should foresee a terrorist using the car to dynamite an embassy. Under the scope-of-the-risk approach, the defendant would not be liable, since the risk that caused the harm was not a risk he should have anticipated when he committed the negligent act.

Similarly, where a driver drives too fast, she should foresee that a collision could follow, injuring another motorist. But only the most bleakly neurotic pessimist who drove too fast would anticipate that her victim would be injured in a hospital fire three days later.

This foreseeability/scope-of-the-risk approach to proximate cause has the virtue that it provides an analytical basis for consistent decision-making. It relates the scope of liability to the faulty aspect of the defendant's conduct, and gives us a question to ask about that conduct rather than relying on a phrase like "direct cause" or an intuitive guess in limiting liability. The judge or jury can ask what unreasonable risks the defendant should have anticipated at the time she acted, and compare those risks to the injury that actually occurred.

Here's a little torts role-play you can use to apply this scope-of-the-risk analysis to proximate cause problems. Imagine that at the time the defendant acted, that obnoxious, self-righteous, odious character, the Reasonable

3. Restatement (Third) of Torts: Liability for Physical and Emotional Harm §29.

Person, was standing next to him. Imagine that the defendant is about to do the unreasonable act that gives rise to the plaintiff's injury. As he presses his foot to the accelerator, or drops the box lid on the sidewalk, or exits his car without taking the keys, what would that odious paragon say to him? In the speeding case, he would doubtless warn the driver that he might cause an accident, with resulting personal injury to himself or others, or property damage from a collision. However, obsessive though he may be, the odious character would not warn him not to speed, because his victim might end up suffering burns in a hospital fire. In the box lid case, the Reasonable Person would warn the storeowner, as he dropped the lid to the sidewalk, that a pedestrian might stumble over it and fall, or drop a valuable package, or even fall down the adjacent stairs. But even the odious character would not say, "Tsk! Tsk! Don't drop that box lid! A pedestrian might fall over it, suffer an injury, end up getting a later train, and be injured in a train wreck!"

VARIETIES OF FORESEEABILITY: *WAGON MOUND AND PALSGRAF*

The two most famous proximate cause cases, *Overseas Tankship (U.K.) Ltd. v. Morts Dock & Engineering Co., Ltd. (The Wagon Mound)*, 1 All E.R. 404 (1961), and *Palsgraf v. Long Island* R.R., 162 N.E. 99 (N.Y. 1928), both exemplify a scope-of-the-risk approach to the proximate cause problem.

In *Palsgraf*, the defendant's conductors were negligent in assisting the rushing passenger onto a moving train, causing him to drop a package. Although there was no reason for the conductors to suspect it, the package contained firecrackers, which exploded, overturning some scales a distance away. The scales fell and injured the reluctantly famous Mrs. Palsgraf.

Although the railroad's employees were found negligent in *Palsgraf*, the railroad argued that their negligence only posed a foreseeable risk of injury to the passenger or his package, not to Mrs. Palsgraf. Justice Cardozo, writing for the majority, held that the duty to avoid injuring others extends only to those risks the actor should anticipate from her negligent act. Here, the unreasonable risk created by the conductors' conduct was that the passenger or his package would be injured, not Mrs. Palsgraf. Since the conductors would not have anticipated injury to her from their conduct, they owed no duty to avoid the injury and were not negligent in relation to her. Since she was an "unforeseeable plaintiff" to whom no unreasonable risk was to be anticipated, Mrs. Palsgraf was denied recovery.[4]

---

4. Another way to look at this is to say that there is no doctrine of "transferred negligence" analogous to that of transferred intent in intentional tort cases. See G. Williams, The Risk Principle, 77 Law Q. Rev. 179, 185-190 (1961).

In *Wagon Mound*, the defendant's oil fouled the waters around the plaintiff's dock, where welding was in progress. Because of its high ignition point, the oil was unlikely to burn, but it did, through a strange concatenation of circumstances found in the case to be unforeseeable. Other injury to the dock, however, *was* foreseeable, and in fact took place: the fouling of the docks by the oil. The dock owner argued that, since the defendant could foresee *some* injury to the dock, it was liable for *all* injury which actually resulted.

The Privy Council held that the plaintiff could only recover for the injuries that the defendant should have anticipated at the time it released the oil into the water. It would be liable for fouling the slips of the plaintiff's dock, a foreseeable consequence of releasing the oil, but not for the unforeseeable fire which destroyed the dock itself.

SOME GUIDEPOSTS IN THE WILDERNESS

Although proximate cause can never be reduced to a test that mechanically resolves all the cases, there are some fairly well-established principles that at least help to narrow the issues.

- *First*, and most fundamentally, if the plaintiff's injury is truly beyond the type of harm to be expected from the defendant's conduct, the plaintiff will virtually always go uncompensated. A basic sense of justice demands that liability should not extend to consequences radically different from those to be anticipated from an act, and courts—whatever language they use—will find a way to reach that result. In the venereal disease hypothetical, for example, the court may dub Carpenter's disease too remote, unforeseeable, or beyond the risk that made the conduct negligent, but one way or another, it will reason to a judgment for the defendant.

  Conversely, it is worth noting that most tort cases pose no legal cause problem because the harm suffered is exactly the type to be expected. In the run-of-the-mill motor vehicle case, for example, there is no question that a collision is the type of harm to be anticipated, and that, if the other elements are proved, the defendant must pay. Like *Erie* problems in civil procedure, the close cases are excruciatingly hard, but the great majority of the cases are not hard at all.
- *Second*, where a particular type of injury to the plaintiff is foreseeable, the defendant is liable for the injury sustained, even though the injury caused is more serious than might have been anticipated. If, for example, Goodhart knocks Gregory down, causing small lacerations, he is liable if Gregory contracts an infection and becomes

seriously ill, or if he is a hemophiliac and dies from loss of blood. If Goodhart injures Bohlen in an auto accident, disabling him for six months, he must pay the value of Bohlen's lost wages, whether he is a day laborer or the CEO of a Fortune 500 company. It is said that the defendant "takes the plaintiff as he finds her." The fact that she is more susceptible to injury than the average person, has a "thin skull," so to speak, is not a defense to liability. If Goodhart could foresee personal injury to Bohlen, he is liable for the personal injury actually caused, not some hypothetical average ordinarily to be expected from the act.

- *Third*, the cases distinguish unforeseeable consequences of a negligent act from consequences that are foreseeable but take place in an unusual manner. This foreseeable-injury-in-an-unforeseeable-manner principle is nicely illustrated by *United Novelty Co. v. Daniels*, 42 So. 2d 395 (Miss. 1949). In *Daniels*, the defendant allowed its employee to clean some machines with gasoline in a small room heated by a heater with an open flame. A rat, drenched with the gasoline, ran from under one of the machines over to the heater, caught fire, and ran back to the machine, causing an explosion which killed the employee. The court concluded that, while the manner in which the accident took place was unusual, an explosion was exactly the type of accident to be anticipated from using a volatile, flammable liquid in a small room with an open flame. The defendant was held liable.

  Consistent with the *Daniels* analysis, courts often affirm that the defendant "need not foresee the details of the accident"—the idiosyncratic facts present in virtually every case—but rather must anticipate the general mechanism of harm that leads to the plaintiff's injury. In *Daniels*, the details of the accident were quirky, to say the least, but the danger that the Odious Character would have anticipated is the very risk that caused the injury.

  There is something to this distinction. The exact sequence of events in every accident is unique, but in most the general nature of the damage threatened was foreseeable. Distinguish from the rat case, for example, the terrorist bombing hypo at the beginning of the chapter. In the rat case, the general nature of the accident threatened by the conduct actually took place. In terms of the risk rule, the risk of an explosion of the vapors, causing personal injury to the employee, was the very risk that made the defendant's conduct negligent. But in the terrorist case, the general nature of the risk to be expected from leaving the keys in the car was far afield from that which injured the passerby at the embassy.

  The trick, of course, is in making the distinction: In many cases the line between unforeseeable consequences and unforeseeable manner is a fine one, if indeed a defensible line can be drawn at all. Consider, for example, *Doughty v. Turner Mfg. Co.*, 1 Q.B. 518 (1964). In *Doughty*, the plaintiff was standing next to a vat of molten liquid when the cover of the vat was negligently knocked into it. Nothing happened at first, but several minutes later there was an explosion within the vat, caused by a chemical reaction of the lid with the liquid. The plaintiff argued that the defendant's employees negligently created a risk that he would be splashed by the liquid, and that, indeed, he *was* injured by splashing (when the explosion threw the liquid out of the vat), though in an unusual manner. The court, however, held that he was injured by a different risk, the risk of an unforeseeable chemical reaction causing explosion, not physical splashing from the dropping of the cover. The case seems rightly decided, but it turns on a nice distinction indeed.

- *Fourth*, an injury does not have to be *likely* or *probable* in order to be foreseeable in proximate cause analysis. Many acts are culpable even though they pose a relatively small risk of injury. If Smith throws a flower pot out a third-story window without looking, there may be only a 3 percent chance that someone will be hit. But this conduct is clearly negligent because it poses an unreasonable risk of injury to passersby. No court in the country would deny liability in such a case on proximate cause grounds. "Foreseeability is not to be measured by what is more probable than not, but includes whatever is likely enough in the setting of modern life that a reasonably thoughtful person would take account of it in guiding practical conduct." Harper, James & Gray §18.2 at 657-659. Similarly, the Reasonable Person stops at a rural railroad crossing, even though it is rarely used: In Hand formula terms, the risk encountering a train may be low, but the extent of injury if it does is great, and the burden of avoiding the harm is slight.

AN ECONOMICS PERSPECTIVE ON THE FORESEEABILITY/SCOPE-OF-THE-RISK APPROACH

Economic analysis provides an interesting defense of the scope-of-foreseeable-risks approach to proximate cause. Economists view tort law as a means to control activity *prospectively*. They advocate rules of liability that will encourage people to act in socially desirable ways. If tort law holds a person liable for certain risks of his conduct, presumably the actor will take care to avert those risks since he will bear their costs if an injury occurs:

> These [liability] rules tell decision makers that, under certain conditions, they will be forced to bear the costs of their activities to others. The effect of such

> rules is to give rational decision makers an incentive to incorporate the costs to others into their decisions about whether to engage in the activity, and hence, to create a situation in which the activities chosen by the rational decision maker are efficient from an aggregate point of view.

B. Zipursky, Rights, Wrongs, and Recourse in the Law of Torts, 51 Vand. L. Rev. 1, 46 (1998). However, the rational actor can only consider the liability consequences of risks that he can foresee. Imposing liability for unforeseeable risks will not affect his choices:

> *Palsgraf* stands for the proposition that the tort law does not require an individual to consider, in selecting her activity, costs to persons to whom harm is not reasonably foreseeable. Unforeseeable harm cannot be internalized because, by definition, the decision maker could not have foreseen it. Imposing liability where there is no foreseeability will "confer no economic benefit; it will merely require a costly transfer payment."

Id. at 46. In economic terms, a rule that an actor must pay for unforeseeable harms will not affect the actor's choices about activities that impose risk. If we make him pay for unforeseeable injuries caused by his conduct, it will not make the world any safer or more efficient: An actor cannot plan his conduct in light of risks he does not anticipate. So, economic analysts argue, there is little point to a liability rule that makes the actor pay damages for such risks.

If you think economic analysis of tort law is a lot of hooey, the basic point can be rephrased in more general normative terms: We impose liability because we think the actor should have acted differently. But we can't really "blame" an actor for acting in a certain way unless he would anticipate that doing so would cause harm. If the injury that results could not be anticipated, it doesn't seem "fair" to hold him liable for it.

HARM INSIDE THE CIRCLE OF FORESEEABILITY

Although courts will find a way to avoid imposing liability for unforeseeable injuries, it does not follow that the converse is always true, that is, that a defendant must pay whenever he causes *foreseeable* harm. In some situations, for various reasons of policy, courts also refuse to hold defendants liable for injuries that could be foreseen.

Consider the case in which the shopkeeper dropped the box lid, delaying the plaintiff, who was later injured in a train wreck. Doubtless, her harm falls outside the circle of foreseeability, at point A on Figure 12-1, and the court will refuse to impose liability for it. The court will likely explain its decision on the ground that the shopkeeper's act was "not the proximate cause" of the injury because it could not be foreseen.

Well enough. But now let's consider some types of cases that pretty clearly fall *inside* the circle of foreseeability, but in which courts still refuse to hold the defendant liable. One example is the case of secondary economic losses as a result of a negligent act. Suppose that Goodhart negligently causes a factory fire that injures Green, an employee, but also shuts down the factory for three months. It is obviously foreseeable that a fire would cause injury to a worker in the factory, and Goodhart will be liable for Green's foreseeable injury. However, while it seems equally foreseeable that the fire could cause a shutdown, so that the employees would suffer lost wages, most courts would deny recovery for the workers' lost wages during the shutdown.

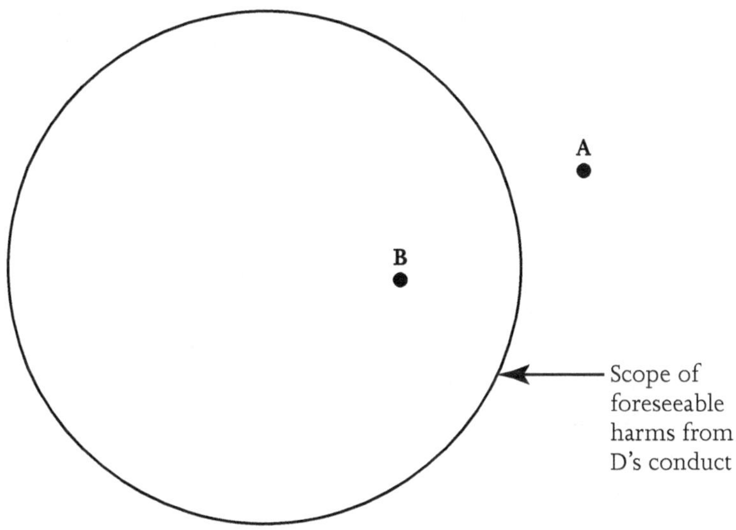

Figure 12-1. The Circle of Foreseeability

This economic loss to the workers pretty clearly falls at point B on Figure 12-1, within the circle of foreseeability, just as Green's personal injury does. Thus, courts that deny recovery for such secondary economic losses cannot credibly do so based on lack of proximate cause. Generally, courts reason that the burden of liability for such secondary economic losses is too great. (Imagine, for example, the potential liability if Goodhart had burned down a bridge, interrupting the business affairs of an entire town.) However, while the denial of recovery in such cases has nothing to do with proximate cause, the cases frequently state that the defendant's conduct was "not the proximate cause" of the secondary losses. The use of proximate cause language in cases like these is unfortunate, but widespread.

New York's early rule limiting recovery for damages by fire provides another example of a court limiting liability, for policy reasons, for harm within the circle of foreseeability. In *Ryan v. New York Central Railroad Co.*, 35 N.Y. 210 (1866), the New York court restricted liability for fire damage to the first adjacent property burned. The *Ryan* court dubbed the burning of further properties "not the immediate but the remote result of the negligence of the defendants." Id. at 212. This conclusory proximate cause analysis, to borrow Dean Prosser's language in a related context, is "moonshine and vapor."[5] Anyone could foresee that a fire would burn beyond the next lot. The true rationale for the rule was the crushing burden such liability would impose, and the general availability of fire insurance as an alternative source of protection:

> To sustain such a claim as the present, and to follow the same to its legitimate consequences, would subject to a liability against which no prudence could guard, and to meet which no private fortune would be adequate . . . To hold that the owner must not only meet his own loss by fire, but that he must guarantee the security of his neighbors on both sides, and to an unlimited extent, would be to create a liability which would be the destruction of all civilized society.

Id. at 216.[6]

Unfortunately, courts that restrict liability for harm *within* the circle of foreseeability, for reasons of policy, often mask their decisions in proximate cause language, as the *Ryan* court did in talking about "remote" and "immediate" causes. Cases involving liability for serving alcohol to intoxicated patrons provide another example of such obfuscatory rhetoric. Early liquor liability cases refused to hold barkeeps liable for serving intoxicated patrons who caused motor vehicle accidents, on the ground that the drunk driving, not the service of liquor, was the "proximate cause" of the injury. Yet few acts are more foreseeable than an inebriated patron driving home from a roadside bar. The real thrust of these cases (since repudiated in many jurisdictions) was a policy decision to place liability for obviously foreseeable harm on the more blameworthy of two negligent parties.

The law of torts would be tidier if the courts would use *duty* analysis when they deny recovery for harm within the circle of foreseeability, for other policy reasons, and use *proximate cause* analysis in cases involving unforeseeable harm. Frequently, courts do use duty analysis to limit liability for foreseeable harm. (See pp. 297–298 for several examples.) But many other cases that deny recovery for policy reasons—as in the economic loss and drunk driving cases—use proximate cause language instead. One of

---

5. Prosser, Proximate Cause in California, 38 Cal. L. Rev. 369, 376 (1950).

6. Most states have rejected the rigid limits of the *Ryan* rule. New York has modified it as well. See Homac Corp. v. Sun Oil Co. 258 NY.462 (1932) (allowing recovery for owner of non-adjacent properly).

the great challenges in reading these cases is to cut through promiscuous foreseeability references to determine whether some other policy is actually driving the decisions.

The following examples illustrate the basic issues involved in proximate cause cases. In analyzing them, assume that the court adopts a scope-of-the-risk approach to the proximate cause issues, unless otherwise noted. After some examples, we will take up the related conundrum known as "superseding cause." (The analysis begins on page 254.)

Examples

Revisionist History

1. Bingham is running for a Long Island Railroad train that is about to pull out of the station. He is carrying a small package wrapped in brown paper. Two conductors, seeing the train start to leave, reach out to help Bingham onto the train, and one clumsily knocks the package onto the tracks. Alas, the package contains an antique music box which Bingham had just had valued at $5,000. The music box is demolished upon landing. Is the railroad liable under a foreseeability/scope-of-the-risk approach?

2. Bingham is running for a Long Island Railroad train that is about to pull out of the station. He is carrying a small package wrapped in brown paper. Two conductors, seeing the train start to leave, reach out to help Bingham onto the train, and one clumsily knocks the package onto the tracks. Alas, the package contains fireworks, which explode upon impact. A certain Mrs. Falsgraf, running to the same train immediately behind Bingham, is injured by the explosion.
   a. Is the railroad liable for her injuries?
   b. Assume, on the facts of Example 2a, that Mrs. Falsgraf sued Bingham, the passenger carrying the package. Would Bingham be liable for her injuries?
   c. Assume that the conductors negligently jostle Bingham, causing him to drop the package to the platform. It explodes, the passengers on the crowded platform panic and run, knocking down Mrs. Falsgraf 30 feet away. Would the railroad be liable to Falsgraf?
   d. Assume, on the facts of *Palsgraf*, that Mrs. Palsgraf had sued the passenger. Would the court have denied recovery on proximate cause grounds?
   e. Suppose that Mrs. Palsgraf tried a different theory against the railroad: She argued that the railroad was negligent because they placed a tall, unstable scale on the platform, where a small force could cause it to fall. Could she then argue that the scale falling over was foreseeable, so that the railroad would be liable?

Judge Fudd Does the Foreseeable

3. The Bentham Construction Company excavates a deep foundation for an office building in downtown St. Louis, immediately adjacent to a main street. Beale, a Bentham crane operator, sets down a load of iron beams in the street, on the edge of the excavation, but his touch is off and the load lands heavily, causing the wall of the excavation to collapse. The landslide breaks a large water main under the street, flooding the foundation. Bentham's employees were not aware that the water main was there.

   The owner sues for the damage caused by the flooding. Judge Fudd instructs the jury, in part, as follows:

   > If you find that the defendant's employees were unaware that the water main was under the street, then you must find that any negligence of Bentham's employees in causing the collapse was not the proximate cause of the plaintiff's damages.

   What is wrong with Judge Fudd's instruction?

4. Consider the distinction discussed in the Introduction between foreseeable injuries that happen through an unusual sequence of events (for which a defendant will be held liable) compared to injuries that happen through an unforeseeable mechanism of harm (for which they often will not). In which category would you put the following cases?
   a. A train collides with a car at a railroad crossing, due to negligence of the engineer. The car is thrown into a track switch, throwing the switch and turning the train onto a side track, where it collides with a boxcar. Fletcher, a passenger, is injured by the collision with the boxcar.
   b. Hill was repairing a "fender," made of piles driven into a stream bed below a bridge. He pried two piles apart and inserted a brace to hold them apart while he was inserting another pile. At this point a tug came along and hit a pile further along the fender, jarring the successive piles, causing the brace to fall out and the piles to spring back together. Hill's leg was trapped between them. He sued for his injuries.
   c. In *Lewis v. Kehoe Academy*, 346 So. 2d 289 (La. App. 1977), a day care center negligently allowed a child to ingest rat poison. As a result, a small bruise the child later suffered was greatly accentuated, leading welfare authorities to conclude that the child had been abused, and to remove the child from the custody of his guardians.

Fudd Tries Again

5. Corletti, a passenger on the way to an Italian festival, is assisted onto a Long Island Railroad train by a conductor. The conductor jostles him

roughly, and he drops a package, which contains fireworks. The package explodes, causing burn injuries to Corletti.

Judge Fudd, who is handling the case, must determine whether the issue of proximate cause should be decided by the judge or the jury.

a. Which party do you think would prefer to have the jury decide the proximate cause question?
b. Suppose that Judge Fudd proposes to send the Corletti case to the jury, with the following instruction:

> If you find that, when the conductor assisted the plaintiff onto the train, he should have foreseen an unreasonable risk of injury to the plaintiff from that act, then you should find that the conductor's negligence was a proximate cause of his resulting injury.

What change would you recommend in the Honorable Fudd's instruction?

The Thin Shell Rule?

6. Keeton is driving along the road when his nose starts to run. He reaches over to the floor of the passenger's seat for a tissue and his car crosses the center line into the path of a gasoline truck. The truck swerves to avoid a collision, hits a wall and springs a leak. Gasoline pours out, percolates down into the public water supply, and triggers a $1 million environmental cleanup by county health officials. The county sues Keeton to recover its costs. Assuming that Keeton was negligent, is his conduct a proximate cause of the cleanup?

Risky Business

7. On March 16, 2014, the Gregory Railroad Company accepts electric motors from Pollack for shipment. Because Pollack needed the motors as components for a finished product, he requested delivery of the goods within ten days. Through the negligence of the railroad, shipment of the goods is delayed for five days. On March 30, while in transit on board a Gregory freight train, the goods are damaged in a flood. Is the railroad liable under the "risk rule"?

8. On October 15, 2014, the Gregory Railroad accepts a shipment of apples to deliver for Pollack. Because the weather is cool and frost could spoil the apples, Pollack requires that the apples be delivered within four days. Gregory delays, and the apples are spoiled by freezing on October 23. Is the railroad liable?

9. In *Johnson v. Kosmos Portland Cement Co.*, 64 F.2d 193 (6th Cir. 1933), workers were working inside the hold of a barge, evidently installing a boiler. The

barge was used for the transport of oil, and was full of gases generated by the oil, which should have been cleared out before the workers began their work. As luck would have it, the barge was struck by lightning, which caused the gases to explode, killing the workers.

a. Is this case like the rat case, a foreseeable kind of harm that happens in a quirky manner, or is it like the vat case, in which the injury results from an unforeseeable mechanism of harm?
b. Reconsider *In re Polemis*, in which the ship's hold was full of fumes, and they were ignited by a board that fell into the hold. The court applied a "direct cause" test in *Polemis*, but if it had applied a foreseeability/scope-of-the-risk test would apparently have held that this accident was unforeseeable. In light of the *Johnson* case, what argument might you make on behalf of the plaintiff in *Polemis*, if the foreseeability/scope-of-the-risk test were used?

SUPERSEDING CAUSE

In a good many proximate cause cases, the defendant argues that, even if she was negligent, a later act supersedes her negligence and "breaks the causal chain." An example from the casebooks is *Derdiarian v. Felix Contracting Corp.*, 434 N.Y.S.2d 166 (1980). In *Derdiarian*, the defendant contractor was working in an excavation in the traveled roadway, and failed to erect a barrier (such as a truck or concrete blocks) to protect workers from traffic. Dickens, an epileptic who had failed to take his medication, suffered a seizure, lost control of his car, and careened into the excavation, throwing Derdiarian into the air, where his body ignited from a kettle of hot enamel in use for the repairs.

Derdiarian involves a typical scenario in which the "superseding cause" argument is raised. *First*, the defendant is negligent (failure to erect the barrier); *second*, some other act happens after the defendant's negligence (Dickens's passing out due to failure to take meds), and *third*, the two acts together lead to an injury to the plaintiff (Derdiarian's accident). The contractor in *Derdiarian* argued that the bizarre subsequent events leading Dickens's car to enter the work area "superseded" its negligence. Consequently, "there was no causal link" (434 N.Y.S.2d at 159) between its failure to erect a barrier and the worker's burns.

In actual cause analysis, of course, this argument does not hold water. The company's negligence in failing to provide a barrier was clearly a "but for" cause of Derdiarian's injury. If the company had provided a proper barrier, Derdiarian would not have been injured, even if Dickens lost control of his car. The contractor's real argument is that Dickens's subsequent negligent act of driving without taking his meds, and the bizarre sequence of events that it engendered, should "cut off its liability," and cause the court to place the loss on Dickens instead of on the contractor.

Such "superseding cause" cases don't require any different analysis than other proximate cause problems. If we apply scope-of-the-risk analysis to *Derdiarian*, the outcome is clear: Working in the middle of a busy street poses a risk that a vehicle will enter the worksite. This is the foreseeable risk that makes it reasonable to put up a barrier. "A prime hazard associated with [omitting the barrier] is the possibility that a driver will negligently enter the work site and cause injury to a worker." Id. at 170. This is the risk that injured Derdiarian. The contractor should be liable—and it was held liable—even though later negligence of Dickens caused the vehicle to enter the worksite. As to the quirky details of the accident—Dickens's epilepsy, the vat of molten enamel—the court correctly noted that "the precise manner of the event need not be anticipated." Id. at 170.

So what kind of later events would a court find a "superseding cause" that "cuts off" the liability of the previously negligent party? Generally speaking, courts will not hold the negligent party liable when bizarre, unforeseeable events give rise to a risk different from the one the defendant should have anticipated. "Highly improbable and extraordinary intervening forces are generally found superseding and preclude liability." J. Diamond, L. Levine & A. Bernstein, Understanding Torts 194 (7th ed. 2023). In other words, these cases are just a special instance of the more general principle, that actors are not liable for truly unforeseeable harm.

The superseding cause argument is frequently raised, but has seldom prevailed. In *Cleveland v. Rotman*, 297 F.3d 569 (7th Cir. 2002), the court refused to hold a lawyer who had allegedly provided negligent tax advice liable for the subsequent suicide of his client, dubbing the suicide "an independent intervening event that broke the chain of causation." Id. at 572. And here's a hypo in which the argument would fly: Ace Taxi Service is called by Costas, waiting at a park for a ride. It negligently fails to send a driver, and Costas is injured by a tornado that strikes the park. The dangers the taxi company should foresee from failing to send a car do not include the risk of tornadoes; assuming none have been predicted! So a court would very likely dub this one a "superseding cause."

The superseding cause argument is frequently made in cases involving subsequent intentional acts by third parties, including criminal acts. In one of the classic superseding cause cases, *Watson v. Kentucky and Indiana Bridge & R.R. Co.*, 126 S.W. 146 (1910), for example, the defendant railroad negligently spilled gas in a street, and it was subsequently ignited by a match thrown by Duerr. The court held that if Duerr had thrown the match negligently, the railroad would be liable for the fire, but if he had done it intentionally, his deliberate criminal act would cut off the railroad's liability since it was "not bound to anticipate the criminal acts of others." 126 S.W. at 151. The argument for this result seems to be that the deliberate act of arson is unforeseeable as a matter of law, and that the greater culpability of a criminal act should lead the court to place the responsibility on the criminal actor rather than the actor whose prior negligence contributed to the harm.

In many circumstances, however, criminal acts are foreseeable, and indeed, are the very risk that require the reasonable person to take precautions. In another of the classic cases, *Hines v. Garrett*, 108 S.E. 690 (Va. 1921), a train passed the plaintiff's stop and the conductors let her off a mile down the line, in an area known to be frequented by vagrants. While walking back to her stop she was assaulted. The court summarily dismissed the railroad's argument that the assault was a superseding cause: "The very danger to which this unfortunate girl fell a victim is the one which would at once suggest itself to the average and normal mind as a danger liable to overtake her under these circumstances." 108 S.E. at 694. When the risk of criminal conduct is foreseeable, it will not "cut off" the liability of a defendant who negligently exposes the plaintiff to that risk.

> If the likelihood that a third person may act in a particular manner is the hazard or one of the hazards which makes the actor negligent, such an act whether innocent, negligent, intentionally tortious, or criminal does not prevent the actor from being liable for harm caused thereby.

Restatement (Second) of Torts §449.[7] This principle is frequently applied in cases involving negligent security at hotels and apartment complexes.

Afterthoughts

10. Consider, in the following cases, whether the later event should be treated as a superseding cause, "cutting off" the original negligent party's liability.
    a. Hart negligently repairs Mendoza's brakes. As Mendoza is driving along a main highway, Ellsworth negligently pulls out without looking, in front of Mendoza. Mendoza applies the brakes, but they fail, and the cars collide. Mendoza sues Hart for her injuries.

---

7. The Third Restatement quite sensibly treats superseding cause as a simple variant of the basic test for scope of liability:

> Restatement (Third) of Torts §34:
>
> > Where a force of nature or an independent act is also a factual cause of harm, an actor's liability is limited to those harms that result from the risks that made the actor's conduct tortious.

b. Mendoza is injured in the accident just described, and taken to the hospital with a broken arm. The arm is negligently set by Dr. Zipursky, causing additional injuries. Mendoza sues Hart and Ellsworth for her injuries, including the injuries from Zipursky's malpractice.

c. In *Merhi v. Becker*, 325 A.2d 270 (Ct. 1973), a union gave a party with unlimited beer, but negligently failed to provide adequate security. Becker drank a lot of beer and got into two fights. A half hour later he got his car and drove it at one of his adversaries, but injured the plaintiff instead.

d. Icarus Airlines negligently fails to fill all the fuel tanks on a passenger plane. Consequently, the plane is forced to land on a Pacific island. Morris, a passenger, is injured when a volcano on the island erupts while they are refueling.

    i. Was the airline's failure to fill the tanks an actual cause of Morris's injury?

    ii. Is the airline's negligence a proximate cause of Morris's injury?

    iii. Suppose that the plane had to land on the island, the runway was short for a large plane, it overshot the runway, and passengers were injured. Would the airline be liable for their injuries?

e. Apex Alarm Company installs a security system in Smith's home. The alarm is designed to sound at the Apex office if the system is activated by an intruder. The Apex employee on duty then calls the police department, which ideally nabs the culprit at the scene of the crime.

    On a balmy June evening, a burglar breaks a window at Smith's home. This should activate the alarm system, but due to negligent rewiring at the Apex office, it fails to go off. The burglar makes off with Smith's valuables, and Smith sues Apex. Apex moves for summary judgment on the ground that the burglar's intentional criminal act supersedes its negligence in wiring the alarm improperly. How should the court rule?

You Be the Judge

11. Consider this case:

> A dredger, though warned of a gas main in the area, negligently breaks it while dredging. A factory a mile away, supplied with gas through the main, suffers damage to its equipment and loss of production due to the sudden loss of power.
>
> Would you characterize this case as one involving unforeseeable harm, or foreseeable harm in an unusual manner, or one inside the "circle of foreseeability" for which liability would be denied anyway?

Explanations

Revisionist History

1. Whether the railroad is liable under the foreseeability/scope-of-the-risk rule depends on how broadly you define the risk the defendant must foresee. Arguably, the presence of an expensive antique was not a risk that the conductors should have foreseen, and therefore they were not negligent for failing to foresee it. But most courts would define the risk more generally. They would conclude that the risk that makes the conductor's act negligent is the risk that either the passenger or his belongings would fall and be injured. When one of those risks causes the injury, the defendant is liable because it is a risk that she should have anticipated and averted.

   The fact that the package contained a valuable antique goes to the *extent* of the risk rather than its nature. The nature of the unreasonable risk that the conductors should have anticipated was damage to personal property from falling, and that was the risk that led to the harm. As in the "thin skull" cases, it should not be a defense for the railroad that the conductors did not know the contents of the package. They could foresee that Bingham would be carrying a package, that it might fall if they were not careful, and that the contents—whatever they were—might be damaged if it fell. Where damage of the general type sustained was foreseeable, courts usually hold defendants liable for the damage *actually* caused, even if that is greater than one might ordinarily expect.

2. a. There are some obvious differences here from the facts of *Palsgraf*. Here, because Mrs. Falsgraf is next to Bingham, personal injury to her is foreseeable: The package could fall on her foot and injure her, or the conductor or the passenger could hit her, causing her to fall to the platform or even under the train. Palsgraf will argue that, on these facts, the conductors could foresee a risk of personal injury to her. Consequently, she is a foreseeable plaintiff and should recover for her injuries.

      However, the court will probably not accept this argument. True, the conductors could foresee personal injury of one sort to Mrs. Falsgraf—from falling or being hit by the package—but they could not foresee injury of the sort that actually occurred—explosion. Most courts would conclude that the injury she suffered arose from a different risk than those the railroad could anticipate, and would therefore deny recovery. See, e.g., the *Doughty* case, described above at p. 243.

      Example 1 illustrates that the proximate cause analysis must avoid defining the foreseeable risk too *specifically*. This example shows that the court may also go awry if it defines the risk too *generally*. If the defendant need only foresee "personal injury" of some sort, the plaintiff who tripped over the box lid, missed her train, and was injured when the later train crashed could recover: The box lid left on the sidewalk created a risk of personal injury, she suffered personal injury, ergo liability. Yet this analysis would be too broad in both cases. The court must focus on the particular types of harm to be anticipated from the defendant's act. At the same time, as Example 1 illustrates, it must avoid getting bogged down in the idiosyncratic "details" of the accident.

b. Mrs. Falsgraf's case against Bingham is distinguishable from her case against the railroad. Since Bingham *knows* that the package contains fireworks, he is aware of the risk of explosion. Most courts would conclude that he is negligent for bringing fireworks into a crowded place, precisely because they might be detonated by some kind of incident such as the scenario here. Since the risk of an explosion is one of the risks that makes his conduct negligent, most courts would hold him liable to those injured when an explosion actually takes place.

c. Under the scope-of-the risk approach, the railroad should probably not be held liable to Mrs. Falsgraf on these facts. When the conductors acted, they could anticipate Bingham falling or dropping his package, but they had no reason to anticipate an explosion that would trigger a stampede among the passengers. Not even that odious character, the Reasonable Person, would warn them of such a consequence from jostling a passenger. Since they could not anticipate the general nature of the risk that injured Falsgraf, they should not be liable to her under the scope-of-the-risk approach.

d. In the *Palsgraf* case, Mrs. Palsgraf was not directly injured by the blast, but by a set of scales some distance from the explosion, which were knocked over on her foot. Yet it does not seem unusual that a bystander, even at some distance, should be injured by flying debris if an explosion takes place. The details are unique—as they always are—but the general nature of the accident is within the scope of the risk to be anticipated.

   Suppose you went up to the Reasonable Person and asked her whether she would anticipate that, if a package of explosives exploded in a public place, a bystander might be injured by an object dislodged by the blast. Doubtless, our odious character would view this as foreseeable, even if she could not tell you that the object would be a set of scales. Since this is a foreseeable risk of carrying explosives in a train station, the passenger would likely be held liable to Mrs. Palsgraf.

e. This is a nice argument. It may not be foreseeable that a passenger would be carrying fireworks, but isn't it foreseeable that something would knock over a heavy, unstable scale? The defendant, after all, doesn't have to anticipate the details of the accident, just the general nature of the risk that injured the plaintiff. The railroad could anticipate a number of things knocking over the scale, such as a passenger running for a train or a worker pushing a large trunk.

Although the argument refocuses the negligence analysis on the scale rather than the fireworks, we should still ask whether the general mechanism that caused the harm was foreseeable. A court would probably hold that the mechanism of harm here was still a fireworks explosion, and that the reasonable person, in thinking about the risks of having the scale on the platform, would not be bound to anticipate that, even though she could anticipate other ways the scale might topple.

Judge Fudd Does the Foreseeable

3. Judge Fudd's instruction requires the jury to find for the defendant if they find that its employees did not know that the water main was there. Presumably, his reasoning is that, if its employees were unaware of the water main, they had no reason to foresee the risk of water damage.

   This is seriously Fuddled reasoning. If actual knowledge were required, a Menlove who threw a flower pot out the third-story window without looking would not be liable if it hit a pedestrian. The important question is what Beale, the employee who dropped the beams, could *foresee* as a consequence of his negligence, not what he knew would happen. Surely, if that odious Reasonable Person had been there when Beale dropped the beams, he would have smugly explained to Beale that underground utilities *might* be under the street and that, if they were, they might rupture if the excavation collapsed. Since this was one of the risks that made Beale's act negligent, he should be liable, even if he was not sure what utilities actually ran under the street.

4. a. In the early case from which this example is drawn,[8] the court denied recovery, based on lack of foreseeability.

   > That an automobile should suddenly appear upon a railroad track and be struck by an approaching train is not a matter of unusual occurrence, and is one that might reasonably be anticipated; but that such a collision should result in the automobile being thrown against a switch stand in such a manner as to open the switch is a possibility so remote as to be beyond the realm of events reasonably to be anticipated. This being true, the independent agency so intervening must be treated as the sole proximate cause of the injuries. . . .

   133 N.E. at 140. However, this court almost certainly was seduced by the quirky "details" of the accident. While the particular sequence of events was certainly bizarre, the general nature of the harm—injury to the passenger when a collision throws him from his seat—is a foreseeable risk of negligently driving the train at a crossing. Most

8. *Engle v. Director General of Railroads*, 133 N.E. 138 (Ind. App. 1921).

modern courts would look to the general nature of the risk threatened by the engineer's negligence, and hold the railroad liable on these facts.

b. This Rube Goldberg scenario seems pretty idiosyncratic. But one of the basic risks of negligent piloting of the tug was that it would hit the fender and injure a worker working on it. That's just what happened. If the defendant had to foresee the particulars, such as the brace getting dislodged and trapping the plaintiff's leg, defendants would seldom be liable, even though they could foresee the general risks of their conduct. This one should go in the foreseeable injury/quirky facts category.

c. This case is best characterized as unforeseeable harm through a different mechanism of harm. The risk the reasonable person would anticipate from exposing the child to poison is the risk of physical injury from poisoning, not the risk of deprivation of custody through misinterpretation of bruising. In addition, the reasonable actor would anticipate harm to the child from leaving the poison around, not to his guardians. As in *Palsgraf*, harm to them from this negligent act is unforeseeable. The complaint in *Lewis* was dismissed for lack of proximate cause.

Fudd Tries Again

5. a. It is frequently said that whether the defendant's negligence was a proximate cause of the plaintiff's injury is a question of fact for the jury. Surely the plaintiff will breathe a sigh of relief if the judge decides that the issue is one of fact, and sends it to the jury. In general, the jury won't have the foggiest idea of what proximate cause means. Imagine yourself, after a few classes on the concept in Torts class, trying to apply the concept effectively to a real case. The jury must do so based on a vague, general instruction such as this:

> A proximate cause of an injury is that which in a natural and continuous sequence, unbroken by an independent intervening cause, produces the injury, and without which the injury would not have occurred. It need not be the only cause, nor the last nor nearest cause. It is sufficient if it occurs with some other cause acting at the same time, which in combination with it, causes the injury.[9]

---

9. Adapted from a prior version of New Mexico Model Jury Instruction UJI 13-305. The reporter's note to §29 of the Restatement (Third) of Torts: Liability for Physical and Emotional Harm offers an instruction that may be clearer to lay jurors:

> You must decide whether the plaintiff's harm was of the same general type of harm that the defendant should have acted to avoid. If you find that it is, you shall find for the plaintiff. If you find that it is not the same general type you must find for the defendant.

Reporter's note to §29 cmt. b.

One study of jurors' understanding of proximate cause instructions concluded that all they take from an instruction like this is that "proximate cause [is] just a fancy way of saying causation." C. Mikell, Jury Instructions and Proximate Cause: An Uncertain Trumpet in Georgia, 27 Georgia St. Bar J. 60, 63 (1990). They have no real concept of it as a separate limit on *legal responsibility* apart from actual causation.

The lesson of this for defense lawyers is that they must win the proximate cause battle in front of the judge, by convincing her that, as a matter of law, the defendant's act was not the proximate cause of the plaintiff's injury. This is a realistic prospect; in many cases the judge will grant summary judgment for the defendant, concluding as a matter of law that the plaintiff's injury was unforeseeable. If she lets the issue go to the jury, the plaintiff has probably won the proximate cause battle.

b. Judge Fudd's instruction misses the mark. He has instructed the jury that if the conductor should have anticipated injury to Corletti from his act, he is liable to him for the injury he sustains. This instruction is too broad, though you could find similar instructions in use in various states today. Surely the conductor could anticipate injury to Corletti from jostling him as he gets on the train: He might fall under the train, or fall down and get a bruise. But the conductor would not foresee explosion injuries, and it is very unlikely a court would hold him liable for them.

Here is a less fuddled instruction:

> If you find that, when the conductor assisted the plaintiff onto the train, he should have foreseen an unreasonable risk of injury to plaintiff *of the general nature that actually took place*, then you should find that the conductor's negligence was a proximate cause of plaintiff's resulting injury.

If Judge Fudd had added the italicized language to the instruction, he would probably have concluded that, as a matter of law, the jury could not find it satisfied. The mechanism of harm that injured Corletti—explosion—was quite different from the risks the conductor might have expected from helping him onto the train.

The Thin Shell Rule?

6. When I used this example on my exam, many students argued that Keeton's negligence was not the proximate cause of the cleanup, on the ground that he would not have anticipated such an expensive consequence of his act. However, it is very doubtful that a no-proximate-cause argument is going to get Keeton off the hook. Certainly, an accident with an oncoming vehicle is exactly the risk the odious Reasonable Person

would announce, "like a town-crier in Pompei,"[10] as he saw Keeton dive for the tissue. And, if such an accident happens, it is entirely foreseeable that one of the vehicles could be damaged and leak. It is unfortunate for Keeton that that vehicle was a gasoline truck, and that the resulting damage is so extensive, but that fact is a detail of the accident. The general nature of the risk that caused the harm is one that Keeton should have anticipated. Let's hope he's well insured.

Consider a slightly less extreme case. Suppose that Keeton's negligence causes an accident with a dump truck carrying construction debris, which overturns onto the plaintiff's property, destroying plantings and a fence. Clearly Keeton would be liable for that. The gasoline truck seems to me equally foreseeable, though its spillage is more toxic.[11]

Risky Business

7. This is a recurring fact pattern that has spawned contradictory holdings in the cases. But the result under the risk rule seems clear. The risk that made the railroad's delay negligent was the risk that Pollack would suffer commercial losses, not the risk that, if the motors were shipped later rather than sooner, they would be damaged in transit by a flood. That risk is presumably the same whether they are in transit from March 16 to March 26, or March 21 to March 31, for all we know from the facts. Thus, the risk of flood was not a risk that made it negligent to delay the shipment. Under the risk rule, the railroad should not be held liable.

8. This example contrasts nicely with the last. Here, the railroad agreed that the apples would be shipped immediately, and was presumably aware, or should have been, that delay posed a risk that the apples would be spoiled by cold weather. Thus, one of the risks that made the delay negligent here was the risk of freezing as the weather got colder, and it was exactly this risk that caused the damage. (Couldn't you just see that self-righteous Reasonable Person wagging her finger at the railroad superintendent and warning, "Those apples may freeze if you don't ship them soon . . ."?) Consequently, the railroad would likely be held liable for the resulting damage. See *Fox v. Boston and Maine Railroad Co.*, 19 N.E. 222 (Mass. 1889).

9. a. Your Humble Author would analogize this case to the rat rather than the vat. Allowing the workers to work in the hold without clearing the gases posed a risk of explosion, and that is what caused their deaths. Yes, it is surprising that lightning set off the explosion, but the type of accident that occurred was precisely that to be anticipated,

---

10. Dylan Thomas, A Child's Christmas in Wales 4 (New Directions 1954).

11. I get e-mails from students protesting my analysis of this example. I haven't been convinced by them yet, but remain open to further enlightenment.

and the defendant need not anticipate "the details" of the accident. The *Johnson* court held as follows:

> Any one of a number of expectable circumstances might have brought about the precise injury which resulted; a lighted match, the flame of the acetylene torch, a heated rivet, a spark produced by friction of a tool or boot, and so on. The danger of the injurious result was over [sic] present, even though the manner in which, or the means by which, such result was brought about may have had in it some aspect of unusualness.

64 F.2d at 197. Based on this reasoning, the barge owner was held liable . . . but there was a dissent on the proximate cause analysis.

b. Isn't there a nice argument to be made for the plaintiff in *Polemis*, based on the result in *Johnson*, that the explosion in *Polemis* was within the scope of the risk the charterer should have anticipated? The risk created by allowing the vapors to accumulate in the hold was that an explosion would take place. And one did, due to the unusual action of the board falling into the hold. This is just like *Johnson* and the rat case. This argument focuses on the general nature of the risk posed—explosion—rather than the peculiar means by which the risk came to pass. If "the friction of a tool or a boot" could cause the explosion, why not the friction of a board falling into the vaporous hold?[12] This focuses on the basic risk in the case—explosion—and characterizes the board as a "detail of the accident" rather than an unforeseeable cause. This is a pretty good argument that might well carry the day if *Polemis* were litigated today under modern proximate cause principles.

Afterthoughts

10. a. This is the typical "joint tortfeasor" case in which two actors are negligent at different times, and the two negligent acts combine to cause the plaintiff's injury. If Hart could argue that Ellsworth's negligence "superseded" his, there would be no law of "joint tortfeasors" in such cases; only the party who was negligent last would be liable, even though the negligence of each was a "but for" cause of the plaintiff's injury.

This is clearly not the law. One of the foreseeable risks of driving is that other drivers will be negligent. Thus, Hart cannot argue that Ellsworth's subsequent negligence "cuts off" his liability—one of

12. "That friction of metal against metal or even wood against wood will produce fire is boy scout knowledge." L. Green, Foreseeability in Negligence Law, 61 Columbia L. Rev. 1401, 1411 (1961).

the primary purposes for efficient brakes is to respond to the foreseeable risk of emergencies due to negligent driving.

b. Clearly, Hart's negligence and Ellsworth's negligence are "but for" causes of Mendoza's malpractice injury. If negligence of a driver on the road is foreseeable, why not negligence of a doctor practicing her profession? Virtually all courts hold that a tortfeasor who causes injury can anticipate that the victim might suffer further injury from medical treatment. Thus, the original tortfeasor is also liable for the subsequent malpractice.

   Of course, Dr. Zipursky is *not* liable for the original injury, since he is not a "but for" cause of that injury. He is liable only for the additional injury caused by his negligent treatment.

c. Surely, one of the risks of supplying unlimited beer to guests at a party is that fights will arise. Most people won't get mad enough to run someone down, but the general risk of aggressive conduct is one of the risks that makes such conduct negligent, absent adequate security (or, probably, with it). In *Merli*, the court noted that

   > neither foreseeability of the extent nor the manner of the injury constitutes the criteria for deciding questions of proximate cause. The test is whether the harm which occurred was of the same general nature as the foreseeable risk created by the defendant's negligence.

   325 A.2d at 273. Here, the general nature of the risk—uncontrolled aggressive conduct—was clearly foreseeable to the union when it planned the bibulous barbecue. The union was held liable though it did not foresee that Becker would resort to using his car as a weapon.

d. i. Of course it was. If the tanks had been filled, the plane would have flown on to its intended destination and never would have been on the island when the volcano erupted. "But for" the failure to fill the tanks, the plane would not have been there and Morris would not have been injured. But we still have to ask the proximate cause question: Should the airline be held liable for this utterly unexpected injury?

   ii. In this example, borrowed from Schwartz, Partlett, Cardi & Lahav, Prosser, Wade and Schwartz's Torts: Cases and Materials 438 (16th ed. 2024), virtually any court would conclude that the airline's negligence was not the proximate cause of Beale's injury. Injury from an erupting volcano is not a foreseeable consequence of failing to fill all the fuel tanks. Under the risk approach, leaving the fuel out creates an unreasonable risk that the plane would have to ditch in the water or make an emergency landing, but not that the plane would land on an island at the time of a volcanic eruption. The court will deny recovery to Beale for this bizarre occurrence.

Many courts would hold that the eruption of a volcano near the airport where the plane was forced down was such an unexpected later event that it "supersedes" the negligence of the airline. But labeling the eruption a "superseding cause" is more a conclusion than a helpful method of analysis. The court must still separate superseding causes from others which do not cut off liability. Most courts do so on the basis of the extraordinary or unforeseeable nature of the subsequent events.

iii. This would be an easy case. Clearly the airline employees should anticipate that the plane would have to make an emergency landing if they failed to fully top off the fuel tanks. Surely they should also foresee that the only place where the pilot could land might have a short air strip, but that the pilot would wisely do so even if she knew that the plane would run out of room and some injuries might result. No superseding cause here.

e. In this example, Apex was negligent in rewiring the system, but a later, deliberate criminal act of a third person leads to the plaintiff's injury. The issue is whether this act "supersedes" the negligence of Apex, so as to cut off its liability for the theft.

Subsequent intentional acts may cut off liability in some cases. A nice example is the owner who allowed a child trespasser into its building, only to have the boy maliciously usher a visitor into an unguarded elevator shaft. See *Cole v. German S. & L. Soc.*, 124 F. 113 (8th Cir. 1903). No one, not even a law professor, would anticipate such a twisted sense of humor. But other intentional acts are entirely foreseeable. Here, Apex was hired to avert the very type of act which caused Smith's loss. It hardly seems appropriate for Apex to take his money to protect him from theft, and then when it fails to do so, to deny that such theft was foreseeable! Since illegal entry by a burglar is the very hazard that makes it negligent to wire the system improperly, Apex's motion for summary judgment should be denied. See Restatement (Third) of Torts §34 (quoted at p. 252).[13]

You Be the Judge

11. In the case from which this example is drawn, the court held that, while injury to persons or property from the escaping gas would be foreseeable, injury to the plaintiff's business was not.

> [T]he damage arising from the loss of natural gas supply, in turn causing the shutdown of electric turbines, in turn causing a loss of electric power vital to the aluminum reduction process, with the ultimate result being

13. Compare *Stahlecker v. Ford Motor Co.*, 667 N.W.2d 244, 253-257 (Neb. 2003) (manufacturer of defective tire that blew out in remote area not liable for murder of stranded motorist).

> substantial damage to equipment and product-in-process, goes beyond the pale of general harm which reasonably might have been anticipated by negligent dredgers.

Consolidated Aluminum Corp. v. C.F. Bean Corp., 833 F.2d 65, 68 (5th Cir. 1987). With all due respect, this conclusion is dubious. It seems eminently foreseeable that the interruption of gas service will cause many commercial losses to nearby businesses. In fact, such secondary economic losses fall so clearly within the circle of foreseeability, and are claimed so frequently in tort cases, that courts have developed the "economic loss doctrine" to address them.

This case is an example of a court misusing foreseeability analysis to limit liability for other reasons. As stated in the introduction, courts often limit liability for clearly foreseeable harm for other policy reasons. Doubtless, the court denied liability because of the extreme burden that liability for secondary economic losses would impose in a case like this: If the dredger were liable to this plaintiff, it would be liable to all those who suffered from the interruption in service. It is certainly understandable that courts will refuse to impose overwhelming liability for secondary consequences of negligence. But it does little for clarity of analysis to mask this policy conclusion in the guise of foreseeability.

Couldn't the court, with stronger justification, have written as follows, relying on the economic loss doctrine:

> It is hardly unforeseeable that severing a major gas supply line (of which the defendant had been informed) will interrupt the flow of energy to a nearby manufacturer dependent upon that supply line, causing injury from the sudden disruption of complex manufacturing sequences and loss of products in process. However, given the magnitude of the losses that could flow from even a single interruption of such service, we think the burden of liability for such secondary losses too great to impose on the negligent tortfeasor.

PART IV

The Duty Element

CHAPTER 13

The Elusive Element of Duty: Two Principles in Search of an Exception

INTRODUCTION

It is hornbook law that the plaintiff in a negligence case must prove four elements in order to recover: duty, breach, causation, and damages. Even if the defendant was negligent, and that negligence caused injury to the plaintiff, the defendant will not be liable unless he also owed the plaintiff a duty of care. This chapter addresses the elusive element of duty.

It hardly seems that this should be a problem: Don't we all owe a duty to *everyone* not to injure them by our own negligence? Such a universal duty of care would simplify negligence law considerably: It would effectively eliminate the duty element from the plaintiff's burden of proof since a duty of care would always exist. Although such a broad rule is tempting, courts have not been willing to impose a universal duty of due care. Courts have often refused to hold defendants liable, even though they have caused clearly foreseeable harm to the plaintiff. Here, for example, are some situations in which many courts would deny recovery even though harm was to be anticipated from the defendant's conduct.

a. Adler visits city hall to pay a traffic ticket. While walking up the stairs, he sees a pen lying on the edge of one of the stair treads. He fails to pick it up, and Skinner later falls on it, breaking a leg.
b. Federal Safety Insurance Company provides fire insurance for industry. To reduce claims, Federal inspects the premises of the companies it insures for fire hazards before issuing a policy. Federal Safety

inspects Rainbow Paint Company's factory, but neglects to enter a small room in which oily rags have been left in a pile. A week later, Skinner, an employee at the plant, is burned in a fire started by those rags. He sues Federal for failing to prevent the fire by seeing that the rags were removed.

c. Reik is driving down a rural highway and witnesses an accident in which White drives into a tree. Unwilling to get involved, she drives on. White is not found for an hour, and his injuries are aggravated by the delay in receiving treatment.

d. Dr. Rogers treats Jung for an infectious form of hepatitis. He is aware that Jung is a professional dancer. However, he makes no effort to warn other dancers who may have contact with Jung. Klein, a member of Jung's dance troupe, contracts hepatitis from Jung.

In each of these examples, the actor was (we will assume) negligent, and that negligence caused the plaintiff's damages. Yet many courts would refuse to allow recovery in these cases, on the ground that the actor did not owe a duty of care to the plaintiff.

WHY COURTS IMPOSE DUTIES, OR REFUSE TO IMPOSE THEM

Tort duties are not like chemistry's Periodic Table of Elements. Nature's elements (they tell me) have a physical existence quite apart from anything we might think about them. Chemists have identified them, but (with perhaps a few high-tech exceptions) they have not created them. Tort duties, on the other hand, do not exist in nature; they are *made up* by judges because they conclude that a duty *ought to* exist under the circumstances. "[L]egal duties are not discoverable facts of nature, but merely conclusory expressions that, in cases of a particular type, liability should be imposed for damage done." *Tarasoff v. Regents of the Univ. of California*, 551 P.2d 334, 342 (Cal. 1976). "[I]t should be recognized that 'duty' is not sacrosanct in itself, but is only an expression of the sum total of those considerations of policy which lead the law to say that the plaintiff is entitled to protection." Prosser & Keeton at 358. If a court concludes that society will be better off if store owners exercise due care to assist injured customers, it will create such a duty; if a court concludes that bystanders should not be legally bound to render aid in an emergency, it will refuse to create a duty to intervene, and so on.

This fundamental fact of tort life is not something to be embarrassed about: Determining the legal rights and obligations of the parties is a fundamental task of judging. On the other hand, it is not particularly satisfying to students simply to tell them that the duty issue is difficult and judges have to decide it. Understandably, you want more guidance about such an important issue.

Though the duty issue is complex, we can at least identify major factors that judges consider in deciding whether to impose a duty in a given case. These factors include the judge's sense of morality, the foreseeability and extent of the likely harm from the defendant's conduct, the burden that the new duty will impose on the defendant, alternative ways of protecting the plaintiff's interest, the increased safety likely to result from imposing the duty, the chilling effect the duty may have on defendants' conduct, administrative problems for the courts in enforcing the duty, problems of proof, and others.

Certainly, the foreseeability of harm weighs heavily in favor of imposing a duty on the actor since it makes basic good sense that a defendant "should" avoid foreseeable injuries to others. For example, it is highly foreseeable that a mental patient who threatens to kill a relative will do so if released from custody, or that a parent will suffer traumatic shock if a negligent driver hits his child. Where resulting harm is so likely to follow, the argument is persuasive that the court should impose a duty of care to prevent it.[1]

The moral argument is also strong in many duty cases. Most people would believe that it is "right" for an employer to go to the aid of an injured worker, or a doctor to take steps to assure that an HIV-infected patient does not engage in unsafe sexual practices. This argument is particularly persuasive if the defendant is uniquely positioned to prevent harm. The psychiatrist who releases a patient who has threatened a relative, for example, may be the only one in a position to warn the relative. The police officer who stops a drunk driver is uniquely placed to prevent that driver from causing an accident.

Other factors, however, weigh against imposing a duty of care, even if harm is foreseeable and avoidable. Courts hesitate to create duties that impose excessive burdens on actors. A court might, for example, refuse to impose a duty on school officials to supervise school children at bus stops. Such a duty would impose an expensive burden on school districts, which can be fulfilled as well, if not better, by parents. Similarly, many courts have refused to impose a duty of care on municipalities to properly inspect private property. Here too, the burden on municipalities would be exceedingly

1. The Third Restatement would deny foreseeability a role in determination of duty, arguing that this is a jury issue relevant to proximate cause, not a factor in legal analysis of duty. See Restatement (Third) of Torts (Liability for Physical and Emotional Harm) §7, cmt. j (2010). See also Dobbs' Law of Torts §256. However, myriad cases hold that the foreseeability of harm is a relevant consideration in determining the existence of a duty. Your (very) Humble Author predicts that judges will continue to find foreseeability of harm an important factor in crafting duties in tort law.

broad, and the risk can be averted by owners. Similarly, a court refused to hold that a hospital has a duty to warn all patients of the risks of medications, on the ground that the duty would be too broad, and that it can be better fulfilled by the patient's doctor. *Kirk v. Michael Reese Hosp. & Medical Ctr.*, 513 N.E.2d 387, 396-397 (Ill. 1987).

Administrative problems of enforcing the duty may also influence the court's judgment. For many years, courts denied liability for infliction of emotional distress on the ground that the risk of fraudulent claims and excessive litigation was too great. Similarly, they rejected claims for injury to fetuses partly on the ground that it would be extremely difficult to prove that the defendant's conduct was the cause of prenatal injury.

In other cases, the chilling effect of imposing the duty has counseled hesitation. In *Eiseman v. State*, 511 N.E.2d 1128 (N.Y. 1987), the court refused to hold that a college had a duty to control the acts of a parolee admitted to a college enrichment program. The court was unwilling to create a duty that would force colleges to place discriminatory restrictions on the very persons the program was meant to assist in reintegrating into society. Similarly, some courts have refused to impose a duty on theater operators to prevent violence by viewers of violent movies, to avoid chilling activity protected by the First Amendment. See, e.g., *Yakubowicz v. Paramount Pictures Corp.*, 536 N.E.2d 1067, 1071-1072 (Mass. 1989).

Policies established by the legislature will also influence the court's duty analysis. Courts that have imposed a tort duty on the police to arrest drunk drivers have noted the firm legislative policy of controlling drunk driving. See *Irwin v. Town of Ware*, 467 N.E.2d 1292, 1302 (Mass. 1984). Similarly, the *Tarasoff* court, in concluding that the psychiatrist had a duty to warn, rejected the argument that it would impair doctor/patient confidentiality in part because a statute rejected the privilege in situations involving danger to third persons. 551 P.2d at 346-347.

Other policy considerations may also be relevant to the duty analysis, depending on the facts of each case. In most, no single factor will be determinative; the judge will balance many to reach a conclusion. See generally Dobbs' Law of Torts §255. As an advocate, you may not always be able to predict that conclusion, but you can learn to identify factors relevant to the duty analysis, and to formulate arguments for or against imposing a duty based on those factors.

In many common situations, decades of precedent have defined fairly clearly the extent to which the courts will recognize a duty of care. The remainder of this introduction addresses common situations in which courts impose such a duty—or refuse to. However, it is important to remember that the duties described are not immutable truths; they are pragmatic policy judgments that may be reconsidered by future judges as society and public attitudes evolve.

FIRST PRINCIPLES: TORTS AND THE COUCH POTATO

I find it useful to analyze tort duties in terms of two basic principles, each liberally qualified with exceptions. The first principle is that courts generally refuse to impose liability for doing nothing. If Adler, a couch potato, spends all of his time on the sofa watching TV, he is in an excellent position to avoid tort liability. Indeed, as a Torts professor, I would advise you to do just that. People get into tort suits in the weirdest of ways, but they have little to fear from being inert.

This long-held view of the common law, that there is no liability for the failure to act, is illustrated by the hypothetical of the callous bystander who watches a blind man walk into a busy street and fails to call out a warning. Our moral sense is repulsed by the illustration, yet in most states the bystander still has no *legal* duty to act to protect another, and therefore is not liable for failing to do so. Similarly, a sunbather who watches a child going under the waves has no duty to dive in the water, throw her a life ring, or even notify a nearby lifeguard:

> The fact that the actor realizes or should realize that action on his part is necessary for another's aid or protection does not of itself impose upon him a duty to take such action.

Restatement (Second) of Torts §314.[2] According to the Second Restatement,

> The origin of the rule lay in the early common law distinction between action and inaction, or "misfeasance" and "non-feasance." In the early law one who injured another by a positive affirmative act was held liable without any great regard even for his fault. But the courts were far too much occupied with the more flagrant forms of misbehavior to be greatly concerned with one who merely did nothing, even though another might suffer serious harm because of his omission to act. Hence, liability for nonfeasance was slow to receive any recognition in the law.

Restatement (Second) of Torts §314 cmt. c.

Although torts scholars usually cite this no-duty-to-act principle with embarrassment, there are some substantial policy arguments to support it. The defendant whose act (misfeasance) endangers the plaintiff has "created a new risk of harm to the plaintiff, while by 'nonfeasance' he has at least made [the plaintiff's] situation no worse, and has merely failed to benefit him by interfering in his affairs." Prosser & Keeton at 373. Other defenders

2. The Third Restatement (§37) takes essentially the same position.

of the principle emphasize the infringement on individual liberty posed by coercing services from unwilling bystanders,[3] and the difficulty of defining the duty if it is to be imposed. For example, how great an effort would the defendant have to make? Would a bystander have to dive in after a drowning child if he could not swim? *Which* bystanders would have the duty—a whole beachful? Would bystanders be required to subordinate important interests of their own to effectuate rescue (e.g., postpone visiting a seriously ill relative to assist at an accident scene)?

These objections are probably not insurmountable; most European countries impose a limited duty to aid, as does the state of Vermont. See Vt. Stat. Ann. tit. 12 §519. Yet most American courts have not rejected the no-duty-to-act rule outright. Instead they have nibbled away at it by carving out exceptions (discussed below at pp. 273–277). For an interesting defense of the no-duty-to-rescue rule, see M. Scordoto, Understanding the Absence of a Duty to Reasonably Rescue in American Tort Law, 82 Tulane L. Rev. 1447 (2008).

SECOND FIRST PRINCIPLES: RISK CREATION AS A SOURCE OF DUTY

The second broad duty principle complements the first: Those who do act, who choose to engage in activities that create a risk of injury to others, *do* have a duty to exercise care to avoid injuring others. If Bruner drives his car negligently and hits Gilligan, he has set loose a dangerous force that creates a risk to others. If Freud is reroofing his garage and drops his hammer on a pedestrian, that also creates a new risk of harm. If Chef Adler bakes a quiche with spoiled ingredients, causing food poisoning, he too has set in motion a new force capable of causing harm. These defendants, unlike the bystander in the nonfeasance cases, have "created new risks" by their activities which have caused injury.

Far and away the largest proportion of negligence cases—perhaps 90 percent—involve situations like these, in which defendants have let loose dangerous forces that have caused injury. In these cases, the defendant's

3. Consider the case posed by Professor Epstein in his defense of the rule:

> X as a representative of a private charity asks you for $10 in order to save the life of some starving child in a country ravaged by war. There are other donors available but the number of needy children exceeds that number. The money means "nothing" to you. Are you under an obligation to give the $10?

R. Epstein, A Theory of Strict Liability, 2 J. Legal Stud. 151, 198-199 (1973).

choice to engage in risk-creating conduct for his own benefit imposes the reciprocal duty to exercise due care toward those who may foreseeably be injured by that conduct. The law tolerates, indeed, encourages, activity, including activities that impose risks of injury on others. But it has long recognized that those who unleash such forces owe a duty to others to keep that risk to a reasonable level.

In most cases, risk creation is the obvious basis of the duty to exercise due care. Duty is probably the least frequently contested element of a negligence claim because most negligence cases arise from active conduct, and it is clear that the actor owed a duty to exercise due care toward those who might foreseeably be injured by it. For example, the duty issue is seldom raised in highway accident cases since we all understand that we owe a duty of due care to others in driving a car. Similarly, it is clear that a utility company that erects a telephone pole owes a duty of care to anyone who might foreseeably be injured if it falls.

In analyzing duty issues, it is important to keep in mind these two divergent first principles—on the one hand, the bystander who has not created any risk and who declines to get involved, and, on the other, the actor whose conduct creates a risk of injury. However, these two paradigms do not, unfortunately, resolve all the cases. For various policy reasons, courts have spawned exceptions to both principles. As discussed below, a person who has done nothing may sometimes be held liable for failing to act. And, at times, a person who has created a risk will *not* be held liable, even though her risk-creating activity leads to foreseeable injury.

EXCEPTIONS TO THE NO-DUTY RULE: DUTIES OF AFFIRMATIVE ACTION

Let's look first at some exceptions to the no-duty-to-act rule. Courts have not hesitated to create "affirmative duties" to act for the protection of another where some policy justifies departing from the no-duty rule. When such a duty of affirmative action is found, the actor may not defend on the basis that "I just didn't want to get involved": The law imposes a duty to get involved.

A. Duty Based on a Special Relationship to the Victim

Courts often impose a duty to aid based on a preexisting relationship between the defendant and the person who needs assistance. See Restatement (Third) of Torts §40. Here are some typical examples in which courts have imposed a duty to act for the protection of another due to a "special relationship" to the plaintiff:

- A train conductor sees a passenger being assaulted by another, but fails to come to the victim's aid.
- A factory owner fails to assist an employee who is trapped in an elevator in the course of his employment.
- School officials note that a child is feverish but fail to seek medical care for the child.
- A prison inmate complains repeatedly to a guard of stomach pains, but the guard fails to take any steps to get him medical help.

In each of these situations, the defendant is not the source of the injury-producing conduct. The school officials, for example, did not cause the child's fever, nor did the train conductor assault the passenger. However, because of the defendant's relationship to the victim in these cases, the courts impose a duty on the defendant to take affirmative steps to minimize or avert the harm. In the factory example, the duty is based on the fact that the employer is uniquely situated to mitigate the harm and that the employee is on the premises for the benefit of the employer. The duty in the school case is based on the fact that school officials take charge of children with knowledge of their need for protection. The duty to prisoners is premised on taking charge of the prisoner and depriving him of the ability to act for his own protection.

B. Duty Based on a Special Relationship to the Perpetrator

A second category of special relationship exceptions to the no-duty rule involves situations in which courts impose a duty to control one person to prevent him from injuring others. Examples include the duty of a parent to control a child in certain circumstances (Restatement (Second) of Torts §316) and the duty of an employer to control an employee. Restatement (Second) of Torts §317. The Restatement imposes a similar duty on one who takes charge of another with "dangerous propensities":

> One who takes charge of a third person whom he knows or should know to be likely to cause bodily harm to others if not controlled is under a duty to exercise reasonable care to control the third person to prevent him from doing such harm.

Restatement (Second) of Torts §319. Accord: Restatement (Third) of Torts: Liability for Physical and Emotional Harm §41. This exception, which applies primarily to those in charge of mental patients or prisoners, reflects the courts' conclusion that the defendant accepts a duty of care by taking charge of a person who poses a risk of injury. The employer's duty to control an employee is presumably based on the benefit the employer derives from the activities of the employee. In addition, as noted above, the defendant in those situations is often uniquely positioned to prevent the harm.

Perhaps the most famous affirmative duty case, *Tarasoff v. Regents of the Univ. of California*, 551 P.2d 334 (1976), was decided on the basis of this special relationship principle. The *Tarasoff* court concluded that the psychiatrist's relationship to a dangerous patient gave rise to a duty to warn the patient's intended victim that the patient had threatened to kill her. This particular application of the special relationship approach has been controversial. Because of the burden this duty imposes on defendants, some courts have refused to extend it beyond situations involving a threat to a particular victim. See *Leonard v. State*, 491 N.W.2d 508, 512 (Iowa 1992) (holding psychiatrist owes no duty to members of general public in discharging patient).

C. Duty Based on Innocent Creation of the Risk

Another set of exceptions to the no-duty rule involves situations in which the defendant, without negligence, creates the risk that causes injury to the plaintiff. See Restatement (Second) of Torts §321, which provides:

> (1) If the actor does an act, and subsequently realizes or should realize that it has created an unreasonable risk of causing physical harm to another, he is under a duty to exercise reasonable care to prevent the risk from taking effect.

The Restatement gives the example of a driver whose truck suddenly becomes disabled on the road and fails to warn oncoming traffic. Restatement (Second) of Torts §321 illus. 3. Under §321, the driver, though not negligent, is the author of the risk, and owes an affirmative duty to warn other drivers of the danger. Similarly, under Restatement (Second) of Torts §322, an actor who has injured another, even without negligence, has an affirmative duty to render assistance to prevent further harm to the injured party. For example, if Freud hits Adler, a pedestrian, with his car and knocks him into the street, §322 requires Freud to take reasonable steps to protect Adler from further injury.[4]

4. This duty is also recognized in the Third Restatement of Torts. See Restatement (Third) of Torts: Liability for Physical and Emotional Harm §39.

These exceptions to the no-duty rule are presumably based on the risk creation rationale. Even though Freud was not negligent, he has, by his risk-creating conduct for his own purposes, placed Adler in a position of danger. To require him to go to Adler's aid "is simply requiring [a person] to minimize the consequences of risks which society gives him a privilege to create." F. James Jr., Note, Scope of Duty in Negligence Cases, 47 Nw. U. L. Rev. 778, 804 (1953).

This duty to help persons injured or placed in peril by the actor without negligence illustrates the way in which duties evolve. Both the Second Restatement and the Third Restatement take the position that innocently placing another in peril gives rise to a duty of care. However, §322 of the First Restatement of Torts limited the duty to persons "made helpless by *tortious* conduct" (emphasis added). What changed in the intervening years to make judges willing to impose a duty to assist, even if the actor had not been negligent? Perhaps the New Deal and the Second World War tempered the rampant individualism of the nineteenth century. Perhaps the increased frequency of automobile accidents played a part. Perhaps the lessening of a moralistic focus on fault, and increased emphasis on risk creation and cost avoidance as bases for liability, have contributed. For whatever reasons, as society has changed, so has the scope of duty.

D. The Gratuitous Services Exception

Another widely recognized exception to the no-duty-to-act principle arises where the defendant, though under no initial duty to do so, goes to the aid of another:

> One who, being under no duty to do so, takes charge of another who is helpless adequately to aid or protect himself is subject to liability to the other for any bodily harm caused to him by
>
> (a) the failure of the actor to exercise reasonable care to secure the safety of the other while within the actor's charge, or
>
> (b) the actor's discontinuing his aid or protection, if by so doing he leaves the other in a worse position than when the actor took charge of him.

Restatement (Second) of Torts §324. This exception is illustrated by the bystander who sees a pedestrian hit by a car, and goes to the pedestrian's assistance, but negligently causes further injury to her by handling her roughly or using clearly inappropriate first aid techniques.

Ironically, this exception to the no-duty principle imposes the risk of tort liability on the bystander who makes the worthy choice to render assistance. Once Smith decides to "get involved," he assumes a duty of care, although, had he simply stood by or walked away, he would have incurred no liability. See Restatement (Second) of Torts §314.[5] Presumably, the rationale is that the actor, while virtuous, is still a risk creator in rendering assistance, and should not be licensed to mishandle the victim with impunity.

EXCEPTIONS TO THE RISK CREATION RULE: DUTY AS A LIMITING FACTOR IN NEGLIGENCE CASES

This introduction began by describing two "first principles." First there is no general duty to act for the benefit of another, and second, those who choose to act owe a duty to others to use due care in such conduct. Then, we explored some exceptions to the no-duty principle, situations in which courts have imposed a duty on one person to act for the benefit of another. Now, let's consider some exceptions to the second "first principle," that persons who choose to engage in risk-creating activity owe a duty of care to others who might foreseeably be injured by that activity.

One school of thought argues that there should be *no* exception to this second "first principle," that actors who engage in risk-creating activities should be liable for all injuries foreseeably caused by their negligence. The argument traces its roots to the following statement in *Heaven v. Pender*, 1881-1885 All E.R. Rep. 35, 39 (1883).

> [W]henever one person is by circumstances placed in such a position with regard to another that any one of ordinary sense who did think would at once recognise that, if he did not use ordinary care and skill in his own conduct with regard to those circumstances, he would cause danger of injury to the person or property of the other, a duty arises to use ordinary care and skill to avoid such danger.

Despite the intuitive appeal of this statement, no court accepts it without qualification.[6] Liability for all foreseeable injury from negligent conduct would impose too heavy a burden on defendants in some situations. Sometimes, the extent of this burden leads courts to restrict liability for

---

5. The Third Restatement has a similar provision—§42—but it is harder to understand, so I have used the Second Restatement provision for illustration purposes. Neither version, of course, is "the law" of any jurisdiction unless adopted by the courts of that jurisdiction.
6. See Restatement (Second) of Torts §302 cmt. a: "In general, anyone who does an affirmative act is under a duty to others to exercise due care of a reasonable man to protect them against an unreasonable risk of harm to them arising out of the act." See also Restatement (Third) of Torts: Liability for Physical and Emotional Harm §7(a) (actor whose conduct creates a risk of physical harm "ordinarily" owes a duty of reasonable care).

foreseeable harm by holding that the defendant "owed no duty" to the plaintiff.

Many casebooks illustrate the point with two classic limited duty problems, duties to the unborn and duties to avoid inflicting emotional distress. In each of these areas, courts have drawn the circle of duty considerably more narrowly than the limits of foreseeable harm. For example, many early cases held that a defendant who injured a fetus (e.g., by negligently hitting the mother with a car), was not liable, because there was "no duty to the unborn." See, e.g., *Magnolia Coca Cola Bottling Co. v. Jordan*, 78 S.W.2d 944, 945-950 (Tex. 1937), *overruled*, *Leal v. C. C. Pitts Sand & Gravel Inc.*, 419 S.W.2d 820, 822 (Tex. 1967). While such injuries are foreseeable, the early cases denied liability for policy reasons, including the difficulties of proving the cause of prenatal injury, reluctance to treat fetuses as "persons" in the absence of statutory authority, and the risk of fraudulent claims.

More recently, many courts have recognized a duty of care to the unborn in at least some circumstances. See generally Liability for Prenatal Injuries, 40 A.L.R. 3d 1222 (1971). This is not because the defendant's conduct is any different or the plaintiff's injury any more foreseeable. Modern courts, for various reasons of policy, are simply more willing to impose a duty in such cases. Doubtless two reasons for the shift are the improved ability to trace the source of fetal injury and the wide availability of insurance for such claims.

Similarly, early cases refused to allow recovery for infliction of emotional distress unless the plaintiff suffered a physical impact. For example, recovery was denied where the plaintiff, narrowly missed by a speeding car, suffered serious fright and a resulting heart attack. Here again, it was often clear that the defendant had created the risk and that the risk had caused foreseeable injury to the plaintiff. Yet the courts refused to recognize a duty here, out of fear of fraudulent claims and greatly increased litigation. Recent cases have broadened this duty as well, but liability for negligent infliction remains considerably narrower in most states than the all-foreseeable-risks principle argued for in *Heaven v. Pender*. See Chapter 14, which analyzes claims for negligent infliction of emotional distress in detail.

Courts have similarly limited the duty of care in many other types of cases, based on policy considerations unique to each situation. Some examples include liability for serving alcohol to intoxicated patrons, liability of lawyers to beneficiaries for negligent drafting of a will, liability of accountants to third parties (other than their clients) who rely on their opinions, liability for secondary economic losses, and the liability of landowners for injury to entrants on their land. In these and other situations, courts often refuse, for policy reasons, to impose liability even though the defendant has caused foreseeable harm to others.

THE RELATION OF DUTY TO PROXIMATE CAUSE

Much confusion exists as to the distinction between the duty element in negligence cases and proximate cause limitations on liability. It may help, however, to distinguish two types of limitations that courts place on liability: First, limiting liability to the foreseeable consequences of the defendant's negligent act, and second, denying liability for consequences that *are* foreseeable, for the types of policy reasons discussed in this chapter.

Courts very frequently use the concept of *proximate cause* to limit liability to the foreseeable consequences of a negligent act. Consider, for example, the hypothetical in which the defendant leaves the ignition key in his car, and it is stolen by a terrorist and used to bomb an embassy. The defendant may well owe a duty not to leave his car open to theft, particularly in an area where teenagers congregate. Yet the result here is so idiosyncratic, so beyond the scope of harm to be expected, that most courts would refuse to hold the defendant liable for the bombing damages. The rationale here is that liability should be limited to the circle of foreseeability, the consequences that the defendant could reasonably anticipate at the time he acted.

By contrast, courts often use the *duty* concept to deny liability for consequences that *are* foreseeable, as in the early emotional distress and fetal injury cases. These courts refused to impose liability for policy reasons, and found the duty concept a proper tool for limiting recovery much more narrowly than foreseeability analysis would.

Unfortunately, this distinction between duty and proximate cause analysis is not consistently honored in the cases. The issue in *Palsgraf*, for example, was foreseeability, yet Justice Cardozo used duty analysis to reject Mrs. Palsgraf's claim, while Justice Andrews's dissent concluded that she was owed a duty and analyzed the case in proximate cause terms. In other cases courts use proximate cause language in placing policy limits on liability for clearly foreseeable harm. For example, earlier cases held that a barkeep who served liquor to an intoxicated patron was not "the proximate cause" of her drunk driving, though nothing could be more foreseeable than a drunk driver causing an accident.

When they make me the King of Torts, my first decree shall be that courts must always use proximate cause analysis to bar liability for unforeseeable harm, and duty analysis to impose policy limits on liability for harm that *is* foreseeable. But in our motley kingdom as it stands today, we have to live with the fact that the two concepts are sometimes used interchangeably. Even if the courts' duty and proximate cause analysis is not always consistent, however, it will still be helpful to keep in mind the above distinction between refusing to impose liability for unforeseeable consequences (the classic proximate cause situation), and refusing, for policy reasons, to impose liability for ones that are foreseeable (the classic duty limitation).

Examples

Matters of Principle

1. On a breezy morning after a storm, Ellis leaves his house to walk to the train station. As he passes the house of his neighbor, Klein, he notices a tree limb in the road in front of her driveway. Pressed for time, he continues on his way to catch his train. Klein is injured when her car hits the limb as she backs out of the driveway. She sues Ellis for failing to warn her of the danger. Ellis moves to dismiss Klein's complaint, on the ground that, as a matter of law, he had no duty to Klein under the circumstances.
   a. Should this case be analyzed under the no-duty principle (and its exceptions) or the risk creation principle (and its exceptions)?
   b. Will the motion be granted?

2. Muller, while tearing down an old shed with a friend, Ehrlich, negligently knocks out a post which supports the upper floor. The floor falls on Ehrlich, who suffers a concussion. She is taken to the hospital and kept for observation overnight. During the night, the hospital wing catches fire, and she is burned. She sues Muller for her injuries.
   a. Is this a risk creation case or a no-duty case?
   b. How should the court rule if Muller moves to dismiss the claim for the burns?

Limited Duties

3. Reik decides to go boating. She goes down to the local marina, rents a rowboat from Lake Rentals, and takes her family out in the boat. An hour after they get out onto the lake, the wind comes up, the boat capsizes, and Reik is drowned.

   Her estate sues Lake Rentals for wrongful death. The complaint alleges that Lake was negligent in failing to supply adequate life vests, in renting a boat that was not seaworthy for the lake, and in failing to warn her that strong winds were expected that afternoon.
   a. Which theory is likely to be challenged on no-duty grounds?
   b. How do you think it will be resolved?

4. Consider the example from the Introduction in which Dr. Rogers treats Jung, a professional dancer, for hepatitis, but fails to warn his dance troupe that he has a disease that can be spread through physical contact. Klein, one of his dance partners, contracts hepatitis and sues Dr. Rogers. Naturally, Klein, in arguing that Rogers owed her a duty of care, relies

on *Tarasoff v. Regents of the University of California*, 551 P.2d 334 (1976), which held that a therapist had a duty to warn a homicide victim that a mental patient had threatened to kill her.[7]

a. You represent Rogers. How would you argue that the duty created in *Tarasoff* should not be extended to this case?
b. You represent Klein. If the court refuses to recognize a duty to warn her, what more limited duty argument might still support recovery?

Her Spouse's Keeper?

5. Antell, an alcoholic, injures Freud while driving drunk. Freud learns that Antell had been drinking at home all day before the accident. Antell's wife had threatened to take away his car keys (usually left hanging on a hook in the kitchen when not in use), but had failed to do so. Freud sues Mrs. Antell for negligence, and she moves to dismiss.
   a. Should this case be analyzed under the no-duty principle (and its exceptions) or the risk creation principle (and its exceptions)?
   b. How should the court rule on the motion?

The Priest and the Levite

6. Dr. Rogers, a doctor in general practice, is driving to work one morning on a quiet country road. He witnesses a single-car accident in which the driver, Jung, hits a tree, opens the driver's side door and falls to the ground. Anticipating a busy morning at the office, he drives on. Jung suffers permanent injuries which would have been considerably less severe if he had received prompt treatment. He brings a negligence action against Rogers.
   a. Did Dr. Rogers cause any injury to Jung?
   b. Will the court dismiss the case for lack of duty if it applies §324 of the Second Restatement (see p. 276)?
   c. Suppose that Dr. Rogers witnesses the accident and calls 911 to report it. He then drives away. Would he then be liable for failing to provide emergency treatment to Jung?
   d. How do you think the court would rule if Rogers recognized Jung as a patient he had treated for ulcers, yet still failed to stop?

7. Assume, on the facts above, that Dr. Rogers *did* stop to help Jung. In an effort to make him more comfortable, he moves Jung over onto the grass. However, because Jung's leg was broken, the move caused serious

7. See, e.g., 551 P.2d at 340, where the court holds that "[w]hen a therapist determines, or pursuant to the standards of his profession should determine, that his patient presents a serious danger of violence to another, he incurs an obligation to use reasonable care to protect the intended victim against such danger. The discharge of this duty may require the therapist to . . . warn the intended victim or others likely to apprise the victim of the danger. . . ."

additional damage to Jung's leg. Jung sues Rogers for negligence. Rogers moves to dismiss on the basis that he owed no duty of care to Jung. How will the court rule on the motion if it applies §324 of the Second Restatement (see p. 276)?

8. Suppose, on the facts of Example 7, that Klein, a stranger, happens by and sees Jung lying unconscious on the ground. She moves Jung off the road and then, realizing that Jung is severely injured, she becomes upset and drives away. Jung suffers serious injuries from loss of blood, which could have been avoided had Klein remained with him and bound up his wound. Would Klein be liable to Jung under §324 of the Second Restatement?

9. While Skinner is driving down a West Dakota street, a mud flap from a truck blows onto his windshield. Skinner instinctively ducks, and his car swerves onto the sidewalk, pinning Ortega, a pedestrian, against a building. Skinner gets out and tries to extract Ortega by pushing the car. Instead, the car rolls farther forward, aggravating Ortega's injury. Ortega sues Skinner for negligently causing the increased injury.

   Skinner moves to dismiss based on West Dakota's Good Samaritan statute, which provides in part that "A person who, without a duty to do so, renders emergency care at or near the scene of an emergency, gratuitously and in good faith, is not liable for any civil damages as a result of any act or omission by the person rendering the emergency care, unless the person is grossly negligent." How should the court rule on Skinner's motion?

Remy's Revenge

10. As the introduction notes, a common duty problem in tort law involves whether a duty of care is owed to unborn children. Early cases generally rejected such a duty, but more recent cases tend to recognize it. For example, most courts today would recognize that drivers owe a duty of care to unborn children, so that a driver who negligently injures a pregnant woman, leading to injuries to the fetus, would be liable for those injuries. See Dobbs' Law of Torts §366.

    Remy v. MacDonald, 440 Mass. 675 (2004), involved a fascinating twist on this problem. In *Remy*, an unborn child was injured in an auto accident, and sued for her injuries. The twist was that she sued her mother, who was driving one of the cars.[8] Fifty years ago, this suit would have been

---

8. Why would she sue her mother rather than the other driver? Most likely, the other driver had limited insurance, so the child (suing through her father) sought to reach the mother's insurance policy as well to obtain full compensation. (There is always the possibility, too, that the accident was caused solely by the mother's negligence.)

barred by parental immunity. But that doctrine has been abrogated in most states, including Massachusetts. If Remy's mother had delivered her, and caused injuries to her while driving home from the hospital, Remy could have recovered from her mother for those injuries. And, as just noted, if she were injured while in utero by the negligence of the other driver in the accident, she could have recovered from the other driver after being born. So why not, putting these two principles together, recover from her mother for her prenatal injury due to the mother's negligence?

a. What principle is in play here, the special relationship principle or the risk creation principle?
b. What are the arguments *against* recognizing that the mother owed her fetus a duty of reasonable care?

11. Bettelheim, a bar owner, is working behind the bar when a distraught passerby runs in to call the police to stop a robbery out on the street. Bettelheim refuses to allow him to use the phone. Couch, the victim of the robbery, is then stabbed by his assailant and sues Bettelheim for his injuries.
    a. Which of our two principles should we start from in analyzing this case?
    b. Should Bettelheim be held liable?

Judge Fudd Does His Duty

12. Jack, a convicted murderer, escapes while being transported to court by Freud, a prison guard, and attacks White on the street while trying to steal his car. White sues Freud for his injuries. Judge Fudd instructs the jury in part as follows:

> If you find that the defendant had charge of Jack at the time of the incident, and that Jack was likely to cause harm to others if not controlled, then you may find that the defendant owed a duty to the plaintiff to prevent the attack by Jack on the plaintiff.

Can you spot two fundamental problems with Judge Fudd's instruction?

Explanations

Matters of Principle

1. a. This case should be analyzed under the first principle, that there is no general duty to act for the protection or aid of another. Ellis has not created a risk to Klein; Mother Nature is responsible for that. The question is whether, for one reason or another, the court will impose a duty on Ellis to take affirmative steps to protect Klein from a risk he did not create.

b. As the introduction suggests, the general rule is that Ellis is not his neighbor's keeper. He is under no legal duty to aid another simply because she may need it, because it would be easy or morally appropriate, or because the risk to the other person is great. Archaic though the rule may seem, it is alive and well. The court will grant Ellis's motion, on the ground that he owed no duty to Klein, unless she can establish some basis for an exception to the no-duty principle.

The facts here do not suggest a basis for such an exception. Ellis has not created the hazard, so the most likely basis for avoiding the effect of the general rule is to argue that a special relationship between him and Klein supports a duty to aid her. The only source of such a relationship in this case is the fact that Ellis and Klein are neighbors. But in a society that puts a premium on individualism, it is very doubtful that a court would transform neighborliness into a legally enforceable duty. Becoming a neighbor is not like taking charge of a pupil or running a train service. People hardly expect that they have assumed any degree of care for their neighbors, whom they may like, loathe, or ignore as the case may be.[9]

While imposing such a duty might lead to a marginal decrease in injuries, it would also create potentially intrusive relationships between abutters who may have no interest in anything but being left alone. Can't you just imagine the busybody next door coming over weekly with a list of dangerous conditions you should abate immediately for your own good? Those dead limbs should come off your trees; that big flower pot on the railing could fall; you need a safer lid on your well; you ought to trim those bushes at the end of your driveway, and so on. It's enough to make the no-duty rule look halfway respectable!

2. a. This case is clearly based on Muller's risk-creating conduct. Muller's active conduct in demolishing the shed has created a risk of injury to Ehrlich, and she has suffered injury from that risk.

b. This example illustrates the distinction between existence of a duty and the *extent* of liability in a situation where a duty clearly exists. Any court would conclude that Muller owed Ehrlich a duty of care in working on the shed, and that he is liable for her concussion. He engaged in risk-creating conduct, and Ehrlich's injury results from it. It was foreseeable that, if the floor collapsed, the collapse would cause personal injury, and it did.

---

9. For a provocative feminist critique of the no-duty rule, clearly rejecting the result in examples like this, see L. Bender, A Lawyer's Primer on Feminist Theory and Tort, 38 J. of Legal Ed. 3, 33-36 (1988).

However, many courts would refuse to hold Muller liable for Ehrlich's burns since the risk that she would be burned in a fire at the hospital was unforeseeable. To me, this is best explained in proximate cause terms, as a refusal to hold a defendant liable for bizarre consequences. Yet many courts would conclude, following Cardozo's approach in *Palsgraf*, that Muller "owed no duty" to Ehrlich to prevent this type of harm since being burned in a hospital fire was not one of the foreseeable risks of knocking out the porch post.

Whichever formula the court uses, the crux of the matter here is that courts are unwilling to extend liability for risk-creating conduct beyond the circle of foreseeable risk. They sometimes draw the liability limit *short* of foreseeability, but very seldom impose liability *beyond* its bounds.

Limited Duties

3. a. The estate's third theory raises the most difficult duty question. Lake Rentals engaged in risk-creating conduct by renting the boat to Reik: It would clearly create unreasonable risks if it rented her a boat that wasn't seaworthy, or that lacked adequate life vests. However, it is more of a stretch to argue that they assumed a duty to warn her about the weather.

   b. While Lake Rentals clearly engaged in risk-creating conduct by renting Reik a boat, there must be some limits to the duty it has assumed. Must it, having rented the boat, instruct Reik in safe methods of rowing? Must it warn her of submerged rocks on the other side of the lake? Must it explain to her that putting all passengers on one side of the boat will cause it to tip, or that in cold water one might die of hypothermia before reaching shore? If the court imposes a duty to warn of the weather, these cases will follow hard upon. At the same time, boaters are in as good a position as Lake Rentals to check the weather before they take to the lake. In the case from which this example is drawn, the court held that the marina had no duty to monitor the weather and warn of expected winds. The court emphasized that the duty would be "unwieldy" and that boaters are equally able to ascertain these matters for themselves. *Leach v. Mountain Lake*, 120 F.3d 871, 873 (8th Cir. 1997). Accord: *In re Aramark Sports & Entertainment Services, LLC*, 831 F.3d 1264, 1279-1284 (10th Cir. 2016).

   Note that here the plaintiff's injury is clearly foreseeable to the defendant. It should hardly be surprising to Lake Rentals that a small boat will founder in high winds, especially if it knew the winds were coming. Liability is denied, not for lack of proximate cause, but because the judicial system is unwilling to impose a duty to prevent the harm.

4. a. There is some force to the argument that *Tarasoff* supports recovery for Klein. Rogers has assumed a duty of care by accepting Jung as a patient, and he was uniquely placed to prevent the harm. Imposing a duty to warn on Rogers would perhaps reduce the risk that Jung would infect others, just as warning Tarasoff might have prevented her death.

However, there is a strong argument that imposing a duty to warn Klein is an unwarranted extension of *Tarasoff.* In *Tarasoff,* the psychiatrist was aware of a risk to a particular person. Here, the risk is to a large, ill-defined class of persons. Would Rogers be required to seek them out or to obtain a list of all possible dance partners? Who else would he be required to warn? In addition, there is a significant difference between Jung in this case and the mental patient in *Tarasoff.* Presumably, Jung has no desire to infect others, and can take steps to avoid doing so. By contrast, the patient in *Tarasoff* had every incentive to conceal the risk he posed from his intended victim.

In addition, imposing a duty to warn would seriously breach the confidentiality of the doctor/patient relationship. Rogers would have to reveal Jung's disease to a large group of persons, not just to one individual.

A few cases have imposed a duty to warn members of a patient's family of a communicable disease. See, e.g., *Safer v. Estate of Pack,* 677 A.2d 1188 (N.J. Super. 1996) (duty to inform member of patient's family of genetic risk). Compare *Lemon v. Stewart,* 682 A.2d 1177 (Md. Ct. Spec. App. 1996) (no duty to inform family members that patient was HIV positive); *Gammill v. United States,* 727 F.2d 950 (10th Cir. 1984) (doctor owed no duty to warn friends who contracted hepatitis while babysitting for children of infected patient); see generally Annot., 3 A.L.R. 5th 370 (1992). But this example entails a considerable expansion of the duty that most courts would hesitate to approve.

b. Since courts are naturally hesitant to create broad new duties, plaintiff's counsel should argue for the narrowest duty that will serve her purpose. Here, Klein can argue that Rogers had a duty to *warn the patient* of the risk of spreading the disease through contact. This duty is not subject to the same objections as the wider duty to warn third parties. It is easily performed while treating the patient, involves no breach of confidentiality, and places no burden on Rogers to identify persons at risk. Consequently, this duty has been much more widely accepted. See, e.g., *Reisner v. Regents of the University of California,* 37 Cal. Rptr. 2d 518 (Cal. App. 1995) (third party later infected by patient may sue hospital for failure to inform patient of HIV infection).

Of course, if Klein relies on this narrower duty, she will face a further problem: causation. She will have to establish that Jung, if warned, would have avoided the contacts through which he gave

Klein the disease. Even if warned, Jung might not have acted on the advice, since his livelihood was at stake.

Her Spouse's Keeper?

5. a. This case should be analyzed under the no-duty principle and its exceptions. This is not a case in which Mrs. Antell has created the risk that injured Freud. The direct risk-creating conduct was her husband's—the supremely antisocial act of driving while intoxicated. If she is liable for it, it will have to be based on some affirmative duty to avert that risk.

   b. This motion should be granted unless some exception to the no-duty principle applies. Naturally, the special relationship exceptions spring to mind as a promising source of such a duty; what relation is "special" if not marriage?

   Marriage is indeed sacred, but it is not an automatic source of vicarious liability for the torts of one's spouse, nor have courts concluded that tying the knot gives rise to a duty to control an errant spouse. Even though it would have been easy and socially beneficial for her to palm the keys, most courts would conclude that Mrs. Antell is not liable to Freud for failing to do so. Cf. *Andrade v. Baptiste*, 411 Mass. 560 (1992) (wife had no duty to prevent husband from storing weapons in home she owned, though she knew of his serious drinking problem). See also *Grover v. Stechel*, 45 P.3d 80 (N.M. App. 2002) (mother supporting adult son owed no duty to protect third party from his violent tendencies). But see *Volpe v. Gallagher*, 821 A.2d 699 (R.I. 2003) (mother liable for failing to act to control conduct of mentally ill son who kept multiple weapons in family home and used one to kill neighbor).

   Plaintiffs in cases like this will have a better chance of recovering under the risk creation principle. Suppose, for example, that Mrs. Antell had provided her husband with keys to her car and he was driving that car at the time of the accident, or she had insisted that he drive to the store for a battery for her laptop. On these facts, she would have participated in the creation of a foreseeable risk, and could be held liable for doing so.

The Priest and the Levite

6. a. Rogers certainly did not cause Jung's injury from running into the tree, but he may be a but-for cause of the aggravation of the injury. If Jung's injuries would have been less severe with prompt treatment, Rogers's failure to stop is a but-for cause of the aggravation. Certainly if Rogers had a duty to help Jung (e.g., if Jung were a student in his charge), a court would have no problem concluding that he had caused the aggravated injuries by his failure to aid.

b. This is also a nonfeasance case, in the sense that the defendant Rogers has not created the risk to Jung or done anything to cause his initial injury. The question is whether a court will impose a duty on Rogers, due to his awareness of Jung's need for assistance or his ability to render it.

Most courts would conclude that this falls squarely under the no-duty principle, that a bystander owes no duty to aid another unless the bystander has placed the victim in peril or has a previous relationship with the victim that supports a finding of duty. Since Rogers, as a doctor, is obviously in a superior position to help Jung, there is a strong moral argument that he should stop. The cases, however, do not find a duty to aid based on the fact that the defendant would be good at it.

If duties are based on public policy, why shouldn't the court jettison the special relationship theory and impose a duty on Rogers frankly based on common sense? Courts can create whatever duties they wish; the special relationship concept is simply a rationale for the court's decision to do so. Imposing a duty on doctors to assist accident victims should lead to an overall increase in societal welfare since more victims would get timely professional assistance—so why not go for it?

Maybe courts should. Maybe they will someday. But most courts remain unwilling to press strangers into service by creating such a duty. Instead, many states have sought to encourage bystanders to assist by passing statutes that limit their liability for injuries they may cause while rendering aid. Typically, such "good Samaritan" laws immunize those who assist in an emergency from liability for negligence, though not for grossly negligent or reckless conduct. See, e.g., Kan. Stat. Ann. §65-2891 (health care providers only).[10]

c. In this example, Rogers takes one step to assist at the scene, but then takes off. Under Restatement (Second) §324, he would not be liable. Under §324(a), he is OK: While he assisted, he acted reasonably, by calling for aid.[11] And §324(b) provides that he may leave without rendering all care that he could, as long as he didn't leave Jung in a worse position. Here he left Jung in the same position, so he is not in violation of the duty created by §324(b). He did something for Jung,

10. Good Samaritan statutes frequently protect health professionals only, not all gratuitous rescuers. Watch for that point on your Torts exam!

11. Jung might argue that Dr. Rogers was "unreasonable" not to help more, given his special skill and Jung's need for help. But accepting that argument would effectively read §324(b) out of the provision. That subsection tells Rogers that he may stop without doing all that he could for Jung, that he does not owe a duty of ongoing care by deciding to render some aid.

but not everything he could do . . . but the section allows Rogers to make that choice.

d. In this example Rogers is still guilty of nonfeasance, so the issue is whether the court would find that his prior treatment of Jung imposes a duty on Rogers to succor him on the roadside. If Rogers were Jung's banker, no court would conclude that he had assumed a duty to aid Jung under these circumstances. But Rogers is Jung's doctor. Shouldn't that support a duty to help him?

   Probably not. It hardly seems that either Rogers or Jung would expect that Rogers had accepted such a duty by his unrelated prior treatment of Jung. Suppose Rogers had treated Jung six years ago? Or suppose Rogers were an allergist; would *that* impose a duty to treat Jung's leg at the accident scene? Or suppose Jung was not physically injured at all, but trapped in his car? On balance, it seems difficult to impose or define a legal duty based on this limited prior relationship.

7. This case is squarely addressed by §324 of the Second Restatement. Once Dr. Rogers decides to intervene, the Restatement takes the position that he must exercise due care in assisting Jung. Because he has assumed a duty of care, the motion to dismiss will be denied. Rogers is now a risk creator, an actor whose negligent conduct may foreseeably injure Jung. It hardly seems appropriate that he should be immune from liability no matter how badly he bungles the rescue. On the other hand, as Prosser so eloquently puts it:

   > The result of all this is that the Good Samaritan who tries to help may find himself mulcted in damages, while the priest and the Levite who pass by on the other side go on their cheerful way rejoicing.

   Prosser & Keeton at 378. Good Samaritan statutes provide a middle ground in such cases, by limiting the rescuer's liability to grossly negligent or reckless conduct.

   Section 324 does not say, however, that Dr. Rogers is liable for *any* injury he causes in rescuing Jung. Rather, it imposes on Rogers a duty of due care in the course of his rescue. If Rogers had no reason to know that Jung's leg was broken, moving him was probably a reasonable choice. If so, he would not be liable to Jung, even though his assistance caused further injury. Similarly, on my exam one year, I had Cleveland, a rescuer, roll an accident victim over to check his breathing. In doing so, he aggravated the victim's cracked rib. However, Cleveland probably made a reasonable choice to roll the victim over if he didn't know about the cracked rib, and maybe even if he did, since breathing is rather important. If Cleveland's conduct was reasonable, he is not liable, even if he caused further injury to the victim.

8. In this case Klein, a bystander with no duty to aid Jung, elects to come to his aid. The Restatement takes the view that Klein's laudable decision

to act gives rise to at least a minimal duty of care to Jung, though she owed him none before. On the other hand, Klein's duty should presumably be limited: Her admirable conduct should not obligate her to pay Jung's hospital bills or take him home and tend to him until he recovers.

Section 324 of the Restatement tries to walk this line, by imposing only a limited duty on the rescuer. Section 324(a) requires her to use reasonable care while she assists Jung, but §324(b) provides that she may stop assisting, even if Jung could use more help, as long as she doesn't leave him "in a worse position that when [she] took charge of him." Here, Klein has not left Jung in a worse position than he was in before; he is in a safer position out of the road.

Jung might argue that Klein did not "secure his safety" (§324(a)) because she did not bind up his wound. Comment g to §324 states that the bystander's choice to intervene "does not require him to continue his services until the recipient of them gets all of the benefit which the actor is capable of bestowing." But the same comment also states that the actor must "act with reasonable consideration for the other's safety."

The drafters probably intended to require Klein to use reasonable care for the victim's safety *while she chooses to continue her aid,* but to leave her free to discontinue her services at any time. This conclusion follows from the basic assumption that the victim's need for services does not create a duty to render them. The opposite reading, that §324 imposes a duty on the rescuer to continue aid until the victim is "safe," would create a positive duty to continue aiding the victim for an uncertain period. Section 324(b) only holds the rescuer who chooses to discontinue aid liable if she leaves the victim in a worse position. The drafters did not intend to impose on a rescuer the duty to continue giving assistance until the victim no longer needs any.

The court should deny the motion. The purpose of Good Samaritan laws is to encourage bystanders who are not obligated to render assistance to do so anyway, by giving them a measure of protection from liability. Such statutes are not intended to grant immunity to persons who *already have a duty* to render assistance. Skinner's risk-creating conduct (driving) caused the original injury to Ortega. Under the Second Restatement, he has a duty to come to her aid, whether or not he was negligent in causing the accident. Restatement (Second) of Torts §322; Restatement (Third) of Torts: Liability for Physical and Emotional Harm §39. Thus, he was not "gratuitously" assisting Ortega, but fulfilling a duty to assist her under the circumstances. The court would probably conclude that he is not protected by the Good Samaritan statute. See, e.g., *James v. Rowe,* 674 F. Supp. 332 (D. Kan. 1987).

Remy's Revenge

9. a. Although there could hardly be a more "special" relationship than that between a mother and her unborn child, this is actually a risk creation case. The child's argument is not that her mother failed to protect or rescue her from some danger from a third party, but rather that she (the child) was injured due to her mother's negligent driving. Remy's mother engaged in risk-creating conduct, did so negligently, and injured the plaintiff. Our second "first principle"—that those who impose new risk on others owe a duty to act reasonably in creating that risk—applies, unless the court makes an exception to it.

   b. On first blush, this case seems like a slam dunk. Relevant case law already established that parents owe a duty of care to their children and are not immune from suit by them. The cases also establish that those who injure children in utero are liable for those injuries. It seems an obvious next step to combine the two principles and hold the mother liable. Indeed, the *Remy* court stated that "[t]here is . . . no question that, had the plaintiff been born at the time of the accident, even if only one hour of age, she would have been able to recover" for injuries suffered due to her mother's negligence. 440 Mass. at 681.

   There are some powerful arguments, however, for refusing to impose a duty in these circumstances. In the *Remy* court's words:

> [D]uring the period of gestation, almost all aspects of a woman's life have an impact, for better or for worse, on her developing fetus. A fetus can be injured not only by physical force, but by the mother's exposure, unwitting or intentional, to chemicals and other substances, both dangerous and nondangerous, at home or in the workplace, or by the mother's voluntary ingestion of drugs, alcohol, or tobacco. A pregnant woman may place her fetus in danger by engaging in activities involving a risk of physical harm or by engaging in activities, such as most sports, that are generally not considered to be perilous. A pregnant woman may jeopardize the health of her fetus by taking medication (prescription or over-the-counter) or, in other cases, by not taking medication. She also may endanger the well-being of her fetus by not following her physician's advice with respect to prenatal care or by exercising her constitutional right not to receive medical treatment.

440 Mass. at 678-679. In view of these considerations, the court feared that recognizing such a duty

> would present an almost unlimited number of circumstances that would likely give rise to litigation. Courts would be challenged to refine the scope of such a duty, including the degree of knowledge expected of a mother in order to pinpoint when such a duty would arise (e.g.,

> at the point of pregnancy; at the point of awareness of pregnancy; or at the point of awareness that pregnancy is a possibility) or the particular standard of conduct to which a reasonably careful pregnant woman, in a single case, should be held.

440 Mass. at 678.

In light of these concerns, the court refused to recognize a duty owed by the mother to her unborn child. The case presents a dramatic example of a court creating an exception, for reasons of social policy, to the second "first principle," that we all owe a duty of care to those injured by our risk-creating conduct. Typically, however, the *Remy* court notes five other cases on the point, two refusing to recognize the duty and three that allowed recovery. See also *Tesar v. Anderson*, 789 N.W.2d 351 (Wis. App. 2010) (allowing claim for injury to fetus based on mother's negligence under Wisconsin's broad approach to duty in negligence cases).

10. a. The analysis here must begin with the no-duty principle. Couch was not injured by any risk created by Bettelheim. The threat is from the assailant, and Bettelheim is asked to act to prevent the harm by helping to summon aid.

b. It is hard to fashion an argument for liability in this case based on the recognized exceptions to the no-duty principle. Bettelheim has no relation to either the perpetrator of the robbery or to Couch. The owner of a bar, a place of public accommodation, might owe a duty to Couch if he were injured in the bar, or if he were a patron, but Couch was not. While the conduct appears gratuitously obnoxious, it does not appear actionable.

The California Court of Appeals, however, ruled otherwise in *Soldano v. O'Daniels*, 190 Cal. Rptr. 310 (Cal. Ct. App. 5th Dist. 1983). The *Soldano* court recognized the prevalence of the no-duty rule embodied in §314 of the Second Restatement, and admitted that it would be "stretching the concept beyond recognition" (190 Cal. Rptr. at 314) to find any special relationship between the barkeep and the injured plaintiff. It then openly rejected the no-duty rule based on an analysis of various policies California cases have considered in determining duty issues.[12]

12. "These factors include: 'the foreseeability of harm to the plaintiff, the degree of certainty that the plaintiff suffered injury, the closeness of the connection between the defendant's conduct and the injury suffered, the moral blame attached to the defendant's conduct, the policy of preventing future harm, the extent of the burden to the defendant and consequences to the community of imposing a duty to exercise care with resulting liability for breach, and the availability, cost, and prevalence of insurance for the risk involved.'" 190 Cal. Rptr. at 315 (quoting *Rowland v. Christian*, 443 P.2d 561, 564 (Cal. 1968)).

> The *Soldono* case may portend the abandonment of the no-duty principle, long tort law's ugly duckling. However, reaction to the case does not suggest any rush to bury the rule. See, e.g., *Clarke v. Hoek*, 219 Cal. Rptr. 845, 852 (Cal. Ct. App. 1st Dist. 1985) (suggesting more limited reading of *Soldono* and that California Supreme Court has reaffirmed the no-duty rule since). Indeed, the ALR annotation on *Soldano* may win the prize for the shortest annotation ever: More than 40 years after *Soldano* was decided, it still included only *one* case—*Soldano* itself! See 37 A.L.R. 4th 1196. If this is the wave of the future, it is still a long way from shore.

Judge Fudd Does His Duty

The first problem with Fudd's instruction is that it tells the jury to decide whether Freud owed a duty to White or not ("[Y]ou may find that the defendant owed a duty. . . ."). Unlike the other elements of a negligence claim, duty is a question of law. It is up to courts to define enforceable legal duties, not juries. If Judge Fudd's language were proper, the jury would be left to create the substantive law of torts in each case, by determining the extent of the defendant's duty anew in every trial. Consequently, there would not be one standard for liability, but a different one for each case. *Au contraire*, the judge should instruct the jury as to the duty owed in each case. If none is owed under the circumstances, the case should never go to the jury at all.

The second problem with the instruction is equally basic: Fudd's language implies that Freud had a duty to *prevent* the attack. This would be a duty indeed, a duty of absolute protection of White no matter what the circumstances. The law seldom imposes such a stringent burden, although it does at times impose greater or lesser duties than the duty of due care. In this situation, as in most, the Restatement describes the duty as a duty to *exercise reasonable care* to prevent injury from the dangerous person. Restatement (Second) of Torts §319; Restatement (Third) of Torts: Liability for Physical and Emotional Harm §41 and cmt. c.

CHAPTER 14

Vicarious Displeasure: Claims for Indirect Infliction of Emotional Distress and Loss of Consortium

INTRODUCTION

Hamlet hit the nail on the head when he complained of the "thousand natural shocks that flesh is heir to."[1] Even in a "civilized" society such as ours, life is fraught with stresses, anxieties, fears, and sorrows. Many are indeed natural shocks, the inevitable concomitants of unfolding human experience from birth to death (and let's not forget adolescence either). Much emotional distress, however, is inflicted upon us by other people as well, either deliberately or carelessly.

We live in a culture that attempts a legal response to most problems, probably too many problems, so it should not prove surprising that courts have been asked to fashion a remedy for emotional distress as well. This chapter considers the approaches courts have taken to one of tort law's most intractable problems, claims for negligent infliction of emotional distress. It then contrasts such claims with another type of claim for emotional injuries, loss of consortium.

Claims for indirect infliction of emotional distress (frequently referred to as "bystander" claims) are based on emotional trauma suffered by one person who witnesses or learns of an injury to another. Here are some examples:

- A worker at a construction site sees a coworker crushed under a dump truck.

1. W. Shakespeare, Hamlet, act 3, sc. 1.

- A father, watching from the living room window, sees his child hit by a car that careens over the curb and onto the front lawn.
- A parent learns by telephone that his son has just suffered a serious injury in a fire negligently caused by the defendant.
- The wife of a comatose patient visits him at the hospital and discovers that he has just been severely bitten by rats.

In each of these cases, the person who suffers *direct* physical injury from the defendant's negligence obviously has a claim for those injuries. However, those who witnessed or soon learned of the injury may also seek damages for emotional distress resulting from the traumatic experience of either witnessing that injury or learning of it. Such claims are referred to as claims for "indirect infliction" of emotional distress because they are asserted by bystanders who suffer emotional injury indirectly due to the direct physical injury to another.

The distress in such cases is often both foreseeable and severe. Thus, the plaintiff will frequently be able to establish that the defendant's negligence was an actual and proximate cause of his emotional damages. Consequently, courts which have sought to limit liability for indirect infliction of emotional distress have usually used duty analysis to do so. Many courts have held that defendants owe *no duty* to avoid inflicting emotional distress on bystanders, or only owe such a duty in very limited circumstances. That is why this chapter, which seems to deal primarily with a type of damages, appears in the duty section of the book.

It is not hard to see why courts are reluctant to impose a duty to avoid indirect infliction of emotional distress. Several important factors relevant to duty analysis suggest caution in creating such a duty. *First*, the very foreseeability of such distress argues for restraint. For every victim who suffers negligent physical injury, a number of bystanders may suffer emotional distress:

> It would be an entirely unreasonable burden on all human activity if the defendant who has endangered one person were to be compelled to pay for the lacerated feelings of every other person disturbed by reason of it, including every bystander shocked at an accident, and every distant relative of the person injured, as well as all his friends.

Prosser & Keeton §54 at 366.

Second, courts are reluctant to impose a duty to persons who have no relationship to the defendant. While the defendant usually has some immediate interaction with the direct victim of his negligence—the child hit by the car, the patient diagnosed, the worker actually hit by the dump truck—he usually has had no contact with bystanders who suffer indirect emotional distress from the negligent act. The defendant may not know who they are, where they are, or how many of them there are.

Third, judges are justifiably concerned about the impact that creating a duty will have on the administration of justice. Recognition of indirect infliction claims could clog the courts with suits over trivial unpleasantries better dealt with by "a certain toughening of the mental hide." C. Magruder, Mental and Emotional Disturbance in the Law of Torts, 49 Harv. L. Rev. 1033, 1035 (1936). In addition, courts have feared the specter of fraudulent claims. It is easy enough for a plaintiff to carry on about how distressed he was by the defendant's conduct, and even to believe it after a while. It is difficult to verify such claims, or to attribute the plaintiff's distress to the defendant's conduct, as opposed to the thousand natural shocks that take their toll on us all.

Thus, for many years courts severely limited indirect infliction claims, lest such claims open a Pandora's box of woes for both courts and defendants. However, the compelling nature of the suffering inflicted on indirect victims has led to a gradual recognition of some claims for indirect infliction of emotional distress. How can a court refuse recovery to a father who watches a driver negligently run down his child and suffers a heart attack on the spot? Many courts, unable to turn such sympathetic plaintiffs away, have created a duty to avoid inflicting emotional distress, at least in limited circumstances.

Once a court opens this box a crack, however, it is very hard to close it on other equally sympathetic indirect victims. The history of the law in this area has been a constant struggle to define some limiting principle that will allow recovery for deserving victims without throwing the courts open to a flood of litigants upset over something that the defendant did to someone else. (Other useful metaphors for the jurisprudence in this area might be a series of defense lines by a retreating army, or successive walls of sandbags holding back a flooding Mississippi.) Indirect infliction claims are a useful study because they vividly illustrate the difficulty of establishing satisfactory limits to a duty once it has been recognized. The effort of courts to limit indirect infliction claims has led to tortured line-drawing, evasive distinctions, and some of the least intellectually defensible doctrine in the annals of tort law. Emotional distress seems to be one of those areas in which courts cannot solve a legal problem, only decide cases.

THE HISTORICAL APPROACH TO EMOTIONAL DISTRESS CLAIMS

Courts have long awarded emotional distress damages in negligence cases if the defendant causes direct physical injury to the plaintiff. For example, if Marat's car knocks DuBarry down, DuBarry may recover for any physical injury sustained and for any emotional distress from the accident as well. Restatement (Second) of Torts §456; Dobbs' Law of Torts §479. This would include pain and suffering resulting from the physical injury, emotional distress resulting from disfigurement or physical impairment (such as a facial scar or a limp), and any other demonstrable emotional damages.

This principle, that recovery for emotional distress was proper if the plaintiff also suffered physical injury, became known as the "impact rule." Emotional distress damages were often described as "parasitic": They could be added on if the plaintiff suffered a traditional physical contact from the defendant's negligence, but could not sustain an action on their own. If Marat's car narrowly missed DuBarry, he could not recover, even if he was badly frightened by the near miss, since he suffered no "impact."

The impact rule was tort law's first effort to keep the flood of emotional distress claims at bay. While it defined a limit, many courts found it an intellectually indefensible one. The plaintiff was allowed full recovery for emotional distress if the defendant barely touched him, but denied recovery if the defendant inflicted the same degree of distress (or much more) but just missed hitting the plaintiff. Even if the emotional distress *led* to a physical illness (e.g., if DuBarry suffered a heart attack from fear of being hit by Marat's car), recovery was barred if there was no physical impact upon which to piggyback the distress damages. The obvious artificiality of this rule invited courts to evade it by literal application. In *Porter v. Delaware, L. & W. R.R.*, 63 A. 860 (1906), for example, the court found the impact requirement satisfied where the plaintiff got dust in her eyes, and therefore allowed full recovery for emotional distress from the accident. A more recent example is *Conder v. Wood*, 716 N.E.2d 432 (Ind. 1999), in which the plaintiff pounded on the side of a truck to alert the driver that her companion had fallen under the wheels. The court concluded that the pounding constituted an impact, making her eligible to recover for emotional distress due to the injury to her companion.[2]

Although the impact rule was no "hymn to intellectual beauty,"[3] it did address some of the policy concerns relevant to duty. It alleviated fears of fraudulent claims, perjured (or at least, exaggerated) testimony and excessive damages based on jury sympathy. It premised liability on an objective fact that could be proved or disproved, and, in a rough sort of way (all right, a *very* rough sort of way), filtered out frivolous claims while allowing the

---

2. *Hunter v. J & M Displays, Inc.*, 203 N.E.3d 518 (Ind. App. 2023) illustrates just how finely the "impact" line may be drawn. In *Hunter*, the plaintiff was in bed when fireworks hit her house. She argued that the impact rule was satisfied because "her bed shook" when the fireworks crashed into the roof. The *Hunter* court—from the same state that decided *Conder*—held that the impact rule was not satisfied and dismissed the claim.

3. "[A]s law is an instrument of governance rather than a hymn to intellectual beauty, some consideration must be given to practicalities." *Newman-Green, Inc. v. Alfonzo-Larrain R.*, 854 F.2d 916, 925 (7th Cir. 1988), *rev'd on other grounds*, 490 U.S. 826 (1989).

most serious ones to proceed. A few courts still apply the rule, at least in some types of cases. See, e.g., *Malibu Boats, LLC v. Batchelder*, 819 S.E.2d 315, 318 (Ga. App. 2018); *Dowty v. Riggs*, 385 S.W. 3d 117 (Ark. 2010).

THE "ZONE-OF-DANGER RULE"

The impact rule bars recovery in most indirect infliction cases because these claims are generally asserted by bystanders who were not directly involved in the accident. Some courts, unwilling to turn all bystander plaintiffs away, have adopted alternative tests to define the duty in indirect infliction cases. Some allow a bystander to recover for emotional distress if he was in the "zone of danger"; that is, if he was close enough to the defendant's negligent conduct to be placed at risk of physical injury, even though he was not actually touched. Under the zone-of-danger rule, a mother walking next to a child hit by a negligent driver would recover for emotional distress due to witnessing injury to her child since she might have been hit herself.

The rationale for the zone-of-danger approach is that the defendant owes these bystanders a duty of care because they are within the area of the risk created by his conduct, and hence injury to them is foreseeable. This rationale derives from Justice Cardozo's proximate cause analysis in *Palsgraf v. Long Island R.R. Co.*, 162 N.E. 99 (N.Y. 1928). Since injury to the bystander is foreseeable, the argument goes, the defendant has a duty to avoid injury—either physical or emotional—to him.

The zone-of-danger rule compensates a limited class of indirect victims, a class that is reasonably likely to be seriously affected by the accident. However, like other limiting principles in this area, it is easier to criticize than to justify. The father who watches from the house as his wife and child cross the street will suffer just as much distress if the child is hit as the mother will. In addition, his presence is foreseeable, though he is not within the zone of risk of physical injury. Yet, because he is out of range of the car, he is barred from recovery under the zone-of-danger rule, no matter how manifest his distress may be. The line drawn is basically arbitrary. In the words of a leading decision on emotional distress, it suffers from "hopeless artificiality." *Dillon v. Legg*, 441 P.2d 912, 915 (Cal. 1968).

LIMITED FORESEEABILITY: THE DILLON RULE

The arbitrariness of the zone-of-danger rule has led other courts to seek a more flexible approach to indirect infliction claims. Many states have found such an approach in the California Supreme Court's decision in *Dillon v. Legg*.

In *Dillon*, a mother suffered emotional distress from seeing her daughter fatally injured by a car while crossing the street. The *Dillon* court held that defendants have a duty to avoid infliction of emotional distress that is reasonably foreseeable, including infliction of such distress on indirect victims. However, the court established three factors to be considered in determining whether such distress was foreseeable:

> 1) whether plaintiff was located near the scene of the accident as contrasted with one who was a distance away from it; 2) whether the shock resulted from a direct emotional impact upon the plaintiff from the sensory and contemporaneous observance of the accident, as contrasted with learning of the accident from others after its occurrence; 3) whether plaintiff and the victim were closely related, as contrasted with an absence of any relationship or the presence of only a distant relationship.

441 P.2d at 920.

Although *Dillon* purports to establish a foreseeability standard based on the above factors, the *Dillon* rule, like the impact and zone-of-danger rules, also bars recovery to many bystanders whose distress is foreseeable. For example, the first factor implies that a close relative would be barred if she was not present at the scene of the accident, though it is virtually inevitable that close relatives will suffer severe distress when a family member is injured. The second factor suggests that a plaintiff who is summoned to the scene after the accident may be denied recovery, though the potential for severe distress is still great. And the third factor suggests that a stranger, friend, or coworker would not recover, though it is surely foreseeable that anyone could suffer traumatic distress from witnessing massive injury to another.

REQUIRING FURTHER CORROBORATION: RESULTING PHYSICAL INJURY

Some courts that apply the zone-of-danger or *Dillon* approaches to indirect infliction claims *also* require that the plaintiff suffer some physical symptoms *as a result* of the emotional distress caused by the defendant's conduct. This "resulting-physical-injury" requirement is intended to provide additional corroboration that the plaintiff's claim is genuine. See *Payton v. Abbott Labs.*, 437 N.E.2d 171, 180 (Mass. 1982) (resulting-physical-injury rule "will serve to limit frivolous suits and those in which only bad manners or mere hurt feelings are involved, and will provide a reasonable safeguard against false claims"). California initially suggested that resulting physical injury must be shown along with the *Dillon* factors, but later abandoned this additional requirement. See *Hedlund v. Superior Court of Orange County*, 669 P.2d 41,

47 n.8 (1983). Other courts have adopted the *Dillon* guidelines for indirect infliction cases without requiring resulting physical injury. See, e.g., *Paugh v. Hanks*, 451 N.E.2d 759 (Ohio 1983).

It is important to distinguish the resulting-physical-injury approach from the impact rule. The impact rule allows a plaintiff who sustains a direct physical impact (from the defendant's car, for example) to recover for emotional distress. The resulting-physical-injury rule, on the other hand, allows the plaintiff who is missed by the car, but frightened by the near miss, to recover for emotional distress if the emotional distress itself leads to some form of physical injury, such as a heart attack.

Some courts have imposed other corroborative requirements along with one of the above approaches. Some require the plaintiff to prove "serious" or "severe" distress in order to recover. *Camper v. Minor*, 915 S.W.2d 437, 446 (Tenn. 1996). Others require expert testimony to establish the existence of the distress. *Kinard v. Augusta Sash & Door Co.*, 336 S.E.2d 465, 467 (S.C. 1985). Some cases have refused recovery, even if the distress is genuine, unless the *direct* victim of the accident suffers serious injury. *Clohessy v. Bachelor*, 675 A.2d 852, 864 (Conn. 1996).

On the other hand, a few courts have adopted very broad standards for indirect infliction claims. Several courts allow indirect plaintiffs to recover if they prove that they suffered objective symptoms of a physical injury or psychic disability as a result of the distress suffered from witnessing injury to the direct victim, without meeting the *Dillon* or zone-of-danger standards. See generally Dobbs' Law of Torts §391. And at least one court has held that indirect infliction plaintiffs may recover simply on a showing that severe emotional distress was reasonably foreseeable from the defendant's negligent act. *Wages v. First Natl. Ins. Co. of America*, 79 P.3d 1095 (Mont. 2003).

A DISTINCTION WITH A DIFFERENCE: DISTRESS DISTINGUISHED FROM DISTRESS

An injury to one person is likely to cause a variety of emotional reactions in others. A bystander who witnesses traumatic injury to a family member may suffer acute emotional shock from the unexpected, wrenching experience of witnessing serious physical injury to a loved one. She may also experience feelings of grief, loss, sympathy, or sadness due to the fact that the immediate victim has been injured or killed.

Although the general term "emotional distress" (or "mental anguish") is often applied to both of these types of injuries, they are meaningfully different. The shock of witnessing the accident is sudden and traumatic, aggravated by the very fact that it is unanticipated, so that one can make no emotional preparation to sustain it. Consider, for example, the gruesome facts of *LeJeune v. Rayne Branch Hosp.*, 556 So. 2d 559 (La. 1990), in which the wife of a comatose patient came into his room shortly after he had been bitten all over by rats. There is a fundamental difference between the impact that kind of horror scene engenders and the grief or sadness one experiences from knowing that a loved one has suffered an injury and must cope with its consequences.

It is the first type of emotional distress—the trauma of witnessing a horrific event or injury—which gives rise to a claim for indirect infliction of emotional distress. This cause of action does *not* compensate for general feelings of grief, loss, or empathy for an injured person. See, e.g., *Frame v. Kothari*, 560 A.2d 675, 678 (N.J. 1989) (claim applies to "the observation of shocking events that do not occur in the daily lives of most people," such as "bleeding, traumatic injury and cries of pain"); *Thing v. La Chusa*, 771 P.2d 814, 828 (Cal. 1989) ("the impact of personally observing the injury-producing event . . . distinguishes the plaintiff's resultant emotional distress from the emotion felt when one learns of the injury or death of a loved one from another, or observes pain and suffering but not the traumatic cause of the injury"). While watching a loved one suffer is surely one of life's most gut-wrenching experiences, it is one of the "natural shocks" that we all must bear when a loved one suffers. Most courts do not allow emotional distress claims for such general grief and suffering of third parties.

Because indirect infliction claims are based on the sudden shock of witnessing injury, factors like those cited in *Dillon*, which emphasize proximity to the traumatic events themselves, make sense as limiting factors. Proximity to the accident, actually witnessing it, and being closely related to the victim, all tend to increase the traumatic impact of witnessing serious injury. By contrast, liability has usually been denied where relatives learn of an injury at a distance, or even observe an injured family member after the fact. Similarly, where relatives of a direct victim suffer emotional distress, but the victim has not suffered a traumatic accident, recovery is usually denied. In *Frame*, for example, the direct victim was allegedly injured due to medical malpractice by the defendants. Although relatives witnessed his suffering, they did not witness a sudden traumatic injury to him. Their claims for indirect infliction of emotional distress were denied. See *Frame*, 560 A.2d at 680 (a misdiagnosis "normally does not create the kind of horrifying scene that is a prerequisite to recovery").

ANOTHER DISTINCTION, AND ANOTHER DIFFERENCE: LOSS OF CONSORTIUM

When one person suffers physical injury due to a defendant's negligence, relatives of the victim will also suffer a third type of emotional damage, "loss of consortium." This term refers to the impairment of a relative's opportunity to relate to the party directly injured by the defendant. The classic loss of consortium claim is brought by the spouse of a person whose physical injury prevents him or her from enjoying the usual satisfactions of the marital relationship. If, for example, Josephine is seriously injured due to Robespierre's negligence, her injury may interfere drastically with her ability to relate to her spouse. The injury may interfere with recreational activities the couple shared, the division of labor within the household, the sexual society they shared, and the comfort, affection, advice, and moral support that ideally flow from marriage. These associational losses, the "constellation of companionship, dependence, reliance, affection, sharing and aid" (*Hopson v. St. Mary's Hosp.*, 408 A.2d 260, 261 (Conn. 1979) (quoting *Brawn v. Kistleman*, 98 N.E. 631 (1912)), which derive from the marital relationship, are generally referred to as "loss of consortium" or "loss of society."

Like indirect infliction, loss of consortium compensates an emotional loss to one party due to a direct injury to another. But the two claims compensate very different losses, and may frequently be brought in the same suit. Loss of consortium does not stem from a sudden traumatic experience, but from the impairment over a period of time—perhaps years or decades—of the opportunity to relate to the injured spouse. While a large component of the loss is emotional, it is not a claim for shock or trauma from witnessing the injury. Indeed, it is entirely immaterial to a consortium claim whether the consortium plaintiff witnessed the accident.

Loss of consortium also differs subtly from grief and sadness. Loss of consortium compensates for the inability to relate to the direct victim, not for general feelings of sadness or empathy for him. While grief and sadness tend to fade over time, the impairment of the relationship may persist as long as the injury does. In theory, a jury should consider only the interference with the relationship in determining consortium damages, not the general grief a spouse feels due to injury to his partner. Obviously, however, it is easier for lawyers to draw conceptual distinctions between these types of emotional losses than it is for juries to separate them in reaching a damage award.

THE EVOLUTION OF LOSS OF CONSORTIUM CLAIMS

The history of consortium claims has not been the common law's finest hour. Under early doctrine the wife owed her husband services. Where injury to the wife impaired her ability to render them, the husband had a cause of action against the tortfeasor for that impairment. The wife, however, had no corresponding claim since at common law the husband had no duty to render services to her. Dobbs' Laws of Torts §392.

Gradually, the concept of "services" was broadened to encompass not only loss of services but also emotional losses, including affection, comfort, companionship, and sexual society. Despite the obvious reciprocity of these emotional blessings of marriage, the claim remained limited to the husband until 1950, when the court in *Hitaffer v. Argonne Co., Inc.*, 183 F.2d 811, 813-819 (D.C. Cir. 1950) rejected the common law analysis and granted consortium recovery to the wife as well. Most courts quickly followed suit in granting equal consortium rights, though a few ironically equalized them by eliminating the husband's right rather than extending it to wives. Prosser & Keeton §125 at 932. In most states today both spouses have a right to full recovery for loss of consortium due to injury to the other.

While spousal consortium claims are well established, there is no consensus on the right of parents or children to claim consortium losses. Historically, the common law accorded a father the right to his children's services, and authorized a claim for the loss of those services where the child was injured. Prosser & Keeton at 934. But no claim existed for interference with the emotional relationship with a child. Since the broadening of spousal consortium rights, some states have allowed claims by parents for loss of "filial consortium" when their child is injured. Many courts, however, have rejected such claims. There is a similar split of authority on claims for loss of consortium brought by children whose parents have been injured by a tortfeasor. Some states have recognized such claims, but the majority of those that have addressed the issue have rejected those claims as well, choosing to restrict consortium recovery to spouses only. See *Mendillo v. Board of Education of East Haddam*, 717 A.2d 1177, 1193-1194 (Conn. 1998) (reviewing the decisions going both ways). *Mendillo* denied recovery for parental consortium, but 17 years later, the Connecticut Supreme Court overruled *Mendillo* and recognized a child's right to recover for loss of parental consortium. *Campus v. Coleman*, 123 A.3d 854, 858-869 (Ct. 2015).

If judges were writing on a blank slate, most would probably find a small child's relationship to a parent at least as worthy of protection as the spousal relationship. It is difficult to imagine a more serious loss than the support, advice, comfort, and education that a parent provides over a child's early years. However, unlike spousal consortium claims, which have been recognized in a limited way for many years, there was no historical precedent for consortium claims for loss of a parent. Approving such claims would represent a new burden on defendants (and insurers). That burden would often be substantial since parents often have several children, while only the most adventurous have multiple spouses. Thus many courts have refused to create a duty to avoid loss of parental society, even though the logical case for doing so may be stronger than for spousal consortium. For the same reason, courts have not extended the consortium cause of action to other close relatives such as siblings.

The examples that follow are intended to help you distinguish the types of claims discussed in this introduction and to understand the varying standards courts have applied to them.

Examples

Unnatural Shocks

1. Marat is shaken up but not injured when the car she is riding in, driven by her husband De Sade, collides with a car negligently driven by Robespierre. De Sade suffers gruesome injuries and is in severe pain. Marat brings suit against Robespierre for the distress she suffers from seeing her husband seriously injured in the accident.
   a. Would Marat recover in a state that applies the impact rule?
   b. Would she recover in a state that applies the zone-of-danger rule?
   c. Would she recover in a state that applies the *Dillon* approach?

2. Assume that Marat was driving to work with a friend, Blanc, instead of her husband when the accident took place. She suffers severe emotional distress from witnessing serious injury to Blanc.
   a. Would she recover under zone-of-danger rule?
   b. Would she recover under the *Dillon* approach?
   c. Would she recover under the impact rule?

3. Cardet, an elementary school student, falls asleep on the school bus on Friday afternoon. The driver completes his route, returns the bus to the parking area, and locks it, without noticing the student. She is not found for almost two days, driving her parents to distraction. Under which of the rules described for indirect infliction claims would her parents recover for their distress?

Hard Cases Make Sad Law

4. As indicated in the introduction, efforts by courts to establish defensible limits on a defendant's duty to avoid indirect infliction of emotional distress have led to arbitrary decisions and seemingly indefensible distinctions. The following examples illustrate some typical problem cases under the various rules. Consider how each should be resolved under the applicable standard.
   a. Roget is walking with his daughter on the sidewalk when a car careens off the road from behind them and hits the girl. Roget sues for his emotional distress from seeing her seriously injured. May he recover under the zone-of-danger rule?
   b. Carnot is visiting his wife in the hospital when she has a cardiac arrest. Two nurses rush to the bedside to attempt to revive her. His

wife is clearly in great pain, although she survives. Later, Carnot learns that the nurses negligently used a type of resuscitation technique that is dangerous for a patient with her illness, thereby greatly exacerbating her pain. He sues for his distress at witnessing the episode. What result if the zone-of-danger rule applies? What result if the *Dillon* standards apply?

c. Cordet hears a crash and comes running out as a small child, evidently her son, is hit by a car, flies through the air, and lands on a lawn across the street. She suffers a cerebral hemorrhage and dies. Her estate sues for indirect infliction. However, it turns out that the child is not her son. How should this case be decided under the *Dillon* approach to indirect infliction?

d. Cordet hears a screech of brakes while weeding the flower beds and turns to see a car careening off the street right at her son. Terrified, she faints. As it turns out, the car missed little Johnny, but she suffers severe traumatic neurosis from the incident and sues the driver. What result under *Dillon*?

e. Carnot hears shouts and sirens from his neighbor's yard, and races over in time to see his son lying beside his neighbor's pool, very close to death from drowning while paramedics struggle to revive him. He collapses in distress and later sues the neighbor (who had left the pool gate open) for negligent infliction. What result if the *Dillon* approach applies?

f. Danton witnesses an accident in which his wife is seriously injured when hit by Roget's car. As a result of the incident, he experiences anxiety, sleeplessness, and loose bowels for several months. He sues Roget for indirect infliction of emotional distress. What result in a jurisdiction that applies the *Dillon* factors, but also requires resulting physical injury?

Consortium Compared

5. DeFarge's adult daughter Belle is seriously injured in an auto accident while driving with DeFarge. Belle is hospitalized for three months, and is left with a permanently disfigured left leg. Which of the following claims will support recovery, and under what theories (i.e., indirect infliction or loss of consortium)?

   a. DeFarge claims damages for the loss of Belle's company during the time Belle is hospitalized.

   b. DeFarge is knocked unconscious from the accident. She wakes up in the hospital and suffers severe distress when told of the extent of her daughter's injuries.

c. DeFarge claims damages due to the fact that Belle is withdrawn, quiet, and unwilling to go out in public due to humiliation at her disfigurement.
d. DeFarge claims damages for Belle's inability to play tennis with her due to her disability.
e. DeFarge claims damages for the depression she suffers as a result of watching Belle trying to cope with the disability caused by the accident.
f. As a result of her injuries, Belle is unable to work, and consequently unable to contribute to the rent of the apartment she shares with her mother. DeFarge claims damages for these lost payments.
g. Marlene, Belle's twin sister, was also in the car at the time of the accident. She is slightly injured, but is extremely upset from seeing Belle seriously injured at the scene. She claims damages for indirect infliction of emotional distress and for loss of consortium due to Belle's inability to participate in many activities they previously enjoyed together.

6. Assume that DeFarge was not in the car with Belle when Belle was injured. Could DeFarge still sue for loss of consortium with Belle?

7. What kinds of evidence will the consortium plaintiff submit at trial to allow the jury to assess damages for a claim for loss of consortium with a spouse?

Another Distinction that Makes Another Difference

8. In what important respect do *all* of the following emotional distress cases differ from the ones previously analyzed in this chapter?
   - Plaintiff was negligently diagnosed with cancer. It turned out that she had an easily treated viral infection.
   - Plaintiff was a passenger in a plane that dove suddenly, 35,000 feet, toward the ground. The pilot regained control at 5,000 feet and landed safely.
   - Plaintiff, a health care worker, was negligently stuck with a used hypodermic needle, and suffered severe distress from fear of contracting AIDS.

An Elementary Example

9. DuBarry is driving down Rue Street when she has a sudden heart attack. Her car careens off the street and hits Louis, who is seriously hurt. Antoinette, Louis's wife, witnesses the accident from the sidewalk and sues for indirect infliction. Will she recover if the jurisdiction applies the *Dillon* approach to indirect infliction claims?

Explanations

Unnatural Shocks

1. a. Although Marat was not injured, she did sustain an impact from the accident. Under the impact rule, a plaintiff who suffered a physical impact to her person was allowed to recover for emotional distress as well as physical injury. However, this example goes a step beyond the usual impact case since the plaintiff who suffered an impact seeks recovery for distress caused by injury to another person.

   The impact rule is based on the premise that physical contact corroborates the likelihood of actual emotional distress. That premise seems justified where the distress is "parasitic" to the impact itself, that is, where the distress is suffered due to the accident and the injury that causes the distress. But it is more attenuated to conclude that Marat has suffered genuine distress due to injury to her husband simply because she also sustained an impact in the accident. The rule seems a poor fit for indirect infliction cases.

   However, some courts have allowed recovery for indirect infliction of emotional distress under these circumstances. In *Binns v. Fredendall*, 513 N.E.2d 278 (Ohio 1987), for example, the court allowed recovery to a passenger who suffered emotional distress due to injuries to the driver. The court noted the difficult proof problem of separating her distress from the accident itself (which is compensable along with her own injuries under the impact rule) from the additional distress she suffered due to the injury to the driver. The court also suggested that since impact is basically a corroborative factor, once it is satisfied the door is open to all emotional damages from the accident, not just those directly flowing from the impact to her. For another case with a full discussion of this twist on the impact rule, see *Pieters v. B-Right Trucking, Inc.*, 669 F. Supp. 1463, 1467-1471 (N.D. Ind. 1987) (also allowing recovery).

   b. Marat was in the zone of danger in this case; that is, she was herself at risk of physical injury from the defendant's conduct. Thus, she can recover for the emotional distress she suffers from witnessing injury to her husband under the zone-of-danger approach. Courts that apply the zone-of-danger rule reason that defendants can foresee injury to persons who are in danger of physical injury from their negligence. Thus, the defendant owes such persons a duty of care and is liable to them even if they only suffer emotional distress.

   However, some states that follow the zone-of-danger approach require that the indirect infliction plaintiff *also* suffer physical injury as a result of the emotional distress. See, e.g., *Rickey v. Chicago Transit Auth.*, 457 N.E.2d 1, 4-5 (Ill. 1983). Marat would not recover in such a state since she did not suffer physical injury from her distress. The *impact* she suffered in the accident would not satisfy this requirement; the physical injury must be caused by the *distress*, not by the accident itself.

However, Marat would probably recover in this state anyway under the impact rule: Most courts view standards like the zone-of-danger rule or *Dillon* standards as an expansion of traditional grounds for recovery rather than a new, exclusive standard. Since Marat satisfies the impact rule, she would likely recover on that ground even in a zone-of-danger state. It is worth remembering this subtle point, that the plaintiff can probably still recover her emotional damages as "parasitic" if she suffers impact, even if she does not satisfy the state's "liberalized" standard for indirect infliction claims *in the absence* of impact.

c. The *Dillon* approach would probably also support recovery on these facts. Marat satisfies all three of the *Dillon* requirements for "foreseeability." She was present at the time of the accident, witnessed it, and is a close relative of De Sade. Robespierre might argue that Marat did not witness the accident unless she was actually looking at her husband at the time of the collision, but it is doubtful that the court would be that rigid about the requirement that the plaintiff observe the accident. Presumably, realizing that the accident was taking place would suffice. See *Bliss v. Allentown Pub. Library*, 497 F. Supp. 487, 488-489 (E.D. Pa. 1980) (rejecting the argument that the plaintiff should be denied recovery because she was looking in the other direction at the moment the accident occurred).

2. a. The zone-of-danger analysis is no different here than in Example 1. However, the driver here is not a member of the plaintiff's family; does the zone-of-danger approach still apply?

Nothing in the zone-of-danger test itself suggests that it only allows recovery to members of the direct victim's family. Nor does the logic of the test, which is based on the fact that the defendant could foresee injury to those near the victim. However, it is very doubtful that recovery would be allowed to non-family members. Even though distress is clearly foreseeable in a case like this, allowing recovery would greatly expand the scope of liability. It is likely that the balance of burdens and benefits (the "practical politics" of tort law Justice Andrews notes in his *Palsgraf* dissent[3]) is likely to weigh against extending a duty to bystanders unrelated to the primary victim. See, e.g., *Hislop v. Salt River Project Agr. Imp. and Power Dist.*, 5 P.3d 267, 269-272 (Ariz. App. 2000) (denying recovery to "co-worker and friend"); see generally Minzer, Nates et al., Damages in Tort Actions §5.03[2][g] (most courts have rejected bystander claims by non-family members under all theories). Similarly, the construction worker who witnesses

3. *Palsgraf v. Long Island R.R. Co.*, 162 N.E. 99, 103 (N.Y. 1928).

a coworker's injury—or, *a fortiori*, a stranger—will likely be denied recovery, even if she was nearly hit herself. See *Pizarro v. 421 Port Assoc.*, 739 N.Y.S.2d 152 (App. Div. 2002) (no recovery for witnessing decapitation of stranger on elevator). Yet, even this levee against the flood may be giving way in some jurisdictions. See *Bray v. Marathon Corp.*, 588 S.E.2d 93 (S.C. 2003), which allowed the plaintiff to recover for distress from witnessing the death of a coworker in a products liability action.

b. Two of the factors established in *Dillon* are clearly met here: Marat witnessed the accident and was at the scene. However, it is not clear that the third factor, a close relationship to the injured party, is met since the plaintiff and the driver were friends, not relatives. Thus, the example poses two issues under the *Dillon* approach. *First*, is each of the factors a *prerequisite* to recovery, or only a consideration in making a case-by-case assessment of the foreseeability of serious emotional distress? And *second*, is friendship a close enough relationship to satisfy the third *Dillon* factor?

The *Dillon* court did not hold that all three criteria must be satisfied to allow recovery. Rather, it suggested that they were relevant "factors" in the foreseeability analysis. 441 P.2d at 921. However, the California Supreme Court subsequently held that each of the *Dillon* factors must be satisfied to support recovery for indirect infliction. *Thing v. La Chusa*, 771 P.2d 814, 829-830 (Cal. 1989). In other words, *Thing* converts the *Dillon* factors from relevant considerations to absolute prerequisites to recovery. Thus, Marat would not recover in California after *Thing*. The court in *Thing* acknowledged that it was "arbitrary" to require each factor, but concluded that "drawing arbitrary lines is unavoidable if we are to limit liability and establish meaningful rules for application by litigants and lower courts." 771 P.2d at 828.

While the California court now requires all three factors to be present, other courts will likely continue to view the *Dillon* factors as relevant rather than essential. See, e.g., *Paugh v. Hanks*, 451 N.E.2d 759, 766 (Ohio 1983). Marat would obviously have a better chance of recovery in a state that views the factors as guidelines rather than absolute prerequisites to recovery.

If a "close relationship" is required, will friendship satisfy it? Most cases involve recovery for family members, and it seems very doubtful that the courts will go beyond the family sphere in allowing recovery. Several California cases have refused to do so. See *Kately v. Wilkinson*, 195 Cal. Rptr. 902, 905-907 (Cal. App. 1983) (emotional distress recovery denied under *Dillon* analysis for witnessing injury to close friend, but allowed on products liability theory); *Elden v. Sheldon*, 758 P.2d 582 (Cal. 1988) (refusing to allow indirect infliction claim resulting from injury to cohabiting lover of accident victim); but see *Dunphy v. Gregor*, 642 A.2d 372 (N.J. 1994) (allowing recovery to unmarried cohabitant fiancée of victim); *Graves v. Estabrook*, 818 A.2d 1255 (N.H. 2003) (same); *Paugh v. Hanks*, 451 N.E.2d at 766-767 (blood relationship not necessarily required).

c. Example 1a indicates that some courts have allowed recovery for distress due to injury to another person under the impact rule. However, it is likely that many courts would refuse to extend indirect infliction claims to cases like this, in which the negligent infliction plaintiff is not a close relative of the injured party, for the same policy reasons already discussed. But, typically, there's a case that allowed recovery on similar facts. See *Condor v. Wood*, 716 N.E.2d 432 (Ind. 1999).

3. Although it is hard to imagine a scenario more likely to inflict emotional distress than this, Cardet's parents are unlikely to recover under any of the common approaches to indirect infliction claims. They have not suffered an impact. They are not within a zone of physical danger. And the *Dillon* factors are not satisfied, since they have not witnessed traumatic injury to their child.

   Cases like this have repeatedly defeated the efforts of courts to develop consistent standards for recovery for emotional distress. After the court establishes a purportedly clear rule such as zone-of-danger or *Dillon*, a case like this comes along which cries out for relief but doesn't fit the rule. Very frequently, the court then writes a confusing decision that blurs the lines but comes out "right."

   For example, some California courts have allowed recovery in indirect infliction cases that don't meet the *Dillon* standards if the defendant owed a "direct" duty to the bystander. See, e.g., *Huggins v. Longs Drug Stores California, Inc.*, 14 Cal. Rptr. 2d 77 (Cal. Ct. App. 1992) (concluding that parents who administered improper dose of medication to infant could recover for distress resulting from injury to infant, despite failure to meet *Dillon* test, since pharmacist owed them direct duty to provide proper dosage).[4] Some cases have purported to use a straight foreseeability standard in hard cases, which certainly would favor recovery here, but would lead to a dramatic increase in such claims, and difficult issues as to the limits of foreseeability. See, e.g., *Masaki v. General Motors Corp.*, 780 P.2d 566, 575-576 (Haw. 1989) (recovery allowed based on foreseeability, though parents did not witness the accident); but see *Kelley v. Kokua Sales and Supply*, 532 P.2d 673 (Haw. 1975) (recovery denied where decedent died of a heart attack in California upon being informed of his relatives' death in Hawaii). See also *Wages v. First Natl. Ins. Co. of America*, 79 P.3d 1095 (Mont.

4. This dubious holding was overruled by the California Supreme Court. 862 P.2d 148 (1993). But many other equally dubious holdings in hard emotional distress cases have not been.

2003) (requiring only that severe distress be foreseeable from the negligent act).

Hard Cases Make Sad Law

4. a. In this example Roget is in the zone of danger but does not know it, since the car approached from behind. Must he be *aware* of the risk to himself in order to recover for distress at the injury to his daughter? The logic of the zone-of-danger test would not seem to require this; the rationale is that the defendant can foresee injury to Roget because he is close to the accident, so it is not unreasonable to hold the defendant liable if Roget suffers emotional distress rather than physical injury.

   This seems like the right answer, and many courts would probably so hold. However, some zone-of-danger cases suggest that the bystander plaintiff must *both* be in the zone *and* fear for his own safety before he can recover for distress at injury to another. See, e.g., *Rickey v. Chicago Transit Auth.*, 457 N.E.2d 1 (Ill. 1983).

   b. A court that sticks by the zone-of-danger rule will provide no relief on these facts. Carnot is simply not in any physical danger. His distress at witnessing his wife's suffering is foreseeable and doubtless severe, but this arbitrary line cuts him out.

   It is unclear whether Carnot would recover if the *Dillon* standards applied. Carnot suffered emotional distress from witnessing his wife's medical crisis, but at the time he was not aware that it resulted from negligence on the part of the nurses. Must he be aware that the injury is being caused by negligence, if he satisfies all the *Dillon* criteria? Logically, such awareness seems unnecessary. The gravamen of the indirect infliction claim is traumatic distress caused by the defendant. This comes from witnessing the injury, whether the bystander realizes that it results from negligence or not. Liability for indirect infliction was upheld on this logic in *Downey v. City of Riverside*, 551 P.3d 11090 (CA 2024).

   Indeed, it seems unnecessary that the indirect infliction victim witness the defendant's negligent act at all. The mother who sees a car hit her child suffers the same degree of distress whether it resulted from the driver's negligence or that of a mechanic who failed to properly repair the brakes two weeks earlier. Yet it is not clear that recovery will be allowed in cases of antecedent negligence. Typically, there are cases going both ways. See *Love v. Cramer*, 606 A.2d 1175, 1178 n.4 (Pa. Super. 1992), *appeal denied, Cramer v. Love*, 621 A.2d 580 (indicating that Pennsylvania law requires bystander to witness the negligent act); compare *Kearney v. Philips Indus., Inc.*, 708 F. Supp. 479 (D. Conn. 1987) (allowing recovery where bystander only witnessed resulting injury, not the negligent act that caused it).

c. This change in the facts challenges the line drawn in *Dillon*. In *Dillon*, the direct victim actually was the bystander's child; here, Cordet mistakenly thought he was. The impact on Cordet could still be traumatic; indeed, in the case upon which this example is based (*Barnes v. Geiger*, 446 N.E.2d 78 (Mass. 1983)), the bystander really did suffer a cerebral hemorrhage and die. If the defendant's duty to bystanders were based solely on foreseeability, it seems clear that this plaintiff would recover. But in this area, as in others, public policy frequently requires that the limits of the defendant's duty be drawn well short of foreseeability. Although the Massachusetts courts use an approach much like *Dillon*, *Barnes* denied recovery, emphasizing the practical need to limit liability:

> Daily life is too full of momentary perturbation. Injury to a child and the protracted anguish placed upon the witnessing parent is, on the scale of human experience, tangible and predictable. Distress based on mistake as to the circumstances is ephemeral and will vary with the disposition of a person to imagine that the worst has happened. We are unwilling to expand the circle of liability . . . to such an additional dimension, because to do so expands unreasonably the class of persons to whom a tortfeasor may be liable.

Id. at 81. Whenever courts draw a line like this, ivory tower academics (who don't have to decide the case) will argue that the line is arbitrary. Such caviling is easy; of course the line is arbitrary. Still, it must be drawn.

d. Here again, foreseeability and practical politics suggest different results. It is obviously foreseeable that a mother would be traumatized by seeing her child nearly killed by a car. Yet allowing recovery would again expand the ambit of liability substantially. The *Barnes* court would deny recovery on these facts: "Whether the mistake be as to the identity of the victim . . . or the gravity of the injury, the anxiety, perforce, is transitory, and a 'fleeting instance of fear or excitement' . . . does not present a set of circumstances against which a tortfeasor can fairly be asked to defend." 446 N.E.2d at 81. Some courts have required that the direct victim suffer serious injury if bystanders are to claim for indirect infliction (see, e.g., *Portee v. Jaffee*, 417 A.2d 521, 527-528 (N.J. 1980)), but others have not. See *Paugh v. Hanks*, 451 N.E.2d at 767 (direct victim need not suffer actual physical harm).

e. This example tests the limits of the *Dillon* requirement that the indirect victim witness the injury. Many cases have turned on whether the relative must be on the scene, see or hear the accident, arrive immediately, or simply see the injured victim in pain. Recovery has usually been denied where relatives learn of an accident later, but this case is closer, since Carnot arrives in the immediate aftermath of the accident.

Here, the parent has suddenly come upon the child in a desperate condition immediately after being pulled from the pool, amid frantic efforts to revive him. This is a sudden, terrible shock. It does no violence to the *Dillon* requirement of witnessing the injury to hold it met here. The court so held in *Nazaroff v. Superior Court*, 145 Cal. Rptr. 657 (Cal. Ct. App. 1978), but *Nazaroff* was overruled in *Thing v. La Chusa*, 771 P.2d at 830, which held that the bystander plaintiff must actually witness the injury-causing event itself in order to recover. Courts have drawn various fine distinctions in applying *Dillon's* "contemporaneous observance" requirement. See, e.g., *Brooks v. Decker*, 516 A.2d 1380 (Pa. 1986) (recovery denied to father who rushed to the scene, saw the ambulance arrive, saw his son's bicycle on the ground, and accompanied his injured son to the hospital); *Stump v. Ashland, Inc.*, 499 S.E.2d 41 (W. Va. 1997) (recovery allowed where plaintiffs were at the scene and knew victims were being harmed by fiery crash, but their view was obscured by flames); *Gabaldon v. Jay-Bi Prop. Mgmt. Inc.*, 925 P.2d 510 (N.M. 1996) (bystander must either be there when the injury occurs or arrive before emergency medical personnel). One of the most liberal cases is *Ferriter v. Daniel O'Connell's Sons, Inc.*, 413 N.E.2d 690 (Mass. 1980) (superseded on other grounds, St. 1985, c. 572 s. 35), which allowed recovery where plaintiffs did not witness the accident but rushed to the hospital and saw the seriously injured victim there.

f. Danton satisfies the three basic *Dillon* factors, but must also show that he has suffered "physical injury" as a result of the distress from witnessing the accident. In most cases the bystander plaintiff does not suffer dramatic physical injury such as a heart attack or cerebral hemorrhage. Yet, if the courts require resulting physical injury, plaintiffs will try to come up with something. Many tedious, unsatisfactory cases consider whether headaches, upset stomach, loose bowels, depression, social withdrawal, insomnia, perspiration, muscle tension, loss of appetite, and other general complaints satisfy the "resulting physical injury" standard.

Because such symptoms are subjective and hard to disprove, the resulting physical injury requirement has failed miserably as a bright line test to corroborate distress. In the same way that skeptical courts turned the impact requirement into a token, they have eviscerated the "resulting physical injury" requirement by finding vague complaints sufficient. See *Sullivan v. Boston Gas Co.*, 605 N.E.2d 805 (Mass. 1993) (discussing range of symptoms that satisfy the requirement, and approving virtually any evidence that corroborates plaintiff's claim of distress). As with the other requirements, however, some courts have taken a tougher line. See, e.g., *Muchow v. Lindblad*, 435 N.W.2d 918, 921-922 (N.D. 1989) (loss of sleep and weight insufficient).

Consortium Compared

5. a. This is a proper element of a loss of consortium claim. DeFarge does not seek damages for the shock of witnessing injury to Belle, but for the interference with her ability to associate with Belle while she is hospitalized *after* the accident. However, this claim is for loss of "filial consortium," that is, for interference with the relationship to a child. As the introduction states, courts are divided on whether parents may recover for loss of consortium with a child. Many have refused to allow such claims.

   b. This is a claim for distress at the thought that Belle has suffered serious injury. In one sense, it looks like an indirect infliction case, since DeFarge is distressed due to the injury of another. But it is not based on sudden shock at the scene of the accident itself, but the distress and grief of learning that her daughter has been injured. She would experience the same grief if she had not been with her at the time of the accident, and learned of it at home. This does not meet any of the usual tests for indirect infliction of emotional distress.

   c. The example here is ambiguous. Does DeFarge seek damages for *Belle's* emotional reaction of withdrawal from social activities, or for the loss of her own (DeFarge's) opportunity to engage in such activities with Belle? If the claim is for Belle's social withdrawal itself, this is an element of *Belle's* negligence claim, not DeFarge's. Plaintiffs who suffer physical injury are always entitled to prove their full damages, including emotional damages like Belle's, that result from or accompany physical injury. Chapter 17, pp. 377–378.

      If DeFarge seeks damages for loss of the opportunity to engage in social activities with Belle as they did previously, or to relate to her due to her emotional withdrawal, this would be a proper element of a loss of consortium claim in states that recognize a parent's right to recover for loss of consortium with a child. Note again that the injury claimed is the ongoing impairment of DeFarge's relationship with Belle after the accident, not the trauma of witnessing the accident itself.

   d. This chapter considers consortium claims together with indirect infliction claims because both are injuries to one person as a result of a separate injury to another. But consortium claims are substantially broader than infliction of emotional distress claims, since loss of consortium compensates a variety of losses due to impairment of the relationship to an accident victim, including interference with social and recreational aspects of the relationship. The loss of the opportunity to play tennis with Belle, while not strictly a form of emotional distress, is a loss the jury may consider in valuing DeFarge's consortium claim.

e. This is not an indirect infliction claim—at least, not in the sense in which the courts have recognized them. It stems from DeFarge's sadness at seeing her daughter cope with a disability, not from witnessing the injury that gave rise to it. Nor is it, strictly speaking, within the ambit of a loss of consortium claim. It is not a claim for Belle's inability to do things with DeFarge, or to relate to her emotionally and socially. It is a form of grief distinct from either of the claims addressed in this chapter.

   As previously noted, the legal distinction between DeFarge's depression from watching Belle struggle with disability and the emotional impairment of their relationship due to Belle's injury may be too subtle for most juries. Their award for emotional damages is likely to be a general one, based on their overall impression of the impact Belle's injury has had on DeFarge.

f. This is obviously not a claim for emotional distress, nor is it properly recoverable on a loss of consortium claim. Even if DeFarge loses rent due to Belle's injury, she may not sue the negligent driver for it. Belle will recover directly for her lost future wages in her negligence action against the other driver. If DeFarge could recover for the contributions Belle would have made to the rent from her future wages, the defendant would be made to pay the same loss twice.

   It is not unusual for third parties to suffer substantial secondary losses as a result of an injury. If Belle is an indispensable executive, for example, her company may suffer serious economic losses from her absence. Generally speaking, however, courts have refused to allow recovery for these types of derivative economic losses to others. Dobbs' Law of Torts §647.

g. Marlene has a better claim than DeFarge for indirect infliction of emotional distress, since she was in the car and saw Belle's injuries at the scene. This would probably state a claim for indirect infliction under the impact rule (see Example la) and the zone-of-danger rule. It would also probably satisfy the *Dillon* factors, since siblings have generally been considered close enough relatives to recover under *Dillon*.

   However, Marlene will almost certainly not recover for loss of consortium, since most courts have denied consortium recovery to siblings. Once again, this has nothing to do with foreseeability; impairment of Marlene's relationship to her sister is highly likely when Belle is seriously injured. It is another example of the practical need to keep liability within manageable limits.

   It is not surprising that most courts have extended indirect infliction claims to siblings but barred their claims for loss of consortium. Cases in which siblings witness traumatic injury to accident victims are unusual. But many seriously injured accident victims will have siblings who suffer loss of consortium. Thus, allowing sibling recovery for indirect infliction does not expand liability substantially, while allowing sibling recovery for loss of consortium clearly would.

6. Yes, she could, if the jurisdiction recognizes claims for loss of consortium with a child. DeFarge's claim is not for the trauma of witnessing the injury; it is for the interference with her ability to relate to Belle caused by Belle's injury. DeFarge suffers this interference equally, whether she witnessed the injury or not. In most cases, consortium plaintiffs will not have witnessed the underlying injury to the direct victim. But this is irrelevant to recovery for loss of consortium.

7. If the jury is to assess damages for loss of consortium, it has to have a sense of what the consortium plaintiff has lost. Thus, evidence about the quality of the relationship between the direct victim and the consortium plaintiff before and after the accident is relevant and admissible. The jury will hear evidence about how the spouses related to each other, their recreational activities together, the closeness of their relationship, their social life and sex life, their division of functions within the home, and the impact the injury has had on all these aspects of their marriage. *Davis v. Caterpillar, Inc.*, 787 So. 2d 894 (Fla. Ct. App. 2001), review dismissed, 817 So. 2d 845 (Fla. 2002), for example, presented the following evidence of loss of consortium:

   > Mrs. Davis worked at a Wal-Mart store at the time of the incident. She visited her husband in the hospital every day for over a month. When he came home, she quit her job for two years to take care of him. She changed his dressings day after day, cleaned his wounds, massaged his leg, bathed him, helped him dress and took him to his numerous doctor's appointments. She designed and sewed pants with a zipper in the leg to make his dressing easier. Mrs. Davis is 70 years old. She continues to work because she now provides the family's sole financial support. Mr. Davis continues to be very dependent upon her. Mrs. Davis has suffered through her husband's irritability, frustrations, sexual dysfunction and nightmares, in addition to her own stresses. She is now the family's sole provider and caretaker.

   The *Davis* court held that an award of $35,000 on these facts was clearly inadequate compensation for her loss of consortium.

   Evidence of consequential losses to the spouse of an injured party, like that in the *Davis* case, is powerful and emotional evidence that may have a significant impact on the jury. And, typically, the consortium claim will be heard with the personal injury claim of the direct victim, in a single trial. No defendant can be enthusiastic about the jury hearing all this. Thus, the assertion of consortium claims ups the ante for the defendant, and may drive up the settlement value of the case.

Another Distinction that Makes Another Difference

8. In each of these cases, the plaintiff suffered emotional distress due to fear of an injury to *herself* rather than fear of or witnessing injury to another. These are often referred to as "direct infliction" cases, as opposed to "bystander" cases, in which the plaintiff seeks recovery after witnessing injury to another. In Example 3, for example, in which Cardet is unintentionally locked in the school bus, she would likely suffer emotional distress as a direct victim, just as her parents would as indirect victims.

   The standards applicable to direct infliction cases are even less clear than those for indirect infliction. Courts have not even consistently made the distinction between direct and indirect infliction, or recognized that standards developed in one context may not work in another. A few courts continue to apply the impact rule to such cases. Some apply the zone-of-physical-danger rule. Some may focus on resulting physical injury, or on whether the defendant owed the plaintiff a preexisting duty. A few appear only to require that distress be foreseeable and serious. See generally Minzer, Nates §5.02.

An Elementary Example

9. This example is deceptively simple. The *Dillon* factors are clearly met, since Antoinette is closely related to the direct victim, witnesses the accident, and is close at hand. However, satisfying the *Dillon* factors merely proves that DuBarry *owed Antoinette a duty* to avoid negligently inflicting emotional distress upon her. It does not show that DuBarry breached that duty of care, and the facts here suggest that she didn't. She did not drive negligently, but was overtaken by a sudden illness that prevented her from controlling her car at all. See, e.g., *Cohen v. Petty*, 65 F.2d 820 (D.C. Cir. 1933) (no liability when driver fainted from sudden illness).

   Students often get so caught up in the special standards for allowing indirect infliction claims that they forget that those standards only address the issue of whether a duty of care is owed. These are still claims for negligence, and that means that all four elements of a negligence claim must be proved to recover. In other words, the special standards for indirect infliction claims are not a separate set of elements which support recovery in themselves, but rather prerequisites to establishing *one* of the usual elements of a negligence claim, duty. If they are met, the plaintiff must still shoulder the burden of proof on the other three as well. Here, DuBarry will fail to establish that old stand-by, Element #2, breach of the duty of due care.

CHAPTER 15

Strict Products Liability: Basic Theories of Recovery

INTRODUCTION

The term *products liability* refers to claims for injuries caused by commercial products. Examples of such cases abound: A plaintiff is injured by a snowblower that lacks an adequate blade guard; a user of a prescription medication suffers an adverse side effect; a passenger in a car is injured when the brakes unaccountably fail; a child is caught under an electric garage door. This chapter addresses the basic theories of recovery available to such plaintiffs, with an emphasis on the cause of action for "strict products liability."

BACKGROUND: PRODUCTS LIABILITY THEORIES OTHER THAN STRICT LIABILITY

The recognition of "strict liability" for injuries due to defective products was one of the most dramatic developments of twentieth-century tort law. But why did it happen? Why weren't negligence law and other traditional remedies deemed adequate to remedy this class of tort claims?

A. Negligence Claims

Plaintiffs have long pleaded negligence claims in actions for injuries caused by products, and still do. But there are some significant hurdles to negligence recovery in products liability cases. For many years, the concept of "privity" barred many negligence claims against manufacturers. The privity requirement, relied on in the oft-cited case of *Winterbottom v. Wright*, 152 Eng. Rep. 402 (Ex. 1852), held that a seller of goods only owed a duty of care to the purchaser of the product. Under *Winterbottom*, if a manufacturer sold a defective stagecoach to a transit company, and a passenger was injured due to a defect in the coach, the manufacturer was not liable. The manufacturer was only "in privity" with its direct buyer, the transit company, and therefore only owed a duty of care to the transit company. The same principle applied if the defect caused the coach to veer off the road into a pedestrian: The lack of privity between the pedestrian and the manufacturer precluded recovery.

However, the privity requirement was rejected in *MacPherson v. Buick Motor* Co., 217 N.Y. 382 (N.Y. 1916), and virtually all courts today would follow *MacPherson*. See Restatement (Third) of Torts: Products Liability §1 cmt. a. Courts now hold that a manufacturer owes a duty of care to all those who may foreseeably be injured by its products. Restatement (Second) of Torts §395 cmt. h, i. So, if that were the only problem with the negligence remedy, courts might not have felt the need to deploy other remedies to deal with product injuries.

But there are other problems with negligence claims for product injuries. It is often difficult to prove that a manufacturer's negligence led to the defect that injured the plaintiff. Even with good quality control, a small number of units of a product may come off the assembly line with defects. Although a plaintiff can invoke res ipsa loquitur in such cases, the jury may deny negligence recovery, accepting the defendant's argument that although it used due care, such defects may still occur.

Another problem with negligence liability is that it will frequently provide no remedy against the available defendant. Suppose that a Colorado manufacturer's table saw is marketed through a chain of wholesalers, and ultimately sold to the plaintiff by a hardware store in Indiana. If the plaintiff is injured using the saw in Indiana, the manufacturer might not be subject to personal jurisdiction there. See *Asahi v. Superior Court*, 480 U.S. 102 (1987). The hardware store, which clearly would be subject to jurisdiction in Indiana, would very likely not be liable in a negligence action. It simply sold a product it bought from a wholesaler, probably without ever taking the saw out of its box or doing anything to prepare it for use. It is hard to see in such a case what act of the retailer falls below the standard of due care.

B. Breach of Express Warranty

Plaintiffs have also invoked several contractual theories of recovery for injuries due to product defects. One such theory is breach of express warranty under Article 2 of the Uniform Commercial Code. Under Section 2-313, a seller warrants the quality of its products if it makes specific representations about those qualities. A buyer who is injured because the product does not live up to those expectations may recover for resulting injuries on a theory of breach of express warranty. However, this theory often provides a very limited remedy to the injured user.

First, it only applies when specific representations were made to the buyer about the product feature that caused the injury. Statutory notice provisions, which require the buyer to notify the seller of the breach within a short time or be barred from recovering on the warranty, may also limit the remedy. See, e.g., *Greenman v. Yuba-Power Products, Inc.*, 377 P.2d 897, 900 (Cal. 1963) (noting notice requirement under California statute). Traditionally, the buyer also had to prove that she had relied on the warranty. Under the Uniform Commercial Code reliance is not required, but a good many courts require that the express warranty form part of "the basic of the bargain." See §2-313 cmt. 3. And, of course, the claim only arises if the feature that was the subject of the warranty causes the injury. If the seller warrants that a vehicle "has excellent brakes," and it doesn't, a plaintiff could sue for breach of the warranty if the brakes fail, but not if some other defect in the product causes her injury.

C. Breach of Implied Warranty of Merchantability

Another, somewhat broader contractual theory supporting recovery for injuries from product defects is breach of the "implied warranty of merchantability." In most states today this remedy is governed by the Uniform Commercial Code, which provides that a seller warrants (among other warranties) that its goods are "fit for the ordinary purposes for which goods of that description are used." U.C.C. §2-314(2)(c). This warranty arises by operation of law; it is not based on any representations of the seller. Thus, a plaintiff may recover by showing that the defendant was a dealer in goods of that kind, sold the goods, that they were not fit for the ordinary purposes for which they were sold, and that she suffered personal injury as a result of their unfitness for that purpose.

The implied warranty remedy approaches a strict liability cause of action since the warranty arise automatically and allows recovery without any showing of negligence or misrepresentation by the seller. However, it also has limitations. First, in some states implied warranties may be disclaimed, if it is done clearly. U.C.C. §2-316. Second, the Code contains alternative provisions that states may adopt concerning who may recover for breach of the implied warranty. One alternative limits recovery to "any individual who is in the family or household of the immediate buyer or the remote purchaser or who is a guest in the home of either . . ." U.C.C. §318 (alternative A). In a state that adopts this version of the section, the class of potential plaintiffs is quite limited. Injured employees, bystanders, or passengers in the buyer's car, for example, would not be within the scope of this warranty. (Other states, however, have adopted broader versions of §318, which effectively allow any reasonably foreseeable plaintiff to recover.) Third, in some states the warranty claim requires timely notice of the breach to the seller.

D. Misrepresentation

Another potential source of recovery for persons injured by products is the tort of misrepresentation. The plaintiff establishes a misrepresentation claim by showing that the defendant made a misrepresentation (either intentionally, recklessly, negligently, or innocently) about a fact material to the transaction, that the plaintiff acted in reliance on that misrepresentation, and that she suffered injury because the product was not as represented by the seller. Restatement (Second) of Torts §402B; Restatement (Third) of Torts: Products Liability §9.

One advantage of the misrepresentation claim is that the plaintiff may recover even if the product is not defective, as long as failure to live up to the representations led to the plaintiff's injury. If an all-terrain vehicle, for example, has a tendency to tip in certain situations, but the seller represented that it would not, the buyer could sue for misrepresentation, even if there was no defect in the vehicle. But the plaintiff must establish that she was actually aware of the seller's representation, and relied upon it in deciding to make the purchase or in using the vehicle.

Like the other remedies described, misrepresentation is a limited remedy. The most obvious limit is that there must have been an inaccurate representation by the seller about the particular characteristic of the product that led to the plaintiff's injury. If no relevant representation was made, the plaintiff has no claim. Another problem with the misrepresentation remedy is that it may not support recovery by third parties such as bystanders.

THE DEVELOPMENT OF STRICT LIABILITY FOR DEFECTIVE PRODUCTS

In the mid-1960s, courts began to recognize a broader approach to products liability—strict liability for product defects. The seminal case was *Greenman v. Yuba Products, Inc.*, 377 P.2d 897 (Cal. 1963), in which Justice Traynor held a manufacturer strictly liable for an injury caused by a defective power tool. *Greenman* held that strict liability was appropriate in order "to insure that the costs of injuries resulting from defective products are borne by the manufacturers that put such products on the market rather than by the injured persons who are powerless to protect themselves." Id. at 901.

Since *Greenman*, courts have articulated several policy reasons for imposing strict liability on manufacturers for injuries caused by their products. The increasing sophistication of products makes it difficult for consumers to assess their risks, emphasizing the need for manufacturers to do so. The lack of any personal relationship between manufacturers and consumers means that buyers cannot rely on such relationships to assure quality. Instead, they must rely on information provided by the distant manufacturer. In addition, manufacturers encourage purchase of their products by extensive advertising. Courts have viewed such aggressive efforts to stimulate sales as fairly involving a quid pro quo: that manufacturers stand behind their products when they cause injuries. Other courts have argued that manufacturers should be held liable for injuries from defective products because they can redistribute that liability, through insurance, to all users of the product. Thus, the price of the product will reflect its true cost rather than "externalizing" accident costs to innocent victims. In addition, the risk of liability will encourage manufacturers to make their products safer and to discover and disclose product risks that the consumer might not recognize. See generally Dobbs' Law of Torts §450.

Shortly after *Greenman*, strict products liability gained momentum when the American Law Institute added §402A to the Second Restatement of Torts. The Restatements of the Law are drafted by the American Law Institute (ALI), an organization of eminent lawyers, scholars, and judges. The goal of the Restatements is to restate and clarify areas of the common law. The ALI, of course, has no authority to pass statutes or decide cases; thus, the adoption of §402A, endorsing strict liability for defective products, did not "create a cause of action" for strict liability. However, the Restatements are frequently influential, and it is doubtful that any provision in a Restatement has had more impact on courts than §402A. The Reporter for the Second Restatement was Dean William Prosser, the dean of torts scholars of his day. His "restatement" of strict products liability in §402A, along with the *Greenman* case, virtually created the tort of strict products liability.

Restatement (Second) of Torts, section 402A.

Special Liability of Seller of Product for Physical Harm to User or Consumer

(1) One who sells any product in a defective condition unreasonably dangerous to the user or consumer or to his property is subject to liability for physical harm thereby caused to the ultimate user or consumer, or to his property, if

(a) the seller is engaged in the business of selling such a product, and

(b) it is expected to and does reach the user or consumer without substantial change in the condition in which it is sold.

(2) The rule stated in Subsection (1) applies although

(a) the seller has exercised all possible care in the preparation and sale of his product, and

(b) the user or consumer has not bought the product from or entered into any contractual relation with the seller.

Let's tease out the elements of the claim created by §402A. It authorizes recovery

1. by a *user or consumer*
2. from *a seller,*
3. who is *engaged in the business of selling the product*
4. for *physical harm*
5. caused by a *defective product*
6. that is *unreasonably dangerous.*

Note that §402A says nothing about how the product came to be defective and dangerous. Fault is not—on the face of §402A, anyway—an element of the claim, which is why the commentary to §402A declares that it creates "strict liability, making the seller subject to liability to the user or consumer even though he has exercised all possible care in the preparation and sale of the product." Section 402A cmt. a. However, courts have subsequently construed §402A to require proof of fault in several categories of liability cases, making many such claims almost indistinguishable from a negligence claim. (More to come on this below.)

The claim for strict products liability defined in §402A was quickly adopted in many states. Some courts simply adopted §402A verbatim as their law of strict products liability. "If ever a Restatement reformulation of the law were accepted uncritically as divine, surely it is section 402A of the Second Restatement of Torts."[1]

---

1. D. Owen, Defectiveness Restated: Exploding the "Strict" Products Liability Myth, 1996 U. Ill. L. Rev. 743, 744 (footnotes omitted). Professor Owen indicates that only five states "never did succumb to the new religion" of strict products liability. 1996 U. Ill. L. Rev. at 745.

In 1998, the American Law Institute promulgated the Third Restatement of Torts: Products Liability, which is entirely devoted to "restating" the tort principles applicable to products liability cases. The Products Liability Restatement, like the Second Restatement, does not become "law" in any state unless that state adopts it by legislation or court decision. In most respects, the Third Restatement's approach is consistent with s. 402A. See page 330 for a comparison of the two Restatements' approaches.

TYPES OF PRODUCT DEFECTS

Under §402A, a manufacturer is liable for injuries resulting from the "defective condition" of its products. Such product defects usually fall into one of three categories: manufacturing defects, design defects, and warning defects.

A. Manufacturing Defects

Cases based on manufacturing defects present the most straightforward type of products liability claims. In these cases, the plaintiff alleges that the product was defective because it did not meet the manufacturer's own specifications for the product. Suppose, for example, that a medical instrument has a structural defect due to contamination in the steel, and breaks while in use during an operation, injuring the patient. The gravamen of the plaintiff's claim is that the instrument was defectively manufactured—it did not come off the assembly line as the manufacturer intended. Or, a computer hard drive is somehow miswired, so that it catches fire when turned on. Again, the problem alleged is that the computer failed to meet the manufacturer's own design, and was consequently defective and dangerous.

Today, manufacturing defect claims are the only true "strict" products liability claims recognized in most states. The plaintiff recovers by showing that the product does not meet the manufacturer's own specifications for the product, and as a result the product was dangerously defective. If the product does not match the product specifications, it does not matter how the defect occurred. The plaintiff need not show that negligence led to the defect, or that the manufacturer should have discovered the defect. She need only establish that the defect existed, made the product unreasonably dangerous, and caused her injury. For example, if it turns out that the steel used in the medical instrument had an undetectable flaw when it was purchased by the manufacturer, the manufacturer would still be liable. The basis of the liability is selling the defective product, not faulty conduct that leads to the defect. It is commonly said that the gravamen of the claim is "the condition of the product, not the conduct of the defendant." See, e.g., *Olson v. A.W. Chesterton Co.*, 256 N.W. 2d 530, 540 (N.D. 1977).

B. Design Defects

A product can also be defective if its design makes it unnecessarily dangerous to the user. A power saw, for example, may be quite safe with a blade guard, but pose a risk of serious injury without one. A punch press with an exposed switch may lead to accidents when it is started inadvertently, while a recessed switch would eliminate the risk. Probably the lion's share of products liability claims are based on the theory that the product was defectively designed because it failed to eliminate the risk of injuries from its use. Frumer & Friedman, Products Liability §11.03[l][c].

Surely, however, a manufacturer should not be liable simply because its product involved *some* risk of injury. If so, automakers would be liable for all motor vehicle injuries, knife manufacturers would pay for all cut fingers, and drug sellers would pay for even the most unexpected and unavoidable side effects of their medications. These products involve some risk of injury, but are often not *unreasonably* dangerous. Since many products cannot be functional without imposing some level of risk, products liability law needs some standard for distinguishing acceptable designs from those that pose unacceptable risks. "The goal of both design engineers and the law should be to promote in products an ideal *balance* of product usefulness, cost and safety." D. Owen, Defectiveness Restated: Exploding the "Strict" Products Liability Myth, 1996 U. Ill. L. Rev. 743, 754 (footnote omitted).

Section 402A provides that a product is "unreasonably dangerous" if it is "dangerous to an extent beyond that which would be contemplated by the ordinary consumer who purchases it, with the ordinary knowledge common to the community as to its characteristics." Restatement (Second) of Torts §402A cmt. i. A good many courts have applied this test, which focuses on the consumer's expectations about the product. Others, however, have used a risk/utility balancing approach to design defect cases. Under this approach, the factfinder decides, applying a number of factors, whether the product's design represents a fair balance between the cost of designing the product to prevent the risk of injury, the effect the redesign would have on the utility of the product, and the extent of the risk that the product poses.

> [I]n evaluating the adequacy of a product's design pursuant to this latter standard, a jury may consider, among other relevant factors, the gravity of the danger posed by the challenged design, the likelihood that such danger would occur, the mechanical feasibility of a safer alternative design, the financial cost

> of an improved design, and the adverse consequences to the product and to the consumer that would result from an alternative design.

Barker v. Lull Engineering, 573 P.2d 443, 455 (Cal. 1978).

The choice between the consumer expectations test and the risk/utility test has been a hotly disputed one. While many courts have applied §402A's consumer expectations test, the ALI's Third Restatement of Torts: Products Liability, adopted in 1997, endorsed the risk/utility test. Restatement (Third) of Torts: Products Liability §2(b) and cmt. d.

Ironically, while plaintiffs' advocates tend to favor the consumer expectations approach, that test does not always support broader liability than the risk/utility approach. Some products might meet consumer expectations but not satisfy the risk/utility test. A consumer might, for example, think a machine with an exposed switch was a reasonable design, or not have thought anything about it one way or the other. However, if the switch could easily be relocated to avoid inadvertent start-ups, the design might fail the risk/utility test. In *Halliday v. Sturm, Ruger & Co.*, 792 A.2d 1145 (Md. 2002), the plaintiff argued that simple design changes in a handgun would have prevented the death of a three-year-old child who was killed playing with the gun. But the court, applying the consumer expectations test, held that the product had functioned exactly as expected, and was not defective, even if a simple redesign would have prevented the accident. The *Halliday* court's choice to invoke the consumer expectations test doomed the plaintiff's case, while a risk/utility test might have gotten the case to a jury.

Yet the consumer expectations test has several advantages plaintiffs embrace. It is more intuitive, leaving more leeway to the jury to make a commonsense evaluation of the product. And, proving a design defect under this approach does not require the plaintiff to demonstrate a safer way to design the product. She need only show that the product was less safe than a reasonable consumer would expect. This may allow the plaintiff to establish her claim without hiring an expensive expert witness to testify about alternative designs that would have eliminated the danger that injured the plaintiff. In some cases, a product may not live up to consumer expectations, even though it cannot be redesigned to be safer. Consumers may reasonably anticipate that a product will function safely (and the manufacturer's advertising may create such expectations), although it in fact poses serious risks that the consumer would not anticipate. An interesting article on the controversy between the tests (H. Bowbeer, T. Cavanaugh & L. Stewart, *Timmy Tumble v. Cascade Bicycle Co.*: A Hypothetical Case Under the *Restatement (Third)* Standard for Design Defect, 30 U. Mich. J.L. Ref. 511 (1997)) offers the example of a dirt bike with a shock absorber that fails in certain circumstances. A consumer might well expect the bike to function more safely than it does, yet be unable to suggest a redesign that would eliminate the risk. If so, it might be defective under the consumer expectations test, even if there is no feasible safer alternative design.

The Third Restatement endorses the risk/utility approach to design defects, but also requires the plaintiff to establish that "a reasonable alternative design" would have eliminated the risk that injured the plaintiff. Restatement (Third) of Torts: Products Liability §2(b). This can be an imposing evidentiary problem, involving evidence of costs of materials, production techniques in a specialized industry, complex price calculations, and analysis of the collateral effects of the hypothetical alternative design on function and marketability of the product.[2] The evidence must show that "the suggested alternatives are not only technically feasible but also practicable in terms of cost and the over-all design and operation of the product." *Wilson v. Piper Aircraft Corp.*, 577 P.2d 1322, 1327 (Or. 1977).

If the plaintiff cannot demonstrate a reasonable alternative design that would eliminate a product risk, then the product is presumably not defective under the Third Restatement approach. Yet it may still pose more danger than consumers would expect. In such cases the design would be defective under the consumer expectations test, but not under the Third Restatement. Some detractors of the Third Restatement argue that the consumer expectations approach is preferable because some products—such as cigarettes and asbestos—may be unreasonably dangerous even if they cannot be designed to be safer. Others endorse the risk/utility test in general, but argue that the plaintiff should be able to prove that a design is defective because it poses excessive risk, even if she cannot demonstrate a feasible alternative design that would eliminate the danger.

Some courts have held that a product is defective if it fails *either* the consumer expectations test or the risk/utility test. See, e.g., *Barker v. Lull Engineering* Co., 573 P.2d 443 (Cal. 1978). If Maryland accepted that position, the *Halliday* plaintiff could have argued that even if the gun was as safe as a consumer would expect it to be, it was defective because it could have been made safer without impairing its function.

Cases since the adoption of the Third Restatement (in 1998), with its strict risk/utility approach to design defect claims, including the reasonable-alternative-design requirement, have been mixed. Some courts have continued to apply the consumer expectations test, rejecting the risk/utility test entirely. See, e.g., *Ford Motor Co. v. Trejo*, 402 P.3d 649, 656-657 (Nev. 2017). A good many others have accepted the Third Restatement standard but also continued to endorse the consumer expectations test as an alternative way of showing design defect. See, e.g., *Izzarelli v. R.J. Reynolds Tobacco Co.*, 136 A.3d 1232, 1244 (Conn. 2016); *Aubin v. Union Carbide Corp.*, 177 So. 3d 489,

---

2. The Third Restatement throws a bone to consumer-expectations advocates, however, by providing that consumer expectations about product dangers are relevant to the risk/utility analysis in a design defect case. Restatement (Third) of Torts: Products Liability §2 cmt. g.

510-512 (Fla. 2016). However, it appears that the majority of states now apply the Third Restatement approach.

Regardless of which test a state adopts, design defect claims will generate a vigorous defense from manufacturers. A manufacturing defect claim alleges that a single unit of a product was defective because something went awry in the manufacturing process. When the plaintiff claims that the product design is defective, a lot more is at stake since a design defect claim asserts that all units of the product are defective. A finding that the product's design is unreasonably dangerous suggests that the product should not be marketed at all, unless it is redesigned to reduce the risk of injury. In addition, such a finding may lead other users injured by the same product to sue for their injuries, and to assert that the manufacturer is estopped from denying that the product was defective.

C. Defects Due to Failure to Warn

The third common type of strict products liability claim involves failure to warn the user of dangers associated with a product's use. Many products are safe if used as intended, but pose risks of injury if not properly used. A hay baler may pose a risk of entangling the user if the gears are not disengaged before clearing obstructions. A drug may pose a risk of adverse reactions if taken with alcohol. A solvent may prove useful and safe if the user wears gloves while applying it, but cause serious allergic reactions to exposed skin.

In such cases, the user is often the "cheapest cost avoider": She can avoid the risk posed by the product at a low cost, by taking precautions in using it, while redesigning the product to eliminate the risk would be considerably more costly—or impossible. However, if the user is to avoid the risk, she must have clear directions and warnings to allow her to do so. Thus, a product may be safe enough with the appropriate warnings and directions, but unreasonably dangerous without them. Plaintiffs frequently allege that a product, though reasonably designed, was defective for failure to provide such warnings of the dangers posed by its use.

What dangers does a manufacturer have the duty to warn users about? Because each case turns on its facts, it is hard to articulate a standard other than that of reasonable care. The manufacturer should consider the extent of the risk, the likelihood that it will arise, the user's likely understanding about the danger, the means available to convey a warning, the likelihood that too many warnings will decrease the effectiveness of each, and other factors in deciding which warnings to give. The Second Restatement suggests that a consumer should be warned if a danger is "not generally known, or if known is one which the consumer would reasonably not expect to find in the product." Restatement (Second) of Torts §402A cmt. j. The Restatement (Third) of Torts: Products Liability throws similar language at the problem: "[W]arnings must be provided for inherent risks that reasonably foreseeable product users and consumers would reasonably deem material or significant in deciding whether to use or consume the product." Section 2 cmt. i; see also id., first paragraph (detailing factors the court should consider in assessing the adequacy of a warning). This language, studded with references to reasonable conduct, suggests that "strict" liability for failure to warn turns basically on a reasonableness standard. "In effect, warning claims are negligence claims, as a number of courts recognize." Dobbs' Law of Torts §464 (footnote omitted).

If a warning is required, it must be an *adequate* warning, that is, one calculated to clearly alert the user to the danger and how to avoid it.

> [T]he warning must plainly describe the *Nature* of the risk; its *Severity*; its *Scope*; and the means of *Avoidance*. . . . To illustrate, the Nature of the risk might be conveyed by language like, "Radioactive," "Live Electricity," "Poisonous." Severity could be described by language such as "2000 Volts," "Severe Burns if Used Without Protective Clothes," "No Antidote." Scope might be stated by, for example, "Unprotected Exposure Causes Chronic Respiratory Illness." Means of Avoidance could be explained by language like "A Facemask Must be Worn," or "If Contact With Skin Or Eyes, Irrigate with Water For 20 Minutes and Seek Medical Attention Immediately."

J. Diamond, L. Levine & M. Madden, Understanding Torts 299-300 (1996). Here again, the jury will likely be instructed to assess the adequacy of the warning under a general reasonableness analysis.

A product may also be defective because it provides inadequate directions for use or assembly. Directions are different from warnings, and both may be required. In *Midgley v. S.S. Kresge Co.*, 127 Cal. Rptr. 217 (1976), for example, a telescope, which was safe if properly assembled, caused injury to the plaintiff's eye because the sun filter was not properly installed. The court held the telescope was defective without proper instructions for installing the sun filter.

THE SECOND AND THIRD RESTATEMENT APPROACHES COMPARED

The Third Restatement of Torts: Products Liability "restates" strict products liability law in somewhat different terms than §402A. First, it explicitly categorizes products liability claims as manufacturing defect claims, design defect claims, or failure to warn claims. Section 2(b). It also adopts the risk/utility test for design defect claims rather than §402A's consumer expectations test. Id. In addition, it requires the design defect plaintiff to establish that a reasonable alternative design was available. Id.

The Third Restatement also takes the position that there should be one unified claim for injury due to product defect, replacing the mélange of claims that courts have recognized based on negligence, warranty, and strict liability. Thus, liability under the Restatement would exist no matter what theory the plaintiff asserted in her complaint, only if the liability standard of Restatement (Third) §2 was met. See §2 cmt. n. This too does not reflect settled law. In many states, a claim for strict products liability, whether based on case law or a state products liability statute, may be asserted along with other claims based on negligence or breach of warranty. See, e.g., *Singer v. Federated Dept. Stores, Inc.*, 447 N.Y.S.2d 582 (N.Y. Sup. 1981); *Brown v. Skecherd Inc.*, 709 W.L. 3/5 7677 (M.D. Fl 2009).

Not all changes in the Third Restatement will be widely accepted. Its standard for design defects, in particular, has met fierce opposition from plaintiff advocates. A good many courts continue to endorse the consumer expectations test, either instead of or as an alternative to the risk/utility test. It is also likely that many courts will also continue to allow plaintiffs to try their cases on negligence, warranty, and strict liability theories simultaneously. Indeed, §402A remains the law in a number of states today, though frequently embellished with local quirks and quiddities.

The Third Restatement has been criticized for attempting to establish a new products liability regime rather than "restating" current doctrine. This criticism may be accurate, but it is also ironic: When Dean Prosser drafted §402A of the *Second* Restatement, it was directly supported by only one case! While Restatements are generally meant to clarify and organize accepted doctrine, they have on occasion pushed the law into dramatically new channels. Section 402A is probably the most striking example of a Restatement taking the law in a new direction rather than summarizing accepted principles.

STATUTORY CHANGES TO PRODUCTS LIABILITY LAW

Several states, in an effort to simplify products liability litigation, have supplemented or displaced their common law principles of products liability by enacting statutes that govern many aspects of products liability law, including definitions of product defect; the relation of product liability claims to other available theories; the effect of plaintiff's fault, misuse, or assumption of the risk; the state-of-the-art defense; privity requirements (or the lack thereof); limitations on the liability of sellers; the nature of the warnings required; limits on particular claims (such as tobacco or firearms cases); punitive damages; the effect of compliance with safety statutes; and many other issues. See, for a review of product liability statutes, Frumer & Friedman §XIII app. C.

Some of these statutes create an *exclusive statutory tort remedy* for injury from defective products which displaces common law theories. See, e.g., Conn. Gen. Stat. §52-572n(a); Kan. Civ. Prac. Code Ann. §60-3302c. *Canty v. Ever-Last Supply Co.*, 685 A.2d 1365 (N.J. Super. 1996) (New Jersey Products Liability Act signaled intention of legislature to replace common law negligence theories in products liability area with statutorily defined cause of action). Under a statute of this type, Gutierriez would have a single claim defined by the statute, and would not be able to also assert claims based negligence, breach of implied warranty, or other product liability theories.

This chapter reviews general principles of products liability doctrine, but remember that in legal analysis the devil is always in the details, and the product liability details may be covered by statute in your state.

HOW STRICT IS "STRICT PRODUCTS LIABILITY"?

If strict liability means that the defendant is liable for causing an injury without fault, only manufacturing defect cases satisfy that definition in most states today. In manufacturing defect cases (almost certainly the least common of the three categories), the manufacturer is liable simply for selling a product that turns out to be defective, without proof of any fault.

In design defect cases, however, the plaintiff must establish that the product design was inadequate, under a standard that looks much like a negligence test. Under a risk/utility standard, the jury must decide whether the manufacturer made a reasonable trade-off, in designing its product, between risk and the expense of preventing that risk. This "Hand formula"-type assessment of the design decision is very close to the reasonable person standard of negligence law. Arguably, design defect liability is "strict" if a court uses the consumer contemplation test, which theoretically only considers the nature of the product sold rather than the defendant's conduct in designing it. But this too can be conceptualized as negligence, the unreasonable choice to market a product that does not satisfy consumer expectations for safety.

Similarly, in warning cases, the question basically comes down to whether the manufacturer made a reasonable choice in deciding not to warn, or in the nature of the warnings it provided. Thus, while courts frequently refer to "strict products liability," a strong case can be made that, in all but manufacturing defect cases, Dean Prosser's dramatic §402A remedy has become a negligence claim with a good many specialized rules, but a negligence claim nonetheless.

In working through the examples below, assume that §402A of the Second Restatement applies, unless otherwise indicated.

Examples

Parameters of Strict Products Liability

1. In each of the following cases, there is an issue as to whether strict liability under Restatement (Second) §402A would apply. Can you spot the problem in each?
   a. Menendez buys an Acme framing machine for use in his picture framing business. For some reason, the machine repeatedly breaks down, leading Menendez to suffer delays and lose business.
   b. Fun & Fitness Gyms provides exercise facilities for busy professionals with fancy jobs. It buys an exercise machine from Ace Equipment Company, but decides it is too small for its purposes and buys a bigger model. It sells the smaller machine to Florio, a client at the gym. Florio is injured when the machine tips over while he is using it in his basement. He sues Fun & Fitness under §402A.
   c. Paramount Construction Company buys a concrete mixing truck directly from Constantine Truck Bodies, a manufacturer of trucks. Due to a design defect, sand added to the mix escapes into the gears that turn the mixer, destroying the mixer. Paramount brings suit against Constantine under §402A.
   d. Merriman goes to Scott Motors, the local Ford dealership, to test-drive a new Ford. She takes it for a spin, but when a car stops short in front of her and she hits the brakes, they fail. She is injured, and sues Scott Motors, claiming a design defect in the brakes under §402A.
   e. Argento Electric installs wiring in Porazzo's house. One of Argento's electricians strips the insulation too far back off a wire, causing a fire that extensively damages the house. Porazzo sues Argento Electric under §402A.

Responsibility Without the Blame

2. Computex Corporation manufactures computers. It sells a computer to Tech Store, a computer products store, which resells it to Gutierriez. She takes it home and plugs it in. It catches fire, and the fire damages her home.

   Investigation reveals tiny teeth marks on the wires inside the computer—mice had evidently gotten in at some point during the manufacturing process and chewed off some insulation, allowing a short circuit that started the fire. Gutierriez sues Tech Store and Computex on a strict products liability theory. Will either defendant be liable to her?

3. Gutierriez, in the case described in Example 2, brings a strict liability claim against Computex, on a manufacturing defect theory. In a second count in her complaint, she seeks recovery on a negligence theory. Is this proper?

4. Assume that investigation reveals that the offending mouse must have gotten in at Tech Store's retail store rather than during the manufacturing process. Which defendant, if either, would be liable to Gutierriez under §402A?

5. Assume instead that the fire resulted from a printed circuit board inside the computer. Computex had bought the circuit board from Allied Wiring Corporation and installed it, without alteration, in the computer. Somehow, the circuit board had been misprinted, leading to the fire. Who would be liable to Gutierriez under §402A?

Designs and Defects

6. In *Pouncey v. Ford Motor Co.*, 464 F.2d 957 (5th Cir. 1972), the blade of a radiator fan broke off, striking Pouncey in the face. Examination revealed (according to the plaintiff's expert, anyway) a high level of impurities in the steel in the blade, which would tend to make it more prone to breakage. Is this a manufacturing defect case or a design defect case? Why do we care?

7. Algren develops a taste for Smirnoff Vodka in college. She becomes an alcoholic, her husband leaves her, and she loses her job. She sues Smirnoff, alleging that its vodka is defective and unreasonably dangerous because it can lead to alcoholism.
   a. Under §402A, how do you think the court would go about rejecting Algren's claim that vodka is defective and unreasonably dangerous?
   b. Algren sues instead for failure to warn that consumption of vodka may lead to addiction. What result?

8. Perini purchased a Honda motorcycle, and was injured in a collision with a car. When he was hit, the motorcycle fell over, and his right leg, under the cycle, was crushed. He sues, claiming that the cycle should have had crash bars that would have protected his legs in a crash of this type.

   If you represented Perini, and had the choice to sue in a jurisdiction that would apply the consumer expectation test to this design defect case, or alternatively, one that would apply the risk/utility test, which would you think preferable for your client's case?

Liability for Failure to Warn

9. Durabrand Power Tools makes a stamping machine for metal fabricators. The machine has an on/off switch away from the stamping area,

but no guard to protect the operator's hands from entering the stamping area. Such a guard could be included, but it would reduce the speed of production somewhat. On the bed of the machine, directly in front of the operator, is a warning label, in large red letters: WARNING: KEEP HANDS FROM STAMPING AREA TO AVOID SERIOUS INJURY OR AMPUTATION! Gainor, using the machine, is distracted by a coworker. She turns, and her hand drifts into the stamping area and is seriously injured. What is the best argument that Durabrand should be liable under principles of strict products liability?

10. Parker purchases an electric hedgeclipper from his local hardware store, Acme Hardware Company. The clipper was purchased fully packaged from Garden Products, Inc., the manufacturer, with directions inside and various warnings on the clipper itself as well as in the directions. Acme never opens the box, but sells the clipper to Parker still in the package. Parker is injured using the clipper when the clipper dips into a puddle and Parker receives a shock. Neither the directions nor the clipper provided any warning about the danger of shock through this type of occurrence.

    Parker sues Acme Hardware, alleging strict liability for failure to warn. Assuming that there should have been a warning about this risk, will Acme Hardware be liable to Parker?

Limits of the Duty to Warn

11. Lawrence Ladder Company makes stepladders. Paoli buys a Lawrence stepladder for use in painting his house. As he is trying to reach a high point on the side of the house, he puts one foot on the next-to-the-top step of the ladder, and the other on the little paint shelf opposite to it. The paint shelf collapses, and Paoli falls. He sues Lawrence, alleging that it failed to warn him of the danger of climbing on the paint shelf. Lawrence argues that it owes no duty to warn consumers of dangers from the *misuse* of its products. Will its argument prevail here?

12. Juarez buys a set of oversized wheels for her pickup truck. The tires bear a label stating that they should not be installed on a truck larger than a certain size. Plaintiff installs the tires on hers, even though it is larger than the specified size. She is injured when the truck rolls over in an emergency stop. Juarez brings a products liability claim, arguing that the warning on the tires was inadequate. Is it?

Material Risks

13. Leahy Pharmaceuticals develops a new drug for depression, called Perzac. Leahy tests the drug thoroughly for three years before placing it on the market, and discovers several side effects, including a 3 percent

risk of a psychotic reaction. It markets Perzac, warning of several side effects but not of the risk that the drug may cause a psychotic reaction. Collier takes Perzac, has a psychotic reaction, and brings suit against Leahy, alleging it is liable for selling Perzac without a warning of the danger of psychotic reactions.[3]

a. Leahy argues that it is not liable because the benefits of the drug justify marketing it, even if it does cause an adverse reaction in some patients. What would Collier argue to counter this argument?

b. Leahy argues that it is not liable because only 3 percent of patients experience the adverse reaction, too small a percentage to merit a warning. How do you think the court would rule on this argument?

Elements, Elements

14. Daniel suffered respiratory injuries when Shroeder, a coworker in a restaurant, poured chlorine bleach instead of cleaning fluid into a deep fat fryer. Shroeder testified that he was in a hurry, grabbed the bottle by mistake, and poured it into the fryer. The chlorine vaporized, injuring Daniel's lungs. She sued the manufacturer of the bleach, alleging that the label on the bleach bottle should have contained a warning against exposing it to heat. What problems do you anticipate Daniel will have in proving her failure-to-warn claim?

Explanations

Parameters of Strict Products Liability

1. a. Section 402A allows recovery for "physical harm" caused by defective products that are unreasonably dangerous. Here, Menendez has not suffered physical harm—meaning, generally, personal injury or damage to property. He has suffered loss of business due to the failure of the machine to perform as expected. Section 402A was not intended to cover this type of claim. Fundamentally, this loss is a commercial loss due to the failure of the goods to live up to contractual expectations. Courts have generally held that the buyer should be left to contractual remedies for the failure of the product to meet contractual requirements. See Frumer & Friedman, Products Liability §13.07[1][a].

b. The problem here is that Fun & Fitness is not "engaged in the business of selling such a product." Its business is providing exercise facilities, not selling exercise equipment; this sale was an aberration rather than

3. Leave aside for the moment the question of *who* must be warned of the risks from the drug. Under the "learned intermediary" doctrine, drug manufacturers can frequently discharge the duty to warn of drug risks by warning the medical providers who prescribe them.

its regular business. Section 402A limits liability to sellers who are in the business of selling the product that caused the injury.

> The basis for the rule is the ancient one of the special responsibility for the safety of the public undertaken by one who enters into the business of supplying human beings with products which may endanger the safety of their persons and property, and the forced reliance upon that undertaking on the part of those who purchase such goods.

Restatement (Second) of Torts §402A cmt. f. Most of the rationales for strict liability do not apply to a situation like this. Fun & Fitness is not in a position to spread the cost of this product injury since it neither regularly makes nor sells exercise equipment. It is not in a position to improve the design of the equipment, in any direct way since it doesn't design them. It doesn't advertise or promote the sale of exercise machines, so it cannot be said to have induced the sale or promoted reliance on its expertise.

c. Here, the damage caused by the product defect is to the product itself. There's a fair argument that this constitutes "physical harm thereby caused to the ultimate user or consumer, or to his property." Restatement (Second) §402A. After all, the defect did cause physical harm to the user's property, the truck itself. However, most courts applying §402A have held that when a defect causes injury to the product itself, rather than to other property, the owner is limited to contractual remedies. The Third Restatement also takes this position. Restatement (Third) of Torts: Products Liability §21 cmt. d.

d. Under §402A it is proper to sue a retailer as well as a manufacturer. Scott Motors is a "seller . . . engaged in the business of selling such product," so it is a proper defendant under §402A. But Merriman's problem here, if it is one, is that there hasn't been a sale. Merriman is a customer, but not yet a buyer when she is injured. Section 402A speaks of "one who sells any product . . ." and here Scott hasn't sold it yet.

   However, it is unlikely that a court would take this literally, when the product was offered for sale by Scott, a seller of Fords. The rationale for strict liability involves the distribution of products that impose risks on users. This product has done that, even though it has not yet been purchased. Requiring sale to the consumer smacks of the old privity requirement; §402A, by contrast, allows recovery by many plaintiffs who never bought anything from the defendant. ("It is not even necessary that the consumer have purchased the product at all. He may be a member of the family of the final purchaser, or his employee, or a guest at his table, or a mere donee from the purchaser." Restatement (Second) §402A cmt. 1.) Thus, Scott probably won't prevail on the argument that it is not liable because the sale never transpired. For a case rejecting the argument, see *Rivera-Emerling v. Fortunoffs of Westbury Corp.*, 721 N.Y.S.2d 653, 654-655 (App. Div. 2001); see also Restatement (Third) of Torts: Products Liability §20(b) cmt. f (definition of seller or distributor includes one who provides car for test-drive).

e. The problem here is that the claim does not arise from the sale of a defective product. It arises from faulty installation, which is the provision of a service. Section 402A creates a remedy for dangerously defective products, not for faulty rendition of services. Porazzo will likely have to look to other remedies, either under contract or negligence law.

The issue would be closer if Argento's electricians installed defective wiring, manufactured by Superior Electric, and a defect in the wire caused the fire. Clearly, Superior would be liable under §402A, as a seller (to Argento) of the defective wire. But would Argento be a "seller" on those facts? Surely the cost of the wire is incorporated into its contract price for the work, so in some sense it is a seller of the wire. But the sale is incidental to Argento's main work—electrical installations. Similarly, a plumber may provide a gasket for sealing gas lines when installing a new gas stove. Doubtless, a charge for this will appear on the plumber's bill, but most courts would hold that the plumber is not primarily "engaged in the business of selling such product" (Restatement (Second) of Torts §402A(1)(A)) and therefore not liable under §402A. See, e.g., *Johnson v. Zimmer Spine Inc.*, 2008 WL 11449246 (D. Nev.) (Aug. 8, 2008) (medical provider not strictly liable for defect in medical device implanted during surgery).

Responsibility Without the Blame

2. Both Computex and Tech Store will be liable to Gutierriez under §402A. They each are in the business of selling computers, and both sold one that was defective and unreasonably dangerous, and led to physical harm to Gutierriez's house. Computex, of course, did not sell it to Gutierriez, but that isn't required under §402A. Manufacturers and intermediate sellers (such as wholesalers) are liable to consumers injured by the products they sell, as well as the retailer who directly deals with the consumer. Privity is not a requirement.

In this case, neither Computex nor Tech Store did anything negligent; the mouse was the guilty party. Although the defect here is neither a failure of the manufacturing materials nor misassembly, the manufacturer and retailer are still liable. It is enough under §402A to establish that the seller sold a defective product. The plaintiff need not establish that the product was defective due to negligence.

This case would come out the same way under the Restatement (Third) of Torts: Products Liability. Under §2(a) of the Products Liability Restatement, sellers are strictly liable for manufacturing defects in their products, "even though all possible care was exercised in the preparation and marketing of the product." Several of the rationales for strict liability support this result, including the manufacturer's ability to spread the cost of accidents from product defects through price, the incentive that liability will give manufacturers to inspect products carefully, and the inability of the consumer to protect herself from such defects.

3. In many states, it is proper to assert multiple tort theories for recovery in a products liability case. The adoption by courts of a cause of action for strict products liability was meant to expand plaintiffs' remedies, not to bar their resort to traditional causes of action that might also apply. A plaintiff might sue for negligence, breach of implied warranty, breach of express warranty, misrepresentation, and strict products liability if the evidence supports each theory.

   The elements of a negligence claim and a manufacturing defect claim are slightly different. On her negligence claim, Gutierriez will have to establish that Computex failed to exercise reasonable care in making or inspecting the computer. As Example 2 illustrates, she doesn't have to show that to recover on a strict liability claim for defective manufacture. Often, there will be little point to asserting the negligence claim if strict liability applies, but in some states statutes of repose or limitations or other defenses might defeat one claim but not the other.

4. In this case, Tech Store would be liable but Computex would not. Computex sold the product, but it was not defective when it left Computex's control. It is not strictly liable for defects that occur later. Similarly, it would not be strictly liable for a defect that arose from shipping or weather damage after the product was shipped. The product was defective, however, when it was sold by Tech Store, so it would be liable to Gutierriez under either §402A or the Third Restatement §2(a).

5. This is another manufacturing defect case, but here the defect is in a component Computex purchased and incorporated into its finished product. Computex will be liable for the fire. The defective component made the finished product defective since it was unreasonably dangerous and led to the fire. Again, Computex did not do anything "wrong," but is strictly liable for the damage caused by its defective product.

   Both Allied Wiring and Tech Store will also be liable to Gutierriez under §402A since they also sold the defective product that led to the fire. Allied sold the defective printed circuit board. As a seller, it remains responsible for damages caused by that product, even if it is incorporated into a finished product and resold to a consumer. See, e.g., *Jenkins*

v. T & N P.C., 53 Cal. Rptr. 2d 642, 645 (Cal. App. 1996); see generally Restatement (Third) of Torts: Products Liability §5 and cmt. b.

Designs and Defects

6. You can't really answer this question without more information. If the blade that broke was like all blades on Ford radiator fans—if they were all fabricated with impure steel—this is a design defect. Pouncey would argue that Ford's design choice to use that type of steel in its fans was inappropriate in light of the risks of failure of the blades. If, however, discovery revealed that the level of impurities in this fan blade was an aberration, the case would be a manufacturing defect case since the fan blade did not conform to Ford's own design specifications for the product.

   Classifying the case matters because if it is a manufacturing defect case, the plaintiff need not shoulder the expensive burden of proving that the design was defective, under risk/utility analysis or a consumer expectations standard. (What consumer really has any expectations at all about this?) It need only show that the fan did not conform to manufacturing specifications, and that the resulting defect led to Pouncey's injury. If that is true, Ford would be "strictly" liable for Pouncey's injury.

7. a. It appears that Algren's claim is based on design defect rather than manufacturing defect. She does not claim that the vodka was adulterated in some way, but that vodka, in its intended form, is unreasonably dangerous. If the claim were accepted, Smirnoff would be liable to all alcoholics since they marketed the product in an unsafe form.

   The court will almost certainly reject Algren's argument based on the fact that vodka, while it has risks, cannot be made safer without fundamentally altering its nature. It would be great if we could have unlimited vodka without hangovers or addiction. But that isn't one of the choices. If products liability law dubs alcohol defective and unreasonably dangerous because it poses risks, it condemns the entire product since it can't be redesigned and still be vodka. While courts might be willing to brand some such products unreasonably dangerous (cigarettes and asbestos are two possible candidates), they have generally been unwilling to assume the role of arbiters of public conduct in this way. Consequently, courts have seldom concluded that products that pose risks, but cannot serve their intended purposes without those risks, are defective.

   > Good whiskey is not unreasonably dangerous merely because it will make some people drunk, and is especially dangerous to alcoholics; but bad whiskey, containing a dangerous amount of 40 oil, is unreasonably dangerous. . . .

Restatement (Second) of Torts §402A cmt. i. The Third Restatement takes a similar position. Restatement (Third) of Torts: Products Liability §2 cmt. d. Under the consumer expectations test, the product passes muster because consumers understand its dangers and accept them as inseparable from the product itself. Under a risk/utility test, vodka is not defective since it can't be redesigned to be completely benign and still be vodka; there is no reasonable alternative design.

b. Since the court will not likely hold that vodka is "defectively designed," Algren tries a failure to warn theory. Even if it is reasonable to market a product that poses risks, a manufacturer may be liable for failure to warn users of risks from its use. But here the risk is so generally known that the court will almost certainly hold that a warning is unnecessary, simply because there is no duty to tell people what they already know. In *Garrison v. Heublein, Inc.*, 673 F.2d 189 (7th Cir. 1982), the court rejected the failure to warn argument in an alcohol case on this theory.

   It might be different if the risk were less generally understood. For example, until recently the effect of alcohol on in utero fetuses was not general knowledge, though it was likely understood by medical personnel and distillers. A claim for failure to warn of potential damage to fetuses might have prevailed in those circumstances. This risk is one that cannot be eliminated. While it may not warrant a ban on alcoholic products, it is appropriate to warn pregnant women of this risk, so they can avoid it.

8. The consumer expectations test very likely would be less favorable in this case. Most consumers would probably recognize the risk that a motorcycle will be knocked over, and that if it is, a rider's leg may be crushed underneath it. They would probably be surprised to learn that cycles can be fitted with crash bars that offer protection against leg injuries. Thus, the cycle without such crash bars probably comports with most consumers' expectations.

   However, a fair case can be made by design experts that the cycle could be made safer with little effect on its operation. In a jurisdiction that applies the risk/utility approach, this evidence might establish that the cycle was defective, even though it was as safe as most consumers would expect it to be. See *Camacho v. Honda Motor Co., Ltd.*, 741 P.2d 1240 (Colo. 1988), in which the court splits on the proper test to use in a case with similar facts.

Liability for Failure to Warn

9. Gainor should argue that a warning was an insufficient response to the danger posed by the machine. Instead, the manufacturer should have

eliminated the risk altogether by designing a guard that would prevent the operator's hands from entering the stamping area. Although a guard would have slowed production somewhat, under a risk/utility analysis this loss in production speed is likely outweighed by the increased safety. It is foreseeable—indeed, almost inevitable—that an operator's hands will end up in the stamping area now and then, due to some form of accident, the temptation to adjust the work despite the danger, or sheer inadvertence, as in Gainor's case. If that is true, the machine is probably defective if it lacks a guard.

Assuming that a reasonable design required a guard, Durabrand's argument that it provided a *warning* of the danger likely will not avoid liability. Interestingly, §402A appeared to endorse the defendant's argument here. See §402A cmt. j (product not defective if a warning was given, and a product could be safely used if the warning was heeded). Courts, however, have generally rejected comment j, as does the Third Restatement. Restatement (Third) of Torts: Products Liability §2 cmt. 1 (when safer design is possible, warning not adequate alternative). The manufacturer should not be able to avoid liability for a defective design by giving notice of the danger it should have designed out of the product. It would frequently be cheaper for the manufacturer to warn of a defect in its product than to redesign the product to make it reasonably safe. If a warning were a defense to design defect liability in such situations, it would undermine the incentive to make products safer. Thus, the court will almost certainly reject the argument that the warning is a proper substitute for a safer design. Accord: *Weigle v. SPX Corp.*, 729 F.3d 724, 738-739 (7th Cir. 2013).

10. Because a reasonableness standard governs products liability claims for failure to warn, some authorities question whether there is really a difference between negligence and strict liability in failure to warn cases. This example illustrates one significant difference. Surely, if Parker sued Acme Hardware for negligence, he would lose. They didn't do anything negligent. They just bought a packaged product from a presumably reputable manufacturer and resold it to a customer. It was Garden Products that packaged the product without adequate warnings. But under §402A, Acme is a "seller," and would be liable if the warning is inadequate. It will likely have an action against Garden Products for indemnification, but Parker will still be able to sue the local seller for his injury. See, e.g., *In Re Shigellosis Litigation*, 647 N.W.2d 1, 5-6 (Minn. App. 2002); see generally Restatement (Third) of Torts: Products Liability §2 cmt. o.

    A number of states now limit the plaintiff's right to sue downstream sellers, either by statute or judicial decision. Indiana, for example, limits products liability claims to the manufacturer of the product or component that caused the injury, unless the manufacturer is not subject to personal jurisdiction in the action. See, e.g., Ind. Code §34-20-2-3, §34-20-2-4.[4] These statutes reflect the view that the manufacturer, who designs the product, fabricates it, and decides what warnings to give, should bear liability for injuries it causes. In states that allow suit against the retailer, the retailer will have a right of indemnification—reimbursement—from the manufacturer if it is held strictly liable to the plaintiff.

Limits of the Duty to Warn

11. The example raises the question of whether manufacturers can be strictly liable for failing to warn a consumer about the dangers of various ways she might misuse their products.

    In *Greenman v. Yuba Power Products, Inc.*, Judge Traynor spoke of strict liability for a product's "intended" use. 377 P.2d 897, 901 (Cal. 1963). Similarly, §402A refers to dangers in "normal handling and consumption." Restatement (Second) of Torts §402A cmt. h. Since consumers can come up with all kinds of ridiculous ways to misuse a product, Lawrence's argument that it should not be required to warn Paoli of the dangers posed by unintended uses is a credible one.

    The case law, however, has generally recognized a duty to warn of *foreseeable* misuses that result from human nature acting upon opportunity. It is highly foreseeable that a user, stretching to reach the top of a window, will be tempted to gain some altitude by putting one foot on that paint shelf. If it is dangerous to do so, that danger can be averted by a warning. Many courts have held that defendants have a duty to warn of such foreseeable misuses. See Frumer & Friedman, Products Liability §12.05; see generally D. Owen, Defectiveness Restated: Exploding the "Strict" Products Liability Myth, 1996 U. Ill. L. Rev. 743, 780-781. It is likely that this approach will continue in jurisdictions that adopt the Third Restatement, which imposes liability for "reasonably foreseeable uses and risks." Restatement (Third) of Torts: Products Liability §2 cmt. 1.

    Of course, Paoli may be *negligent herself* for trusting her weight to the paint shelf without inquiry. If so, her negligence can be taken into account under principles of comparative negligence or assumption of risk rather than concluding that the manufacturer had no duty to warn of this misuse. If the manufacturer can avoid serious and foreseeable accidents from such foreseeable misuse by printing a warning on the shelf, products liability standards should encourage it to do so.

12. This notice is almost certainly inadequate. Arguably, it isn't a warning at all; it's an instruction about how to use the product. It is frequently

4. Some statutes bar *any* strict products liability claim against the retailer or wholesaler. See, e.g., Neb. Rev. St. §25-21,181; S.D.C.L. §20-9-9.

insufficient to simply instruct consumers not to use a product in a particular way. A true warning should inform the consumer of the nature and extent of the risk posed by ignoring the instructions. As one court stated,

> it may be doubted that a sign warning, "Keep off the Grass," could be deemed sufficient to apprise a reasonable person that the grass was infested with deadly snakes. In some circumstances a reasonable man might well risk the penalty of not keeping off the grass although he would hardly be so daring if he knew the real consequences of his failing to observe the warning sign. . . ."

Post v. American Cleaning Equip. Corp., 437 S.W.2d 516, 520 (Ky. 1968). Without a sense of the reason for obeying instructions, people have a human tendency—whether reasonable or not—to ignore them if obedience is inconvenient. To really affect consumers' behavior, a warning must convey the nature and gravity of the risk of ignoring instructions. "Warning! Use of these tires on trucks heavier than 2,000 pounds may cause serious injury or death from rollover accidents!" would be an obviously more effective warning.

Material Risks

13. a. This argument is easily refuted. Leahy Pharmaceuticals argues that the benefits Perzac provides to most users make it reasonable to market the drug, even if a few users suffer side effects. But Collier hasn't challenged Leahy's decision to market Perzac. He claims that while it was reasonable to market the drug despite the small risk of psychotic reactions, users *should have been warned* about that risk. When a drug is widely beneficial, yet presents risks to some users that cannot be eliminated, warnings give users the information they need to make choices about the product. If Collier had been warned of the risk of psychotic episodes, she could have made an informed decision whether to run that risk or avoid the product. Because the drug had no warning of the risk of a psychotic reaction, Collier was unable to make that choice.

    So, Leahy can't defend the failure to warn claim on the ground that its choice to market Perzac, despite the risk, was a reasonable one. A manufacturer must be reasonable both in choosing to market a drug that poses risks, and in informing users about the risks it cannot eliminate from that product. See Restatement (Third) of Torts: Products Liability §2 cmt. k.

    b. Leahy's argument here is that it had no duty to warn of the risk because it was a small one. Many cases consider whether a risk was sufficiently substantial to merit a warning. In deciding whether a warning of a particular hazard should be given, courts have taken a general reasonableness approach, considering such factors as the gravity of the risk, how likely it is, whether the user will already be aware of it, and whether adding another warning to the product would decrease the effectiveness of *other* warnings. See generally Dobbs' Law of Torts §464. Because warnings are easy to provide, they will usually be warranted if the risk is one the ordinary consumer would want to know about. While the need for a particular warning is usually a question of fact, it is likely that a manufacturer should warn of a serious reaction suffered by 3 percent of users.

In the medical malpractice area, some courts hold that a patient should be warned of all risks she would consider material in deciding whether to undergo the procedure. See, e.g., *Scott v. Bradford*, 606 P.2d 554 (Okla. 1979). Logically, a similar standard might be applied to products liability failure to warn claims, but has apparently been invoked only occasionally. See Dobbs' Law of Torts §464.

Elements, Elements

14. One problem Daniel faces is convincing a jury that this type of misuse of the product is sufficiently likely that the defendant should have warned about it. Manufacturers can't warn about *everything*, since excessive warnings tend to undercut the impact of each one.[5] Nor can manufacturers anticipate every preposterous manner in which people will, in the fullness of time, misuse their products.

    Assuming that Daniel could convince a jury that a warning of this risk was needed, she faces another elemental problem: causation. From Shroeder's testimony it appears that even if the label had warned about this risk, Shroeder never would have read it, since he grabbed the bottle in haste and poured without examining the label. Products liability plaintiffs, like other tort plaintiffs, must establish that the defendant's defective product was a "but for" cause of her harm, that is, that the injury would not have happened if the product had not been defective. See Chapter 10, pp. 192-193 ff. Here it seems likely that the injury would have happened the same way even if the manufacturer had provided an adequate warning to keep the bleach away from heat since Shroeder would not have read it. Don't lose sight of the fact that causation must always be proved in a products liability case, as in other tort cases.

5. The defensive tendency to overwarn in order to limit liability has been referred to as "warnings pollution." D. Owen, Defectiveness Restated: Exploding the "Strict" Products Liability Myth, 1996 U. Ill. L. Rev. 743, 766.

Defendants frequently raise this argument when the plaintiff admits that she did not read the label or directions on a product. Courts have sometimes resolved the problem by creating a presumption that an adequate warning (perhaps with exclamation points, red capital letters, or a skull and crossbones, prominently placed) *would* have been read. But even this helpful presumption may be rebutted when the evidence indicates—as it probably does here—that an adequate warning would not have come to the user's attention.

CHAPTER 16

More Products Liability: Common Defenses to Strict Products Liability Claims

INTRODUCTION

The previous chapter explained that strict products liability allows an injured party to recover against a *seller* for *personal injury or property damage* caused by *defective* products. We also saw that proof that a product was defective depends on the type of defect alleged. A plaintiff who claims injury from a manufacturing defect may recover by proving that the product was dangerously defective, but need not prove that negligence by the manufacturer led to the defect. However, in design defect and failure to warn cases, the plaintiff must make a showing that looks very much like negligent conduct by the manufacturer.

This chapter considers four common defenses to products liability claims. Several of these are true affirmative defenses, including comparative negligence and assumption of the risk. But others, such as the state-of-the-art "defense," the argument that a danger was "open and obvious," and the "defense" of misuse, might better be characterized not as defenses, but as challenges to the plaintiff's ability to make a prima facie case of product defect.

While the issues reviewed in this chapter arise in products liability cases in every state, their treatment varies considerably from one state to another. For example, a plaintiff's negligence may bar a products liability recovery entirely in one jurisdiction, reduce it in others, and have no effect at all in others. This chapter emphasizes basic arguments that defendants commonly raise in products cases to avoid liability, and the various approaches the states have taken in analyzing those arguments. Remember that tort law is state law, so every state makes its own. Thus, states may, and do, take different approaches to defenses in strict products liability cases.

THE EFFECT OF PLAINTIFF'S NEGLIGENCE

Let's start with a true affirmative defense, contributory or comparative negligence. In strict products liability cases, as in traditional negligence cases, defendants frequently argue that the plaintiff should be barred from recovering because her own negligence contributed to her injury. For example, suppose that Accu-Cut Corporation makes a saw with a blade that tends to stick if used to cut stock that is thicker than one inch. Ramirez, the plaintiff, uses the saw and senses that something isn't right, but continues to work. On one cut, the saw sticks and the board kicks back, injuring Ramirez. The saw may well be defective, because it tends to throw the work back (or because of failure to warn not to use it for thicker cuts). However, Ramirez may also have contributed to his injury by continuing to cut the stock despite this problem.

A. The Background: Treatment of Plaintiff's Fault in Negligence Cases

In cases brought on a negligence theory, such "contributory negligence" by a plaintiff barred her entirely from recovery in most states until the 1960s. Since then, however, contributory negligence has been replaced in most states by comparative negligence. Under comparative negligence, a plaintiff whose negligence contributed to an injury may still recover, but her recovery will be reduced by the percentage of fault the jury attributes to her. If, for example, Ramirez sued Accu-Cut on a negligence theory, and the jury concluded that Ramirez was 30 percent at fault for continuing to use the saw for thick cuts, his damages would be reduced by 30 percent. In a good many states, Ramirez would be barred from any recovery if his negligence reached a certain level—either 50 or 51 percent. For a full discussion of comparative fault, see Chapter 24.

B. Evolution of Treatment of Plaintiff's Fault in Strict Products Liability Cases

When §402A was added to the Restatement (Second) of Torts in 1965, the drafters concluded that contributory negligence should not bar recovery on a strict products liability claim. Restatement (Second) of Torts §402A cmt. n. Strict liability was thought of as a different type of liability, intended to place the risk of injury from defective products on the seller, even if the plaintiff's negligence was also a cause of her injury. Early cases under §402A followed comment n, refusing to bar plaintiffs in strict products liability cases even if their negligence was a factor in causing their injury. See Prosser & Keeton at 712.

However, as states abandoned the complete bar of contributory negligence in negligence cases in favor of comparative negligence, litigants inevitably began arguing that comparative negligence principles should apply to strict products liability claims as well. Indeed, in many products liability cases, the plaintiff asserts both a negligence claim and a strict products liability claim, based on the same underlying conduct of the defendant. It seems odd that the plaintiff's negligence would reduce her recovery on the negligence count, but be ignored on the strict liability count in the same case.

One argument against applying comparative fault to products liability claims is that it requires the jury to compare apples and oranges. In a negligence case, the jury compares the defendant's negligence to the plaintiff's. But how do you compare a defendant's *strict liability* for selling a defective product to the plaintiff's *negligence* in using it? These are conceptually different types of conduct: The defendant's liability arises without any fault at all (at least, in manufacturing defect cases), while the plaintiff's fault is based on negligence.

On the other hand, reducing recovery for a plaintiff's fault furthers several goals of tort law. It encourages care by plaintiffs, and causes negligent plaintiffs to share the loss caused in part by their negligence. The common sense of this approach has led many states to apply comparative fault to products liability claims as well as negligence claims. Dobbs' Law of Torts §470. In these states, the jury is instructed to assign a percentage of causal responsibility to the seller-defendant for selling the defective product, and to the plaintiff for her negligence in using the product. If the jury finds the seller 70 percent responsible, for example, and the plaintiff 30 percent responsible, the plaintiff will recover 70 percent of her damages. Although it may be a bit conceptually messy to assign percentages of "responsibility" to these different types of conduct, experience indicates that juries manage to do it reasonably well, and apportioning responsibility in such cases probably serves the goals of tort law better than ignoring the plaintiff's fault entirely.

Because the jury compares strict liability to negligence in such cases, some states now call their statutes comparative "responsibility" statutes rather than "comparative negligence" statutes. See, e.g., Tex. Civ. Prac. & Rem. Code Ann. §33.001 ("proportionate responsibility"); see also Restatement (Third) of Torts: Apportionment of Liability, Topic 1 (entitled

"Basic Rules of Comparative Responsibility"). Others still call their statutes "comparative fault" schemes, but define fault broadly to include the sale of a defective product. The Arkansas comparative fault statute, for example, applies to "any act, omission, conduct, risk assumed, breach of warranty, or breach of any legal duty which is a proximate cause of any damages sustained by any party." Ark. Code Ann. §16-64-122(c). The broad phrase "breach of any legal duty" surely includes strict liability for selling a defective product. Similarly, the Maine comparative fault statute applies (in addition to negligence claims) to a "breach of statutory duty or other act or omission that gives rise to a liability in tort or would, apart from this section, give rise to the defense of contributory negligence." 14 Me. Rev. Stat. Ann. §156. This too would include a products liability claim.

Note that adopting comparative negligence in products liability cases has a very different impact than adopting it in negligence cases. States switched to comparative negligence in negligence cases to allow plaintiffs *some recovery*, even if they were partly responsible for their own injury. Under comparative negligence, a negligent plaintiff now recovers reduced damages. But switching to comparative negligence for strict products liability claims often leads to a smaller recovery for plaintiffs. Under the approach of §402A cmt. n, the products ability plaintiff *recovered fully despite her negligence*. Switching to comparative responsibility principles in strict products liability cases means that a negligent plaintiff will recover less than before, because her negligence (ignored before) will reduce her damages.

Today, the effect of a plaintiff's negligence in a strict products liability case varies from state to state. A few states still adhere to the approach of comment n of the Second Restatement, that a plaintiff's negligence is irrelevant to a strict products liability claim. In these states, a negligent plaintiff recovers fully despite her negligence in using the product. "A strong majority"[1] of states, however, now treat such negligence as a partial defense to a strict products liability claim. A negligent plaintiff's damages will be reduced by the percentage of fault the jury assigns to her. If the applicable comparative fault statute bars a plaintiff from recovery if she is 50 percent or more at fault, the same rule is applied to strict products liability claims. See generally Restatement (Third) of Torts: Products Liability §17. Last, at least one state, North Carolina, treats contributory negligence as a full defense to a strict products liability claim. Any negligence of the plaintiff bars her from recovery entirely. See *Nicholson v. American Safety Utility Corp.*, 488 S.E.2d 240, 244 (N.C. 1997). See now N.C. Gen. Stat. §99B-4(3).

1. Restatement (Third) of Torts: Products Liability §17 cmt. a.

ASSUMPTION OF THE RISK

Just as the adoption of comparative negligence has spread from negligence cases to products liability cases, it has also affected the treatment of another traditional defense, assumption of the risk. To understand current approaches to assumption of the risk in products liability cases, we need to recall how that defense has evolved in negligence cases.

A. The Background: Treatment of Plaintiff's Assumption of Risk in Negligence Cases

Fifty years ago, most courts held that a plaintiff who recognized a risk and made a deliberate choice to encounter it was barred from recovering from the defendant who created the risk, even if the defendant was negligent in creating the risk. See Restatement (Second) of Torts §496A. Suppose, for example, that Quentin, an obviously intoxicated driver, offered Tanaka a ride, and Tanaka accepted and was later injured due to Quentin's negligent driving. Under assumption of the risk, a negligence claim by Tanaka would be barred by his deliberate choice to accept the risk of driving with Quentin. See id., illus. 2. The idea was that the plaintiff's deliberate choice to proceed in the face of clear knowledge of the danger constituted a kind of consent to the risk posed by the defendant's conduct, even if it had been negligently created by the defendant. See generally Chapter 23.

The advent of comparative negligence has altered the treatment of assumption of the risk in negligence cases. Today, many states that have comparative negligence regimes treat a plaintiff's assumption of a risk as a form of negligent conduct. Thus, the jury will be instructed to assign the plaintiff a percentage of fault for deliberately encountering the risk, just as they do for other forms of plaintiff's negligence. Consequently, assumption of the risk, like other forms of plaintiff's negligence, becomes a partial defense to a negligence claim rather than a complete bar to recovery. In the drunk driving case, for example, the jury might find Tanaka 30 percent at fault for choosing to ride with Quentin, and Quentin 70 percent at fault for driving while intoxicated. If so, Tanaka would recover 70 percent of his damages. In states that treat a plaintiff's deliberate choice to engage in the risk as comparative negligence, the separate defense of assumption of the risk is abolished. See, e.g., Mass. Gen. Laws ch. 231, §85.

A few states, however, continue to treat conscious assumption of the risk as a separate and full defense to a negligence action, even though they otherwise apply comparative negligence to account for a plaintiff's negligence. See, e.g., *Kennedy v. Providence Hockey Club, Inc.*, 376 A.2d 329 (R.I. 1977);

see generally Dobbs' Law of Torts §470. This is now clearly a minority position in negligence cases.

B. Evolution of Treatment of Assumption of the Risk in Strict Products Liability Cases

With assumption of the risk, as with plaintiff's negligence, the evolution of the law in negligence cases has affected products liability claims as well. When the American Law Institute adopted §402A, it took the position that a plaintiff's deliberate assumption of the risk (unlike contributory negligence) should bar her from recovery entirely on a strict products liability theory.

> [T]he form of contributory negligence which consists in voluntarily and unreasonably proceeding to encounter a known danger, and commonly passes under the name of assumption of risk, is a defense [to liability] under this Section as in other cases of strict liability. If the user or consumer discovers the defect and is aware of the danger, and nevertheless proceeds unreasonably to make use of the product and is injured by it, he is barred from recovery.

Restatement (Second) §402A cmt. n. Strict products liability cases initially followed this approach. See, e.g., *Johnson v. Clark Equipment Co.*, 547 P.2d 132 (Or. 1976); Annot., Products Liability: Contributory Negligence or Assumption of Risk as a Defense under Doctrine of Strict Liability in Tort, 46 A.L.R.3d 240 §5 (1972).

In recent years, however, a good many states that have adopted comparative negligence, and treat assumption of risk as a form of negligence in *negligence* cases, have adopted the same approach for *products liability* claims as well. That is, they now treat a plaintiff's conscious choice to encounter the risk posed by a defective product as a form of comparative fault. See, e.g., Iowa Code Ann. §668.1 (applying comparative negligence to "unreasonable assumption of risk"); Utah Code Ann. §78B-5-817(2) (defining fault to include assumption of the risk). The Restatement (Third) of Torts: Products Liability adopts this position—that assumption of the risk should be treated as a form of plaintiff's "responsibility" that reduces rather than bars recovery. "The majority position is that all forms of plaintiff's failure to conform to applicable standards of care are to be considered for the purpose of apportioning responsibility between the plaintiff and the product seller or distributor." Restatement (Third) of Torts: Products Liability §17 cmt. d.

Once again, however, the law is not uniform on the point. Some states have continued to treat a plaintiff's conscious assumption of the risk as a complete defense in strict products liability cases. See, e.g., *Tafoya v. Sears Roebuck & Co.*, 884 F.2d 1330, 1341 (10th Cir. 1989) (applying Colorado law); see generally Restatement (Third) of Torts: Products Liability §17, reporter's note to cmt. d. So, though it is frustrating to students, who would like to know "what the law is," the law again varies from state to state. A plaintiff's conscious assumption of the risk posed by a defective product will reduce her recovery in many states, but in a few it still stands as a complete defense. In these latter states, a plaintiff who recognizes the danger and proceeds to use the product will recover nothing.

THE "DEFENSE" OF MISUSE

While cases sometimes refer to a "misuse defense," misuse of a product may affect a products liability claim in several ways. Sometimes misuse defeats the plaintiff's prima facie claim, because it indicates that the product was not defective; in other cases, it constitutes a form of plaintiff misconduct that reduces or bars recovery.

Let's start with misuse that defeats the plaintiff's initial proof of a products liability claim. Sometimes people use a product in truly unforeseeable ways, ways so unusual that the manufacturer, when it made the product, would not reasonably have anticipated them. In these cases, a court (or a jury) may find that the product was not defective, even though it was dangerous when used as the plaintiff did, because it was never designed to be put to that use. In *Venezia v. Miller Brewing Co.*, 626 F.2d 188 (1st Cir. 1980), for example, the plaintiff sued the manufacturer of a beer bottle that shattered when he threw it against a telephone pole, injuring his eye. The court held that the manufacturer could not be held liable for the plaintiff's injury, because beer bottles are not designed to withstand such "use."[2] A court might hold the same way if the plaintiff inhaled spark plug cleaner to get high, or used a revolver to drive a nail.[3] In these examples, the plaintiff's "misuse" is not an affirmative defense, but rather prevents the plaintiff from establishing a prima facie case. She cannot establish that the product was defective, since she does not show that it was used for a purpose the manufacturer intended or should have foreseen. Such a use is "so unusual that the average consumer could not reasonably expect the product to be designed and manufactured to withstand it." *Findlay v. Copeland Lumber Co.*, 509 P.2d 28, 31 (Or. 1971).

---

2. See also *May v. Gillette Safety Razor Co.*, 464 N.E.2d 401 (Mass. App. Ct. 1984). In *May*, the plaintiff swallowed a razor blade. His estate sued Gillette, alleging that it was not (as it was represented) made of stainless steel, and therefore did not show up on an X-ray! The court refused recovery on the ground that a razor blade is not defective even if it will not show on an X-ray. Gillette was not bound to design a razor blade with this use in mind.

3. See *Jimenez v. Sears, Roebuck and Co.*, 904 P.2d 861, 872 (Ariz. 1995) (Martone, J., concurring).

It is conceptually tidier to view such misuse as defeating the plaintiff's proof of her prima facie case rather than as an affirmative defense—the plaintiff simply cannot prove that the product was defective. However, courts often hold that the plaintiff loses in such cases due to a "misuse defense," and several states have adopted statutes that expressly make "misuse" an affirmative defense. See, e.g., Ariz. Rev. Stat. §12-683(3). It is important to recognize, however, that in cases like this the plaintiff loses entirely since the manufacturer was not bound to make its product safe for an unforeseeable use.

In other strict products liability cases, the plaintiff's injury may be caused by a defect in the product, but also by her own misuse of it. Take, for example, the plaintiff who stands on the paint shelf of a stepladder. This is not the intended use of the shelf, but it is a foreseeable one. Consequently, the maker of the ladder probably has a duty to warn against that use. The plaintiff may well convince a jury that the ladder was defective without a warning of this. But it is also true that the reasonable person should know better than to stand on the paint shelf. Doing so is a negligent misuse by the user.

In cases like this ladder example, the plaintiff has used the product in a foreseeable manner, and may be able to prove that it was defective without a warning. The defendant, however, pleads the plaintiff's negligent misuse as an affirmative defense. ("Even if the ladder was defective for lack of a warning about standing on the paint shelf, you were negligent too since the reasonable person would realize that it was dangerous to stand on it.") The treatment of this type of misuse varies, as explained above in discussing comparative negligence. A clear majority of states today treat such negligent misuse by a plaintiff as a form of comparative fault, and reduce her recovery to account for it. In those states, the plaintiff would be assessed a percentage of fault for misusing the shelf as a step, and her recovery would be reduced by that percentage.

But suppose that the plaintiff fully appreciated the danger of misusing the product, and proceeded to misuse it that way anyway? For example, the plaintiff realizes that a table saw should have a guard, and that hers does not, but uses it anyway, confident that she can avoid injury. Here, the plaintiff's "misuse" could be characterized as conscious assumption of the risk, the deliberate choice to encounter a risk created by the defective product. And here again, the effect of such deliberate misuse will vary from state to state. Some states still treat such deliberate misuse as a complete defense, as §402A recommends. Other states—now most—treat it as a form of plaintiff's fault.

Misuse of a product may undermine a plaintiff's products liability claim in yet another way: She may misuse a product in such an unexpected way that she loses based on ordinary proximate cause analysis. Here's a classic example. In *Daniell v. Ford Motor Co.*, 581 F. Supp. 728 (D.N.M. 1984), the plaintiff deliberately locked herself in a car trunk, intending to commit suicide. She then changed her mind, but was unable to get out, because the trunk lid had no inside release. The car may have been defective for lack of a release, but the court held that even if it was defective, Ford would not be liable for such an unforeseeable occurrence as the plaintiff's failed suicide attempt. In this case, the bizarre nature of the plaintiff's misuse barred recovery even if she proved that the product was defective.

Products liability law would be conceptually cleaner if courts stopped treating the concept of "misuse" as a separate defense in products liability cases. The term adds little that isn't better accounted for by other concepts. When the plaintiff uses a product for an unforeseeable purpose, courts could simply hold that she has failed to prove that the product was defective. When the product is defective, but the plaintiff contributes to her injury through negligent or deliberate misuse, courts could address that conduct through the affirmative defense of plaintiff's fault or assumption of risk. If the misuse led to a completely unforeseeable type of harm (as in the *Daniell* case), the court could resolve the case under traditional proximate cause analysis. See generally Dobbs' Law of Torts §471.

However, under current products liability law, the term *misuse* is frequently invoked in each of the contexts discussed above. The term is enshrined in statutes in some states as well. So the concept is certain to remain important in strict products liability cases. To understand its use, you need to recognize the different roles that the plaintiff's misuse may play: that it may defeat proof of defect, establish an affirmative defense to the claim (or partial defense), or establish that the resulting harm was unforeseeable.

THE OPEN AND OBVIOUS DANGER "DEFENSE"

Another argument defendants raise in product liability cases is that the danger that injured the plaintiff was "open and obvious." Suppose that a cook gets cut while using an Accu-Cut knife, and sues Accu-Cut for failing to warn him of the danger of cuts. Accu-Cut will no doubt argue that it is not liable for failure to warn because the risk of being cut by a knife is open and obvious. This is another phrase that is loosely used. Sometimes the fact that a danger is obvious is no defense at all. In other cases in which a danger is obvious and cannot be eliminated from the product, obviousness defeats a plaintiff's prima facie case for failure to warn since there is no need to warn people of dangers they fully understand.

Distinguish two types of open and obvious dangers: ones that can't be designed out of a product, and ones that can. Suppose Sno-Begone Company markets a snow blower on which the snow-throwing blades are completely exposed. The owner stumbles against the blades and is injured.

The danger of the exposed blades may be obvious, but the snow blower is still unreasonably dangerous, because this obvious danger *should have been designed out*. Because it is easy to add a shield over the blades, this design fails either the consumer expectations test or the risk/utility test. Since that is true, Sno-Begone cannot avoid liability by claiming that the danger was open and obvious. Although the danger is obvious, it should not be there at all. Sno-Begone cannot avoid liability by arguing that while its product design was unreasonably dangerous, it was obviously so. If this argument worked, manufacturers would not have a duty to design reasonably safe products. And the more egregiously dangerous the design was, the less risk the manufacturer would run of being held liable. When the danger can be eliminated at a reasonable cost, it should be, whether it is obvious or not.

Compare the knife case. The danger of cutting a finger with a sharp knife is obvious. But here, the risk is not the result of a design flaw; to do its job, a knife must be sharp. Although the knife poses a risk of cuts, it is not an unreasonable risk, and can't be eliminated without undermining the utility of the product. So the design of the knife is not defective, despite the danger of cuts.

However, the plaintiff may argue that even if the knife had to be sharp, it should have included a warning of the risk of cuts. "If you couldn't design this risk out of the knife, at least you *could have warned me about it*." In other words, the plaintiff is thwarted on her design defect theory, and tries a failure-to-warn theory instead. Here, the obviousness of the danger plays a different role. If a danger is obvious, there is no need to warn about it, because people know about obvious dangers (whichever they are, but they surely include cuts from knives). So, the plaintiff will lose on her *design defect* claim, because the danger is inseparable from the product, reasonably designed. And she will lose on her *failure to warn* claim, because the manufacturer has no duty to warn people of dangers they already understand. If the danger is *not* obvious, however, the user may not understand it, and the manufacturer may be liable on a failure to warn claim if it does not warn of it.

JUST ONE MORE: THE STATE-OF-THE-ART "DEFENSE"

Here's one more "defense" that is probably not logically a defense at all. During the formative period of strict products liability law, the 1960s to the 1980s, a hotly disputed issue was whether a product was defective if it posed dangers that were unknown at the time of sale, and could not reasonably have been discovered through investigation and testing. Suppose, for example, that a drug manufacturer marketed a drug, after reasonable testing, without any reason to anticipate that it might cause an allergic reaction.

However, after widespread use by large numbers of patients, it became clear that the drug leads to an allergic reaction in a small percentage of users. If a user who suffered a reaction brought suit on a strict products liability theory, the manufacturer would argue that given the state of the art at the time it sold the drug—that is, the state of scientific knowledge about its risks—it had no reason to anticipate this type of injury. It would be unfair, the manufacturer argued (and will still argue, vehemently), to hold it liable for marketing a drug that posed a risk it could not recognize when it marketed it.

Under a negligence standard, this seems right. But in those heady days when §402A swept the nation, the thinking was that strict liability was *not* negligence liability; it was *strict* liability, based on the seller's distribution—with or without fault—of a defective product. Arguably, if the drug lacked a warning of a dangerous side effect, or if its design entailed an unacceptable risk of injury, it was defective, whether or not the seller could have known of the defect.

While one treatise suggests that rejecting the state-of-the-art defense would impose a duty that "could only be met, perhaps, by hiring Merlin, the magician of Arthurian legend, who lived backwards,"[4] several of the rationales for strict liability support liability for such unknowable defects. These include the ability of the manufacturer to insure and distribute the loss, reliance by consumers on the safety of products, and the incentive that liability provides to ferret out product risks. In the early days of §402A, several courts, convinced by these arguments, rejected the state-of-the-art defense in strict products liability cases, holding instead that manufacturers were liable for failure to warn of unknowable dangers of their products. See, e.g., *Beshada v. Johns-Mansville Products Corp.*, 447 A.2d 539, 546-547 (N.J. 1982).

However, most recent cases have rejected this position, concluding that manufacturers are not liable for failing to warn of a danger unless they knew or should have known of the need for a warning. *Vassallo v. Baxter Healthcare Corp.*, 696 N.E.2d 909 (Mass. 1998); *Fibreboard Corp. v. Fenton*, 845 P.2d 1168 (Colo. 1993); F. Vandall, Constricting Products Liability: Reforms in Theory and Practice, 48 Vill. L. Rev. 843 (2003). Even New Jersey, which started the brouhaha by rejecting the state-of-the-art defense in *Beshada*, subsequently endorsed it in *Feldman v. Lederle Labs.*, 479 A.2d 374 (N.J. 1984). Once again, however, there are contrary holdings. See, e.g., *Sternhagen v. Dow Co.*, 935 P.2d 1139 (Mont. 1997), a comprehensive opinion rejecting the defense despite its recognition in the Third Restatement of Torts.[5]

While the state-of-the-art argument is frequently referred to as a defense, it may be conceptually clearer to conclude that the manufacturer

4. Frumer & Friedman, Products Liability §12.02[4].

5. See Restatement (Third) of Torts: Products Liability §2, reporter's note at 104-107.

has not committed a tort by selling a product that poses an unknowable risk of injury. This characterization matters, because if this is an element of the plaintiff's prima facie case rather than a defense, she will have the burden to establish that the manufacturer should have been aware of or discovered the danger before selling the product. Once again, the state of the law is mixed: Some states have treated it as a defense, and others have placed the burden on the plaintiff to establish that the risk could have been discovered by the seller. See G. Robb, A Practical Approach to Use of State of the Art Evidence in Strict Products Liability Cases, 77 Nw. U. L. Rev. 1, 7 (1982). See generally Framer and Friedman ch. 8.04 (6).

There are many other interesting defensive issues in products cases, including preemption of state products liability law by federal law, the "learned intermediary" doctrine, the government contractor defense, and others. Those, however, are grist for an advanced products liability course. For now, let's focus on sorting out the five basic issues discussed above.

Examples

Some Apples and Oranges

1. Ortney sues Pretoria Motor Company for injuries she suffered when the brakes on a Pretoria sedan she was driving suddenly locked, causing an accident in which she was injured. Prior to the accident, Ortney had noticed that the brakes seemed "a little sticky," but had not taken the car in to have them checked. Ortney's complaint asserts a strict liability claim based on defective design of the brakes. Pretoria claims that Ortney was negligent since she did not have the car serviced after noticing brake problems.
   a. If the jury found that the brakes were defectively designed, but also that Ortney was negligent for failing to have them checked, what judgment would the court enter, in a jurisdiction that applied §402A of the Second Restatement of Torts?
   b. How would this case be submitted to the jury in most jurisdictions today, and how would the judgment be fashioned based on the jury's findings?

2. Suppose, in Ortney's case, that Pretoria had raised the defense that Ortney had assumed the risk of the defective brakes. Assume that the jury concluded that Ortney fully understood the risk posed by the brakes and chose to use the car anyway.
   a. What judgment would result if the approach of §402A applied?
   b. What judgment would result in most jurisdictions today?

3. On the same facts, Ortney sues Pretoria on two theories. In Count One, she alleges that Pretoria negligently designed the brakes. In Count Two, she alleges that Pretoria is strictly liable for selling the car with defective brakes.
   a. Is it possible that she could recover on both theories?
   b. Assume that Pretoria pleads, as a defense to each of Ortney's claims, that she was contributorily negligent for failing to have the brakes checked. The jury finds that the brakes were defective, but that Ortney was also negligent. If the approach of §402A applied to the strict liability claim, what judgment would result on each of Ortney's claims?

A Tough Question and a Tough Choice

4. Hedgepeth drives an oil delivery truck for a home heating oil business. When he tries to make a delivery to a West Dakota customer one morning, the pump on his truck doesn't function properly. He climbs on top of the truck and loosens the cap on the fill pipe, to allow some air into the tank to facilitate pumping. As he does so, he slips on the rounded surface of the tank and falls. He sues TankCraft, the manufacturer of the tank, for his injuries, claiming that the tank was defectively designed because there is no flat surface on top to walk on when servicing the tank. TankCraft claims that Hedgepeth, who testified in his deposition that the surface of the tank was sometimes "real slick" from spilled oil, assumed the risk of slipping when he climbed onto the tank.

   Assume that, since TankCraft does business in both West and East Dakota, Hedgepeth's lawyer could file his suit in either state. Assume that West Dakota treats assumption of the risk as a full defense to a strict products liability claim, but does not bar or reduce recovery if the plaintiff is negligent. Assume that East Dakota treats both assumption of the risk and plaintiff's negligence as forms of comparative fault that reduce recovery. Hedgepeth's lawyer concludes that whichever state hears the case would probably choose to apply its own products liability law to the case. In which state should Hedgepeth's lawyer file suit?

Use and Misuse

5. Pahti, an unhandy fellow, buys a can of paint to paint the living room of his apartment. When he gets home he realizes that he doesn't have a screwdriver to open the lid. So he uses a paring knife instead. Unfortunately, the blade of the knife breaks as he pries at the lid, and a piece goes into his eye. He sues Accu-Cut, the manufacturer of the knife, on a strict liability/design defect theory. What is the manufacturer's best argument to avoid or reduce liability?

6. Carlino bought a pair of pajamas and glued white cosmetic puffs all over them to make a Halloween costume. While wearing the costume, she reached up above the stove and was burned when the puffs ignited.
   a. What liability theory might Carlino assert in an action against Acme Cosmetics, the manufacturer of the puffs?
   b. What defenses should Acme assert? How would you expect the court to rule on them?

The "Open and Obvious" Defense

7. Clancy is riding in the cargo area of a Ford pickup truck when it collides with another vehicle. The back gate of the pickup is open, because it is carrying several long pieces of lumber. He is thrown from the truck and injured. He sues Ford, claiming that the truck bed should have included a warning that persons riding in the truck bed could be injured when thrown from the vehicle in a collision. What argument will Ford make to defeat the claim?

8. Let's revisit the situation in Example 9 from Chapter 15, in which Durabrand designed a stamping machine without a guard to prevent the operator's hands from getting caught in the machine, although a guard was feasible. Suppose that Durabrand did not provide a warning of the risk of injury to the user's hands from entering the stamping area. Gainor's hand drifted into the stamping area, she was injured, and she sues Durabrand on a products liability theory. She asserts that the product was defectively designed, and that Durabrand was liable for failing to warn her of the danger posed by the open stamping area.
   a. Durabrand argues that the design of the stamping machine was not defective, because the danger from putting her hands in the work area was "open and obvious." Consequently, since Gainor was clearly aware of the danger, Durabrand is not liable when she ignores the danger and suffers injury. Assuming that the danger is obvious to an ordinary user, does this prevent Gainor from proving a *design defect* claim?
   b. Durabrand moves for summary judgment on Gainor's *failure to warn* claim, arguing that it had no duty to warn her of a danger that was obvious to the user. How should the court rule?

Unknowable Dangers

9. Let's revisit another example from Chapter 15, Example 13, in which Leahy Pharmaceuticals marketed Perzac for depression, without warning of the danger of a psychotic reaction. It subsequently turns out, after wide use by hundreds of thousands of patients, that it can cause such a reaction in a very small number of patients. Leahy argues that it is not liable for failing to warn of this risk, because it did not know about it,

despite reasonable care in making and testing Perzac. How is the court likely to rule on this argument?

The State of Judge Fudd's Art

10. Pollard sues General Motors Corporation, claiming that he was injured in an accident driving a GM car because it did not have an airbag. GM argues that airbag technology had not been developed at the time Pollard bought his car, so it could not have been used to reduce collision injuries.
    a. How is GM's state-of-the-art argument here different from the state-of-the-art argument in the last example?
    b. Assume that Judge Fudd instructs the jury as follows:

    > If you find that at the time the defendant marketed the car that was involved in the plaintiff's accident, no manufacturer provided airbags in its sedans, then the defendant is not liable for failing to provide airbags.

    If you represented the plaintiff, why would you argue that Judge Fudd's instruction is defectively designed?

11. Bernstein's hair catches fire while using a Holden Products hair dryer. Investigation reveals that the solder on an electrical connection in the hair dryer was contaminated, melted, and caused a short circuit, causing the temperature of the hair dryer to increase dramatically. In Bernstein's products liability action, Holden argues that such contamination can happen in the manufacturing process but that it is exceedingly rare, and that there is no known process for detecting it. Judge Fudd instructs the jury that if the defect could not have been detected under the state of the art at the time of the sale, Holden is not liable for Bernstein's injury. What is wrong with the Honorable Fudd's instruction?

Fish or Fowl? A Too Hard Hypothetical

12. Acme Chemical sells a solvent used for removing oil from metal. The solvent causes a serious rash if it comes in contact with the skin. However, the risk of this rash can't be eliminated if the solvent is to do its job. Acme places a boldface warning on the container that the user should always wear rubber gloves to avoid the risk of a serious rash. Trask reads the label, but he can't find his rubber gloves. In a hurry to finish a job, he uses the solvent without gloves and suffers the rash. He sues Acme for his injury. The state applies comparative fault principles in strict products liability claims, and treats a plaintiff's conscious assumption of the risk as a form of comparative fault. If you represented Acme, what would you argue to defeat recovery?

Explanations

Some Apples and Oranges

1. a. Under §402A, the plaintiff's negligence—unless it constituted conscious assumption of the risk—was not a defense to a strict liability claim. Thus, Ortney would recover her full damages, despite her negligence in failing to have the brakes checked. For a dramatic example of this approach, which ignores the plaintiff's fault on a products liability claim, see *Kimco Development Corp. v. Michael D's Carpets*, 637 A.2d 603, 605-607 (Pa. 1993). In *Kimco*, a store ordered carpet backing and piled it all the way up to the ceiling. It ignited from the heat of the lights, leading to a serious fire. The jury found the store 80 percent at fault in causing the fire, but also found that the seller had failed to warn that the product was flammable. The court held that the store could recover fully for its fire loss since the store's negligence was not a defense to its strict products liability claim for failure to warn.

   b. In most jurisdictions today, the jury would be asked to find whether the brakes were defectively designed and also whether Ortney was negligent in failing to have the brakes checked. If they found that the design was defective, but that the plaintiff was also negligent in failing to have the brakes checked, they would assign percentages of fault to Pretoria for selling the defective product and to Ortney for her negligence. A judgment would then be entered based on these percentages of fault. For example, if they found Ortney 20 percent at fault and Pretoria 80 percent, Ortney would recover 80 percent of her damages.

2. a. Section 402A ignored a plaintiff's contributory negligence, but treated assumption of the risk as a complete defense to a strict liability claim. Thus, if Ortney fully appreciated the dangerous condition of the brakes, but chose to take a chance and use the car anyway, she would be barred from any recovery under the §402A approach. Needless to say, this made a rather subtle distinction—between a negligent failure to check the brakes and a clear appreciation that they posed a particular danger—critical in a products liability case. If the jury found only the first—negligent conduct but no deliberate choice to encounter the risk—the plaintiff recovered fully. If they found that the plaintiff understood the risk and consciously encountered it, she lost entirely.

   b. Today, in most jurisdictions, even full appreciation of the danger posed by a defective product is not a complete defense to liability. The jury would be asked to assign a percentage of fault to Ortney for her choice to drive with knowledge of the danger. (Naturally, they might assign a higher percentage of fault for such a deliberate choice than they would for driving with vague concerns about the brakes.) Ortney's damages would be reduced to reflect her fault in deliberately using the car with awareness of the risk posed by the defective brakes.

3. a. Yes, it is possible. A product will frequently be defective due to negligence of the manufacturer in designing it. Indeed, if the risk/utility test applies to the design defect claim, a finding that the design was defective (because the manufacturer had not properly balanced risk and utility) would usually support a finding that the manufacturer was negligent as well. If the jury finds that the design was unreasonably dangerous, they presumably also would find that Pretoria was negligent for using that design.

   b. If the jury found that the brakes were defective because Pretoria was negligent in designing them, Ortney would recover in most jurisdictions, but her negligence would reduce her recovery on the negligence claim. For example, if the jury had found Ortney 20 percent negligent, she would recover a judgment for 80 percent of her damages on the negligence count. (In a contributory negligence jurisdiction, she would lose entirely.)

   However, the jury's finding that she was negligent would have no effect on the strict liability count. Under the approach of §402A, contributory negligence was not a defense to a strict liability claim, so Ortney would recover fully on the strict liability claim. The judge should enter judgment on the negligence claim for 80 percent of Ortney's damages, but on the strict liability count for 100 percent of those damages. Of course, the plaintiff could not recover twice (or almost twice) by recovering on two theories. But she could choose to enforce the liability judgment for her full damages and thus recover fully despite her negligence.

   This anomaly—that the same events could lead to judgments for different amounts based on the same conduct—is eliminated in jurisdictions that apply comparative fault to strict products liability claims. The plaintiff's negligence is treated the same way on the liability count and the negligence count, as a damage-reducing factor rather than as a full defense.

A Tough Question and a Tough Choice

4. This is the kind of tactical decision that litigators often face in trying to serve their clients' interests. The problem is that it is not clear whether Hedgepeth will be found to have assumed the risk of his injury by climbing on the tank, even though it was sometimes "real slick." If the jury concludes that he fully appreciated this danger, and chose to encounter it, he will lose entirely under West Dakota law, based on the assumption of risk defense. If, on the other hand, the jury concludes that he was

simply negligent for disregarding a risk that the tank would be slippery, he would recover fully, with no deduction for his negligence since West Dakota does not reduce recovery in products liability cases based on a plaintiff's contributory negligence. So West Dakota is either the best or the worst choice, depending on the subtle factual distinction between consciously assuming a specific risk and acting negligently without fully appreciating the consequences of that choice.

If Hedgepeth sues in East Dakota he will probably recover something. The assumed East Dakota law treats plaintiff's fault as a damage-reducing factor, whether the jury characterizes his conduct as assumption of risk or negligence. So this is the conservative choice. But, the jury might find him pretty careless for walking on top of the tank, so this could mean a substantially reduced recovery.

There is no "answer" to this question. It is a difficult judgment to make, based on counsel's assessment of the likelihood that a jury would label Hedgepeth's conduct as assumption of the risk. Adventurous lawyers might "roll the bones" by suing in West Dakota. The more timid would likely opt for the safer course and sue in East Dakota.

Use and Misuse

5. The knife manufacturer might argue that Pahti was negligent to use a paring knife to open a can of paint. However, in some jurisdictions, a plaintiff's negligence is not a defense at all, and in most, it is only a partial defense, under comparative negligence rules. A better argument would be that Pahti had used the knife for an unforeseeable purpose for which it was never intended. If the court (or the jury) finds that this is true, Accu-Cut would not be liable at all. To recover on a strict products liability theory, Pahti must prove that the knife was defective when used for the purpose for which it was intended, or at least for a purpose that Accu-Cut should have anticipated that it would be used. If this is an unforeseeable misuse (which it probably is), the knife is not defective, even though it was unfit for that use.

   Surely this limitation on strict liability makes sense. Accu-Cut, in designing knives, can't be expected to contemplate its use for a screwdriver, a splint, or other idiosyncratic uses that might occur to a buyer. They are entitled to focus on the risks and utility of the knife as a knife, and perhaps for other closely related, foreseeable uses. A knife can't be all things to all people; if manufacturers had to design products for all possible uses, they could never design a decent knife.

6. a. Carlino might argue that the puffs were defectively designed because they were flammable. However, it seems doubtful that cosmetic puffs, generally used individually for applying or removing cosmetics from

the skin, are defective even if they are flammable. A stronger argument (though still somewhat shaky) is that Acme could foresee this type of misuse, and therefore should have included a warning with the puffs of the danger that they would catch fire. Acme need not design its puffs for that use, the argument goes, but it should at least warn people of the danger of that foreseeable misuse.

b. Acme might argue that Carlino was contributorily negligent for using the puffs for a Halloween costume. This argument would be based on misuse as a form of negligence. However, a jury might find that she *wasn't* negligent for doing so, in light of the low risk of igniting one's clothes. And, if she was negligent, that would not necessarily reduce her recovery, since in some states contributory negligence is not a defense to products liability claims. (In other states, however, her negligence would reduce recovery in proportion to her fault.) Acme might also argue that Carlino was negligent for getting too close to the stove. If she was, the effect of that negligence, as just stated, varies from state to state.

However, Acme's best argument is that gluing the puffs onto a Halloween costume is not a foreseeable misuse of the product. Again, this is not really an affirmative defense, but an argument that Carlino cannot establish an element of her prima facie case: that the puffs were used for a purpose for which they were intended, or a foreseeable misuse. If they are put to some truly bizarre alternative purpose, they are not defective if they fail to serve that purpose safely. In *Trivino v. Jamesway Corp.*, 539 N.Y.S.2d 123 (N.Y. App. Div. 1989), on which this example is loosely based, the trial court granted summary judgment for the manufacturer, but the appellate court reversed, holding that it was a jury question whether this use of the puffs was an unforeseeable misuse.

Last, Acme might argue that the danger of the puffs igniting was obvious. If so, a warning would not be necessary, since users would be aware of it. The *Trivino* court held that this, too, was a jury question, so the plaintiff survived the summary judgment motion.

The "Open and Obvious" Defense

7. While manufacturers have a duty to warn users of the dangers of their products, including the dangers of misuse, they do not have to warn of dangers that the user would already know about. It is probably foreseeable that consumers will misuse the cargo area of a pickup truck as a passenger compartment, but surely the danger of being thrown from the open bed of a pickup truck is "open and obvious." The duty to warn extends to dangers that the consumer would not readily understand from her common knowledge. Here,

the obviousness of the danger obviates the need to warn of it, because the user very likely already knows about it

Naturally, there will be close questions as to when a danger is obvious. Does the manufacturer, for example, have a duty to warn of the danger of choking on a marshmallow? A Montana trial judge held that this danger was obvious, but in *Emery v. Federated Foods, Inc.*, 863 P.2d 426 (Mont. 1993), the appellate court reversed, on the ground that whether the danger was obvious was a jury question. A Michigan appellate court held that a manufacturer had a duty to warn of the risk of diving into the shallow end of its pool (see *Glittenburg v.Wilcenski*, 435 N.W.2d 480 (Mich. App. 1989)) but was reversed by the Michigan Supreme Court. It held (but with a dissent!) that the manufacturer owed no duty to warn of this danger, because it was open and obvious. *Glittenburg v. Doughboy Recreational Industries*, 491 N.W.2d 208 (Mich. 1992).

8. a. In this example Durabrand designed a machine that posed an unreasonable risk of injury to users. Since the danger could be substantially eliminated by a guard, the design is defective. Durabrand argues, however, that it is not liable because the danger posed by the machine was "open and obvious" to users.

   In Example 9 from Chapter 15, Durabrand warned of the danger of hands getting caught in the machine. However, this warning did not avoid liability, since the danger could have been eliminated by a better design. If it was liable in that case, it surely should be liable here too, where its design is unreasonably dangerous and it does not warn of the danger. The machine is defective because the danger should not exist at all: The machine should be designed with a guard that eliminates the danger. Durabrand should not be allowed to defend a design defect claim by arguing that it designed an *obviously* dangerous product. If Durabrand's argument were accepted, it would mean that the more egregious the danger of its product, the greater the protection it would enjoy from design defect liability.

   b. Durabrand's "open and obvious" defense to the failure to warn claim is more credible. There is no duty to warn of obvious dangers; if the danger here was indisputably obvious, Durabrand might get summary judgment on the failure to warn claim. In many cases, however, whether the danger was obvious will be a factual question appropriate for the jury to decide.

   So here, the open and obvious defense might defeat a failure to warn claim, but the obviousness of the danger does not defeat the claim for defective design, based on the theory that the danger should have been designed out of the product. Indeed, the obviousness of the danger strengthens the argument that it was defectively designed.

Unknowable Dangers

9. As the Introduction indicates, some cases have held that a product is "defective" if it lacks warning of a danger, even if the manufacturer had no reason to know of that danger when it marketed the product. See, e.g., *Beshada v. Johns-Mansville Products Corp.*, 447 A.2d 539, 546-547 (N.J. 1982). The logic for this is that products liability is based not on the conduct of the manufacturer, but on the unreasonable risk posed by the product. If such a danger turns up, the consumer has been exposed to it whether or not the manufacturer could have anticipated it.

   However, most courts today would accept Leahy's argument that it is not liable for "unknowable" dangers posed by its product, as long as it had conducted reasonable testing before marketing the drug. These courts hold that if the risk could not have been anticipated based on the state of scientific knowledge and reasonable testing at the time of sale, the manufacturer is not liable for injuries resulting from that risk. See, e.g., *Potter v. Chicago Pneumatic Tool Co.*, 694 A.2d 1319 (Conn. 1997); *Barton v. Adams Rental, Inc.*, 938 P.2d 532, 539 (Colo. 1997); Restatement (Third) of Torts: Products Liability §2 cmt. a (product only defective if dangers reasonably foreseeable at time of distribution). Acceptance of the state-of-the-art defense is one of several ways in which "strict" products liability has converged with negligence law in the post-§402A era.

The State of Judge Fudd's Art

10. a. In this case, the manufacturer's argument is that given the technology available at the time the defendant sold the car, it was not feasible to design an effective airbag. Just as it should not be liable for failing to warn of risks it could not anticipate, the manufacturer argues, it also should not be held liable for omitting safety devices that were not technologically feasible at the time of manufacture. This argument is based on the premise that the limits of scientific and technical knowledge should be considered in determining the manufacturer's liability for product injuries.

    Courts that accept the state-of-the-art defense are likely to accept it in both the warning and design contexts. It seems axiomatic that a state that follows the Third Restatement of Products Liability would accept the state-of-the-art defense in design defect cases. The Third Restatement requires the plaintiff, in order to prove a design defect, to show that a reasonable alternative design existed that would have eliminated the danger. Restatement (Third) of Torts: Products Liability §2(b). The essence of the state-of-the-art argument in this context is that no safer design was feasible at the time of manufacture.

b. Judge Fudd's instruction tells the jury that the manufacturer is not liable if no manufacturer was including airbags in sedans. However, if airbags were feasible at the time, GM may be liable for failure to include airbags even if no other manufacturer was doing so.

This argument that "no manufacturer would have been aware of the need for this, or been able to provide it," is quite different from the argument that "no manufacturer *was doing it* at the time I sold the product." As Judge Learned Hand opined in a different context, "a whole calling may have unduly lagged in the adoption of new and available devices." *The T.J. Hooper*, 60 F.2d 737, 740 (2d Cir. 1932). The state-of-the-art argument is that an adequate safety device *could not* reasonably have been provided at the time of sale, not that no manufacturer was doing so.

11. The problem here is that Judge Fudd has imported the state-of-the-art defense from the design defect/warning context and applied it to a manufacturing defect case. The gist of the state-of-the-art defense is that a manufacturer cannot be faulted if the design of its product is reasonably safe, in light of the technology available at the time it designed and sold the product. Similarly, the trend in the cases applies the state-of-the-art defense to failure to warn claims as well: A manufacturer does not have a duty to warn of product risks it could not have discovered, in the exercise of reasonable care and pre-sale investigation, before it sold the product.

Here, however, Holden's argument is that there was no technologically feasible way to detect this type of manufacturing defect, and consequently, it should not be held liable for failing to detect it. The argument isn't a bad one; Holden is in some sense just as "blameless" for failing to detect this problem as it would be for failing to institute a design that wasn't technologically feasible. Yet, manufacturing defect cases, are, after all, the last bastion of "true" strict liability in the products area. Holden's argument would probably not prevail in most jurisdictions. However, several products liability statutes appear to apply the state-of-the-art defense even to manufacturing defect cases. See Iowa Code §668.12; Ky. Rev. Stat. §411.310 4(2).

Fish or Fowl? A Too Hard Hypothetical

12. Here, Trask has misused the solvent by ignoring the warning. What effect should Trask's misuse have on his claim? Should it bar it, or reduce his recovery? Acme should argue that Trask cannot show that its solvent was defective, because used as directed it is safe. It could not design the risk of the rash out of the product, and it warned users of that risk. It will argue that it has the right to expect users to use products according to adequate instructions and warnings. If the product is safe when so

used, Acme argues, the product is not defective, so Trask cannot make a prima facie case products liability case. And the necessary warning was given. What more can it do? If, in spite of all that, it is liable for Trask's injury, it seems like a form of absolute liability; it is held liable no matter what it does if the product causes injury.

Most courts would hold, I think, that when Acme provides a product that is reasonably safe when used as directed, and warns of dangers that cannot be designed out of the product without undermining its function, the product is not defective. On this logic, Trask should lose entirely. Otherwise, Acme is liable despite offering a reasonably safe product, and providing adequate warnings of the irreducible dangers associated with its use.

> Where warning is given, the seller may reasonably assume that it will be read and heeded; and a product bearing such a warning, which is safe for use if it is followed, is not in defective condition, nor is it unreasonably dangerous.

Restatement (Second) of Torts §402A cmt. j. See *Uptain v. Huntington Lab. Inc.*, 723 P.2d 1322, 1326 (Colo. 1986). Some states also have statutes that deny recovery if the plaintiff ignores adequate product directions or warnings. See, e.g., Ariz. Rev. Stat. §12-683(3); N.C. Gen. Stat. §99B-4(1).

However, a few cases have treated the plaintiff's failure to follow directions in such circumstances as a form of comparative fault. See, e.g., *Malen v. MTD Products, Inc.*, 628 F.3d 296, 313 (7th Cir. 2010) (applying Illinois law).

PART V

Damages for Personal Injury

CHAPTER 17

Personal Injury Damages: The Elements of Compensation

INTRODUCTION

Plaintiffs bring lawsuits for a variety of reasons, but when the cause of action is in tort, the reason is almost always to obtain monetary compensation for the injury.

We might well pause for a moment to ask whether this makes sense. If Krutch runs down Gray, breaking Gray's leg, why should the legal system respond by ordering Krutch to pay money to Gray? Aren't there other responses that would make more sense? Perhaps the court should order Krutch to perform services for Gray, take a driving course, or publicly acknowledge responsibility. Or maybe the court should provide social services to Gray, or retraining, or visits from neighbors, or who knows what.

Such responses to personal injury might be more creative than the impersonal transfer of dollars from the defendant (or his insurer) to the plaintiff. But the fact is that the usual balm the law provides to personal injury plaintiffs is money. Such payments are called "compensatory damages," and it is sometimes said that they are intended to "repair[] plaintiff's injury or . . . mak[e] him whole as nearly as that may be done by an award of money." Harper, James & Gray §25.1 at 493.

Clearly this goal is an idle dream in many cases: No amount of money could possibly compensate an active, healthy adult rendered paraplegic in an auto accident, a child disfigured by severe burns, or a patient brain-damaged by excessive anesthesia. These plaintiffs can never be put back in their pre-injury position, and none of us would incur their injuries for any sum. However, while money damages may seem an inadequate response to such injuries, they do help. A paraplegic with a two-million-dollar trust fund is a lot better off than he would be with no money and impaired earning power, and a remedy that provides the trust fund is, if imperfect, still a good deal better than nothing. And so tort law endeavors to provide the injured plaintiff a sum of money adequate to *compensate* him, though certainly not to *restore* him to his pre-injury position.[1]

THE SINGLE RECOVERY RULE

Perhaps the most fundamental point to grasp about tort damages is that the plaintiff must seek compensation for all his losses from the tort in a single trial. That is, he must prove both past damages and any future losses he is likely to experience from the injury—such as future medical expenses, lost wages, or medical complications—at the time of trial. The rationale for the rule is not hard to discern. Without it, cases would have to be reopened every time the plaintiff incurred further losses due to an injury, to allow recovery for those additional losses. There is simply no way the judicial system could entertain such repeated claims; it is hard enough to provide even a single hearing for the numbers of cases that confront the courts today.

While this "single recovery rule" makes administrative sense, it places the plaintiff in a difficult, at times untenable position. As the sage has noted, "the art of prediction is very unpredictable . . . particularly when it pertains to the future."[2] It is often very difficult to anticipate whether the plaintiff will need future operations, have his work-life expectancy shortened, or incur a further disability due to his injury. Under the single recovery rule, however, the plaintiff must make just such predictions about events that may lie far in the future—and prove them by a preponderance of the evidence.

Even if such future problems *may* arise, they may not be sufficiently likely to support a damage award under the single recovery rule. Most courts hold that the plaintiff can recover for future consequences of an injury if he proves that they are a reasonable *probability* (Minzer, Nates, eds., Damages in Tort Actions §9.06[6][b]), but an award may not be based on "mere conjecture or speculation." Id. If the plaintiff might need future surgery, but probably will not, most courts would not allow him to recover damages

1. Two other types of damages, nominal damages and punitive damages, are not addressed in this chapter. Nominal damages may sometimes be granted if the plaintiff proves the elements of a tort but has suffered no actual damages. Punitive damages are sometimes awarded in tort cases to punish the defendant for particularly egregious conduct, and to deter such conduct in the future. Punitive damages may be awarded in addition to compensatory damages.
2. This bon mot, like so many others, has been attributed to Yogi Berra, but I don't have an official citation.

for it. If, then, he does later require the surgery, he will be barred by the single recovery rule from bringing a second suit for the losses associated with that surgery. Similarly, if the plaintiff cannot prove that the injury will prevent him from working, he will not receive damages for future lost earning capacity. If in fact he is unable to return to work, that loss will go uncompensated.

Of course, this can work both ways: The plaintiff might prove that he is likely to require future surgery, and recover damages for it, but then do better than expected and not require surgery. If so, he will have received damages for a loss he ultimately did not incur, but will not have to return the damages recovered for that future risk.

THE ELEMENTS OF COMPENSATORY DAMAGES

The three usual components of compensatory damages are medical and related expenses, lost earnings and earning capacity, and pain and suffering. Let's examine each of these in a little more detail.

A. Medical Expenses

The plaintiff is entitled to compensation for all medical costs of diagnosing and treating the injuries resulting from the tort, such as doctor and hospital bills, medicines and special therapeutic equipment, rehabilitation therapy, travel for medical treatment, and ongoing nursing care. These services are incurred to cope with the consequences of the accident, and their cost should be shifted to the tortfeasor who caused the injury rather than borne by the victim.

Past medical expenses are often fairly easy to calculate. The plaintiff can submit medical and hospital bills and offer expert testimony to prove the reasonable value of these losses. But even such tangible economic losses as medical costs become extremely difficult to calculate if they will extend for a significant period into the future. Under the single recovery rule, the plaintiff must offer proof of what his future medical expenses will be, years or decades before they occur, and the jury must attach dollar sums to these future expenses based on the evidence before them.

For example, if the jury concluded that the plaintiff would probably require future surgery to relieve muscle problems related to a burn injury, they would have to determine the proper sum to compensate him for the medical expenses of that operation, even though it might occur 20 years down the road. They would also have to value the associated pain, any resulting loss of earnings, the costs of rehabilitation, and so forth. Needless to say, any sum the jury awards for such future contingencies would be charitably viewed as a rough approximation. Measuring such damages may not be "a leap in the dark, but it is certainly a leap into the deep dusk of twilight." D. Dobbs, Law of Remedies, Practitioner Treatise Series, vol. 2, §8.1(1) at 361 (2d ed. 1993).

B. Lost Earnings and Earning Capacity

The second component of compensatory damages is lost earnings and earning capacity. Lost earnings refers to *past* income losses due to the injury, that is, earnings lost between the time of injury and the time of trial. Clearly, if the plaintiff was out of work for ten weeks because of the injury, the tortfeasor should compensate him for the wages lost as a result. Lost earning *capacity* refers to loss of *future* earning potential. If the injury will prevent the plaintiff from going back to work for a period of time, it has affected his ability to continue to earn money in the future. Under the single recovery rule, he must be compensated at trial for this future loss.

Lost earnings, like past medical expenses, can usually be calculated fairly accurately, based on the plaintiff's earnings record for the period immediately prior to the accident, evidence of his likely advancement had he not been injured, and evidence concerning changes in the salary structure of his employer up to the time of trial. But future earning capacity is seldom so easily assessed. First, the jury will have to determine how long the plaintiff would have worked if he had not been injured. This may depend on the type of work he did, his life expectancy, state of health *prior to* the injury, and level of interest in his work. Other factors that might have led him to retire early must also be considered, such as a spouse's retirement, an unrelated medical condition which could cause him to move to a different climate, or an anticipated inheritance.

Second, the jury will have to determine what type of work the plaintiff would have done if he had not been injured. For plaintiffs with a long-established work history, this may be clear, but in other cases it is not. Maybe the plaintiff was working as a secretary for a year to pay off some loans, but planning to enter business school the year after. Maybe he graduated magna cum laude from Berkeley, but was working as a truck driver for a while as a lark. Maybe he was earning $250,000 as a partner in a law firm, but hated his work passionately and would not have lasted another six months. (Imagine the difficulty defense counsel would have proving that crucial but subjective fact.) To compound the problem, suppose that he was not working at all when injured, but likely would have returned to the work force at some point. Or consider the case of a plaintiff five years old at the time of the injury, with no work history, educational history, or other basis for estimating his future income potential.

Even if it is reasonably clear what work the plaintiff would have undertaken, the jury will have to decide what his salary would have been during those years. Ideally, this projection would include such factors as prior advancement in his job, the projected future fortunes of his employer, the general state of the sector of the economy in which he worked, the prospects that he would have been promoted or moved to a more lucrative position with another employer, possible alternative employment he may be able to find after his injury, and doubtless many others unique to each plaintiff's circumstances.

In addition, if the plaintiff is really to be fully compensated for future lost earnings, the jury should consider fringe benefits, such as health insurance, a company car, educational credits, bonuses, and stock options. And how about retirement? If the defendant's tortious conduct has deprived the plaintiff of the opportunity to build a retirement fund partially funded by the company, this benefit should also be calculated. Here again, in assessing such damages, the jury is called upon to make judgments that would intimidate the most experienced actuary.

C. Pain and Suffering

The third component of damages, "pain and suffering," can cover a lot of ground. It certainly includes physical pain from the impact of an accident, but it also includes ongoing pain from a wound, or long-term discomfort from a permanent condition such as a limp or weakened back. It also includes the pain of medical procedures (such as surgery, grafting, or physical therapy) to treat the injuries.

Beyond these obvious connotations, the phrase also includes many other types of mental suffering from the consequences of the injury, such as the humiliation, anguish, or embarrassment suffered from living with permanent disfigurement, the frustration of dealing with disability caused by the injury, the fright associated with a traumatic accident, fear of a recurrence of the accident, or depression induced by the injury and its consequences. Thus, "pain and suffering" is a catch-all term that can encompass almost any kind of subjective reaction to the accident or its consequences. "[T]he unitary concept of 'pain and suffering' has served as a convenient label under which a plaintiff may recover not only for physical pain but for fright, nervousness, grief, anxiety, worry, mortification, shock, humiliation, indignity, embarrassment, apprehension, terror or ordeal." *Capelouto v. Kaiser Found. Hosp.*, 500 P.2d 880, 883 (Cal. 1972).

Obviously, such sensations are highly subjective; there is no scale or mathematical process jurors can use to reach a dollar figure to compensate the plaintiff for them. They must simply pick a number based on their sense of the severity of the loss the plaintiff has suffered. The judge might give the jury an instruction like this on assessing damages for pain and suffering:

> In assessing damages, if you have occasion to do so, the law allows you to award to plaintiff a sum that will reasonably compensate him for any past physical pain, as well as pain that is reasonably certain to be suffered in the future as a result of the defendant's wrongdoing.
>
> There are no objective guidelines by which you can measure the money equivalent of this element of injury; the only real measuring stick, if it can be so described, is your collective enlightened conscience. You should consider the evidence bearing on the nature of the injuries, the certainty of future pain, the severity and the likely duration thereof.
>
> In this difficult task of putting a money figure on an aspect of injury that does not readily lend itself to an evaluation in terms of money, you should try to be as objective, calm and dispassionate as the situation will permit, and not to be unduly swayed by considerations of sympathy.

G. Douthewaite, Jury Instructions on Damages in Tort Actions 274 (1988). Basically, this instruction throws the matter to the jury without guidance, but with a plea for them to be objective even if there are no objective guidelines to apply.

LOSS OF ENJOYMENT OF LIFE

In addition to the unpleasant sensations and emotions usually associated with the concept of pain and suffering, tort victims also frequently suffer loss of the opportunity to engage in many of life's pleasurable activities. If his leg is maimed in the accident with Gray, Krutch will doubtless suffer the physical pain and mental anguish generally associated with such injuries. But he may also lose the ability to play tennis, to take walks in the woods, to carry his son to school, to dance, or to enjoy many of life's other common, pleasurable experiences. These functional impairments go beyond the usual connotations of "pain and suffering," but are also common consequences of serious injuries.

Such impairments are often profound—perhaps the most profound—consequences of physical injury. Imagine, for example, that Krutch's most cherished activity is playing the violin, and that he suffers a hand injury that prevents him from doing so. Or suppose that the accident destroys his sense of sight or taste. Certainly, these are grievous losses above and beyond the sensation of physical pain or fear immediately stemming from the injury.

Many courts describe these losses, aptly enough, as "loss of enjoyment of life." All courts recognize that such losses are compensable, but the cases are split over whether damages for loss of enjoyment fall into the general category of "pain and suffering" or constitute a separate element of compensatory damages. Some courts treat loss of enjoyment as a form of pain and suffering: the mental suffering that comes from the plaintiff's realization that he can no longer engage fully in life's pleasures. Courts that take this approach will refuse to give the jury a separate instruction on "loss of enjoyment" damages, on the ground that it duplicates the pain and suffering instruction and invites the jury to compensate the plaintiff twice for the same losses. See, e.g., *McDougald v. Garber*, 536 N.E.2d 372, 375-377 (N.Y. 1989).

Other courts have recognized loss of enjoyment as a distinct category of compensable damages. See, e.g., *Thompson v. National R.R. Passenger Corp.*, 621 F.2d 814, 824 (6th Cir.), *cert. denied*, 449 U.S. 1035 (1980), in which the court concluded that "pain and suffering compensates the victim for the physical and mental discomfort caused by the injury; and loss of enjoyment of life compensates the victim for the limitations on the person's life created by the injury." See also *McGee v. A C and S, Inc.*, 933 So. 2d 770 (La. 2006) (allowing separate item on special verdict slip for loss-of-enjoyment damages); courts that take this view allow the trial judge to instruct the jury separately on loss of enjoyment of life. Plaintiffs' counsel naturally prefer such a separate instruction since it emphasizes the distinct nature of loss of enjoyment damages and invites the jury to consider them apart from a general pain and suffering award.

It is probably not of great consequence whether loss of enjoyment is characterized as part of pain and suffering or as a separate component of compensatory damages. The important thing is that everyone—the lawyers, the judge, and the jury—understands that, whatever called, such restrictions on the plaintiff's "ability to function as a whole person" (*Canfield v. Sandock*, 563 N.E.2d 1279 (Ind. 1990)) are proper elements in the assessment of damages. Plaintiff's counsel may introduce evidence of all the ways in which the plaintiff's injury has impaired his ability to engage in activities he previously enjoyed. Where such evidence is offered, the judge should explain to the jury that they are entitled to compensate the plaintiff for these losses, in addition to the physical pain and emotional distress traditionally associated with "pain and suffering."

THE ELUSIVE CONCEPT OF "DISABILITY"

Although all states recognize the basic categories of damages discussed above, some courts may use different terms, such as "disability" or "permanent impairment" in discussing compensatory damages. These terms often overlap with several concepts already discussed, particularly loss of enjoyment and lost earning capacity.

In its strictest sense, "disability" or "permanent impairment" refers to the injured party's *condition*, not to the losses suffered as a result of that condition:

> Disability and permanent injury refer to states of ill health that preclude an injured person from carrying on normal activities of life in the manner which would have been possible had the injury in question not occurred.

Minzer, Nates §4.02[2][cJ. While this definition sounds similar to loss of enjoyment, it is more accurate to view loss of enjoyment as the *consequence* that flows from the plaintiff's disabled condition. For example, the loss of a leg is an impairment or disability. The loss of the opportunity to engage in activities as a result of that disability—running marathons, hiking, or whatever—constitutes a consequential loss of enjoyment for which damages may be awarded.

However, many courts use the terms "disability" and "permanent impairment" loosely as the equivalent of "loss of enjoyment of life." These courts will instruct the jury that they may assess damages for the plaintiff's "disability," but will not instruct separately on loss of enjoyment damages: It would frequently allow double counting to instruct the jury to award damages for both disability and loss of enjoyment. See P. Hermes, Note, Loss of Enjoyment of Life—Duplication of Damages Versus Full Compensation, 63 N.D. L. Rev. 561, 579 (1987).

There is also frequent confusion between "disability" and lost earning capacity. Here again, the *condition* of being disabled leads to the *consequence* of lost earning capacity. If the jury is instructed to award damages for lost earning capacity, the instructions should make clear that they should not award the same losses under a separate "disability" instruction, even though the earnings loss stems from the disability. On the other hand, it is quite possible to have disability without loss of earning capacity: If Krutch is a computer programmer who loses a leg in an accident, for example, he might return to work in a few weeks with little or no loss of salary. Yet clearly he has suffered a permanent, serious disability—in the sense of interference with enjoyment of life—that should be compensated.

ECONOMIC vs. NONECONOMIC DAMAGES

The elements of damages discussed above are often grouped into *economic* and *noneconomic* damages. Lost earnings, lost earning capacity, and medical and other out-of-pocket expenses are considered *economic* or *tangible* damages since they are actual dollar losses that can be calculated. By contrast, pain and suffering and loss of enjoyment are *noneconomic* or *intangible* damages which the jury has no mathematical or accounting basis for valuing. Infliction of emotional distress and loss of consortium also fall into this category.

The distinction between economic and noneconomic damages has become increasingly important in recent years. A good many legislatures, reacting to large increases in insurance costs, have enacted caps on noneconomic damages such as pain and suffering and loss of consortium. For example, Idaho Code §6-1603 provides:

> (1) In no action seeking damages for personal injury, including death, shall a judgment for noneconomic damages be entered for a claimant exceeding the maximum amount of two hundred and fifty thousand dollars ($250,000).[3] . . .

Other states have enacted caps on noneconomic damages in particular types of cases, such as medical malpractice. See, e.g., Miss. st. §11-1-60 ($50,000 cap on noneconomic damages in actions against health care providers). Needless to say, statutes of this type do not warm the hearts of the plaintiff's bar, since they reduce plaintiffs' recoveries and counsel's contingent fees. They represent a legislative compromise between the ideal of full compensation and the reality of limited resources. The debate about such compromises has been heated, and continues to be. A major indictment of damage caps is that they limit the recovery of those who need it most: Plaintiffs with lesser injuries recover fully for their intangible damages, while those most seriously injured may recover only a fraction of their intangible damages. A good argument can be made that a *floor* on intangible damages would be fairer. This approach would bar recovery for intangible losses where the economic loss (and therefore, presumably, the underlying physical injury itself) is minor, but preserve full recovery to victims of catastrophic injury.[4]

While the terminology courts use in analyzing compensatory damages may vary, the fundamental inquiry does not. The jury must assess the plaintiff's situation after the injury compared to his situation before. They must consider his physical and emotional suffering from the injury, his lost opportunities, both economic and personal, as a result of the injury, and the economic costs of dealing with the injury. From this analysis they are to distill a sum of money damages to "compensate" him for all losses he has suffered or will suffer in the future from the injury. The examples below explore these damage issues in the context of particular cases.

---

3. Section 6-1603 provides for annual adjustments to the cap to reflect general changes in wage levels.

4. A common problem with statutory damage caps is that legislatures enact them and forget them. Over time, inflation radically decreases the value of the award allowed by the cap. The Mississippi limit, for example, was enacted in 2002, and has not been raised in the ensuing 23 years.

Examples

The Art of Prediction

1. Mendel, a 25-year-old truck driver, is injured in a traffic accident and rendered permanently paraplegic. He sues the other driver. If you represented Mendel, for what types of future medical and therapeutic expenses would you seek compensation?

2. Assume that Mendel only suffers a concussion in the accident. He has minimal medical expenses, but testifies that he has developed tinnitus, or ringing in the ears, as a result of the impact. Tinnitus is a recognized medical condition, but it is very hard to corroborate its existence by medical tests. Mendel testifies that the ringing is always there, that it is a constant irritant, that it has made him irritable and difficult with his family. He continues to work as a construction worker, but the condition interferes with his ability to concentrate on many leisure activities, such as card playing or reading. It also makes it very difficult for him to get to sleep, so he is always tired.

   Assume that liability is clear, and that medical costs and lost earnings are negligible. The defendant's insurer offers $35,000 to settle Mendel's claim. If you represented Mendel, would you take it?

3. Audubon, a 42-year-old naturalist, is seriously injured in an accident involving his car and Darwin's. The evidence at trial indicates that Audubon is totally disabled. Due to his injury, his life expectancy has been shortened from 31 years to 20 years, and his work-life expectancy from 25 years to zero. Stated another way, before the accident Audubon could have expected, based on statistical tables, to live to the age of 73, and work to the age of 67. However, due to his injuries he will now likely live only to the age of 62, and will not return to work. The evidence also indicates that he will continue to endure pain, embarrassment, and other psychic injuries from the accident until his death.
   a. If Darwin is found liable, for what time period should the jury assess damages for Audubon's lost earning capacity?
   b. Assuming that Audubon will continue to experience pain and mental anguish from the accident as long as he lives, for what period should the jury assess damages for pain and suffering?
   c. Should the jury award damages to Audubon for the shortening of his life span?
   d. For what period should the jury award damages for loss of enjoyment of life?

The Single Be-Fuddlement Rule

4. Muir, a shipyard worker, contracts asbestosis, a respiratory disease caused by exposure to asbestos. He sues General Yards, the shipyard, for

negligently failing to warn him of the danger of working with asbestos. At trial, he produces evidence of the pain and suffering he suffers from the disease, his medical expenses, and his impaired earning capacity. He also offers expert testimony that 20 percent of those who contract asbestosis later go on to develop cancer as well, and of the likely medical effects of this type of cancer. Counsel for General Yards objects to all evidence relating to the cancer risk. What is the basis of the evidentiary objection and how should Judge Fudd rule on it?

Unpredictable Predictions

5. Beebe is a college graduate with a degree in economics. She is also a mother of three. She worked as an administrative assistant at a college until her first child was born. Now, she has three children and does not work outside the home. She is injured in an auto accident and permanently disabled. If she sues the other driver, should she recover for lost earning capacity?

6. Thoreau, a 12-year-old child, is thrown from an off-road vehicle and sustains serious injuries. As a result, he is left with a limp and permanent weakness in his right arm and leg. Thoreau had never worked prior to the injury.
   a. In an action against the manufacturer of the vehicle, could Thoreau recover for loss of earning capacity?
   b. Assume (though it is unlikely on these facts) that the jury found that Thoreau would be unable to work at all due to the injury. What evidence would be relevant to ascertaining the value of his lost earning capacity?
   c. Assume that the jury concludes that Thoreau would have earned $900,000 as a laborer over his work-life expectancy, had he not been injured, and that, due to his injury, he will not be able to do any kind of heavy work. Should they award him that sum as damages for lost earning capacity?

Missing Elements

7. Agassiz, a 79-year-old retired botanist, is hit by a concrete block which falls from the fifth floor of an apartment house. He is rendered permanently unconscious by the blow, and is maintained in a comatose state by various invasive procedures such as breathing and feeding tubes. Prior to the accident, Agassiz lived on his pension and Social Security, which he continues to receive. The medical bills for his treatment are truly impressive; luckily, they are covered by Medicare and his supplemental health insurance.
   a. Should Agassiz recover for pain and suffering?
   b. Should he recover for loss of enjoyment of life?

c. Should Agassiz recover for the medical expenses for treatment of his injury?
d. Should he recover for lost earning capacity?

An Emotion Motion

8. Watson is seriously burned in an intersection accident between a car in which he is riding as a passenger and a dump truck driven by Muir. One of the two vehicles ran a red light, causing the collision. As a result of the accident, he is hospitalized for many months, is severely disfigured, and suffers ongoing pain and a variety of humiliating and depressing side effects of his injuries. He will also require continuing treatment, including many operations, for the rest of his life. He sues for his injuries.

   As trial approaches, one of the lawyers moves to "bifurcate" the trial, that is, to try the issue of liability first, and have the jury decide whether Muir negligently caused the accident before presenting evidence to the jury on Watson's damages.
   a. Which lawyer probably made the motion, and why?
   b. What are the arguments in favor of granting the motion?
   c. What are the arguments against granting the motion?

9. Assume that Watson's case goes to trial on liability and damages. At trial, Watson's counsel seeks to introduce evidence that Agassiz, a plaintiff in another recent lawsuit, received a jury award of $5.3 million in damages for burns. Should the evidence be admitted?

Explanations

The Art of Prediction

1. You are probably not an expert in the medical treatment of paraplegia—though you might become one if you represented Mendel. But it is not hard to imagine the wide variety of medical problems that may result from paraplegia, and are likely to continue or worsen throughout the patient's life. Mendel, at 25, has a very long life expectancy, even if it is diminished somewhat by the injury. Over the years, he will likely require operations to cope with the consequences of his immobility, including, perhaps, plastic surgery to deal with sores on his body. He will need long-term physical therapy to preserve as much mobility as possible. He will need vocational training and counseling, sexual counseling, home care, special equipment, and home modifications to accommodate his condition. He will likely be hospitalized from time to time for more intensive care. He will need continuous medical monitoring and prescription medications, and may develop a variety of diseases that must be treated as well. He is likely to require psychotherapy as well to assist

in adjusting to his disability. For a fuller discussion of the medical consequences of paraplegia, see Minzer, Nates, ch. 126.

Naturally, Mendel himself knows little or nothing of all this, and probably does not want to think about it. His counsel must develop the proof based on Mendel's past treatment, current condition, and expert medical and actuarial testimony. Counsel must learn a great deal about the day-to-day effects of her client's condition, including such unglamorous realities as bowel and bladder control, bed sores, and muscle atrophy. Medical specialists will testify about the likely course of treatment his condition will require over the years, the probable prognosis for his long-term health, likely complications and corrective surgery, and the types of ongoing nursing and therapeutic services and medicines he will need. An accountant or economist will also testify as to the likely costs of such care, extrapolating out years or decades into the future, depending on the plaintiff's life expectancy.[5]

The defendant will likely present opposing experts on these issues, who reach substantially different conclusions concerning the required treatment and its projected cost. Ironically, the members of the jury, probably unschooled in either medical care or accounting, will then have to assign a sum to this element of damages based on their assessment of the evidence.

2. This is typical of the type of judgment attorneys must make all the time about the value of tort cases. Actually, it is simpler than most: Since negligence is admitted, Mendel's counsel does not have to consider the risk that he will be unable to establish that crucial element. In addition, since earnings and medical costs are negligible, the only real issue is the value of the intangible damages for tinnitus.

   Of course, Mendel's counsel does have to consider whether the jury will believe his client. Since the symptoms cannot be corroborated by objective measures, Mendel's testimony will be critical. If the jury concludes that he is making up the injury, they may find against him even though the defendant admits negligence: You have to prove all four elements to recover for negligence, including damages.

   If we assume that Mendel is credible, and that the testimony of family and coworkers corroborates his story, the question then becomes what the injury is "worth." As the introduction states, there is no objective measure for such intangible damages, so it becomes very difficult to predict the number a jury will attach to it. Any settlement will be based

5. These experts will command substantial fees for their assistance in trial preparation and for their testimony. In the ordinary case, the fee will be advanced by plaintiff's counsel as part of the costs of suit. Ultimately the plaintiff will have to reimburse her counsel for these expenses (ranging sometimes into five figures) out of the judgment or settlement the defendant pays.

on educated guesses of counsel as to what would happen if they went to trial. As an indication of how uncertain the damages may be, I gave the facts of Mendel's case to my Torts class, and asked the students to decide, individually, what they would award if they were on the jury. Their figures (offered about 25 years ago) ranged from $20,000 to over $500,000.[6]

If Mendel's counsel concludes that the jury would award $50,000 for this, he might still settle for $35,000. He has to consider the costs of trial and the risk that the jury will disbelieve his client. On balance, it might be a reasonable choice to accept. Obviously, if counsel expects a considerably higher verdict at trial—as the figures from my class suggest he might—he should hesitate to accept the insurer's offer.[7]

3. a. The goal of tort damages is to "place the victim in the same position he would have been in if he had not been injured." If Audubon had not been injured, he would have had income up until the age of 67. Due to the accident, all of those earnings are lost. Most courts would hold that Audubon can recover for lost earning capacity based on his *pre-accident* work-life expectancy, even though he is not now able to work.

   Arguably, calculating the future wages for the entire period overcompensates Audubon somewhat. If he had not been injured, he would likely have had his income for his full work-life expectancy but would also have expended a large part of that on his living expenses. For the period from age 62 to 67, however, Audubon will not incur those expenses, due to his premature death (again, statistically speaking). It would be more accurate to require the jury to deduct the living expenses for that period from the earnings. Sounds a bit cold-blooded, though, doesn't it? Darwin's counsel may hesitate to raise the argument since it sounds like he is trying to take advantage of the fact that the accident has shortened Audubon's life expectancy.

   b. Damages for pain and suffering compensate the victim for having to endure physical and psychic pain, humiliation, and anguish caused by the injury. The award should be based on the period during which he will actually experience pain and suffering. In Audubon's case, he will have to endure these (again, statistically speaking) for 20 more years. Pain and suffering damages should be awarded for his 20-year

6. A fair number of students reached their awards by calculating a sum for each minute, hour, or day that Mendel must live with the problem. One student gave two cents per minute; another allotted $10,000 per year; a third, a dollar an hour. The resulting awards were in the $300,000 to $500,000 range given Mendel's life expectancy.

7. These days the defendant's $35,000 offer would likely be rejected. Your Humble Author's contacts with personal injury lawyers who have litigated tinnitus cases suggest that settleents well into six figures are not uncommon.

post-accident life expectancy, not based on his pre-accident life expectancy.

c. This is an interesting issue. It is hard to deny that the loss of 11 years of life is grievous. It seems that Audubon ought to be compensated for that. On the other hand, if Audubon had been killed in the accident, he would have received no compensation for his lost years: Wrongful death actions compensate the *survivors* for their losses, not the decedent for his. See Chapter 18. But then, one of the rationales for the rule in death cases is that you cannot compensate the dead. Audubon is still alive. If we award him damages for his lost years, he can at least live out the years he has left a bit more pleasurably.

   The courts are split on whether loss of life expectancy is a proper element of damages. English courts have allowed limited recovery for reduced life expectancy, but most American courts have denied it. See Minzer, Nates, §8.07[9]. Several cases have recognized this as compensable, however, and there may be a trend in this direction. See, e.g., *Alexander v. Scheid*, 726 N.E.2d 272, 280 (Ind. 2000); *Morrison v. Stallworth*, 326 S.E.2d 387, 393 (N.C. Ct. App. 1985).

   Even courts that deny recovery for lost life expectancy per se will often allow the jury to consider, as a part of pain and suffering, the mental anguish the plaintiff suffers from the *realization* that he will likely die before his time. In addition, since Audubon's lost earning capacity is assessed on the basis of his pre-accident life expectancy, this element of his "lost years" will be considered in assessing damages.

d. Loss of enjoyment damages compensate the plaintiff for her inability to participate in activities that she enjoyed prior to the accident. The types of losses included are legion, from walks in the park to playing softball with the kids to sky diving to bocci to sitting on the front porch and watching the world go by. Had the accident not taken place, Audubon would have engaged in whatever activities he fancied for as long as he was able, in many cases up to the end of his life. Due to the accident, he can no longer do so. The loss of enjoyment damages should be assessed with regard to his pre-accident life expectancy, not his reduced expectancy after the accident.

   If a court accepts this view and allows damages for loss of enjoyment based on Audubon's pre-accident life expectancy, this recovery will also partially substitute for a separate award for the lost years themselves. Naturally, a large part of the value of Audubon's lost 11 years is the enjoyment of the activities and sensations of life during that period. If the jury can compensate for this loss, they are effectively invited to compensate for the lost years themselves. There may be a technical distinction—they are not supposed to give an award for the loss of life per se—but it is one which is likely to elude most juries.

The Single Be-Fuddlement Rule

4. Doubtless, General Yards has objected to the evidence because it only indicates a 20 percent chance that Muir will develop cancer. Most courts hold that plaintiffs are entitled to recover for future injuries that are "reasonably probable," but 20 percent does not meet this standard. If Muir's evidence is insufficient to prove that cancer is a probable consequence, the jury should not hear it.

   Obviously, Muir is in a very difficult position here. If he sues for his asbestosis damages, he will not recover any cancer damages in that action, and under the single recovery rule, he may be barred from bringing a second suit if he develops cancer later. Some courts have reached this conclusion under the single recovery rule. See, e.g., *Gideon v. Johns-Mansville Sales Corp.*, 761 F.2d 1129, 1136-1137 (5th Cir. 1983) (under Texas law, plaintiff must recover for present harm and all future consequences that will probably develop in the future). If Judge Fudd presides in such a jurisdiction, he should deny admission of the cancer evidence and Muir would recover nothing for this risk.[8]

   Other courts, however, have recognized an exception to the single recovery rule in asbestos cases on the ground that cancer is a separate disease giving rise to a separate cause of action. See, e.g., *Pustejovsky v. Rapid-American Corp.*, 35 S.W.3d 643, 647-654 (Tex. 2000) (declining to follow *Gideon*). These courts would allow Muir to sue again if he contracts cancer in the future. If the Honorable Fudd presided in a state that takes this view, he would *still* deny admission of the cancer evidence in the initial action, but Muir would be able to recover for cancer in a later suit if he develops it.

   This latter approach relieves the plaintiff from the difficulties of proof posed by the single recovery rule, but it has several serious implications. First, it will multiply litigation since plaintiffs who have already sued for asbestosis will be entitled to sue again. In addition, this approach seriously erodes the single recovery rule since plaintiffs will make the same argument in other types of cases where further complications of an injury arise that were not compensated in the original suit.[9]

---

8. Even in such a jurisdiction, Muir may be able to recover for the present fear that he will contract cancer in the future. Some courts have viewed this as a separate form of mental distress which, if reasonable, is compensable. See generally Minzer, Nates §13.05.

9. Your Humble Author's dire prediction that cases like *Pustejovsky* would undermine the single recovery rule has yet to prove true. It is very hard to find cases taking this approach outside the asbestos context. See, e.g., *Faulkner v. Caledonia County Fair Assoc.*, 869 A.2d 103 (Vt. 2004). In *Faulkner*, the plaintiff suffered a head injury and recovered damages from the defendant. Eight years later she was diagnosed with epilepsy, allegedly due to the same blow. The court rejected the plaintiff's argument (based on the asbestos/cancer cases) that she could bring a second action. I guess Berra is right.

Unpredictable Predictions

5. Although she was not working outside the home prior to the accident, Beebe certainly should receive damages for lost earning capacity. The fact that she was not working at the time does not mean that she would not have worked later. The odds are very good that a woman in her position would return to the work force when her children were older, if only to help with the staggering cost of college. Beebe's capacity to do so has been destroyed, and she is entitled to compensation for that. Estimating her lost earning capacity, of course, will be difficult since she has little in the way of a track record on which to predict her earning potential. The jury will simply have to do their best based on testimony about her background, interests, and opportunities, and economic testimony concerning wage trends for the type of work she would likely have undertaken in later years.

   Beebe would be entitled to an award for loss of earning capacity even if she testified that she had no intention to work in the future since the injury has deprived her of the *option* to work, should circumstances require her to do so. "The theory is that the injury has deprived the plaintiff of a capacity he would have been entitled to enjoy even though he may never have profited from it." *Hunt v. Bd. of Supervisors of the La. State Univ.*, 522 So. 2d 1144, 1152 (La. Ct. App. 1988).

6. a. Surely Thoreau should not be denied recovery for loss of earning capacity simply because he has no earnings history. It would make no sense to refuse recovery to a child plaintiff who is injured before starting to work, and perhaps loses *all* his potential earnings, while an adult who only lost part of his would be fully compensated for that loss. The jury should compensate Thoreau for his lost future earning capacity, even though it is exclusively a *future* loss and he has no earnings history.

   While it is clear that Thoreau has a right to recover for lost earning capacity, it is less clear whether he has actually lost earning capacity, and, if so, how much. His partial disability would certainly interfere with his earning capacity if he were likely to become a manual laborer, but the interference might be minimal if he becomes a computer programmer or a stock broker. At the time of trial, Thoreau had no earnings history, no profession, and probably no special skills or interests upon which to base a prediction of what work he would have chosen absent the injury. Thus, it will be very difficult for the jury to determine whether he has lost earning capacity. Yet they must decide, and might well conclude that an injury of this magnitude is likely to reduce his earning power. If they do, they may award damages, in some roughly appropriate amount, to compensate for the loss.

b. In arriving at a figure, the jury must decide what Thoreau was likely to have earned if he had not been injured, which turns on the kind of work he would have chosen. To predict this, the jury may consider such factors as Thoreau's character, his health and physical skills, his record in school, his IQ, his background (including his parents' occupations and education), the likelihood that he would have finished high school and gone on to college, and his interests, as well as government statistics about earnings for different occupations and education levels. On the basis of such factors, the jury must determine Thoreau's pre-accident earning capacity. The result will of course be a gross approximation, but on balance preferable to denying compensation for a very serious economic loss.

Ironically, Thoreau's award may be higher if the evidence shows that he was academically deficient or less intelligent. If he shows strong intellectual ability, he may have lost little earning capacity since he can still perform the work he would likely have chosen if he had not been injured. By contrast, a plaintiff with weaker academic skills would more likely make his living through some form of manual labor. If so, a disabling injury would have a greater impact on his earning capacity and lead to a greater award.

c. The jury's calculation of Thoreau's loss begins rather than ends with the determination of what he would have earned. Thoreau's lost earning capacity cannot be measured solely by what he could have earned *before* the injury. The jury must make a separate assessment of what he can earn *after* the injury. While Thoreau won't be able to do heavy manual labor, he may still be able to perform many other kinds of work. If he can work, his award for lost earning capacity should be based on the difference between his earning potential before and after the injury. Thus, the jury should consider what type of work Thoreau will be able to do with his disability, and determine the amount he is likely to earn from that work. They should then subtract that amount from the $900,000 he would have earned to determine the damages for lost earning capacity.

Once the jury has determined an amount for lost earning capacity, they will have to reduce this figure to "present value." Since Thoreau will receive the award today to compensate for losses over a number of years, the amount must be reduced to account for the interest Thoreau can earn on the award over the years.[10]

10. For example, if the jury concludes that Thoreau will lose $40,000 in salary in the tenth year after trial, it may significantly overcompensate him to award $40,000 to replace that year's earnings. If Thoreau gets $40,000 today and invests it, it could well double in ten years.

Missing Elements

7. a. Agassiz has suffered a very serious injury, but a number of the usual elements of compensatory damages will not apply to his case. The facts suggest that he was rendered unconscious immediately by the blow. If so, he has not suffered any conscious pain and suffering. Most courts hold that a plaintiff must be conscious to recover for pain and suffering since pain and suffering compensates subjective discomfort resulting from the injury, and unconscious patients do not experience these symptoms.

   This basic fact of damages doctrine has led to strained, sometimes unseemly efforts by plaintiffs' counsel to prove that the victim was conscious, if only for a second, since such proof opens the door for the jury to award damages for this highly subjective element.

   b. Agassiz has lost the ability to enjoy virtually all of life's pleasures. If that isn't loss of enjoyment, what is? Interestingly, the cases are divided on the question of whether a comatose patient can recover for loss of enjoyment. A leading New York case denies recovery, on the ground that the unconscious patient cannot benefit in any way from an award for loss of enjoyment, and consequently such an award would serve no compensatory purpose:

   > Simply put, an award of money damages in such circumstances has no meaning or utility to the injured person. An award for the loss of enjoyment of life "cannot provide [such a victim] with any consolation or ease any burden resting on him . . . He cannot spend it upon necessities or pleasures. He cannot experience the pleasure of giving it away."

   McDougald v. Garber, 536 N.E.2d 372, 375 (1989) (quoting *Flannery v. United States*, 718 F.2d 108, 111 (4th Cir. 1983)), *cert. denied*, 467 U.S. 1226 (1984).

   This holding has been controversial. For one thing, there can be no doubt that the plaintiff has suffered a grievous loss: Basically, he has lost *all* of life's enjoyment, whether he is aware of it or not. Had the plaintiff been totally disabled, but remained aware of it, he would have received full compensation for loss of enjoyment. It hardly seems appropriate that an even more seriously injured plaintiff should receive nothing for this loss. In addition, tort victims sometimes do obtain recoveries that they cannot enjoy, as where the estate of a decedent recovers damages in a survival action for predeath pain and suffering.

   Other courts have allowed loss of enjoyment damages to comatose plaintiffs, on the theory that the loss of life's pleasures is an objective loss suffered by the plaintiff, whether or not he subjectively comprehends or experiences it. See, e.g., *Eyoma v. Falco*, 589 A.2d 653,

658-662 (N.J. Super. 1991); *Flannery v. United States*, 297 S.E.2d 433, 438-439 (W. Va. 1982).

c. This fairly simple question requires a complex answer. There is in the law of damages a quizzical doctrine called the "collateral source rule," which frequently holds the defendant responsible for losses to the plaintiff even though those losses are actually paid by a third party. For example, if a plaintiff incurs $5,000 in medical bills, but her health insurer pays most of it, she is still entitled, under the collateral source rule, to collect the full $5,000 from the defendant. Similarly, if plaintiff loses $30,000 in wages, but is compensated by his disability insurance policy for the loss, the defendant must still pay $30,000 for the loss.

   This bewildering rule is often justified on the ground that the defendant should not obtain a windfall from the plaintiff's foresight in obtaining (and paying for) insurance protection against these losses. See generally Minzer, Nates, §17.01. Whether or not this rationale is convincing, the rule has been applied to many types of collateral source payments, including Medicare, private insurance, continuation of wages by the plaintiff's employer, unemployment compensation, worker's compensation, and others. See generally Minzer, Nates, §§17.03-17.06.

   Although the collateral source rule has been very widely applied, it has also been widely criticized since it compensates plaintiffs for losses that they do not actually incur. Many recent statutes have limited the rule in an effort to control insurance costs, at least for certain types of cases or certain types of collateral benefits. See, e.g., Mich. Laws Ann. §600.6303 (requiring reduction of damages for collateral payments, adjusted for premiums plaintiff paid to obtain collateral source protection). If Agassiz's case were governed by the Michigan statute, he would recover very little despite the very substantial expense of his medical care.

d. Although lost earnings and earning capacity are basic elements of tort damages, Agassiz will presumably not recover anything for this category of damages. Agassiz has not lost his pension or Social Security income: They are still paid to him after his injury, just as they were before, and at 79, he would be unlikely to go back to work. If he has not suffered a loss of these items due to the accident, the defendant need not compensate for them.

   Even if the collateral source rule applies in Agassiz's jurisdiction, Agassiz will still have no claim for his lost pension or Social Security. Agassiz is entitled to be paid his pension and Social Security regardless of his state of health, and will continue to be paid them despite the injury. Thus he hasn't lost these benefits; the collateral source rule is irrelevant to this element of his damages.

In the final analysis, Agassiz's case is troubling. He has suffered catastrophic injury, yet most of the big-ticket elements of compensation—pain and suffering, loss of enjoyment, and lost earnings—will hardly figure at all in his damages. Depending on the status of the collateral source rule, he may not even be compensated for medical costs.

An Emotion Motion

8. a. The motion will virtually always be made by the defendant's counsel. If the trial is bifurcated, and liability is tried first, the jury will hear the evidence about the collision, the relative positions of the vehicles, the skid marks, the speed, and so on, and then go out and deliberate on the issue of which party ran the red light. If they find that Muir was not negligent, the trial will be over: Watson can't recover if Muir wasn't negligent. Defendant's counsel would very much prefer that the jury decide this relatively mundane issue without hearing the emotionally charged evidence about Watson's frightful injuries and continuing suffering. Who could hear such testimony and not want to do something for him? Who could dispassionately consider closely conflicting liability evidence without visions of the debilitated Watson haunting the deliberations? Jurors understand that Watson will go away empty handed if they find that Muir was not negligent. It seems almost too much to ask of them to set aside the testimony about Watson's injuries in deciding that question.[10]

   b. There are several strong arguments for bifurcating trials in such circumstances. The first has already been suggested, that the jury will be more objective about the liability issues if they have not heard extensive testimony about Watson's grievous injuries. Another is that trying liability first can save a great deal of time. The damages testimony in Watson's case will be extensive, probably including expert witnesses, treating physicians and other health professionals, medical actuaries, and Watson himself. If the jury finds that Muir was not negligent, all the time devoted to hearing that extensive damages testimony will be saved. Further time will be saved in closing arguments and

---

10. "Plaintiff in this case seeks damages for physical injuries, death and pain and suffering on behalf of himself and his deceased wife and children. In support of such damages, he will offer detailed evidence of extreme pain and suffering, including burning flesh and screams of pain. Courts in this Circuit have recognized that 'evidence of harm to a plaintiff, regardless of the cause, may result in sympathetic jurors more concerned with compensating plaintiff for his injury than whether or not defendant is at fault.'" *Zofcin v. Dean*, 144 F.R.D. 203, 205 (S.D.N.Y. 1992) (quoting from *Buscemi v. Pepsico, Inc.*, 736 F. Supp. 1267, 1272 (S.D.N.Y. 1990)).

in instructing the jury if the trial is bifurcated since only the liability issues need be considered and argued during the liability phase of the trial.[11]

c. One argument against bifurcation is that the same witnesses may testify on both liability and damages issues—for example, the plaintiff and the eye witnesses to the accident. The trial may lose coherence if these witnesses are called, examined on liability issues, and then recalled later to testify on damages. In addition, the plaintiff's injuries are sometimes relevant to the liability issues. For example, the location of Muir's injuries may assist the jury in deciding how the collision took place. In a surgical malpractice case, the nature of the plaintiff's neurological injuries may assist the jury in determining whether she received excessive anesthesia.

   The decision to bifurcate the trial rests in the discretion of the trial judge, which is unlikely to be reversed on appeal. Traditionally, many judges favored letting plaintiffs try their cases as they please, and then sending the whole case to the jury. In an age of judicial management and overcrowded dockets, however, the efficiency and fairness arguments for bifurcation have begun to find more favor in the courts. See, e.g., 22 N.Y. Uniform Trial Ct. Rules §202.42(a) (judges encouraged to bifurcate liability and damages issues in personal injury cases).

9. The introduction to this chapter emphasizes the subjective, unguided nature of the jury's decision on the intangible aspects of damages. Wouldn't it reduce this subjectivity somewhat if juries were able to compare awards made by other juries in similar cases? Perhaps it would, but the evidence will almost certainly be excluded. To understand why, ask yourself what Muir's counsel would do if the judge admitted this evidence of the damages awarded in Agassiz's case. Naturally, she would want to distinguish Agassiz's case from Watson's, by showing that Agassiz's injuries were worse than Watson's, for example, or that he had a longer life expectancy than Watson. She would also cast about for other burn cases in which juries had awarded substantially *less*. Each party would expect the other to reveal the cases they planned to use before trial, and the parties would then do discovery and prepare evidence about them all. Pretty soon, the court would be trying not one burn case, but twenty.

   Even if Agassiz's case were closely comparable to Watson's, the damage award in Agassiz's case is not an objective measure of the proper award. It is simply *another jury's* effort to value an inherently ambiguous

11. Even if the jury finds the defendant negligent, bifurcation can save time since, once liability is established, the likelihood of settlement increases dramatically.

loss. It is difficult to see why the Watson jury should give it any more credence than they would give their own judgment on the point.

On the other hand, giving the jury guidance about a reasonable range of verdicts would certainly improve the system; currently, they receive essentially no guidance in determining intangible damages. The only method of controlling damage verdicts is for judges to order a remittitur—to give the plaintiff a choice between accepting a lesser amount or facing a new trial. This provides some protection against extreme awards, but still leaves a wide range of discretion to the jury. A number of commentators have suggested that juries should receive a list of verdicts in similar cases, with information about the injuries in those cases and the amounts awarded. See, e.g., O. Chase, Helping Jurors Determine Pain and Suffering Awards, 23 Hofstra L. Rev. 763 (1995). See *Jutzi-Johnson v. United States*, 263 F.3d 753, 759-760 (7th Cir. 2001) (suggesting that judge, as trier of fact should consider awards in similar cases to avoid "standardless, unguided exercise of discretion"); but see *Jentz v. ConAgra Foods, Inc.*, 2013 WL 498736 (refusing to consider other awards in diversity case governed by Illinois law and tried to a jury).

CHAPTER 18

Compensating Somebody: Wrongful Death and Survival Actions

INTRODUCTION

We think of "the olden days" as full of dangers, and thank our stars that we live in a "civilized" era. But no one can emerge from the course in Torts without a sobering sense of how dangerous industrialized society is. A few generations back, the major risks were natural ones: disease, natural disasters, and unruly fellow creatures. Today, these have been surpassed by human contrivances, especially that very mixed blessing, the internal combustion engine.

Too often, the products of human genius cause catastrophic injury and untimely death. This chapter addresses two distinct but related types of claims arising from such deaths. First is the *wrongful death* claim, which is a claim for damages for tortiously causing the death of another. Second is the *survival* claim, which is an action brought by the representative of the estate of a deceased person (called in legal parlance a "decedent") for injuries suffered by the decedent before her death.

Although these actions both arise because of the death of the tort victim, they are quite different. Wrongful death statutes usually allow damages for the losses suffered by surviving relatives, such as the loss of economic support or society of the decedent. The survival action, by contrast, allows the estate of a decedent to enforce a tort claim for damages suffered by the decedent *before* death, which she could have enforced personally had she lived.

Suppose, for example, that Mozart and Haydn are listening to a symphony at the local concert hall when a chandelier, negligently installed by Handel, falls from the ceiling. Mozart is killed instantly. Haydn suffers serious injuries, is hospitalized for seven months, and finally dies of his injuries. At common law, the estates of these decedents would have had no remedies for their injuries, regardless of whether they were negligently inflicted. Under modern tort law, however, Mozart's death would give rise to a claim for wrongful death. Haydn's would support both a survival claim for his predeath losses (such as pain and suffering, medical expenses, and lost wages) and a wrongful death claim since he ultimately died of his injuries.

THE ACTION FOR WRONGFUL DEATH

Let's first consider the claim arising from Mozart's death. Mozart died instantly; his estate has no claim for predeath pain and suffering, hospital bills, or disability caused by the accident. The sole injury to be recompensed is the death itself. The issue raised is whether Mozart's estate or his surviving relatives have any claim against Handel for negligently causing his death.

Under the English common law, the answer for five or six centuries was "no." Lord Ellenborough put it clearly in *Baker v. Bolton*: "In a civil court, the death of a human being could not be complained of as an injury." 170 Eng. Rep. 1033 (1808). If the rule was clear, the reasons for it were less so. The scholars suggest that it was rooted in the early English "felony-merger doctrine," which barred civil suits to recover damages for acts that constituted a felony. Felonies were punishable by death and forfeiture of the felon's property to the crown. Since causing the death of another, either intentionally or negligently, was a felony, there would be no defendant left to sue for wrongful death, and no property from which to collect a judgment. See *Moragne v. States Marine Lines, Inc.*, 398 U.S. 375, 382 (1970). So there was no point to such a claim.

Other reasons for the common law position were grounded in policy rather than history. Some cases argued that allowing claims for wrongful death would lead to "runaway" damages from sympathetic juries, or that it is somehow immoral to put a price on human life. S. Speiser, Recovery for Wrongful Death and Injury §1:5 (hereinafter "Speiser").

Whatever the rationale for the common law rule, the result was that "it was cheaper for the defendant to kill a person than to scratch him." Prosser & Keeton at 942. Prosser's treatise notes the wry suggestion that this rule explains "why passengers in Pullman car berths rode with their heads to the front" and that "the fire axes in railroad coaches were provided to enable the conductor to deal efficiently with those [sic] were merely injured." Prosser & Keeton at 942, n.24. Such speculations make the point well enough: It is manifestly indefensible to allow recovery for personal injury, but bar recovery entirely where the victim suffers the ultimate injury, death.

Although it is easy to criticize the early common law rule, most American courts initially followed it without question. In the American states, as in England, it has been the legislatures, not the courts, which have established the right to recover for wrongful death. England reversed course in 1846, when Lord Campbell's Act authorized a cause of action for wrongful death. Since that time, all American states have enacted statutes (often referred to as "Lord Campbell's Acts") that authorize recovery for wrongful death.

THE STATUTORY RIGHT TO SUE

Because actions for wrongful death are based on statutes, they differ from state to state. However, many still track quite closely the language of Lord Campbell's Act. The North Dakota statute, for example, provides:

> Whenever the death of a person shall be caused by a wrongful act, neglect, or default, and the act, neglect, or default is such as would have entitled the party injured, if death had not ensued, to maintain an action and recover damages in respect thereof, then and in every such case the person who, or the corporation, limited liability company, or company which, would have been liable if death had not ensued, shall be liable to an action for damages, notwithstanding the death of the person injured or of the tort-feasor, and although the death shall have been caused under such circumstances as amount in law to felony.

N.D. Cent. Code §32-21-01. Statutes like this allow recovery for wrongful death if the decedent would have had a cause of action herself had she been injured instead of killed. Thus, an "action for wrongful death" is not a separate tort in itself; it is an action for a recognized tort—such as battery, negligence, or a products liability claim—in which the victim is killed rather than injured. In a wrongful death claim based on negligence, for example, the plaintiff must prove the same elements as in a personal injury negligence claim: duty, breach, causation, and damages. The proof of the first three elements will be the same as in an injury case. The major difference between a wrongful death case and other negligence cases involves the last element, damages.

WRONGFUL DEATH DAMAGES: WHO GETS COMPENSATED?

Damages in personal injury cases compensate the injured person herself for the losses resulting from the accident, such as medical expenses, lost wages, or pain and suffering. Wrongful death statutes, however, do *not* compensate the decedent herself; it is obviously impossible to compensate the decedent for anything. The best the law can do is to compensate survivors who were close to the decedent for the losses *they* suffer as a result of the decedent's death. Thus, wrongful death statutes authorize damages for the economic or emotional losses to the survivors of the decedent, not the loss suffered by the decedent herself.

Assessing the damages to the survivors raises two thorny questions: Which survivors, and for what losses? As to the first question, most wrongful death statutes limit the recovery to the losses suffered by close relatives as a result of the decedent's death. For example, the Virginia statute provided until 1992[1] that the recovery is for the benefit of

> (i) the surviving spouse, children of the deceased and children of any deceased child of the deceased or (ii) if there be none such, then to the parents, brothers and sisters of the deceased . . . or (iii) if the decedent has left both surviving spouse and parent or parents, but no child or grandchild, the award shall be distributed to the surviving spouse and such parent or parents.

Va. Code §8.01-53. South Carolina's statute is a little different:

> Every such action shall be for the benefit of the wife or husband and child or children of the person whose death shall have been so caused, and, if there be no such wife, husband, child or children, then for the benefit of the parent or parents, and if there be none such, then for the benefit of the heirs of the person whose death shall have been so caused. . . .

S.C. Code §15-51-20.

Provisions of this type authorize damages to general classes of relatives likely to be closest to the decedent. If there are none in the closest class, the next group is considered, and so on. Like all efforts to deal generally with human relationships, these legislative classifications may miss the mark in particular cases. Mozart might be survived by a live-in lover to whom he was very close, and a son who had ignored him for 30 years. Under the Virginia statute, the son's losses would be the measure of damages. Or, Mozart might leave no close relatives. Surely, the gravity of his death is just as profound in such a case, but under the South Carolina statute the only loss to be compensated in such a case would be the losses of remote heirs, who perhaps never saw or cared about Mozart and will consequently be unable to prove substantial damages. However, in most cases the beneficiaries named in the

1. The statute was amended in 1992. This is the pre-1992 version, used for illustration purposes. The current version is discussed in the analysis of Example 3.

statutes—husbands and wives, children, parents, and siblings—are the ones likely to suffer most from the death of the decedent.[2]

Under many wrongful death statutes, the beneficiaries do not bring suit themselves. The executor or administrator of the estate is empowered to bring the action, but the damages are measured by the losses to the statutory beneficiaries and are distributed by the personal representative to them. Many statutes provide that the recovery does not become part of the decedent's estate. See, e.g., Ala. Code Tit. 6-5-410(c); R.I. Gen. Law 10-7-10. The major consequence of this is that the recovery does not go to pay the decedent's creditors. Even if the victim dies in debt, the wrongful death damages will go to the survivors the action is meant to compensate rather than to pay the decedent's debts.

MORE ON DAMAGES: WHAT LOSSES ARE COMPENSATED?

The second thorny question is what losses of the survivors are compensable under wrongful death statutes. The death of a loved one entails many losses. Some are concrete and quantifiable, such as loss of financial support or household services rendered by the decedent. Others are intangible, such as the loss of companionship, sexual consortium, advice, and emotional support, the same types of losses which are compensated as "loss of consortium" when the victim survives. See Chapter 14, pp. 302–304. In addition to these long-term losses from the death of the decedent, the survivors also suffer tangible immediate losses (funeral and burial expenses) and intangible immediate losses (the grief and mental anguish of learning of the death).

Historically, many wrongful death statutes limited damages to the "pecuniary losses" resulting to the specified survivors, that is, direct financial contributions or services the decedent would have rendered to the survivors. The New Jersey wrongful death statute, for example, provides that the jury may give damages for "the pecuniary injuries resulting from such death, together with the hospital, medical and funeral expenses incurred for the deceased. . . ." N.J. Stats. §2A:31-5. The reason for this limitation is historical: Although Lord Campbell's Act provided that the jury should award the statutory beneficiaries "such damages as they may think proportioned

2. For an excellent example of a court allocating a wrongful death recovery among various relatives under the Virginia wrongful death statute, see *Meeks v. Emiabata*, 2015 WL 6760491 (W.D. Va. 2015). The court in *Meeks* allocated small awards to two relatives with distant relationships to the decedent, and very substantial awards to two other relatives with very close relationships to him.

to the injury," the Act was early held to authorize only pecuniary damages. *Blake v. Midland, Ry. Co.*, 118 Eng. Rep. 35 (1852). Many of the American statutes either explicitly incorporated the "pecuniary loss" measure of damages (as the New Jersey statute does) or were initially interpreted to authorize only such damages. Under such statutes, damages for intangible losses such as loss of the society, sexual relationship, or advice and counsel of the decedent were not compensable.

Unless the decedent leaves a dependent spouse or children, the "pecuniary loss" standard, strictly construed to include only economic contributions the decedent would have made to the beneficiaries, is highly restrictive. In many cases, actual pecuniary losses in the nature of lost financial contributions from the decedent will be impossible to prove. If Mozart is survived by his parents only, who are financially secure, they would likely suffer no compensable damages under a strict "pecuniary loss" standard, and hence recover only funeral and burial expenses. The same may be true if he is survived by adult children or siblings who are financially independent.[3] And, of course, the standard—if literally applied—provides no recovery for the primary loss the survivors suffer: the loss of the opportunity to be with, learn from, and receive solace and emotional support from the decedent.

The inadequacy of the pecuniary loss standard is most glaring when the decedent is a young child. In such cases, the emotional loss to the parents is frightful, yet there is seldom evidence or likelihood of actual financial loss to the survivors. Such compelling cases have led many courts to evade the strictures of the pecuniary loss standard by tortured interpretation. In *Green v. Bittner*, 424 A.2d 210 (N.J. 1980), for example, the New Jersey Supreme Court allowed recovery under a "pecuniary loss" standard for the pecuniary value of the companionship and advice a daughter would have provided to her parents as they grew older. See also *Clymer v. Webster*, 596 A.2d 905, 914 (Vt. 1991) (loss of comfort and companionship of adult child "is a real, direct and personal loss that can be measured in pecuniary terms").

Clearly, *Green* and *Clymer* have stretched the concept of pecuniary loss far beyond its ordinary meaning. Such cases have deliberately blurred the distinction between a financial loss and a noneconomic loss that can be compensated—in some sense—by an award of money, in order to allow substantial damages in cases in which the survivors suffer little financial

---

3. Some states interpret their wrongful death statutes to allow recovery for loss of inheritance. See Speiser §12:35. This would allow some recovery for pecuniary loss even if the decedent was making no contributions to the statutory beneficiaries before he died. Presumably, the plaintiff would still have to show that the beneficiary would have inherited the decedent's estate, *and* that he or she was in the class of beneficiaries eligible to take under the wrongful death statute.

loss but great emotional loss as a result of the death. This parallels the modern trend to allow recovery for loss of consortium in injury cases, at least to the spouse of the direct victim, and sometimes to her children or parents. It hardly makes sense to allow consortium recovery for *impairment* of these relationships when the direct victim is injured, but to deny recovery for similar losses (by strict interpretation of the term "pecuniary loss") when the relationship is completely *destroyed* because the direct victim is killed.

Some legislatures have responded to this incongruity by amending their statutes to provide that the term "pecuniary loss" *includes* such elements as loss of companionship or mental anguish. See, e.g., Ark. Stat. 16-62-102(f)(l) (including spouse's loss of services and companionship and mental anguish as pecuniary loss). Others have simply amended their wrongful death statutes to authorize recovery for intangible damages *as well as* more typical pecuniary losses such as financial contributions and services by the decedent. The Kansas statute, for example, allows the "heirs at law" to recover pecuniary losses, as well as the following:

> (1) Mental anguish, suffering or bereavement;
> (2) loss of society, companionship, comfort or protection;
> (3) loss of marital care, attention, advice or counsel;
> (4) loss of filial care or attention;
> (5) loss of parental care, training, guidance or education; and
> (6) reasonable funeral expenses for the deceased.

Kan. Stat. Ann. §60-1904(a). This statute clearly allows recovery for many types of intangible emotional losses due to the death of the decedent. It even allows damages for grief, which is usually barred in actions for loss of consortium, and is barred under many wrongful death statutes as well. However, a separate section of the Kansas statute tempers the liberality of this damages provision by limiting the nonpecuniary damages to $250,000. Kan. Stat. Ann §60-1903(a). Other statutes, however, authorize unlimited damages for pecuniary and consortium damages alike. The Hawaii statute, for example, provides that:

> such damages may be given as under the circumstances shall be deemed fair and just compensation, with reference to the pecuniary injury and loss of love and affection, including (1) loss of society, companionship, comfort, consortium, or protection, (2) loss of marital care, attention, advice or counsel, (3) loss of care, attention, advice, or counsel of a reciprocal beneficiary as defined in Chapter 572C, (4) loss of filial care or attention, or (5) loss of parental care, training, guidance or education, suffered as a result of the death. . . .

Haw. Rev. Stat. §663-3(b).

AN ALTERNATIVE APPROACH

A few states take a different approach to wrongful death damages, focusing on the loss to the decedent's *estate* from his premature death. See, e.g., N.H. Rev. Stat. Ann. §556:12, which allows the jury to consider (as to damages caused by the death itself) "the reasonable expenses occasioned to the estate by the injury, the probable duration of life but for the injury, and the capacity to earn money during the deceased party's probable working life." Under statutes of this type, damages are frequently measured by calculating the decedent's future earnings, subtracting the amount the decedent would have spent on his own living expenses, and reducing the net figure to "present value." The rationale for this measure is that whatever the decedent saved from his income would have gone either to support his family while he was alive or into his estate and been distributed to his heirs or legatees after death.

The loss-to-the-estate rule provides a purely economic measure of damages, and shares some of the problems of the strict pecuniary loss rule. The loss-to-the-estate formula might not support any damages for the death of a retired person who lives on her current income. Similarly, there would be no loss to the estate of even a young person whose earnings did not exceed her living expenses. It seems likely that in many cases where strict application of the loss-to-the-estate standard or pecuniary loss standard would lead to no recovery, juries have ignored such instructions on the measure of damages and assessed a reasonable figure according to their own sense of justice.[4]

SURVIVAL STATUTES: PRESERVING CLAIMS FOR PREDEATH DAMAGES

So much for the erstwhile Mozart; now let's consider Haydn's case. He also died as a result of Handel's negligent act. Consequently his estate or survivors will have a cause of action for wrongful death. But he suffered other injuries as well from Handel's negligence: He lingered for seven months, suffered pain and suffering, incurred medical expenses, and was out of work and unable to enjoy his usual activities. Had he recovered at the end of those seven months, instead of dying, he would have had a right to sue for

4. The New Hampshire statute includes a separate provision for recovery of consortium losses *in addition to* the pecuniary loss-to-the-estate measure.

these losses. Shouldn't his estate be able to sue for these predeath damages, even though he died?

The common law took a hard line on these cases as well. Tort cases were classified as "personal" actions, and under the common law personal actions could only be prosecuted by the injured person herself. Speiser §1:14.[5] Haydn could sue for his injuries while alive, but no one else could do it for him. If he died before bringing suit, the estate had no right to pursue the claim. If he brought suit but died before the suit went to a verdict or judgment, most courts held that the action "abated" and could not be prosecuted further. The principle applied to the defendant as well. If a person caused an injury, a tort action had to be brought against her personally; if she died before suit was brought, the plaintiff could not sue her estate.

This hoary common law principle, like the bar on recovery for wrongful death itself, has been supplanted by statute. Most states now have "survival" statutes which provide that causes of action "survive" rather than abate at the death of either the tortfeasor or the injured party. Note that it is the *claim itself* that survives, not the plaintiff or defendant: The very point of a survival statute is that the party need not survive for suit to be brought. Typically, where the injured party dies, the statute authorizes the decedent's personal representative (executor or administrator) to bring suit (or continue one already in progress) to recover for the decedent's injuries. While the statutes vary, the Maine survival provision is simple and representative:

> No personal action or cause of action is lost by the death of either party, but the same survives for and against the personal representative of the deceased. . . .

Me. Rev. Stat. Ann. 18-C §3-817. Under a provision such as this, Haydn's estate could still recover for Haydn's predeath injuries, whether or not suit had been brought before Haydn died. If Haydn had not brought suit before his death, the personal representative of his estate could file suit. If Haydn had sued but died before the case was decided, his personal representative would be substituted as the plaintiff and continue the litigation.

A simple diagram may help to distinguish survival actions from wrongful death actions. Figure 18-1 is a timeline, running from the point of Haydn's injury forward. At common law, Haydn had to bring suit himself, while alive, to recover for any damages he incurred during Period A, the period after the injury but before his death. If he did not sue, or died before a suit went to judgment, no recovery was allowed for the predeath damages. Under a survival statute, however, Haydn's estate is authorized to bring an action, after Haydn's death, for such damages. These damages will include

---

5. Like so many issues, the common law dealt with this one by throwing a little legal Latin at it: "actio personalis moritur cum persona," translated "a personal action dies with the person." Speiser §1:14 n.l.

medical expenses, lost wages, and pain and suffering Haydn sustained from the date of the accident until his death.[6] Since Haydn died from his injuries, the wrongful death statute also authorizes a separate action for damages caused by the death itself, that is, losses incurred by his survivors during Period B, after Haydn's death.

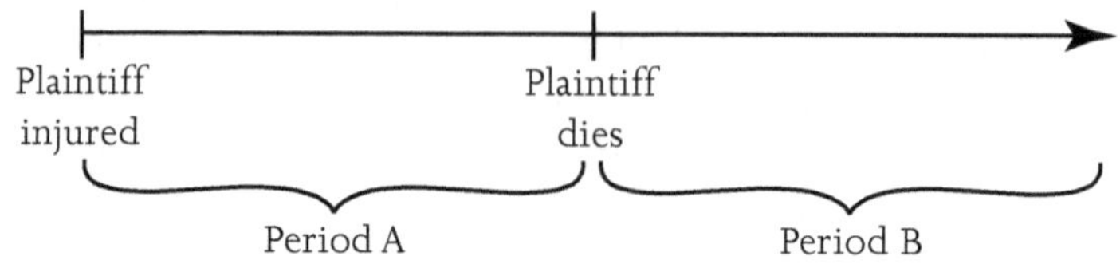

Figure 18-1

The rationale for allowing causes of action to survive where the tort victim dies is not far to seek. Although a survival action, like a wrongful death action, cannot compensate the decedent, the recovery usually goes into the decedent's estate and passes to her heirs. Though the decedent takes no direct benefit from the action, she may at least take solace before death in the knowledge that *somebody* will be compensated for the tort, and that those somebodies will be of her choosing. In addition, there is an obvious anomaly between allowing recovery if a tort suit goes to judgment a day before the victim dies, but not if judgment is entered the day after.

Survival statutes similarly allow recovery in cases where the *tortfeasor* dies. At common law, the plaintiff was out of luck if the tortfeasor died before she sued for her injuries. However, under a survival statute, the plaintiff may bring suit against the decedent's estate for the tort. The plaintiff in such cases is as much in need of compensation whether the defendant lives or dies. If the defendant leaves substantial assets, it seems reasonable that they should go to compensate the victim. In addition, in many cases the decedent's insurer is effectively the defendant since it will defend the action and pay any damages awarded. It seems inappropriate that the insurer should get a windfall and the injured person go uncompensated if the negligent person fortuitously dies before recovery is awarded.

Although often associated with wrongful death statutes, survival statutes do not apply only in cases where the defendant's negligence causes death. Under a statute like Maine's, Haydn's damage claim survives whether he dies of the injuries suffered in the accident or of an unrelated cause. Similarly, his claim would survive if Handel died from the accident or any other cause. Handel's personal representative would simply be substituted as the defendant in the action.

---

6. Some survival statutes do not allow recovery by the estate for predeath pain and suffering. See, e.g., Ariz. Rev. Stat. §14-3110.

Because wrongful death and survival claims are based on statutes, there is a good deal of variation on the approaches discussed above. However, the basic patterns are fairly uniform. The following examples illustrate those patterns. For an example of a complaint that asserts claims under both a survival statute and a wrongful death statute, see Chapter 19, p. 432.

Examples

A Dandelion from the Bluebook Garden

1. The following statement sometimes sprouts, weedlike, in my spring bluebooks:[7] "If the plaintiff cannot prove a claim for negligence, she may be able to recover damages for Smith's death under the applicable wrongful death statute." Can you articulate the misconception that underlies this statement?

Laws of Relativity

2. Purcell is run down and killed instantly. He is survived by his parents, whom he has not seen for 30 years, and a disabled sister, for whom he is the sole source of support.
   a. Who would be entitled to damages under the Virginia statute quoted at p. 400?
   b. Who would be entitled to damages under the South Carolina statute quoted at p. 400?

3 Assume that Purcell is survived by an adult son, his disabled sister, and his elderly parents, with whom he has a close relationship. Who would be entitled to damages for his death under the version of the Virginia statute quoted at p. 400?

4. Assume the same facts given in Example 3, but that the case arose under the Hawaii statute, which authorizes damages for both pecuniary and intangible damages "suffered as a result of the death of the person; by the surviving spouse, reciprocal beneficiary, children, father, mother, and by any person wholly or partly dependent upon the deceased person." Haw. Stat. §663-3. Who will recover, and how will the damages for each beneficiary be ascertained?

5. What will be the result under the South Carolina statute (p. 400) if Purcell dies without leaving any close relatives?

---

7. Do any of you know what a bluebook is anymore? Back in the day nervous law students wrote their exams in them. They had blue covers.

6. Brahms, a highly successful musician, dies leaving an adult daughter with a large income, a six-year-old son, a wife who does not work outside the home, and an elderly mother whom he frequently helps out financially. What damages could each recover if the Virginia beneficiary provision quoted at p. 400 applied and
   a. the measure of damages was limited to pecuniary loss, strictly construed?
   b. the applicable measure of damage was the same as the Kansas statute quoted at p. 404?
   c. the "loss to the estate" measure of damages applied?

"The Lawsuit Was a Success but the Plaintiff Died"

7. Verdi and Vivaldi are seriously injured when Strauss drops a tuba from a scaffold above the stage. Verdi survives for a year in constant pain and is unable to work. He then dies of his injuries. Vivaldi suffers a broken arm, is out of work for three months, and suffers permanent reduction of function in the arm.
   a. What causes of action would Verdi and Vivaldi have against Strauss under early common law?
   b. If the Maine survival statute quoted at p. 405 applied, what damages could Verdi's estate recover in the survival action?
   c. If Verdi's personal representative sought damages under the survival statute, could he also sue for wrongful death?
8. Assume that Verdi suffers a broken hip from the accident and is laid up in bed. Six months later, he dies of an unrelated stroke, without having brought any suit against Strauss for his tuba injury. What actions may his personal representative bring against Strauss, if any?

Consorting with Confusion

9. On the facts in Example 8, could Jane Verdi, his widow, bring an action against Strauss for loss of consortium under the survival statute?
10. Assume that Verdi dies instantly when the tuba falls on him, leaving his widow, Jane, who is appointed as personal representative of his estate. Six months later, before suit is brought against him, Strauss dies.
    a. What statute is implicated here, the wrongful death statute or the survival statute?
    b. Assume that the applicable wrongful death statute only authorizes recovery for pecuniary loss and is strictly construed to encompass solely economic losses. Jane's complaint includes a count for wrongful death, and a second count for loss of consortium with her husband due to his death. What is the problem here?

c. Assume that Jane, still hoping to recover for consortium losses due to her husband's death, adds a third count in her complaint, asserting a "claim for negligence" and asking for consortium damages on that claim. What is the problem with this count?

Substance and Procedure in the Law of Wrongful Death

11. Mahler, a student from North Dakota studying at the University of Kansas, is killed in an accident on a school trip. The accident takes place in Tennessee. His parents retain you to bring an action to recover for his death. What crucial strategic question will you need to confront at the outset in representing them?

Judge Fudd on an Off Day

12. Assume that Mendelssohn, a drummer, gets knocked off the stage by Brahms during a performance. He dies immediately from his fall, and his estate sues Brahms for wrongful death. Brahms pleads as a defense that Mendelssohn was contributorily negligent for standing behind Brahms at the edge of the stage during the crescendo. Assume that contributory negligence is a complete defense to a negligence action in the relevant jurisdiction. Assume also that the language of the applicable wrongful death statute is the same as the North Dakota wrongful death provision quoted on p. 399. At trial, the Honorable Fudd instructs the jury as follows:

> If you find by a preponderance of the evidence that the decedent was contributorily negligent, and that his negligence was a proximate cause of the accident which led to his death, then you must find for the defendant.

Is Fudd's instruction proper?

Explanations

A Dandelion from the Bluebook Garden

1. This statement is based on the premise that there is a distinct "cause of action for wrongful death" apart from the traditional torts live plaintiffs can recover for. That isn't so. Wrongful death statutes typically allow recovery if the decedent would have had a right to recover if she had lived. See, e.g., the language in the North Dakota statute, p. 399. If the injured party could have recovered for negligence, had she lived, the personal representative may recover if the negligence caused the decedent's death. If the decedent would have had a battery claim had she lived, the representative may recover when the battery causes death. And so on. In other words, there is no separate tort called "wrongful death." Wrongful

death statutes create a remedy for existing torts when those torts lead to the death of the victim.

Laws of Relativity

2. a. The Virginia statute allows recovery to siblings and parents if the decedent does not leave a spouse, child, or grandchild. That is true here, so both the sister and the parents are eligible to receive damages for the death. However, it appears unlikely that the parents will be able to prove substantial damages since they have been cut off from Purcell for many years. Thus, if the damages are assessed to the sister and parents according to their actual losses, she will receive a substantial award and they will receive little or nothing.
   b. Under the South Carolina statute, the action is "for the benefit of the parent or parents" if there is no spouse or child. Thus, it appears that only they would be entitled to damages, while the sister, who suffered compelling losses, would not be entitled to recover.

3. In this example, Purcell is survived by a number of close relatives, all of whom may have suffered compensable losses, at least if the measure of damages includes consortium losses such as companionship, advice, and comfort. However, the version of the Virginia statute quoted on p. 400 limits the recovery to the son. He falls within the class of beneficiaries in clause (i) of the statute, and the statute apparently denies recovery to parents and siblings if there are clause (i) beneficiaries. Cf. *Carroll v. Sneed*, 179 S.E.2d 620, 623 (Va. 1971) (suggesting that presence of a child precludes any recovery to parents under the Virginia statute).

   Obviously, specifying classes of beneficiaries in this way can lead to pretty unsatisfactory results. Although it is likely in this case that the heaviest losses, both pecuniary and emotional, were suffered by the elderly parents and dependent sister, they would obtain no compensation, while the lesser losses of the son will be the sole measure of damages. One wonders if courts haven't found some way around such results, despite apparently clear statutory language. See Prosser & Keeton at 947 and accompanying notes (suggesting that some cases have winked at the statutory limits, but others have not).

   The Virginia legislature later amended the wrongful death statute to allow recovery for dependent relatives in some cases. It now allows recovery for

   > (i) the surviving spouse, children of the deceased and children of any deceased child of the deceased, and the parents of the decedent if any of such parents, within 12 months prior to the decedent's death, regularly received support or regularly received services from the decedent for necessaries, including living expenses, food, shelter, health care expenses, or

> in-home assistance or care, or (ii) if there be none such, then to the parents, brothers and sisters of the deceased, and to any other relative who is primarily dependent on the decedent for support or services and is also a member of the same household as the decedent or (iii) if the decedent has left both surviving spouse and parent or parents, but no child or grandchild, the award shall be distributed to the surviving spouse and such parent or parents or (iv) if there are survivors under clause (i) or clause (iii), the award shall be distributed to those beneficiaries and to any other relative who is primarily dependent on the decedent for support or services and is also a member of the same household as the decedent or (v) if no survivors exist under clause (i). (ii), (iii), or (iv), the award shall be distributed in the course of descents as provided for in §64.2-200. . . .[8]

It isn't clear that Purcell's sister will fare any better under this amended version. Is she included in the first tier or the second tier? It isn't clear whether the phrase "and to any other relative who is primarily dependent on the decedent for support or services and is also a member of the same household as the decedent" modifies only clause (ii) or both clauses (i) and (ii). If it only modifies the second clause, Sis is out of luck since Purcell did leave a son. Even if the phrase including other relatives applies to clause (i), Sis would still have to live with Purcell to be eligible for recovery.

4. The Hawaii statute avoids the problem illustrated in Example 3 because it authorizes damages for close relatives who suffer loss from the decedent's death without setting priorities that exclude other beneficiaries. (A fair number of statutes now take this approach. See generally Speiser §3:1.) Thus, Purcell's son, parents, and sister would be entitled to recover. Presumably, their awards would depend on the actual pecuniary and consortium losses each proves at trial. If, for example, the son is estranged from the decedent, the jury would likely award him minimal damages, while the dependent sister's damages would presumably be very substantial.

   This statute obviously provides greater flexibility in assessing the wrongful death damages of various survivors, but it is also quite open ended, leading to greater exposure. If the victim is J.S. Bach, who has 20 children, a close relationship to his parents,[9] and several live-in siblings, the defendant may be hit with a very substantial verdict.

5. The last clause of the South Carolina statute provides that, if there are no statutory beneficiaries, the recovery will go to those who inherit the decedent's estate. Thus, if Purcell leaves no close relatives, the wrongful

---

8. Va. Stat. §801.53.
9. He actually did have 20 kids.

death recovery will be distributed to his heirs, probably collateral relatives such as cousins, nieces and nephews, and aunts and uncles.

However, the damages assessed will still have to be based on actual damages suffered by these collateral relatives. The more distant these survivors are, the more difficult it will be for them to prove substantial damages—either economic or emotional—as a result of Purcell's death.

6. a. Under the Virginia beneficiaries provision, the wife and children would recover, but presumably the mother would not, since she is not in the first class of beneficiaries. Under a strict pecuniary loss standard, the wife and children would recover damages for the lost financial contributions and household services Brahms would have rendered to them. As to the adult daughter, this is likely to be small, but it will clearly be substantial as to the wife and son, who were entirely dependent on Brahms for support.

   It should include, for example, the cost of maintaining the son for 12 years at home, and quite likely four more years of college. If the evidence supports it, the damages might also include four more years in medical school or seven studying mathematical linguistics in graduate school. There might also be proof that Brahms would have made monetary gifts to his children over the years, for tax reasons or maybe even out of the goodness of his heart. The wife's damages might include the cost of her support for the balance of her life expectancy, and perhaps the loss of the inheritance she would have received had Brahms accumulated a substantial estate and predeceased her. Funeral and burial expenses would also be recoverable under a pecuniary loss standard.

   b. If the Kansas damages provision applied, Brahms's survivors would recover fully for the pecuniary losses discussed above, and up to $250,000 for grief, mental anguish, and consortium losses.

   In a jurisdiction that authorized unlimited recovery for consortium losses, the eligible beneficiaries would all be entitled to full recovery for the loss of society, care, counsel, and guidance that they suffered due to Brahms's death, in addition to proven pecuniary loss. However, if a provision like the Virginia statute applied, limiting the eligible beneficiaries, the mother would not recover anything for economic or consortium losses, since she is not within the first tier of beneficiaries.

   c. Under the loss-to-the-estate theory, the damages are often calculated by determining how much the decedent would have earned, subtracting the amount he would have spent on his own maintenance, and then discounting the resulting figure to present value. This figure represents the excess income the decedent could have contributed to his survivors or left to them in his estate.

Obviously, this measure provides nothing for consortium losses, and will not support a substantial award if the decedent had little income. In other cases, however, the loss-to-the-estate measure of damages will yield a much higher award than the loss-to-survivors approach. Consider a case in which the decedent is survived by his elderly parents. Under the loss-to-survivors approach there will likely be little in the way of provable financial loss to the parents. Even if the relevant statute allows recovery for consortium losses, they will be limited due to the parents' relatively short life expectancy. Thus the award in a loss-to-survivors state is unlikely to approach the loss-to-the-estate measure, which considers the decedent's future income stream over decades.[10]

The analysis of this example must go one step further, however, because the example asks how much *each* beneficiary would receive. In a jurisdiction that uses the loss-to-the-estate measure of damages, the *estate* will recover the decedent's lost income, minus personal consumption. But how will the recovery then be distributed to the actual beneficiaries? Here, for example, it is clear that Brahms's minor son has suffered a greater loss than the adult daughter.

"The Lawsuit Was a Success but the Plaintiff Died"

7. a. This example illustrates the anomalous effects of the common law abatement rule. Under that rule Vivaldi would recover in full for his injuries since he lived, and is personally able to bring this "personal" cause of action. At common law, however, Verdi's claim abated at his death unless he obtained judgment against Strauss before he died. His estate had no right to sue for his predeath losses, such as the pain and suffering, lost wages, and disability he experienced during the year before he died. Nor did Verdi's estate have a cause of action for wrongful death since the common law barred wrongful death claims as well.
   b. In Maine, as in most states today, Verdi's claim would survive his death and could be enforced by the representative of his estate. But remember that the survival action is for Verdi's *predeath* losses from the tort. It is not a claim for wrongful death; rather, it is for the losses Verdi suffered before death that he could have recovered himself had he lived. Thus, his personal representative could recover for his predeath pain and suffering, lost wages, medical bills, and other compensable damages suffered during the year that he lingered.
   c. Absolutely. The right to sue under the survival statute for losses suffered by the victim before death does not bar the right to sue for

10. However, the parents should only recover for the decedent's future accumulations up to the date of their own life expectancy, a significant limit as well.

wrongful death. The two actions address distinct injuries, and may benefit different parties. The survival action compensates Verdi's estate for damages he suffered before death that he could have recovered himself if he had lived. The wrongful death action (in most jurisdictions) compensates the survivors (whichever are eligible under the statute) for their losses as a result of the death.

8. In this case, Verdi had a claim against Strauss for his injuries in the accident, but he died of an unrelated cause before bringing suit to enforce it. Under a survival statute the right survives to his estate, regardless of the cause of his death. The rationale for survival statutes is that the tortfeasor should compensate the victim's estate for the damages the victim suffered before dying, even though the victim dies before suing for those injuries herself. This rationale applies equally, whether the victim dies of injuries inflicted by the tortfeasor or from an unrelated cause. Thus, Verdi's estate may recover under the survival statute for the medical expenses, lost wages, and pain and suffering from the time of the injury until his death, even though the hip injury did not cause his death.

   However, Verdi's personal representative would not have a wrongful death claim in this example. Verdi died of a stroke, not the broken hip suffered in the accident. Under basic negligence law, Strauss cannot be held liable for damages he didn't cause.

Consorting with Confusion

9. Verdi's widow has a claim against Strauss for loss of consortium, but the survival statute has nothing to do with it. Survival statutes allow a decedent's estate to bring a claim *the decedent* could have brought before death. The consortium claim is Jane's own claim for her consortium losses as a result of Verdi's injury, suffered during the period when he was incapacitated. She is seeking recovery for her own loss, the inability to relate to Verdi in the same way she did before, due to his injury. This is her own claim, and she will bring it in her own name.

   Her consortium claim will be limited to the impairment of her relationship with Verdi during the six months he was incapacitated by the accident. The relationship was then cut off entirely by his death from an unrelated cause.

10. a. Both the wrongful death and the survival statute come into play here. Verdi's estate has no "survival claim," because he did not suffer any predeath damages; he died instantly. However, the survival statute is still implicated because *the tortfeasor* died. Under the old common law approach, tort claims abated if the tortfeasor died. So, at common law, neither Verdi nor his estate could have sued Strauss's estate; the negligence claim would die with Strauss. However, most states now

have survival statutes that allow a claim to survive against the estate of a tortfeasor. See, e.g., the Maine survival statute quoted at p. 405.

So Jane, as personal representative of Verdi's estate, will be able to sue Strauss's estate. Her claim is for the wrongful death of Verdi, under the relevant state wrongful death statute, but it is the survival statute that provides that this claim "survives" the death of Strauss, allowing Jane to bring that claim against his estate. Her suit will be an action for wrongful death, and will be entitled *Jane Verdi, as Personal Representative of the estate of Angelo Verdi v. Estate of Strauss.*

b. In this case, the applicable wrongful death statute only authorizes recovery for the actual economic losses Jane suffers as a result of Verdi's death (because the "pecuniary loss" provision is strictly construed). It makes no provision for the consortium losses she sustains as a result of the destruction of her relationship to her husband. So Mrs. V. has simply asserted a separate count in her complaint for loss of consortium as well.

This creative effort to circumvent the limits of the wrongful death statute will fail. Because Verdi died instantly, Jane's loss of consortium claim is for the loss of his company, companionship, advice, support, and society *after* death. It is, in other words, a claim for damages resulting from the death. But these damages are *not* allowed under the applicable wrongful death statute, which has been construed to limit recovery to "pecuniary loss" in the strict sense. Since the right to recover for wrongful death is defined by the statute, the court will confine recovery to that allowed by the statute itself, and dismiss Jane's second claim.[11]

There is certainly a strong policy argument for Jane's position, however. Had Verdi survived, she would have been entitled to recover for the impairment of her relationship with him while he was incapacitated, under a count for "loss of consortium." See Example 8. Why shouldn't she have the same right when the relationship is completely cut off by his death? Does it make sense to retain the pecuniary loss measure of damages for wrongful death where much broader compensation is provided for consortium losses when the direct victim is merely injured?

---

11. At least one court has refused to follow this reasoning. See *Giuliani v. Guiler*, 951 S.W.2d 318 (Ky. 1997), which *did* recognize a common law loss of consortium claim due to the death of a parent, even though the relevant wrongful death statute did not allow consortium damages for the death of a parent. A strong dissent argued for the position in the text above. Compare *Bratcher v. Galusha*, 417 Mass. 28, 30-31 (1994) (rejecting similar claim made by parents of the decedent; court declined to "rewrite or ignore the plain language of the statute"). As Oliver Wendell Holmes once said, "No generalization is worth a damn, including this one."

This argument has led many states to amend their wrongful death statutes to authorize broad consortium damages in wrongful death cases. For example, if the Kansas provision on p. 403 applied, Verdi's widow could recover damages for loss of society, companionship, advice, counsel, and so forth, the same elements compensated under loss of consortium where the direct victim is merely injured.

c. The problem here is that the claim for negligence is really no different from the claim for wrongful death. A wrongful death claim must be based on a recognized tort that the decedent could have asserted had he survived. Here, that claim would be negligence, for carelessly dropping the tuba on Verdi. The wrongful death action is simply a negligence action in which the injury resulting from the defendant's negligent act is death. Verdi's wife has a claim under the wrongful death statute, but no separate right to assert a common law negligence claim against Strauss for causing Verdi's death. Thus, her third count does not state a claim for which relief can be granted.

Substance and Procedure in the Law of Wrongful Death

11. This chapter illustrates that the extent of the damages available for wrongful death varies dramatically from state to state. For the most part, tort law is state law, and each state is free to create its own rules, whether by statute or judicial decision, without regard to what the rules are in another state. Some states inevitably will have more generous rules than others.

    A corollary of this basic tenet of tort law is that a plaintiff may fare a lot better under one state's tort law than under another state's. In the case on which this example is based,[12] Kansas imposed (at the time) a \$100,000 cap on intangible damages, while North Dakota had no cap. Since the case involved the wrongful death of a college student, who was probably not making financial contributions to his parents, the intangible damages were probably the major item of damages. Thus, the case would be "worth" a lot more under North Dakota law than under Kansas law. (No one argued for Tennessee law, another candidate.)

    So, as counsel for Mahler's family, you might choose to sue in North Dakota, on the premise that it would be likely to apply its own statute to the wrongful death of a North Dakota domiciliary. But there might not be personal jurisdiction over all of the defendants in North Dakota for a Tennessee accident.

    Alternatively, you might sue in Tennessee or Kansas, but argue that the court should *apply North Dakota law to the case*. In every case involving multi-state contacts, the court must decide which state's law to apply

12. *MacDonald v. General Motors Corp.*, 110 F.3d 337 (6th Cir. 1997).

to the case. Every state has pesky "choice-of-law" rules about this, and they do not always lead courts to apply their own law. In this instance, the court in Tennessee concluded that the North Dakota statute should apply since the claim was for the death of a North Dakota domiciliary.

The point is that, given the wide variation in tort rules, and the often broad reach of personal jurisdiction, there is room for creative lawyers to maximize their clients' opportunities by choosing a favorable forum. So, before bringing suit, you should consider the wrongful death statutes of the states in which suit might be brought, and the choice-of-law rules of those states, in order to maximize the chances of having the case decided under the most favorable wrongful death statute.

Judge Fudd on an Off Day

12. Fudd is only "off" here because he's right on. The North Dakota statute, like many wrongful death acts, authorizes wrongful death recovery for claims that "would have entitled the party injured, if death had not ensued, to maintain an action and recover damages in respect thereof. . . ." If Mendelssohn had lived and brought suit, he would not have been entitled to "recover damages in respect thereof," since his contributory negligence would have been a complete defense (the example assumes). Consequently, the wrongful death suit is barred as well.[13]

---

13. In a comparative negligence jurisdiction, the decedent's negligence will reduce recovery in a wrongful death case, just as it would have if the decedent had survived. Prosser & Keeton at 955.

An argument can (as always) be made to the contrary. The wrongful death recovery is for the benefit of the survivors. If *they* have not been negligent, arguably their recovery should not be reduced. But most courts have considered themselves bound by statutory language like North Dakota's, or by the obvious fact that the decedent's conduct would have barred recovery if he had survived.

PART VI

Interlude: Pleading a Personal Injury Case

CHAPTER 19

Some Legal Anatomy: Thinking Like a Tort Lawyer

INTRODUCTION

If you had chosen medical school, your course in human anatomy would probably have been broken down into topics, like the brain, the circulatory system, the digestive system, the skeletal system, and so on. But bodies don't operate that way; they function as a unified system in which all elements interact to form a living organism.

Similarly, while most of the chapters in this book, like the Torts course itself, focus on particular elements or types of tort claims, cases do not arrive in lawyers' offices in such neat categories. Accidents present complex, miscellaneous, unorganized facts that lawyers must reconceptualize in terms of the theoretical framework of tort law. The challenge of a torts practice is to fit these unorganized real-world facts into the recognized elements and defenses of a negligence claim. This chapter provides a brief opportunity to look at tort claims the way a practitioner does, to reason from raw data to legally supportable claims for damages.

To begin with, remember that the plaintiff must prove all the basic elements of a negligence claim in order to recover. If Bernhart is injured in a boating accident, the fact that she is seriously injured and needs compensation is not enough to support recovery. She must also prove that the pilot of the other boat was negligent, and that her negligence caused the accident. If Terry sells stock at a serious loss after an inaccurate financial statement is published by the corporation's accountants, she will still not recover if the court concludes that the accountants owed her no duty, or that the drop in value of the stock was not caused by the accountants' negligence. A torts chain is only as strong as its weakest link; you have to examine the whole chain to give a realistic assessment of the chances of recovery.

In addition, while we often speak broadly of a "claim for negligence," many types of negligence claims require more specific analysis. A plaintiff cannot recover for infliction of emotional distress, for example, simply by showing that the defendant's negligent conduct caused her distress. Courts have imposed additional requirements to limit emotional distress claims, such as physical contact, the *Dillon* standards, or presence in the "zone of danger." See generally Chapter 14. Similarly, plaintiffs seeking recovery for loss of consortium must show more than negligence, causation, and damages: Courts generally conclude that a defendant only owes a duty to avoid loss of consortium if a close relationship exists between the plaintiff and the direct victim. See Chapter 14, pp. 302–304. Similarly, in wrongful death cases, only certain parties are allowed to recover. See Chapter 18. Counsel must analyze such cases with a view to these constraints on recovery for negligence.

Third, counsel must consider carefully what damages are recoverable in a negligence case. The fact that a defendant is liable does not necessarily mean that she is liable for every loss the plaintiff has suffered. This may be true because the law limits the types of damages recoverable (as in wrongful death cases), because the defendant did not cause all the plaintiff's damages (as in some multiple tortfeasor situations), or because, as a matter of policy, the law refuses to shift the loss for certain damages, under a proximate cause or duty analysis.

Without further ado, let's explore some of these limitations on negligence recovery based on the facts of this relatively simple accident case:

> Isadora Garfield was a famous opera star. On March 1, 2018, she and her husband, Booth, were pulling out of their driveway on to Main Street in the town of Elkton, West Dakota. Burton came speeding around a curve and hit their car broadside. Isadora, who was three months pregnant at the time, was severely injured. John, son of Isadora and Booth, was playing basketball in the driveway, about 25 feet from the point of the accident, heard the collision, and ran to the scene immediately. Isadora suffered the loss of sight in one eye and multiple internal injuries, and was hospitalized in serious condition. The baby suffered fetal distress and cardiac arrhythmia from the trauma of the accident, and was stillborn a week later. Four months later, on July 1, Isadora died as a result of her injuries.
>
> Booth suffered minor facial lacerations. John was extremely upset by the accident. He subsequently became withdrawn, suffered a severe decline in his high school grades, and more or less "dropped out." Lydia, a married daughter of Isadora, was also seriously affected by the accident. She became tense, impatient with her husband, cried a lot, and had difficulty sleeping. She became

difficult to work with and was skipped over for promotion. She also missed her mother.

Garrick was Isadora's costar in many important productions and a close personal friend. He was extremely upset by her injury, suffered a nervous breakdown, and never quite fully recovered. Unable to find a comparable costar, his career was limited thereafter to minor supporting roles.

Burton, the other driver, was also seriously injured. He died a year later of unrelated causes.

The following examples consider the elements, special requirements, and limitations on relief for the different types of claims that may be asserted based on the Garfield accident. In analyzing the claims, focus on the claims that the plaintiffs could raise, even if some claims may be vulnerable to legal or factual challenge by the defendant or appear strategically dubious. Assume that West Dakota has a survival statute, a wrongful death statute that authorizes pecuniary and loss of consortium damages for survivors, and that it recognizes claims for spousal consortium in personal injury cases but has not decided whether children can recover for loss of parental consortium.

Examples

Setting the Stage

1. Assume that Isadora did not initiate suit before her death. Booth, the personal representative of her estate, comes to you after her death, to inquire about potential claims for damages as a result of her physical injuries.
   a. What would you advise Booth about the effect of Isadora's death on the right to recover for her injuries?
   b. What would you advise Booth about the effect of Burton's death on Isadora's claims?

Act One

2. Booth retains you to bring an action against Burton for damages for Isadora's injuries. Which of the following elements of damages would you claim in a *survival* action for predeath losses suffered by Isadora?
   a. pain and suffering
   b. lost future earning capacity
   c. loss of enjoyment of life
   d. medical bills
   e. loss of consortium with members of her family

3. Assume that Booth also wishes to assert a *wrongful death* claim resulting from Isadora's death. Which of the following elements of damages would you seek in the wrongful death claim?
   a. pain and suffering
   b. lost earning capacity
   c. loss of enjoyment of life
   d. loss of consortium suffered by Booth and other family members due to Isadora's death

Act Two

4. Booth also inquires as to claims he may assert on behalf of the deceased child Isadora was carrying at the time of the accident. What would you advise him as to the prospects of recovery for the child's death, and the elements of damages?

5. Booth also inquires as to the claims he may assert on his own behalf as a result of the accident.
   a. What would you advise Booth as to the elements of damages for his own physical injuries?
   b. What would you advise Booth as to his right to assert claims for loss of consortium?
   c. What would you advise Booth concerning other claims he might have?

6. Booth brings John with him. John is also interested in asserting claims against Burton's estate. What claims may he have, and what problems do you anticipate in recovering on them?

7. A week after your interview with Booth and John, Lydia comes in to inquire about possible claims against Burton. What claims may she have, and what problems do you anticipate in recovering on them?

Supporting Actors

8. Next to come in is Garrick, Isadora's costar in the opera. What would you advise him as to his rights against Burton arising from the accident?

Putting the Show on the Road

9. Draft a complaint seeking relief on behalf of Isadora's estate, Booth, John, and Lydia. Assume that the West Dakota law allows both survival and wrongful death claims and recognizes fetal wrongful death claims, but has not yet addressed claims for loss of consortium on behalf of parents or children. Assume also that it is unclear what the standards are in West Dakota to state an adequate claim for negligent infliction of emotional distress.

Explanations

Setting the Stage

1. a. The right to recover for Isadora's injuries depends on the applicable survival and wrongful death statutes, which vary from state to state. Thus, you might advise Booth, as lawyers frequently do, that you don't know whether suit can be brought, but will find out. However, if you were an experienced West Dakota practitioner, you would probably be familiar with the local law on these issues.

   As Chapter 18 explains, virtually all states have modified the common law doctrine denying recovery for wrongful death. Here, for example, West Dakota's wrongful death statute authorizes recovery of pecuniary and consortium damages suffered by Isadora's survivors as a result of her death, and the survival statute authorizes Booth, as Isadora's executor, to recover for predeath losses Isadora suffered as a result of the accident.

   b. The question here is whether Isadora's claims "survive" the death of Burton, the tortfeasor. Most states now provide by statute that tort claims survive the tortfeasor's death and may be brought against the tortfeasor's estate. This is true regardless of the cause of the tortfeasor's death. Thus, it makes no difference here that the cause of Burton's death was unrelated to the accident.

Act One

2. a. Most survival statutes allow recovery by the estate of a deceased tort victim for losses suffered by the decedent prior to death. Under these survival statutes, the estate recovers any damages the plaintiff sustained from the date of the accident until her death, and which she could have recovered herself if she had survived.

   Had Isadora survived and filed suit herself, she could have recovered for pain and suffering. Thus, the physical pain and emotional anguish she sustained during this four-month period as a result of her injuries should be proper elements of damages in the survival action.

   Of course, any recovery under the survival claim will not compensate Isadora for having suffered it; she is beyond compensation in any worldly sense. Consequently, a few states view recovery for pain and suffering as a "windfall to the heirs" (see Prosser & Keeton at 943) and bar recovery for pain and suffering in survival actions. See, e.g., Ariz. Rev. Stat. Ann. §14-3110. Most states, however, allow recovery for the decedent's predeath pain and suffering: If these damages are not allowed in the survival action, the *defendant* will get a windfall due to the victim's death. Although these damages cannot benefit her, at least her survivors, through her estate, can receive the benefit of the recovery.

b. Lost future earning capacity refers to the tort victim's loss of the ability to earn money in the future, that is, after the trial. See Chapter 17, pp. 377–379. Under most survival statutes, this is not a proper element of a survival claim, which only encompasses losses suffered prior to death. Minzer, Nates §21.03. Only her *predeath* lost earnings, for the four months from the accident until her death, would be properly sought under the survival claim. Her future earning capacity will be taken into account in assessing the damages for wrongful death. See Example 3b.

   Here again, there are statutory variations. In a few states, lost earning capacity *is* allocated to the survival claim. See, e.g., *Wetzel v. McDonnell Douglas Corp.*, 491 F. Supp. 1288 (E.D. Pa. 1980). In a state with a statute of this type, the court must be very careful to assure that these same damages are not assessed again under the wrongful death claim.

c. All states recognize that an injured plaintiff's loss of the ability to enjoy normal activities and pleasures of living is a compensable element of damages in tort actions. As Chapter 17 indicates, some states view this as included in pain and suffering, while others treat "loss of enjoyment of life" as a distinct element of damages. Presumably Isadora's estate would recover for her loss of enjoyment of life during the four months she survived since this is a loss she suffered prior to death, for which she could have recovered herself had she lived. However, as with her earnings, she cannot recover for *future* loss of enjoyment in a survival action.

   As noted above, a few states specifically bar claims for pain and suffering in survival actions. If the Garfield case arose in one of these states, counsel for Burton's estate would doubtless argue that the exclusion for pain and suffering damages also bars recovery for the related loss of enjoyment damages.

d. Isadora's medical expenses incurred prior to death would be included in the survival claim. These are losses she suffered prior to death as a result of the defendant's negligence. Had she lived, she would have been able to sue for them herself. The estate steps into her shoes for purposes of enforcing this predeath claim.

e. This is a tricky question. Isadora does not have a claim for loss of consortium as a result of her *own* injuries. Consortium claims are claims by family members of an injured person, alleging that the injury has impaired the injured person's ability to interact with those family members. Booth, John, and Lydia may have consortium claims based on the impairment of Isadora's ability to relate to them as a result of her injury, but Isadora will not. Her claim for impairment of her ability to relate to others caused by her injuries is a "loss of enjoyment" claim, which is part of the survival claim for her predeath damages. See Example 2c.

3. a. Neither Isadora's estate nor her survivors would have a claim for future pain and suffering because Isadora, due to her death, will not experience any. Had she lived and sued, she might well have had such a claim since she would have faced the prospect of continued suffering. (As Example 2a indicates, the claim for her predeath pain and suffering would be part of the survival claim in most states.)

   b. Under most wrongful death statutes, the decedent's survivors may recover for pecuniary support they would have received from the decedent. See generally Chapter 18, pp. 401–402. This recovery will not exactly equal Isadora's lost earning capacity; it only includes that part of her future earnings that would have gone to support the survivors. Certainly John would have a substantial claim since he was still at home and dependent on his parents for support. Booth might also recover such damages under the wrongful death statute. Because Isadora was very successful, her income doubtless contributed substantially to the family's lifestyle. The loss of this income is a pecuniary loss to Booth, even if he is still able to support himself in the food-and-shelter sense of the term without it.

   Lydia, however, will have a harder time making out a claim for pecuniary losses due to Isadora's death since she was financially independent. However, if she could prove that Isadora made gifts to her from time to time (as wealthy, tax-conscious parents are known to do), she might claim that she has also suffered pecuniary losses compensable under the wrongful death statute.

   c. If Isadora had lived but been disabled, either temporarily or permanently, she would have had a claim for future loss of enjoyment of life caused by any impairment she sustained as a result of the accident. For example, if she survived the accident but lost an eye, this would interfere with Isadora's enjoyment of life as long as she lived. However, since she died as a result of the accident, there will be no claim for loss of enjoyment of life for any period after her death. Recovery for any damages due to her death is governed by the wrongful death statute, which compensates survivors for their losses due to the decedent's death, not the decedent for hers. While there is surely no greater loss of enjoyment than the loss of life itself, this is a loss to Isadora, not her survivors.

   d. Under many wrongful death statutes, immediate survivors of the decedent are entitled to compensation for consortium-type damages—their loss of the comfort, companionship, advice, society, and counsel of the decedent—for the period after the decedent's death. See, e.g., Kan. Stat. Ann. §60-1904, quoted at Chapter 18, p. 403. Since the West Dakota wrongful death statute authorizes recovery for these emotional damages (the Introduction tells us), Booth and Isadora's children will recover for this loss for the future years they otherwise would have enjoyed their relationship with Isadora.

Act Two

4. For many years, the courts barred claims for injury or death of a fetus, on the theory that no *duty* was owed to an unborn child. Prosser & Keeton §55 at 367. More recently, many states have allowed such claims, but others have held that the term "person" in their wrongful death statutes does not apply to a fetus, and passed the buck to the legislature to change the rule. See, e.g., *Witty v. American Gen. Capital Distrib., Inc.*, 727 S.W.2d 503 (Tex. 1987).[1] Thus, whether there is a claim for the unborn child's death will turn on how the court interprets West Dakota's wrongful death statute.

   If the wrongful death statute allows recovery for causing the death of a fetus, the damages will depend on the terms of the wrongful death statute. Many such statutes authorize damages for both pecuniary and consortium losses to closely related survivors such as parents and siblings. Naturally, assessing the monetary contributions this child would have made to her parents in the future, or the quality of the relationship that would have developed between the child and her family, is a surreal process. Certainly, the losses could be great since the relationship is destroyed from the outset and all monetary contributions the child might have made are lost. If this claim is allowed, it will introduce a very emotional and uncertain element into the trial that will doubtless have great settlement value from the plaintiffs' point of view.

   Are there any other claims you might assert on behalf of the deceased child? The facts indicate that Isadora miscarried a week after the accident, and that during that period the baby suffered fetal distress and cardiac arrhythmia. This suggests that the baby, though in utero, suffered pain and suffering prior to the miscarriage. Advancing medical knowledge suggests that fetuses have a good deal more awareness than previously thought. As plaintiff's counsel in this case, you might draw on this advancing medical knowledge to argue for a new type of claim for "fetal pain and suffering."

   Presumably, such claims would be asserted under a survival statute, as an injury suffered by the child prior to death. It is highly doubtful that

1. See now Tex. Civ. Prac. & Remedies Code §71.001(4), enacted in 2003, which defines an "individual" to include an unborn child for purposes of the Texas wrongful death act.

a state that rejects fetal wrongful death claims would recognize a claim for its predeath pain and suffering, but the argument might be accepted in a jurisdiction that allows fetal wrongful death claims.

Issues like fetal suffering prior to death are grim to contemplate. As plaintiff's counsel, however, it is your job to contemplate them, and to seek compensation for such losses if they may be allowable. It is through such constant probing of the boundaries by creative plaintiff's counsel that tort law grows.

5. a. You would advise Booth that he is entitled to sue for his medical bills, pain and suffering, and lost wages, and for property damage to the car if he owned it. However, you would also advise him that these damages are not likely to be great since he suffered minor injuries. Clearly, the substantial claims available to Booth are for his intangible damages—his emotional distress and loss of consortium claims arising from the serious injuries sustained by Isadora.

   b. Booth's loss of consortium claims will be based on the injuries to other family members that impair their ability to relate to Booth. Booth would certainly have a loss of consortium claim resulting from the injury to Isadora, his wife, since her serious injuries impaired her ability to relate to Booth as she had before. However, this consortium claim will be limited to the four-month period prior to her death. The loss of Isadora's consortium suffered by Booth *as a result of* her death is part of the wrongful death claim discussed earlier. Since the West Dakota wrongful death statute authorizes damages for loss of the relationship with the decedent, Booth will recover loss of consortium damages for this post-death loss. But he will do so under the wrongful death statute, and will have no separate "loss of consortium" claim for the post-death period. If he were allowed to sue for post-death "loss of consortium," and for the same losses under the wrongful death statute, he would recover twice for the same loss.

   Booth has also lost the ability to relate to his unborn child due to the child's death. However, this claim is also a claim for post-death loss of consortium, and will be compensable, if at all, under the wrongful death statute. See Example 4.

   c. Booth will likely have a claim for indirect infliction of emotional distress. He witnessed traumatic, serious injury to Isadora and was himself injured in the same accident. If West Dakota followed the zone-of-danger rule, Booth would recover for indirect infliction of emotional distress since he was within the zone of danger created by Burton's negligence. If the *Dillon* factors applied, he would also recover since he was present and witnessed injury to his wife. Even in a jurisdiction that retains the impact rule, it is likely that Booth could assert this claim. He suffered an impact in the accident, which opens the door to related emotional distress, probably including distress from witnessing injury to Isadora. See p. 14, Example 1a.

6. John suffered no direct impact or physical injury in the accident. However, he did rush to the scene immediately and witness the traumatic impact of the accident on members of his family. Whether he can recover for this depends on West Dakota's law on indirect infliction of emotional distress. Courts following the impact rule would deny recovery. Under the zone-of-danger approach, John's claim would turn on whether John was close enough to the collision to be endangered by it (how about flying debris?). Under the *Dillon* approach, John will state a claim if the court concludes that he "witnessed" injury to close family members by hearing the crash, even though he did not see it. (See Chapter 14, Example 1c for a discussion of this issue.) Some jurisdictions also require resulting physical symptoms in order to recover for indirect infliction. The facts indicate that John became withdrawn and his grades went down. Although it would be hard to characterize these as physical symptoms, some courts might find such dubious "physical injuries" sufficient. See Chapter 14, Example 4f.

   John may also have a claim for loss of consortium with Isadora for the four-month period prior to her death. Clearly her injuries impaired her ability to relate to John. Many jurisdictions do not allow children to sue for loss of consortium with their parents, but some do. The result will turn on how West Dakota decides this issue. However, John's claim for loss of the relationship with Isadora for the period after her death is compensable, if at all, under the wrongful death claim.

   Last, John, as an eligible beneficiary under the wrongful death statute, will be entitled to recover pecuniary losses he has suffered due to Isadora's death. These losses could be substantial, including the cost of his present support and a future college education. They are separate from his consortium losses and must be based on separate proof of Isadora's expected financial support of John.

7. Lydia suffered no physical injuries, but apparently did experience a great deal of emotional distress. However, it is highly doubtful that she can recover on an indirect infliction claim. Most jurisdictions limit indirect infliction claims to those who are in the zone of danger or witness the accident or its immediate aftermath.

   Lydia might seek recovery for loss of consortium. Like John's claim, the result will depend on whether West Dakota allows children to recover for loss of consortium due to injury to their parents. If such claims are recognized in West Dakota, Lydia's recovery on this claim will be limited to the four months during which Isadora survived. Her claims for loss of consortium with Isadora for the period after her death, like John's, will be governed by the wrongful death statute. Even states that deny loss of consortium claims for an *injured* parent may allow the children to recover for consortium losses under their wrongful death statutes if the parent is killed.

Even if the wrongful death statute allows damages for consortium losses, the court will probably not allow the jury to award consortium losses for such extended consequences as Lydia's missed promotion. Loss of consortium is meant to compensate for the interference with the relationship with the directly injured party, not for collateral economic consequences of that interference. The defense would doubtless argue that such attenuated consequences were not "proximately caused" by Burton's negligence.

Supporting Actors

8. Garrick has suffered serious injury due to the negligence of Burton, but it is very unlikely that he will recover damages from Burton's estate. Certainly, Garrick has no indirect infliction claim since he is not related to Isadora, did not witness traumatic injury to anyone, suffered no impact, and was not in the zone of danger. Nor does he have a loss of consortium claim: Such claims are limited to family members, not operatic partners.

   But doesn't he have a just plain "negligence" claim? Burton had a duty to drive carefully, he didn't, and his negligence caused injury to Isadora and consequent damages to Garrick. This is true, but most courts would hold that Burton's *duty* to drive with due care was owed to other drivers, perhaps to family members, but not to others who suffer secondary emotional or economic losses as a result of the accident. Other courts might reach the same result by holding that Burton's negligence was not the "legal cause" or "proximate cause" of the consequential injuries suffered by Garrick. Even if Garrick's injuries are foreseeable, the court must draw the line on secondary damages at some point, as a matter of policy. See generally Chapter 12, pp. 244–246. Whether on duty or proximate cause grounds, virtually all courts would reject Garrick's claim.

Putting the Show on the Road

9. The complaint below is an example of the type of complaint that might be filed in the *Dunton* case. In reading the complaint, consider how the various claims for relief have been drafted to allege the elements necessary to support the claims. After the complaint are some notes on the reasoning underlying it.

STATE OF WEST DAKOTA

SUPERIOR COURT CHEYENNE COUNTY	CIVIL ACTION NO. 25-1341
BOOTH GARFIELD, Individually and as the Administrator of the estates of ISADORA GARFIELD and BABY DUNTON, JOHN GARFIELD and LYDIA GARFIELD PLAINTIFFS v. ELIZABETH BURTON, executrix of the estate of ROBERT BURTON, DEFENDANT	COMPLAINT AND DEMAND FOR JURY TRIAL

PARTIES

1. Isadora Garfield is an individual, formerly residing at 43 Keane Drive, Elkton, West Dakota, who died on July 1, 2024 of injuries suffered in the motor vehicle accident which is the subject of this action.

2. Baby Garfield is the child of Isadora and Booth Dunton, who died on March 8, 2024 of injuries suffered in the motor vehicle accident which is the subject of this action.

3. The plaintiff Booth Garfield is an individual residing at 43 Keane Drive, Elkton, West Dakota. He is the widower and duly appointed administrator of the estates of Isadora Garfield and Baby Garfield.

4. The plaintiff John Garfield is the minor son of Isadora and Booth Garfield. He resides at 43 Keane Drive, Elkton, West Dakota.

5. The plaintiff Lydia Garfield is the daughter of Isadora and Booth Dunton. She resides at 1138 Lankton Boulevard, Elkton, West Dakota.

6. The decedent Robert J. Burton is an individual, formerly residing at 12 Lake Street, Burns, West Dakota, who died on February 15, 2025.

7. The defendant Elizabeth Burton is the daughter and duly appointed personal representative of the estate of Robert J. Burton.

FACTS

8.On March 1, 2024, the decedents Isadora Garfield and Baby Garfield were passengers in a 2015 Volvo station wagon, driven by the plaintiff, Booth Garfield.

9.At approximately 11:05 a.m.,Booth Garfield started the car in the family driveway at 43 Keane Drive, Elkton, West Dakota, and began to back out of the driveway onto Keane Drive, in order to proceed in an easterly direction on Keane Drive.

10. As the car backed into Keane Drive, a Ford Taurus, driven by the decedent Robert J. Burton, came around the corner, traveling east at an excessive speed and without keeping a proper lookout, in violation of West Dakota St. Ann. Tit. 32, §§90 and 93.

11. As a result of his negligent driving, the decedent Robert J. Burton was unable to stop his vehicle or avoid colliding with the plaintiffs' vehicle backing out of the driveway at 43 Keane Drive.

12. As a direct and proximate result of the negligence of the decedent, Robert J. Burton, his vehicle collided violently with the Garfield vehicle, demolishing the Garfield vehicle and causing serious personal injuries to Isadora Garfield, Booth Garfield, and Baby Garfield.

13. As a direct and proximate result of the accident, the decedent Isadora Garfield suffered multiple internal traumas and extensive damage to her left eye, causing permanent blindness. She was taken to Elkton General Hospital, where she remained in the intensive care unit until her death on July 1, 2024 from injuries suffered in the accident.

14. As a direct and proximate result of the accident, the decedent Baby Garfield suffered traumatic injuries, resulting in fetal distress and cardiac arrhythmia. On March 8, 2024. Isadora Garfield miscarried, causing the death of Baby Garfield.

15. As a direct and proximate result of the accident, Booth Garfield suffered multiple lacerations requiring medical treatment, experienced pain and suffering, extreme emotional distress and temporary disability, and lost wages in excess of $2,000.

16. At the time of the accident, the plaintiff John Garfield was standing in the driveway at 43 Keane Drive, in the immediate vicinity of the collision. He witnessed the accident, rushed to aid the injured members of his family and observed his mother and father covered in blood and suffering from extreme shock and pain.

17. As a result of the accident and the injuries suffered by her parents, the plaintiff Lydia Garfield has suffered serious emotional distress, inability to sleep, difficulties at work, and other damages.

18. At all times relevant to the events in this action, the plaintiffs and their decedents were in the exercise of due care.

FIRST CLAIM FOR RELIEF:
WRONGFUL DEATH OF ISADORA GARFIELD

19. The plaintiff repeats and realleges the allegations in paragraphs 1 to 18 of the complaint.

20. As a result of the collision proximately caused by the decedent Robert Burton's negligence, Isadora Garfield suffered extensive personal injuries which led to her death on July 1, 2024, at the age of forty-three.

21. As a result of the death of Isadora Garfield negligently caused by the decedent Robert Garfield, her husband Booth Garfield and her children John and Lydia Garfield have been deprived of both the financial support and the comfort, companionship, advice, society, and counsel they would have received from Isadora Garfield had she lived.

Wherefore, the plaintiff Booth Garfield, in his capacity as administrator of the estate of Isadora Garfield, seeks damages under the West Dakota Wrongful Death Statute, West Dakota St. Ann. Tit. 12 §143, on behalf of Booth Garfield, John Garfield, and Lydia Garfield, for the loss of financial support, comfort, companionship, advice, society, and counsel of the decedent Isadora Garfield, and for funeral and burial expenses, together with interest and costs of suit.

SECOND CLAIM FOR RELIEF:
SURVIVAL CLAIM FOR PREDEATH DAMAGES OF ISADORA GARFIELD

22. The plaintiff repeats and realleges the allegations in paragraphs 1 to 18 of the complaint.

23. As a result of the collision proximately caused by the decedent Robert Burton's negligence, Isadora Garfield suffered extensive personal injuries, emotional distress, pain and suffering for a period of four months prior to her death, suffered loss of the normal pleasures and enjoyment of life over the four month period, lost substantial earnings from her work as a soloist with the West Dakota Civic Opera, and incurred great medical and other expenses for her care, all of which she would have been entitled to recover in an action against the defendant had she survived.

Wherefore, the plaintiff Booth Garfield, in his capacity as administrator of the estate of Isadora Garfield, seeks damages under the West Dakota survival statute, St. Ann. Tit. 12 §147, on behalf of the estate of Isadora Garfield, for her lost earnings, medical expenses, pain and suffering, and loss of enjoyment of life from March 1, 2024 until her death on July 1, 2024, together with interest and costs of suit.

THIRD CLAIM FOR RELIEF:
WRONGFUL DEATH OF BABY GARFIELD

24. The plaintiff repeats and realleges the allegations in paragraphs 1 to 18 of the complaint.

25. At the time of the accident, the decedent Isadora Garfield was pregnant with a baby girl, the decedent Baby Garfield,

26. As a result of the collision proximately caused by the decedent Robert Burton's negligence, Isadora Garfield suffered extensive personal injuries which led to the death and miscarriage of her child, Baby Garfield, on March 8, 2024.

27. As a result of the death of Baby Garfield negligently caused by the decedent Robert Burton, the plaintiffs Booth Garfield, Lydia Garfield and John Garfield have been deprived of both the financial support and the comfort, companionship, advice, society, and counsel they would have received from Baby Garfield had she lived.

Wherefore, the plaintiff Booth Garfield, in his capacity as administrator of the estate of Baby Garfield, claims damages under the West Dakota Wrongful Death Statute, West Dakota St. Ann. Tit. 12 §143, on behalf of Booth Garfield, for the loss of financial support, comfort, companionship, advice, society, and counsel of the decedent Baby Garfield, as well as for funeral and burial expenses, together with interest and costs of suit.

FOURTH CLAIM FOR RELIEF:
SURVIVAL CLAIM FOR PREDEATH DAMAGES OF BABY GARFIELD

28. The plaintiff repeats and realleges the allegations in paragraphs 1 to 18 of the complaint.

29. As a result of the collision proximately caused by the decedent Robert Burton's negligence, Isadora Garfield suffered extensive personal injuries which caused the child Baby Garfield to suffer cardiac arrhythmia and extreme fetal distress from the date of the accident until her death, injuries for which she could have recovered herself had she lived.

Wherefore, the plaintiff Booth Garfield, in his capacity as administrator of the estate of Baby Garfield, claims damages under the West Dakota survival statute, St. Ann. Tit. 12 §147, on behalf of the estate of Baby Garfield, for the pain and suffering she experienced from March 1, 2024 until her death on March 8, 2024. together with interest and costs of suit.

FIFTH CLAIM FOR RELIEF:
BOOTH GARFIELD'S CLAIM FOR PERSONAL INJURIES

30. The plaintiff repeats and realleges the allegations in paragraphs 1 to 18 of the complaint.

31. As a result of the collision proximately caused by the decedent Robert Burton's negligence, Booth Garfield suffered facial lacerations, incurred lost wages and medical bills, experienced pain, and suffering, and was temporarily disabled.

Wherefore, the plaintiff Booth Garfield, suing in his individual capacity, seeks damages from the defendant for pain and suffering, medical expenses, lost wages, and loss of the enjoyment of life suffered as a result of his injuries, together with interest and costs of suit.

SIXTH CLAIM FOR RELIEF:
BOOTH GARFIELD'S CLAIM FOR LOSS OF CONSORTIUM
WITH ISADORA GARFIELD

32. The plaintiff repeats and realleges the allegations in paragraphs 1 to 18 of the complaint.

33. As a result of the collision proximately caused by the decedent Robert Burton's negligence, Isadora Garfield suffered extensive personal injuries which led to her death on July 1, 2024.

34. As a result of the serious personal injuries suffered by Isadora Dunton, the plaintiff Booth Garfield suffered the loss of his wife's comfort, companionship, advice, society, and counsel from the date of the accident until her death on July 1, 2024.

Wherefore, the plaintiff Booth Garfield claims damages from the defendant for loss of consortium with his wife, Isadora Garfield.

SEVENTH CLAIM FOR RELIEF:
JOHN AND LYDIA GARFIELD'S CLAIMS FOR
LOSS OF CONSORTIUM WITH ISADORA GARFIELD

35. The plaintiffs repeat and reallege the allegations in paragraphs 1 to 18 of the complaint.

36. As a result of the collision proximately caused by the decedent's negligence, Isadora Garfield suffered extensive personal injuries which led to her death on July 1, 2024.

37. As a result of the serious personal injuries suffered by Isadora Garfield, her children Lydia Garfield and John Garfield suffered the loss of their mother's comfort, companionship, advice, society, and counsel from the date of the accident until her death on July 1, 2014.

Wherefore, the plaintiffs Lydia and John Garfield claim damages from the defendant for loss of consortium with their mother, Isadora Garfield.

EIGHTH CLAIM FOR RELIEF:
BOOTH GARFIELD'S CLAIM FOR
NEGLIGENT INFLICTION OF EMOTIONAL DISTRESS

38. The plaintiff repeats and realleges the allegations in paragraphs 1 to 18 of the complaint.

39. As a result of the collision proximately caused by the decedent's negligence, Isadora Garfield suffered extensive personal injuries which led to her death on July 1, 2024. Booth Garfield was also present and sustained personal injuries in the accident.

40. Immediately after the collision, Booth observed his wife in extreme pain, shock and distress from the injuries suffered in the accident.

41. As a result of the terrifying experience of observing the accident and its aftermath, Booth Garfield suffered immediate emotional trauma and permanent psychic damage, as well as direct physical injury.

Wherefore, the plaintiff Booth Garfield claims damages from the defendant for negligent infliction of emotional distress.

NINTH CLAIM FOR RELIEF:
JOHN GARFIELD'S CLAIMS FOR
NEGLIGENT INFLICTION OF EMOTIONAL DISTRESS

42. The plaintiff repeats and realleges the allegations in paragraphs 1 to 18 of the complaint.

43. As a result of the collision proximately caused by the decedent's negligence, Isadora Garfield suffered extensive personal injuries which led to her death on July 1, 2024.

44. At the time of the accident, John Garfield was standing in the immediate vicinity of the collision, and immediately became aware that his parents had been involved in a serious accident.

45. Immediately after the collision, John Garfield rushed to the scene and observed his mother and father in extreme pain, shock and distress from the injuries suffered in the accident.

46. As a result of the terrifying experience of observing the accident and its aftermath, John Garfield suffered both immediate emotional trauma and long term psychological damage. Since the accident, he has become withdrawn and uncommunicative, has received low grades, lost touch with his friends, and shows other signs of post traumatic stress syndrome.

Wherefore, the plaintiff John Garfield claims damages from the defendant for negligent infliction of emotional distress.

TENTH CLAIM FOR RELIEF:
BOOTH GARFIELD'S CLAIM FOR PROPERTY DAMAGE

47. The plaintiff repeats and realleges the allegations in paragraphs 1 to 18 of the complaint.

48. As a result of the collision proximately caused by the negligence of the decedent, Robert J. Burton, the 2015 Volvo station wagon in which the Garfield family was riding was damaged beyond repair.

Wherefore, the plaintiff Booth Garfield, as owner of the vehicle, claims damages from the defendant for its fair market value, together with the costs of substitute transportation incurred as a result of the collision.

The plaintiffs claim trial by jury on all issues in this action.

Allison Barrymore
Attorney for Plaintiffs
132 Hayes Boulevard
Elkton, West Dakota 11111
(419) 832-1239

Comments on the Garfield Complaint

Barrymore, the Garfields' counsel, has put a lot of thought into drafting this complaint based on the facts of the Garfield accident. Doubtless, there are problems with some of the claims, either because it is not clear that they are legally sufficient, or because of difficulties of proof. Barrymore's job at this stage is to determine which claims may be legally and factually supportable, not to determine which will actually prevail at trial.

The comments below reflect some of the analysis which went into drafting this negligence complaint.

1. Barrymore has broken down the various claims both by parties and by the particular types of claims. As the Introduction suggests, she has taken these miscellaneous facts and reconceptualized them in terms of legally recognized claims for tort damages. For example, the First Claim for Relief seeks damages for wrongful death of Isadora, and the Second for the predeath damages to Isadora. Even though these claims are both based on injuries to the same person and are both asserted by the same plaintiff, it facilitates an understanding of the claims to set them forth separately because negligence law analyzes the claims differently.

2. Barrymore has included some claims in the complaint even though it is unclear whether they are legally sufficient. For example, the Second Claim for Relief seeks damages for Isadora's loss of enjoyment of life for the period from the accident until her death. It may be unclear under West Dakota law whether such damages can be recovered in the survival action. As long as the estate *may* be entitled to such damages, the estate may properly assert them; nothing requires them to confine their claims to those which are absolutely certain to be recognized as legally valid. See Fed. R. Civ. P. 11(b)(2) (authorizing assertion of claims which are supported by existing law or a nonfrivolous argument for extension or changes in existing law).

   Similarly, the Seventh Claim for Relief alleges loss of consortium claims on behalf of John and Lydia, though it is unclear whether West Dakota law will recognize claims for loss of parental consortium. Barrymore has also included the frontier theory of a survival claim on behalf of Baby Garfield, though this one is a very long shot indeed. If such claims were clearly not viable, it would be improper to assert them, but where there may be a right to recover on these claims, Barrymore is entitled to present them and let the court decide whether they are legally cognizable.

   Although Barrymore may have given considerable thought and research to these various unresolved issues, the complaint holds no hint of the doubts she may entertain about the strength of these claims. Defendant's counsel will have to assess their viability and challenge those which she concludes are legally unsound.

3. Other parts of the complaint reveal how the Garfields' counsel crafted the allegations to reflect the substantive requirements of each theory of relief. For example, the Ninth Claim for Relief, seeking recovery for negligent infliction of emotional distress upon John, alleges that John immediately arrived on the accident scene and viewed his injured relatives in a sorry state. Paragraph 45. Barrymore may anticipate that West Dakota will adopt the *Dillon* approach to indirect infliction claims, which focuses on the immediacy of the event, the nearness of the bystander to the accident, and the closeness of the relationship of the bystander to the injured victims.

   The allegations in Paragraph 44 lay the groundwork for an indirect infliction claim under the zone-of-danger rule as well. Barrymore has alleged that John was in the "immediate vicinity" of the accident. It is not entirely clear that he *was* in the zone of danger: The facts indicate that he was 25 feet from the collision. But it is not clear that this is too far away either, so the allegation leaves the door open to litigate the issue. Similarly, she has alleged symptoms that John suffered as a result of his emotional distress which might suffice to establish "resulting physical injuries" if West Dakota law turns out to require this.

   Similarly, in Booth's count for negligent infliction of emotional distress, Barrymore realleges that Booth was a direct victim of the accident. See para. 39. Should West Dakota stick with the requirement of impact to support an emotional distress claim, this allegation will lay the groundwork for an argument that he can sue for *indirect* infliction because he suffered an impact. See Chapter 14, Example la.

   Barrymore's complaint does not specifically allege that any one of these standards for recovery applies. It is not necessary to allege the exact legal standard in the complaint, but it is important to allege facts that demonstrate that the legal standard—whichever one the court ultimately applies—can be met.

4. Barrymore has given thought to other problems of proof as well. For example, she has alleged that Burton's driving violated several West Dakota statutes. Presumably, she has included these allegations to lay the groundwork for an instruction to the jury that Burton was "negligent per se" for violating these statutes. See Chapter 8.

5. The damage allegations in the various claims also reflect Barrymore's analysis of the substantive law. For example, the wrongful death claims seek damages for the financial support and consortium losses of the survivors, presumably echoing the language of the West Dakota wrongful

death statute. See the "wherefore" clauses in the First and Third Claims for Relief. (Note that recovery is sought in the First Claim for Relief on behalf of Booth, John, and Lydia, for wrongful death of Isadora. But recovery is only sought on behalf of Booth in the Third Claim for Relief for wrongful death of Baby Garfield. This presumably reflects the fact that parents and children, but not siblings, are in the "first tier" of beneficiaries under the West Dakota wrongful death statute.) The survival claims, by contrast, seek damages for losses suffered prior to death. Note also that Barrymore has been careful to assert the various claims on behalf of the proper plaintiffs. The survival and wrongful death claims are asserted by Booth as administrator of the estates of Isadora and Baby Garfield, while the other claims are asserted on behalf of the individuals named in each claim.

6. Naturally, the questionable claims in Barrymore's complaint will not go unnoticed. Burton's counsel will likely challenge the legal sufficiency of some claims, such as the claim for prenatal pain and suffering and John and Lydia's claims for loss of parental consortium.

   She will also probe, through discovery, the plaintiffs' ability to prove their allegations. For example, damages for the wrongful death of Baby Garfield will be very difficult to establish, not to mention the creative claim for her pain and suffering prior to death. Indeed, proof problems led the Garfields' counsel to omit one claim entirely, Isadora's claim for indirect infliction of emotional distress for witnessing injury to Booth. Without her testimony it would be very difficult to establish this claim.

   Burton's counsel will also challenge the plaintiffs' ability to prove causation on some claims. Even if John is entitled to recover for infliction of emotional distress, for example, he will have to establish that his withdrawal and poor performance in school were caused by witnessing the injury to Isadora rather than other causes, such as the usual catatonia of the teenage years.

7. A colleague with a wealth of litigation experience suggests that a very practical consideration would figure heavily in this case: Because of Isadora's success, and the wrongful death claims, the potential damages in this case are great, probably much greater than Burton's estate, even with insurance, will be able to pay. This has several implications. First, it may make sense to leave out some lesser or dubious claims in order to focus the jury on the big ticket issues in the case since the entire judgment will not likely be paid anyway. Second, since the judgment is not likely to be fully paid, conflicts may arise among the various plaintiffs concerning the allocation of any payments received. Counsel will have to be very careful to make sure that all plaintiffs are aware of this problem

from the outset of the case and to consider the possibility that conflicts among the plaintiffs might call for separate representation.

A third implication is that counsel will surely want to look for other potential defendants, to tap their resources as well. If, for example, poor road design contributed to the accident, counsel should consider a claim against the city or town that maintains the road. Or, if brake problems contributed, a claim against the repair shop or manufacturer could also increase the potential recovery.

8. Just to make litigation life more difficult, let's consider one more twist in the Garfield case. Is it possible that negligence by Booth Garfield was partially responsible for the accident? If Booth may have been negligent in pulling out into the street, Barrymore would have a conflict of interest in representing him as a plaintiff along with the other family members. Barrymore would have to have another party appointed as the personal representative of the estates of Isabella and Baby Garfield, consider whether to add Booth as a defendant in the action, and advise Booth that he must look elsewhere for legal representation. If Barrymore had already had significant discussions about the case which included Booth, she would likely have to withdraw from the case entirely. This could introduce a dramatic legal complexity into the litigation and an emotional trauma for members of the family as well.

PART VII

Liability of Multiple Defendants

CHAPTER 20

Joint and Several Liability: The Classic Rules

INTRODUCTION

We saw in the chapters on causation that a plaintiff will frequently have claims against more than one tortfeasor, where several have contributed to causing her injury. This chapter, and the next, address the manner in which tort law distributes the damages in such cases. This chapter deals with the traditional common law rules governing the liability of "joint tortfeasors." The next analyzes principles of contribution, the right of a tortfeasor who has paid the plaintiff's claim to seek partial reimbursement from other defendants liable for the same injury.

JOINT TORTFEASORS DISTINGUISHED FROM JOINT CONDUCT

First, let's distinguish the case of "true" joint tortfeasors from the much more common type of joint and several liability discussed in this chapter. True joint tortfeasors are parties who agree to engage in a course of tortious conduct. Suppose that Kelvin and Curie go looking for Marconi, planning to beat him up. They find him, and Curie breaks his jaw. Because Kelvin and Curie acted in concert to injure Marconi, both are liable to him, even though it was Curie who administered the blow. Although Kelvin didn't hit

Marconi, he encouraged and participated in the common scheme to injure Marconi. Tort law traditionally held—and still holds—actors involved in such joint conduct liable for the acts of either, in much the same way that conspirators are criminally responsible for the acts of other conspirators. See Restatement (Third) of Torts: Apportionment of Liability §15. Similarly, if Ford and Hudson decide to race their cars on the highway, they are both liable if one of their cars hits Lenoir since they jointly engaged in the negligent conduct that led to Lenoir's injury.

Such "true" joint tortfeasor cases, in which parties agree to engage in tortious conduct, are relatively rare. It is much more common for the independent conduct of two actors to combine to injure the plaintiff. Suppose, for example, that Fermi was a passenger in Joule's car, which collided with a truck driven by Edison due to negligence by both drivers, and that Fermi suffered a broken collar bone. Here, Edison and Joule did not act together, probably did not know each other, may not even have known of the other's presence. However, their independent acts have contributed to cause a single injury. As we saw in the discussion of causation, the negligence of each is a "but for" cause of the harm, even though they did not act together.

The traditional common law rule was—and still is in a good many states today—that each tortfeasor in a case like Fermi's is liable to the plaintiff for her full damages since his negligence was a "but for" cause of the plaintiff's injury. Courts generally refer to the defendants in such cases as "joint tortfeasors." This is clearly loose language, though universally used. Fermi and Edison did not do anything "jointly," in the sense that Kelvin and Curie did in the battery example, since they acted separately, without agreement. It is the resulting *injury* that is joint, not the actions of the defendants. The phrase "joint tortfeasors" simply means that the defendants both contributed to a single, indivisible injury to the plaintiff and are each fully liable for that injury.

Here is another example to drive home the point. Watt, a worker on a construction site, negligently leaves an excavation unguarded, and Planck, an oblivious jogger, bumps Curie and knocks her into it, breaking her leg. Here again, Curie would have negligence claims against both Watt and Planck for her injuries since the negligence of each defendant contributed to causing the harm. Watt and Planck are, in the common parlance, joint tortfeasors, each fully liable for Curie's injury.

It is often said that the defendants in cases like the Fermi and Curie examples are "jointly and severally liable" for the injury. This means that each is liable for the full amount of the plaintiff's damages, and may be sued for those damages either singly or along with the other tortfeasors. If the plaintiff prevails in an action against joint tortfeasors, she is (under the classic rules of joint and several liability) entitled to a judgment against each for her full damages. For example, if the jury found both Joule and Edison liable for Fermi's injury, and found Fermi's damages to be $27,000, the court would enter judgment against both Joule and Edison for $27,000. Fermi would obtain a judgment like that in Figure 20-1, on p. 448. Alternatively, had she sued Fermi alone she would have gotten a judgment against him for the full $27,000.

Joint and several liability did not apply, however, if the defendants caused separate damages. Suppose that Farmer Jones and Farmer Smith both decided to burn the stubble off their fields on a windy day, and both fires got away. If Farmer Jones's fire burned two acres on the west side of Doe's property, and Farmer Smith's burned five acres on the east side, it stands to reason that Jones would pay for the two-acre fire but not for the five-acre fire caused by Smith. Jones's negligence caused the two-acre fire, but (assuming that Jones and Smith acted independently) was not a "but for" cause of the five-acre fire, so Jones was not liable for it. The same was true for Smith, who was liable for the five-acre fire but not the two-acre blaze. In such cases, where the damages could rationally be apportioned separately to the tortfeasors, the courts would do so. Restatement (Second) of Torts §881.

SATISFACTION OF JUDGMENTS

Under the judgment in Figure 20-1 (p. 448), Fermi would be entitled to collect his $27,000 from either Edison or Joule. Of course, he could not get $27,000 from each of them, for a total of $54,000. The plaintiff was entitled to one full "satisfaction" of his damages from joint tortfeasors, but no more. Thus, if Joule paid Fermi $27,000, the judgment was deemed satisfied, and Fermi could not collect any additional amount from Edison. Similarly, if he obtained a judgment against Edison and Edison paid, Fermi could not collect from Joule for the same injuries. Dobbs' Law of Torts §488.

Suppose, however, that Fermi sued Edison alone and obtained a judgment for $27,000, but Edison was unable to satisfy the judgment. Early cases held that once Fermi obtained a judgment against one tortfeasor, the judgment extinguished his claim against all the tortfeasors, so that he could not sue Joule separately if Edison failed to pay. The theory was that the plaintiff had a single, indivisible claim, which could only be sued upon once. Dobbs' Law of Torts §491. However, courts later came around to the position that, as long as Fermi's judgment had not been *satisfied*, he was entitled to sue Joule for the same injury, and try to collect from him instead. Or, if Edison had a $10,000 insurance policy, and paid that much, Fermi could seek a separate judgment against Joule and collect the remaining $17,000 from him.

Suppose that Joule was a close friend of Fermi's (or his boss) and Fermi, understandably reluctant to sue Joule, sued Edison only. At common law if a joint tortfeasor like Edison were found liable and paid the judgment, he had no right to force other tortfeasors to "contribute" to the judgment. Edison was liable for the damages, was justly made to pay them, and had no complaint if Joule got off without paying. The courts refused to adjust the loss as between the wrongdoers, just as it refused (under the doctrine of contributory negligence) to adjust a loss between a negligent plaintiff and a negligent defendant. This classic no-contribution rule is no longer the law in most states, but it was for many years. See Chapter 21, which analyzes the basic principles of contribution among joint tortfeasors, and Chapter 25, which illustrates some of the current variations.

STATE OF WEST DAKOTA

COOK COUNTY, SS;	CIVIL ACTION NO. 24-1305
ENRICO FERMI, Plaintiff	
v.	JUDGMENT
MAX JOULE THOMAS EDISON, Defendants	

This action came on for trial before the Court and a jury, Honorable Constance Pallotta, presiding. The issues having been duly tried and the jury having rendered its verdict, it is Ordered and Adjudged

That the plaintiff Enrico Fermi recover from the defendants Thomas Edison and Max Joule the sum of $27,000 with interest thereon at the rate of 7% as provided by law, and his costs of action.

Dated at Cody, West Dakota, this 25th day of May, 2025.

Justice — Clerk of Court

Figure 20-1

SETTLEMENT AND RELEASE OF CLAIMS

Other issues arose if Fermi settled his claim against one tortfeasor and then sued the other. Suppose, for example, that Fermi settled with Joule, agreeing to release his tort claim against Joule for $13,000. When the plaintiff settled with a tortfeasor, he would ordinarily give that defendant a "release" in exchange for payment of the settlement amount. The release would waive all of the plaintiff's claims against that defendant arising out of a particular accident or dispute. Figure 20-2 is a simple example of a release.

A Practical Question

1. If Joule, as a joint tortfeasor, is fully liable for the entire injury to Fermi, and the likely damages are close to $30,000, why would Fermi let him off the hook for $13,000? (Explanations begin on p. 455.)

RELEASE AND SETTLEMENT OF CLAIM

In consideration of thirteen thousand dollars ($13,000), receipt of which is hereby acknowledged, I, Enrico Fermi, of Saginaw, West Dakota, on behalf of myself and my heirs, legal representatives and assigns, hereby release Max Joule of Johnstown, West Dakota, or his heirs or representatives, from all liability, claims, demands, rights or causes of action incident to property damage and personal injury sustained by me in an automobile accident that occurred on May 4, 2024 at Johnstown, West Dakota, involving an automobile driven by Max Joule. This release covers all claims which I had, now have or may have in the future against Max Joule, his heirs or representatives arising out of the May 4, 2024 accident.

By executing this instrument, I do not waive any claim or claims that I may now or hereafter have against any person, firm or corporation other than Max Joule, the releasee named herein. I understand that Max Joule does not, by making the payment set forth above, admit any liability or responsibility for the above-described accident or the consequences thereof.

In witness whereof, I have executed this release at Saginaw, West Dakota, on July 29, 2025.

Signature Enrico Fermi

Figure 20-2

At common law, giving one tortfeasor a release was a tricky business because the early cases held that a release to one tortfeasor released the plaintiff's claims against *all* joint tortfeasors. If Fermi gave a release to Joule, he was deemed to have released Edison, Watt, and any other possible defendants as well, regardless of the amount Joule paid for the release. Historically, there were several reasons for the rule. First, the plaintiff was considered to have a single cause of action for her injuries, even though each defendant was fully liable on that cause of action. *Cooper v. Robert Hall Clothes, Inc.*, 390 N.E.2d 155, 157 (Ind. 1979); Dobbs' Law of Torts, §491. By giving a release to any tortfeasor, Fermi relinquished the cause of action itself. Thus, he was barred from bringing a subsequent suit on that cause of action against another tortfeasor.

A second, less formalistic rationale for the common law rule that a release barred suit against other tortfeasors was the concern that the plaintiff would settle successively with each tortfeasor and collect more than the value of her claim. Since each tortfeasor was liable for the full amount of the plaintiff's damages, a plaintiff could divide and conquer by extracting substantial settlements from each. Fermi, for example, might settle with Joule for $18,000 and with Edison for $18,000. Both might have the incentive to accept the settlement since it is $9,000 less than the (assumed) $27,000 value of the claim. If they both settled, Fermi would be overcompensated by $9,000 ($36,000 − $27,000). The rule that a release barred suit against the other tortfeasors prevented this: Once Fermi gave a release to Joule, Edison would have no incentive to settle since the release barred suit against Edison as well as Joule.

The release rule applied even if the plaintiff tried to limit the release to the settling tortfeasor. Thus, the second paragraph of Fermi's release in Figure 20-2, which states that it does not affect his claims against any other joint tortfeasor, was given no effect. Under the common law view, Fermi was trying to have his cake and eat it too, that is, to continue to prosecute a cause of action that had been surrendered by the release.

Another Practical Question

2. Did the common law release rule encourage or discourage settlements?

This early rule that a release of one tortfeasor released them all was later abandoned, for several reasons. First, the formalistic view that the claims against Joule and Edison constitute a single, indivisible cause of action is no longer accepted. In recent decades, courts have recognized that, even if Fermi's *damages* are indivisible, he has independent claims for those damages against each tortfeasor. Consequently, it is no longer logical to infer that he abandons claims against one tortfeasor by settling with another.

Second, the release rule prevented settlements with individual tortfeasors who were willing to pay a part of the plaintiff's damages, but not to pay enough to induce the plaintiff to release her entire claim. This led to creative efforts by lawyers to find a way of settling with one tortfeasor without relinquishing the right to sue others. The most common device for evading the common law release rule was the "covenant not to sue," by which the plaintiff covenanted (agreed) not to sue the defendant on the claim. In theory, she had not surrendered her claim, but merely promised that she would not bring a lawsuit to enforce it against the settling defendant; for example, a covenant not to sue might provide that the plaintiff

> "covenants with Max Joule, of Saginaw, West Dakota, his heirs, legal representatives and assigns, to never institute any suit or action at law or in equity against Max Joule by reason of any claim I now have or may hereafter acquire relating to an accident that occurred on May 4, 2024, at Johnstown, West Dakota. . . ."

This was fighting formalism with formalism. The actual effect of the covenant not to sue was the same as the release: Plaintiff gave up her claim against the defendant in exchange for a money payment. But, since it did not technically "release" the claim, plaintiffs argued that they were still entitled to sue other joint tortfeasors on the claim.

Because the release rule was an obstacle to sensible settlement of tort claims, some courts sanctioned its evasion through the covenant not to sue. In these states, the common law rule that a release barred any further suit against other tortfeasors became a dead letter. Counsel simply styled the settlement agreement as a covenant not to sue instead of a release, thus achieving settlement with one tortfeasor without waiving the right to sue others. Defendants went along with the practice because they also benefited from such settlements: They could settle legitimate claims without having to pay more than their fair share of the plaintiff's damages. Thus a kernel of common sense was rescued from a shell of outdated legal doctrine.

Other courts, rather than endorsing evasion of the release rule through the covenant not to sue, have overruled it outright. In these jurisdictions, a release or covenant not to sue given to one tortfeasor does not release other parties, unless the release so stipulates. See Restatement (Third) of Torts: Apportionment of Liability §24(b). Under this approach, the release in Figure 20-2 would preserve Fermi's right to sue Edison since it not only shows no intent to release Edison, but affirmatively states that it does not.

Through one of these avenues, most states have arrived at the same basic approach to settlements: The plaintiff may settle with one tortfeasor, and go to trial against others. Under the traditional joint and several liability rules, any judgment she obtained against the remaining defendants would be reduced, dollar for dollar, by the amount paid to her by the settling tortfeasor.

These joint and several liability rules have been changed in many states over the past 40 years or so. Some states now apply "several liability," under which individual tortfeasors pay only a part of the plaintiff's damages. Others apply joint and several liability in some circumstances, but several liability in others. These variations are explored in Chapter 25. However, no matter where you practice, it is important to understand the traditional joint and several liability rules. First, these rules continue to apply to all cases in some states, and to some cases in most states. Second, you have to understand the basic doctrines to grasp the elegant variations state legislatures have recently grafted onto them.

Examples

Sue and Sue Alike

3. Bell is driving home late at night when her car dies. She pulls into the breakdown lane, but fails to put on her hazard lights or put out flares. Marconi negligently fails to see her, drifts into the breakdown lane, and hits Bell's car, injuring Thatcher, a passenger in Bell's car. Thatcher sues Marconi for damages. If the jury concludes that Bell and Marconi were both negligent, and assesses Thatcher's damages at $60,000, what verdict should it render against Marconi, assuming it has been properly instructed on the principles of joint and several liability (and understood them!)?

4. Suppose that Thatcher had sued both Bell and Marconi, the jury found both negligent, and assessed the damages at $60,000.
   a. What verdict should the jury render?
   b. How much could she collect from each defendant?

5. Whiting and Hahn, two employees of an electrical contractor, are working together to install wiring in Pringle's house. They agree that Whiting will stop in the basement to cut off the power to an exposed junction box on the wall, but Whiting forgets to do it. An hour later, Shattuck, a plasterer, negligently swings his ladder into the junction box, causing a short circuit and resulting fire. Pringle's house sustains $50,000 in damages.
   a. Which of the three are liable for the damage?
   b. How much is each liable for?
   c. Assume that Pringle settled with Whiting for $40,000, and gave her a release. She then sues Shattuck for her injuries. In a jurisdiction that applied the strict common law release rule, what would the court do?
   d. What would the court do if Whiting paid Pringle $40,000 in settlement and Pringle gave Whiting a covenant not to sue, in a jurisdiction that allowed evasion of the common law release rule through a covenant not to sue?

6. In the Edison/Joule example in the Introduction, the negligence of Edison and Joule caused Fermi $27,000 in damages. Without regard to history, one sensible and seemingly fair solution would be to split the damages, that is, to hold Edison liable for $13,500 and Joule for the same amount.

a. Why would this solution appear illogical to a traditional common law judge?
b. Suppose, in a jurisdiction that applies joint and several liability, a bill came before the legislature to introduce this approach to the liability of multiple tortfeasors. Who would oppose it, plaintiffs or defendants?

Dissatisfaction of Judgments

7. Erg sues Kelvin for negligence in causing a fire and recovers a judgment for $16,000. Kelvin, who is bankrupt, does not pay. Can Erg now sue Volt, whose negligence also caused the fire, to recover for the fire damage?

8. Suppose that Erg settles his claim against Kelvin for damages arising from the fire, for $7,000, the amount of Kelvin's insurance coverage. Now he sues Volt for the same injuries.
   a. If the jury finds that Erg's damages are $16,000, and a judgment is entered against him for that amount, how much will Volt have to pay?
   b. Suppose that Kelvin settles for $7,000. Volt is held liable for $16,000 at trial, but only has $5,000, and pays that. Can Erg sue Planck, another tortfeasor who allegedly caused the fire?
   c. Assume that Erg sued Volt, after settling with Kelvin for $7,000, and the jury determined that Erg's total damages were $4,500. What would Volt have to pay?
   d. Assume that Erg settled with Kelvin for $4,000, and in a subsequent action against Volt the jury determined his damages to be $16,000. How much must Volt pay to Erg? How much must Kelvin pay to Volt?

9. Erg settles with Kelvin for $7,000, and then goes to trial against Volt. At the close of trial, Volt asks the judge to instruct the jury that Erg has already received $7,000 in compensation for his injuries.
   a. Should the jury be told this?
   b. If they are, what else should they be told as well?

Joint and Several Liability

10. Bethune is driving a backhoe during the construction of a storm drain. She negligently backs up without looking or sounding her beeper and hits Maltby, a passing pedestrian, breaking her leg and knocking her over next to the excavation. DeWolfe, a construction worker down in the pit, negligently throws a large stone up out of the excavation without looking. The stone hits Maltby on the head, causing a severe concussion. She sues them both for her injuries.
    a. Are they jointly and severally liable to Maltby?
    b. Suppose that this case goes to trial against both Bethune and DeWolfe. The jury finds them both negligent. The jury verdict slip requires the jury to specify the total damages suffered by Maltby. The jury

finds that Maltby's damages are $60,000. What judgment should the judge enter against each defendant?

Bewitched, Bewildered, and BeFuddled

11. Assume that Fermi suffered a serious back injury in his accident with Joule and Edison. The undisputed evidence shows that he was out of work for six months, suffered $26,000 in lost wages, paid $21,000 in medical bills, and sustained serious pain and suffering, as well as some permanent disability.

    At trial, Judge Fudd instructs the jury as follows:

    > If you find that the defendants were both negligent, and that the negligence of each defendant was a cause of the plaintiff's injuries, then you must find the defendants liable for the full amount of damages suffered by the plaintiff.

    The jury comes back with the verdict in Figure 20-3. Fermi's attorney is amazed that the jury could have awarded only $50,000 in damages, which allows a mere $3,000 over the proven economic losses to compensate Fermi for pain and suffering and disability. Something, she suspects, has gone amiss in the jury's deliberations.

STATE OF WEST DAKOTA

COOK COUNTY, SS; ENRICO FERMI, Plaintiff v. MAX JOULE THOMAS EDISON, Defendants	CIVIL ACTION NO. 24-1305 VERDICT

We the Jury, find for the plaintiff against defendant Joule for $50,000. (Strike out if inapplicable)

We find for the plaintiff against the defendant Edison for $50,000. (Strike out if inapplicable)

~~We find for the defendants.~~ (Strike out if inapplicable)

Benjamin Franklin

Jury Foreperson

Figure 20-3

a. What do you think the jury did, and how did Judge Fudd's ambiguous instruction lead them to do it?
b. How should the plaintiff have avoided the problem?

Joint Sheepfeasors

12. Farmer Jones's prize field of Kentucky bluegrass is eaten clean when Herder's and Shepherd's sheep escape from their pens. Investigation reveals that both Shepherd and Herder were negligent and that 30 of Shepherd's sheep got into Jones's field and 10 of Herder's got in. Are Shepherd and Herder jointly and severally liable to Jones?

Explanations

A Practical Question

1. There are many reasons why a plaintiff might settle a claim against one tortfeasor for less than the full value of her damages. She might have doubts about her ability to prove that the particular party is liable, and therefore settle for less than the full value of her claim to account for the risk that she would lose entirely at trial. (The reasonable risk-averse client would presumably prefer $13,000 in hand to a 25 percent chance of collecting $27,000.) The plaintiff might know that the party is unable to pay more than the insurance coverage available, so there is little point in obtaining an unenforceable judgment for more. She might not want to try the case against a particular party, due to jury sympathy or an anticipated aggressive defense by that party. It might also cost more to pursue the case against that defendant than she gives up by settling, perhaps due to the need for expensive expert testimony to prove negligence by that defendant.

   In addition, tort claims often involve intangible damages such as pain and suffering or disfigurement. In such cases, neither party knows what value the jury will place on the plaintiff's injuries. Thus even a plaintiff who expects to win at trial may settle for less than the apparent full value of the claim, to avoid the risk that a jury will return a meager verdict. Thus, a settlement against Joule for $13,000 may make good sense for Fermi, even if he believes that a jury would give him a $27,000 verdict. It makes particularly good sense if Fermi *retains his right to sue Edison* since he may still collect the balance of his damages from him. The $13,000 he collects from Joule would be credited against the later judgment, but he would still be made whole despite his settlement with one of the tortfeasors.

Another Practical Question

2. The common law release rule discouraged settlements. Because a release barred the plaintiff from suing any other party on the same claim, a

plaintiff would only settle with one of several tortfeasors if the amount offered came close to the amount she would likely recover if she tried the case against them all. In other words, the settlement against one had to be good enough to induce the plaintiff to abandon her claims against everyone; she couldn't settle with one tortfeasor for part of her damages with the hope of recovering more from someone else. Since the common law rule forced the plaintiff to set a high price on settlement, individual defendants in a multidefendant case would be less likely to ante up the amount necessary to settle the case.

Sue and Sue Alike

3. The jury should render a verdict against Marconi for $60,000. His negligent driving was a "but for" cause of the harm. Consequently, he is a tortfeasor. (Under joint and several liability he is liable to Thatcher for her full damages.)

   It is true that Bell is a tortfeasor too since her negligence was another cause of the accident. Under principles of joint and several liability, Thatcher was free to sue either of the tortfeasors and recover her full damages. She could, of course, have sued them both. But she didn't have to. She could choose . . . and it was not uncommon for a plaintiff like Thatcher to choose *not* to sue the driver of the car she was in.

4. a. If Thatcher sued both drivers, and both were found liable, she would get a verdict against each for $60,000.
   b. Thatcher could collect $60,000 from either defendant. Each was jointly and severally liable for the whole damages she suffered, so either could justly be made to pay the entire judgment. Of course, if she collected it from one, she could not seek $60,000 more, or any amount more, from the other. Once her judgment was satisfied, she had no further rights against either tortfeasor.

5. a. In this case, Whiting was negligent in failing to cut off the power, and Shattuck was negligent in swinging the ladder into the junction box. Their independent acts together caused the fire. Thus, they are joint tortfeasors in the sense that their separate negligent acts concurred to cause indivisible harm to Pringle. Both are liable to her.

      What of Hahn, who was working with Whiting? The facts do not indicate that she was negligent, since she was not responsible for cutting off the power. Nor is she liable for Whiting's negligence simply because she was working on the same job with her. (That would be a tough rule indeed, making employees liable for the torts of any coworker.)

      It is true that she and Whiting agreed that Whiting would turn off the power. But agreeing to split up the work in a particular way is quite different from agreeing to engage in tortious conduct. This is not a "joint tort" situation, like the concerted action example in which two drivers engage in a drag race. There, two actors consciously engaged in negligent conduct together, which they knew created unreasonable risks to others. Here, while Hahn and Whiting were both engaged in the construction work, Hahn did not agree to engage in any negligent course of conduct with Whiting. Thus, Hahn is not liable for the negligence of Whiting.[1]

b. Under traditional causation analysis, both Whiting and Shattuck were causes of the fire since the negligence of each was a but-for cause leading to it. Thus, each caused the plaintiff's entire loss, and was held liable for that entire loss. As joint tortfeasors, Whiting and Shattuck would each be liable for $50,000.

c. Under the strict common law release rule, a party who gave a release of her claim to any tortfeasor surrendered her right to sue all possible defendants on that claim. Thus, Pringle would be barred from bringing any further suit on the same claim against Whiting or Shattuck. If this rule applied, Pringle's suit would be dismissed.

d. In a jurisdiction that held that a covenant not to sue did not waive any rights against other tortfeasors, Pringle would still be entitled to bring a separate suit against Shattuck. However, if she recovered a judgment for $50,000, the $40,000 already paid by Whiting in settlement of the claim against her would be credited against the judgment. Shattuck would only have to pay $10,000.

6. a. Logically, there is no reason why the multiple tortfeasor problem could not be dealt with by dividing the plaintiff's damages in this way. If there were two tortfeasors, each would be liable for half the damages; if there were seven, each would be liable for a seventh, and so on.

However, this pragmatic solution was antithetical to the conceptual approach of the common law, which viewed both Edison and Joule as having caused *all* of Fermi's damages, not half. But for Edison's negligent driving, no accident would have taken place, and Fermi would have suffered no injury. Because of Edison's negligence (helped along, admittedly, by Joule's as well), Fermi suffered $27,000 in damages. The same was true of Joule. Because both defendants had caused the full harm, courts refused to divide the damages in half.[2]

---

1. As another example, suppose they agreed that Whiting would go to the hardware store for supplies while Hahn started work, and Whiting had an accident on the way. Clearly, Whiting alone would be liable for the accident.

2. On the other hand, once courts accept the concept of contribution between joint tortfeasors, essentially the same division may ultimately result, if one tortfeasor pays the full judgment and sues the other for contribution.

b. Plaintiffs would resist this Solomonic solution fiercely. Under the traditional rules of joint and several liability, both Edison and Joule were fully liable. If Edison were insolvent, Joule would still have to pay the full damages under the classic rules. By contrast, if the rule were changed so that each was "severally" liable for half the damages, Fermi would collect $13,500 from Joule and nothing from an insolvent Edison. Thus, Fermi would be the loser if Edison were unable to pay. Under joint and several liability, however, *Joule* takes the risk of Edison's insolvency, and the plaintiff has twice the chance of being fully compensated for his injuries.

Dissatisfaction of Judgments

7. Under the earlier cases, the answer to this question was "no." A judgment was treated like a release of all tortfeasors; that is, getting a judgment on a tort cause of action was deemed to extinguish the underlying cause of action, leaving the judgment instead. But that rule later gave way to the more recent common law rule stated in the introduction, that a judgment against one tortfeasor did not bar suit against another, unless the first judgment was satisfied. Thus, Erg could still sue Volt, get a second judgment for her damages, and hopefully collect it from Volt.

8. a. Because no plaintiff was entitled to more than one full satisfaction of his damages, Volt would get a credit against the $16,000 judgment for the $7,000 Erg has received in settlement from Kelvin. Thus, he would have to pay $9,000 to Erg.
   b. At this point, Erg has received $7,000 in settlement from Kelvin and $5,000 from Volt under the judgment. He is still short $4,000. Since he has not yet received full satisfaction of his damages, he can still bring suit against Planck to recover the remaining $4,000.
   c. In this example, Erg settled with Kelvin for more than the jury ultimately determines Erg's damages to be. Volt would get a credit for the settlement, and that would more than cover the judgment amount. Volt would pay nothing. On the other hand, Kelvin would not get anything back either. A deal is a deal; he bought his peace, and he cannot later claim that he paid too much for it.
   d. Here again, Volt gets a credit for the settlement amount. He will be liable to Erg for $12,000 (the $16,000 judgment minus the $4,000 paid by Kelvin in settlement). He will have paid more than half of the damages, but at common law this did not give him any right of contribution from Kelvin. As stated previously, the common law had no trouble requiring Volt to pay the full $16,000 in damages he had caused. Thus, courts were not troubled if, on facts like these, he paid some lesser amount but still more than his "share." Even today, many

jurisdictions protect settling tortfeasors like Kelvin from claims for contribution.

9. a. Usually, there is no reason to tell the jury that Erg has received some compensation by settling with Kelvin. The jury's job is to determine Erg's damages and to decide whether Volt is liable for them. The mention of a settlement figure is only likely to distract them from that task. They might, for example, infer that $7,000 is the value the plaintiff places on her claim, which may not be the case at all. (See Explanation 1, which suggests a number of reasons why a plaintiff will settle low with one tortfeasor.)

   In most cases, the better course is to tell the jury nothing about the settlement, and to let the judge adjust the resulting verdict to give Volt a credit for the settlement. If the jury finds Erg's damages to be $24,000, for example, the judge would apply the dollar-credit rule by entering judgment against Volt for $17,000.

   b. If the jury is told of the settlement, they ought to be told what to do about it: They should be told to determine the plaintiff's damages without regard to the settlement, and then to render a verdict by reducing the damages by the settlement amount. It will be less confusing, however, if the judge tells the jury nothing about the settlement and simply reduces the verdict to account for it herself.

Joint and Several Liability

10. a. In this example, Bethune and DeWolfe are joint tortfeasors as to part of Maltby's injuries, but not as to all of them. The negligence of both Bethune and DeWolfe caused the concussion. Maltby would not have been hit by the stone if Bethune had not knocked her into harm's way, or if DeWolfe had not negligently thrown the stone out of the pit. It is a case of successive negligent acts that together cause the harm. So long as DeWolfe's subsequent negligence is foreseeable, it does not insulate Bethune from liability. As to Maltby's concussion, Bethune and DeWolfe are joint tortfeasors.

   However, DeWolfe is not a joint tortfeasor with Bethune in causing Maltby's broken leg. DeWolfe's negligence had no part in causing the broken leg, which happened before DeWolfe entered the picture. Thus, Bethune would be solely liable for this injury, but both would be liable for Maltby's concussion damages.

   b. The problem here is that the jury's general verdict does not separate the leg damages from the concussion damages. As to Bethune, it doesn't matter, since she is liable for both. The judge should enter a judgment against her for $60,000. But DeWolfe should only be held liable for the concussion damages, and the jury's verdict doesn't indicate how much of the $60,000 is to compensate for that.

The court should avoid this problem by using a special verdict form that asks the jury to specify the amount of damages the plaintiff has suffered from the leg injury and the amount attributable to the concussion. Then the judge can enter judgment against Bethune for the total damages and against DeWolfe for the separate amount attributed to the concussion.

Bewitched, Bewildered, and BeFuddled

11. a. It is very likely that the ambiguity in Judge Fudd's instruction led the jury to render a verdict that does not convey their intended meaning. The jury in this case probably found Fermi's damages to be $100,000 (a more likely figure given the extent of his cumulative injuries), and thought it was rendering a verdict that would require *each* defendant to pay $50,000, for a total of $100,000.

Unfortunately, under principles of joint and several liability, the jury's verdict slip only makes Joule and Edison jointly liable for a *total* of $50,000. Fermi can collect that amount from either, or part from each, but cannot receive more than a total of $50,000. (Compare the judgment in Figure 20-1 at p. 448) Judge Fudd's instruction was open to this misinterpretation since it required the jury to find "the defendants" liable for the plaintiff's full damages, not *each* defendant liable for the plaintiff's full damages.

The verdict slip in Figure 20-3 compounded the judge's error. The verdict slip simply indicates which defendants are found liable, and how much each is liable for; it does not clearly state the plaintiff's total damages or that the jury must find each defendant liable for the plaintiff's full damages.

b. The plaintiff could have avoided this problem by pointing out the ambiguity in the judge's instruction before he gave it. Counsel for all parties will be given a chance to review proposed jury instructions before the judge instructs the jury, so that they may object to instructions that wrongly state the applicable law. If plaintiff's counsel had realized the problem, she could have asked Judge Fudd to revise the instruction along the following lines:

> If you find that both defendants were negligent, and that the negligence of each defendant was a cause of the plaintiff's injuries, then you must find each defendant liable for the full damages suffered by the plaintiff.

The distinction between this instruction and Judge Fudd's is not very great, but the difference in the effect of the two is dramatic. If the jury understood the instruction, and it actually intended the plaintiff to recover $100,000, this instruction would clearly require them to return a verdict for $100,000, not $50,000, against each defendant.

A cogent criticism of jury trial is that juries often do not understand the subtleties of their instructions. Their verdict must be based on instructions on complicated principles that they are given once, often orally. To put the matter in perspective, consider whether you, after brief treatment of joint and several liability in your Torts class, would feel prepared to go into a jury room and apply these rules accurately to an actual case.

Fermi's lawyer could also have reduced the risk of jury misunderstanding by asking the court to use a special verdict form like that in Figure 20-4, which requires the jury to make specific factual findings on negligence and damages. Under this verdict, the jury does not have to fully understand the governing liability rules. So long as they answer the factual questions accurately, the court can enter an appropriate judgment under joint and several liability principles. If the jury had rendered the verdict in Figure 20-4, the judge would have clearly understood that the jury intended Fermi to recover $100,000, and would have entered judgment against each defendant for that amount.

Joint Sheepfeasors

12. As the Introduction states, defendants are held jointly and severally liable for the plaintiff's damages if the damages cannot rationally be apportioned among them, if they are "indivisible." Here, it is doubtless impossible to determine which sheep ate which blades of grass, but there is a basis for a rough apportionment of the damages based on the number of sheep of each defendant that joined the repast. Assuming a sheep is a sheep when it comes to appetite, it is a fair inference that Shepherd's sheep ate about three-quarters of the grass, and Herder's ate the other quarter. Most courts would apportion the damages between Shepherd and Herder on that basis rather than holding them jointly and severally liable. Restatement (Second) of Torts §433A cmt. d.

    While courts will endeavor to make such apportionment, even where it requires some approximation, it is worth reiterating that in most cases that is simply not possible. When two negligent acts combine to cause a broken back, a fatal heart attack, or a fire that burns the plaintiff's barn, it is simply not possible to ascribe part of the injury to one defendant's negligence and part to the other's. In this large class of cases, joint and several liability has been the classic rule because apportionment is not a feasible alternative.

STATE OF WEST DAKOTA

COOK COUNTY, SS; CIVIL ACTION NO. 2024-1305

ENRICO FERMI,

Plaintiff

v. VERDICT

MAX JOULE
THOMAS EDISON,

Defendants

1. Do you find that the defendant Max Joule was negligent?
   Yes ✓ No___
2. Do you find that the defendant Thomas Edison was negligent?
   Yes ✓ No___
3. If the defendant Max Joule was negligent, was his negligence a proximate cause of the plaintiff's damages?
   Yes ✓ No___
4. If the defendant Thomas Edison was negligent, was his negligence a proximate cause of the plaintiff's damages?
   Yes ✓ No___
5. If you find that either defendant was negligent, and that his negligence was a proximate cause of the accident, what amount do you find will fairly and reasonably compensate the plaintiff for the injuries caused by the accident?
   $100,000

E. Isaac Newton
Jury Foreperson

Figure 20-4

CHAPTER 21

Honor Among Thieves: Basic Principles of Contribution

INTRODUCTION

The last chapter explored the common law rules governing the liability of joint tortfeasors. As that discussion indicates, where joint and several liability applies, each tortfeasor who contributed to an indivisible injury is fully liable for the plaintiff's damages. This reflects the fundamental policy choice underlying joint and several liability, that the plaintiff should be fully compensated as long as at least one of the tortfeasors is able to pay the judgment.

However, the rule of joint and several liability can lead to unfair results. Suppose that Nash negligently left his bicycle in the road, and Benchley, not looking where he was going, drove into it, lost control of the car, and injured Twain. Under the common law, Twain could sue either Nash or Benchley for his injuries. The plaintiff was in control, and could choose to impose the full loss on either of the joint tortfeasors. If Benchley was his brother-in-law, Twain could keep peace in the family by suing Nash instead. If he sued Nash and recovered, Nash would have to pay Twain's full damages, and Benchley would pay nothing, even if he also caused the accident.

Of course, in many cases the plaintiff took the prudent course of suing all possible defendants since he might only prove that one was negligent, or that the negligence of one had caused the injury. But even if Twain sued both Nash and Benchley in our example, and recovered judgment against both, he could still choose to *collect* the judgment from either one. So he could still target Nash and let Benchley off the hook entirely if Nash was able to pay.

For many years, courts held that if Nash did pay, he had no right to force Benchley to "contribute to the judgment," that is, to reimburse him for part of the damages he had paid to Twain. The common law, with its somewhat moralistic view of these matters, had no problem with the fact that Nash ended up paying the entire judgment. Nash was a wrongdoer, had caused Twain's injuries, and could fairly be made to pay. Justice was done between the plaintiff and the defendant, and that was that. Nash would not be heard to complain that Benchley had gotten off scot-free, so long as Nash had actually caused the damages he was forced to pay.

Although the common law rule denying contribution from joint tortfeasors was widely applied for many years, it was also widely criticized. Prosser sums up the attack with his usual incisiveness:

> There is an obvious lack of sense and justice in a rule which permits the entire burden of a loss, for which two defendants were equally, unintentionally responsible, to be shouldered onto one alone, according to the accident of a successful levy of execution, the existence of liability insurance, the plaintiff's whim or spite, or the plaintiff's collusion with the other wrongdoer, while the latter goes scot free.

Prosser & Keeton at 337-338. Most critics of the no-contribution rule accepted the basic proposition that each defendant should be fully liable to the *plaintiff.* However, they argued that a defendant who paid the plaintiff's damages should be able to redistribute the loss by making the other tortfeasors contribute to the payment of the common liability.

Most states have responded to such criticism by creating a right to contribution among joint tortfeasors, either by statute or by judicial decision. Many statutes creating the right to contribution were modeled closely on the Uniform Contribution Among Tortfeasors Act, a model contribution statute drawn up in 1955.[1] This chapter introduces the basic principles of contribution, using the Uniform Act as an example. The relevant sections of the Uniform Act are set forth on pp. 473-474 below.

1. Uniform Contribution Among Tortfeasors Act, 12 U.L.A. 201 (2008). The Uniform Contribution Among Tortfeasors Act has since been withdrawn because its principles are now included in the more comprehensive Uniform Apportionment of Tort Responsibility Act (2003). The 1955 Act is used here because it provides a straightforward example of contribution principles and has been the model for contribution statutes in a number of states.

THE RIGHT TO CONTRIBUTION

The Uniform Act starts out by creating the right to contribution among joint tortfeasors:

> 1(a) Except as otherwise provided in this Act, where two or more persons become jointly or severally liable in tort for the same injury to person or property or for the same wrongful death, there is a right of contribution among them even though judgment has not been recovered against all or any of them.
>
> (b) The right of contribution exists only in favor of a tortfeasor who has paid more than his pro rata share of the common liability, and his total recovery is limited to the amount paid by him in excess of his pro rata share. No tortfeasor is compelled to make contribution beyond his pro rata share of the entire liability. . . .

These provisions of the Uniform Act allow a negligent tortfeasor[2] who has paid more than his "pro rata" share of the plaintiff's damages to recover contribution from other tortfeasors who are liable for the same injury. Suppose, for example, that Twain recovered a judgment of $20,000 against Nash for his injuries in the auto accident, and Nash paid the judgment. Section 1(a) of the Uniform Act authorizes Nash to recover contribution from Benchley, if Benchley was "jointly or severally liable in tort for the same injury. . . ." Thus, to establish his right to contribution, Nash would have to show that Benchley was also liable to Twain for his injuries in the accident.

Section 1(b) determines *how much* Nash can seek from Benchley. It authorizes Nash to seek contribution for amounts above his (Nash's) "pro rata" share. In this context, "pro rata" means equal. If there are three tortfeasors, the pro rata share of each is one-third; if there are five, it is one-fifth, and so on. Since there are two tortfeasors in the example, Nash's pro rata share is one-half. Thus, if he paid the $20,000, he could recover one-half the judgment, or $10,000, from Benchley. If there were four tortfeasors, the pro rata shares of each would be $5,000. On those facts, if Nash paid the $20,000 to Twain, he would only be entitled to $5,000 from Benchley since §1(b) limits each tortfeasor's liability for contribution to his pro rata share. Nash would have to go after the other two tortfeasors for their shares to obtain

2. The Uniform Act, like most contribution statutes, bars contribution claims by an intentional tortfeasor. See §1(c), quoted at p. 470. The Restatement of Torts: Apportionment of Liability, however, would allow intentional tortfeasors to seek contribution. Restatement (Third) of Torts: Apportionment of Liability §23 cmt. l. The discussion in this chapter assumes that all claims are based on negligence.

full contribution. If all three paid their shares to Nash, Nash would collect $15,000 in contribution and end up paying $5,000 of the judgment, his own pro rata share.

ENFORCING THE RIGHT TO CONTRIBUTION

Suppose that Twain had sued Nash alone and recovered his $20,000 judgment. As indicated above, Nash could not simply demand $10,000 from Benchley. Under §1(a), Benchley is only liable for contribution if he is a joint tortfeasor. Thus, before he could recover contribution from Benchley, Nash would have to prove that Benchley was *also liable to Twain* for the damages Nash had already paid.

The simplest way for Nash to do this would be to bring Benchley into the original suit when Twain sued him. Most states allow a defendant in Nash's position to "implead" a joint tortfeasor for contribution, that is, to make him a party to the original suit. See, e.g., Okla. Code of Civ. Proc. tit. 12 §2014 (allowing defendant to implead a person who may be liable to him for all or part of plaintiff's claim against him); Ct. R. Super. Ct. Civ. §10-11 (same). If Nash impleaded Benchley, the court would determine in a single trial whether Benchley and Nash were liable for Twain's injury. If both were found liable and Nash then paid the judgment (remember, he is still fully liable to *Twain* based on the principle of joint and several liability), he would make a motion in the original suit for contribution from Benchley. Section 3(b) of the Uniform Act expressly authorizes such orders for contribution in the original suit.

Suppose, however, that Twain sued Nash only, and Nash did not (or could not)[3] implead Benchley. If Nash were found liable, and paid the judgment, he could then bring a separate action for contribution against Benchley. This is a new lawsuit. Nash is the plaintiff, Benchley is the defendant, and the claim is for recovery of Benchley's pro rata share of the judgment which Nash has paid. Section 3 of the Uniform Act authorizes such separate suits for contribution (see §3(a)) and establishes limitations periods for them (§3(c), (d)). Figure 21-1 is a simple example of a complaint for contribution.

3. Nash might not be able to implead Benchley, for example, if the court in which Twain brought suit lacked personal jurisdiction over Benchley.

Like all pleadings, Nash's complaint is basically commonsensical. Since Benchley was not a defendant in the original action, it has never been determined that he is in fact liable for Twain's injuries. Thus, to obtain contribution Nash must allege and prove that Benchley is liable to Twain for the accident due to his negligence. See paras. 8, 9. He also alleges each of the further requirements for contribution established in the statute: that he (Nash) has been sued by the injured plaintiff and held liable for the same injury (paras. 3-6), that he has paid more than his pro rata share (paras. 7, 10), and that he is entitled to pro rata contribution under the statute (para. 10). The relief demanded in the last paragraph of the complaint is, of course, Benchley's pro rata share of the judgment.

EFFECT OF SETTLEMENT ON THE RIGHT TO CONTRIBUTION

It is not unusual for the plaintiff to settle with one tortfeasor and proceed to trial against others.[4] Suppose that Twain settles with Nash for $2,000, releasing his claim against Nash only, and then recovers a judgment against Benchley for $20,000. What is the effect of Nash's settlement with Twain on Benchley's right to recover contribution from Nash?

Here are the relevant provisions of the Uniform Act:

> 4. When a release or covenant not to sue or not to enforce judgment is given in good faith to one of two or more persons liable in tort for the same injury or the same wrongful death:
>
> (a) It does not discharge any of the other tortfeasors from liability for the injury or wrongful death unless its terms so provide, but it reduces the claim against the others to the extent of any amount stipulated by the release or the covenant, or in the amount of the consideration paid for it, whichever is the greater; and,
>
> (b) It discharges the tortfeasor to whom it is given from all liability for contribution to any other tortfeasor.

4. Some of the reasons for doing so are explored in Chapter 20, Example 1.

STATE OF WEST DAKOTA
SUPERIOR COURT

GALLATIN COUNTY, SS: | CIVIL ACTION NO. 24-0129

OGDEN NASH,

Plaintiff

v.

ROBERT BENCHLEY,

Defendant

COMPLAINT FOR CONTRIBUTION

1. The plaintiff Ogden Nash is an individual residing at 14 Stow Street, Sutter, West Dakota.

2. The defendant Robert Benchley is an individual residing at 2116 Twelfth Street, Bridger, West Dakota.

3. On March 11, 2023, Mark Twain commenced a civil action, captioned Twain v. Nash, Civil Action No. 23-219, against Ogden Nash in the Superior Court for Glacier County, West Dakota.

4. The claim in Twain v. Nash arose out of an accident which took place on Maple Street in the town of Sutter, West Dakota, on June 7, 2022. Twain was injured in that accident when a collision between a bicycle owned by Ogden Nash and a car driven by Robert Benchley caused the Benchley car to swerve into him.

5. The plaintiff in Twain v. Nash alleged that his injuries resulted from the negligence of Nash in leaving his bicycle in the road.

6. On November 7, 2023, the court entered judgment against Ogden Nash in Twain v. Nash, in the amount of $20,000 plus interest and costs.

7. On December 15, 2023, Nash, the contribution plaintiff in this action, satisfied the judgment in Twain v. Nash by paying $20,279 to the plaintiff in that action, including $63 in post-judgment interest and $216 in costs.

Figure 21-1

8. At the time of the accident which gave rise to the judgment in Twain v. Nash, Benchley, the contribution defendant, was also negligent in failing to keep a proper lookout. As a result of his negligence, he drove into the bicycle, swerved and ran into Twain. Such negligence was a proximate cause of the accident.

9. As a result of his negligence, the contribution defendant Benchley is a joint tortfeasor fully liable for the injuries sustained by Twain.

10. Plaintiff in this action has satisfied the judgment in Twain v. Nash in full. Thus, he has paid more than his pro rata share of the common liability and is entitled to contribution from Benchley under the provisions of West Dak. Stat. Tit. VII, §1(a) and (b) (the West Dakota Contribution Among Tortfeasors Act), in the amount of one-half of the judgment.

11. The plaintiff in this action has demanded payment from Benchley of his pro rata share of the judgment, but he has refused to pay.

WHEREFORE, the plaintiff demands judgment against the defendant in this action in the amount of $10,139.50, plus costs of suit.

____

By his attorney
Angela Wu
42 River Street
Sutter, West Dakota 68534
(123) 335-8895

Figure 21-1 **(*Continued*)**

The first clause of §4(a) reverses the common law rule that releasing one tortfeasor released them all. Under §4(a), Twain may still sue Benchley even though he gave a release to Nash. However, if Benchley is found liable, §4(a) provides that Benchley will get a credit against the judgment for the amount Nash paid in settlement. This codifies the equitable principle that the plaintiff is entitled to full satisfaction of her judgment, but no more. In this example, if Twain recovered a $20,000 judgment against Benchley, Benchley would only have to pay $18,000 after the credit for the $2,000 Nash paid in settlement.

However, §4(b) of the Uniform Act *bars Benchley from recovering contribution from Nash,* the settling tortfeasor. Thus, on these facts Benchley will pay $18,000 of Twain's damages, while Nash pays only $2,000. Naturally, this provision has little appeal for Benchley. If Nash had not settled, and both he and Benchley had been found liable, Benchley could still have been forced to pay $20,000 to Twain, but he would have had the right to recover $10,000 in contribution from Nash (the amount Benchley had paid in excess of his pro rata share). Thus, he would only have been out $10,000. Why should he have to pay an extra $8,000 simply because Twain made a deal with Nash? Isn't this provision grossly unfair to the remaining defendant?

There are several arguments in favor of barring contribution from a settling tortfeasor. *First,* the purpose of settling a lawsuit is to buy one's peace, to extinguish the liability, close the file, and get on to other things. If Benchley is free to come back against Nash for contribution, Nash has gained little by settling. He is still exposed to $10,000 in liability (his pro rata share), and has simply paid $2,000 of it early. If contribution from the settling tortfeasor is not barred, there is little incentive to settlements, which are generally encouraged as a civilized, less expensive alternative to litigation.

Second, Benchley is free to settle too. Indeed, the risk of paying an outsized share encourages him to do so. Thus, the settling tortfeasor's immunity promotes settlements. In many cases the plaintiff will settle with all tortfeasors rather than risk a loss at trial. In a sense, everyone wins in this scenario.

Third, it may turn out that Nash settled for *more* than his pro rata share. When Nash settles, he does not know how much a jury will award in damages. In our hypo, they awarded Twain $20,000 for his injuries, but personal injury damages are very difficult to predict; they might have given $50,000. To avoid that risk, Nash might pay $16,000 to settle the case instead of $2,000. If he did, and the jury later assessed the damages at $20,000 in Twain's suit against Benchley, Benchley would only have to pay Twain $4,000—the $20,000 judgment minus the $16,000 Nash paid in settlement (Benchley gets a credit for the settlement under the Uniform Act, §4(a), second clause). As you can see, these possibilities make settlement an interesting business for all parties involved.

Fourth, the statute contains a good faith requirement. Uniform Act §4. If the court is convinced that Twain and Nash colluded by settling for an insufficient amount, it need not bar contribution from Nash.

PRO RATA CREDITS FOR SETTLEMENTS

An alternative way to take account of a settlement with one tortfeasor would be to give the remaining tortfeasor a pro rata credit for the settlement instead of a dollar credit. Under this approach, Twain would be viewed (since there are two tortfeasors) to have sold half of his cause of action to Nash by settling with him. Thus, he could only recover from Benchley on the other half. Suppose, for example, that Nash settled for $2,000, and Twain later recovered a $20,000 judgment against Benchley. Under the pro rata credit approach, Twain would be viewed as having sold half of his claim for the $2,000. Obviously, if the jury determines later that his damages are $20,000, that half of the claim was worth $10,000, and Twain badly undersold it. Under the pro rata credit approach, he would be entitled to collect only one-half of the judgment, or $10,000 from Benchley. He would receive only $12,000 in total. By contrast, under the dollar credit approach he would get $18,000 (the judgment amount minus the amount of the settlement) from Benchley and $20,000 altogether.

Let's do one more example of the pro rata approach to accounting for settlements. Assume that there were three tortfeasors in Twain's case, and that he settled with Nash for $2,000. Under the pro rata approach, Twain would be viewed as selling one-third of his claim for that amount. When he later obtained a judgment against the other two tortfeasors for $20,000, it would be reduced by one-third ($6,666) to account for the settlement. He could then collect $13,333 from either of the remaining defendants. He would thus collect a total of $15,333 ($2,000 in settlement from Nash and $13,333 under the judgment).

The pro rata method of accounting for settlements has gained renewed popularity under comparative negligence, with the important modification that the pro rata shares are not equal, but proportional to the percentage of negligence ascribed to the tortfeasors at trial. Under this approach, if Nash settled for $2,000, and he was later found to be 40 percent at fault in causing Twain's damages, the other tortfeasors would get a 40 percent credit against the judgment to account for Nash's settlement. Again, the logic is that Twain has sold that part of the common liability represented by Nash for the settlement amount. We'll explore this approach in more detail in Chapter 25.

A Tactical Question

1. Accounting for the settlement under this pro rata approach seems more equitable. Twain gets what he bargained for from Nash, as well as Benchley's fair share of the damages from him. What is the disadvantage of this variation? (Explanations begin on p. 477.)

CAN A SETTLING TORTFEASOR SEEK CONTRIBUTION?

Now let's look at the other side of the equation. Suppose that Twain settles with Nash for $16,000, and gives Nash a release of his liability. Later, Nash is surprised to learn that the jury in the suit against Benchley assessed Twain's damages at $20,000. Benchley has lucked out: Under §4(a) of the Uniform Act, which provides for a dollar credit for Nash's settlement, he will only have to pay Twain $4,000. Can Nash, the settling defendant who overpaid, recover $6,000 in contribution from Benchley? The Uniform Act says no:

> 1(d) A tortfeasor who enters into a settlement with a claimant is not entitled to recover contribution from another tortfeasor whose liability for the injury or wrongful death is not extinguished by the settlement. . . .

Under §1(d), Nash has no right to seek contribution from Benchley since Twain only released Nash, not both defendants. Since Nash made an unfavorable settlement (at least, unfavorable in retrospect), he ends up paying more than he would have if he had lost at trial and paid half the judgment. Even here, however, he may still "win" in some sense. He has saved the expense of trying the case, and he has avoided the risk—always difficult to assess—that the jury would award much higher damages, say, $100,000. If Nash had not settled, and the jury had done that, he would have paid at least $50,000, and perhaps $100,000 if Benchley were insolvent.

Since the adoption of comparative negligence, many states have modified the basic contribution principles of the Uniform Act. Some of the current permutations are explored in Chapter 477. However, it is important to master the basic principles of contribution, both because they remain applicable in many cases and because it is impossible to understand varying approaches to contribution without appreciating the basic concepts from which they have evolved. In analyzing the following examples, assume that the Uniform Act applies unless otherwise stated. The relevant provisions of the Act are as follows:

Uniform Contribution Among Tortfeasors Act

(1) (a) Except as otherwise provided in this Act, where two or more persons become jointly or severally liable in tort for the same injury to person or property or for the same wrongful death, there is a right of contribution among them even though judgment has not been recovered against all or any of them.

(b) The right of contribution exists only in favor of a tortfeasor who has paid more than his pro rata share of the common liability, and his total recovery is limited to the amount paid by him in excess of his pro rata share. No tortfeasor is compelled to make contribution beyond his pro rata share of the entire liability. . . .

(c) There is no right of contribution in favor of any tortfeasor who has intentionally . . . caused or contributed to the injury or wrongful death.

(d) A tortfeasor who enters into a settlement with a claimant is not entitled to recover contribution from another tortfeasor whose liability for the injury or wrongful death is not extinguished by the settlement. . . .

(2) In determining the pro rata shares of tortfeasors in the entire liability (a) their relative degrees of fault shall not be considered; (b) if equity requires the collective liability of some as a group shall constitute a single share; and (c) principles of equity applicable to contribution generally shall apply.

(3) (a) Whether or not judgment has been entered in an action against two or more tortfeasors for the same injury or wrongful death, contribution may be enforced by separate action.

(b) Where judgment has been entered in an action against two or more tortfeasors for the same injury or wrongful death, contribution may be enforced in that action by judgment in favor of one against other judgment defendants by motion upon notice to all parties to the action.

(c) If there is a judgment for the injury or wrongful death against the tortfeasor seeking contribution, any separate action by him to enforce contribution must be commenced within one year after the judgment has become final by lapse of time for appeal or after appellate review.

(d) If there is no judgment for the injury or wrongful death against the tortfeasor seeking contribution, his right of contribution is barred unless he has either (1) discharged by payment the common liability within the statute of limitations period applicable to claimant's right of action against him and has commenced his action for contribution within one year after payment, or (2) agreed while action is pending against him to discharge the common liability and has within one year after the agreement paid the liability and commenced his action for contribution.

(e) The recovery of a judgment for an injury or wrongful death against one tortfeasor does not of itself discharge the other tortfeasors from liability for the injury or wrongful death unless the judgment is satisfied. . . .

(f) The judgment of the court in determining the liability of the several defendants to the claimant for an injury or wrongful death shall be binding as among such defendants in determining their right to contribution.

(4) When a release or covenant not to sue or not to enforce judgment is given in good faith to one of two or more persons liable in tort for the same injury or the same wrongful death:

(a) It does not discharge any of the other tortfeasors from liability for the injury or wrongful death unless its terms so provide; but it reduces the claim against the others to the extent of any amount stipulated by the release or the covenant, or in the amount of the consideration paid for it, whichever is the greater; and,

(b) It discharges the tortfeasor to whom it is given from all liability for contribution to any other tortfeasor.

In analyzing the examples below, assume that joint and several liability and the Uniform Contribution Act apply.

Examples

Burning Issues

2. Rogers, owner of a small business, gives a Fourth of July barbecue for his employees behind the building. Impatient for the barbecued chicken, Dunne throws gasoline on the coals, and Thurber throws a lighted match into the grill. The resulting fire causes extensive damage to the building. Rogers brings a negligence suit against Dunne for the damage, and gets a judgment for $42,000.
   a. Could Dunne obtain contribution from Thurber at common law? If so, how much?
   b. Could Dunne obtain contribution from Thurber under the Uniform Act? If so, how much?

3. Dunne is held liable for $42,000. He pays Rogers $21,000, and refuses to pay any more, arguing that Thurber is responsible for the other $21,000. Will the court order Dunne to pay Rogers any more?

4. Rogers gets a judgment against Dunne for $42,000, but Dunne does not pay. Could Rogers bring a separate action against Thurber for the damage if the Uniform Act applied?

Fudd Fudges the Figures

5. Rogers sues Dunne and Thurber, and gets a judgment against them both for $42,000. Dunne pays Rogers $34,000, all he is able to. He then makes a motion for contribution from Thurber, and Judge Fudd orders Thurber to pay Dunne $17,000. What is wrong with Fudd's order?

Permutations

6. Assume that Rogers sued both Dunne and Thurber, and the jury found Thurber liable, but not Dunne. After paying Rogers the $42,000 judgment, Thurber seeks contribution from Dunne. May he recover contribution, and, if so, how much?

7. Assume that Rogers sued both Dunne and Thurber, and the jury found them both liable. After paying Rogers $42,000, Thurber seeks $21,000 in contribution from Dunne. Dunne, however, argues that White, another guest at the picnic, was *also* negligent in starting the fire because he placed the grill much too close to the building and left the trash sitting next to it. How much must Dunne pay in contribution?

8. Rogers sues Dunne, Thurber, and White for their negligence in starting the fire. He recovers a judgment against all three for $42,000 and tries to collect it from White. Unfortunately, White has no money and pays nothing, so Rogers demands payment from Dunne, who pays the entire judgment. Dunne then seeks contribution from Thurber. How much will he get?

Some Unsettling Cases

9. Rogers sues Dunne and Thurber for the fire damage. Dunne offers to settle with Rogers for $12,000. Rogers accepts, and releases Dunne from liability in exchange for payment of that amount. Rogers then recovers a judgment for $42,000 against Thurber. (In analyzing this example, assume that Dunne and Thurber are the only tortfeasors.)
   a. How much will Rogers collect from Thurber if the Uniform Act applies?
   b. After paying Rogers, Thurber seeks contribution from Dunne. How much will he recover if the Uniform Act applies?
   c. How much would Rogers collect from Thurber if the relevant contribution statute gave Thurber a pro rata credit for Dunne's settlement instead of a dollar credit?

10. Assume that Rogers settled with Dunne for $35,000 and gave Dunne a release of his liability only. Subsequently, Rogers sues Thurber. The jury finds Thurber liable for the fire and assesses $42,000 in damages.

a. Assuming that the Uniform Act applies, how much must Thurber pay Rogers?
b. After the judgment is entered and Thurber satisfies it, Dunne sues Thurber for contribution. How much would he receive under the Uniform Act?
c. Assume that this settlement took place in a jurisdiction that gives the remaining defendant a pro rata credit for settlements by other tortfeasors. How much would Rogers collect altogether?

Confusion Worse Confounded

11. Porter, driving a Reliable Furniture Company truck, collides with Simon's car. The car is thrown onto the sidewalk, injuring Allen. Allen sues Porter, Simon, and Reliable Furniture Company (on the ground that it is liable for Porter's torts in the scope of employment). The jury finds that the negligence of both drivers caused the accident, and awards Allen $60,000 in damages. Simon pays the judgment. How much can he obtain in contribution from Porter? From Reliable?

12. Assume, after the accident described in Example 11, that the parties exchange papers at the scene, fill out accident reports, and go their separate ways. Simon, a patent lawyer and a worrywart, looks up the statute of limitations for torts and discovers that it is two years. He worries daily for two years, waiting for the process server to serve him with papers in a lawsuit by Allen. The process server never shows; the magic date passes without incident. Simon breathes a deep sigh of relief.

    Not so fast, Simon. Why should he continue to worry?

A Sense of Proportion

13. Assume that Allen, on the facts of Example 11, sued Simon and Porter in a jurisdiction that applies comparative negligence. At trial, the jury finds that Simon was 20 percent at fault in causing the accident, and Porter was 80 percent at fault. It determines that Allen's damages are $100,000.
    a. If Porter pays the judgment, what could he get in contribution from Simon under the Uniform Act?
    b. What might be a more logical way to redistribute the judgment between the two tortfeasors?

Explanations

A Tactical Question

1. Under the pro rata credit approach, plaintiffs have less incentive to settle than under the dollar credit approach. In a state that applies the dollar credit approach, Twain can still recover his full damages, even if he settles with Nash for less than Nash's full share: Benchley is still liable for the entire judgment, and will only get a credit for the amount Nash actually paid. For example, if Twain's damages are $20,000, he can settle with Nash for $5,000 and recover $15,000 from Benchley.

   However, under the pro rata credit approach, Twain gives up 50 percent of his claim when he settles with Nash. If he settles for $5,000, and the jury assesses his damages at $20,000, he will end up with only $15,000, five from Nash and ten from Benchley (the $20,000 judgment minus Nash's pro rata share). Here is a comparison of the results under the two approaches:

	Settlement w/Nash	Jury Award at Trial	Benchley Pays	Plaintiff Receives
Dollar credit approach:	$5,000	$20,000	$15,000	$20,000
Pro rata credit approach:	$5,000	$20,000	$10,000	$15,000

Thus, under the pro rata credit approach, a plaintiff is unlikely to sell half of his claim for much less than half its value.

Burning Issues

2. a. As the introduction indicates, there was no right at common law to demand contribution from a joint tortfeasor. If Dunne paid the judgment, he had no recourse against Thurber and was stuck with the entire liability, simply because Rogers chose to sue him instead of Thurber.

   b. Dunne has no right to contribution under the Uniform Act. Surprised? Well, this answer is a little bit cute. The facts do not indicate that Dunne has paid anything to Rogers. The right to contribution arises in favor of a tortfeasor who has *paid* more than his pro rata share, not one who has merely been found liable. Uniform Act §1(b). The difference between incurring a judgment for $42,000 and paying over $42,000 is dramatic; it is the difference between a bird in the hand and a bird in the bush.

Assuming that Dunne paid the $42,000 to Rogers, he would have a right to pro rata contribution from Thurber under the Uniform Act. He would be entitled to recover $21,000 from Thurber, if he proved that Thurber was also liable to Rogers for negligently causing the fire. Since Rogers only sued Dunne, Thurber has never been adjudged liable for the fire. Thus, Dunne would have to bring a contribution action against Thurber and prove Thurber's negligence in that suit before he could recover contribution.

3. Assuming that joint and several liability applies, the court will order Dunne to pay the entire judgment. The Uniform Act does not alter the fundamental premise that each tortfeasor is *fully liable* to the plaintiff. The plaintiff may still sue whichever tortfeasor he chooses, and collect the damages from whichever he chooses.

   Contribution only deals with adjusting the payment of the damages among the defendants, after one has paid more than his share of the judgment. Dunne may pay Rogers $42,000 and seek $21,000 from Thurber, but he cannot pay $21,000 and force Rogers to chase Dunne for the balance. That, in essence, would make the two tortfeasors "severally" liable for their pro rata shares rather than "jointly and severally" liable for the plaintiff's full damages.[5] The very purpose of joint and several liability is to assure the plaintiff's right to collect fully from any one of the tortfeasors.

4. At early common law, a judgment against one tortfeasor barred suit against others who might also be liable. The rationale was that a tort claim was a "single cause of action." Once sued upon, it was extinguished and replaced by the judgment. See Chapter 20, p. 447. The courts later abandoned that approach, however, replacing it with the rule that a plaintiff could bring a second action against another party responsible for his injuries, so long as the prior judgment had not been fully satisfied. Section 3(e) of the Uniform Act codifies this later approach, which allows a plaintiff who has obtained a judgment against one tortfeasor to sue other tortfeasors until his claim is fully satisfied. Under §3(e), Rogers's judgment against Dunne does not bar him from suing Thurber, since the judgment has not been paid.

Fudd Fudges the Figures

5. The Uniform Act allows a tortfeasor who has paid "more than his pro rata share" of the liability to recover contribution. Section 1(b). Dunne's

5. Many states have now switched from joint and several liability to several liability, at least in limited classes of cases. Some examples are given in Chapter 25, pp. 569–570.

pro rata share would be $21,000, one-half of the judgment. Since he has paid more than that, and Thurber has been held liable for the injury as well, Dunne is entitled to contribution. Fudd was right in awarding him contribution. His error was in determining the amount.

You can see the logic for Fudd's order; it makes Thurber absorb half of Dunne's payment. The Uniform Act, however, provides otherwise. Under §1(b), Dunne can recover from Thurber "the amount paid by him [Dunne] in excess of his pro rata share." Dunne's pro rata share is $21,000. Since he has paid $34,000, he can recover $13,000 in contribution from Thurber.

The logic of the Uniform Act provision is illustrated by considering what would happen if Fudd's order were upheld. Thurber would pay $17,000, but he would still be liable to Rogers for $8,000, the part of Rogers's judgment that he has not yet collected. If Thurber paid $17,000 to Dunne and Rogers then demanded $8,000 more from him, he would end up paying $25,000, $4,000 more than his pro rata share, while Dunne paid $17,000, $4,000 less than his.

The Second Restatement of Torts took the position that a tortfeasor could not seek contribution at all until the plaintiff had been fully paid. See §886A(2) and cmt. f. Presumably, the logic for this position is that, if Thurber only has limited funds, Rogers should get first crack at them: Thurber should not pay contribution to Dunne and be left unable to satisfy the remainder of Rogers's judgment. However, §1(b) of the Uniform Act does not include a similar requirement.

Permutations

6. Since Dunne is not liable to Rogers, he is not liable to Thurber for contribution. A tortfeasor may only recover contribution from someone who is liable to the plaintiff. See Uniform Act §1(a) (authorizing contribution "where two or more persons become jointly or severally liable in tort"). He can hardly be liable for contribution as a joint tortfeasor if he isn't a tortfeasor at all, and that's what the jury decided in this case. See Uniform Act §3(f) (providing that the findings as to the liability of the various defendants in the plaintiff's suit are binding in a subsequent contribution action).

7. Under the Uniform Act, any person who "becomes jointly liable in tort for the same injury" is liable to contribute to the damages. Although White was not sued in the original action, he may still be a joint tortfeasor. Rogers might have decided not to sue him for myriad reasons; that decision does not necessarily mean that he is not "liable" for the injury. If his negligence contributed to the accident, he should be counted in calculating the pro rata shares of each tortfeasor. Thus, when Thurber seeks contribution, the court will have to determine whether White was also

negligent in order to calculate Dunne's pro rata share. If it determines that White was also a tortfeasor, it will order Dunne to pay one-third of the judgment to Thurber ($14,000) instead of one-half.

8. Clearly, Dunne is entitled to contribution from Thurber. If White were solvent, Dunne could recover $14,000 from Thurber and $14,000 from White. Since White cannot pay, shouldn't Thurber pay $21,000? However, Section 1(b) of the Uniform Act suggests that Dunne would only recover $14,000 since it provides that "[n]o tortfeasor is compelled to make contribution beyond his pro rata share of the entire liability." Thurber's pro rata share is one-third, or $14,000; under §1(b), Thurber can argue that he is only required to pay that to Dunne. If this is the answer, Dunne, having paid $42,000, will end up $28,000 out of pocket because he cannot collect contribution from White. The burden of White's insolvency would fall on him.

   Most courts view contribution as an equitable doctrine; on facts like these they would likely require Thurber to pay $21,000 in contribution to Dunne. See Restatement (Second) of Torts §886A cmt. c (when one tortfeasor is insolvent, court may "do what is fair and equitable under the circumstances" in ordering contribution). This flexibility to account for the circumstances is preserved in §2(c) of the Uniform Act, which provides that, in determining the pro rata shares, "principles of equity applicable to contribution generally shall apply." Under this provision, the court would likely require Thurber to pay $21,000 in contribution to Dunne, despite the language of §1(b).

Some Unsettling Cases

9. a. Thurber is still liable for the full judgment, but he receives a dollar credit for the amount of the settlement with Dunne. Uniform Act §4(a). Thus, he will have to pay Rogers $30,000. As this example illustrates, once Dunne has settled, Thurber risks paying more than half of the damages unless he settles as well.
   b. As the introduction indicates, §4(b) of the Uniform Act bars contribution from a settling tortfeasor. Thurber will not be able to force Dunne to pay anything above the $12,000 he paid to settle with Rogers. This gives defendants a strong incentive to settle cases. If Dunne can induce the plaintiff to settle for less than half of the likely damage amount, he will avoid paying his full "share" of the liability.

      Thurber might argue that the settlement is so low that it is not "in good faith," that Rogers and Dunne have conspired to force Thurber to bear the brunt of the damages by settling for an unreasonably low amount. However, many factors affect the parties' judgment about how much a claim is worth, and many of these factors are quite subjective, such as the risk that the settling defendant's negligence cannot be proved at trial, or the adverse effect of having a sympathetic defendant before the court. Due to such factors, it is doubtful that the court will find that the settlement was in bad faith simply because Dunne paid less than his pro rata share of the plaintiff's damages.

c. Under a pro rata credit approach, Rogers effectively sells half (his pro rata share) of his claim to Dunne by settling with him. He would then be entitled to collect one-half of the damages verdict from Thurber. If the total damages found by the jury are $42,000, Rogers would collect $21,000 from Thurber, and $12,000 from Dunne, for a total of $33,000. Naturally, this approach makes plaintiffs cautious about settling with the first tortfeasor.

10. a. Under joint and several liability, Thurber is liable for the full amount of Rogers's damages, but gets a dollar-for-dollar credit for the amount paid in settlement. He must pay Rogers $7,000 ($42,000 − $35,000).

b. Dunne is barred from seeking contribution from Thurber by §1(d), which provides that a settling tortfeasor cannot obtain contribution unless he has obtained a release of the other tortfeasor's liability as well as his own. The example indicates that Dunne received a release of *his* liability, but not Thurber's; thus, he cannot ask Thurber to contribute. Dunne cannot undo his bargain by seeking contribution if his settlement turns out to be higher than his share of the damages awarded. If Dunne had settled for *less* than half the damages assessed, he would not have had to pay contribution to Thurber. See Example 9b. Under the Uniform Act it works both ways, or, more accurately, neither way. If Dunne makes a good deal, he shifts more than half of the damages to Thurber. If he makes a bad deal, as he did here, he ends up paying more than half himself.

c. In a pro rata jurisdiction, Rogers is viewed as having sold half of his claim to Dunne by settling with him. Thus, he may collect only the other half of the $42,000 judgment from Thurber, or $21,000. This amount, together with the $35,000 he obtained in settlement from Dunne, comes to $56,000 for a case in which the jury has determined the damages to be $42,000. Under the pro rata credit approach, the *plaintiff* gets the advantage of a favorable settlement; she collects more than the jury's damage award. Compare Example 10a, which illustrates that the *nonsettling defendant* gets the benefit from a high settlement in a dollar credit jurisdiction.

Confusion Worse Confounded

11. At first glance, it seems that there are three tortfeasors, so that Simon should get $20,000 from Porter, another $20,000 from Reliable, and end up paying $20,000 himself. However, there really aren't three tortfeasors in this example, only two. Simon was negligent and Porter was negligent. Reliable is not a tortfeasor itself; rather, it is a party responsible to pay any amount that Porter is liable for.

    Under the doctrine of respondeat superior, Reliable can be made to pay for Porter's tort. For example, Allen could demand $60,000 from Reliable under this judgment since Porter is liable for the full damages under joint and several liability. Consequently, Reliable is liable to Allen for that amount under respondeat superior. If Simon paid the full judgment to Allen, he would be entitled to $30,000 in contribution from Porter because Simon and Porter are the two tortfeasors. Under respondeat superior, Reliable would be liable to Simon for Porter's $30,000 contribution share (as would Porter). Simon could demand it from either one. However, while Reliable is liable for Porter's share, Reliable is *not* a third tortfeasor; it is a party which the law holds liable, for policy reasons, for Porter's tort. See §2(b) of the Uniform Act, which provides that, where equity so requires, "the collective liability of some as a group shall constitute a single share."

12. If Simon were a tort lawyer, he would realize that he isn't off the hook. Maybe Allen didn't sue him, but maybe she *did* sue Porter. If she did, and if she wins, and if Porter pays, he can then come after Simon for contribution *within one year after he loses to Porter.*[6] In other words, a losing defendant can seek contribution against another tortfeasor long after the original plaintiff is barred from suing that tortfeasor directly. This provision is necessary: Otherwise, Allen could defeat Simon's right to contribution by suing Simon alone, just before the limitations period ran.

    Figure 21-2 illustrates how Porter could come knocking on Simon's door some four-and-a-half years after the statute of limitations had run on a direct claim against Simon.[7]

---

6. See Uniform Act §3(c).

7. As a practical matter, if Allen sues Porter, Simon is likely to find out. One of the parties will doubtless want to depose him in the action, and he will likely be called to testify at trial as well.

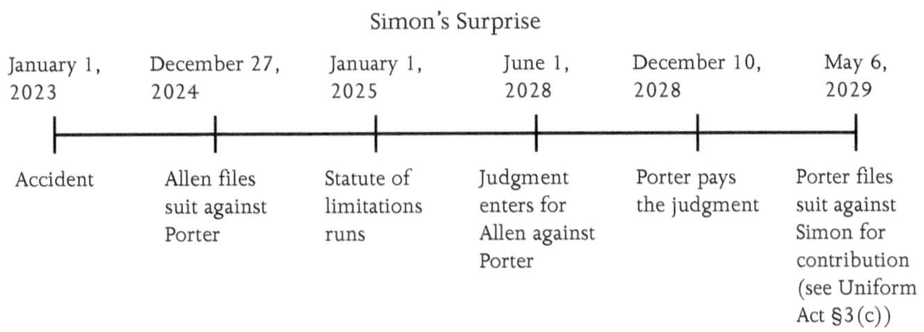

Figure 21-2

A Sense of Proportion

13. a. Under the Uniform Act, Porter would receive one-half, or $50,000 in contribution from Simon.

    b. Wouldn't it make more sense to redistribute the judgment in proportion to the fault of the parties? Under this approach, since Porter was 80 percent at fault and Simon 20 percent, Simon would pay Porter $20,000 in contribution (20% of $100,000 judgment). Had Simon paid the judgment, he would have obtained $80,000 in contribution from Porter. This proportional approach to contribution has rapidly gained popularity in comparative negligence jurisdictions.[8] It is analyzed in more detail in Chapter 25.

8. Some states have switched from pro rata contribution to comparative or proportional contribution simply by dropping the word "not" from §2(a) of the Uniform Act. In these states, the defendants' "relative degrees of fault shall be considered" in determining contribution, so each ends up contributing to the judgment in proportion to her fault. See, e.g., Mich. Comp. Laws §600.2925b.

CHAPTER 22

Please Pass the Liability: Respondeat Superior and Nondelegable Duties

INTRODUCTION

The last two chapters have considered the allocation of liability in cases involving "joint tortfeasors." As those chapters indicate, when more than one party's negligence contributes to an injury, each negligent party is liable, but may be able to seek contribution from other tortfeasors. This chapter addresses the related situation in which one defendant incurs liability, not due to his own negligence, but due to the negligence of another. We focus on two common examples of such "vicarious liability": liability of an employer for the torts of its employees, and liability of one who employs an independent contractor for torts committed by the independent contractor.

RATIONALES FOR IMPOSING VICARIOUS LIABILITY ON EMPLOYERS

The common law has long accepted the premise that employers should be liable for the torts of their employees in the scope of employment. The premise is sufficiently entrenched to merit its own legal Latin, "respondeat superior," which is loosely translated, "let the master respond." While virtually all jurisdictions impose liability on employers for the torts of their employees, the rationales for the respondeat superior doctrine have varied.

It is sometimes said that the employer should pay because she can select and control her employees, and thereby prevent injuries due to negligence. It is doubtless true, as a general matter, that employers can reduce accidents by requiring their employees to exercise care, and that making employers liable for employees' torts gives them an incentive to enforce careful conduct. However, employers frequently have no realistic chance of preventing a particular negligent act by an employee, as when an employee drives alone to pick up a package or goes out alone to repair an elevator. Employers cannot hover over their employees from minute to minute, and, as an actuarial matter, even employees who are carefully selected and supervised will be negligent on occasion, despite the employer's most rigorous efforts to promote safety. When they are, the employer is liable even if it took stringent measures to prevent accidents. This liability, in other words, is truly vicarious; it flows automatically from the employee's tort, regardless of the care the employer exercised in selecting or supervising him.

More skeptical observers have suggested that respondeat superior liability is simply a device to provide a "deep-pocket" defendant able to pay the plaintiff's damages. Prosser & Keeton at 500. Certainly it serves this purpose in many cases, since employers are more likely to have the resources to pay judgments than their employees. Yet, if vicarious liability is imposed solely to assure a deep pocket, it might equally well be imposed on *any* party with substantial resources: We could make millionaires vicariously liable for torts, or any insurance company with a headquarters building over 25 stories, or—what the heck—how about the government? Clearly, while assuring compensation is a factor, respondeat superior is intended to assure that such compensation comes from a party that is fairly made to pay it.

Another rationale cited for the doctrine is that employers are in a position to spread the costs of accidents by purchasing liability insurance and raising the price of their products to reflect the inherent accident costs of the enterprise. This argument, like economic analysis of tort law in general, looks at the issue not as a matter of individual fairness or blame, but rather as a question of the overall societal impact of placing the cost of accidents in one place or another. Respondeat superior encourages employers to insure; the cost of insurance gets incorporated into the price of the product, which consequently reflects more accurately the actual costs of producing it, including the accident costs. This argument makes sense, but, like the deep-pocket argument, courts would probably not accept it if they did not view respondeat superior as inherently fair as well.

Perhaps the most basic rationale for the doctrine is that the employee acts for the master in the performance of the master's work. In the course of that work, he creates risks to further the master's goals, including the risk of injuries due to negligence. Where such risks are created for the master's benefit, it seems intuitively fair to ascribe the conduct to the party for whose benefit it was undertaken. As stated in an early English case, "the reason that

I am liable is this, that by employing [an employee] I set the whole thing in motion; and what he does, being done for my benefit and under my direction, I am responsible for the consequences of doing it." *Duncan v. Findlater*, 7 Eng. Rep. 934, 940 (H.L. 1839). On the simplest level, if the master did not have the work done by another, he would have to do it himself, and would be liable for any torts committed in doing so. Under respondeat superior, the acts done at the master's bidding are treated, for liability purposes, as though he had performed them himself.

THE MEANING OF "EMPLOYEE"

An employer is only liable for the torts of a worker if the worker is its employee and acts in the scope of his employment. In many cases it is unclear whether a party who acts for another is an employee or instead acts as an independent contractor. Suppose, for example, that Bogart hires Bacall to maintain his yard. Bacall could be an employee or an independent contractor, depending on the particular facts of the relationship. If Bogart provides all the tools, pays Bacall by the hour, determines when she will work and exactly what she will do, Bacall would likely be characterized as an employee. On the other hand, if Bacall works with her own truck and tools, comes whenever she chooses, is paid by the season, provides her own insurance, and decides for herself what needs to be done to make the yard sparkle, she would likely be characterized as an independent contractor.

It is often stated that a person is an employee (or, in common law parlance, a "servant") if the employer has the right of control over the person in the performance of the work.

> An employee is an agent whose principal (i.e., employer) controls or has the right to control the manner and means of the agent's performance of work.

Restatement (Third) of Agency §7.07(3). However, this control test does not clearly resolve close cases, since even independent contractors are subject to some degree of control. Doubtless Bogart would have the authority to tell Bacall not to use chemical fertilizer, or to trim the rose bushes in the fall rather than the spring, even if Bacall's business was independent in most respects. Thus, courts have elaborated a number of factors that they consider in determining whether an actor is an employee. The Third Restatement of Agency, for example, lists the following factors:

- **The extent of control which the master is authorized to exercise over the details of the work.** Clearly, the more supervisory authority the employer has to specify how the work will proceed, the more likely it is that the worker will be viewed as an employee.

- **Whether the actor is engaged in a distinct occupation or business.** If Bogart employs a handy person to work around the house, she will more likely be viewed as an employee than if he calls in a computer repair person or an electrician.
- **Whether the type of work is customarily performed under the employer's supervision or by a specialist without supervision, and the extent of the skill required.** If the work involves a skilled task typically hired out to a specialized contractor, it will more likely be viewed as a contract situation. If Bogart hires Greenstreet to move his house, Greenstreet is more likely to be viewed as an independent contractor than if he is hired to wash it.
- **Who supplies the tools, other equipment, and place of work.** If Bacall goes to Bogart's place of business every day to sew shirts and uses Bogart's sewing machines and material, she will probably be viewed as an employee. On the other hand, if she does piecework at home on her own machine, she may be an independent contractor.
- **The length of time for which the person is employed.** Frequently, persons hired for a single purpose and a brief period look more like independent contractors, since there is less of a relationship and a greater likelihood that she was called in to perform a specific task in her own manner. However, like the other factors, this one does not always help. If Bogart hires Bacall for a fall afternoon to rake leaves, she will likely be viewed as an employee. If he hires her for a season to maintain the grounds, she may well be a landscaping contractor.
- **Whether the person is paid on a time basis or by the job.** Workers hired by the hour or the week tend to be viewed as employees, since they are at the employer's "beck and call" on a regular basis. By contrast, contractors are typically hired to accomplish a given end result—such as building a house or repairing a bridge—without detailed supervision during the process, and paid a flat sum to accomplish that result.
- **Whether the employer is in business, and whether the work is part of the employer's regular business.** If Bogart is a jeweler, and hires Bacall to cut diamonds, a court is likely to infer that she is an employee. On the other hand, if he hires her to renovate his jewelry store, the more likely inference is that she is an independent contractor hired on a one-time basis to accomplish a particular task.
- **The parties' belief as to the nature of the relation.** It is relevant, though not dispositive, that the parties view the relation as an employment relation, or otherwise. This belief may be reflected in various arrangements. For example, an employer is likely to pay employment and worker's compensation taxes, to provide insurance,

> and to comply with various other regulatory requirements regarding employees. The fact that the employer has treated the worker as an employee is suggestive that the master/servant relation actually exists.

See Restatement (Third) of Agency §7.07 cmt. f. This multifactor test for determining employment status is widely accepted, not only in the context of tort liability, but in others as well. See, e.g., §3121(d)(2) of the Internal Revenue Code (stating that common law test applies in determining employment status under the Internal Revenue Code). Like so many legal standards these days, this test is hardly cut and dried, and will often pose questions of fact for the jury. On the other hand, while ambiguous cases arise, in most cases it is pretty clear whether the individual is an employee or an independent contractor.

ACTING IN THE SCOPE OF EMPLOYMENT

Even if the court concludes that Bacall was Bogart's employee at the time that she negligently injured the plaintiff, Bogart will only be liable for her negligence if she acted in the scope of her employment. Bogart obviously is not liable for private acts of Bacall, but only those properly attributable to her employment.

Isn't the law tiresome in the way it finds interpretive problems around every corner? Perhaps so, but these interpretive problems arise from the necessary process of determining the outer limits of a principle. Unless we are to hold Bogart liable for everything Bacall does, we must define the limit of his responsibility. He should not be liable if Bacall gets in a motor vehicle accident over the weekend, because her driving is unrelated to her work for Bogart. Even if she gets in the accident on her lunch hour, Bogart should probably not be liable. This trip is for her own purposes, outside of Bogart's premises and control. On the other hand, Bogart clearly would be vicariously liable if Bacall hit a passing pedestrian with a ladder while working as a house painter for Bogart's painting company. Since this act took place in the course of and for the furtherance of the employer's work, it seems fair that it should pay.

The Third Restatement of Agency offers the following definition of "scope of employment":

> An employee acts within the scope of employment when performing work assigned by the employer or engaging in a course of conduct subject to the employer's control. . . .

Restatement (Third) of Agency §7.07(2). This definition works well enough in the easy cases, but is less helpful in the close ones, such as acts that are incidental to the work experience but do not directly further the work. Suppose, for example, that Bacall starts a fire while smoking on the job or bumps into a visitor while on the way to the bathroom. These acts do not directly arise from the performance of the work, but they are normal incidents of the work experience.

Although early cases limited "scope of employment" to acts intended to directly further the employer's business, the tendency in more recent cases is to hold incidental acts in the course of the work (such as lunch or smoking breaks) within the scope of employment. They take place at the employer's place of business, during working hours, and are related in a general way to the accomplishment of the work. If the rationale for vicarious liability is that the risks engendered by an enterprise should be absorbed and distributed by that enterprise, it seems supportable to hold the employer liable for such incidental risks. *George v. Bekins Van & Storage Co.*, 205 P.2d 1037, 1043 (Cal. 1949); see Restatement (Third) of Agency §7.07 cmt. d (personal acts during the workday within scope of employment as "incidental to the employee's performance of assigned work").

VICARIOUS LIABILITY FOR INTENTIONAL TORTS

Another difficult problem is determining when employers will be held vicariously liable for intentional torts by employees. Intentional torts require, by definition, a deliberate decision by the actor to invade another's rights. In almost all cases, such deliberate invasions are unwanted, discouraged, and probably forbidden by the employer. There is some force, therefore, to the employer's argument that he should not be held liable for such acts in clear contravention of his wishes.

Despite these arguments, courts do hold employers liable for at least some intentional torts by their employees. For example, courts have fairly consistently held employers liable where an employee commits an intentional tort in order to serve (however misguidedly) the employer's purposes. Dobbs' Law of Torts §429. An employee of a repossession company who assaults an owner while repossessing his car is clearly trying to do her job. Similarly, a bouncer who uses excessive force in evicting a patron from a bar is motivated to serve his employer, albeit overzealously. He is probably not doing it the way the employer wants him to, but neither is an employee who is negligent. Once again, if the basis for respondeat superior is that the employer's business has created the risk, these cases appear to be good candidates for application of the doctrine.

A second category of cases involves brawls that arise in the course of the work. For example, Bacall, while delivering pizzas for Bogart, might get into a dispute with another driver at a traffic light and punch him, or two assembly-line workers might argue about the proper way to do the job, causing one to hit the other with a wrench.

Bacall's punch is arguably in the scope of employment, since the altercation occurs while she is making a delivery for her employer. The fight is not meant to accomplish the work, but the dispute arises during and because of the work done for the employer.

The cases tend to impose vicarious liability in this scenario, on the theory that the tort is incidental to the work, in the same sense that a smoking break or a trip to the bathroom is. See R. Brill, The Liability of an Employer for the Wilful Torts of His Servants, 45 Chi.-Kent L. Rev. 1, 11-14 (1968). One court suggests that vicarious liability applies in this class of cases if the assault arises "in response to the plaintiff's conduct which was presently interfering with the employee's ability to successfully perform his duties." *Miller v. Federated Department Stores, Inc.*, 304 N.E.2d 573, 580 (Mass. 1973).

Even under a broad test of this type, some scenarios will not support liability even though they occur during the employee's work. Suppose that Bacall, while delivering the pizza, saw Stewart, an acquaintance who owed her money, stopped the car and punched Stewart for refusing to pay. This may have happened "when performing work assigned by the employer" (Restatement (Third) of Agency §7.07(3)), but most courts would not impose liability on the employer for this act of personal pique. Here's a nice statement of this ambiguous line between intentional torts that invoke respondeat superior and those that do not:

> the line separating a master's *respondeat superior* liability from a servant's individual responsibility for the latter's on-duty assault is drawn somewhere between a servant's venting purely personal spleen on a third party and the point at which the servant continues to press the master's interest with mistaken vigor and in an inappropriately aggressive manner.

Baker v. St. Francis Hosp., 126 P.3d 602, 609 n.3 (Okla. 2005) (Opala, J, concurring and dissenting in part).

A third common scenario involves sexual misconduct in the course of medical care or psychotherapy. See, e.g., *Lisa M. v. Henry Mayo Newhall Memorial Hosp.*, 907 P.2d 358 (Cal. 1995) (sexual assault by ultrasound technician during examination); *Birkner v. Salt Lake County*, 771 P.2d 1053 (Utah 1989) (social worker engaged in sexual activity with patient during counseling). The acts in these cases clearly do not serve the employer's purposes, but they are a peculiar risk of certain kinds of work. Few courts would have held an employer liable for these torts 50 years ago; today, the cases are mixed. Some courts, taking a broad view of the costs an enterprise should absorb, will impose liability. See, e.g., *Fahrendorff v. North Homes, Inc.*, 597 N.W.2d 905 (Minn. 1999); *Plummer v. Center Psychiatrists, Ltd.*, 476 S.E.2d 172 (Va. 1996). Others, emphasizing the personal motivation of the tortfeasor, deny recovery. See, e.g., *Birkner*, 771 P.2d at 1058-1059 (citing a gazillion cases).

The Restatement of Agency would resolve intentional tort cases based on the distinction between serving the employer's purposes and "an independent course of conduct not intended by the employee to serve any purpose of the employer." Restatement (Third) of Agency §7.07(2). This test appears to narrow the ambit of liability somewhat. For example, under this test, a fight after a traffic accident would likely not be held in the scope of employment. Although the employment provides the occasion for the employee's assault, the assault hardly serves a purpose of the employer. See id. illus. 7-9.

A related issue arises when an employee's official position facilitates commission of an intentional tort. In *Lo v. Superior Court*, 79 Cal. Rptr. 2d 561 (Cal. Ct. App. 2d Dist. 1998), for example, a judge threatened a defendant with adverse treatment in sentencing if she did not engage in sexual acts with him. Even courts that would generally deny recovery for such assaults may find the employer liable in these cases, based on the special authority vested in the tortfeasor that created a unique risk of abuse. See Restatement (Second) of Agency §219(2)(d) (employer liability when agent is aided by the agency relationship in committing tort); see also *Doe v. Forrest*, 853 A.2d 48 (Vt. 2004) (sheriff's department could be liable under §219(2)(d) for acts of police officer who used his authority to force store clerk to perform sexual acts).

In another common scenario, the employee's tort has no relation to accomplishing the master's purpose, but the employment simply furnishes the opportunity for a completely unrelated tort. For example, a waiter might steal money from a customer's purse. In this scenario, the intentional tort is *related* to the employment, in the "but for" sense that the job creates the opportunity for the tort, but the tort is not motivated by the work or by any work-related purpose. See, e.g., *Effort Enterprises, Inc. v. Crosta*, 391 S.E.2d 477 (Ga. Ct. App. 1990) (employer not liable where employees stole jewelry while moving other items into plaintiff's house). Virtually all courts deny recovery against the employer in these cases.

Courts that take a broad approach to vicarious liability may formulate broader tests than the traditional "motivation to serve" or Third Restatement approach. Some courts have held that the employee's act must be foreseeable in the sense that it is "not . . . so unusual or startling that it would be unfair to include the loss caused by the injury among the costs of the employer's business." *Leafgreen v. American Family Mut. Ins. Co.*, 393 N.W.2d 275, 280-281 (S.D. 1986). Others have simply required the conduct to be foreseeable or incidental to the work. *Martinez v. Hagopian*, 227 Cal. Rptr. 763, 766

(Cal. Ct. App. 1986). Such tests, while broader than the traditional test, are too malleable to help much with the hard intentional tort cases. The Third Restatement rejects a foreseeability test as too broad and unfair to employers. Restatement (Third) of Agency §7.07 cmt. b.

Ultimately, the disparate results in the intentional tort cases "represent differing judgments about the desirability of holding an employer liable for his subordinates' wayward behavior." *Faragher v. City of Boca Raton*, 527 U.S. 755, 798 (1998). In other words, the outcome is a policy choice upon which courts differ. Such opposite outcomes in similar cases tend to frustrate students—and professors—who would like to see all the cases cleanly resolved by a single rule. Unfortunately no such universal rule exists, nor will there be one as long as we have 50 different states entitled to make their own tort law.

THE CONSEQUENCES OF INDEPENDENCE

While employers are generally liable for the torts of their employees in the scope of employment, they generally are *not* liable for torts of an independent contractor, even though they arise from the contractor's work for the employer. Restatement (Second) of Torts §409. (For the sake of clarity, I will call the party who hires an independent contractor the "owner," rather than the "employer" throughout this chapter.) This "rule of insulation" from tort liability (C. Morris and C. Morris Jr., Morris on Torts 256 (2d ed. 1980)) will often influence the way parties structure their business relationships. Owners may choose to hire independent contractors to perform work rather than using their own employees, simply to insulate themselves from tort liability. Of course, where the owner knows he is avoiding a potential liability, the contractor knows that he is assuming it. Consequently, the cost of insuring against tort liability will be considered in setting the price of the work.

EXCEPTIONS TO THE RULE: NONDELEGABLE DUTIES

While hiring an independent contractor usually insulates an owner from liability for torts in the course of the work (Restatement (Third) of Torts: Liability for Physical and Emotional Harm §57), it will not always do so. In some situations, courts have refused to allow owners to insulate themselves from liability, *even* if they use a contractor to do the work. In such situations, it is often said that the owner's duty of care is "nondelegable," so the owner remains liable for tortious injury from the performance of the work, even though the tort was committed by an independent contractor.

The phrase *nondelegable duty* is something of a misnomer. The owner *has* delegated the work to an independent contractor in these cases. What the courts mean is that the owner may delegate the *work* but cannot delegate away the *liability* for tortious acts in the course of the work. Like the employer under respondeat superior, the owner is liable in these cases *vicariously* for the torts of the independent contractor.

The Third Restatement of Torts specifies a number of situations in which vicarious liability is commonly imposed on the party hiring an independent contractor. For example, courts often hold a duty nondelegable (so that the hiring party is vicariously liable for negligent performance) if the contract work involves "a peculiar risk" of physical harm during performance. Restatement (Third) of Torts: Liability for Physical and Emotional Harm §59. The Restatement offers an example in which the plaintiff is injured by high-voltage electricity. Id. at illus. 2. Working with high-voltage electricity poses a serious risk of injury, so much so that courts will hold the owner liable when negligence in the performance of that work causes injury, even though the owner has hired a competent independent contractor to perform the work. For another example, see *McMillan v. United States*, 112 F.3d 1040 (9th Cir. 1997) (clear-cutting of large trees held nondelegable because inherently dangerous). The evident rationale for imposing vicarious liability on the hiring party in such cases is that she should be aware that special precautions are necessary in such activities, and should assure that they are taken or incur liability if they are not.

Similarly, vicarious liability will likely be imposed on a party who hires a contractor to perform construction or repair on instrumentalities that involve unusual danger, such as transmission of high-voltage electricity or blasting. Restatement (Third) of Torts: Liability for Physical and Emotional Harm §60. Here again, the unusual danger inherent in the work, which necessarily imposes a risk of injury and is done for the owner's benefit, supports holding the owner liable for the contractor's torts in the course of such activities.

Courts have also held owners vicariously liable for negligence of their contractors in the course of work done in a public place. Restatement (Third) of Torts: Liability for Physical and Emotional Harm §64. Under this exception an electric company would be liable, for example, if it hired an independent tree surgeon to trim trees along its power lines over the sidewalks, and the tree surgeon caused an accident by cutting a branch down in the path of the plaintiff's car. Similarly, owners are vicariously liable for torts of their independent contractors in maintaining highways and other public property and in maintaining premises open to the public for business purposes. Id. at §64(b). Vicarious liability in these cases is presumably based on the wide risk created by work done in public places and the obvious need to encourage due care to protect the public from injury.

It has been said repeatedly that "the rule [insulating the owner from liability for an independent contractor's torts] is now primarily important as a preamble to the catalog of its exceptions." *Pacific Fire Ins. Co. v. Kenny Boiler & Mfg. Co.*, 277 N.W. 226, 228 (Minn. 1937). However, this catchy phrase is a bit of an overstatement. In many garden-variety cases independent contractors are solely liable for their torts. If Bogart hires Bacall to resurface his driveway, and she backs into the street causing an accident, most likely she alone will bear the liability. If he hires an electrical contractor to rewire his office, most likely the contractor alone will be liable if she negligently starts a fire in the course of the work.

It is not possible to catalog here all situations in which courts have applied the nondelegable duty doctrine. For a full discussion of categories of nondelegable duties, see the Restatement (Third) of Torts: Liability for Physical and Emotional Harm §§57-65. The central point of this discussion is to illustrate that the contractor's independence does not always absolve the owner of responsibility, since courts often refuse, for policy reasons, to allow owners to wash their hands of the matter by hiring out the work.

LIABILITY FOR THE OWNER'S OWN NEGLIGENCE

The nondelegable duty theory will frequently allow a plaintiff injured by a contractor's negligence to recover from the owner who hired the contractor, even though the owner has exercised due care. However, it is important to remember that owners can be negligent too; frequently, a plaintiff will have a claim against the owner based on his *own* negligence in connection with the contract work.

An owner may be negligent in various ways even though the work is delegated to an independent contractor. He may hire a contractor who is clearly incompetent to perform the type of work required. He may fail to properly supervise the contractor. He may fail to require the contractor to take necessary precautions, or specify that the work be done in an inappropriate manner. He may fail to inspect the work after it is done, or negligently perform work over which he retains control. See generally Restatement (Second) of Torts §§410-415 (detailing bases of liability for owner's negligence in connection with contract work); see now Restatement (Third) of Torts §55. In such cases, the owner is liable for his *own* negligence, not vicariously liable for negligence of the contractor.

Frequently, a plaintiff will assert claims against the owner based on both the owner's own negligence and on vicarious liability theories, but it is important to distinguish these two bases for holding the owner liable. Even if there is no basis for holding the owner vicariously liable, he must still be liable for negligence in his own conduct in connection with the work.

The examples below illustrate the nature and the limits of vicarious liability, both for the acts of employees and of independent contractors.

Examples

Respondeat Inferior

1. Grant, an employee of Metro Studios, is sued by Bergman, a passerby, for injuries arising from an accident caused by Grant in the course of making a movie. Grant answers the complaint, denying liability on the ground that he was acting in the scope of his employment for Metro at the time of the accident. Bergman moves to strike the defense as insufficient. Should the motion be granted?

2. Based on the accident, Bergman sues Grant and Metro (on a respondeat superior theory) for her injuries. Both are held liable for Bergman's injury, for which the jury awards $50,000 in damages.
   a. If Grant pays Bergman $50,000, how much can Bergman collect from Metro?
   b. Grant pays the judgment and seeks contribution from Metro. What result?
   c. Assume that Metro pays the judgment. How much should it be entitled to collect from Grant?

3. Assume, on the facts of Example 1, that the movie was a Western. Grant, while waiting for a scene to begin, was sitting on his horse, Trigger, who bolted when a tourist unexpectedly exploded a firecracker. Bergman, another tourist watching from the sidelines, was knocked down by Trigger. Would Metro be liable to Bergman under respondeat superior?

Expert Employment

4. Kildare, a physician with a general practice, is hired to conduct physical exams for Apex, a large manufacturing company. Apex specifies which employees will be examined, what the examinations will entail, what lab tests will be required, and how long Kildare has to submit his reports. The parties agree that Kildare will examine the patients at his office, will conduct a minimum of 20 exams per month, and that he will be paid a set amount for each exam. Kildare negligently injures Garbo during a physical, and she sues Apex. Is Apex liable on the basis of respondeat superior?

5. Freud, a psychiatrist, is hired by Columbia Hospital, a mental health facility, to conduct psychotherapy with inpatients at the hospital. Freud agrees to spend ten hours per week at the hospital, to treat patients designated by Columbia, and to accept one-fourth of a full-time salary

and associated benefits for her work. The parties agree that Freud shall have sole authority over the method of treatment of the patients she sees; however, she is subject to the general administrative regulations of the hospital concerning such matters as treatment notes, guidelines for medicating patients, informed consent, and others. Jones, one of Freud's Columbia patients, commits suicide, and his survivors sue Columbia for alleged negligence of Freud in failing to take steps to prevent the suicide. Should Freud be found to be an employee of Columbia for respondeat superior purposes?

Forewarned and Forearmed

6. Rogers is a sales clerk for the Wild West Gun Shop, which sells firearms and ammunition. Evans, his boss, repeatedly reminds him that he is not to sell to minors. Garner, a 15-year-old, comes into the shop, and Rogers (who is aware of Garner's age) sells him a box of cartridges. Garner is injured using the cartridges and sues Wild West. Would respondeat superior apply?

The Master's Business?

7. Larry, a house painter for Beta Construction Company, is painting an office with an electric paint sprayer when Curley, a fellow employee, happens by. Larry, in a spirit of horseplay, chases Curley around the room, aiming the sprayer at him and threatening to paint him blue. Unfortunately, he pulls the spray hose too far, knocking over the spray pump and spilling paint on the floor. The paint seeps through the ceiling and ruins office equipment in Moe's office below. Is Beta liable for the damage?
8. Grimsley, a pitcher for the Baltimore Orioles, is harassed by fans while warming up in the bullpen. Thoroughly annoyed, he finally heaves the ball at the fans, injuring Flynn. Flynn sues the Baltimore Orioles Baseball Club. If you represented Flynn, which of the tests below concerning the scope of respondeat superior liability would you prefer to see the court apply?
    - an act motivated by a purpose to serve the employer
    - abuse of a position of authority based on the employment
    - an act that responds to a present interference with the performance of the employer's work
    - an act that is foreseeable and incidental to the performance of the employer's work.
9. Hyde, a childcare worker at Child Haven Day Care Center, secretly abuses three children who are cared for at the center. The children sue Child Haven for damages. Which of the various tests for holding the employer liable for an intentional tort would be most favorable to the plaintiffs?

10. Jones, a teacher in a program for severely mentally disabled children, beats one of the children with a ruler for urinating in his pants. The school rules specifically forbid corporal punishment. Can the school district be liable under respondeat superior?

Respondeat Judge Fudd

11. Charles Electronics tries to make employees feel appreciated. Often, on Friday afternoon, Loy, the assembly supervisor, would buy beer for the crew, and they would all tip a few before heading home for the weekend. One Friday, Nick, one of the assembly workers, had five beers before leaving, and then headed downtown to meet his wife for dinner. On the way, he injured Nora in an accident. She sues Charles Electronics for her injuries.

    At trial, after the above facts are proved, Judge Fudd indicates that he will give the following instruction:

    > If you find that, at the time of the accident, Nick was not in the course of his work for the defendant, and was not acting to further the purposes of the defendant, then you must find for the defendant.

    What objection should Nora raise to the proposed instruction?

Déja Vù

12. Tracy hires Hepburn Construction Company to rebuild the fire escapes on its apartment building, which immediately abuts Main Street. In the course of the work, a Hepburn employee negligently attaches a load of iron railings to a crane cable, and they fall, injuring Stewart, a passerby. Stewart sues Hepburn, the contractor, which denies liability. It argues that the duty of care was nondelegable because it involves a risk of injury unless special precautions are taken, so that Tracy is liable for the tort. Is this a good defense?

13. Stewart sues both Hepburn Company and Tracy, and both are found liable for Hepburn's negligence. Hepburn pays and seeks contribution from Tracy. What result?

Nondelegable Nonnegligence

14. Assume, on the facts of the Hepburn example, that the load of iron railings was not negligently attached, but fell when the crane's hoisting cable snapped. Although the cable was new, subsequent metallurgical analysis revealed that it had an undetectable defect, which caused it to snap under a normal load. Is Tracy liable for Stewart's injury?

Delegable Duties

15. Tracy hires Hepburn Construction Company to build a garage for him. In the course of the work, Cagney, a Hepburn employee, is required to cut two-by-fours on a table saw. He fails to use the blade guard, and the force of the blade throws a piece of wood into the air, injuring Stewart's eye as he passes by on the street. Is Tracy liable?

16. Assume that Tracy hires Hepburn Construction to rebuild the fire escapes on its high-rise. A Hepburn employee left a short metal pipe on the sidewalk next to the building. Colbert trips over it and is injured. Is Tracy, the building owner, liable for her injury?

Explanations

Respondeat Inferior

1. The judge should grant the motion to strike this defense. Grant is evidently under the impression (as many of my students are initially) that an employee is not personally liable for his torts in the scope of employment, since the employer is liable under respondeat superior. On the contrary, while respondeat superior provides *another*, potentially more solvent target for the plaintiff, the doctrine does not bar suit against an employee for his own tortious conduct. Both may be sued, and frequently both will be.

2. a. Bergman cannot collect anything further from Metro. Metro, as Grant's employer, is liable along with Grant for the judgment. Bergman could try to collect it from either the tortfeasor or the vicariously liable employer, but cannot collect it twice. Once Grant pays, Bergman's judgment has been "satisfied."
   b. Contribution statutes allow a tortfeasor who has paid a judgment to recover part of the judgment from other tortfeasors. It does not apply between Grant and Metro, however, because they are not joint tortfeasors. Metro is not a tortfeasor at all, but rather is vicariously liable for the tort of someone else. Although Metro is liable to Bergman under respondeat superior, it need not reimburse Grant, who caused the injury, if he pays the judgment. Respondeat superior exists to assure that the *plaintiff* can collect from Metro; it is not intended to insulate the actual tortfeasor from incurring the loss. If Grant pays, he will not recover any reimbursement from Metro.
   c. Most courts hold that an employer who pays the damages caused by his employee is entitled to indemnity—full reimbursement—from the employee, since the employee's negligence actually caused the

injury and gave rise to the liability. Indemnity, unlike contribution, involves situations in which one party is liable for another's tort, yet is able to seek reimbursement for the *entire* damages from the other. (Another common example of indemnity is a retail seller who is held liable without fault for selling a defective product, but has a right of indemnity from the manufacturer who actually produced the product.)

Although employers held liable under respondeat superior have a right of indemnity from the negligent employee, it is seldom exercised. An action for indemnity would frequently be futile, since the employee is unable to pay. In addition, such losses are often paid by an insurance policy covering both the employer and employee. And, of course, such actions do not make for positive employee relations.

3. Respondeat superior makes the employer liable for torts committed by its employees in the scope of employment. This question does not suggest that Grant did anything negligent. If he did not, he is not a tortfeasor. Since he would not be liable to Bergman, neither would Metro.

   Put another way, respondeat superior liability is not strict liability; it does not make employers liable for all *injuries* caused by their employees in the scope of employment. It makes them liable for *torts* committed by employees in the scope of employment. If Bergman's injury is a pure accident, caused by the unforeseeable act of the tourist, Grant is not liable and neither is Metro.

Expert Employment

4. Although Apex exercises some control over Dr. Kildare's work, the court will very likely conclude that he has acted as an independent contractor. Kildare is a practicing physician, a professional whose business is entirely distinct from that of Apex. He is hired to perform a task it requires, but that is not a normal part of its business. He works at his own office, using his own tools and equipment, and is paid on a per capita basis. He doubtless schedules the exams according to his own availability and continues to see other patients as well.

   It is true that Apex has specified in detail what it wants Kildare to do, but this is true in many contract situations. On a complex road construction job, for example, there will be hundreds of pages of specifications, yet it is clear that a contractor is being hired to perform the entire job for a fixed price. While Apex has specified particular aspects of the exams, it will clearly not hover over Kildare to control his detailed performance of the exams. Apex has contracted for a specified result; it has not hired Kildare to work for it on a day-to-day basis, subject to detailed supervision.

5. Although Freud, like Kildare, is a physician, she will likely be held an employee of Columbia on these facts. Freud comes to Columbia to deliver services that are part of the hospital's basic function. She is paid as a salaried employee. True, she only works part-time, but nothing in the test for employment suggests that part-time workers cannot be employees. Columbia assigns Freud her patients, provides her work space, and treats her like an employee for benefits purposes. She is also subject to Columbia's general administrative supervision while working there.

   On the other hand, if the fundamental test for employment is the right to control the details of the work, Freud has an argument that she cannot be an employee: As a doctor, she is bound by the ethical code of the medical profession to exercise independent medical judgment in the treatment of patients. If Columbia cannot control her in the performance of her central task, the treatment of patients, how can she be an employee?

   If this argument were accepted, virtually any professional or skilled worker would have to be viewed as independent. Accountants, lawyers, clergy, and psychologists, for example, frequently work for institutions, and look in virtually all other respects like employees, yet are bound by codes of conduct. Similarly, architects and engineers, as well as pilots, plumbers, electricians, and myriad other skilled workers are subject to statutory codes that prevent their employers from exercising complete control over their work. Yet their employers do exercise broad control over the administrative aspects of their work life: when they work, where they work, what projects they undertake, how they are paid, their general conduct, their benefits, and many others. In such cases, courts have held professionals employees if the employer exercises control over these other aspects of their work. See Restatement (Third) of Agency §7.07 cmt. f (skilled professionals may be employees despite wide discretion in performance of the work).

Forewarned and Forearmed

6. The issue here is whether Rogers's act is in the scope of employment where Wild West expressly prohibited it, but Rogers sold to a minor anyway. Since one of the rationales for vicarious liability is that the employer can control negligence of its employees, you might think that where the employer exercised that control but the employee was negligent anyway, the employer would avoid respondeat superior liability.

   The cases generally hold otherwise: The employer is liable despite its exercise of care to prevent negligence by its employees. See Restatement (Third) of Agency §7.07 cmt. c and illus. 2. This result actually makes a good deal of sense. *First*, while it may seem unfair in the particular case, across-the-board liability will provide an incentive for Wild West to continue to work to prevent injuries. Perhaps it will discipline Rogers or increase employee education efforts. *Second*, as a practical matter, allowing the employer to avoid liability by offering evidence of its care to prevent accidents would introduce a broad new issue—the employer's general quality-control measures—into the suit. *Third*, inducing employers to minimize injuries is only one of the rationales for respondeat superior. Others, such as encouraging loss spreading, internalizing the costs of an enterprise, and placing the loss on the party for whose benefit the risk was created, still support application of the doctrine in this case.

The Master's Business?

7. Although horseplay of this sort is common in the course of many jobs, it obviously does not further the purposes of the employer; Beta hardly pays Larry to chase other workers with the spray gun. On the other hand, smoking does not further the employer's purposes either. Like smoking, a certain amount of joking among coworkers is a foreseeable part of the ordinary course of the work experience, takes place in the workplace and during the course of the work, and serves to relieve the tedium of repetitive work.

   Acts of horseplay have been held "in the course of employment" in worker's compensation cases on the following rationale:

   > Men do not discard their personal qualities when they go to work. Into the job they carry their intelligence, skill, habits of care and rectitude. Just as inevitably they take along also their tendencies to carelessness and camaraderie, as well as their emotional make-up. In bringing men together, work brings these qualities together, causes frictions between them, creates occasions for lapses into carelessness, and for fun-making and emotional flare-up . . . [t]hese expressions of human nature are incidents inseparable from working together.

   Hartford Accident & Indem. Co. v. Cardillo, 112 F.2d 11, 15 (D.C. Cir. 1940); see *Varela v. Fisher Roofing Co. Inc.*, 572 N.W.2d 780 (Neb. 1998) (worker who fell from roof while arm wrestling with coworker in scope of employment). However, this rationale has not been generally accepted in respondeat superior cases involving horseplay, which frequently deny recovery against the employer on the ground that horseplay does not further the work in any way. See, e.g., *Bryant v. CSX Transp., Inc.*, 577 So. 2d 613, 615-616 (Fla. Dist. Ct. App. 1991); *Thomas v. Poole*, 262 S.E.2d 854, 857 (N.C. Ct. App. 1980).

   Liability would likely be imposed for horseplay under broader scope-of-employment tests. It is certainly a "foreseeable risk" of the employment, clearly "incidental" to the work, and would satisfy a test that imposes liability for acts that are "an outgrowth" of the performance of the work. The test suggested in the Third Restatement of Agency, however, denies recovery for "an independent course of conduct not intended . . . to serve any purpose of the employer." Restatement (Third) of Agency §7.07(2). This formula would likely deny recovery in most horseplay situations, though the result seems dubious.

8. Flynn would likely lose under a more traditional test, such as whether the act was motivated in part by a desire to serve the employer. Grimsley's act is motivated by annoyance, not any effort to prepare to enter the game. Nor would Grimsley be viewed as having a position of authority that facilitated this intentional tort. On the other hand, his act certainly does appear motivated by "present interference" with the ability to serve the master's purposes, since the heckling interfered with his concentration while warming up.[1] A fuzzy foreseeability test would also probably get Flynn to the jury, since this kind of harassment and retaliation is increasingly common in an age of declining manners. The Third Restatement of Agency would likely bar recovery, since heaving baseballs at fans is hardly intended to serve any purpose of the employer. See id. at §7.07(2).

9. Most of the tests for imposing respondeat superior liability for intentional torts would not support liability on these facts. Surely it does not further the employer's purposes or stem from present interference with the accomplishment of the work. The best argument would be that Child Haven has placed Hyde in a position of authority over the children that creates a unique risk of the intentional tort. The opportunity to commit the tort in this case arises from Hyde's work with children, and his position of authority over them assists him in doing so.

   If respondeat superior is meant to assure that enterprises internalize the costs of risks they create, liability on these facts may be warranted. Although child abuse is the last thing any day care center wants, its activity does create the risk of such abuse. However, many courts, swayed by the repugnant nature of the conduct, the purely personal motivation of the employee, and the obvious damage the conduct does to the employer's interests, would deny recovery. See, e.g., *Worcester Ins. Co. v. Fells Acres Day Sch., Inc.*, 558 N.E.2d 958, 967 (Mass. 1990).

10. This example is based on *Tall v. School Commissioners*, 706 A.2d 659 (Md. Ct. App. 1998). The *Tall* court held that the teacher's intentional tort fell outside the scope of employment, relying heavily on the fact that corporal punishment was forbidden by the district's rules.

---

1. In the case upon which this example is based, the court held that the Orioles could be liable under this test. See *Manning v. Grimsley*, 643 F.2d 20, 24-25 (1st Cir. 1981).

The decision reflects a very narrow view of respondeat superior. First, as Example 6 indicates, it is well established that an act is not necessarily outside the scope of employment because it violates an employer's rules. Second, there are some strong arguments for respondeat superior liability in this case. Jones may have been acting in the scope of employment even under the most traditional test: His act was likely intended to serve the district's purpose by disciplining a student for disruptive behavior. See Restatement (Third) of Agency §7.07(2) (conduct within scope of employment "when performing work assigned by the employer or engaging in a course of conduct subject to the employer's control"). Alternatively, the beating may have arisen from the employee's frustration created by the work, like the traffic argument cases discussed in the introduction. Many cases support respondeat superior liability in such situations. Although Jones's conduct was unauthorized, even reprehensible, its connection to the employment activity is still strong, much stronger, for example, than the child abuse in Example 9.

Respondeat Judge Fudd

11. Judge Fudd's mistake here is to focus on Nick's driving as the sole basis for imposing respondeat superior liability on Charles. Nora's counsel should hasten to point out to him that the negligent act of another employee—Loy—may also subject Charles to liability.

    Even if Charles is not vicariously liable for Nick's driving, since the workday was over and Nick was on his way to dinner, it very likely *is* liable for the negligence of Loy in furnishing alcohol to Nick. Many courts would find that this act was in the scope of Loy's employment. Doubtless, such efforts to maintain employee morale, while peripheral to the physical production of the company's products, are intended to further the work of the employer in a general way, as do company picnics, the firm dinner dance, and similar happy occasions. Thus, if Loy was negligent in providing too much alcohol to Nick, this will provide a separate basis for holding the employer liable. Nora should explain to Judge Fudd that his instruction is insufficient because her claim against Charles Electronics is based not only on Nick's negligence but also on Loy's.

Déja Vù

12. It is entirely likely that the duty here is nondelegable since lifting heavy objects with a crane above the sidewalk poses an obvious risk to the perambulating public unless special precautions are taken. Restatement

(Third) of Torts §§59, 63. However, finding the duty nondelegable would not relieve Hepburn, the independent contractor, of liability. Just as respondeat superior does not bar suit against a negligent employee, the fact that an owner is vicariously liable in nondelegable duty situations does not bar the plaintiff from suing the contractor for its negligence. It simply means that the owner is liable for it as well. Thus, the fact that the duty is nondelegable is not a proper defense for Hepburn.

13. Here again, as in the analogous circumstances of Example 2, Tracy is not liable to the contractor for contribution. He is not a joint tortfeasor, or any other kind of tortfeasor; he is vicariously liable for damages caused by Hepburn's tort. Because his liability arises from Hepburn's negligence, he is entitled to indemnity from Hepburn if he pays the judgment, but Hepburn has no right to contribution or indemnity from Tracy.

    If Tracy, the building owner, pays the judgment, it is much more likely to seek indemnity in this context than in the employer/employee situation. A contractor is more likely to have adequate resources and insurance to cover the loss. Indeed, Tracy's lawyer should be careful to include a clause in the contract requiring evidence that Hepburn is fully insured, so that this right of indemnity would protect his client from absorbing losses caused by Hepburn's negligence.

Nondelegable Nonnegligence

14. This accident did not result from negligence by Hepburn's employees, since the defect was undetectable. If its employees were not negligent, Hepburn would not be liable for Stewart's injury. If so, Tracy would not be liable either. Declaring a duty "nondelegable" does not mean that the owner is strictly liable for *any* accident that occurs in the course of the work. It only means that he is vicariously liable for his contractor's *tortious* conduct. Tracy, as the owner, would be liable if Hepburn was negligent in failing to take necessary precautions, but if Stewart was injured without negligence, he has no claim against Hepburn, and therefore none against Tracy either.

    Although Hepburn's employees were not negligent in causing the cable to snap, Stewart's counsel should consider whether they may have failed to take other appropriate precautions. It may be, for example, that if the worksite was properly cordoned off, Stewart would not have been within range of the railings. If such special precautions were necessary, and Hepburn failed to take them, Tracy could be held vicariously liable for that negligence.

Delegable Duties

15. Sawing two-by-fours may well be dangerous if the special precaution of putting the safety guard down is not taken. On the other hand, virtually *any* activity other than bookkeeping or playing chess involves some risk of injury if it is not done cautiously. If a duty is nondelegable whenever some appropriate precaution is omitted, the owner would be liable under the peculiar risk exception whenever its contractor is negligent. The exception would swallow the general rule that the contractor, not the owner, is liable for his torts.

    Clearly, the special precautions exception is meant to apply to a narrower class of cases involving unusual risks.

    > The situation is one in which a risk is created which is not a normal, routine matter of customary human activity, such as driving an automobile, but is rather a special danger to those in the vicinity, arising out of the particular situation created, and calling for special precautions.

    Restatement (Second) of Torts §413 cmt. b. The examples offered by the Restatement, demolishing a building or digging an excavation (see §413 cmt. c), clearly involve unusual dangers not encountered in sawing boards to build a garage.

16. As the Introduction notes, courts often hold that activities involving peculiar risk give rise to "nondelegable duties." This means that, while an owner can hire an independent contractor to conduct the work, the owner remains liable for tortious injuries that result from the unusual risks the work poses. For example, a building owner can't hire a contractor to take down a skyscraper and avoid liability if, due to the contractor's negligence, falling debris injures a passerby. This is dangerous work, done for the owner's benefit. Declaring the duty of care in the course of such work "nondelegable" means that, even though the owner contracts out the work, it can be sued for injuries negligently caused by the contractor, much as if it had done the work with its own employees.

    However, the owner's vicarious liability in these nondelegable duty cases only applies to the particular risks that led the court to impose vicarious liability, not for any negligent act that takes place in the course of the job. Suppose, for example, in the skyscraper case, that the contractor sent an employee to the hardware store, and she had an accident on the way. The contractor would be liable for that, but the owner of the building would not. While a building demolition contract may require driving, demolition gives rise to a "nondelegable" duty because of the risk of damage from falling debris, not from driving, an ordinary activity that may take place in any kind of work.

Similarly, in this example, the risk that makes the work nondelegable is the risk of falling objects if special precautions are not taken, not the risk that a slippery pipe would be left on the sidewalk. This is "collateral negligence" that could take place in any kind of construction. Hepburn will be liable for Colbert's injury, but not Tracy. See Restatement (Second) of Torts §426; Restatement (Third) of Torts §57 cmt. f.

PART VIII

The Effect of Plaintiff's Conduct

CHAPTER 23

The Once and Future Defense: Assumption of the Risk

INTRODUCTION

The late nineteenth century was the formative era of the common law of negligence. It was a time of rugged individualism, which emphasized freedom of action, personal initiative, and the right of self-determination. The ideal was the Horatio Alger type, the self-made entrepreneur who grasped the myriad possibilities of an expanding nation through strong character and hard work. Doubtless, the reality of most people's lives had little to do with this ideal, but it still conditioned the thinking of the time, including legal thinking.

It is not surprising that judges steeped in such ideas should accept the principle that the individual is master of his own fate, with the right to choose a course of action and the responsibility to accept the consequences of the choice. The concept of contributory negligence, that a plaintiff whose careless acts contributed to his injuries should bear the consequences, is an example. Another example, also with roots in the nineteenth century, is the doctrine of assumption of the risk.

The basic premise of assumption of the risk is that a person who is aware of a risk, and knowingly decides to encounter it, accepts responsibility for the consequences of that decision, and may not hold a defendant who created the risk liable for resulting injury. The premise was articulated in nineteenth-century terms by Professor Bohlen:

> The maxim *volenti non fit injuria* [that to which a person assents is not deemed in law an injury] is a terse expression of the individualistic tendency of the

> common law, which, proceeding from the people and asserting their liberties, naturally regards the freedom of individual action as the keystone of the whole structure. Each individual is left free to work out his own destinies; he must not be interfered with from without, but in the absence of such interference he is held competent to protect himself . . . the common law does not assume to protect him from the effects of his own personality and from the consequences of his voluntary actions or of his careless misconduct.

F. Bohlen, Voluntary Assumption of the Risk, 20 Harv. L. Rev. 14 (1906). Based on this individualistic premise, assumption of the risk became an established shield to negligence liability, just as the analogous privilege of consent avoids liability for intentional torts.

Many of the early cases applying assumption of the risk arose in the context of injuries to workers on the job. A worker might accept employment in a factory with unguarded vats of molten metal, or requiring work on high scaffolds without railings. If he fell into the vat or off of the scaffold, the employer would argue that, by taking the job with knowledge of the working conditions, he had assumed the risk of injury from the known conditions of employment, and could not complain of the consequences of that choice.[1] Other cases arose in the context of injuries on land of another, where a guest or other licensee suffered injury due to an openly dangerous condition, such as an unfenced quarry or icy steps. As in the employee cases, the owner would argue that the plaintiff who chose to enter the premises with knowledge of open and obvious dangers accepted responsibility for possible injuries from those known risks.

In these and other contexts, courts accepted the argument that the plaintiff's knowing choice to encounter danger relieved the defendant of responsibility for resulting injury, even if the defendant *negligently created the risk* that caused it. Assumption of the risk became a companion defense along with contributory negligence. It differed, of course, in that assumption of the risk required a showing that the plaintiff actually knew of a danger and chose to proceed. If the plaintiff should have known of a risk, but did not, contributory negligence would apply but assumption of the risk would not.

An example may help to illustrate the relationship between assumption of risk and contributory negligence. Suppose that Newman lent his car to Knieval, and told him that the brakes didn't work. If Knieval shrugged and said he would go slow and use the emergency brake, he assumed the risk of injury from the defective brakes. He might well be negligent in making

1. "Assumption of risk . . . developed in response to the general impulse of common law courts at the beginning of this period [the industrial revolution] to insulate the employer as much as possible from bearing the 'human overhead' which is an inevitable part of the cost—to someone—of the doing of industrialized business. The general purpose behind this development in the common law seems to have been to give maximum freedom to expanding industry." *Tiller v. Atl. Coast Line R.R.*, 318 U.S. 54, 58-59 (1943) (footnotes omitted).

such a conscious choice; if so, he both assumed the risk and was contributorily negligent. On the other hand, if Newman did not tell Knieval about the brakes, but Knieval noticed that the pedal felt loose before he started the car and didn't investigate before driving, he was probably contributorily negligent but did not assume the risk of the defective brakes. He was negligent because he should have checked the brakes when he noticed a problem. But he did not assume the risk of defective brakes, because he did not make a deliberate choice to drive without brakes with full knowledge of the risk.

The assumption of risk principle is confusing in practice because it has been applied in a variety of situations. Some of these overlap negligence analysis, while others are confusingly similar to contributory negligence. In addition, courts have not been consistent in the way they classify assumption of risk cases. See C. Gaetanos, Essay—Assumption of Risk: Casuistry in the Law of Negligence, 83 W. Va. L. Rev. 471, 473 (1981) (noting five different classification schemes adopted by various torts scholars). Despite this confusion, it is important to come to grips with assumption of the risk because, unlike contributory negligence, assumption of the risk is clearly *not* a wave of the past. In at least some of its incarnations, the doctrine is recognized today and will continue to be in the future.

This chapter is intended to give you an understanding of the basic situations in which courts have applied the concept of assumption of the risk, and of the areas in which it remains a "once and future defense."

EXPRESS ASSUMPTION OF THE RISK

Perhaps the clearest assumption of the risk cases are those in which the plaintiff expressly agrees that she will not hold the defendant liable for injury she suffers from a risk created by the defendant. Suppose, for example, that Knieval decides to try skydiving, and hires Newman to teach him the sport. Newman may agree only if Knieval consents in writing not to hold Newman liable for any resulting injuries. Or, Newman might agree to let Knieval use his land for motorcycle-jumping practice, conditioned on a similar promise not to sue for any resulting injuries.

As a general matter, such express agreements to assume a risk, even a negligently created risk, are enforced by the courts. Restatement (Third) of Torts: Apportionment of Liability §2. The nineteenth-century belief in individual initiative and freedom of choice persists, including the right to make silly choices, or even dangerous ones, and accept the consequences. Some people prefer that life should be interesting rather than safe, and such venturous souls may claim substantial accomplishments, such as discovering America and going to the moon. To a great extent, our culture continues to support such choices, even where there is little social value gained by accepting the risk.[2] Allowing participants to agree in advance to accept the risk of injury from high-risk activities (that is, to agree *not* to sue if such injuries occur) promotes the availability of exciting and varied opportunities, by insulating providers from the high cost of injuries resulting from the activity.

While the principle of express assumption is generally accepted, it has been hedged around with some qualifications. *First,* it is essential that the consent to accept the risk is freely given: A consent extracted from a party with little bargaining power is inconsistent with the free-choice principle underlying the doctrine, and will not be honored by the courts. For example, courts have struck down contractual "consents" to unsanitary living conditions in public housing or negligent treatment in local hospitals, on the theory that the plaintiff has no meaningful alternative, and therefore has not really consented at all. Similarly, courts have held that providers of quasi-monopolistic public services, such as rail or electric service, cannot condition service on the passenger's acceptance of the risk of injury. Restatement (Third) of Torts: Apportionment of Liability §2 cmt. e. Here again, the lack of choice makes the consumer's "consent" illusory. Interestingly, although assumption of the risk doctrine developed in the employment context, it is now generally held that the inequality of bargaining power inherent in the employment relationship bars express assumption of the risk by employees. Restatement (Second) of Torts §496B cmt. f.

A second qualification, which also follows from the rationale of assumption of the risk, is that the plaintiff must clearly consent to accept the particular risk that led to the injury. For example, some courts have held that a provision releasing the defendant from "all claims for personal injury" does not waive recovery for injury due to *negligence* of the defendant, since it does not sufficiently bring home to the plaintiff the extent of the risks she is accepting. See, e.g., *Hyson v. White Water Mtn. Resorts*, 829 A.2d 827, 830-832 (Ct. 2003). Other courts, however, will enforce releases that don't explicitly specify that claims for negligence are being waived, if the language of the release is sufficiently broad. See *Boyce v. West*, 862 P.2d 592, 598 (WA Ct App. 1993) (release held to encompass negligence though it did not specifically refer to negligence). Generally, contractual clauses assuming risk (also called waiver of liability or exculpatory clauses) are drafted by the party providing the risky activity—the skydiving school, the quarry owner that allows rock climbing for a fee, the horseback riding ranch. Such releases are construed against the drafter, and must be clear in stating the risks allocated to the participant.

Contractual assumptions of risk are also limited by general contractual principles concerning the understanding of the parties. Thus, an agreement

2. For an interesting defense of the socially constructive role of risk-taking in self-actualization, see D. Judges, Of Rocks and Hard Places: The Value of Risk Choice, 42 Emory L.J. 1, 11-26 (1993).

to assume the risk of injuries will not extend to collateral risks beyond their contemplation. For example, if Ruth signs a general waiver of liability for injuries from playing in a baseball game, he would realize that he was assuming the usual risks of playing baseball, such as being hit by the ball or another player. But he would not have in mind the risk of a sinkhole in the base paths. If he fell into one, he would probably not be barred by express assumption of the risk, since the parties did not have this risk in mind at the time of contracting.[3]

Last, there is an important limit on enforcement of releases that warms the hearts of plaintiffs' lawyers. Most courts will not enforce an advance release of tort liability if the defendant's conduct in causing the injury was grossly negligent, reckless, or willful, or wanton. See Dobbs' Law of Torts §232. Whether a defendant's conduct was simple negligence *or really* negligent is often one of fact—which means a jury question. Thus, many plaintiffs have survived the inevitable motion to dismiss based on the release by arguing that a jury must decide whether the defendant's conduct was worse than simple negligence. In a tort case it is always good to live to fight another day.

IMPLIED ASSUMPTION: INHERENT RISK CASES

A plaintiff may also accept risks simply by engaging in an activity with knowledge that it entails certain risks. Many activities involve a risk of injury even if conducted with due care. In such cases participants assume the risks of injuries from the inherent dangers of the activity. Here are a few examples:

- The plaintiff, after watching patrons at a fair try to maintain their balance on an inclined, moving belt called "The Flopper," buys a ticket, steps on the belt, and is thrown off, fracturing his kneecap.
- The plaintiff decides to take wilderness survival training in Minnesota in midwinter. The plaintiff gets lost in a snowstorm and suffers serious frostbite.
- The plaintiff goes skating at the defendant's skating rink, is hit by a poor skater who loses control, and is injured when she hits the wall of the rink.
- The plaintiff takes rock climbing instruction and is injured when a seemingly solid rock is dislodged by a climber and falls on her.

3. Express assumption may also be barred in situations where it would undermine legislative intent. For example, if a statute mandated certain safety standards for public stadiums (such as number of exits or a maximum number of patrons), a court would likely refuse to enforce a release on the plaintiff's ticket accepting risks of injury due to negligence covered by the statute. See Dobbs' Law of Torts §234.

In each of these cases, the defendant has offered an activity to the plaintiff, which he is under no duty to offer, and which the plaintiff is under no duty to attempt. That activity cannot be conducted without certain unavoidable risks of injury ("a risk that goes with the territory" Dobbs' The Law of Torts §237), even if conducted with due care, and the plaintiff has chosen to engage in the activity. As in the express assumption cases, the plaintiff considers the trade-off worthwhile, and accepts the possibility of injury because she enjoys the activity.

As in the express assumption cases, courts have honored the choice to encounter risk in implied assumption cases too. Plaintiffs who choose to engage in unavoidably risky activities assume the inherent risks of the activity, and have no claim for injuries resulting from those risks. Although this is often described as assumption of the risk of injury, the defendant has actually not breached the duty of due care in such cases. It is not negligent to organize a flag football league, to run a horseback riding ranch, or to offer hang gliding instruction, even though these activities involve some risk of injury. The plaintiff who knowingly engages in such sports impliedly accepts the inherent risks they entail, and cannot sue the defendant who offered it to her simply because those inherent risks lead to injury.

Because primary assumption of the risk is based on the fact that certain risks are inherent in the activity and unavoidable at a reasonable cost, primary assumption only applies where that is in fact the case. If Henne goes ice skating, she accepts the risk that she may be hit by other skaters. This is an obvious danger inherent in the sport. It does not result from negligence of the operator, and it cannot be eliminated at a reasonable cost. However, Henne would not assume the risk of a dangerous condition in the ice or a broken handrail along the edge. These risks are not inherent in the activity itself; they are dangers created by negligent operation of the rink. The plaintiff does not impliedly accept these risks by merely deciding to go skating.

Dobbs, Hayden & Bublick argue that the term "assumption of risk" should not apply to inherent risk situations at all; they are simply situations in which the defendant acted reasonably and the plaintiff suffered injury from a reasonable risk of the activity. Dobbs, Hayden & Bublick §238. This makes good sense; the plaintiff in these cases cannot prove her prima facie case of negligence, because the defendant has not breached the duty of due care. It would be clearer to ask in these cases whether the defendant violated the duty of care than to use assumption of the risk terminology. *See Blackburn v. Dorta*, 348 So. 2d 287, 291 (Fla. 1977). However, courts frequently analyze these as "primary assumption of the risk" or "primary implied assumption of the risk" cases. As a result, these situations (in which there is no negligence because the risk the defendant created was reasonable) are frequently confused with other cases (discussed immediately below) in which assumption of risk is properly viewed as a defense.

SECONDARY IMPLIED ASSUMPTION: THE NEGLIGENT DEFENDANT AND THE VENTUROUS PLAINTIFF

In the situations discussed immediately above, the defendant created reasonable risks that plaintiffs chose to encounter. However, a plaintiff may also encounter risks created by a defendant's *unreasonable* conduct. Here are some examples:

- The defendant lends plaintiff his car. She notices that the car swerves sharply to the left while braking, but proceeds anyway, and is injured when she brakes for a light and swerves into an oncoming car.
- The defendant is setting off fireworks in the public street. Plaintiff, anxious to see the show, stands next to him and is injured when a firecracker explodes.
- The defendant waxes part of the floor of his store while open for business. The plaintiff sees the wet floor, but anxious to get a box of Wheetabix for breakfast, walks on the wet floor and falls.
- The defendant's riding stable provides the plaintiff an unruly horse. The plaintiff, after watching the horse start and buck, decides to try to ride it anyway.

In each of these cases, unlike the inherent risk cases discussed above, the defendant breached the standard of due care by creating an unreasonable risk. If that negligence injured the plaintiff before she became aware of the risk, the defendant would be liable. For example, if the plaintiff who borrowed the car was injured the first time she applied the brake, she could sue because it is negligent to lend someone a car without informing the person of known defects that may cause injury. Similarly, if the plaintiff in the fireworks example was an unsuspecting passerby, she could recover for her injury in the explosion since it is negligent to explode firecrackers in the immediate vicinity of others.

However, in these cases the plaintiff, after becoming aware of the unreasonable risk created by the defendant, chooses to encounter it and suffers injury as a result. This type of case is often called "secondary assumption of the risk" or "secondary implied assumption," presumably because the plaintiff's choice is secondary to (comes after) the negligence of the defendant. In secondary assumption situations the plaintiff has been injured due to the defendant's negligence, but the defendant argues that the plaintiff's conscious choice to encounter the negligently created risk should bar her recovery.

Arguably, the defendant should still be liable in these cases: He has created a risk through his negligence that injured the plaintiff. On the other hand, the plaintiff has freely chosen to encounter it for her own purposes, be it enjoyment of the fireworks display, immediate access to Wheetabix, or available but unsafe transportation. Just as the plaintiff's acceptance of deliberate invasions of her person prevents liability for an intentional tort (under the consent privilege), plaintiff's choice to encounter a negligently created risk should arguably avoid liability as well.

True to its individualistic assumptions, the common law held that the plaintiff, by knowingly encountering a danger created by the defendant's negligence, "assumed the risk" of resulting injury, and was barred from suing for that injury. Restatement (Second) of Torts §496C. Under secondary assumption of risk, the courts honored the plaintiff's willingness to confront negligently created risk, just as they honored her willingness to encounter inherent risk under the related doctrine of primary assumption of the risk. However, in secondary assumption cases, the doctrine really was an affirmative defense since it barred the plaintiff from recovering even though she could establish a prima facie case of negligence by the defendant.

REASONABLE AND UNREASONABLE ASSUMPTION

In secondary assumption cases, the plaintiff's decision to encounter the risk may be either reasonable or unreasonable. The decision to stand next to an adolescent playing with fireworks will virtually always be unreasonable. It might be reasonable to drive a car with bad brakes to get a heart attack victim to the hospital, but not to get to a poker game on time. A rescuer's decision to rescue a child from a fire is eminently reasonable, though it knowingly subjects the rescuer to a risk of injury.

Where the plaintiff's decision to encounter the risk was unreasonable, assumption of the risk overlapped with contributory negligence: By definition, the reasonable person does not voluntarily encounter unreasonable risks. At common law, both defenses could be pleaded. If the plaintiff's choice to encounter the risk was an unreasonable one, that choice would constitute both contributory negligence and assumption of the risk. Either defense sufficed to bar the plaintiff's recovery.

Where the plaintiff *reasonably* assumed a risk, contributory negligence would not bar recovery, because the plaintiff was not negligent. *However*, assumption of the risk still did. The basis for the defense was individual choice, not fault. Even if the plaintiff chose to encounter the risk for good reason, the courts still "honored" the choice by denying recovery.

NINE LIVES: ASSUMPTION OF RISK IN THE COMPARATIVE NEGLIGENCE ERA

The advent of comparative negligence has sparked some controversy about the continued role of secondary implied assumption of the risk. Under comparative negligence, the plaintiff's negligence reduces her recovery, but does not usually bar it. Suppose, however, that the plaintiff's negligence consists of unreasonable but knowing assumption of the risk (secondary implied assumption). Should it bar or reduce recovery? For example, assume that the defendant owns a warehouse without a fire alarm or sprinkler system. Gallo knows this, but decides to store her goods there because it is cheaper. This decision may well be negligent. It is also, however, a deliberate, knowing acceptance of the risk.

At common law, this case posed no problem: *Either* contributory negligence or assumption of the risk barred recovery entirely. In a comparative negligence state, however, if Gallo's conduct were treated as negligence, it would reduce her recovery rather than bar it entirely. On the other hand, if unreasonable assumption of the risk persists as a separate defense, *she would still be fully barred*. There is an argument for the latter result since assumption of the risk is based on consent to encounter a risk, not on fault. If Gallo has accepted the risk with full knowledge, arguably the long-standing assumption of risk rule denying recovery should continue to apply.

Despite this argument, most comparative negligence jurisdictions conclude that secondary *unreasonable* assumption of the risk should be treated as a form of negligence. Under this approach, the jury assigns a percentage of negligence to Gallo's unreasonable choice to accept the risk, and her recovery is reduced by that percentage. Some comparative negligence statutes specifically require this result.[4] In other states, this same sensible result has been reached by judicial interpretation. See *Blackburn v. Dorta*, 348 So. 2d 287 (Fla. 1977); see generally Schwartz, Comparative Negligence §9.04[b].

It is fairly easy to conclude that comparative negligence displaces unreasonable secondary assumption of risk because unreasonable assumption is by definition a form of negligence. It is more difficult to decide how *reasonable* secondary assumption should be meshed with comparative negligence. Suppose, for example, that the warehouse without a sprinkler was the only place within 75 miles of Gallo's home, and she was required to go away on business for three months. The decision to take the small risk of a fire loss

4. The Washington comparative negligence statute, for example, defines "fault" to include "unreasonable assumption of risk." Wash. Rev. Code Ann. §4.22.015. The evident purpose of such a provision is to treat unreasonable assumption as a damage-reducing factor rather than a complete bar to recovery.

might well be reasonable on such facts. If so, how should the decision affect her recovery under a comparative negligence statute?

Arguably, her knowing choice to take the risk should not affect her recovery at all since it was (by definition) a reasonable choice, and recovery is only to be reduced for negligence. Some cases have taken this position. See *Rini v. Oaklawn Jockey Club*, 861 F.2d 502, 508-509 (8th Cir. 1988) (a well-reasoned case applying Arkansas law), see also Restatement (Third) of Torts: Apportionment of Liability §3 and cmt. c. However, a few have argued that reasonable secondary assumption should completely bar recovery. Comparative negligence statutes only address the effect of the plaintiff's *fault*, but the rationale for assumption of risk as a defense is knowing *consent* to take a risk, not fault. Arguably, the passage of a comparative negligence statute, which modifies the effect of plaintiff's *negligence*, should not affect the defense of reasonable assumption of risk. See, e.g., *Siglow v. Smart*, 539 N.E.2d 636, 640-641 (Ohio Ct. App. 1987). Restatement (Second) of Torts §496A cmt. (c)(3).

The 1980s, the era of Ronald Reagan and the collapse of communism, witnessed a renewed emphasis on the nineteenth-century values of individual responsibility and freedom of choice. This megatrend has even found expression in obscure corners of tort law like assumption of risk. While it appeared that secondary assumption of the risk would fade away with the advent of comparative negligence, some cases and articles have argued for retaining reasonable secondary assumption as a complete defense. See, e.g., *Ford v. Gouin*, 266 Cal. Rptr. 870 (Cal. Ct. App. 1st Dist. 1990), *aff'd by a divided court*, 834 P.2d 724 (Cal. 1992); P. Rosenlund & P. Killion, Once a Wicked Sister: The Continuing Role of Assumption of Risk Under Comparative Fault in California, 20 U.S.F. L. Rev. 225, 278-283 (1986); R. Spell, Stemming the Tide of Expanding Liability: The Coexistence of Comparative Negligence and Assumption of Risk, 8 Miss. C. L. Rev. 159 (1988).[5]

The major anomaly of this approach, of course, is that it totally bars recovery by a plaintiff who made a *reasonable* choice to assume a risk, while a plaintiff's unreasonable assumption only reduces recovery under comparative negligence. Those who advocate a separate defense of reasonable assumption of risk argue that this is not inconsistent since the defense is

---

5. The following passage from the Spell article, for example, is reminiscent of the nineteenth-century arguments for assumption of the risk:

> Notions of choice do not go so far as to afford the plaintiff, who once stood at the threshold of action armed with both knowledge of the risks ahead and the opportunity to avoid those risks, the ability to cast back upon the defendant the cost of his choice. The more equitable approach is to enforce the "fundamental principle" of assumption of risk that "where the plaintiff has voluntarily and intelligently consented to relieve the defendant of liability for certain known risks, the plaintiff's choice should be enforced."

8 Miss. C. L. Rev. at 171 (quoting from the Rosenlund & Killion article at 255).

based on consent, not on fault. However, if plaintiff's "consent" to encounter the risk bars recovery where her decision is reasonable, it seems logical that it should *also* bar recovery where it is unreasonable. Yet, under most comparative negligence regimes, unreasonable assumption of the risk is treated as a form of plaintiff's negligence, which reduces a plaintiff's recovery rather than barring it. Since that is true, it seems consistent to treat a plaintiff's reasonable choice to encounter a risk negligently created by the defendant as nonnegligent conduct, which should not reduce or bar her recovery from the defendant.

AN ATTEMPTED SUMMARY

All of this is a bit confusing, partly because the courts are inconsistent in the way they analyze the various assumption of risk situations. In some cases, it is clear that the judges themselves did not fully grasp the distinctions, or could not agree with their colleagues about the proper approach to choose. Here is an attempt to describe the current state of the law on assumption of the risk:

- Express assumption of the risk, that is, the waiver by advance agreement of the right to sue the defendant for her negligence, remains a viable defense. Such waivers will not be enforced in certain contexts involving essential services, and they may be construed narrowly, but usually they will be honored by the courts.
- Implied primary assumption of the risk, properly construed, reflects the idea that an activity may entail risks of injury even when carefully conducted by the operator. If a participant is injured due to those inherent risks, she will lose an action against the operator because she will not prove negligence. A skier hit by another skier, or a spectator hit by a foul ball at a baseball game, will likely lose because it was not negligent to offer the activity, even though such injuries occasionally happen. Courts may still declare in such cases that the "plaintiff assumed the risk" of injury, but the real basis for rejecting the claim is that the operator was not negligent.
- Cases of secondary assumption of risk arise when the defendant *was* negligent, and that negligence created a dangerous situation. The plaintiff became aware of the negligently created risk, encountered it, and suffered injury.
  - If the plaintiff's choice to encounter the risk was an unreasonable one, this is negligent conduct. Most courts that apply comparative negligence treat this form of assumption of risk as a type of plaintiff's fault. Thus, the jury will be instructed to assign a percentage

of fault to the plaintiff if they find that she negligently chose to encounter the risk. In this type of jurisdiction, there is no separate defense of secondary assumption of the risk, so the jury will be told nothing about it. See, e.g., *Davenport v. Cotton Hope Plantation Horizontal Property Regime*, 508 S.E.2d 565 (S.C. 1998).

  - A few jurisdictions continue to treat secondary assumption of the risk as a separate defense.[6] In these jurisdictions, the defendant's deliberate choice to encounter the risk will bar her recovery rather than be treated as a form of comparative negligence.

- If a plaintiff makes a knowing choice to encounter the risk negligently created by the defendant, and that choice is a reasonable one, most courts today that apply comparative negligence would allow the plaintiff to recover fully since her conduct was not faulty and should not reduce recovery.[7] A few, however, may still analyze this as a matter of choice rather than fault, and bar such plaintiffs from recovery entirely.
- Jurisdictions that continue to apply contributory negligence may still recognize secondary implied assumption of the risk as a complete defense. See, e.g., *Morgan State University v.Walker*, 919 A.2d 21 (Md. 2007).

Hopefully, the following examples will help you to understand the basic situations in which the assumption of risk issue arises, and the different ways each may be resolved.

Examples

False Assumptions

1. Killey decides to ski the Big Mountain Ski Bowl. He arrives at the ski area, buys a small lift ticket that attaches to the lapel of his ski jacket, and starts to ski. While riding in the chairlift up to the expert trails, he is injured when the chair separates from the drive cable and falls to the ground. When he threatens to sue Big Mountain, its lawyer points out the following language printed on the back of the lift ticket: "The purchaser assumes all risks of injury from any source whatever, arising in the course of the activities authorized by this ticket, whether due to the negligence of the ski operator or third persons, or any other cause." Is Killey barred by express assumption of the risk?

6. See, e.g., *Kennedy v. Providence Hockey Club*, 376 A.2d 329 (R.I. 1977); see generally V. Schwartz, Comparative Negligence §9.03.

7. See, e.g., *Rini v. Oaklawn Jockey Club*, 861 F.2d 502, 508-510 (8th Cir. 1988) (applying Arkansas law).

2. Assume the same facts, except that before he began skiing, Killey was required to read and sign a form containing the following language: "The undersigned acknowledges that skiing is a hazardous sport; that bare spots, ice, changing snow, bumps, stumps, stones, trees, and other hazards exist in any ski area. By purchasing this ticket, the purchaser recognizes such dangers, whether marked or unmarked, accepts the hazards of the sport and the fact that injury may result therefrom, and agrees to assume all risk of such injuries." Is Killey barred from recovering for his chairlift injury by express assumption?

3. Gavin decides to go skydiving and signs up for lessons with Freeflight Skydiving Inc. Freeflight requires him to sign the following release:

    > I understand and acknowledge that skydiving is a dangerous sport involving a serious risk of injury. By engaging in the sport, I recognize the risk of injury from skydiving, assume all risk of injury from doing so, and agree not to sue Freeflight Skydiving Inc. for any injury that may result from my participation in it.

    On his first dive, Gavin suffers a punctured eardrum as a result of the rapidly changing air pressure. Although he had realized that he might suffer broken bones or even death from a failed parachute, Gavin never understood that there was a risk of injuries to his ears from skydiving. He sues for damages, and Freeflight raises the release as a defense. Has Gavin assumed the risk?

Negative Implications

4. On the facts of Killey's ski lift accident, is he barred from suing Big Mountain by primary implied assumption of the risk?

5. Killey skis the expert slopes at Big Mountain. While coming down a particularly steep slope, he is hit by another skier who had negligently failed to notice a turn in the trail and lost control. Killey's leg is broken. Is he barred from suing Big Mountain by primary implied assumption of the risk?

6. Rogers, a novice at horseback riding, goes to the Circle-R Ranch to ride. While he is out on the trail a rattlesnake glides across the trail, startling Rogers's horse. The horse rears, throwing Rogers to the ground and injuring him. Rogers sues the Ranch for his injuries, and the Ranch pleads assumption of the risk as a defense. Rogers claims that the defense does not apply because he did not know that snakes would cause a horse to rear and throw a rider.
    a. What form of assumption of the risk, if any, is implicated in this case?
    b. Assuming that Rogers really did not know of this risk, is he barred from recovery?
    c. In what way has Circle-R "pleaded wrong" in raising its defense?

Taking Negligence to Newcastle

7. Hermit, who lives on a little-traveled rural road, hitches a ride to town for supplies with a passing driver. It is apparent to Hermit that Driver has been drinking heavily. However, Hermit climbs aboard, and is injured when Driver swerves into a ditch.
   a. What type of assumption of risk, if any, applies here?
   b. What would be the effect of Hermit's conduct in a jurisdiction that applies common law contributory negligence and assumption of risk doctrine?
   c. How would his conduct affect his right to recover in a comparative negligence jurisdiction?

8. Farmer, who also lives on a little-traveled rural road, suffers a serious leg injury while harvesting wheat. He hails a passing car and beseeches the driver, Hillary, to take him to the hospital. Hillary says, "Look, my brakes are acting up, but if you're willing to chance it, I'll take you." Farmer agrees and is injured when the brakes lock at a traffic light and the car is hit from behind. Which type of assumption of risk, if any, applies in this case?

9. Assume that Hillary said nothing about the brakes. However, Farmer watched Hillary apply the brakes several times during the ride, and observed that they locked abruptly as soon as applied. Anxious to get medical help, Farmer stays aboard.
   a. What type of assumption of the risk, if any, would this entail?
   b. Assume that, after Farmer realizes that the brakes are bad, they lock at the light and Farmer is injured. Would Farmer be barred from recovery in a jurisdiction that applies the common law contributory negligence and assumption of risk doctrines?
   c. On the same facts, would assumption of the risk bar recovery in a comparative negligence jurisdiction?

Judge Fudd Assumes the Risk

10. Dewey, a teacher in a West Dakota high school, agrees to participate in a "donkey basketball" game for the school scholarship fund. The players play basketball while riding donkeys provided by the Buckeye Donkey Basketball Company. It is really very funny and a lot of students would gladly pay to see their teachers make such asses of themselves. Before the game, an employee of Buckeye explains to the teachers that the donkeys sometimes stop short and lower their heads, and there is a small risk of falling off. In the middle of the game, Dewey's donkey executes such a maneuver, and Dewey is thrown, suffering a dislocated shoulder. He sues Buckeye for his injuries. West Dakota has adopted a comparative negligence statute that provides for reducing plaintiff's damages to account for his fault. The statute also provides that "the defense of

assumption of the risk is abolished." At trial, Buckeye's lawyer asks Judge Fudd to instruct the jury that they should find for the defendant if they conclude that Dewey assumed the risk of being thrown. Judge Fudd responds, "Counsel, I don't see how I can grant that instruction. It says right in the statute that assumption of the risk is abolished." Is Fudd right in rejecting the assumption of the risk argument?

Legal Shape-Sorting

11. Try to fit the following examples into the categories discussed in the Introduction.
    a. Mansfield rents a rustic cabin sight unseen, for his family's summer vacation in the North Woods. When they arrive, they discover that the cabin is not quite finished, and there is no railing on the stairs to the second floor. On the fifth day of their stay, Mansfield stumbles on the stairs and falls off due to the lack of a railing.
    b. Bohlen borrows a table saw from Wade to use in putting a porch on his house. The saw had a kill switch on the side which, when engaged, would cause the blade to stop if the wood going through the saw was pushed too hard. This prevents the wood from kicking back and injuring the user. Wade had disabled the kill switch, however, by "hot-wiring" around it because it slowed down the work when the kill switch engaged. Bohlen is not very familiar with table saws, does not realize the switch has been disabled, and is injured when a piece of wood is thrown back at him by the blade.
    c. James, an experienced mason, is working on a scaffold three stories above the street, putting the brick facade on a new building. When he goes to break for lunch, he remembers that another worker borrowed the ladder that he had used to climb the scaffold, but has not returned it. Impatient to get to lunch, he starts to climb down the angled supports of the scaffolding, and is injured when he slips off.
    d. Dobbs sees a small child playing obliviously in the path of a driver backing out of a driveway without looking. He rushes to rescue the child and is hit by the car.

Risk Twist

12. Story and Holmes attend a football game together. They have a few beers. Well, they have *quite* a few beers. After the game they get in Story's car, and Story drives off. Ten minutes later they have an accident, when Cardozo pulls out of a side street without looking and broadsides Story's car. Holmes, the passenger, sues Cardozo for his injuries.
    a. What brand of assumption of risk is implicated by Holmes's conduct?
    b. What effect should his conduct have on his right to recover from Cardozo?

Explanations

False Assumptions

1. As the Introduction states, parties can assume risks, including the risk of another's negligence, by an express agreement to do so. And the language in this release clause is certainly broad enough to cover the accident Killey suffered since it specifically refers to injury "from any source whatever" and includes negligence of the operator. If Killey has accepted the release clause, he would be barred.

   However, the gravamen of assumption of risk is the plaintiff's choice to assume the risks. Courts are wary of applying the doctrine of express assumption unless the party clearly chose to accept the risks that were being allocated to her. Killey will argue that he did not assume the risk of injury because he never knowingly agreed to the terms of the release. Since the terms were placed in fine print on the back of the lift ticket, where most people would not even read them, the court is likely to agree. See Restatement (Second) of Torts §496B cmt. c: "it must appear that the terms were in fact brought home to him and understood by him, before it can be found that he has accepted them." See also Restatement (Third) of Torts: Apportionment of Liability §2 cmt. d (size of print a factor in determining whether release is enforceable).

2. Clearly not. While he has assumed many of the risks of skiing itself by signing this form, it contains no language assuming the risk of negligent maintenance of the facility. The purchaser would not contemplate such negligence as one of the inherent hazards of skiing. In fact, by enumerating various natural risks, the form tends to confirm that other risks, such as negligent maintenance of the equipment, were not within the contemplation of the clause. Consequently, because the language does not clearly include this risk, Killey has not assumed it.

3. This is an interesting problem. On the one hand, Gavin has expressly agreed to assume responsibility for injuries resulting from skydiving, and Freeflight provided the service with an understanding that this allocation of the risks would protect it from liability. On the other hand, if assumption of the risk turns on knowing acceptance of the risk, Gavin did not assume this risk, since he did not realize (whether he should have or not) that ear problems might result. This case would likely turn on the basic contracts concept of the intent of the parties. If it is clear from the language of the release and the circumstances that Gavin understood that he was assuming the risk of *any* injury, anticipated or not, the release would probably be enforced. Express assumption usually honors the parties' choice in allocating the risk. If the parties clearly allocated this one to Gavin, he is likely to be barred by his express assumption of it, even

though he did not know what the risk was. See Restatement (Second) of Torts §496D cmt. a (plaintiff may expressly assume unknown risk if agreement so intends); Prosser & Keeton at 489 (plaintiff may "consent to take his chances as to unknown conditions").

Perhaps, as a matter of good lawyering, Freeflight's counsel should draft the release to reveal as many potential risks as possible. A release that specifically refers to the risk of ear damage clearly demonstrates that this risk was within the parties' contemplation at the time of contracting. (A release that described in detail all the risks involved might, of course, have a depressing effect on business.) The release should also specify that the plaintiff assumes the risks of the activity, even if he is not aware of them. This strengthens the argument that the plaintiff has chosen to accept all the risks, not just the ones she expected to encounter.

Negative Implications

4. Primary assumption applies where the defendant has not breached a duty of due care, since the risk that injures the plaintiff is inseparable from the activity itself. The defendant is not liable in such cases because it is not negligent, even though the activity it offered involves some risk. Primary assumption would bar Killey from suing if he were injured from the inherent risks of skiing, such as patches of icy snow, sharp drops in expert trails, trees along the side of the trail, bare spots, and others. But he does not assume the risk that the chairlift will fall off the cable. That is not an inherent risk of the sport if it is conducted with due care.

5. The issue here is whether negligent acts of other skiers are an inherent risk of skiing that skiers assume by engaging in the sport. I would think so. Just as a quarterback can expect some overzealous hits, and a jockey some aggressive jockeying for position on the track, a skier should expect that there will be a few overconfident hot dogs on the expert slopes who will fail to keep a proper lookout or attempt maneuvers beyond their skills. It appears likely that, by choosing to ski the expert slopes, Killey assumes the risk of this accident. Stated another (and, I think, clearer) way, it is likely that Big Mountain is not negligent in conducting a ski operation, even though it entails this risk.

6. a. The question here is whether primary implied assumption of the risk applies; that is, was Circle-R reasonable in offering horseback riding even though it entails a risk that a snake might cause a horse to start and throw a rider? If such events are rare, and generally do not result in riders being thrown, it may be reasonable to offer horseback riding to the public despite this risk. Thus, the basic issue is the traditional Hand-formula question as to whether, in light of the magnitude of the risk and the extent of injury to be anticipated from snake-starting,

Circle-R was reasonable to offer the activity (or to offer it without some special precaution, such as a snake eradication program along its trails).

Although I don't know much about horseback riding—or snakes—I'll guess that Rogers's accident is a pretty rare occurrence, so that Circle-R would not be deemed negligent for subjecting its patrons to this risk. If so, many courts would say that Rogers "assumes the risk" of snakes causing a horse to buck, and deny him recovery for his injury. But it would be analytically clearer to reach the same result on the simple ground that Circle-R was not negligent.

b. If Rogers didn't know about the snake-starting risk, how can he assume it? If the premise underlying assumption of the risk is *subjective acceptance* of the risk, the doctrine shouldn't apply to Rogers, and he ought to recover. However, in primary implied assumption cases, the real premise for denying recovery is lack of negligence, not the plaintiff's choice. Plaintiffs like Rogers lose because Circle-R's conduct was reasonable, not because they consciously accepted the risk of snakes. Similarly, a first-time skier hit by another would doubtless be denied recovery, even if she did not understand the risk of a collision.

Although this makes sense, the case law often obscures the point by using assumption-of-the-risk language, which seems to require that the plaintiff actually perceives and appreciates the risk. Rogers will rely on such language to argue that he isn't barred if he didn't actually know the risk. The confusion in this area is such that he might even win on this argument. But, analytically, he shouldn't.

c. If the issue here is whether Circle-R acted reasonably in offering horseback riding, it can raise the issue in its answer simply by denying negligence; there is no need to plead an "affirmative defense" of assumption of the risk in this type of case. Indeed, pleading "no negligence" has an important advantage to Circle-R, since, if the issue is negligence, *Rogers* will bear the burden of proof on it; whereas, if the issue is an affirmative defense, Circle-R will.

However, careful counsel, knowing of the confusion in this area, will doubtless throw in assumption of the risk as an additional defense, out of concern that—if the judge thinks of it as a defense—they will have waived the issue. Thus, the confusion gets perpetuated.

Taking Negligence to Newcastle

7. a. Hermit has not expressly agreed in advance to assume the risk here. Nor is this implied primary assumption: Drunk driving is not an inherent risk of accepting a ride in a car. This is an example of secondary implied assumption of the risk. Hermit becomes aware of negligent conduct of Driver which poses a risk of injury to him, yet,

fully appreciating the risk, chooses to encounter it. More specifically, this is *unreasonable* secondary assumption since Hermit need not get to town immediately and should have waited for a more suitable chauffeur.

b. At common law, assumption of a risk barred recovery entirely, even if the risk was negligently created by the defendant. The gist of the action, as reiterated before, was consent and free choice, and here Hermit made a misguided but informed choice to proceed despite the risk. The common law "honored" Hermit's right to choose by barring him from recovering from Driver.

   Since Hermit's choice was unreasonable, it would constitute contributory negligence as well. At common law Hermit would have been barred from recovery by either defense.

c. Under most comparative negligence regimes, Hermit's unreasonable decision would be treated as negligent conduct, and would be compared to the negligence of the defendant in assessing liability. If, for example, the jury concluded that Hermit was 33 percent responsible for his injuries for riding with a drunk driver, they would reduce his damages by 33 percent. Thus, unreasonable secondary assumption reduces damages under most comparative negligence statutes, but no longer acts as a complete bar. But, as the Introduction indicates, a few states continue to treat it as a full defense analogous to consent.

8. Hillary clearly is negligent for driving with defective brakes; he would, for example, be liable to the driver of the other car in this case. But Farmer has *expressly* assumed the risk in this case. Hillary has no duty to take Farmer into town, but has offered to do so if Farmer is willing to accept the risk of injury due to the defective condition of the brakes. The principle of free choice says parties can make such arrangements to assume the risk. Farmer has agreed in advance not to hold Hillary liable for the risks to which he is exposed. While express assumption is usually by contract, it need not be, and consideration is not essential to make the assumption binding. See Restatement (Second) of Torts §496B cmt. a.

   It is true that this case looks a good deal like reasonable implied secondary assumption as well. Hillary is negligent for driving with defective brakes, and Farmer decides, for a compelling reason, to take the risk. However, since Farmer agrees in advance to relieve Hillary of a duty of care, it is best classified as express assumption. Note that the characterization makes a big difference in the outcome of the case: If it is express assumption, Farmer will be barred; if it is secondary implied assumption, he probably would not be. See Example 9c.

9. a. This is probably an example of reasonable implied secondary assumption of the risk. Secondary assumption arises when the defendant negligently subjects the plaintiff to a risk, and the plaintiff becomes

aware of the risk yet chooses to encounter it anyway. Hillary owes Farmer a duty of due care, and violates that duty by giving him a ride in a car with faulty brakes. However, when Farmer becomes aware of the risk posed by Hillary's negligence, he stays aboard because of the exigency caused by his injury. Although he signals no agreement to Hillary, he accepts the risk for his own sufficient reasons.

b. Assuming that Farmer's decision was reasonable under the circumstances, contributory negligence would not bar his recovery. However, in a jurisdiction that applied traditional common law principles, he would still be barred by assumption of the risk, since he understood the risk and chose to encounter it. The basis for the defense was individual choice, whether reasonable or unreasonable. So long as the choice was made with full understanding of the risk, the defense applied. Note the symmetry under the common law approach between express assumption and reasonable secondary implied assumption. Whether the plaintiff agreed in advance to take on the risk, as in Example 8, or impliedly agreed by staying on board, as here, the result was to bar recovery despite the defendant's negligence.

   The best argument for avoiding assumption of the risk in a case like this would be that Farmer did not fully comprehend the nature of the risk posed by the brakes. Because secondary assumption turns on appreciation of the specific risk that causes injury, the defense only applies if the risk is fully understood. Many courts have rescued plaintiffs from the assumption of risk defense by holding that they did not appreciate the *exact* risk that led to the injury. See, e.g., *Gault v. May*, 79 Cal. Rptr. 858 (Cal. Ct. App. 1969) (although plaintiff was aware that roller skate pulled to left, she did not know of defective wheel, which caused injury). Here, Farmer might argue that, though he realized there was *something* wrong with the brakes, he did not realize that they would lock completely, and therefore did not assume the risk.

c. The result in a comparative negligence jurisdiction depends on the way the jurisdiction treats reasonable secondary assumption. As the Introduction indicates, most states conclude that reasonable secondary assumption of the risk should not reduce or bar the plaintiff's claim. In these states, if the jury found that Farmer's decision was reasonable, Farmer would recover fully, despite his understanding of the risk posed by the brakes. In a few states, however, secondary assumption—whether reasonable or unreasonable—remains a complete defense. In these states, Farmer would lose because he chose to encounter the risk, even if that was a reasonable choice.

   As the Introduction notes, a few states, even after the adoption of comparative negligence, may still treat assumption of the risk as a full defense, on the theory that the plaintiff has made her choice and should be bound by it. This approach seems dubious. It seems anomalous that Hermit, in Example 7, should recover substantial (albeit reduced) damages while Farmer takes nothing. In addition, if reasonable assumption of risk is a bar, Farmer's lawyer is placed in the bizarre position of trying to prove that Farmer was negligent, but only a little: Since unreasonable assumption of risk is treated as damage-reducing conduct under the comparative negligence statute, a minimally negligent plaintiff will recover most of her damages. But if plaintiff argues that her conduct was completely reasonable, and the jury agrees, she recovers nothing!

Judge Fudd Assumes the Risk

10. Although the comparative negligence statute here appears to broadly eliminate assumption of risk, this provision almost certainly was intended to make the plaintiff's choice to encounter a negligently created risk a damage-reducing factor rather than a complete bar to recovery. In other words, it calls for treating the *defense* of secondary implied assumption like negligence by the plaintiff.

    However, Buckeye's argument is not based on the *defense* of assumption of the risk. Buckeye is arguing that it was not negligent to offer donkey basketball, even though it entails a small risk of injury. In other words, its argument is based on *primary* implied assumption of the risk, or, more clearly, the simple argument that Buckeye was not negligent. This is not a "defense" at all, but challenges the plaintiff's ability to establish an element of her prima facie case—breach of the duty of due care.

    A number of comparative negligence statutes include language abolishing the "defense" of assumption of the risk. See, e.g., Mass. Gen. Laws ch. 231 §85. Only by fully understanding the different ways in which the phrase "assumption of the risk" has been used can you clearly evaluate the effect—and the limits—of a provision such as this. Here, if Buckeye's counsel had phrased his argument in terms of due care, he could have avoided confusing Judge Fudd with assumption of the risk concepts entirely, and sidestepped any implication that his argument was based on a "defense" that had been abolished.

Legal Shape-Sorting

11. a. The owner is negligent to rent out a cabin with dangerous stairs, so Mansfield can probably make a prima facie case for liability. However, the owner will assert as a defense that Mansfield assumed the risk by using the stairs anyway. The reasonable person would probably not turn around and go home just because the stair lacked a railing; likely she would just be a bit more careful negotiating the stairs. Thus, this is probably reasonable secondary assumption by Mansfield. Whether

Mansfield's decision bars recovery will depend on how the jurisdiction treats reasonable assumption of risk.

b. This is not assumption of risk at all. Bohlen did not knowingly decide to take the risk of operating the saw without the switch; he never knew the switch existed or appreciated the risk of using the saw without it. He may be contributorily negligent for failing to learn more about a dangerous power tool before using it, but he has not deliberately chosen to encounter the risk that caused his injury.
c. This is unreasonable secondary assumption of the risk. The other worker was negligent in failing to return the ladder, but James has deliberately encountered the resulting unreasonable risk. As an experienced mason, James is aware that it is dangerous to climb on these supports, but he decides to do so anyway rather than wait for someone to return with the ladder. This was an unreasonable choice, a negligent choice, but it was also knowing assumption of the risk. In most comparative negligence jurisdictions, it would be treated as a damage-reducing factor like other negligence by the plaintiff.
d. You may have already come across the "rescue doctrine" in Torts class. The doctrine holds that injury to a rescuer is foreseeable, and therefore the negligence of the person who made the rescue necessary is a proximate cause of resulting injury to the rescuer. See, e.g., *Wagner v. Intl. Ry. Co.*, 133 N.E. 437 (N.Y. 1921). But why aren't these cases resolved under assumption of risk doctrine instead? They appear to be the very paradigm of reasonable implied secondary assumption of the risk: The plaintiff becomes aware of a risk negligently created by the defendant, and makes an eminently reasonable choice to encounter it.

   A few courts *have* barred recovery to a rescuer on the ground of assumption of the risk. See, e.g., *Siglow v. Smart*, 539 N.E.2d 636 (Ohio Ct. App. 1987). See also *Eckert v. Long Island R.R. Co.*, 43 N.Y. 502 (1871) (Allen, J., dissenting) (arguing that rescuer should be barred by assumption of the risk). The Second Restatement avoids this harsh result, however, by concluding that rescue is not "voluntary":

   > The plaintiff's acceptance of a risk is not voluntary if the defendant's tortious conduct has left him no reasonable alternative course of conduct in order to . . . avert harm to himself or another.

   Restatement (Second) of Torts §496E(2)(a). This is a laudable result, but it raises a fundamental question about the meaning of secondary assumption of the risk. If Dobbs's choice here is not voluntary, is a plaintiff's choice to confront a negligently created risk ever voluntary? In most cases, the plaintiff does not *prefer* to be confronted with the risk negligently created by the defendant; she would rather that the defendant had not been negligent in the first place. Here Dobbs would prefer not to have confronted the risk created by the driver's negligence. Similarly, in the vacation home example, the vacationer would have preferred that the stairs have a railing.

The plaintiff in these cases reluctantly goes forward to meet the danger, but in a sense her decision is not "voluntary," since she would prefer not to have been put to an unpalatable choice of alternatives in the first place. See K. Simons, Assumption of Risk and Consent in the Law of Torts: A Theory of Full Preference, 67 B.U. L. Rev. 213, 218-224 (1987), which argues that the doctrine should only apply where the plaintiff "fully prefers" to encounter the risk created by the defendant rather than be placed in a position of having to choose between several unpalatable alternatives.

Risk Twist

12. a. Holmes deliberately chose to drive with Story, even though he knew he had been drinking heavily. As in Example 7, this would be secondary implied assumption of the risk. That is, after recognizing Story's negligent conduct, Holmes has elected—by getting into the car with him—to take the risk created by it.

    b. In most comparative negligence jurisdictions, a plaintiff's conscious, unreasonable choice to encounter a risk like this would be treated as a form of negligence, which would reduce the plaintiff's recovery. However, Holmes's conduct should have *no effect* on his recovery in this case. Holmes unreasonably chose to accept the risk of negligence by Story in driving while intoxicated. But Holmes was not injured by that risk—as far as the example indicates, Story's driving was fine. Holmes was injured by negligent driving *by Cardozo*. Thus, whether we call Holmes's conduct negligence in riding with Story or voluntary acceptance of that risk, that conduct was not the proximate cause of his injury. It isn't negligent to drive with a drunk driver because *some other driver* might drive carelessly and cause a collision. Consequently, Holmes's choice should not affect his recovery from Cardozo at all.

CHAPTER 24

Casting the Second Stone: Comparative Negligence

INTRODUCTION

Somewhere in the Bible lies the telling maxim: "Let he who is without sin cast the first stone." A rich understanding of human experience lies behind this phrase, for few of us are so pure that we can forswear responsibility for life's vicissitudes or piously condemn others without considering our own failings.

For many years, the common law refused to account for this basic truth in tort cases. The contributory negligence doctrine reflected the absolutist moral view that the plaintiff who was blameless was entitled to full vindication in a court of law, but that one who shared the taint of sin in any degree must be sent forth to languish in the wilderness. Today we are less pious and more pragmatic about accident causation. This more "modern" view is reflected in the widespread adoption of comparative negligence, which replaces the all-or-nothing approach of contributory negligence with a system that reduces a party's damages to account for her fault.

I hesitate to call this a "modern" view because there is nothing new about it, really. Comparative negligence was apparently known to those most practical of lawmakers, the Romans, and has prevailed widely in civil law countries since the nineteenth century.[1] American admiralty practice also adopted a rough form of comparative negligence: Under the " equal

1. See E. Turk, Comparative Negligence on the March, 28 Chi.-Kent L. Rev. 189, 239-244 (1950).

division rule," if two ships were at fault in a collision, the court divided the damages equally, regardless of their relative degrees of fault. Suppose, for example, that the *Queen Mary* collided with the *Queen Elizabeth*, and sustained $200,000 in damage. If both ships were partly at fault in causing the collision, the owners of the *Queen Mary* would recover $100,000. This was true even if the *Queen Mary*'s skipper was 1 percent at fault and the *Queen Elizabeth*'s was 99 percent to blame. This may seem like a crude system, but it was a substantial retreat from contributory negligence: Under contributory negligence, the *Queen Mary*'s owners would have recovered nothing at all.

Dissatisfaction with the all-or-nothing feature of contributory negligence also led several states to experiment with a *slight/gross* comparative negligence system. Under an early Nebraska statute, for example, a plaintiff whose negligence was "slight" compared to that of the defendant was allowed to recover, but her recovery was reduced "in proportion to the amount of contributory negligence attributable to the plaintiff." Neb. Rev. Stat. §25-21,185 (repealed by NE. Laws 1992, L.B. 262 §19). This provision changed the result in those cases in which contributory negligence operated most harshly: where the plaintiff was only minimally negligent. However, even under the slight/gross system, if the jury found that plaintiff's negligence was more than "slight," the traditional contributory negligence rule applied, and plaintiff lost entirely.[2]

Such early systems showed that the contributory negligence rule was not immutable, but it was not until the nineteen sixties that this trickle of reform turned into a flood. Since then, most states have replaced contributory negligence with one form or another of comparative negligence. In some states the change has come from the courts—since contributory negligence is a judicial doctrine, some courts have abandoned it by judicial decision. In many, however, comparative negligence has been introduced by statute. At this writing, only four states retain the contributory negligence doctrine.

PURE COMPARATIVE NEGLIGENCE

Most states have adopted either *pure comparative negligence* or one of several common variations (called "modified comparative negligence"), which are described below. Under pure comparative negligence, advocated by most scholars, an injured party may recover, regardless of her degree of fault, but her recovery is reduced by her percentage of fault. For example, the Washington (state) statute provides in part:

2. This Nebraska statute was replaced by a modified comparative negligence statute for cases arising after February 8, 1992. See now NE Stat. Ann §25-21, 185.09.

> In an action based on fault seeking to recover damages for injury or death to person or harm to property, any contributory fault chargeable to the claimant diminishes proportionately the amount awarded as compensatory damages for an injury attributable to the claimant's contributory fault, but does not bar recovery. . . .

Wash. Rev. Code Ann. §4.22.005. Assume that the *Queen Mary*'s skipper was 40 percent at fault in causing the collision. Under a pure comparative negligence statute like Washington's, the owners of the *Queen Mary* would recover, but their damages would be reduced by 40 percent to reflect the *Queen Mary*'s contribution to the accident. Thus, they would recover 60 percent of their damages, or $120,000. If the *Queen Mary* was only 1 percent at fault, they would recover 99 percent of their damages. If the *Queen Mary* was 99 percent at fault and suffered a million dollars in damages, its owners would recover $10,000 (1 percent of $1,000,000).

While there is a pleasing symmetry about pure comparative negligence, it has had its critics too. It may not seem "fair" to pay damages to one who is the overwhelming cause of his own misfortune. If the *Queen Mary*'s skipper was 99 percent at fault, the *Queen Elizabeth*'s owners may be understandably reluctant to pay its owners a penny, much less $10,000, which is one million pennies.

MODIFIED COMPARATIVE NEGLIGENCE

Many states have compromised between the extremes of contributory negligence on the one hand and pure comparative negligence on the other. The slight/gross system was an early example, but it proved hard to apply, due to the difficulty in defining "slight" negligence and controlling jury verdicts based on such an amorphous standard. A more popular approach, particularly in states that have switched to comparative negligence by statute rather than judicial decision, has been *modified* comparative negligence. Modified comparative negligence systems, like the slight/gross system, bar the claimant from any recovery if her negligence reaches a certain level, but they set the level at the point where the plaintiff's negligence either equals or exceeds that of the defendant.

The Kansas comparative negligence statute, for example, provides that a party's negligence will not bar her recovery

> if that party's negligence was less than the causal negligence of the party or parties against whom a claim is made, but the award of damages to that party must be reduced in proportion to the amount of negligence attributed to that party.

Kan. Stat. Ann. §60-258a(a). This statute is typical of the *not-as-great-as* form of modified comparative negligence. Under this approach, the plaintiff recovers her damages, reduced by her percentage of fault, so long as her fault was not as great as that of the defendant or defendants. A plaintiff who was 45 percent at fault would recover 55 percent of her damages under this type of statute, but a plaintiff who was 70 percent negligent would recover nothing. In the frequent scenario in which the jury concludes that the parties were equally at fault, the plaintiff loses since her fault is "as great as" that of the defendant.

The other common system of modified comparative negligence allows the plaintiff to recover reduced damages so long as her negligence was *not greater than* that of the defendant:

> Contributory negligence shall not bar recovery in an action by any person or his legal representative to recover damages for negligence resulting in death or injury to person or property, if such negligence was not greater than the negligence of the person against whom recovery is sought or was not greater than the combined negligence of the persons against whom recovery is sought. Any damages sustained shall be diminished by the percentage sustained of negligence attributable to the person recovering.

N.J. Stat. Ann. §2A:15-5.1. This approach is the same as the not-as-great-as system in every case except where the plaintiff's negligence is equal to the defendant's. While the plaintiff loses in the 50/50 case in a not-as-great-as state, she recovers 50 percent of her damages in a not-greater-than state like New Jersey. Since juries frequently conclude that the parties are equally at fault, this can change the result in quite a few cases.

Modified comparative negligence is perhaps less logically defensible than pure comparative negligence. Suppose that Hobbes is 51 percent at fault in causing an accident and suffers $100,000 in damages. Suppose also that Mill, the other driver, is 49 percent at fault, suffers $100,000 in damages and counterclaims for his injuries. In a modified comparative negligence jurisdiction, Hobbes recovers nothing; he will absorb all of his own loss, and pay Mill $51,000 as well (since Mill is only 49 percent at fault and thus entitled to recover his damages reduced by 49 percent). This disparity in recovery hardly seems justified on the basis of a 2 percent difference in the negligence of the parties. By contrast, under pure comparative negligence, Hobbes would recover $49,000 from Mill, and Mill would recover $51,000 from Hobbes.[3]

Despite examples like this, most states that have adopted comparative negligence by statute have chosen one of the modified forms. Perhaps the best explanation, other than pure political compromise between contributory

3. See R. Keeton, Comment on *Maki v. Frelk*, 21 Vand. L. Rev. 906, 911 (1968).

and comparative negligence, is that of a sponsor of the New Hampshire statute, whose "sandlot instinct" rebelled against allowing recovery to a party who is primarily to blame for her own injury.[4]

Under both pure and modified systems, the seeming precision of the calculations is obviously illusory. It is people—usually ordinary people sitting as jurors—who apply the comparative negligence rules to actual cases. Affixing exact percentages of negligence in complex accidents at a trial four or five years after the fact is a dubious business. However, as Dean Prosser persuasively notes, any system of assigning damages in negligence cases is inherently imprecise:

> [A] division of the plaintiff's damages [on the basis of comparative fault] is at least more accurate than one based on the arbitrary conclusion that 100 percent of the responsibility rests with the plaintiff and none whatever with the defendant, or, if the last clear chance is applicable, 100 percent with the defendant and none with the plaintiff—both of which are demonstrably wrong. Nor is such an estimate in itself any more foolish, or more difficult, than the one which assigns $2,000 as fair value and compensation for the pain of a broken leg, or the humiliation of a disfigured nose, to say nothing of estimates based on a prognosis of speed of recovery, future earnings or permanent disability.

W. Prosser, Comparative Negligence, 51 Mich. L. Rev. 465, 475 (1953).

WHO IS COMPARED?

Some practical problems arise in applying comparative negligence to specific cases, especially under modified comparative negligence. A basic question is who gets compared to whom. For example, assume that Rousseau's car collides with Locke's and Rousseau suffers $100,000 in damages. He sues Locke for negligent driving and the City of Paris for leaving a pothole in the road, which contributed to causing the accident. At trial, the jury concludes that Rousseau was 45 percent at fault, Locke 15 percent, and the city 40 percent. In a modified comparative negligence jurisdiction (of either type) Rousseau will lose if his fault is compared to that of each defendant *individually* since his negligence is greater than either of theirs. However, if his fault is compared to the *total negligence* of the defendants together, he can still recover 55 percent of his damages since 45 percent is less than their combined total of 55 percent.

4. D. Nixon, The Actual "Legislative Intent" Behind New Hampshire's Comparative Negligence Statute, 12 N.H.B.J. 17, 24-25 (1969).

Some states take the harder line on this issue, comparing the plaintiff's negligence to that of each defendant individually. These states bar the plaintiff from recovering from any defendant who is less negligent, though he may recover from others who are more negligent. Most modified comparative negligence states, however, compare the plaintiff's negligence to the combined negligence of the defendants. See V. Schwartz, Comparative Negligence §3.05[c][i].

There are cogent arguments for both approaches. Comparing Rousseau's negligence to all defendants combined seems unfair since Locke will be held liable to Rousseau for $55,000 (55 percent of $100,000), even though he was only 15 percent to blame and Rousseau's fault was three times greater. That result looks like pure comparative negligence since a party more at fault recovers from one less at fault. On the other hand, comparing the plaintiff's negligence to each defendant's individually places a plaintiff at a disadvantage if there are multiple parties: She may lose even if her negligence is substantially less than 50 percent. It also leaves defendants who are found more negligent than the plaintiff holding the bag for others who contributed to the accident but were less negligent than the plaintiff. For example, if Rousseau were 35 percent at fault, the city 40 percent, and Locke 25 percent, the city would be liable for 65 percent of Rousseau's damages (since it is more negligent than he is), while Locke would not be liable at all if his negligence is compared separately to Rousseau's.

WHAT IS COMPARED?

Another basic issue in applying comparative negligence is what is compared among the parties: Is it the *negligence* of each party, or the degree to which each party's negligence *caused* the plaintiff's injury? This problem is conceptually difficult: How do you distinguish causation from the extent of negligence? It is hard to think about degrees of causation: Either the negligence contributed to the accident or it didn't. Suppose, for example, that Montesquieu makes a left turn without putting on his turn indicator, and is hit head-on by Milton, who is doing 75 m.p.h. in a 35 m.p.h. zone. Most jurors would find Milton more to blame, but that both acts equally "caused" the harm. If the goal of comparative negligence is to place the greater burden on the more culpable party, it seems that Milton should be found substantially more responsible than Montesquieu.

Changing the example a bit, assume that Montesquieu was driving while severely intoxicated and made the same left turn without looking, leading to the same accident with the speeding Milton. On these facts, as in the first example, both parties contributed to causing the accident, but the relative culpability of the parties is more nearly equal, and most juries would ascribe a higher percentage of fault to Montesquieu than in the first example.

Dean Prosser was emphatically of the view that it is the degrees of negligence of the parties that is compared. See W. Prosser, Comparative Negligence, 51 Mich. L. Rev. 465, 481-482 (1953). Many statutes appear to take this position since they require the jury to consider the comparative "fault" or "negligence" of the parties. However, the Uniform Comparative Fault Act explicitly requires the jury to consider both:

> In determining the percentages of fault, the trier of fact shall consider both the nature of the conduct of each party at fault and the extent of the causal relation between the conduct and the damages claimed.[5]

As a practical matter, it probably doesn't matter in most cases which approach is taken. Assessing fault is not a scientific process; the jury makes an intuitive judgment about the culpability of each party without focusing on the technical distinction between negligence and causation. However, one thing can be said with certainty: If the plaintiff's negligence was not an actual cause of the injury, the jury should not consider it. If the plaintiff is hit from behind while stopped at a light, irrelevant negligence in failing to get her brakes checked should not reduce her recovery.

CAVEAT: A FUNDAMENTAL FUNDAMENTAL OF COMPARATIVE NEGLIGENCE

A final, fundamental point should be made here, and it is one that is easily missed. Comparative negligence regimes allow a plaintiff who is partly at fault to recover reduced damages, and provide a formula for calculating those reduced damages. But the adoption of comparative negligence, by itself, does *not* change the basic rule of joint and several liability, under which each defendant is liable for the entire judgment awarded to the plaintiff. Nor does adoption of comparative negligence, of itself, change the basic contribution rules governing the redistribution of damages among the defendants.

For example, if Rousseau recovers from Locke and the city in the example on page 539, he will be entitled to 55 percent of his damages, or $55,000. If traditional joint and several liability principles are still followed in the

5. Uniform Comparative Fault Act §2(b), 12 U.L.A. 45 (Supp. 1994). The Uniform Comparative Fault Act is a model act, written by the National Conference of Commissioners on Uniform State Laws, an organization devoted to encouraging uniform state legislation on issues of general applicability. See also Restatement (Third) of Torts: Apportionment of Liability §8 (also noting relevance of causation in assessing percentages of fault).

relevant jurisdiction, both Locke and the city would be liable to Rousseau for $55,000. Put another way, the adoption of comparative negligence does *not* mean that the plaintiff's judgment will be apportioned to the defendants in proportion to their negligence. In the Rousseau case, the city will not be ordered to pay $40,000 of the judgment, and Locke only $15,000. Judgment will enter against each for $55,000 because, under joint and several liability, each defendant who is liable to the plaintiff is liable for the entire judgment. Rousseau will be entitled to collect $55,000 from either Locke or the city.[6] If Locke pays he can seek contribution from the city, or vice versa, under applicable principles of contribution. See Chapter 21.

Since the adoption of comparative negligence, many states have also changed the traditional principles of joint and several liability and contribution. Chapter 25 explores some of the changes to contribution principles and joint and several liability that have been prompted by the adoption of comparative negligence. But it is important to understand that the adoption of comparative negligence *does not in itself change these principles,* and some states that have adopted comparative negligence still apply traditional approaches to both contribution and joint and several liability.

The following examples illustrate the application of the various types of comparative negligence to actual cases. Assume in analyzing them that joint and several liability applies. After the examples and explanations, there is a short discussion of special verdicts, with several examples to illustrate how comparative negligence issues are usually submitted to the jury.

Examples

Comparing Comparative Negligence

1. Paine is injured when his hand is caught in a printing press operated by Burke. He sues Burke for negligence. The jury finds that Paine has suffered $60,000 in damages, and that each party was 50 percent at fault.
   a. How much would Paine recover in a jurisdiction that applies a not-as-great-as form of comparative negligence?
   b. How much would Paine recover in a not-greater-than jurisdiction?
   c. How much would Paine recover under a pure comparative negligence approach?
   d. How much would Paine recover in a jurisdiction that retains contributory negligence?

6. No, he cannot collect $110,000. If Locke pays the judgment, Rousseau could not collect anything from the city; it would plead "satisfaction" of the judgment, that Rousseau had been fully paid. That defense would bar any further recovery from the city.

2. Assume that Paine sued both Burke and Calkins, who had recently repaired the press. The jury finds that Paine was 65 percent negligent in causing his own injuries, that Burke was 15 percent negligent, and that Calkins was 20 percent negligent. Paine's damages are again $60,000.
   a. Would Burke or Calkins be liable to Paine if the suit were brought under pure comparative negligence?
   b. How much would Burke or Calkins be liable for in a pure comparative negligence jurisdiction, if anything?
   c. Assume that the accident takes place in a state that applies the "not-as-great-as" approach. Who would be liable to Paine?
   d. Who would be liable under the "not-greater-than" approach?

3. Assume that the jury found Paine 33 1/3 percent negligent, Calkins 33 1/3 percent negligent, and Burke 33 1/3 percent negligent. Paine's damages are again $60,000.
   a. How much would Paine recover from each defendant under pure comparative negligence?
   b. How much would he recover under the not-as-great-as version of modified comparative negligence?
   c. How much would he recover under the not-greater-than approach?

Judgments, More or Less

4. Descartes sues Mill, Calkins, and Newton for injuries arising from a boating accident. The jury concludes that Descartes was 25 percent at fault, Mill was 10 percent at fault, Calkins was 25 percent at fault, and Newton was 40 percent at fault. They assess Descartes's damages at $100,000. Assume that the suit is brought in a "not-as-great-as" jurisdiction which compares the negligence of the plaintiff to that of each defendant individually.
   a. Who may Descartes recover from?
   b. Will Descartes recover $75,000, $61,538, or $40,000?
   c. Assume that the applicable comparative negligence statute allows recovery if the plaintiff's negligence was not as great as that of the defendant or defendants, and that the plaintiff's negligence is compared to the defendants as a group. Assume further that Newton is insolvent. How much could Descartes recover from Mill?

5. Suppose, on the same facts, that Descartes had sued only Mill. How much, if anything, would he recover from her?

Judge Fudd Redux

6. Pascal sues Hume for negligently dropping a board on him from a ladder. Hume claims that Pascal was also negligent, for philosophizing under the ladder during construction. The case is tried before the

indomitable Fudd, sitting in a pure comparative negligence jurisdiction. The Honorable Fudd instructs the jury as follows:

> If you find that the plaintiff was negligent, then you must reduce the damages awarded in the proportion that the plaintiff's negligence bears to the defendant's.

The jury finds that Pascal suffered $60,000 in damages, that he was 20 percent at fault, and that Hume was 80 percent at fault.

a. How much should the jury award to Pascal under Judge Fudd's instruction?
b. What is wrong with the instruction and how much did the error cost Pascal?
c. What should the instruction be?

7. Assume, on the facts of Example 6, that Pascal claims that Hume had the last clear chance to avoid the injury by warning him that the board was falling. In a contributory negligence jurisdiction, this, if proved, would require the jury to disregard Pascal's negligence. See generally Prosser & Keeton at 462-468. Should the judge instruct the jury to disregard Pascal's negligence if they find that Hume had the last clear chance to avoid the accident?

8. Assume that Hume was also injured in the foregoing fiasco, when Pascal jumped back, knocking over the ladder. He counterclaims against Pascal in the suit for his own injuries, and the jury assesses his damages at $200,000. They assign the same percentages of negligence to Pascal (20 percent) and to Hume (80 percent).
   a. What judgments would result in a contributory negligence jurisdiction?
   b. What judgments would result in a pure comparative negligence jurisdiction?

Comparing Apples and Outrages

9. Hamilton, a tenant in the Philosophers' Corner condominium complex, was assaulted in his unit when Sly, a burglar, broke in through the front door. (Unfortunately, the lock was loose but Hamilton had not had it repaired.) Hamilton sues Spencer Security Co., the company that provided security for the complex, claiming that they failed to adequately patrol the premises.
   a. Assume that the case takes place in a jurisdiction that requires the jury to consider the fault of all tortfeasors, not just the parties before the court. What will Spencer Security argue should be done in apportioning fault?
   b. What is the best argument that the jury should be told to ignore Sly in apportioning fault?

c. What is the best argument that the jury should be told to include Sly in apportioning fault?
d. Why would Spencer care whether Sly is included in apportioning fault?

Explanations

Comparing Comparative Negligence

1. a. Paine will not recover at all in a "not-as-great-as" jurisdiction, since his negligence was as great as that of Burke. This form of comparative negligence bars a plaintiff from recovery if her fault equals (or exceeds) the defendant's.
   b. In a "not-greater-than" jurisdiction, Paine would recover \$30,000. He is not barred from recovery, because his fault was not greater than Burke's. However, his damages will be reduced by his percentage of negligence (.50 × \$60,000).
   c. The result in a pure comparative negligence jurisdiction is the same as in the last example. Paine may recover, but his fault reduces his recovery proportionally, to \$30,000.
   d. Paine would recover nothing in a contributory negligence jurisdiction since his negligence contributed in part to causing the accident. Under contributory negligence, a plaintiff whose fault contributed to the accident could not recover, even if the defendant was more faulty.

2. a. Both Burke and Calkins are liable to Paine under pure comparative negligence since both were negligent. The fact that Paine was *more* negligent than either of them does not bar him from recovering under a pure comparative negligence statute. It will, however, reduce the amount he recovers proportionally.
   b. In a pure comparative negligence jurisdiction, Paine's judgment will be reduced by 65 percent to reflect his negligence. He will therefore recover \$21,000 (\$60,000 – (.65 × 60,000) = \$39.000 reduction). As the Introduction indicates, in some jurisdictions Burke and Calkins will both be liable to Paine for this amount since they are jointly and severally liable for the damages their negligence contributed to causing. Even though each was considerably less at fault than Paine, each is liable to Paine for \$21,000.
   c. Neither defendant is liable to Paine under the "not-as-great-as" form of comparative negligence since Paine's negligence was greater than that of the defendants. This case, in which the plaintiff is primarily at fault, demonstrates the most marked difference between pure and modified comparative negligence systems. Under pure comparative negligence, plaintiff recovers, with a reduction for his percentage of

negligence. Under modified comparative negligence, he loses entirely if his fault reaches a certain level.

d. Paine loses under the not-greater-than approach too since his negligence was greater than that of the defendants. Both forms of modified comparative negligence bar the plaintiff from recovery if he is more than 50 percent at fault.

3. a. In a pure comparative negligence jurisdiction, Paine would recover his full damages, \$60,000, reduced by his own percentage of fault, or \$40,000 (\$60,000 − (.333 × 60,000)). Each defendant would be liable for the \$40,000 judgment, assuming that joint and several liability applies.[7]

b. The answer here depends on whether the jurisdiction compares Paine's negligence to that of Burke and Calkins individually, or to the total negligence of all defendants. Most comparative negligence statutes provide for comparison to the combined negligence of all defendants. Under this approach, Paine's negligence would be compared to the combined negligence of Burke and Calkins. Paine would recover since his negligence (33 1/3 percent) is less than that of Burke and Calkins combined (66 2/3 percent). His recovery would be reduced by 33 1/3 percent, to \$40,000, to account for his negligence.

If the traditional rules of joint and several liability apply, Paine will get a judgment for \$40,000 against each defendant. Note again, as in Example 1, that pure and modified comparative negligence systems reduce Paine's damages in the same manner. The difference is that under modified comparative negligence, Paine loses entirely if his fault reaches a certain percentage.

If this case were tried in a state which applies the "not-as-great-as" approach, but compares the negligence of *each defendant individually*, Paine would lose entirely since his fault is as great as that of each of the other defendants.

c. Under the "not-greater-than" approach, Paine would recover even if his negligence were compared to Locke's and Calkins's individually. Because his negligence is not greater than that of either defendant, he is entitled to recover. His recovery will be reduced by his percentage of fault, so he would recover a judgment for \$40,000 against each defendant, assuming joint and several liability applies.

Judgments, More or Less

4. a. Since the case arises in a state that compares the plaintiff's negligence to each of the defendants individually, Descartes may recover against

7. Of course, Paine could only collect a total of \$40,000. See n. 6, p. 542.

Newton because his negligence was not as great as Newton's. But he cannot recover from Calkins, since his negligence equals Calkins's. And, *a fortiori*, he cannot recover from Mill, who was less at fault.

b. Descartes will recover $75,000 from Newton, his total damages reduced by his own percentage of negligence. This may seem unfair to Newton since it makes Newton bear the damages (adjusted for Descartes's negligence), even though two other parties who contributed to it are not liable at all. Wouldn't it be fairer to ignore the negligence of the other defendants, and compare Descartes's negligence (25 percent) to the combined total of his and Newton's (25 percent + 40 percent, or 65 percent), the only liable defendant? That's how I got the $61,538 figure, which reduces Descartes's damages by 25/65ths of $100,000. Alternatively, it may seem appropriate to make the one liable defendant pay only his percentage of negligence. This approach would yield the $40,000 figure.

   Maybe that would be fairer, but a good many comparative negligence statutes do not change the basic principle that those defendants who are liable are liable for the plaintiff's damages, reduced only by her percentage of fault. They do *not* limit a defendant's liability to her own percentage of negligence (unless the jurisdiction has adopted several liability). If the rule seems unfair, remember that under the common law approach, every defendant who was found negligent at all was *fully* liable to the plaintiff, even if other tortfeasors also contributed to the injury. In this case, Newton at least has his liability reduced to account for Descartes's contribution to the accident. But if Mill and Calkins are not liable (because they are less negligent than the plaintiff, and they are each compared to the plaintiff individually), Newton will end up holding the bag. He will have to pay the $75,000 judgment without getting any contribution from them (since they are not liable at all), even though their negligence also contributed to the accident.

c. If we compare Descartes's negligence to that of the defendants combined, his is less than theirs (25 percent versus 75 percent). So he is entitled to a judgment for his damages, reduced by his percentage of negligence, against all three defendants. Descartes would get a judgment for $75,000 against each defendant.

   Newton, the example assumes, can't pay. However, if joint and several liability applies, Descartes could collect $75,000 from Mill (or Calkins). After paying, Mill may be able to get some of the judgment back from Calkins, under contribution principles, but won't get any back from Newton.[8] Thus, the example illustrates that a fairly minor

8. Under the bedrock principle that you can't get blood out of a stone.

player in the accident can end up bearing substantial liability, if the jurisdiction compares the plaintiff's negligence to that of the defendants as a group.

Under this version of modified comparative negligence, more plaintiffs will recover since their negligence is less likely to exceed that of all defendants together. More defendants will end up splitting the damages since they will be liable even if they were less negligent than the plaintiff. The judgment will likely then be spread among them through contribution.

5. This example introduces a perplexing problem. In assessing percentages of negligence, should the jury only consider the parties to the lawsuit, or should they consider all persons who may have contributed to causing the accident? Here, if only Descartes and Mill are considered, and the jury must make their causal negligence add up to 100 percent, they might well assign Descartes more than 50 percent of the negligence. If they do, Descartes loses, even though, if all the actors involved in the accident were assigned percentages, his would drop below 50 percent.

Clearly, this gives Descartes an incentive to sue all potential defendants. By divvying up the liability among more parties, he will probably drive his percentage of fault down, which means his judgment will be bigger. And, if we assume the jurisdiction compares his negligence to that of the defendants as a group, by suing more defendants he increases the chance that their collective fault will exceed his. On the other hand, it is not always possible to sue all tortfeasors. Some may be bankrupt, immune from suit, never identified (as in the case of a hit-and-run driver), or not subject to personal jurisdiction.

Approaches to this problem vary. Some courts have held that the plaintiff's negligence should only be compared to that of the parties before the court at trial. See, e.g., *Shantigar Foundation v. Bear Mountain Builders*, 441 Mass. 131 (2004). This seems somewhat artificial—Calkins and Newton were involved in the accident, may have been the major causes of it, but the jury is required to ascribe 100 percent of the fault to Mill and Descartes. This may also make Descartes's recovery turn in part on procedural factors, such as whether some tortfeasors have filed for bankruptcy or can't be sued in a particular state.

Other jurisdictions require the jury to consider all actors who may have contributed to the accident in assigning negligence percentages. In these states, the parties before the court will litigate the negligence of other tortfeasors who are not present at trial. Although this can be awkward, it allows a more realistic assessment of the percentages of fault of the parties since all contributors to the accident are considered. In other states, some absentees but not others (such as immune tortfeasors) are considered. See generally V. Schwartz, Comparative Negligence §15.05.

Judge Fudd Redux

6. a. Under Judge Fudd's instruction, the jury should reduce Pascal's award by 20/80, or 25 percent, "the proportion that his negligence bears to the defendant's." He would recover $45,000.
   b. The judge's error has cost Pascal $3,000. The problem with the instruction is that it asks the jury to relate the plaintiff's negligence to the defendant's rather than to the total negligence of all parties. The proper method would be to reduce Pascal's award by 20/100, to $48,000.
   c. Jury instructions frequently require the jury to "reduce the total amount of plaintiff's damages by the proportion or percentage of negligence attributable solely to the plaintiff." It would be even clearer to instruct as follows:

   > If you find that the plaintiff was negligent, then you must reduce the damages awarded to the plaintiff by the proportion which her negligence bears to the total negligence of all parties.

   This instruction makes it clear to the jury that the Pascal's recovery is to be reduced by his percentage of fault (20%), not just compared to that of the defendant.

   If the judge uses a special verdict form, she may avoid having to instruct the jury at all on the proper method for calculating the plaintiff's recovery. The jury makes simple factual findings, and the judge fashions a judgment by applying the comparative negligence rules of the state to those findings. Use of special verdicts is discussed at p. 552 ff. in this chapter.

7. The issue posed here is whether the last clear chance doctrine applies in a jurisdiction that has changed over to comparative negligence. The last clear chance doctrine provided a means of avoiding the harshest applications of contributory negligence. The court would find for the plaintiff, despite her negligence, if the defendant had the last chance to avoid the accident (and hence was at least arguably the more negligent party). Here, Pascal argues that, since Hume had the last clear chance to avoid the accident, his (Pascal's) negligence should be ignored entirely, as it was before the adoption of comparative negligence.

   Once comparative negligence is adopted, there is no need for a doctrine that ignores the plaintiff's negligence simply because the defendant was (arguably) more negligent. If the defendant is more negligent, she can be assigned a higher percentage of negligence, but the plaintiff's negligence can still be taken into account. On this rationale, most courts have concluded that the last clear chance doctrine does not apply under comparative negligence. See Schwartz §7.02 (discussing both positions);

see also Restatement (Third) of Torts: Apportionment of Liability §3 cmt. b (advocating abrogation of last clear chance under comparative fault). If the court adopts the majority position, Pascal would still be assigned a percentage of negligence, which would reduce his damages, even though Hume had the last chance to avoid the accident.

As Chapter 23 explains (see pp. 519–521), many jurisdictions have similarly concluded that secondary unreasonable implied assumption of the risk should not be a complete bar to recovery once comparative negligence is adopted. Instead, the plaintiff's unreasonable decision to encounter a risk should be considered a form of "fault" that the jury uses in assessing her percentage of negligence.

8. a. In a contributory negligence state, neither party would recover since each was partially at fault. The court would enter a judgment dismissing each party's claim against the other.
   b. There is nothing to prevent an injured defendant from recovering from a plaintiff under comparative negligence. After all, if Hume had gone to court first, he would have been the plaintiff; he shouldn't be prejudiced by merely losing the race to the courthouse. Thus, if both parties are injured, and both are negligent, each may be entitled to some recovery in a pure comparative negligence jurisdiction. Here, Pascal would recover $48,000 from Hume ($60,000 reduced by his 20 percent of fault), and Hume would recover $40,000 from Pascal ($200,000 reduced by 80 percent).

Comparing Apples and Outrages

9. a. Spencer will argue that the jury should apportion the fault among Hamilton, Spencer, and Sly, the burglar. If the jury is so instructed, they will presumably assign a large percentage of fault to Sly, the intentional tortfeasor, and a lesser percentage to Spencer, which merely failed to prevent the criminal act.
   b. The title of this chapter is "comparative negligence." The doctrine arose as a substitute for the earlier doctrine of contributory negligence, which applied where both the plaintiff and the defendant were negligent. Traditionally, contributory negligence was *not* a defense to an intentional tort. So there is a strong argument that legislatures that enacted "comparative negligence" statutes never intended that intentional conduct should be compared to negligence, as Spencer argues here.
   c. In a state that generally requires the jury to consider the fault of all tortfeasors (including absent tortfeasors), ignoring Sly (the party with the lion's share of the fault) seems totally artificial. If an absent party whose conduct was merely negligent will be considered, it is hard to

see why a more faulty party—the intentional tortfeasor—should be ignored.

Cases like this may arise in many contexts. A school district might be sued for negligently hiring a bus driver who sexually abuses a child. A psychiatrist might be sued for failing to warn of a dangerous patient who assaults a family member. A hotel might be sued for negligent security after a guest is assaulted in the parking garage. In such cases, the liability of the negligent defendant may depend on how the intentional tortfeasor is treated in allocating fault.

Some of the cases on the point have turned on the wording of the state's comparative negligence statute. In *Welch v. Southland Corp.*, 952 P.2d 162 (Wash. 1998), for example, the court looked at the definition of "fault" in the Washington comparative fault statute, and concluded that the legislature had not intended comparison of negligent and intentional conduct. Other courts, however, have held that intentional tortfeasors should be compared, noting the artificiality of making the comparison in these cases without including them. "To penalize the negligent tortfeasor in such circumstances not only frustrates the purposes of the [comparative fault] statute, but violates the commonsense notion that a more culpable party should bear the financial burden caused by its intentional act." *Weidenfeller v. Star*, 2 Cal. Rptr. 2d 14, 16 (1991). Accord: *Liberty Ins. Corp, v. Techlan, LLC.*, 289 A. 3d 429 (N.J. 2023). The Restatement (Third) of Torts: Apportionment of Liability would allow apportionment to intentional tortfeasors. See §1 cmt. b, c. However, it is hard to view this as a "restatement" of the law since the cases are sharply divided on the issue. See *Whitehead v. Food Max of Mississippi, Inc.*, 163 F.3d 265, 281-282 (5th Cir. 1998) (citing numerous cases taking both positions).

d. Maybe Spencer wouldn't care. If joint and several liability applies, assigning a percentage of fault to Sly will not reduce Spencer's liability: It will be liable for the plaintiff's damages, reduced only by the plaintiff's percentage of fault. In fact, including Sly in the apportionment might have the effect of driving down the plaintiff's percentage of fault. For example, if the jury only considers the fault of Hamilton and Spencer, they might find Hamilton 25 percent at fault, for failing to repair the lock, and Spencer 75 percent at fault, for failing to patrol. If they consider Sly as well, however, they might assign Hamilton 10 percent of the fault, Spencer 20 percent, and Sly 70 percent. On these assumptions, and the further assumption that joint and several liability applies, Spencer pays more—90 percent of Hamilton's damages instead of 75 percent—if Sly is considered.

On the other hand, if the jurisdiction has moved to *several liability*,[9] under which each defendant only pays in proportion to its fault, including Sly makes a dramatic difference in the outcome. Spencer now pays 20 percent of Hamilton's damages if fault is apportioned to Sly, but 75 percent if Sly is ignored. Since Sly probably can't pay his part of the judgment, Hamilton loses big-time if Sly's fault is considered. Naturally, it has been plaintiffs who argue vehemently against including intentional tortfeasors in the apportionment of fault.

SPECIAL VERDICTS: GUIDING THE JURY IN APPLYING COMPARATIVE NEGLIGENCE

While comparative negligence may be fairer than the all-or-nothing contributory negligence rule, it is more complicated for a jury to apply. Under contributory negligence, the jury's role was clear. If it found that the plaintiff was negligent, it rendered a verdict for the defendant since any negligence barred the plaintiff from recovery. If it found that the plaintiff was not negligent, but that the defendant was, it decided how much the plaintiff should be awarded in damages to compensate her for her injuries, and came back with a verdict for the plaintiff for that amount.

Under comparative negligence, by contrast, the jury must decide the percentage of negligence of each party, including the plaintiff, and perhaps of absent tortfeasors as well. It must then determine the value of the plaintiff's damages, and apply the comparative negligence statute to reduce those damages and render a verdict for the reduced damages against the appropriate defendants. Since the jurors presumably know little about comparative negligence, they must be fully instructed as to how to compare the negligence of the parties, the effect of the plaintiff's negligence, and how the damages are to be reduced.

These instructions will be complicated. If the jury simply renders a general verdict ("verdict for plaintiff for $50,000" or "verdict for the defendant"), it will be impossible to know whether they understood and followed the instructions. Many states address this problem by authorizing or requiring the use of special verdicts, which ask the jury to make factual determinations about the negligence of each party and damages and leave it to the court to apply the comparative negligence statute to fashion a proper judgment. For example, if the Rousseau case (described on p. 553) were tried in a pure comparative negligence jurisdiction, the court might use a special verdict form like that in Figure 24-1 (see p. 24).

9. For an analysis of several liability, see Ch. 25, pp. 568–569.

STATE OF WEST DAKOTA

SUTTER COUNTY

SUPERIOR COURT
NO. 24-3217

JOHN J. ROUSSEAU,
Plaintiff,
v.
JOHN LOCKE,
CITY OF PARIS
Defendants

SPECIAL VERDICT

We, the jury in the above entitled case, find the following special verdict on the issues submitted to us:

Issue #1: Were the defendants, or either of them, negligent? (Answer ''yes'' or ''no'')

Answer: Defendant John Locke YES

Defendant City of Paris NO

[If you answered ''yes'' as to either defendant, then answer the next issue]

Issue #2: Was the negligence of the defendant, or either of them, a proximate cause of the injury to the plaintiff? {Answer ''yes'' or ''no'')

Answer: Defendant John Locke YES

Defendant City of Paris —

[If you answered ''yes'' to Issue #2 as to either defendant, please answer Issue #3]

Issue #3: Was the plaintiff negligent? (Answer ''yes'' or ''no'')

Answer: YES

[If you answered ''yes'' to Issue #3, then answer the next issue]

Figure 24-1

Issue #4: Was the plaintiff's negligence a proximate cause of his injury? (Answer ''yes'' or ''no'')
Answer: YES

[If you answered ''yes'' to both Issue #1 and Issue #2, then answer the next issue]

Issue #5: Without taking into consideration the question of reduction of damages due to the negligence of the plaintiff, if any, what is the total amount of damages suffered by the plaintiff?

Answer: $40,000

[If you have answered Issues #1, 2, 3 and 4 ''yes,'' then answer the following issue]

Issue #6: Assuming that 100 percent represents the combined negligence of the plaintiff and of the defendant[s] whose negligence contributed as a proximate cause to plaintiff's injury, what proportion of such combined negligence is attributable to the plaintiff and what proportion is attributable to each defendant?

Answer:		
	To plaintiff:	55%
	To defendant Locke	45%
	To defendant City of Paris	0%
	Total:	100%

J. Stuart Mill
Jury Foreperson

Figure 24-1 (continued)

A special verdict form like Figure 24-1 allows the court to ensure that the more complex comparative negligence rules are properly applied. The jury is simply instructed to make the necessary factual findings concerning the negligence of each party and the plaintiff's resulting damages. The jury fills in these findings on the special verdict form. After the jury renders the special verdict, the judge applies the comparative negligence statute to its findings by reducing the plaintiff's damages to account for her negligence and entering judgment against the defendants who are liable under the statute, or if the statute requires, entering a judgment for the defendant. The special verdict procedure simplifies the jury instructions since the judge does not have to explain to the jury how to compare the negligence of the various parties in fashioning a final judgment.

For example, if the Rousseau case were tried under pure comparative negligence doctrine, and the jury rendered the special verdict in Figure 24-1, the judge would enter judgment for Rousseau against Locke for $18,000 (45 percent of $40,000), but dismiss the claim against the city since the jury did not find it negligent. If the case had been tried in a modified comparative negligence state, the judge would enter judgment for both defendants since the plaintiff was more than 50 percent negligent.

Examples

Verdicts and Judgments

10. Assume that the jury returned the special verdict shown in Figure 24-2 (see p. 556), in a not-greater-than state that compares the plaintiff's negligence to the aggregate negligence of the defendants.
    a. What judgment should the judge render?
    b. What if the jurisdiction compared plaintiff's negligence to each defendant individually? (See p. 558 for analysis.)

11. One of the advantages of the special verdict is that the jury need not be given complicated instructions on the effect of their factual findings. For example, they do not need to know that the plaintiff will lose if she is more negligent than the defendant in a modified comparative negligence state. All they need do is find the actual percentages since the judge fashions the verdict based on their findings. However, a good many states require the judge to inform the jury of the effect of finding the plaintiff more negligent than the defendant, even though logically it is unnecessary—or perhaps even an impediment to objective decision-making—for them to know. See, e.g., Iowa Code Ann. §668.3(5). Under such a statute, the judge would give an instruction like this in a state which applies the 50 percent bar rule:

STATE OF WEST DAKOTA

SUTTER COUNTY

SUPERIOR COURT
NO. 24-3217

JOHN J. ROUSSEAU,

Plaintiff,

v.

JOHN LOCKE,
CITY OF PARIS

Defendants

SPECIAL VERDICT

We, the jury in the above entitled case, find the following special verdict on the issues submitted to us:

Issue #1: Were the defendants, or either of them, negligent? (Answer ''yes'' or ''no'')

Answer: Defendant John Locke YES

Defendant City of Paris YES

[If you answered ''yes'' as to either defendant, then answer the next issue]

Issue #2: Was the negligence of the defendants, or either of them, a proximate cause of the injury to the plaintiff? (Answer ''yes'' or ''no'')

Answer: Defendant John Locke YES

Defendant City of Paris YES

[If you answered ''yes'' to Issue #2 as to either defendant, please answer Issue #3]

Issue #3: Was the plaintiff negligent? (Answer ''yes'' or ''no'')

Answer: YES

[If you answered ''yes'' to Issue #3, then answer the next issue]

Issue #4: Was the plaintiff's negligence a proximate cause of his injury? (Answer ''yes'' or ''no'')

Answer: YES

[If you answered ''yes'' to both Issue #1 and Issue #2, then answer the next issue]

Figure 24-2

Issue #5: Without taking into consideration the question of reduction of damages due to the negligence of the plaintiff, if any, what is the total amount of damages suffered by the plaintiff?

Answer: $100,000

[If you have answered Issues #1, 2, 3 and 4 ''yes,'' then answer the following issue]

Issue #6: Assuming that 100 percent represents the combined negligence of the plaintiff and of the defendant[s] whose negligence contributed as a proximate cause to plaintiff's injury, what proportion of such combined negligence is attributable to the plaintiff and what proportion is attributable to each defendant?

Answer:		
	To plaintiff:	45%
	To defendant Locke	50%
	To defendant City of Paris	5%

Total: 100%

J. Stuart Mill
Jury Foreperson

Figure 24-2 (continued)

> If the plaintiff's negligence is as great as or greater than the negligence of the defendant, she may not recover. If the plaintiff's negligence is less than that of the defendant, she may recover her damages, reduced in proportion to her negligence in causing the accident.

Who wants the jury to be given this instruction, the defendant or the plaintiff?

12. Assume that the relevant state applies pure comparative negligence. The jury fills out the form as shown in Figure 24-3 below at p. 559.
    a. What mistake did the jury make?
    b. What should the judge do about it?

Explanations

Verdicts and Judgments

10. a. The judge should enter judgment for Rousseau for $55,000 against both Locke and the City of Paris. Rousseau is entitled to recover since his negligence is not greater than that of all defendants combined, but his $100,000 in damages will be reduced by 45 percent. If joint and several liability applies, both defendants are liable for the resulting judgment of $55,000, despite the disparity in their degrees of negligence.
    b. If the jurisdiction compared the plaintiff's negligence to each defendant's individually, the judge would enter a judgment for Rousseau against Locke for $55,000, and a judgment dismissing Rousseau's claim against the City of Paris since Rousseau's negligence is greater than the city's negligence.

11. Naturally, the plaintiff will seek this instruction since it alerts the jury to the fact that, if they find the plaintiff as faulty as the defendant (or more at fault), she will lose entirely. Realistically, this is likely to influence a jury in a close case to find the plaintiff 49 percent negligent instead of 50 percent (or 55 percent, or 60 percent for that matter). Statutes that require an instruction like this recognize the practical reality that juries often structure their findings to divide the damages in close cases, and that in a practical torts world there is nothing particularly shocking about that.

STATE OF WEST DAKOTA

SUTTER COUNTY — SUPERIOR COURT NO. 24-3217

JOHN J. ROUSSEAU,

Plaintiff,

v.

JOHN LOCKE,
CITY OF PARIS

Defendants

SPECIAL VERDICT

We, the jury in the above entitled case, find the following special verdict on the issues submitted to us:

Issue #1: Were the defendants, or either of them, negligent? (Answer ''yes'' or ''no'')

Answer: Defendant John Locke YES

Defendant City of Paris YES

[If you answered ''yes'' as to either defendant, then answer the next issue]

Issue #2: Was the negligence of the defendant, or either of them, a proximate cause of the injury to the plaintiff? (Answer ''yes'' or ''no'')

Answer: Defendant John Locke YES

Defendant City of Paris NO

[If you answered ''yes'' to Issue #2 as to either defendant, please answer Issue #3]

Issue #3: Was the plaintiff negligent? (Answer ''yes'' or ''no'')

Answer: YES

[If you answered ''yes'' to Issue #3, then answer the next issue]

Figure 24-3

Issue #4: Was the plaintiff's negligence a proximate cause of his injury? (Answer ''yes'' or ''no'')

Answer: YES

[If you answered ''yes'' to both Issue #1 and Issue #2 , then answer the next issue]

Issue #5: Without taking into consideration the question of reduction of damages due to the negligence of the plaintiff, if any, what is the total amount of damages suffered by the plaintiff?

Answer: $100,000

[If you have answered Issues #1, 2, 3 and 4 ''yes,'' then answer the following issue]

Issue #6: Assuming that 100% represents the combined negligence of the plaintiff and of the defendant[s] whose negligence contributed as a proximate cause to plaintiff's injury, what proportion of such combined negligence is attributable to the plaintiff and what proportion is attributable to each defendant?

Answer:		
	To plaintiff:	10%
	To defendant Locke	75%
	To defendant City of Paris	15%

Total: 100%

J. Stuart Mill
Jury Foreperson

Figure 24-3 (continued)

12. a. The special verdict here indicates that the jury has failed to follow its instructions. If the city's negligence was not a proximate cause of the accident, as the answer to the second question indicates, the jury should not have included it in assigning the percentages of negligence at the end. The jury may have concluded that, as long as *some* defendant's negligence caused the accident, both could be liable. Or, perhaps the jurors misunderstood proximate cause (now really, how could they?) to mean the most important cause, and they answered "no," since they found Locke much more negligent. For whatever reason, the jury's factual findings are inconsistent; it has assigned negligence percentages to all parties despite its finding that the city's negligence was not a proximate cause of Rousseau's injuries.

    b. If the jury comes back with this verdict, the judge can reinstruct them on proximate cause and send them back to deliberate further and clarify their verdict. This may well "save the trial" if the jury comes back with a consistent verdict after the supplemental instruction.

    Consider what would have happened if the jury had simply been asked to render a general verdict in this case. If it mistakenly considered the city's negligence, even though it did not cause the injuries, it probably would have come back with a verdict against each defendant for $90,000 (Rousseau's damages reduced by his 10 percent negligence). This would look on the surface like a perfectly permissible verdict, even though in fact it was based on a misunderstanding of the law. The general verdict often hides such mistakes. That is its virtue or its vice, depending on how you look at it.

    Interestingly, although the special verdict appears to make so much sense in comparative negligence cases, not all states favor them. Some require the court to use a special verdict; others permit them, and one or two, remarkably, *bar* them entirely, despite their obvious utility in revealing the jury's reasoning process. See, e.g., Vt. Stat. Ann. tit. 12 §1036 (requiring use of general verdict).

CHAPTER 25

The Fracturing of the Common Law: Loss Allocation in the Comparative Negligence Era

INTRODUCTION

Until recently, negligence doctrine developed largely through case law. Successive court opinions refined basic principles such as duty, breach, and causation, and affirmative defenses such as assumption of the risk and contributory negligence. Throughout this formative era, there was never any doubt that legislatures had the power to change such common law principles. Indeed, dramatic changes were made by statute in certain areas, such as workers' compensation and wrongful death. But these were exceptions; for the most part, negligence law was common law.

In recent decades, however, legislatures have gotten heavily into the business of restructuring the common law of torts. A prime example, of course, is comparative negligence, which has been adopted by statute in many jurisdictions. Many states have also enacted statutes placing caps on noneconomic damages, creating screening panels for medical malpractice cases, and limiting the scope of the collateral source rule.

Legislatures have been especially tempted to tinker with two traditional doctrines governing the allocation of negligence damages: joint and several liability and contribution. Recent statutes have fractured these fairly straightforward doctrines into a profusion of idiosyncratic approaches, many applicable only in a single state. These legislative changes to the principles allocating damages among tortfeasors illustrate a movement, found in many areas of the law, from general principles that work well in the broad run of cases (but may operate unfairly in some), to more precise, detailed rules that may be "fairer" but also introduce administrative complexities.

This chapter illustrates some of the changes legislatures have made to basic doctrines governing liability of multiple tortfeasors. It is not intended to make you an expert in the details of any state's doctrine, but rather as a case study of the extent to which legislatures have fractured previously monolithic common law principles in the search for greater equity.

COMPARATIVE NEGLIGENCE: THE CATALYST FOR CHANGE

As earlier chapters explain, before comparative negligence the defendants' responsibility for damages was determined by principles of joint and several liability and contribution. Each tortfeasor was fully liable for the plaintiff's damages. A tortfeasor who paid the plaintiff was usually entitled to collect "pro rata" contribution from the other tortfeasors. That is, the tortfeasors shared the damages equally; if there were two tortfeasors, the one who paid the judgment would recover half in contribution from the other; if there were six, each tortfeasor paid a sixth, and so forth.

In most states, these principles were well established before the advent of comparative negligence. While the adoption of comparative negligence did not automatically change them, it provided new information about the relative fault of the parties, which suggested that the classic principles were too blunt.

Suppose, for example, that Nell sued Fagan and Twist for negligence, and the jury found Nell 20 percent at fault, Fagan 70 percent at fault, and Twist a mere 10 percent at fault. If Nell's damages were $100,000, she would be entitled to recover $80,000, her full damages reduced by her percentage of negligence. Under joint and several liability, Fagan and Twist would each be liable for the $80,000, the plaintiff's damages adjusted to account for her negligence.[1] Under traditional contribution doctrine, whichever defendant paid that amount would recover a pro rata share, or $40,000, from the other, assuming the contributing tortfeasor was able to pay.

However, in light of the parties' percentages of negligence, these results appear inequitable. Twist, who was found only 10 percent at fault, will argue that he should not be liable to Nell (who was twice as faulty) for $80,000, as he would be under joint and several liability. Similarly, he will argue that if Fagan pays the judgment, Fagan should get much less than half of it

1. This assumes that Nell's negligence is compared to the defendants' combined negligence, as it is in most modified comparative negligence jurisdictions. See generally pp. 539–540.

(which he would get under pro rata contribution) back from Twist since Twist was only one-seventh as faulty as Fagan.

LOGICAL IMPLICATIONS: PROPORTIONAL CONTRIBUTION

Perhaps the most obvious implication of comparative negligence is that contribution among tortfeasors should be in proportion to their degrees of fault. Under this approach Fagan would contribute seven-eighths of the judgment ($70,000) and Twist would contribute one-eighth ($10,000). Because the defendant's relative degrees of fault are determined in comparative negligence cases, this appears both simple and fair: The proportions can be calculated from the jury's verdict, and tortfeasors who are more "faulty" will pay more than those who are less so. If each defendant is able to pay, each will end up contributing to the judgment in proportion to the fault assigned by the jury.[2]

Some tinker-prone legislatures have adopted such "proportional" or "comparative" contribution. The Rhode Island contribution statute, for example, provides:

> The right of contribution exists among joint tortfeasors; provided however, that when there is a disproportion of fault among joint tortfeasors, the relative degree of fault of the joint tortfeasors shall be considered in determining their pro rata shares.

R.I. Gen. Laws §10-6-3. Under a statute like this, after the plaintiff has been paid, the judgment will be redistributed among the defendants through contribution in proportion to the tortfeasors' percentages of fault rather than equally.

While proportional contribution distributes the loss in proportion to the fault of the parties, calculating the defendants' shares is more complex under proportional contribution than it is under pro rata contribution. Instead of simply dividing by the number of tortfeasors, judges and juries have to deal with fractions. In the example, Twist should bear 10/80ths of the judgment ($10,000) and Fagan 70/80ths ($70,000). (The proportions can be calculated by adding the defendants' percentages of negligence together to form the denominator of the fraction; each individual tortfeasor's percentage will form the numerator for that tortfeasor.) If Fagan paid Nell her $80,000 (remember that he is liable for the whole judgment

2. So does the plaintiff, in a sense, since 20 percent of her damages is deducted from her recovery to account for her negligence.

under joint and several liability), he would receive 10/80ths ($10,000) from Twist, and absorb 70/80ths ($70,000) of the judgment himself.

These fractions don't seem so bad; this amount of increased complexity is clearly worth it for the gain in fairness. As the following examples illustrate, however, applying proportional contribution not only requires judges to dust off their math skills but also raises administrative problems. In considering these examples, don't get bogged down in the math; the concept of proportional contribution, and the complexities it can raise, are the main point. (The explanations begin on p. 572.)

Examples

Out of Proportion

1. Flite sues Micawber, Heap, and Murdstone for negligence. The jury finds Flite 20 percent at fault, Micawber 50 percent, Heap 20 percent, and Murdstone 10 percent. They find Flite's damages to be $60,000.
   a. Assume that the case takes place in a modified comparative negligence jurisdiction which compares the plaintiff's negligence to that of all defendants combined. Assume further that joint and several liability and the Rhode Island proportional contribution statute apply. How much would Flite be entitled to collect from Heap?
   b. If Heap paid the judgment, how much would he recover in contribution from Murdstone if proportional contribution applies?
   c. Assume that the case takes place in a modified comparative negligence jurisdiction that compares the plaintiff's negligence to that of each defendant individually, and allows her to recover from any defendant as long as she was not more negligent than that defendant. If Heap paid the judgment, and proportional contribution applied, how much would he recover from Micawber in contribution?

2. Suppose that Heap pays the judgment and seeks contribution from Turveydrop, who allegedly was *also* negligent in causing the accident, but wasn't sued by Flite. How should Turveydrop's liability for contribution be determined?

MORE LOGICAL IMPLICATIONS: PROPORTIONAL CREDIT FOR SETTLEMENTS

Once comparative percentages of fault are established, another logical implication is to give a proportional or comparative credit for a settlement with one tortfeasor, instead of the traditional dollar credit provided in the

Uniform Contribution Among Tortfeasors Act (see §4(a), p. 474). Suppose, for example, that Nell sued Fagan and Twist, and settled with Fagan for $25,000. She then tries her case against Twist, in a jurisdiction that requires the jury to assign percentages of negligence to all tortfeasors (including Fagan). The jury comes back with a finding that Nell was 20 percent at fault, Fagan 70 percent, and Twist 10 percent. It finds Nell's damages to be $100,000.

In a jurisdiction that retains joint and several liability, Twist would be liable to Nell for $80,000, her damages reduced by 20 percent to account for her negligence. If the jurisdiction applied the Uniform Act's dollar credit for settlements, Twist would pay $55,000 to Nell, after the dollar credit for Fagan's settlement payment.

Now, let's consider what Twist would owe in a jurisdiction that gives him a proportional credit for Fagan's settlement. Under this approach (advocated in the Restatement (Third) of Torts: Apportionment of Liability §16), Fagan is viewed as selling his proportion of the ultimate judgment to Nell for the agreed settlement amount. Thus, Twist would get a $70,000 credit against the judgment for Fagan's proportion of their combined fault—70/80ths of the $80,000 judgment. Twist would end up paying $10,000 to Nell under this approach, instead of $55,000 under the dollar credit approach.[3]

Another example may help. Assume that Nell had settled for $3,000 with Twist, and the jury returned the same $100,000 verdict when Nell went to trial against Fagan. Fagan would get a 10/80ths credit against the $80,000 judgment. He would end up paying $70,000 to Nell.

Example

Credit Transactions

3. Take the facts of Example 1, in which the jury found Flite (the plaintiff) 20 percent at fault, Micawber 50 percent, Heap 20 percent, and Murdstone 10 percent. They find Flite's damages to be $60,000. Assume that Flite settles with Heap for $22,000 before trial. Assume that the jurisdiction applies joint and several liability, compares plaintiff's fault to the combined fault of the defendants, and gives a proportional credit for settlements.
   a. How much is Murdstone liable for, before considering any credit for Heap's settlement?
   b. How much will Murdstone actually have to pay, after he gets a proportional credit for Heap's settlement?
   c. How much will Flite collect altogether?

3. Of course, when they settled, the parties did not know what percentages of negligence the jury would assign to them. So Twist may do better if Fagan settles, but also may do worse.

ULTIMATE IMPLICATIONS: SEVERAL LIABILITY

The adoption of proportional contribution does not change the principle of joint and several liability. It only changes the rules for *reallocating* the loss once one of the tortfeasors has paid the judgment amount to the plaintiff. Thus, proportional contribution still requires a two-step process: a suit by the plaintiff that establishes her right to recover damages, followed by a second action for contribution by the tortfeasor who pays those damages (or a motion for contribution in the original action). Similarly, giving a proportional credit for settlements requires the entry of a judgment, followed by a proportional adjustment for the settlement.

Logically, wouldn't it be simpler to make the defendants separately liable to the plaintiff for their *respective shares of the judgment*? In Nell's action, for example, Fagan would be liable to Nell for 70/80ths of her adjusted damages ($70,000), and Twist would be liable for 10/80ths ($10,000). Nell would recover $80,000 (her raw damages reduced by her percentage of negligence) just as she did under joint and several liability, but each defendant would only be "severally" liable for her own portion of the damages.

Obviously, one great advantage of this approach is that it eliminates the need for contribution entirely: None of the defendants need seek contribution since none pays in excess of his "share" of the damages. However, several liability has a great *disadvantage* from the plaintiff's point of view: It casts the burden of the insolvent tortfeasor on her. If Fagan cannot pay, Nell will only recover $10,000 under several liability because Twist is not liable for Fagan's share. Under joint and several liability, by contrast, both tortfeasors would be liable to Nell for the entire judgment. If Fagan were insolvent, Nell could collect his share from Twist. Of course, this advantage of joint and several liability to the plaintiff carries a corresponding *disadvantage* to defendants: Under joint and several liability, Twist could end up paying the entire judgment if Fagan is insolvent, even though he was only 10 percent at fault.[4]

An increasing number of states have adopted several liability, either for all cases or for some situations. Utah's comparative negligence statute, for example, provides

> No defendant is liable to any person seeking recovery for any amount in excess of the proportion of fault attributed to that defendant under Section 78B-5-819.

Utah Code Ann. §78B-5-818(3). Similarly, Vermont's statute provides that

> Where recovery is allowed against more than one defendant, each defendant shall be liable for that proportion of the total dollar amount awarded

4. This assumes that Nell's fault is compared to the *combined* negligence of the defendants.

as damages in the ratio of the amount of his or her causal negligence to the amount of causal negligence attributed to all defendants against whom recovery is allowed.

Vt. Stat. Ann. tit. 12 §1036.

The following examples illustrate how Flite's case would come out under several liability. Assume in each example that the jurisdiction applies comparative negligence of the "not greater than" variety, compares the plaintiff's fault to the combined fault of all defendants, and has switched to several liability. Again, the examples illustrate that the attempt to make the rules more equitable carries its own problems of administration.

Several Examples

4. Assume the same facts as in Example 1: Flite sues Micawber, Heap, and Murdstone for negligence. The jury finds Flite 20 percent at fault, Micawber 50 percent, Heap 20 percent, and Murdstone 10 percent. They find Flite's damages to be $60,000.
   a. If all defendants are solvent, how much will Flite recover from each defendant under several liability?
   b. If Micawber pays the judgment against him, how much can he get in contribution from Murdstone?

5. Assume that Flite's case was litigated in a state that requires the jury to assign percentages to all tortfeasors, including tortfeasors who are not before the court at trial. Assume that Flite settled with Micawber for $9,000 before trial. The jury assigns 20 percent to Flite, 50 percent to Micawber, 20 percent to Heap, and 10 percent to Murdstone. The damages are again assessed at $60,000. How much should Heap and Murdstone pay to Flite?

One Among Several

6. Suppose that Flite sued Micawber only, that under the applicable statute the negligence is apportioned only to the parties at trial, and the jury determined that Flite was 25 percent at fault and Micawber was 75 percent at fault.
   a. Assuming again that the damages are $60,000, how much would Micawber be liable for?
   b. Could Micawber implead Heap and Murdstone in the action, to assure that their negligence is considered in allocating percentages?

7. It is sometimes said that several liability makes more sense because it allocates the loss according to the amount of damage caused by each tortfeasor. What would a classic old common law judge like Judge Fudd think about this reasoning?

8. Assuming that it appears that Murdstone's negligence was a relatively minor factor in causing the accident, how would you expect the switch to several liability to affect the dynamics of settlement negotiations between him and Flite?

POTPOURRI: A SAMPLING OF COMPARATIVE APPORTIONMENT STATUTES

All of this fine-tuning makes the classic liability rules look like pretty blunt instruments, though perhaps blissfully so. Yet recent statutes illustrate even more idiosyncratic variations on the basic allocation rules. Here are three statutes that illustrate the variety of statutory approaches to apportioning damages under comparative negligence.

Let's start with a fairly straightforward several liability statute. The Indiana comparative fault statute provides:

> (1) The jury shall determine the percentage of fault of the claimant, of the defendants, and of any person who is a nonparty. . . . In assessing percentage of fault, the jury shall consider the fault of all persons who caused or contributed to cause the alleged injury, death, or damage to property, tangible or intangible, regardless of whether the person was or could have been named as a party. The percentage of fault of parties to the action may total less than one hundred percent (100%) if the jury finds that fault contributing to cause the claimant's loss has also come from a nonparty or nonparties.
> (2) If the percentage of fault of the claimant is greater than fifty percent (50%) of the total fault involved in the incident which caused the claimant's death, injury, or property damage, the jury shall return a verdict for the defendants and no further deliberation of the jury is required.
> (3) If the percentage of fault of the claimant is not greater than fifty percent (50%) of the total fault, the jury shall then determine the total amount of damages the claimant would be entitled to recover if contributory fault were disregarded.
> (4) The jury next shall multiply the percentage of fault of each defendant by the amount of damages determined under subdivision (3) and shall enter a verdict against each defendant . . . in the amount of the product of the multiplication of each defendant's percentage of fault times the amount of damages as determined under subdivision (3).

Ind. Code Ann. §34-51-2-8(b).

The Iowa comparative fault statute retains joint and several liability only for defendants found at least 50 percent at fault. Even for them, joint and several liability only applies to economic damages, not to intangible or "noneconomic" damages:

> In actions brought under this chapter, the rule of joint and several liability shall not apply to defendants who are found to bear less than fifty percent of the total fault assigned to all parties. However, a defendant found to bear fifty percent or more of fault shall only be jointly and severally liable for economic damages and not for any noneconomic damage awards.

Iowa. Code Ann. §668.4.

Last, here's one that Oregon tried for a while, but was later replaced by another complex provision!

> (2) In any civil action arising out of bodily injury, death or property damage, including claims for emotional injury or distress, loss of care, comfort, companionship and society, and loss of consortium, the liability of each defendant for noneconomic damages awarded to plaintiff shall be several only and shall not be joint.
> (3) The liability of a defendant who is found to be less than 15 percent at fault for the economic damages awarded the plaintiff shall be several only.
> (4) The liability of a defendant who is found to be at least 15 percent at fault for the economic damages awarded the plaintiff shall be joint and several, except that a defendant whose percentage of fault is less than that allocated to the plaintiff is liable to the plaintiff only for that percentage of the recoverable economic damages.

Or. Rev. Stat. §18.485 (superseded under 1995 Or. Laws ch. 696).

These statutes illustrate that the monolithic common law approach to allocating liability has yielded to a good many experiments in the "laboratory" of the states.[5] While these statutes fine-tune the liability rules in an effort to make the punishment fit the crime, they are also more complex for courts and parties to apply. Consider how the following case would come out under these fractured approaches to allocating liability.

Compound Fractures

9. Jingle sues Weller and Snubbin for negligence. After trial, the jury finds Jingle 20 percent at fault, Weller 60 percent, and Snubbin 20 percent. The jury further finds, by special verdict, that Jingle's economic damages are $20,000, and his noneconomic damages are $60,000.
   a. How much would Jingle recover from Weller under each statute?
   b. How much would he recover from Snubbin under each statute?

5. *New State Ice Co. v. Liebmann*, 285 U.S. 262, 311 (1932) (Brandeis, J., dissenting).

Explanations

Out of Proportion

1. a. Because Flite's negligence is less than the total negligence attributed to the defendants, she would recover a judgment of $48,000, her raw damages reduced by 20 percent. Under joint and several liability, each defendant, including Heap, would be liable for that amount. Proportional contribution does *not* change the principle of joint and several liability to the plaintiff; it simply changes the rules for reallocating the judgment after one of the tortfeasors pays it.

   b. To determine Murdstone's liability for contribution, it is necessary to calculate his proportion of the judgment. As the introduction indicates, Murdstone's proportion can be calculated by taking the total of the negligence percentages of all defendants as the denominator (here 80) and Murdstone's percentage (10) as the numerator (10/80). Multiply that fraction times the judgment amount, which is $48,000. If Heap paid $48,000 to Flite, he should recover 10/80ths of it from Murdstone, or $6,000. He'll get 50/80ths ($30,000) from Micawber, and absorb 20/80ths ($12,000) himself.

   c. The problem here is in determining the proportional shares. Since the jurisdiction compares the negligence of the plaintiff to that of each defendant individually, Flite cannot recover from Murdstone, who was less negligent. She can recover from Micawber, and from Heap, whose negligence was equal to hers. If joint and several liability applies, Heap and Micawber are still liable to Flite for $48,000, 80 percent of her damages. Heap pays the $48,000, and now seeks proportional contribution from Micawber.

      Since Murdstone is not liable to Flite, he is also presumably not required to contribute to the judgment: It doesn't seem logical that a defendant should recover contribution from Murdstone when the plaintiff can't recover anything from him. Contribution statutes typically provide for contribution among parties "jointly liable in tort," or "liable for the same injury." Since Murdstone is not liable, he presumably cannot be forced to contribute.[6]

      So, Heap and Micawber should contribute proportionally to the $48,000 judgment. Between them, they account for 70 percent of the fault. Presumably Heap should pay 20/70ths and Micawber should pay 50/70ths. Thus, Heap will recover 50/70ths of 48,000 ($34,286)

6. Most cases have so held. See, e.g., *Horton by Horton v. Orbeth, Inc.*, 342 N.W.2d 112, 113-114 (Minn. 1984) (refusing contribution on similar facts since there was no "common liability"); but see *Otis Elevator Co. v. F.W. Cunningham & Sons*, 454 A.2d 335 (Me. 1983) (despite plaintiff's inability to recover, considerations of fairness support contribution from the less negligent tortfeasor).

in contribution from Micawber. He ends up paying $13,714, which is 20/70ths of $48,000.

2. Our theme is simplicity versus fairness. It is probably more equitable to make contribution proportional, but this example illustrates the price that must be paid in terms of increased complexity of administration. If all tortfeasors are parties to the first action, proportional contribution is fairly simple to administer: The jury's findings can be applied to redistribute the judgment according to the defendants' percentages of negligence. But the plaintiff need not sue every tortfeasor. Here, for example, Flite did not sue Turveydrop, and no negligence percentage was assigned to him. Heap, who paid the judgment, should be entitled to contribution from Turveydrop, but it is not clear how to calculate the proportion of the judgment Turveydrop should pay.

   Some courts require the jury in comparative negligence actions to assess percentages of negligence for *all* tortfeasors, even if the plaintiff has not made a claim against them and they are not before the court. (Others restrict the jury to assessing percentages for the parties before the court at trial.) However, even if Turveydrop were assigned a percentage in Flite's initial suit, it would not bind him, since he has not had the opportunity to litigate his proportion of negligence. See J. Glannon, Civil Procedure: Examples and Explanations 599-600 (9th ed. 2023), Example 1 (explaining leniency of surly myrmidons toward parties who have not litigated issue in prior action). Alternatively, some comparative negligence statutes require the defendant to implead other tortfeasors in the original suit to obtain contribution from them. However, this has problems too since there may not be personal jurisdiction over all tortfeasors in the plaintiff's initial action.

   Since Turveydrop was not a party to the first action, it appears that the court in the contribution action would have to make a new finding of the relative percentages of negligence of all the parties, including Turveydrop. Turveydrop would be liable for the percentage allocated to him in the contribution action, but presumably the other tortfeasors would pay according to the percentages assessed against them in the original action. This is awkward—somehow, the accounting is not going to work out right—and imposes an additional burden on the court in the contribution action.

Credit Transactions

3. a. Under joint and several liability, Murdstone is liable for Flite's damages, $60,000, reduced by her 20 percent of fault, or $48,000. But he will get a credit against this amount for Heap's settlement.
   b. Murdstone is entitled to a proportional credit for Heap's settlement. The credit should be 20/80ths, or 1/4 of the $48,000. (It is

calculated by putting Heap's percentage over that of all defendants as a group (20/80), and then taking the credit against the judgment amount—not the raw damages.)[7] So Murdstone owes $36,000 to Flite.

c. Flite collects $58,000, the $36,000 he gets from Murdstone plus the $22,000 Heap paid in settlement. This is $10,000 more than the jury decided she should get since Flite made a good deal with Heap, who paid well in excess of his "share" of the fault. The Restatement (Third) of Torts: Apportionment of Liability approves this result. "Since the plaintiff bears the risk of an inadequate settlement (in which case the plaintiff will recover less than the damages determined by the factfinder), the plaintiff should also obtain the benefit of a favorable settlement." §16 cmt. e.

   Of course, when Heap paid his $22,000 he didn't know what the jury would ultimately do, so he may have made a reasonable decision (even leaving legal fees and costs of going to trial aside). And remember, so long as joint and several liability applies, he could have ended up paying the whole $48,000 if he didn't settle and the other defendants were insolvent.

   Although Flite made out well in this example, she could also end up collecting less than $48,000 if the court uses the proportional credit approach. If Heap had settled for $5,000, Flite would have collected a total of $41,000 ($36,000 from Murdstone or Micawber and $5,000 from Heap). These possibilities make settlement an interesting exercise for all parties.

Several Examples

4. a. Flite should recover a total of $48,000 if all defendants pay their several shares. Micawber is liable for 50/80ths of the damages after adjustment for Flite's negligence, or $30,000. Heap pays 20/80ths of the adjusted judgment, or $12,000. And Murdstone owes 10/80ths of $48,000, or $6,000. Their three several shares together total $48,000.

   Thus, Flite recovers the same amount as she would under joint and several liability, as long as everyone is solvent.[8] The difference is

7. Yes, you can reach the same result by taking a 20 percent credit against the raw damages. But I find it clearer to think of Heap having sold his portion of *the judgment*, and therefore using the judgment as the figure against which to take the credit.

8. Some states that have adopted *several* liability include provisions to soften the blow to the plaintiff if one of the tortfeasors is insolvent. They provide for the reallocation of the uncollectible share among the other tortfeasors (or among the other tortfeasors and the plaintiff) in proportion to their *fault*. See, e.g., Ariz. Stat. Ann. §12-2508 (reallocation among other defendants).

that each defendant pays according to his proportion of negligence, instead of being liable for the full judgment. And, of course, Flite must *do the collecting* from each defendant; she cannot collect the full judgment from one and leave him to seek contribution from the other defendants. Since collecting judgments can be an arduous and expensive process in itself, this is a significant shift in the burden on the parties.

b. Micawber recovers nothing in contribution from Murdstone. The judgment against Micawber will be for his share ($30,000) but no more, since he is only liable to Flite for his share. Thus, he has no right of contribution from any other tortfeasor because he never pays more than his "share." Nor does anyone have a right of contribution from him. This is an obvious advantage of several liability.

5. Under several liability, a tortfeasor who settles simply extinguishes liability for his share. There is no need to give anyone else a credit for the payment because they are only separately liable for their own shares. If Micawber had not settled, his share would have been $30,000, but Flite settled this share for $9,000. The remaining tortfeasors are only liable for their shares. Heap would pay 20/80ths of $48,000, or $12,000, and Murdstone would pay 10/80ths, or $6,000.

   Thus, Flite would recover $27,000 altogether ($9,000 from Micawber, $12,000 from Heap, and $6,000 from Murdstone). She would collect less than her full judgment because she sold Micawber's share ("worth" $30,000 [50/80ths of $48,000]) for $9,000. Of course, when she settled with Micawber, she did not know how the jury would allocate fault, so her choice was at best a guess.

One Among Several

6. a. Here is another example that illustrates that several liability, while arguably more equitable, is also more complicated than it first appears. While several liability is meant to confine each defendant's liability to his share, the plaintiff has a good deal of control over what that share will be since a tortfeasor's share depends on whose fault is considered. Here, since Micawber is the only defendant, and absent tortfeasors' negligence is not considered in this jurisdiction, he will be liable for 75 percent of the damages, or $45,000. Yet, in a several liability jurisdiction he will have no right to contribution since he is only paying his share. Had Flite sued Heap and Murdstone as well, Micawber's percentage would presumably have been considerably smaller since they were also partially at fault.

   It would seem that the logical way to address this problem would be to require the jury to assign shares to all tortfeasors, whether or not they are made parties to the action. Under this approach, Micawber could reduce his share by proving that Heap and Murdstone were also negligent (and therefore assigned percentages of fault by the jury), even though they are not defendants. However, some jurisdictions that have moved to several liability only allow apportionment among the parties present at trial. See, e.g., Vt. Stat. tit. 12 §1036 (a); *McCormack v. State*, 553 A.2d 566, 569 (Vt. 1988).

b. Since the jurisdiction only allows the jury to consider the negligence of the parties to the suit, Micawber would clearly like to bring the other tortfeasors in as third-party defendants so that their negligence would also be considered. However, many impleader rules only allow a defendant to bring in other parties who may be liable to *him*, that is, to the defendant, not to the plaintiff. See, e.g., Fed. R. Civ. P. 14(a). Typically, other tortfeasors are brought in for contribution, but in a jurisdiction that applies several liability, there is no contribution. See Example 4b.

   Some comparative negligence statutes authorize a defendant to prove that other tortfeasors were also partly at fault in causing the plaintiff's injury, even though they are not made parties. See, e.g., Ind. Code Ann. §34-51-2-8(b). This approach can be awkward, however, since the nonparties' negligence is being assessed, but they are not there litigating the issue before the jury. Any percentage of fault attributed to such an absent tortfeasor could not bind her if the plaintiff later sued her separately.

   Other statutes deal with this problem, that a defendant sued alone risks disproportionate liability, by allowing that defendant to join other tortfeasors as additional defendants in the action, even though those tortfeasors would only be liable to the plaintiff, not to the original defendant for contribution (since there is no contribution under several liability). See, e.g., Conn. Gen. Stat. Ann. §52-102b (allowing defendant to join in the action a nonparty who is or may be liable for a proportionate share of the plaintiff's damages). One problem with this approach, however, is that it may not be possible to join the absent tortfeasor, because she was never identified, has settled, or is not subject to personal jurisdiction in the action.

7. Judge Fudd would think this was arrant nonsense. Under traditional causation analysis any person whose act is a but-for cause of the harm has caused *all* the harm, not a part of it. That is still true under comparative negligence: The jury still must find that each defendant's negligence caused indivisible harm to the plaintiff before that defendant is liable. (If they caused divisible harm, they would be separately liable for that harm only. See Chapter 20, Example 12.)

   Thus, the jury does not assign a party a 15 percent share of the negligence because she only caused 15 percent of the plaintiff's damages.

When juries assign percentages of negligence, they are making findings as to how *faulty* each defendant was in causing the single, indivisible harm the plaintiff suffered. In finding one defendant 15 percent at fault and another 85 percent, they are saying that the one was considerably less negligent than the other, even though each was a but-for cause of *all* of the plaintiff's resulting damages.

8. Under several liability, Murdstone's potential damage exposure is much less than it is under joint and several liability because he is only liable for his percentage share of the total damages. He will therefore take a harder line in settlement negotiations than he could under joint and several liability, which exposes him to liability for the plaintiff's full damages. Under joint and several liability, plaintiff could argue, "Look, as long as the jury finds you negligent at all—even one percent—you are liable to me for the entire judgment." This is a forceful argument in many cases because, even though a plaintiff like Murdstone has a theoretical right of contribution from more negligent tortfeasors, they are often unable to pay.

   Under several liability, this sword of Damocles is removed; Murdstone is only at risk for the share of fault that the jury assesses to him. If this is likely to be small, defendants like Murdstone are likely to be a good deal more stingy in considering settlement.

Compound Fractures

9. a. *Indiana:* Indiana's modified comparative negligence statute (subsection 3) allows the plaintiff to recover as long as her negligence is 50 percent or less. If this is true (as it is in Jingle's case), each defendant is severally liable in proportion to his percentage of fault. Jingle gets a judgment against Weller for 60 percent of his total damages ($80,000), or $48,000.

   Iowa: Under Iowa's statute, a defendant who is more than 50 percent at fault is jointly and severally liable for the economic damages only. This distinction is sometimes found in comparative negligence regimes. Retaining joint and several liability for the "hard" losses like medical expenses and lost earnings makes it likely that these out-of-pocket losses will be paid. At the same time, imposing several liability for intangible damages, such as pain and suffering and loss of consortium, limits the exposure of defendants. The distinction may suggest that there is something less real about the intangible consequences of a serious injury. Or, it may reflect simple doubt that these intangible consequences can actually be recompensed by a money award.

   Under the Iowa statute, Weller is liable for $16,000 for Jingle's economic damages. You take the $20,000 in economic damages and reduce it for Jingle's fault, to $16,000, Weller is jointly and severally liable for this under the statute since his fault is more than 50 percent. Weller is also severally liable for 60 percent of Jingle's $60,000 in noneconomic damages, or $36,000. So Jingle could collect a total of $52,000 from Weller.

Oregon: Under Oregon's (now superseded) statute, defendants are severally liable for noneconomic damages. But a defendant more than 15 percent at fault is jointly and severally liable for the economic damages (after reduction for the plaintiff's fault), if his percentage of fault is greater than the plaintiff's. Weller is more than 15 percent at fault, and his fault is greater than Jingle's, so subsection (4) of the statute applies. Weller is jointly and severally liable for Jingle's economic damages ($20,000) reduced by Weller's percentage of fault to $16,000. He is also severally liable (under subsection (2) for 60 percent of Jingle's $60,000 in noneconomic damages, or $36,000. He owes Jingle $52,000.

b. *Indiana:* Under the Indiana statute Snubbin is severally liable for 20 percent of Weller's $80,000 in damages, which is $16,000. That statute makes no distinction between economic and noneconomic damages.

Iowa: Since Snubbin is less than 50 percent at fault, his liability is several. He would owe Jingle $16,000, 20 percent of his $80,000 in total damages.

Oregon: Under subsection 4 of the Oregon statute, Snubbin's liability for economic damages would be joint and several. His percentage of fault is at least 15, and he is not less faulty than Jingle. His liability for noneconomic damages is several, under subsection 2. So he is liable for $16,000 for the economic damages[9] and $12,000 (20 percent of $60,000) for the intangible damages, for a total of $28,000.

I find these variations intriguing, but they drive my students crazy.

9. Jingle's $20,000 in economic damages must still be reduced to account for his fault, which brings them down to $16,000. Snubbin is jointly liable for this amount under subsection 4.

PART IX

Taking a Torts Essay Exam

CHAPTER 26

The Pot at the End of the Rainbow: Analyzing Torts Issues on an Essay Exam

Most of this book has dealt with the substance of tort law, analyzing the liability standards courts apply to claims for personal injury. This Part has a different goal: to introduce you to the type of analysis you will be expected to perform in answering an essay question on your Torts exam.

A major goal—in fact, *the* major goal—of the first-year curriculum is to develop students' analytic skills, to teach you to "think like lawyers." And the primary way in which we determine whether students have absorbed that skill is through essay exams. Most students have never encountered essay exams quite like the typical law school exam. It seems appropriate to give you some explanation of the logic behind these exams, together with examples of the type of analysis we expect you to produce.

This Part includes three chapters on the nature of the legal analysis expected on a Torts exam. This chapter discusses the basic analytic approach required on a Torts essay, by pulling single issues out of an essay and illustrating how to address them. The next chapter comes at the problem from the other direction. It provides examples of the typical mistakes students make in answering essay questions. These can be kind of fun, and the explanations should help you to avoid these pitfalls and highlight the proper approach. The last chapter includes several essay questions, with sample answers and some suggestions about how to approach the questions.

I should offer a disclaimer here. While I believe the approach in these chapters would be endorsed by a large majority of your professors, some may draft their exams differently. Your Torts professor may have taken a heavily philosophical approach to the course, engaging in extended discussion of economic analysis, critical legal studies perspectives, or feminist legal analysis. If so, she may write an exam that emphasizes high-altitude policy perspectives more than effective application of doctrine to facts, as I do. On the other hand, even a professor who luxuriated all semester in philosophical speculations may surprise you with an exam that looks much like mine, since analytic skills are fundamental and are easier to test than more freewheeling policy analysis.

THE BASICS: APPLYING LAW TO FACT

On the most basic level, what your professor wants to see you do on a Torts essay is to apply the law, as insightfully as possible, to the facts of the question she has set before you. She wants you to recognize a legal problem, grasp the relevant rule of law that a court will use to resolve it, explain how the court will resolve that issue given the peculiarities of the facts in the question, and most important, explain *why* the court will reach the conclusion you predict. Call it IRAC (Issue/Rule/Application/Conclusion) if you like, or whatever; the important thing is that you *do it*, that you explain why, on the facts presented, the court will reach a particular outcome.

Enough generalities; let's get down to cases. Consider this short snippet from one of my exams:

> Jackson, a trucker, picked up a load of construction debris to be hauled to a landfill. She took off, without securing the tarpaulin over the load, as required by statute for all debris hauling.
>
> Later, Jackson stopped for coffee at a rest area on the turnpike. Since there were no parking spaces she started to back into an area behind the restaurant, marked No Parking—Tow Zone. Behind a fence was a large tank. Jackson backed into the space. Somehow, the truck hit the tank, which exploded and threw a large plank out of the back of Jackson's truck. The plank flew 200 feet and hit Polk, knocking him face down on the ground. Cleveland, a stranger, ran over and rolled Polk over to check his breathing. Because Polk had suffered several broken ribs, this caused internal bleeding.
>
> Jackson was shaken up by the blast, but managed to get out of her truck. She saw Polk on the ground. Although she was trained as an emergency medical technician, she did not immediately go to help Polk.

Let's focus on a single issue raised by these facts. When you saw that phrase "as required by statute," it should have set off a small alarm bell in the torts corner of your brain. "Aha! He's setting up a violation-of-statute-as-negligence issue." Indeed I was. So let's pull this small issue out and take a look at it.

As Chapter 8 illustrates, a court will sometimes find a party negligent for violating a safety statute. Sometimes, but not always: The court will only "borrow" the statute if it was enacted to protect persons like the plaintiff from the type of harm that the plaintiff suffered. That is all you need to know to respond to the statutory issue here:

> Polk may argue that Jackson can be found negligent for violating the statute requiring a tarpaulin over the load of debris. However, a court will only find negligence due to the violation if the statute was meant to avoid the type of harm Polk suffered. Here, the tarpaulin statute was probably enacted to prevent debris from blowing out of the truck on the highway and hitting or obstructing other vehicles. It is farfetched indeed to argue that legislators, when they enacted this statute, had in mind protecting pedestrians from debris thrown out of trucks by an explosion. Thus, the court will not find Jackson negligent per se for violating the tarpaulin statute.

This is fairly straightforward. But the writer has shown her ability to see an issue ("whether Jackson will be negligent per se for violating a statute"), state the applicable rule ("a court will only hold a party negligent per se for a statutory violation if the statute was intended to protect against the type of harm suffered by the plaintiff"), apply the law to the facts ("this statute was aimed at debris blowing out during travel, not explosions throwing planks out of trucks"), and explain the result the court will reach ("the court will not find Jackson negligent for violating the statute"). In IRAC terms: issue, rule, application, and conclusion.

A couple of points about this. First, law students talk a lot about "issue spotting," but if you content yourself with spotting the issues on your exams you should resign yourself to getting low Cs at best. It isn't very hard to spot issues, and, more important, it doesn't demonstrate the skill we are trying to test: your ability to analyze and predict the outcome of cases. Consider this response to the Jackson negligence per se issue:

> There is an issue here as to whether Jackson will be held negligent per se for violating the tarpaulin statute. If the court applies the negligence per se doctrine, Jackson will be found negligent, because she did not put on the tarpaulin.

As my seven-year-old daughter used to say, "*Pah-leeese!*" All this writer says is that there's an issue about negligence per se, and that if the doctrine applies, it applies. Sure, the student has "spotted the issue," but she has not done the real work of the exercise: to explain the governing rule and apply it insightfully to the facts. You've got to do more than parrot back the issues I wrote into the exam. You have to analyze how the court will resolve them and tell me why it will resolve them that way.

Just to nail down the point, imagine that you were a practicing lawyer, and that Jackson came to you for advice on her liability to Polk. Imagine that you advised her as follows:

> Well, Jackson, there's an issue here as to whether the court will find you negligent per se for violating the tarpaulin statute. If the court applies the negligence per se doctrine, you will be found negligent, because you did not put on the tarpaulin.

What would Jackson say to you after hearing this pithy oration? She would have the good sense to ask, "Well, *will* the court apply the negligence per se doctrine or not?" She came to you for solutions, or at least educated judgments, not just for a restatement of the problem. To show your ability to advise Jackson, you must go beyond spotting the issues.

Second, even if you go beyond the issue to state the relevant rule of law, you still may not have tackled the real job your professor expects of you. Consider this response to the negligence per se issue:

> There is an issue here as to whether Jackson will be held negligent per se for violating the tarpaulin statute. Courts will find a party negligent per se for violating a statute if the plaintiff is in the class of persons the statute was enacted to protect, and if the statute was intended to protect against the type of harm the plaintiff suffered. If the court finds the tarpaulin statute was enacted to protect against the type of injury Polk suffered, Jackson will be negligent per se.

This writer has gone beyond spotting the negligence per se issue: She has stated the legal principle the court will use to resolve it. Good! . . . You can't *apply* a legal principle effectively if you don't know what it is. But the real goal of the exam is *not* to test your memory of legal principles. We are not primarily trying to teach you rules, and we are not content to see that you remember what the rules are. We want to teach you—and, therefore, to test you on—*legal judgment*, the ability to make sophisticated predictions about how a court is likely to apply a principle to a new case. Consequently, about 80 percent of the IRAC job is in the "A": applying the principle to the facts. Can you see that the writer of this excerpt has contented herself with the "I" and the "R," but avoided shouldering the main burden these elements lead up to?

Somehow this doesn't seem fair. You spend all that time learning principles of tort law, like the negligence per se rules, and it doesn't get you anywhere! But it does get you somewhere: Stating the rule puts you in the position to analyze the facts and apply the rule to them. And, without doubt, the more sophisticated your understanding of the rules, the better job you will do in applying them to the new facts in the question. But no, we are not testing you primarily on your knowledge of the rules, and simply regurgitating the rules will not serve you well in the merry month of May.

On the other hand, it's a dirty little secret that you really don't have to know an awful lot of law to do well on a first-year exam. Sure, you need to study the material and have a good grasp of the basic doctrines you studied. But most of the issues—even those much more difficult than the Jackson issue—involve sophisticated application of *basic doctrine* rather than encyclopedic knowledge of the furthest reaches of the torts landscape. Most students spend inordinate amounts of time learning more and more rules, and very little time practicing the skill of applying the fundamental rules to new facts. You would be wiser to spend less time memorizing rules and more time applying them. That's why Chapter 28 offers example essays to work with (and also why there are examples in every chapter in this book).

ANOTHER SNIPPET—AND ANOTHER RULE

Let's illustrate the basic point again, with another snippet from a different exam:

> Phelps bought a used bike and started riding home on the sidewalk (a practice forbidden by statute). As he passed Jill's house, Jill was on her lawn with her dog Woof. They had just come back from a walk, during which Jill had kept Woof on his leash, as required by the town leash ordinance. However, as she reached her lawn, Jill took off the leash and started throwing a ball for Woof to retrieve. Woof, a frisky adolescent, took off and ran right at the front wheel of Phelps's bike. Woof hit the wheel, knocking the bike over and sending Phelps flying over the handlebars into the street.
>
> Phelps landed hard, and scraped his leg on a parking meter stub as he landed, tearing his pants and suffering a serious laceration. Phelps was knocked out by the impact, and lay bleeding from his wound. Jill saw the accident, but did nothing to help Phelps.

This short passage raises a number of issues (including several negligence per se issues). But let's focus for the moment on the issue raised by the fact that Jill did nothing to help Phelps after the accident.

Clearly, there is a duty issue here, and, on the facts given, it is not a very hard one. Although there is some ambiguity as to whether Jill was negligent, you should recognize that under tort law she has a duty to assist Phelps whether she was negligent or not. Courts impose a duty on an actor whose act causes bodily injury to another to go to the victim's assistance, even if the actor caused the injury without negligence. Restatement (Third) of Torts: Liability for Physical and Emotional Harm §39. Here's a response that analyzes Jill's liability appropriately:

> Jill may be liable to Phelps for failing to aid him after Woof knocked him off the bike and injured him. Where a party causes injury to another, even without negligence, she has a duty to go to the injured party's aid. Thus, whether or not Jill was negligent (for violating the ordinance or under general reasonable care analysis), she had a duty to help Phelps, since her act of releasing Woof caused the injury. If Phelps suffered any additional injury from Jill's failure to assist him, Jill may be liable for the additional injury.

Again, this is a very basic example; seeing that Jill has a duty on these facts is not rocket science. Other issues will be more complex. But the basic process is much the same, even for more sophisticated issues: explaining your educated judgment about how an issue will be resolved on a given set of facts.

MORE LAYERS OF THE ONION

Individual issues like the ones illustrated above are the basic building blocks of a law school essay question. Your exam will have plenty of them, probably more than you can fully address in the time allotted. Some will be straightforward, like those above. Professors put some relatively easy issues on their exams to make sure students can do basic legal analysis—the few students who flub these are headed for the door. The students who handle these competently—but only these—will scrape by in the lower part of the class.

Other issues in the exam will be considerably more complex, and will require consideration of multiple principles to resolve effectively. Professors put these more complex issues in the exam in order to make distinctions among the stronger students, to decide who gets the *A*s and who gets the *B*s. The more sophisticated the problem, the more clearly the exams break down into categories. I like to think of it in terms of layers of an onion. The mediocre student will only see the outer layer; a better student will peel off another layer of the problem; but the student who has really mastered the analytic technique will keep going, peeling more and more layers, showing that she understands the true elegance of the problem.

Let's try another negligence per se example, which shows how an effective analysis of the issue becomes more complex as you consider more issues. This example is not a killer, but involves a few more layers of the onion.

> Holmes went to a football game with his friend, Cardozo. As they were driving home, somewhat tipsy from the beers they had had at the game, Holmes noticed that Cardozo was driving about ten miles over the speed limit. He said nothing. Suddenly the right front tire blew out, sending the car spinning across the opposite lane of traffic, toward the far side of the road.
>
> Brennan was driving a flatbed truck coming the other way. The truck was loaded with steel reinforcing rod—in fact, it was overloaded. Although a statute limited truck loads to 40,000 pounds, Brennan had 46,000 pounds on his. (Almost all truckers in the state *did* violate the weight limits—it was pretty widely known that the police wouldn't give you a hard time unless loads were about 25 percent above the limit.) Brennan jammed on his brakes as he saw Cardozo's car swerve across his path. Cardozo, seeing the truck barreling toward him, jerked the steering wheel to the left, away from the truck, just as the car skidded into a phone pole on the side of the road. Holmes was thrown against the windshield and injured. Brennan's truck barely missed hitting Cardozo's car.

Once again, there's a statute in the fact pattern. Doubtless, it's in there for a reason—you've probably heard that every word in the law school essay question is there for a reason. This may not be literally true, but it's a fair working assumption that most of the facts in the question are pertinent to some issue to be addressed. And, again, the obvious issue is negligence per se. The statute establishes a weight limit, and Brennan violated it. Will he be found negligent for doing so?

This one is a little more subtle than the first. Some students argued that the weight limit is irrelevant to Holmes's injury:

> Although Brennan violated the statutory weight limit, this will not make him negligent per se, because the statute was not meant to protect plaintiffs like Holmes from the type of injury he suffered. Weight limits are meant to protect against excessive wear on the roads, not traffic accidents.

But others recognized that a weight limit may have more than one purpose, and that one may be to protect plaintiffs like Holmes:

> Holmes faces several problems in asserting a claim against Brennan for his injuries. First, if he tries to establish that Brennan was negligent per se for violating the weight statute, he will have to show that the statute was enacted to protect against traffic accidents such as his. If the statute was intended solely to protect against excessive wear on the roads, Holmes would not be able to establish negligence per se based on the violation. However, it seems likely that the legislature <u>also</u> had in mind the fact that overweight trucks are more difficult to control and to stop. Holmes has a strong argument that Brennan's violation of the weight limit is relevant, since the legislature meant to assure adequate ability to control trucks, and Brennan's excess weight likely affected his ability to do so.

Wouldn't you agree that the second answer has peeled more layers off of the onion? This student went beyond the first-level answer to a more comprehensive analysis of the issue. Imagine that you represented Holmes, who wanted advice on whether to sue Brennan. "No, Holmes, don't bother to make a negligence per se claim against him; the statute's irrelevant." This would not be effective representation, would it? The situation is more complicated than that, and your advice should recognize that there is more to it. On the exam, we want you to show us that you can go beyond the superficial to a more sophisticated application of law to facts.

Let's take this example a bit further because another aspect of onion peeling is to recognize the interrelatedness of various issues in the course. Suppose that the statute *was* intended to protect against accidents, so that Brennan may be found negligent per se for violating it. A good onion peeler should recognize that Holmes faces several further hurdles to establish that Brennan is liable for violating it. First, courts allow a violator to offer evidence of excuse, so the student will have to consider any indication of an excuse in the fact pattern.

> Assuming that the statute was intended to protect against traffic accidents, Brennan might raise the excuse that truckers customarily violated the statute, and that the police did not generally enforce it. This is a weak argument. It is the legislature that sets the policy, not the public or even the police. As a matter of policy, the courts ought not authorize either truckers or the police to overrule the statute by ignoring it. (Distinguish the role

> of custom where there is no statute; it is relevant evidence of due care in that context, but courts would very likely reject it where it contradicts the statute.) The court will likely hold, as a matter of law, that this is not an adequate excuse.

This is a nice little issue. I had never discussed the relationship between negligence per se and custom in class, so the student was not given "the answer" to this before seeing the issue on the exam. Does this seem unfair? I don't think so; legal analysis is about extrapolating what you *do* know to new situations. This twist requires the student to think about the relation between two doctrines, negligence per se and custom. If she really understands the rationales of the two rules, the answer should be fairly clear. Admittedly, the exercise is more sophisticated than basic IRAC. The better students will do it better; some won't do it at all. So, the issue helps me to separate the exam books.

Let's keep going with some more layers of the onion. Even if no acceptable excuse is available, Brennan might still escape liability for his negligence:

> Even if Brennan is negligent for violating the statute, he will only be liable if his negligence caused Holmes's injury. Although Brennan's truck never hit Cardozo's car, his violation of the weight limit might still be found to be a cause of the accident. If his truck had not been overloaded, he could have slowed it more quickly. If he had, Cardozo might not have jerked the wheel to the left, and might have missed the pole. Thus, it may be that "but for" Brennan's negligence in overloading the truck, Cardozo would have avoided hitting the pole, and Holmes would not have been injured.
>
> However, the facts suggest that Cardozo was about to hit the pole when he saw Brennan and turned the wheel. If he was that close, he presumably would have hit the pole whether he turned the wheel to avoid Brennan or not. If this is true, Brennan's negligence would not be a "but for" cause of Cardozo hitting the pole . . . he would have hit it whether Brennan's truck was overloaded or not.

How's that for onion peeling? This student has recognized that proving Brennan's negligence only establishes breach of the duty of due care, that there are three other elements to the claim, and that the facts suggest a serious problem in proving causation. If I were Brennan, I would want to be represented by this student. She's going down each branch of the decision tree, to predict the issues that will arise in the case and the various defenses to be asserted on my behalf. That's good lawyering; showing that you can do it is good exam writing.[1]

Let's reconsider the first answer, from the student who concluded that the statute was irrelevant. She certainly gets some credit for her answer: She has recognized the problem and applied the appropriate rule, though in a conclusory manner. This isn't a flunker, but if all issues were addressed on this level, she would end up pretty low in the pack. *More importantly*, by failing to recognize that the statute may be relevant, she has failed to peel the other layers of the onion, to spin out the implications of a claim against Brennan.[2] Compare the two analyses of Brennan's liability:

Student #1:

> Although Brennan violated the statutory weight limit, this will not make him negligent per se, because the statute was not meant to protect plaintiffs like Holmes from the type of injury he suffered. Weight limits are meant to protect against excessive wear on the roads, not traffic accidents.

Student #2:

> Holmes faces several problems in asserting a claim against Brennan for his injuries. First, if he tries to establish that Brennan was negligent per se for violating the weight statute, he will have to show that the statute was enacted to protect against traffic accidents such as his. If the statute were solely to protect against excessive wear on the roads, Holmes would not be able to establish negligence per se based on the violation. However, it seems likely that the legislature also had in mind the fact that overweight trucks are more difficult to control and to stop. Holmes has a strong argument that Brennan's violation of the weight limit is relevant, since the legislature meant to assure adequate ability to control trucks, and Brennan's excess weight likely affected his ability to do so.
>
> Assuming that the statute was intended to protect against traffic accidents, Brennan might raise the excuse that truckers customarily violated the

1. We still haven't peeled the last layer of this simple little scenario. For example, Holmes knew that Cardozo had been drinking, but drove with him anyway. Could Brennan assert an assumption of risk defense if sued by Holmes? Presumably not; Holmes may have assumed the risk of injury due to Cardozo's intoxication, but he did not assume the risk of *Brennan's* negligent driving.

2. This student might still address those issues if she recognizes that negligence per se is *only one way of proving a defendant negligent*. Brennan may be negligent under common law reasonable care analysis for overloading his truck. If the student realized this, she should still discuss the causation and assumption of the risk issues.

> statute, and that the police did not generally enforce it. This is a weak argument. It is the legislature that sets the policy, not the public or even the police. As a matter of policy, the courts ought not authorize either truckers or the police to overrule the statute by ignoring it. (Distinguish the role of custom where there is no statute; it is relevant evidence of due care in that context, but courts would very likely reject it where it contradicts the statute.) The court will likely hold, as a matter of law, that this is not an adequate excuse.
>
> Even if Brennan is found negligent, he will only be liable if his negligence caused Holmes's injury. Although Brennan's truck never hit Cardozo's car, his violation of the weight limit might still be found a cause of the accident. Had the truck been lighter, he could have stopped sooner, and Cardozo might not have turned the wheel to avoid Brennan. However, the facts indicate that Cardozo swerved as he was about to hit the pole. If he was that close, he presumably would have hit the pole whether he swerved or not. If this is true, Brennan's negligence did not cause the harm.

Looking at the two side by side, it isn't hard to see which answer will receive the better grade.

LET'S DO IT AGAIN

Peeling the onion is important enough that I want to illustrate it again, using the duty issue from the Jackson exam on p. 582. The first step, of course, is to recognize that there is an issue as to whether Jackson owes a duty of care to Polk, the bystander injured by the explosion. If you don't see the issue, you can't show your onion-peeling prowess. On the other hand, when I grade an essay, I do not knock students down for missing a few issues. There are always too many to discuss fully, so I don't assign grades by tallying up points for issues seen or missed. If the student sees the important issues and discusses them effectively, she can do very well even though she has not seen some others. Some professors may take a more mechanical issue-counting approach. But even issue counters will give credit for the quality of analysis as well as the number of issues seen, so peeling the onion remains important in taking their exams as well.

Let's look first at several responses to this issue that fail at the most basic level—understanding the legal rules themselves.

> Although Jackson did not go to Polk's aid, she will not be liable for failing to do so. Under §314 of the Restatement, a bystander has no duty to give aid to another simply because the other is in need of assistance. Even though Jackson is an EMT, she owes no duty to Polk.

This response falters on the "R" in IRAC. The student doesn't know the basis rule that Jackson has a duty to assist Polk based on the fact that her conduct—whether negligent or not—led to Polk's injury. See Chapter 13, pp. 275–276. The student's failure to see this hurts in two ways: First, it makes me think the student doesn't know the basic doctrine. Second, it means that she will not go on to consider whether Jackson fulfilled her duty toward Polk.

Here's another answer that reveals problems at the "R" level:

> Jackson will be liable for failing to aid Polk after the injury. Jackson is an EMT, with special training in providing emergency care to injured persons. Thus, she has a duty to assist as a reasonable EMT would under the circumstances.

This response misses the mark because the mere fact that a person possesses special training that would make her a good rescuer does not impose a legal duty to assist. See Chapter 13, Example 6b. Both of these students are headed for trouble because they simply don't know the rules. If all their responses looked like this, they would likely fail.

Most students *do* know the rules, however, and state them adequately on the exam. They survive the "R" and falter at the "A" stage, by failing to apply the principle effectively to the facts. Here's a student who knows the rule, but still provides an unpeeled answer to the duty issue:

> Jackson has a duty to assist the injured Polk, because she caused injury to him. (This is true whether Jackson was negligent in causing the explosion or not.) Therefore, since she did not go to Polk's aid, she is liable to Polk.

As I already reiterated, the name of the game is not just knowing the rule, but applying it intelligently to the facts. This student states the basic rule, but her application to the facts is totally conclusory. If *you* represented Jackson, would you give up this easily? If so, you aren't representing her effectively because Polk faces several serious problems in holding Jackson liable for failing to aid. This student's analysis places her in the C range.

Here's a student who takes the analysis of Polk's liability a step further:

> Because Jackson's driving caused the injury to Polk, she has a duty to go to his assistance (whether she negligently or innocently caused the explosion). However, Jackson's duty is to exercise reasonable care to aid Polk, not an absolute duty to help regardless of her own injury in the accident. Here, Jackson was shaken up, and stumbled out of her truck. A reasonable person in those circumstances would probably not be able to rush over and render aid. Thus, while Jackson owed a duty to Polk, she may not have breached it.

That's true, isn't it? When negligence law imposes a duty, it's a duty of reasonable care, not an absolute duty no matter what the circumstances. If Jackson did as well as the reasonable person would have under similar circumstances, Polk will fail to establish element #2, negligence. By peeling off the breach issue as well, this student shows that she recognizes that duty is the beginning of the analysis, not the end of it. This answer is moving into the B range, depending on the quality of the discussion.

Of course, there's more. Even if Jackson owed a duty and was negligent, she may yet escape liability:

> Should the court find that Jackson owed a duty to aid Polk, and that a reasonable person in her circumstances would have rushed to Polk's aid, Jackson may still not be liable. A person who owes a duty to aid is liable for the additional injury suffered as a result of the failure to aid, so Polk will have to show that Jackson's failure to aid caused him further injury. The facts indicate that Polk was 200 feet away from the truck. It is extremely unlikely that the most diligent rescuer in Jackson's position would have reached Polk before Cleveland rolled him over. Thus, even if Jackson had a duty to aid and breached it, we cannot say that "but for" her failure to aid Polk, Polk would not have suffered the internal bleeding.

This student is on an onion-peeling roll. I said above that we want to watch you *think like a lawyer*, and this student is really thinking in a comprehensive way about the problems in establishing Jackson's liability. She's in the high-B/low-*A* range if she keeps this up. Maybe a straight *A*, depending on the quality of her explanation.

This Jackson issue works well for testing onion peeling. There are even a couple more layers to peel. For example, even if Jackson had a duty, *and* breached, *and* could have reached Polk before Cleveland, she might have rolled him over, *just as Cleveland did*, since Jackson probably would not have known that Polk had broken ribs. And, even if Jackson could tell that Polk had broken ribs, breathing is important stuff; it might be perfectly reasonable to roll Polk over anyway to clear the airway. Last, you could round out the discussion nicely by pointing out that, if Jackson was negligent in causing the explosion that knocked Polk down (and if the flying plank was foreseeable), the whole duty-to-aid issue is moot: She would be liable for all of Polk's injuries anyway, including those from Cleveland's foreseeable rescue effort, as the initial tortfeasor!

SUMMING UP

If all this seems too much to ask, remember that your professors don't expect you to belabor every issue in the fact pattern, and to spot every permutation. They expect you to do the best you can in the time allotted. You will be graded relative to what a good first-year law student can do. The more you see the ramifications of the facts, and the more insightfully you explain them, the better you will do.

If you get the hang of this basic analytic technique, it will serve you well over your entire law school career (and after). The following examples should help to drive the point home. The explanations begin on p. 598.

Examples

Stretched on the IRAC

1. Consider the following short essay question:

> While King was driving north on a two-lane rural road, his tire blew out, causing the car to pull sharply to the right. King turned the wheel back to the left to avoid going off the road; the car then swerved into the southbound lane. Phil, traveling south, ran into it. King's car rolled off the road and down an incline. Debris from the crash was scattered in the southbound lane, including the tailpipe and muffler from Phil's car.
>
> Phil ran to King's assistance. Queen was traveling north behind King, on her way to an important meeting. She stopped and picked up some of the debris, but not the tailpipe, which was quite hot. Then she left to make her meeting. Deuce, an off-duty emergency medical technician, passed the accident, saw the debris in the road, and drove on. Trip, King's partner in a

house-painting business, was driving behind King in their truck; they were going to start a job that morning. Trip did not stop.

Ace came around the curve, going south at 40 m.p.h. in a 30 m.p.h. zone, and saw the tailpipe in the road. He decided that it would be safer to drive over it rather than swerve to avoid it. When he did, the truck went out of control. Ace suffered serious injuries.

Discuss the claims Ace may assert based on these facts, and the major issues he will face in establishing liability of the possible defendants. *Explain fully how you expect the issues to be resolved and why.*

a. What claims should you *definitely not* discuss in writing this essay?
b. What major issues do you see in the fact pattern?
c. Which issue gets your vote for the easiest issue in the question?
d. Which issue do you think is the most complex?

2. Consider the following three responses on the duty of Trip to stop and assist at the accident scene. In IRAC terms, what is missing from each?

a

There is an issue here as to whether Trip will be liable to Ace for failing to stop and clear the debris from the roadway after the initial accident. Here, because Trip did fail to stop, and Ace ran into the tailpipe, Trip has breached his duty to aid, and will be liable to Ace for his injuries.

b

Trip may be liable to Ace if he owed a duty to stop and assist at the scene of the accident. Ordinarily a person does not owe a duty to stop and assist, simply because a dangerous situation exists. However, a duty may be imposed if the person either created the risk that threatens injury (in this case, the debris in the road) or has a special relationship that imposes a duty to assist. Here, since Trip did not stop and assist, he will be liable to Ace for his injuries.

c

Trip may be held liable to Ace if he had a duty to stop and help but failed to do so. Here Trip owed a duty, since he was King's partner in the painting business. Thus, he will be liable to Ace for his injury.

3. Draft a more effective analysis of Trip's liability.

Onion Rings

4. Assume that you conclude that Trip did owe a duty to assist after the initial accident. What further layers would you peel off the onion in assessing his liability to Ace?

5. Let's round out the discussion by peeling the layers off a rather subtle issue. Consider this excerpt from one of my past exams, which raises an intentional tort issue.

> Alou, a pedestrian, was hit on the head by a flower pot that fell from an apartment building. As he lay groaning in the street (a pedestrian way closed to all but emergency traffic), Sanchez rushed up. Alou, who was having trouble breathing, cried, "Don't touch me!" However, Sanchez could see a fire truck rushing down the street, and thought it might hit Alou unless he was moved. Thus, he grabbed Alou by the arm and dragged him toward the curb. At this point, the fire truck pulled up in front of them and two firefighters jumped out; they were responding to a call from a neighbor informing them of Alou's accident.
>
> The firefighters rushed Alou to the hospital, where he was diagnosed with a concussion and a broken rib, which had somehow punctured a lung.

The following three analyses address the question whether Sanchez battered Alou by dragging him from the street. Please grade them, on a scale from *D* to *A*. Assume that the authors had all read *Clayton v. New Dreamland Skating Rink, Inc.*, 82 A.2d 458 (N.J. 1951), in which a woman broke her arm while skating, and the attendant set the arm over her protests to leave her alone. The court held that the attendant committed a battery by doing so.

Student #1:

> Sanchez may have committed battery when he grabbed Alou and pulled him out of the street, since Alou told him not to touch him. A contact can be tortious even if it is well intended—a virtuous motive won't protect Sanchez if he intentionally made a harmful or offensive contact with Alou. (See skating rink case.)
>
> Here, however, Sanchez was acting to protect Alou from the danger of the oncoming fire truck. A reasonable person would do the same thing, even if Alou said not to. The privilege of necessity applies where a person inflicts an unwanted contact in order to prevent a greater harm. That is exactly what Sanchez did here, so he will not be liable to Alou, even if he caused additional injury to Alou by pulling him.

Student #2:

The facts here raise a question as to whether Sanchez battered Alou when he grabbed him and dragged him by the arm. Even though Alou said not to touch him, Sanchez pulled him out of the road anyway. A person commits a battery when he intentionally makes an unconsented contact that the reasonable person would find harmful or offensive. This protects people's autonomy and prevents unwanted contacts. The law of battery is meant to protect people from contacts that they don't want, even if they are not harmful. The contact must be intentional; that is, it must be done with a purpose to cause the contact or with knowledge to a substantial certainty that it will cause one.

Here, Sanchez knew that Alou did not want to be touched, because Alou said so. Thus, he made a tortious contact when he pulled Alou out of the street after Alou told him not to. This was a deliberate, offensive contact with Alou. When he acted he knew that Alou did not want him to touch him. Therefore Sanchez is liable for battery, since he went ahead and did it anyway.

Student #3:

Sanchez will probably not be liable to Alou for battery. Sanchez committed a prima facie battery when he grabbed Alou after Alou said not to touch him, since he knew Alou did not want to be touched. This contact would be battery, even if he did it to help. Compare the case where the attendant set the woman's arm against her protest.

However, Sanchez may have a privilege to act despite Alou's refusal. If both Sanchez and Alou possessed all the facts, Sanchez would not have a privilege, even if he thought the touching was necessary. Alou would have the right to refuse the contact even if the reasonable person would accept it. But here Alou may not be aware of the fire truck coming at him. If this is true, his refusal is given without all the relevant facts. Just as a consent without all the relevant facts may not be valid (e.g., consent to sex with a partner who does not reveal a sexually transmitted disease), a court would likely allow Sanchez to ignore Alou's refusal if he were ignorant of a fact crucial to his decision (the fire truck).

This is not inconsistent with the skating rink case. There, both parties had the same information, and the attendant simply ignored the patron's wishes. Here, Sanchez can reasonably infer that Alou would consent if he knew about the truck, and act accordingly. (The more accurate analogy to the skating rink case would be if the Zamboni were bearing down on the patron and she didn't know it.)

As it turned out, Sanchez was wrong; the truck would not have hit Alou since it was coming to rescue him. However, the court would doubtless accord him a privilege anyway if his mistake was reasonable under the circumstances.

Explanations

Stretched on the IRAC

1. a. Please, in writing a law school essay, answer the question that is asked. You'd be amazed how often students ignore this maxim! One reason students complain about insufficient time to write their essays is that they discuss all sorts of issues they don't have to. Here, the closing paragraph is explicit: discuss *Ace's* claims. If you spend half your time on claims King or Phil might assert, you have wasted half your writing time. I can't give you credit for this. It would be unfair to the students who followed my directions to grade you on this irrelevant discussion.

   b. Needless to say, this small vignette is replete with interesting torts issues. Let's pull out the major ones, in order of their occurrence in the facts.

1. Breach: Can we establish negligence of King based on the fact that his tire blew out, using res ipsa loquitur?
2. Breach: Was King negligent in swerving back across the road after the tire blew out?
3. Duty: Did Phil (or King) have a duty to clear the debris out of the roadway?
4. Breach: If Phil did have a duty to clear the debris, was he negligent in performing the duty? (He went to help King instead.)
5. Duty: Did Queen owe a duty to Ace to stop and clear the road? If not, did she assume one by stopping and doing part of the job? If she had a duty, did she breach it?
6. Duty: Did Deuce, the E.M.T., owe a duty to assist at the accident scene? If he did, did the duty extend to clearing the debris?

7. Duty: Did Trip, King's partner, owe a duty to stop and assist?
8. Actual Causation: If Trip owed a duty and breached by failing to stop, did that breach cause the accident that injured Ace?
9. Proximate cause: Was injury to Ace from running into the debris foreseeable? If so, was it foreseeable to Queen, to Phil, or to everyone?
10. Breach: Was Ace negligent in driving over the tailpipe instead of swerving? Was he negligent in driving over the speed limit?
11. Negligence per se/Proximate cause: Assuming that Ace was negligent per se for speeding, was the speed limit aimed at preventing the kind of accident he suffered when he ran over the tailpipe?

    Students often ask me how they should structure their essay answers. Most students address the issues sequentially as they arise in the fact pattern. I have no problem with that, or with any other clear organizational principle for that matter. Dealing with the issues as they appear in the question helps you to make sure you address them all, and is generally fairly easy for the reader to follow.

c. I vote for the duty of Deuce as the easiest issue. The law is clear that Deuce has no duty to aid. As a stranger to the events that caused the accident, the somewhat callous no-duty-to-aid rule allows him to drive by with impunity. See Chapter 13, pp. 271–272. The fact that he has some medical training, which would make him a competent rescuer, does not impose a duty to aid. Even if it did, any claim by *Ace* would be based on the failure to stop and clear the road, not the failure to stop and render medical assistance. Deuce's medical training is doubly irrelevant to that claim.

d. Perhaps you picked proximate cause as the most complex issue since proximate cause tends to be puzzling. However, there is little doubt that a person who leaves debris in the road can anticipate that it will cause an accident to another driver who comes along. It is also foreseeable that a driver will speed, so Ace's speed may make him comparatively negligent, but does not make injury to him unforeseeable.

    A much more subtle and interesting issue is the duty of Trip to stop and assist. Trip is King's partner, and they are engaged in a joint enterprise at the time—or at least, they are *on their way to* a joint enterprise, the paint job. Does this impose a duty on Trip to stop and assist? If so, does he owe that duty to Ace? At least one court has imposed duties on persons engaged in a joint venture to assist *each other*, based on their relationship. See *Farwell v. Keaton*, 240 N.W.2d 217 (Mich. 1976). That rationale would support a duty for Trip to assist King, though perhaps not a duty to act to avoid injury to Ace.

Most courts would hold that King, since he caused the accident that created the risk, owes a duty to do what he can to mitigate that risk, whether he was negligent or not. Restatement (Third) of Torts: Liability for Physical and Emotional Harm §39. Isn't there an argument to be made here that Trip, who engaged in risk-creating conduct with King by driving to the job, owes a duty to act to mitigate the danger caused by their joint activity?

I don't know the "answer" to this issue, if there is one. But the student who sees this issue and analyzes it effectively, based on analogous principles studied in the course, shows me that she can get to the heart of the onion, to mix a few metaphors.

2. a. In IRAC terms, this excerpt states the issue, and gives a conclusion, but leaves the reader guessing as to what legal principle the writer has applied, and why that principle leads her to the conclusion she has reached.

Issue	There is an issue here as to whether Trip will be liable to Ace for failing to stop and clear the debris from the roadway after the initial accident.
Conclusion	Here, because Trip did fail to stop, and Ace ran into the tailpipe, Trip has breached his duty to aid, and will be liable to Ace.

From the grader's point of view, the "I" and the "C" are the least important parts of the exercise, bookends for the much meatier matter in between: the explanation of the applicable legal principle and the analysis of how it will apply to the facts. Stating the issue simply sets up the "R" and the "A." If you state the applicable principle and apply it effectively, it will be abundantly clear what the issue is. And, if you discuss insightfully how a court is likely to apply a principle to the facts, the conclusion will also be perfectly clear. So the "C" is a mere coda; you could skip it entirely and lose little.

b. This student is batting three for four, but she left out the most important part of the job. The excerpt states the issue and describes applicable duty principles, then jumps to the conclusion without explaining her reasoning. Again, let's break it into components:

Issue	Trip may be liable to Ace if he owed a duty to stop and assist at the scene of the accident.
Rule	Ordinarily a person does not owe a duty to stop and assist, simply because a dangerous situation exists. However, a duty may be imposed if the person either created the risk that threatens injury (in this case the debris in the road) or has a special relationship that imposes a duty to assist.
Conclusion	Here, since Trip did not stop and assist, he will be liable to Ace for his injuries.

The writer leaves us wondering whether she reached her conclusion through guesswork or inexorable reasoning. In my grading process you get little credit for reaching the "right" conclusion . . . on the juicy issues, I often don't know what the "right" conclusion is. It is the quality of your reasoning I want to assess, and if you *do it in your head only*, as this student has, I can't give you points for it.

Often, students come in to go over an exam and are able to explain to me why they put a certain conclusion in their answer. ("Professor Glannon, that's exactly what I meant," they say.) But I can only grade you on what you explain on the exam, not the private ruminations that led you to a conclusion. If you decline to share your reasoning (the "A" in IRAC) with me in your answer, I can't give you any credit for it.

c. This answer states the issue, and makes a passing effort at analysis. However, it is impossible to follow the student's reasoning.

Issue	Trip may be held liable to Ace if he had a duty to stop and help but failed to do so.
Analysis	Here Trip owed a duty, since he was King's partner in the painting business.
Conclusion	Thus, he will be liable to Ace for his injury.

In this excerpt, not only is the "A" much too brief, but the student's failure to state what principle of tort law she is applying—the "R" in IRAC—makes it impossible to evaluate the reasoning. Are partners always liable for their partners' torts? Are they vicariously liable? What is the nature of the duty Trip owed? Why is it breached on these facts? Remember that I want to *watch you think*, not just compare your conclusions to mine. This answer gives me very little on which to evaluate the writer's reasoning.

3. Here are two responses that grapple effectively with the duty issue.

Answer #1:

> If Ace asserts a claim against Trip, King's partner, for failing to stop and clear the roadway after the accident, Ace will have a major problem establishing that Trip owed him a duty to assist. Usually courts impose a duty to aid where the defendant created the risk that threatens injury, or where the defendant has a special relationship to the injured person. Trip has no relationship to Ace, so the only potential source of duty would be creating the risk. It might be argued that Trip jointly created the risk with King, because they were partners driving to the same job site. However, the two were not actually working together; they were simply driving to the job. It seems unlikely, on these facts, that the court would impose a duty on Trip to respond to an accident caused independently by King.

Answer #2:

> If Ace sues Trip for failing to stop and clear the debris, he will have to show that Trip owed him a duty to do so. Ordinarily, there is no duty to assist a stranger, but this case may be distinguishable. Trip was engaged in a joint venture with King, who created (either innocently or negligently) the danger from the debris in the road. Courts have held that even innocent risk creators have a duty to assist to avert a danger they have created. And, at least one case (the one involving the two teenagers who went cruising and got in a fight) imposed a duty on one actor engaged in a joint venture to aid the other. It would be a small step to regard King and Trip's driving to the job as joint risk creation, and impose a duty on Trip to help avert the risk created by King. The joint venture argument would be stronger if they were driving from one job site to another rather than if they were independently commuting from home.

Note several things about these answers. First, although they reach opposite conclusions, both students have gone to the heart of the matter. They have seen the duty problem, and focused on the risk-creation argument as the one likely to resolve it. They have explained why, based on the applicable legal principle, they conclude that the court would or would not impose a duty. Both are good answers.

Now, I naturally have my own views about what the court would do. I would be disingenuous to suggest that those views have *no* effect on the grading process. But I can say with conviction that well-reasoned analysis that focuses on the relevant issue and gives detailed reasons for the writer's prediction of the outcome always fares well, even if the writer doesn't reach the same conclusion I would.

Second, these answers are a little longer than the inadequate answers given in Example 2. True, good answers tend to be longer because it takes more words to go into one's reasons for a conclusion. But that does not mean that longer is always better. Some students manage to go on at length without providing meaningful analysis. Others manage to get to the heart of the matter in relatively few words. Believe me, when facing 70 or 80 exams, I value such economy!

Third, a quick note about the way the second student has used a case in her answer. The second answer notes that the duty issue here is somewhat like that in a case she had read,[3] and then explains how finding a duty here

3. The case referred to is *Farwell v. Keaton*, 240 N.W.2d 217 (Mich. 1976). In *Farwell*, the decedent and the defendant were out drinking together, talked to some girls, and then were chased by the girls' friends. The decedent was badly beaten. The defendant put him in his car, put ice on his head, drove around for a few hours, then left the decedent in the back of the car at his grandparents' house. The boy died of his injuries, and the defendant was sued for failing to obtain further medical assistance for him.

would extend the principle in that case. It is always helpful to draw analogies in analyzing an issue: Analogical reasoning is one of the primary tools of a legal system based on precedent. Often, cases read for class furnish useful analogies, so it is appropriate to use them to explain your reasoning. But don't worry about the case names. It's the limits of the principles we want to test, not the names of the cases that exemplify them. Identifying the case as the cruising teenagers case is fine with me.

Onion Rings

4. Even if Trip owed a duty to stop and clear the debris left by the initial accident, there are other problems in establishing his liability for Ace's injury. First, there is a subtle factual issue that might absolve Trip. The facts indicate that King's car was thrown down an incline, so Trip may not have seen it. Would Trip have a duty to avert the hazard if King, his joint venturer, had created it but Trip *did not know that he had*? It is hard to imagine that a court would find Trip liable for failing to stop and assist unless he realized (or, perhaps, should have realized) that his partner was involved in the accident. This issue is very subtle. If a student even *saw* this issue I'd be impressed. I'd be bowled over if she offered a reasoned judgment about how it should be resolved.

   Second, Trip might get off for lack of actual causation. If he had a duty to clear the debris, it was a duty to exercise reasonable care, not an absolute duty regardless of the circumstances. If Ace came barreling along before Trip would have been able to reach the tailpipe, then his failure to stop would not be an actual cause of Ace's accident.

   There are some other issues, too. Trip might argue that, had he stopped, he reasonably would have gone to King's assistance before dealing with the debris. If his joint venture gave rise to a duty to respond to King's accident, it probably also gave rise to a duty to aid his joint venturer. If this is so, he could make another argument that his failure to stop was not a "but for" cause of Ace's injury: If he had stopped, he would have reasonably helped King first instead of clearing the debris. (There is, of course, a counterargument: Phil was already helping King, so arguably the reasonable person in Trip's position would have dealt with the debris instead.)

   There is also a proximate cause issue, though this one seems like a slam dunk: Surely Trip can foresee Ace's accident if he is negligent in failing to deal with the tailpipe.

5. Let's talk first about Student #2's response. This is the weakest because the student talks on about the meaning of battery, but never gets to the hard issue in the case. Basically all she says is that Sanchez is liable because he touched Alou without his consent, and an unconsented touching is a battery. However, while Sanchez committed a prima facie

battery by ignoring Alou's words, the more complex question is whether Sanchez may have a privilege defense to the battery. This answer, while it is well written, stops with the easy issue, beats it over the head, and misses the opportunity to grapple with the tough one. This can't get better than a C+. Student #1's response is better. The student went beyond the first layer to recognize that Sanchez will raise a privilege defense, based on the risk of greater harm to Alou. The student suggests a reason why the court would accept the defense: As in the necessity cases, the court accepts a lesser harm caused by the actor in order to avert a greater one. This is a solid response—I'd give it a B– or a B—but it fails to really knock heads with the underlying dilemma: Would the court allow Sanchez, by comparing the two harms, to *displace Alou's expressed choice* with his own judgment about what is "good for him"? The law is pretty clearly to the contrary. For example, it is established that a rational patient may refuse a blood transfusion, even at risk of death. How do we reconcile this autonomy principle with our gut feeling that Sanchez ought not to be held liable?

The third student's response really peels the problem to the core: The crux of the matter here is the apparent difference in what Sanchez and Alou understand about the facts. Sanchez may well believe that Alou has refused without understanding his danger, and that his choice would be different if he understood the facts as Sanchez does. Yet there is no time to debate the matter; Sanchez has to act before the truck arrives. It seems likely that the court would allow Sanchez to view Alou's refusal as ineffective in these circumstances, and act instead on his reasonable perception (even if Sanchez was wrong about the danger).

To emphasize the point, change (or, rather, clarify) the facts a little. Suppose Alou was looking down the street, saw the fire truck, believed it was coming to help, and also could tell that he had an internal injury that could be aggravated by movement. If he communicated all *that* to Sanchez, it seems clear that Sanchez would no longer have a privilege based on his own perception of the greater or lesser harm. The crux of the matter is not Sanchez's right to displace Alou's choice, but to make one for him where Alou has not really made a knowing decision based on all the facts.

This is a very subtle issue, more subtle than most. Class provided no "answer" to it; the student must extrapolate from various battery principles we *did* study to predict the outcome of a case with a new twist. When you practice law, many of your cases will have such twists. Your ability to predict how those twists will be resolved by a court is your stock in trade. We have a right to test this ability. The more insightfully you rise to the challenge, the better you will do. This student gets an *A*.

CHAPTER 27

Dandelions in the Bluebook Garden: Six Classic Exam Writing Mistakes

The last chapter explored the type of analysis most law professors want to see on first-year law essay exams. It is a skill you can learn, once you recognize what we want. Once you grasp the basic approach, you can continue to improve at it through practice.

This chapter comes at the topic from the other direction: the classic mistakes students make, year after year, in answering essay questions. These mistakes reflect basic misconceptions students have about the nature of legal analysis and the exam process. If you learn to recognize these misconceptions before taking your finals, you will be able to avoid these dandelions, and to focus on the type of analysis we *do* want, as illustrated in the previous chapter.

Here's a question from one of my old exams, which I will use to illustrate the various dandelions to be rooted out of your exam-taking strategy.

> The football season at Grumbling State was the high point of the year. In recent years, Grumbling had become a football power, and games had almost always been sold out. Officials made every effort to cram as many paying spectators as possible into the 50-year-old stadium, to fund those lavish athletic scholarships.
>
> This year, before the season began, Allen, the athletic director, noticed some weakness in section C of the stadium stands. He wondered if the supporting structure was sound, and decided to hire a contractor to look it over. He called in Munoz Construction Company to inspect the section and perform any necessary repairs.
>
> Upon examination, Brian, a Munoz supervisor, determined that several of the vertical wooden beams supporting section C had deteriorated. He ordered

Griffin, an employee, to replace them with metal "I" beams. Although "I" beams would have been stronger, Griffin replaced the beams with new wooden beams he had on hand, identical to the ones he removed. Other Munoz employees then bolted the new beams in place to the horizontal girders.

The tenth game of the season, against Texas Agricultural, a traditional rival, was a thriller. The fans were on their feet, doing the "wave" and cheering wildly. All of a sudden section C collapsed completely, sending the fans down into the bowels of the stadium. The entire section was reduced to splinters. Jane Aragna, sister of the Grumbling quarterback, was injured. The Grumbling mascot, Sticky (an absurd-looking porcelain porcupine which had cost the athletic department $25,000), was smashed to smithereens. Hal Aragna, the Grumbling quarterback, heard the noise, froze, and looked for his sister, who had disappeared when the stands collapsed. At that moment, a Texas player tackled him from behind, injuring his throwing hand and ending a promising football career. (Aragna had been seriously scouted by the Atlanta Falcons of the National Football League.)

Please discuss the claims that Jane, Hal, and Grumbling University might assert against the possible defendants. What problems do you see with the plaintiffs' claims and how do you think the court is likely to rule on them? What defenses will the defendants raise, and how are they likely to be resolved? *Explain your reasoning fully; this is more important than your "bottom-line" conclusions on the various issues.*

This chapter does not include an "answer" to the Grumbling problem since the goal here is to provide examples of typical ways in which students go astray in responding to questions like this. However, in some cases I have rewritten the examples to illustrate a better approach.

So, let's proceed to some dandelions.

DANDELION #1: THE ABSTRACT EXPRESSIONIST

Let's begin with one of the most common mistakes students make. Consider the following excerpt from the Expressionist's answer:

> This fact pattern raises issues of negligence liability. Tort law provides that parties can be held liable for their negligence under certain conditions. However, defendants are not always held liable simply because they cause injury. Sometimes they are not liable even if they negligently cause injury. In order to recover, the plaintiff must establish that the defendant owed her a duty of care, breached that duty of care, that is, was negligent, and that the defendant's negligence caused resulting injury to her. If all these elements are satisfied, the plaintiff may recover in tort from the defendant.

> Negligence is determined by comparing the defendant's conduct to that of the reasonable person under the same circumstances. If the defendant acted in an emergency, for example, his conduct will be compared to that of the reasonable person acting in a similar emergency. Or, if the defendant was acting as a professional, such as a doctor, her conduct will be compared to the conduct of the reasonable doctor under the circumstances, or even of the reasonable doctor in the same specialty as the defendant. There are special standards for persons acting under disability, such as those with physical disabilities—someone who is blind or deaf, for example—and for children, who are held to the standard of a reasonable child of like age, intelligence, and experience under the same circumstances.
>
> However, most jurisdictions do not apply a special standard to persons with mental disabilities. And no special allowance is made for the person who has poor judgment. In Vaughan v. Menlove, for example, the defendant argued that he should only be held to the standard of having acted in good faith to the best of his judgment, even if his judgment wasn't very good. The court rejected the argument and applied the usual reasonable-person-under-the-circumstances test.
>
> Even if a person is negligent, he will not be held liable if he did not owe a duty to the plaintiff. Duties may be imposed on parties who create a risk that injures the plaintiff. In other cases, a court may hold that the defendant owed a duty to the plaintiff because he had a special relationship to the plaintiff, such as an innkeeper, or a jailer, or even a psychiatrist who treated a patient. Other special relationships courts have recognized include . . .

This one really is a classic. Any law professor will recognize it as a common weed in the bluebook garden. If you read it through, however, it doesn't sound bad. In fact, there is nothing "wrong" with the Expressionist's description of the relevant law. The problem is that she has *not answered the question*. Instead, having stuffed a great deal of tort doctrine into her head, the Expressionist is determined to show me that she did, so she launches into an abstract dissertation on tort rules.

This would be a fair answer if the question were different. Here's the question the Expressionist evidently thinks that I wrote:

> Describe the principles of tort law, including the elements of a claim for negligence and the various defenses available to an action for negligence.

This unimaginative question asks the student to regurgitate general information to see if she did her homework. *This isn't going to happen on your law school exams.* We aren't testing your memory of the rules: We want to watch you *apply* those rules to the facts in the question. This student hasn't done that; she has already written several pages and hasn't even mentioned the question! Where are Hal and Jane? Where are Sticky, Grumbling, and Munoz Construction? Isn't it obvious that the student could have written this answer without ever reading the question?

One of the goals of a good exam question is to determine whether the student can separate relevant tort rules—those a court would use in resolving the issues raised—from the irrelevant. The Expressionist's answer refuses to take the gambit. It includes all kinds of general doctrine of no relevance to the question. There's no child in the Grumbling question. There's no doctor. No one acted in an emergency. No one has argued that she should be judged by the *Menlove* subjective standard.

Usually, students who indulge in abstract expressionism (about 20 percent of my students do) eventually go on to tackle the issues in the question. Five or six pages in, I get to a sentence that starts, "In Hal and Jane's case . . ." That's where I start to pay attention. The long wind-up I skim with annoyance. By the time the Expressionist gets down to the real business at hand, she has wasted valuable time on an exercise that gets little, if any, credit. Students always claim they don't have enough time on exams, but frequently this is because they waste time disgorging general information before they go for the jugular: analyzing the facts of the case.

Don't get me wrong. I don't mean to suggest that you should never state principles of law in writing a law school essay. You should, but you should state the principle in the course of applying it to specific issues in the question. For example, in addressing the liability of Griffin, you will want to state basic negligence principles in order to discuss Griffin's liability:

> Griffin acted as a risk creator by repairing the stands. Consequently he has a duty to act with reasonable care and will be liable if he failed to act like a reasonable person when he used the wooden beams instead of the metal "I" beams. In this case, Griffin was probably not negligent under the reasonable person standard, even though he ignored his supervisor's instructions. The wooden beams he used were identical to those that had held up the stadium for 50 years . . .

This opening shows that the writer recognizes the source of a duty owed by Griffin, and that he will only be liable if he failed to use reasonable care under the circumstances. Then, the writer proceeds to the crucial step: measuring his conduct against this standard. The writer shows that she knows the law by stating the particular legal principle that applies to the issue she is addressing. She doesn't shoot with buckshot, as the Abstract Expressionist does, but aims right at the target.

The cure for abstract expressionism is to read the instruction paragraph of the question (usually the closing paragraph), read it again, and then make sure that you *do what the professor has asked you to do*. Usually, that last paragraph will resemble the one in the Grumbling question. "Please evaluate the claims the plaintiffs may assert, and the various defenses the defendants are likely to raise," or some such language. Your answer should focus right in on that task. A good first sentence in answering the Grumbling question might be, "The first claim Jane might raise would be a negligence claim against . . ." Skip the generalities and get down to cases, or more particularly, the Grumbling case.

DANDELION #2: THE ANTIPHONALIST

The "antiphonal" answer is another way students avoid doing the real work of an essay exam. The name of this dandelion comes from early music. In the medieval churches there were often two choirs; one would sing, then the other would answer, back and forth.

> In this case, Jane will argue that Allen was negligent for failing to inspect the stands after the repairs were completed. Allen will argue, however, that he had no duty to inspect the stands, and that, even if he had, he would not have discovered the defect that caused the collapse.
>
> Jane will argue that Griffin was negligent, because he replaced the wooden beams with new wooden beams instead of with the metal "I" beams. Griffin will argue, however, that he was not negligent, because the beams were the same as the ones that had been used before. Jane will also argue that he was negligent in disregarding his instructions from Brian, but Griffin will argue that he is not liable, even though he did disregard his instructions, if he used a reasonable method of supporting the stands.
>
> Jane will argue that she can prove negligence of Griffin by invoking res ipsa loquitur, since stadium seats do not ordinarily collapse unless someone was negligent in constructing or repairing them. Griffin will argue that he was not the only one who worked on the stands, and they could have collapsed from another problem, so that the negligence was not necessarily his.
>
> Hal will argue that he can sue Griffin for negligent infliction of emotional distress, since he witnessed the incident and was very upset. Griffin, however, will argue . . .

It is important to recognize the fallacy involved in the antiphonal response. Students often repeat the old saw that you should "argue both sides" on law exams, and think that what the student did above is what is wanted. It is not. The Antiphonalist has not argued *either* side. She has set up the pieces on the chessboard, but refused to make any moves. All she has done is to state that the plaintiff will argue for one result, and the defendant for the opposite. She has nicely avoided the real work of the exam—*evaluating* the strength of the arguments. Oliver Wendell Holmes once said that "the science of law is the prediction of what a judge will do." The Antiphonalist has nicely avoided making and explaining her predictions about the Grumbling case.

Suppose that you represented Jane, and she came to you for advice on whether to sue Griffin. Could you really send Jane a bill for telling her that she will argue that Griffin was negligent in replacing the beams, and that he will argue that he wasn't? Of course not. That's just restating the problem, not offering a judgment about the outcome.

Consider this rewrite of one issue touched on in the antiphonal response:

> Jane may sue Griffin for using the wooden beams instead of "I" beams, arguing that he was negligent for disregarding his boss's instructions. However, the court will probably not be persuaded by this argument. Griffin's conduct will be tested under the reasonable person standard: whether the reasonable construction worker under the circumstances would have used wooden beams, not whether Griffin did as he was told. (If Griffin had been told to use inadequate beams, and had done so, I doubt that the court would treat his boss's orders as a defense!)
>
> There is a strong argument that Griffin was not negligent under the reasonable person standard. He used new beams of a type that had sufficed for 50 years, and continued to hold the rest of the stadium. The evidence might very well show that this was reasonable care. At any rate, the court will focus on that issue, not whether he was instructed otherwise or whether "I" beams would have been stronger.
>
> Jane might argue that those beams were not adequate because more people are being allowed to occupy the stands these days. However, it is not clear that more people do come to the games than used to. Even if they do, only section C collapsed, although all sections had the same beams. This suggests that the problem may not have been the beams at all. For example, the other employees may have failed to bolt the beams in place. . . .

This student does a lot more than indicate what the parties will argue. Unlike the Antiphonalist, she grasps the opportunity to show that she can think like a lawyer. She states the relevant rule, uses the facts effectively, and explains her reasons, based on those facts, for predicting that the court will accept one argument over the other.

DANDELION #3: THE REITERATOR

Here's another problem that is more common than you would think.

> In this case, Allen, the athletic director, noted problems with section C and hired Munoz Construction to inspect and repair the section. When Brian found weakened beams in section C he ordered Griffin to replace the beams with metal "I" beams, but Griffin used wooden beams like the old ones instead. Later, that section of the stands collapsed, and Jane Aragna was injured in the collapse. Her brother Hal, the captain of the football team, was also injured when a player tackled him from behind. Sticky, an unusual team mascot worth $25,000, was also broken when the stands collapsed. . . .

This one hardly requires explanation. The writer has simply restated the facts. This drives me nuts. I *wrote* the facts. Why does the Reiterator insist on telling me what they are? More important, how can I possibly give her any credit for it? I'm not testing the ability to read a paragraph and restate it; I'm testing the ability to explain how the facts will influence the outcome of the case. Facts are indeed important, but you need to tell me *why* they are important, not just what the facts are.

For example, the fact that Sticky cost $25,000 is an important fact; clearly I stuck that in there (excuse the pun) for a reason. Restating the fact that Sticky is expensive gets you no credit, but recognizing why that fact is (or is not) relevant gets you lots. Consider this excerpt, which *analyzes* the relevance of Sticky's value rather than simply reiterating it.

> In this case, Sticky is a highly unusual and valuable piece of personal property. The defendants may argue that they are not liable for the loss of Sticky, because it is unforeseeable that a $25,000 porcelain porcupine would be in the stands. However, where a defendant negligently causes injury to property, she need not foresee the exact nature of the property in order to be held liable. As long as she can foresee damage of the general nature that took place, she will be liable for whatever damage actually occurs. The defendants in this case could foresee injury to objects in the stands if they collapsed. And it hardly seems surprising that the team mascot would be in the stands at a football game. Thus, the no-proximate-cause argument is likely to fail here.

Like Abstract Expressionists, Reiterators usually get on eventually to actually answering the question. However, before they do they lose valuable time telling me what I wrote. As a result, they often don't finish answering the question. When I see "Out of Time" written at the end of these answers, I have little sympathy.

DANDELION #4: THE TANTALIZER

Tantalus, an unfortunate figure of Greek mythology, was doomed to stand in water that receded when he tried to drink, and beneath ripe, hanging fruit he could not reach. When I read answers like the example below I share a little of his frustration.

> Jane might try to prove that Munoz Construction was negligent using the doctrine of res ipsa loquitur. If Jane can prove that the accident that happened to her was the type of accident that does not ordinarily happen without negligence, and that, if someone was negligent, it was probably Munoz Construction, then she can recover on a res ipsa theory.
>
> Jane might also try to recover from Allen, the athletic director, for failing to inspect section C after the work was done. If Allen owed a duty to inspect the stadium after completion of the repairs, he could be held liable for her injury.
>
> Hal may sue Munoz Construction for negligent infliction of emotional distress. If Hal can show that he satisfies the Dillon standards for a negligent infliction claim, or whichever standard applies in the relevant jurisdiction, he will recover. . . .

Can you see why I call this writer the Tantalizer? There hangs a nice juicy legal issue, just waiting to be plucked. The Tantalizer notes the issue, states a relevant principle of law, but never sinks her teeth into the analysis. It is true that Jane can use res ipsa if she can prove that the accident would probably not have happened without negligence, and that the negligence was likely Munoz's. But *can she prove those things?* Does res ipsa apply on these facts, and if so, why? Similarly, it is true that Allen may be liable for failing to inspect if he owes a duty to inspect, but *does he owe such a duty, and why?* Please don't hide your light under a bushel; share with me your views on these matters, and your reasons. These are what I will grade you on.

Basically, the Tantalizer suffers from "A"-aversion, unwillingness to apply the law to the facts. We discussed the importance of the IRAC "A" in the last chapter, but I repeat it here because failure to apply the law to the facts in a meaningful manner is the most common failing in student answers. Explaining why res ipsa does or does not apply to Jane's case is where you can really show your stuff. Don't miss your chance—as the Tantalizer has—by giving me the wind-up (issue and rule, if you like) but failing to deliver the pitch.

Consider this rewrite of part of the Tantalizer's answer:

> Since the stands were badly damaged, Jane will have a problem proving what caused them to collapse. However, she may well be able to invoke res ipsa loquitur against Munoz Construction Company. First, this is the type of accident that does not ordinarily happen without negligence: Stands in a stadium do not fall in if properly built and maintained, especially stands recently examined and repaired. (Note that no section other than C collapsed, though all were presumably crowded.) Second, the facts fairly clearly point to negligence of Munoz. They had recently repaired section C. The fact that that section collapsed suggests that they made some mistake in repairing the stands. We don't know exactly what it was—or which Munoz employee did it—but it is a fair inference that negligence during the repair caused the problem. As long as the evidence permits a reasonable inference that some Munoz employee negligently caused the collapse, Munoz can be held liable under res ispa and respondeat superior.
>
> A problem for Jane will be that the stands collapsed ten weeks after Munoz repaired them. Munoz was not "in control" of the stands at that point. But the control test is too restrictive: The real question is whether the general facts about the accident point to negligence of Munoz. Here, a jury could reasonably conclude that they do.

This analysis states the basic res ipsa requirements, but it goes well beyond that, to explain how the writer predicts that they would be applied by a court, and why.

DANDELION #5: THE FLYSWATTER

Here's an excerpt from an answer that sounds pretty good, but has serious problems in terms of exam-taking strategy.

> Jane may decide to sue Munoz Construction Company for negligence in repairing the stands. However, courts do not always hold negligent actors liable in tort. The defendant must also owe a duty to the plaintiff. Munoz will only be liable if it owed a duty to Jane to exercise care in doing the inspection and repairs. Generally parties owe a duty of care to others who might foreseeably be injured from conduct that creates a risk of injury to others. For example, in driving a car we create the risk of an accident to those around us; thus, we owe them a duty to drive with reasonable care.
>
> A second source of duty arises from special relationships between the victim and the defendant. In many situations actors assume a duty of care, as by taking a patient or a client, or by taking charge of a person in need of assistance.
>
> In this case, Munoz engaged in risk-creating conduct by undertaking to repair the stands. By working on the stands, it created risks of injury if the repairs were faulty. They could foresee injury to patrons at the game if they negligently supported the stands or otherwise failed to exercise due care. It isn't surprising that, if the beams aren't strong enough, or the bolts are left out, they will collapse, and that with all that weight in the stands someone might be injured. Having all those people in the stands creates a risk of injury if the stands aren't sufficiently strong. Munoz should know this. Thus, a court would very likely hold that Munoz owed a duty of care to patrons at the game, including Jane.

Everything said in this excerpt is true. The problem, however, is that the writer has used a sledgehammer to swat a fly. She has belabored the obvious, spent a lot of valuable time arguing at great length a proposition that is quite clear. Everyone should know that Munoz has a duty to exercise due care in doing the repairs. I can't give you a lot of credit for recognizing that fact.

In the heat of an exam, it is a relief to see an issue you know you can handle. "Great," says the Flyswatter, "I've got this one nailed down. The answer to some of those other issues is really unclear, so I'll spend my time on the issue I know I can answer. Watch my dust."

This is bad strategy. Even though it is disconcerting to deal with issues to which you don't know "the answer," it is just those issues, the tough, ambiguous issues, where the answer is anything but obvious and creative reasoning is needed, that give you the chance to shine. In answering the exam, you have to learn to recognize which issues are clear, and to dispose of them quickly so you can concentrate on the tough ones. Consider this rewrite:

> Munoz owes a duty to exercise reasonable care in repairing the stands, since it created a foreseeable risk of injury if it negligently repaired the stands. The real problem will be proving that Munoz, or someone who worked for it, was negligent. Jane may be able to establish negligence by . . .

The writer disposes quickly of the easy question, and turns immediately to the more difficult negligence question. In the process, she saves all that time the Flyswatter spent going into unnecessary detail on the duty question.

Very frequently, it is the first issue in the exam that evokes fly swatting. Instead of assessing which issues to spend the most time on before starting to write, the student launches in, beats the first issue to death, and then discovers as she goes along that she doesn't have time to adequately address more sophisticated ones. I'm not a great fan of outlining exam answers, but you should at least make a list of major issues to make sure you spend the most time on the issues that have the most substance.

The trick, of course, is learning to recognize which issues are meaty and which are straightforward. I don't have a magic formula that will help you do that: Developing such judgment is what the first year of law school is about. However, practice will help a lot. The next chapter offers a chance to do just that. It provides several sample questions, offers you the chance to practice spotting the harder and easier issues in those questions, and gives some illustrative answers with comments.

DANDELION #6: THE EDITOR

I include this one mostly for fun, but I do find that it crops up fairly frequently in my exams. Here's a short sample from the Editor's answer:

> Jane may try to sue Munoz Construction for her injuries. If Munoz's employees had replaced the beams with smaller beams which were too weak to do the job, they would be found negligent and could be held liable for her injuries.
>
> Grumbling may try to recover the value of Sticky from Munoz. If Munoz had been told that Sticky was kept in section C, and that he was worth $25,000, they would foresee injury to Sticky from negligent repair and could be liable for it.

> Hal may sue Munoz and Griffin for negligent infliction of emotional distress. He would be entitled to recover for such distress under the Dillon standards if he had been sitting with Jane in the stands and had actually seen her fall.

Do you see what the Editor has done? Perhaps in doubt that she can answer the tough issues posed by my question, she has rewritten it to make the issues easy, and then answered her own question! Of course Munoz would be negligent if it used beams too small for the job. Of course Munoz would foresee injury to Sticky if they knew they were building the stands to hold Sticky. Of course the *Dillon* standards would apply if Hal sat next to Jane and saw her fall.

I purposely designed the facts to make the issues tougher, so that I can watch you do more sophisticated analysis. The Editor has missed her chance to shine, by ignoring the tough issues. Not only that, in the process she has made me mad. You should know by now that law professors are very egotistical: When we write an exam, we want you to answer *our* question, not rewrite it to suit yourself.

Another syndrome similar to the Editor's is to address a bunch of issues raised by the facts that the question does not ask you to address. Often, the instruction paragraph in the question will ask you to discuss a subset of the possible claims. For example, my closing paragraph in the Grumbling question asks you to evaluate the claims of Jane, Hal, and Grumbling. Please, don't go off on a discussion of Brian's contribution claims against Griffin, or other claims not called for in the question. When you become a law professor, you can write your own question; for now, remember that the professor sets the agenda.

Where students do address issues I didn't ask for, I will do my best to ignore the discussion of those issues. I owe it to my students to evaluate each on the same material. It wouldn't be fair to let one student essentially analyze a different—perhaps easier—question while the rest of the class labors away on the Sisyphean task I asked them to undertake. Consequently, the time students spend addressing claims I didn't raise are a waste of that most valuable resource on an exam—time.

The dandelions reviewed above appear not because students lack the ability to answer law exams, but from basic misconceptions about what is expected. It is worth your time to learn to recognize these misconceptions now, and train yourself to avoid them in your own exam writing. For some practice, try the next chapter.

CHAPTER 28

Practice Makes Perfect: Examples and Explanations

INTRODUCTION

This may sound like heresy, but the plain fact of the matter is that most students spend entirely too much time studying for their first-year exams.

Let me clarify what I mean. Most students study for their finals by reviewing their notes, rereading material from the casebook, writing outlines, and memorizing the legal doctrines studied in the course. All this is very well, and should be done, but learning every minute rule in the Torts course is not the best way to assure a strong performance. The best way to prepare for your law exams, once you have mastered the basic legal rules, is to take some law exams. There's a big difference between reading about chess and playing the game. If you were going to a chess tournament, you would prepare by playing a lot of chess. Similarly, there's a big difference between learning legal rules and using them effectively to answer an essay question. If you want to develop a facility for clearly applying the law you have studied to new facts, the best way to do it is to practice at it.

This chapter is meant to facilitate that process, which should help you on all your first-year exams. If you're going to practice, you need some sample questions to practice on. So this chapter presents two Torts essay questions covering basic concepts taught by most Torts professors. Once you have outlined, read, and studied, you should sit down and take the first exam, in the allotted time, without looking at my suggested answer.

Then, you should read my comments about the question, and my suggested answer.

Then, do it again, using my second question. Practice really does make perfect. Again, be honest; don't peek. Much of the learning takes place from trying your own hand at the question, and then comparing your analysis to mine. If you just passively read the question and my answer, you will lose the benefit of working through the process yourself. Then, you'll have to do it for the first time in the exam room. Certainly, you would not want to play your first game of chess at the chess finals.

You needn't wait until you have finished studying for the Torts final to do this, but you should do a basic review of your outline before sitting down to answer the first question. One of the virtues of writing practice answers is that the process will highlight the issues you need to study further. If you get to a duty issue in the question, for example, and are unsure how to address it, you will realize that you need to spend more time studying the duty material. Then, when you go back to do so, you'll go back with a purpose, so your further study will be much more effective.

After you read the question, jot down the issues that you see before you start to write. Make a tentative choice about the order in which you will discuss the issues. Any sensible order that works for you will probably be acceptable to your professor. Some students take the facts line by line and discuss the issues as they arise. Another reasonable approach to organizing your answer is to first discuss the elements of the torts that might be claimed, and then discuss defenses, vicarious liability, and other peripheral issues. Often, the question will dictate the organization. If the question asks you to analyze the claims of Mary Smith and the defenses to those claims, do just that. Always focus ruthlessly on the instructions in the question to make sure you answer the question the professor has posed.

EXAMPLES

McGee's Bad Day

1. Read the first practice question below. Write out quickly the issues you see. Put an asterisk next to the ones you think are most important or complicated, to make sure you leave the time necessary to address them adequately.

2. Now, start the clock and give yourself 90 minutes to write out an answer. If you aren't able to spend 90 minutes on it, spend 45 on half the issues. Remember that you are not only trying to learn how to answer a question like this; you are trying to learn how to do so under exam conditions. So writing out the answer at your leisure would be useful, but not nearly as useful as doing it under time constraints.

   If you are tempted just to read the question and then read the sample answer, resist the temptation. Painful as the process of taking the exam may be, spending the time to do this will easily be worth more than three or four hours of regular study time. Then look at Explanation # 2 and the suggested answer.

McGee's Bad Day (1 hour and 30 minutes)

The ventilating system at Elston General Hospital was giving out. Elston retained Climatrol Corporation, an established company with a AAA safety rating, to rebuild the system. The plan was to replace the large blowers on the roof first, and then to empty one ward at a time to rebuild the duct work in the individual rooms.

The first blower arrived at about 10:00 a.m. on a gusty Monday morning, weighing in at about 7,000 pounds. Archer, an employee of Climatrol, began rigging a cable from a crane to the blower to hoist it up to the roof. McGee, a mechanical engineer on his way to the hospital to visit his wife, stopped to watch. He stood about 30 feet back from the crane, even though the crane had signs on it saying, "Warning! Danger! Stay 100 feet back!" McGee was surprised to see Archer rig the blower with single-braided cable since he knew that triple-braided cable was usually used on such jobs. Archer's boss had suggested using triple-braided cable, but the crane was equipped with single-braided cable, which was rated for 14,000 pounds anyway, so Archer rigged the blower with that. He then got into the cab and started to hoist the blower up to the roof.

He got the blower up to the level of the roof, but as it rose above the roof a sudden gust of high wind started the blower swinging back and forth. Archer, fearing that the blower would smash against the building, quickly swung the crane away from the building. Unfortunately, as it swung out, the blower hit the edge of the roof, tipped, snapped one of the cables, and tumbled to the pavement below.

To make matters worse, a ChemHaul Company truck was delivering a large cylinder of potentially explosive acid to the hospital at the time. The acid should have been delivered the night before (state law required all hazardous chemicals to be transported outside of normal working hours). The truck had just finished depositing the cylinder in the acid storage area, and hooked it up for service, when the blower landed. The concussion from the blower hitting the pavement caused the cylinder, some 70 feet away, to explode. The force of the explosion threw McGee to the ground, puncturing his eardrum and causing a concussion.

Alas, McGee's wife, who was in the hospital for serious heart surgery, was watching out the window and witnessed the accident. Several minutes later, she suffered heart failure and died, without moving or uttering a word. Her sister Maria was in the room at the time and thought she had fallen asleep. A few minutes later she went to wake her, realized Mrs. McGee was dead, and suffered extreme emotional distress.

Please evaluate the personal injury claims that might be brought based on this unfortunate chain of events, and the defenses you would expect to be asserted. Discuss the problems you see in establishing the various claims and defenses. Explain your reasoning fully; this is more important than your bottom-line conclusions as to who will win or lose on particular issues.

Do it Again: Bad Day at the Mall

3. After taking the McGee practice question, go off and do other things. Then, a few days later, try your hand again at this process, focusing on the Bad Day at the Mall question below. It tests much the same material as the McGee question, so you should be able to focus on the process itself. Once again, start by reading the question and taking a few minutes to list the issues you see, noting the ones that you think will require more time to discuss. My list is at p. 623.

4. After doing your issues list, answer the exam question in the time allotted. I know, it's bad enough to take exams once without doing it multiple times. All I can say is that this exercise will help you more than anything else you can do to prepare for the Big Day. A sample answer to this question is found at page 628.

Bad Day at the Mall (1 hour and 30 minutes)

Sammy and his friends, all seventh graders, were fooling around in a mall parking lot early one January morning before school. Paul dared Sammy to throw his sneakers up over the electrical cables that served the parking lot lights for the mall. Sammy whipped off his sneakers, tied them together, and gave 'em a heave. A perfect shot; they wrapped themselves around two cables, pulling the cables together and causing a short circuit. The mall lights went out. The boys took off.

Someone from the mall management called Emerson Electric Company, an electrical contractor, to repair the lines. A state statute barred "maintenance work on electrical installations during business hours," but Emerson sent out a truck, with three workers, Rodansky, Chu, and Perkins. They parked the bucket truck beneath the wires and swung the mechanical arm with the bucket on the end up toward the lines. Rodansky was in the bucket.

Suddenly Kent, a shoplifter, ran across the parking lot, pursued by Moreno, a store manager. Redstone Management had a security officer patrolling the mall in a car, but she had gone into a shop to get a cup of coffee to go. Darley, backing out of a parking space opposite the bucket truck, suddenly saw Kent running behind his car and went to hit his brake, but hit the accelerator instead. His car shot across the parking lot into the bucket truck. The impact swung the bucket up against the power line.

The bucket truck had rubber tires so that it wouldn't conduct electricity if the bucket contacted a power line. However, Perkins, standing next to the truck with a ladder, had leaned the ladder against the truck so he could chase Kent. Brice, a friend of Rodansky who worked for another electrical contractor, came across the lot just at that moment and saw the ladder there. He realized the danger that the ladder might conduct power from the lines down into the truck and the ground, but did not move the ladder or warn Rodansky.

The collision with Darley's car caused the bucket to contact the line, and electric power jumped from the power line to the bucket truck and through the ladder into the ground, knocking out Rodansky in the bucket. Chu was still inside the truck. He had seen Perkins lean the ladder against the truck, and was about to get out and move it, but was making an entry in the work log first. He received a massive shock and was also knocked unconscious. Brice saw Chu slumped in the seat and was able to pull him from the truck, but suffered a serious shock when he did so.

Perkins, returning from chasing Kent, did not go to assist Chu. Instead, he grabbed the ladder and tried to reach Rodansky in the bucket. Swensson, a bystander, did go to the unconscious Chu's aid. Swensson had been trained years ago in emergency resuscitation techniques. He feared that Chu was not breathing, so he began resuscitation on Chu, alternately pounding Chu's chest and giving mouth-to-mouth resuscitation. Unfortunately, Chu had burns on his chest and the pressure from Swensson's pounding tore the burned areas of skin. As Swensson did this, Chu's wife came out of a store and saw Chu on the ground with Swensson working on him. She was so upset that she suffered a minor stroke. Twenty minutes later, an ambulance arrived. However, Chu was found to have died.

Please discuss the tort claims that the injured parties might bring based on this set of facts. Don't discuss the store's claims against the shoplifter for the initial theft or any claims by or against the shoplifter. Disregard the possible effect of any worker's compensation statute. Explain the problems you see with the various claims, the defenses you would expect to be raised, and especially your reasoning as to how you would expect a court to resolve these issues, and why.

No rest for the weary.

5. Here's another question from one of my past exams. Take the question with a couple of classmates and then discuss your analysis of the issues together. No answer this time . . .

Skipping School

(1 hour and 30 minutes)

Largo and Felder, two 14-year old ne'er-do-wells, decided to skip school and spend the day skateboarding. So at 8:50 a.m. (15 minutes after school started), they met on Main Street and took off down the sidewalk. A state statute banned skateboarding on downtown sidewalks during business hours, but they didn't know or care about that. Back at school, Simmons, the school truant officer, learned that they had not signed in for their first class. She was pretty sure where they were but didn't go after them; she knew it would be a hassle to drive down and drag them back to school.

Five blocks down the street the boys came to the Jewelers' Building, which housed jewelry stores of various specialties. Although a town ordinance banned leaving obstructions on the sidewalk, Wordin, who had a window cleaning business, had a ladder standing on the sidewalk leaning against the Jewelers' Building. He was up on the ladder cleaning the second-story windows. Wordin had been instructed not to start work until 9:00 a.m., when the building opened and Rodriguez, the security officer, would be on duty. But Wordin had two other jobs scheduled for the day, so he started at 8:15.

As they approached Wordin, the boys were speeding, jostling for position and pushing each other away. Largo pushed Felder, who lost his balance and careened into Wordin's ladder. The ladder bounced against the building wall and fell, taking Wordin with it. He landed on top of Largo, who had stopped when Felder crashed into the ladder. Both Wordin and Largo suffered serious injuries in the accident.

Inside the building, Chang, a jeweler, was cutting a diamond for an expensive wedding ring. (She wasn't supposed to enter the building until 9:00 a.m. but had slipped in to start work early.) The impact of the ladder against the building shook her desk, and her hand slipped, ruining the rare diamond she was cutting.

Gomez, a lawyer, was walking down Main Street, on his way to court to represent Abrams, a criminal defendant. When Gomez saw Largo and Wordin fall to the pavement, he rushed across the street toward them, without looking for traffic. Ruggles was driving down Main Street and texting at the same time. She saw Gomez jump into the street, but she was too close to brake in time and she hit Gomez. Ruggles stopped immediately but did not get out of her car; instead, she looked for a place to hide her cell phone, so it would not look like she had been texting at the time of the accident.

At this point (9:05 a.m.) Rodriguez arrived for work, a bit late.

Gomez was lying in the street in obvious pain. Kildare, an emergency medical technician, was walking her dog, Hoover, along Main Street and saw the accident. Surprised, she dropped Hoover's leash and Hoover ran off. Even though the relevant jurisdiction has a Good Samaritan statute that protects medical providers from negligence liability for assisting in an emergency, Kildare ran after Hoover. Neither Wordin, Largo, nor Felder went to Gomez's assistance. Gomez, who had ruptured a lung, suffered severe pain during the 20 minutes between the injury and the arrival of an ambulance, which had been called by another bystander.

Meanwhile, without counsel at court, Abrams was denied bail, though Gomez had several good arguments that he should be granted bail.

Please discuss the various tort claims that might be brought based on these facts. Evaluate the problems you anticipate each plaintiff would have in establishing liability, the defenses you would expect to be raised, and how you conclude the court would rule on the various issues. Explain your reasoning fully.

Explanations

McGee's Bad Day

1. The McGee question raises lots of issues, more issues than you can fully explore in the time allotted. Here's my own list of issues in the McGee question:
    1. Vicarious liability of Elston and Climatrol for negligence of Archer
    *2. Negligence in using single-braided cable (relevance of custom to use triple-braided)
    3. Causation—did single-braided cable cause the harm?
    4. Proximate cause—high wind as unforeseeable
    5. Emergency doctrine—Archer's reaction to swaying of blower
    6. Duty—McGee's failure to say anything about use of lighter cable
    *7. Negligence of McGee in standing nearby
    *8. Assumption of the risk by McGee in standing nearby
    *9. Causation—did McGee's negligence in standing too near cause the harm?
    *10. Superseding cause—explosion of acid tank
    * 11. Negligence per se—violation of statute by delivering acid during the day
    12. Negligence of Elston—working while hospital open
    *13. Negligent infliction of emotional distress on Mrs. McGee (duty, causation, thin skull problem)
    14. Negligent infliction on Maria

    These may not be all the issues in the question, but they are the main ones. If you hit these, or most of them, you will do fine. In jotting down the issues, it is worth using some quick system—like my asterisks—to flag the issues that you think are more complex so that you can plan to spend more time on them. Remember, as discussed in Chapter 26, that the more complex the issue, the better you can show your ability to perform effective legal analysis. So don't shy away from these!

2. Despite preaching about the value of practice questions, I must confess that I have seldom given out sample essay answers to my students. One reason for this is that my answer might be wrong, and the students might expose me as a fraud. (Most law professors secretly harbor this fear, no matter how much they may deny it.) But there is a more respectable reason as well. In giving out a model answer, I have two choices. First, I could hand out an answer typical of what a good student can produce in the time allotted. However, no student or professor can produce a perfect and complete analysis of a problem like McGee's in 90 minutes, so this type of model answer will doubtless miss some issues and analyze some others ineffectively. So this sample answer could be misleading.

Alternatively, I could hand out an answer I deem "right"—whatever that means—in its analysis of all the issues. Doubtless, I would slave for about a week to write that answer, to avoid the fraud-exposure risk mentioned above. Obviously, this type of model won't give students a realistic sense of what I expect from them either.

The answer below is a bit of a compromise between the two extremes. It is meant to illustrate a basically sound analysis of the issues, but at a level of sophistication that a good student could produce in an exam setting. Thus, it is representative of good student analysis, but probably more consistently so than I would see, even from a strong student, on a timed exam. Overall, it should give you a good sense of the type of analysis your professor is looking for.

So, herewith, is a sample answer to the McGee question.

Sample Answer: McGee's Bad Day

Let's start with whether Archer was negligent. McGee may argue that Archer was negligent in rigging the crane with single-strand cable. The issue is whether Archer acted as the reasonable crane operator would in rigging up the blower. McGee's surprise (as an engineer with relevant experience) that Archer used single-strand cable, and Archer's boss's suggestion to use triple, suggest that most riggers use triple. Usual practice is certainly admissible on the question of Archer's reasonableness, but not dispositive. The cable was "rated for 14,000 pounds," so it may have been reasonable to use it even if triple would have been stronger. Archer doesn't have to use the strongest cable, or even the usual cable, so long as he made a reasonable choice.

It may be that single-strand cable would hold 14,000 pounds if it just had to hold the weight, but not if it was going to be raised and swung, which puts more stress on the cable. This depends on facts we don't have about what it means to "rate" the cable for that amount of weight. McGee will need an expert to testify on this issue.

Archer's decision to swing the blower away from the building due to the wind may have been reasonable. The sudden gust suggests an unanticipated emergency—if so, Archer's decision will be evaluated in light of the need to make a quick decision. However, since the day was "gusty," Archer should have anticipated this risk. If so, he may not be negligent for his reaction to the wind, but may be for creating the emergency by doing the job at all on a windy day or without more precautions. In addition, even if he responded reasonably to the emergency, he could still be liable based on the initial negligent act of using inadequate cable. Maybe triple-strand would have held if subjected to the jolt of hitting the building.

Depending on how gusty it was, Archer might argue that, even if he was negligent in using single-strand cable, the sudden wind is an unforeseeable event, so his negligence is not a proximate cause of the fall. However, crane operators should probably anticipate winds, including sudden winds, when they raise objects high in the air. This argument will likely fail.

Archer might also argue that even if his use of single-strand cable was negligent, it was not the actual cause of the accident. If even triple-braided cable would have broken when the blower jolted against the building, his use of weaker cable would not be a "but for" cause of the harm. We don't have enough information to evaluate this argument. Expert testimony would be needed on the point. Archer might assert a cross-claim against the company that supplied the cable, arguing that it should not have broken under a 7,000-pound load. This claim would also raise technical questions about what it means for a cable to be "rated" at 14,000 pounds, information not supplied in the question.

Archer will argue that the explosion of the acid cylinder is a superseding cause that avoids liability to McGee. McGee was injured due to the blast, not being hit by the blower itself. If Archer could not have anticipated the explosion, he may avoid liability on proximate cause grounds. However, the facts indicate that there was an acid storage area nearby, and that a truck had just delivered a cylinder of acid there. Archer probably would have realized that dangerous chemicals were stored in the area. He may not have known that they were explosive, but he probably should have anticipated that they might be, and that is all that is required. However, even if this is true, he may still have not reasonably anticipated that the concussion from dropping the blower would cause the tank to explode. The blower did not drop on the tank and cause the explosion; the concussion is a different, unusual mechanism of harm that Archer can at least argue he had no reason to anticipate causing explosion.

Archer will likely argue that McGee was negligent for standing too close to the crane, especially as an engineer with relevant knowledge. The crane company can't define reasonableness by telling people how far back to stand, but McGee may still have been too close for safety. However, even if he was, this negligent act is not the actual cause of his harm: The blower didn't fall on him; it triggered the explosion that knocked him down. It may well be that McGee, had he obeyed the 100-foot warning, would have been closer to the tank and injured more! Thus, depending on the facts, McGee's negligence, if any, in standing too close to the crane is probably not an actual cause of his injury.

Archer might argue that McGee should have said something about the cable. However, McGee, as a bystander, owed no duty to intervene in Archer's work, even if he has relevant knowledge as an engineer.

Archer will also argue that McGee "assumed the risk" of the injury by standing near this heavy work. However, assumption of the risk probably doesn't apply, even if the jurisdiction still recognizes the traditional assumption of the risk defense. To assume a risk created by the defendant's negligence, McGee would have to be fully aware of the specific risk. The standard is not what McGee should have known, but what he actually subjectively knew. McGee may have assumed the risk of the blower falling on his head, but it hardly seems that he was fully aware of the risk that the blower would trigger an explosion. In addition, most jurisdictions now treat a plaintiff's negligent choice to encounter a risk (secondary implied assumption) as comparative negligence, so if the defense applied it would only reduce recovery.

McGee might sue ChemHaul for violating the statute requiring deliveries outside of working hours. The statute was probably aimed at preventing deliveries of volatile chemicals during busy periods when accidents would be more likely to happen, so it may establish a relevant standard of care. However, the violation was not a "but for" cause of the accident. ChemHaul had already hooked the tank up when the accident happened, so presumably the accident would have happened the same way if the tank had been delivered during the night instead of ten minutes before. Thus, McGee probably cannot show that, but for ChemHaul's violation of the statute, McGee would not have been injured.

If Archer is liable to McGee, Climatrol will be as well, as Archer's employer. Under respondeat superior, the employer is liable if Archer's act was in the scope of employment. Raising the blower here clearly was, even if Archer ignored his instructions about the cable.

The personal representative of Mrs. McGee's estate might assert a wrongful death claim, arguing that Archer's negligence led to her distress which caused her death. Recovery for Mrs. McGee's distress at witnessing the accident will depend on the jurisdiction's standard for indirect infliction claims. She was probably not in the zone of danger (though if the explosion was big enough, perhaps she could argue this) but might satisfy the Dillon standards. She's a close relative and saw the accident. True, she was not that physically close, but seeing the accident might suffice since actually seeing the injury is the source of the traumatic emotional reaction. The heart attack would satisfy a "resulting physical injury" requirement (if the jurisdiction requires that) if it was caused by the emotional distress.

Mrs. McGee's estate will have a difficult causation problem on the emotional distress claim. Since she was recovering from "serious heart surgery," she may have died from her cardiac illness, not from the shock of witnessing the accident. Her estate will have to establish that the trauma of seeing her husband injured caused the death, not the underlying heart condition. If the estate proves this, it could recover under the "thin skull" rule even if a normal person would not have suffered substantial injury from the emotional distress.

Maria will not recover for indirect infliction. Although she may have been watching when her sister died, she did not know at the time that Mrs.

McGee had died. Her distress is from learning later that her sister had died. Even if Archer's negligence caused Mrs. McGee's death, indirect infliction claims are based on witnessing a shocking, traumatic injury to the direct victim, not general distress at another's injury.

Some Comments on the McGee Answer

Note that there is very little abstract statement of legal principles in the McGee answer. Instead, concepts like proximate cause and negligence, assumption of the risk, and indirect infliction are discussed as they apply to the facts of the question. The answer is not an abstract exposition of tort law; it is more like a memorandum to a partner detailing the likely outcomes of issues that both the writer and the reader basically understand. It isn't meant to tell an uninitiated reader general principles about the law of torts; it's meant to explain to another lawyer how tort concepts you both understand would likely be applied to a new set of facts, and why.

If you go over this answer, and list the torts concepts you need to understand to write it, you'll see that the question tests the basic, central issues that most professors focus on in the course. Some professors may test more fringe stuff, but most will zero in on the core issues emphasized in class—issues like intent, the negligence test, statutory duty, actual cause, proximate cause, and comparative negligence. Since this is true, skill at applying such central concepts will serve you better than an encyclopedic knowledge of more esoteric rules touched on in the course.

Note, too, that the analysis in the answer does not mechanically tick off each element of each tort discussed. It focuses on the problems the writer expects in proving each claim. For example, the answer doesn't discuss McGee's damages. It is clear that he suffered damages—the concussion—and that if Archer is liable, McGee would collect for it. Similarly, it's clear that Archer owed McGee a duty of care in lifting the blower. The problems in proving McGee's claim lie in the causation and negligence elements, so the answer focuses on these.

Out of curiosity, I did a word count on this sample answer: It contains about 1,400 words. This is fairly realistic for a 90-minute question: I checked a number of old exam answers and found that the average number of words for a 90-minute answer was closer to 1,600. So you do have time to write a full answer: The important thing is to avoid spending your time writing the wrong stuff.

4. Do it again. Sample answer to Bad Day at the Mall

Bad Day at the Mall

Let's start by analyzing whether the electrical workers (and as the employer, Emerson Electric) were negligent for violating the statute barring "maintenance work on electrical installations during business hours." There is a strong argument that this statute does not apply to an emergency repair. The legislature probably meant to bar ordinary maintenance, which could be done at any time, from interference with business operations, not to prevent the electric company from fixing an electrical outage. Although the lights would not be needed until evening—which would come early in January—the lights would be needed before business hours were over. So it seems likely that the statute was not meant to apply to this emergency repair. If it did, the workers would likely have an excuse for violating it due to the danger of the mall parking lot without lights.

Perkins was negligent to leave the ladder against the truck. Arguably, he acted in an emergency created by the shoplifter running across the lot. But it seems likely that he was negligent even under the emergency standard, which still requires reasonable conduct in the emergency. It would have taken little time to drop the ladder on the ground instead. And it's not clear how much of an emergency it was anyway: Perkins didn't know why the shoplifter was being chased, and why would he be a better chaser than the store manager anyway? Perkins was clearly negligent.

How about Darley, who negligently hit the accelerator? There's another question about the emergency doctrine since Darley suddenly saw the shoplifter and sought to avoid hitting him. But a jury could still find Darley negligent—even though it's an emergency—to hit the accelerator instead of the brake. After all, the brake is there for emergencies, and a driver ought to be able to find it when one occurs.

Darley might argue that the shoplifter being chased in the parking lot is unforeseeable, but that argument is a loser—Darley did not have to foresee the shoplifter. *He did see him* and must act reasonably in light of the situation. Darley might argue that the presence of the electric company truck in the parking lot is unforeseeable, but will lose on this proximate cause argument too. A court would look at the general risk of causing an accident in a busy parking lot. Darley can foresee that, even if not the detail that it was a repair truck behind him.

Brice will not be liable for doing nothing about the ladder when he saw it. As an electrician he recognized the danger. And, he is a friend of Rodansky. But the notorious "no duty" rule will bar liability for failing to intervene since he did not create the risk and a court would not be likely to impose on him a duty to act just because he knows one of the workers.

When Brice goes to Chu's aid he acts as a rescuer. He would probably not be found negligent for proceeding even though he risked a shock when he touched the truck. If a reasonable person would go to the rescue as he did, then he would not be found negligent. However, in a jurisdiction that still recognizes assumption of the risk as a full defense, he might — weirdly — be barred from recovery for his shock injury because he deliberately chose to encounter a risk — electric shock — which he fully understood.

Because Perkins was a cause of the injury to Chu and Rodansky, he has a duty to go to their aid. He had to choose one to help first, so if he reasonably chose to check Rodansky first, he would likely be found to have fulfilled his duty even though Chu needed help too. However, Perkins is likely liable for their injuries regardless of his care in giving aid — because his initial act of placing the ladder against the truck is a cause of the other workers' injuries.

Chu saw the ladder leaning against the truck but stayed in the truck. This was negligent, but it is also a conscious choice to encounter a recognized danger, which would probably have constituted assumption of the risk at common law. In most jurisdictions today it would be treated as comparative fault, so that Chu's recovery would be reduced instead of barred. Under most wrongful death statutes, his negligence will reduce the recovery for his survivors.

Swensson went to Chu's aid and may have caused additional injury by pounding on his chest. However, he may have made a reasonable choice to do so. Perhaps his C. P. R. would have kept Chu alive, so it may have been reasonable to attempt it even if it aggravated the burns. If his conduct was reasonable, he would not be liable even if he did cause additional injury. It is also possible that Chu had already died when Swensson went to his aid, so that his conduct did not cause any compensable injury.

The injured workers might argue that the security officer was negligent for going for coffee. However, it is probably reasonable for a security guard to duck inside to get coffee — especially a coffee to go! The guard was probably not negligent to do so. Even if she was, how would the events have been different if the guard had been out in the lot? The chance that she would have been right at the scene of the accident and been able to do something to prevent it is very small, so there probably is no actual causation here. She clearly could have been anywhere else in the lot when the events took place.

Mrs. Chu clearly suffered negligent infliction of emotional distress when she saw her injured husband. Clearly, Swensson would not be liable for that. Her distress stems from her husband's condition, not from Swensson's aid. If she sued Darley for it, recovery would depend on the jurisdiction's approach to indirect infliction. She would not recover in a zone-of-danger jurisdiction, because she arrived after the accident. In a strict Dillon jurisdiction she might also lose since she did not actually see the injury take place.

How about the liability of Sammy? Sammy committed an intentional tort, probably trespass to property, for intruding on the mall property. Paul is probably equally liable since he encouraged Sammy to do so. Even applying a child standard of care, these kids are old enough to recognize that this act would intrude on the mall's property: their wires. There is also no doubt that Sammy's act was the actual cause of all the subsequent events.

It is often said that there is no proximate cause limit on liability for intentional torts, so arguably, even if Sammy would not anticipate the accident that resulted, he would be liable for all the resulting injuries. The Third Restatement suggests that an intentional tortfeasor's liability should reflect the reprehensibility of the conduct and the likelihood that the harm would flow from the tort. Here, the conduct is pretty tame, though it does involve electricity, a dangerous instrumentality. But I think that Sammy would be liable: It seems quite foreseeable that an electric company employee would be injured fixing the lines Sammy damaged. The fact that the accident was precipitated by a fleeing shoplifter may be quirky, but it seems that the type of accident that occurred is very much the type of accident to be expected from Sammy's act.

For those compulsives who really want to get the most out of this exercise, I'll offer one more suggestion. After writing out answers to these questions, and reading the sample answers, try taking one of them again. Writing out the answer with some foreknowledge of the analysis will allow you to concentrate on the process of organizing and expressing your analysis, and further your understanding of how to write an effective answer.

OK, that's that. Hope it helps. Thanks for listening.

Index

Index

www.ingramcontent.com/pod-product-compliance
Lightning Source LLC
LaVergne TN
LVHW082008200926
848481LV00010B/2822

9798889062691